Introduction to Global Politics

A Reader

Introduction to Global Politics

A Reader

Edited with Introductions by

John S. Masker
Temple University

New York Oxford
OXFORD UNIVERSITY PRESS

Oxford University Press, Inc., publishes works that further Oxford University's objective of excellence in research, scholarship, and education.

Oxford New York
Auckland Cape Town Dar es Salaam Hong Kong Karachi
Kuala Lumpur Madrid Melbourne Mexico City Nairobi
New Delhi Shanghai Taipei Toronto

With offices in
Argentina Austria Brazil Chile Czech Republic France Greece
Guatemala Hungary Italy Japan Poland Portugal Singapore
South Korea Switzerland Thailand Turkey Ukraine Vietnam

For titles covered by Section 112 of the US Higher Education Opportunity Act, please visit www.oup.com/us/he for the latest information about pricing and alternate formats.

Published by Oxford University Press, Inc.
198 Madison Avenue, New York, New York 10016
http://www.oup.com

Library of Congress Cataloging-in-Publication Data

Introduction to global politics : a reader / edited with introductions by John S. Masker.
p. cm.
Includes bibliographical references and index.
ISBN 978-0-19-979625-0 (acid-free paper)
1. International relations. 2. International relations—Philosophy.
3. World politics—1989- I. Masker, John Scott.
JZ1242.I5872 2011
327—dc23

2011041254

9 8 7 6 5 4 3 2 1

Printed in the United States of America
on acid-free paper

For Graham

BRIEF CONTENTS

CONTENTS

PREFACE

"Globalization" has become a buzzword in recent years. We talk about *global* security threats, *global* trade, *global* banking, *global* warming, but we often come up short when we try to make connections across the disciplines or subfields that study each of these topics. This can create a dilemma for those of us who teach undergraduates, often non-majors: which readings best present this concept of globalization while still complementing a basic international relations textbook? This anthology goes at this quandary from three directions.

First, the choice of readings. We selected a mix of classic pieces that have become the core of the international relations canon. You will find many of the readings that we all first saw as undergraduates. However, we wanted to add non-Western voices that have been overlooked or undervalued in the field. The goal is to create an anthology that is genuinely "global" so that students can read, evaluate, and draw their own conclusions about the authors' work. We selected academic, policy, and news media sources from around the world in our attempt to reach this goal.

A second goal was to choose readings from a range of theoretical perspectives. As with including non-Western voices, we wanted readings beyond certain token selections from the "leading authors" in a specific tradition. To give an example, we picked a Harry Magdoff chapter because his was an important voice within the Marxist/socialist tradition that is left out of anthologies, perhaps for reasons more political that scholarly. Unfortunately, because of space restrictions it was simply not possible to include the many valuable suggestions that our panel of anonymous reviewers made.

A concluding point is important. Whether we believe that globalization is the best organizing concept to apply to our field, we have to acknowledge that globalization, as a phenomenon, is occurring. This anthology will show our students the many ways that we are all connected to the world, and the ways in which various parts of the world are interconnected. As the Behera and Tang extracts in Part Two demonstrate, the dominant international relations theories heavily influence how the field is taught in Asia. Or, international relations specialists may dispute the importance of non-governmental actors, but this class of actor undeniably shapes international activities, as the readings in Parts Three and Four show. Finally, all of the topics we present in Part Four significantly affect our daily lives, and all have globalized aspects. The media and op/ed extracts show how policy-making and academic opinions meet.

ACKNOWLEDGMENTS

The author thanks all the people at Oxford University Press who worked on this project, especially Jennifer Carpenter, Executive Editor for Politics, and Maegan Sherlock, Editorial Assistant. Jennifer provided guidance at all stages of the work; without Maegan's efforts it is unlikely I would have met any of the production deadlines. Several colleagues and friends read drafts, offered advice on reading selections, or provided encouragement and a cup of tea. This list includes Steven Lamy, Mark Pollack, Donald Hafner, Daniel Chomsky, and Sharon White. I would also like to thank the following reviewers for their feedback: Linda S. Adams, Baylor University; Michael E. Allison, The University of Scranton; John R. Dreyer, South Dakota School of Mines and Technology; Cynthia Enloe, Clark University; William Felice, Eckerd College; Vincent Ferraro, Mount Holyoke College; Stefan Fritsch, Bowling Green State University; Jeannie Grussendorf, Georgia State University; Jeneen Hobby, Cleveland State University; Joyce P. Kaufman, Whittier College; Remonda Kleinberg, University of North Carolina Wilmington; Paul MacDonald, Williams College; Anas Malik, Xavier University; Bob Mandel, Lewis & Clark College; Mary Manjikian, Regent University; Mary M. McCarthy, Drake University; Michael Nojeim, Prairie View A&M University; Emily Rodio, Saint Joseph's University; Robert Schulzinger, University of Colorado, Boulder; Meredith Weiss, University at Albany; Yi Edward Yang, James Madison University.

PART I

Introduction

Take a moment to look at the "made in" label in your shoes. Where were they manufactured? Did you eat some fruit at lunch today? If you are reading this in the Northern Hemisphere's winter, it is a safe bet that your apple, raspberries, or avocado came from some place warmer than Minnesota or Vermont in January—maybe Jamaica? Mexico? These are but two obvious ways that you might be connected to the rest of the world through a process often called globalization. There are other, more subtle ways that we forget sometimes. Apple Computer is based in California, but its products are normally made somewhere in Asia. New automobiles offered for sale in the United States must have so-called domestic content labels that attest to what percentage of the car is made in which country. Did you purchase your car on the basis of that sticker, or by how it felt on the road? Did you take an airplane to get to your new university? The exhaust fumes from the engines of your plane added to transboundary air pollution and therefore contributed to the store of greenhouse gases in the Earth's atmosphere. At the airport the full-body scan that the TSA workers gave you was intended to stop terrorists from destroying your aircraft.

These are but a few of the ways we are all connected to the rest of the world—international relations specialists often call this globalization. There are much less depressing ways: for example, you can join an online action group that promotes the protection of human rights in other countries. Perhaps you did this during the protests in Egypt and received nearly instantaneous updates from demonstrators confronting troops. After the earthquake struck Haiti in January 2010, you could have used your mobile telephone (made in Shanghai, China) to send a text message to the International Committee of the Red Cross (based in Geneva, Switzerland) giving that non-governmental organization (NGO) ten dollars. Maybe you recently took an eco-tourism vacation out of the country and spent your hard-earned cash eating in a restaurant in Mexico, or splurging for a hotel in Costa Rica, while waiting to hop in your kayak to explore endangered mangrove swamps. These actions provided desperately needed income to people living in those countries by giving them employment, thanks to the tourist dollar.

This book will introduce you to global politics through a selection of readings from academic and media sources on the main topics of the international relations: security, political economy, human rights, and the environment. All of these topics have become linked through the concept known as globalization, but there are other ways to see these events: power politics, international regimes, and exploitation are but a few of the terms that we could use. The term *globalization* is meant to suggest that issues that were once local or regional now have impacts that can be seen around the Earth. The following parts of the book contain readings on theories of international relations, international actors, and global issues. Each part begins with an essay that provides some background on the central features on the topic that specialists debate. After each introductory essay you will find several readings excerpted from academic sources and media outlets. There are guiding questions before each reading to provide you with clues to the important aspects of the extract. We have highlighted key terms and names that we define for you in the glossary.

We will develop the concept of globalization and its effects in later parts of this book. Right now we provide an overview of the central features of the academic debate about the phenomenon. The central nub of the economic aspects of globalization is this: is the phenomenon good or bad for people? Like many aspects of human interaction, how you respond to this question is often the result of your own life experience, or to put it another way, your "worldview."

The question about negative and positive aspects of globalization is primarily a moral judgment. Critics of globalization say the process creates a "race to the bottom" in which firms outsource work to countries and facilities where labor costs are lowest; health and safety laws are weak or nonexistent, and environmental problems are ignored. Globalized production, runs a nationalist criticism, also robs workers in the more developed world, North America and Europe, of meaningful employment.

Advocates of the process, such as former U.S. President Bill Clinton, often assert that all people will benefit from products that are made in a globalized economy. Firms will move production to countries where wages are low, thus cutting costs and creating products for sale at lower prices for consumers. Some advocates of globalization acknowledge the potential for exploitation of workers in countries with developing economies, but contend that pressure from social groups and countries of the developed world will bring about improved working conditions globally.

A secondary debate about globalization asks: is the phenomenon a new creature, or is it simply a continuation of a centuries-old process? This remains essentially an academic debate, although one with policy implications. Those writers who maintain that it is a new phenomenon point to the rapid spread of the so-called Anglo-American model of capitalism after the end of the Second World War in 1945. A source of this diffusion of a specific business model can be found in the United States, where, for a variety of reasons, political leaders believed that their government should create incentives for American businesses to shift their operations out of the country. (We will learn more about this trend in Part Four.)

Writers who believe that globalization is not a new trend point to the long history of international trade and finance, in some academic studies examining events of the early 800s, the "Dark Ages" of Europe, when long-distance trade was the norm in Asia and Africa. This school of writers occasionally calls the enthusiastic focus on the post-1945 international economy "Globaloney."

We can find the policy aspect of the globalization debate played out in the actions of three international organizations that the United States, with assistance from the United Kingdom, created to manage this post-1945 business model. They were the International Monetary Fund, the International Bank for Recovery and Development (also called the World Bank), and the International Trade Organization (ITO). Political opposition in the United States led to the demise of the ITO in 1947 before it began operations; the General Agreement on Tariffs and Trade (GATT), initially a small recordkeeping facility, took its place. The World Trade Organization (WTO) superseded GATT in 1995. Critics of globalization often point to the economic harm that the actions of the IMF, the World Bank, and the WTO—often called "the Washington Consensus"—cause in developing countries. For example, to gain access to the organizations' economic assistance for national development, national leaders in the Global South must accept often-intrusive and burdensome conditions on the price of basic goods like food and cooking oil. As a result, impoverished people around the world suffer because of decisions made in developed countries. For instance, some commentators blame in part the policies of the IMF and World Bank for the protests that led to the overthrow of Tunisian President Zine el-Abidine Ben Ali in January 2011.

The political aspects of globalization are reflected in the increasingly penetrated nature of domestic systems by international events. Like countries' economies, political systems have been interdependent for decades, even centuries. For example, in the eighteenth century Western European states fought the War of Spanish Succession to determine who would be the next monarch of Spain. Modern political globalization has eroded the power of states in other ways. As we will see in several of the reading extracts in this book, international organizations, such the United Nations, European Union, and African Union, and non-state actors, such as transnational corporations, transnational social movements, and even transnational terrorist groups, have all eroded the authority and sovereignty of states.

The following sections of this book will expand upon these topics. When you reach the end of the text, you should be able to give an account of the nature of the contemporary international system. We live in interesting times—we hope that this book will provide you with the tools to better understand our world.

Useful Internet Resources

Asian Development Bank, http://www.adb.org/
Canadian International Council, http://www.canadianinternationalcouncil.org/
G-8 Information Centre, http://www.g7.utoronto.ca/
International Atomic Energy Agency, http://www.iaea.or.at/
International Monetary Fund, www.imf.org
Multinational Monitor, http://multinationalmonitor.org/monitor.html
One World Online, http://us.oneworld.net/
United Nations Research Institute for Social Development, http://www.unrisd.org/
Women in International Security, http://wiis.georgetown.edu/
World Trade Organization, www.wto.org

Discussion Questions and Activities

1. Make a list of the ways in which you are "globalized" in your daily life.
2. Is the United States losing its ability to control global events? Give examples to support your answer. If you answered yes, what do you think caused this change?
3. What does the growing global assertiveness mean for the United States?
4. The concept of globalization implies different kinds of power. How have international power relationships changed since 1945? 1989? 2001? 2011?

Theories and Perspectives

When you saw the title of this chapter, did your heart sink? Have you always been better with "facts" than with "theories"? In this chapter we will try to demystify the concept of theory as it applies to the study of international relations. Our goal is to introduce you to some of the ways in which IR researchers use theories to guide and structure their work. For our purposes right now, a theory—sometimes called a "perspective" or a "research tradition"—is best understood as an idea or conceptual tool that helps us to determine what information matters as we seek to understand the international system and the actors that make up that system.

The readings in this part represent academic work from the five leading IR research traditions. At this point we are not asking you to make a judgment about which tradition is "the best." Indeed, your college professors go to conferences and argue about that. We would like you to be open to what you are about to read. Think of the five theories as eyeglasses you can put on to help you see better: you might need reading glasses, glasses for distances, or maybe sunglasses. Remember, also, that there are more than just these five. If you continue in the study of IR you will most likely learn about several others.

The Realist and Liberal perspectives tend to dominate the study of international politics at universities in North America, Europe, and many other parts of the world, including—as we will see later—India. This dominance results from several factors. Both have been around since the early 1900s, when scholars formed the first two departments of IR at the University of Wales in the city of Aberystwyth and Clark University in Worcester, Massachusetts. Realism and Liberalism also represent two basic views of human nature. Realists tend to argue that we can depend only upon ourselves because ultimately people cannot be trusted. Advocates of the Liberal model are inclined to agree that people might not be trustworthy, but that we can learn to cooperate for the common good. The critical idea for us to remember is that within each of the five academic IR perspectives there are differences of opinion; all Realists, for instance, do not agree with each other all the time.

The Marxist, Constructivist, and Feminist traditions are often collectively labeled "alternative" in textbooks. This may result in part from the minority status each has within some academic departments. However, the Marxist perspective has been around since long before 1948, when Hans Morgenthau published the book that contains the principles of realism excerpt we will read below. In the 1840s Karl Marx and Friedrich Engels were already writing the fundamental texts that eventually would guide political leaders, workers, and students around the world in their thinking about government, and the relationships between government and the people. The Constructivist and Feminist perspectives on IR are much more recent, gaining increasing academic popularity in the 1970s and 1980s. Like with Realism and Liberal perspectives, there are also questions about both of these approaches as well as deep divisions within each of these schools of thought.

Table 2.1 Some Perspectives on the International System

	Realist	Liberal, Institutionalist	Marxist	Constructivist	Feminist
Primary Unit	State	States, NGOs, MNCs, TNCs, individuals	State	Various: states, social groups, NGOs, etc.	Various: states, social groups, NGOs, etc.
International system is...	Anarchic, dangerous	Self-interestedly cooperative	Based upon capitalist exploitation	Various: global society; sum of ideas; a fiction	Various, but gender-biased
Leaders are...	Rational actors	Rational actors	Capitalists	Biased by personal perspectives, experiences	Gendered while: Rational actors, capitalists, or biased by personal perspectives, experiences

Table 2.1 provides a visual representation, or typology, of the ways in which IR theories address three central concepts. There are other ways to represent the similarities and differences between the theories. If you keep it in mind as you read,

this typology will help you as you proceed through the rest of this book. As you can see, there are some areas of agreement between and among some of these academic perspectives. For instance, a Feminist writer might work within the Liberal, the Marxist, the Constructivist, or even the Realist perspective, while looking for examples of the ways in which gender helps to explain behaviors and results. In the same manner, an advocate of the Liberal model might use the language of inequality found in the Marxist tradition.

To a certain extent a researcher's personal experiences and psychological make-up influences how that person perceives the international system. This is an over-simplification, of course, but if you believe that interpersonal relationships are a "zero–sum game" in which if one person wins another must lose, you are also likely to see the international realm the same way. As Table 2.1 indicates, the various advocates of the IR perspectives see the world in different ways. These perceptions of the world directly influence the ways in which each IR thinker interprets events, and has a direct impact on the advice that people in academia give to policy-makers. Therefore, if political leaders listen to advocates of the Liberal perspective, then public policy might favor long-term international cooperation through institutions. U.S. Presidents Woodrow Wilson and Bill Clinton fit this model. On the other hand, if politicians seek advice from advocates of the Realist lens, then public policy might look very different. Here we often think of President Richard M. Nixon and his Secretary of State, Henry Kissinger. We turn now to a discussion of how advocates of the theories respond to the three concepts.

Realism

Realists contend that the state is the sole legitimate authoritative actor in the international system. This position results, in part, from the term "international" itself: it implies relations between *states*, not individuals or corporations. It is not that other actors do not matter, only that they have a lesser role in IR. Some Realists also believe in the concept of sovereign equality that developed as a result of the Peace of Westphalia that ended the Thirty Years' War in 1648. States are supposed to respect the right of other states to organize their domestic political systems in the manner they wish without outside interference. This concentration on the role of the state has certain important ramifications, like the belief that some problems, arms races for instance, matter more than others, such as transboundary air pollution. We often call this dichotomy "high politics/low politics." The terms, which developed in the 1700s and 1800s, are meant to convey the notion that a state's power, prestige, and preservation are more important than other issues that do not directly affect that state's survival. However, as we will see in readings in Part Four, since the 1960s there has been a growing awareness that issues that seem to be "low politics"—greenhouse gas emissions, to name one—can in fact directly imperil a state's existence. The high politics/low politics intellectual dichotomy also resulted in the creation of an international hierarchy of states in the Realist model: "Great Powers" have global interests that matter, but "Small States" do not. By that logic, Small States and Middle Powers should accommodate their foreign policies to the needs of the Great Powers.

The most important concept for the Realist school of thought is the notion of "anarchy." In simple terms, anarchy in this case refers to the lack of a central authority to enforce agreements. This is an idea that Realists such as Morgenthau and Waltz take away from their interpretation of the seventeenth-century English writer Thomas Hobbes. Anarchy is the touchstone for Realists, who rely upon it as the justification for a range of actions, such as building a large military and being suspicious of the motivations of leaders of other states. If there is no central power or authority that governs the actions of the international system, then states must take it upon themselves to maximize their own power, in order to protect themselves.

Many proponents of Realism and the other schools of thought share the notion that leaders are rational actors. In political science this means something slightly different than in other fields, for it suggests that leaders follow a series of steps when they make decisions. Built into this concept, as you can see in the Olson extract, is the idea that leaders make choices and that they themselves have control over the government apparatus. Then, if a policy fails, the reasons can be found in the way in which leaders reached that decision. We could look for those reasons in several places: the way in which they collected information before selecting an option; in the manner in which the bureaucracy operated and implemented policy; or in what are sometimes called "unintended consequences." The most important difference between Realist thinking and that of Liberalism is the tendency among the former to give greater weight in their research to state actors, bureaucrats, and leaders than to non-state actors like NGOs, transnational corporations (TNCs), and private individuals, which emerge as important in Liberal thought.

Liberalism

The Liberal perspective developed at roughly the same time as the Realist model; as a result they share certain features. For instance, many advocates of the Liberal approach agree with Realists that the international system is anarchic. But while Realists propose building large armies to defend and protect the state, Liberals like Doyle tend to propose building webs that involve international economic cooperation and social collaboration. As these webs develop, leaders will see the need for more cooperation, and this, in turn, will enhance security. In this approach, slowly the fear of an Unknown Other will subside, thereby reducing international anarchy.

It is not that simple, of course, and the process is a long one, with occasional setbacks. However, Liberals argue, it is possible.

Advocates of the Liberal and the other perspectives do not share Realists' belief in the centrality of the state as the primary actor in global politics. Instead, researchers might look at the ways in which non-state actors like TNCs or peace movements apply pressure to members of governments. Analysts might also examine the effects of "interdependence" on a Great Power/Small State dyad to determine the ability of the less powerful state to get its way. As you will see in the readings below, writers apply a range of techniques in their work.

Marxism

With the Cold War over, it is easy to dismiss the relevance of Marxism. It is important to remember, however, that at one time Marxist socialism in different forms was a viable alternative to Western-style capitalism. Socialism and social welfare programs remain important in countries around the world.

Karl Marx and his followers saw the world as a struggle between rival economic classes. Marx himself wrote very little about IR, but Lenin and others of his followers applied the concept to the interactions of states. States themselves were in a globalized class struggle with a capitalist center and a proletariat periphery. Therefore, in the Marxist worldview, states and their governments are the equivalent of the chief operating officer of a corporation: it is their job to make certain that the ruling economic class receives a return on its investment.

Constructivism

We can find the roots of the Constructivist perspective on IR in philosophy and sociology. Constructivists like Wendt argue persuasively that meanings of words are not fixed in concrete, that over time the definition of a word changes. We can see this if we examine the term "anarchy." Did you notice how often a phrase such as "Realists (or Liberals) tend to argue..." appeared above? This is because scholars do not—perhaps cannot—agree on what a term like *anarchy* means. We can agree that in a world of sovereign and equal states there is no policing authority, yet we can all think of cases in which one state or another acted as the "global police force." We have a term for that state: the hegemonic state. The excerpt below from Wendt's path-breaking essay says much more about this idea.

Feminism

There is more than one feminist lens. Researchers in this school of thought might write from an angle that could sound like the Liberal, Marxist, or Constructivist perspective. Indeed, it is difficult to find any published work written in the style of Realist Feminism. The Tickner and Sylvester excerpts give you a flavor of this variety of feminist approaches to global politics. The Feminist research perspective in IR examines the ways in which ideas of "proper" gender roles influence public policy decision-making. As Cynthia Enloe famously wrote, "where are the women?" becomes the guiding question. For Enloe herself this has taken her from the study of ethnic soldiers in the former English colonial armies, to Nike sneaker factories in South Korea, to Abu Ghraib prison in U.S.-occupied Iraq, as you will see in Part Four.

READING SELECTIONS

Six Principles of Political Realism

HANS J. MORGENTHAU

Morgenthau's *Politics Among Nations* is often the first book IR specialists cite when they discuss the Realist perspective. This extract presents a parsimonious statement of the perspective, with its focus on power, national security, and the state. Can you think of modern cases that rebut Morgenthau's assertions? Are there states that do not seek to maximize their power resources? How does Realism account for non-state actors, such as TNCs, religious movements, or globalized groups, that use terror as a weapon?

1. Political realism believes that politics, like society in general, is governed by objective laws that have their roots in human nature. In order to improve society it is first necessary to understand the laws by which society lives. The operation of these laws being impervious to our preferences, men will challenge them only at the risk of failure.

Realism, believing as it does in the objectivity of the laws of politics, must also believe in the possibility of developing a rational theory that reflects, however imperfectly and one-sidedly, these objective laws. It believes also, then, in the possibility of distinguishing in politics between truth and opinion—between what is true objectively and rationally, supported by evidence and illuminated by reason, and what is only a subjective judgment, divorced from the facts as they are and informed by prejudice and wishful thinking.

Human nature, in which the laws of politics have their roots, has not changed since the classical philosophies of China, India, and Greece endeavored to discover these laws. Hence, novelty is not necessarily a virtue in political theory, nor is old age a defect. The fact that a theory of politics, if there be such a theory, has never been heard of before tends to create a presumption against, rather than in favor of, its soundness. Conversely, the fact that a theory of politics was developed hundreds or even thousands of years ago—as was the theory of the balance of power—does not create a presumption that it must be outmoded and obsolete. A theory of politics must be subjected to the dual test of reason and experience. To dismiss such a theory because it had its flowering in centuries past is to present not a rational argument but a modernistic prejudice that takes for granted the superiority of the present over the past. To dispose of the revival of such a theory as a "fashion" or "fad" is tantamount to assuming that in matters political we can have opinions but no truths.

For realism, theory consists in ascertaining facts and giving them meaning through reason. It assumes that the character of a foreign policy can be ascertained only through the examination of the political acts performed and of the foreseeable consequences of these acts. Thus we can find out what statesmen have actually done, and from the foreseeable consequences of their acts we can surmise what their objectives might have been.

Yet examination of the facts is not enough. To give meaning to the factual raw material of foreign policy, we must approach political reality with a kind of rational outline, a map that suggests to us the possible meanings of foreign policy. In other words, we put ourselves in the position of a statesman who must meet a certain problem of foreign policy under certain circumstances, and we ask ourselves what the rational alternatives are from which a statesman may choose who must meet this problem under these circumstances (presuming always that he acts in a rational manner), and which of these rational alternatives this particular statesman, acting under these circumstances, is likely to choose. It is the testing of this rational hypothesis against the actual facts and their consequences that gives meaning to the facts of international politics and makes a theory of politics possible.

2. The main signpost that helps political realism to find its way through the landscape of international politics is the concept of interest defined in terms of power. This concept provides the link between reason trying to understand international politics and the facts to be understood. It sets politics as an autonomous sphere of action and understanding apart from other spheres, such as economics (understood in terms of interest defined as wealth), ethics, aesthetics, or religion. Without such a concept a theory of politics, international or domestic, would be altogether impossible, for without it we could not distinguish between political and nonpolitical facts, nor could we bring at least a measure of systematic order to the political sphere.

We assume that statesmen think and act in terms of interest defined as power, and the evidence of history bears that assumption out. That assumption allows us to retrace and anticipate, as it were, the steps a statesman—past, present, or future—has taken or will take on the political scene. We look over his shoulder when he writes his dispatches; we listen in on his conversation with other statesmen; we read and anticipate his very thoughts. Thinking in terms of interest defined as power, we think as he does, and as disinterested observers we understand his thoughts and actions perhaps better than he, the actor on the political scene, does himself.

The concept of interest defined as power imposes intellectual discipline upon the observer, infuses rational order into the subject matter of politics, and thus makes the theoretical understanding of politics possible. On the side of the actor, it provides for rational discipline in action and creates that astounding continuity in foreign policy which makes American, British, or Russian foreign policy appear as an intelligible, rational continuum, by and large consistent within itself, regardless of the different motives, preferences, and intellectual and moral qualities of successive statesmen. A realist theory of international politics, then, will guard against two popular fallacies: the concern with motives and the concern with ideological preferences.

To search for the clue to foreign policy exclusively in the motives of statesmen is both futile and deceptive. It is futile because motives are the most illusive of psychological data, distorted as they are, frequently beyond recognition, by the interests and emotions of actor and observer alike. Do we really know what our own motives are? And what do we know of the motives of others?

Yet even if we had access to the real motives of statesmen, that knowledge would help us little in understanding foreign policies, and might well lead us astray. It is true that the knowledge of the statesman's motives may give us one among many clues as to what the direction of his foreign policy might be. It cannot give us, however, the one clue by which to predict his foreign policies. History shows no exact and necessary correlation between the quality of motives and the quality of foreign policy. This is true in both moral and political terms.

We cannot conclude from the good intentions of a statesman that his foreign policies will be either morally praiseworthy or politically successful. Judging his motives, we can say that he will not intentionally pursue policies that are morally wrong, but we can say nothing about the probability of their success. If we want to know the moral and political qualities of his actions, we must know them, not his motives. How often have statesmen been motivated by the desire to improve the world, and ended by making it worse? And how often have they sought one goal, and ended by achieving something they neither expected nor desired?

Neville Chamberlain's politics of appeasement were, as far as we can judge, inspired by good motives; he was probably less motivated by considerations of personal power than were many other British prime ministers, and he sought to preserve peace and to assure the happiness of all concerned. Yet his policies helped to make the Second World War inevitable, and to bring untold miseries to millions of men. Sir Winston Churchill's motives, on the other hand, have been much less universal in scope and much more narrowly directed toward personal and national power, yet the foreign policies that sprang from these inferior motives were certainly superior in moral and political quality to those pursued by his predecessor. Judged by his motives, Robespierre was one of the most virtuous men who ever lived. Yet it was the utopian radicalism of that very virtue that made him kill those less virtuous than himself, brought him to the scaffold, and destroyed the revolution of which he was a leader.

Good motives give assurance against deliberately bad policies; they do not guarantee the moral goodness and political success of the policies they inspire. What is important to know, if one wants to understand foreign policy, is not primarily the motives of a statesman, but his intellectual ability to comprehend the essentials of foreign policy, as well as his political ability to translate what he has comprehended into successful political action. It follows that while ethics in the abstract judges the moral qualities of motives, political theory must judge the political qualities of intellect, will, and action.

A realist theory of international politics will also avoid the other popular fallacy of equating the foreign policies of a statesman with his philosophic or political sympathies, and of deducing the former from the latter. Statesmen, especially under contemporary conditions, may well make a habit of presenting their foreign policies in terms of their philosophic and political sympathies in order to gain popular support for them. Yet they will distinguish with Lincoln between their "*official* duty," which is to think and act in terms of the national interest, and their "*personal* wish," which is to see their own moral values and political principles realized throughout the world. Political realism does not require, nor does it condone, indifference to political ideals and moral principles, but it requires indeed a sharp distinction between the desirable and the possible—between what is desirable everywhere and at all times and what is possible under the concrete circumstances of time and place.

It stands to reason that not all foreign policies have always followed so rational, objective, and unemotional a course. The contingent elements of personality, prejudice, and subjective preference, and of all the weaknesses of intellect and will which flesh is heir to, are bound to deflect foreign policies from their rational course. Especially where foreign policy is conducted under the conditions of democratic control, the need to marshal popular emotions to the support of foreign policy cannot fail to impair the rationality of foreign policy itself. Yet a theory of foreign policy which aims at rationality must for the time being, as it were, abstract from these irrational elements and seek to paint a picture of foreign policy which presents the rational essence to be found in experience, without the contingent deviations from rationality which are also found in experience.

The difference between international politics as it actually is and a rational theory derived from it is like the difference between a photograph and a painted portrait. The photograph shows everything that can be seen by the naked eye; the painted portrait does not show everything that can be seen by the naked eye, but it shows, or at least seeks to show, one thing that the naked eye cannot see: the human essence of the person portrayed.

Political realism contains not only a theoretical but also a normative element. It knows that political reality is replete with contingencies and points to the typical influences they exert upon foreign policy. Yet it shares with all social theory the need, for the sake of theoretical understanding, to stress the rational elements of political reality; for it is these rational elements that make reality intelligible for theory. Political realism presents the theoretical construct of a rational foreign policy which experience can never completely achieve.

At the same time political realism considers a rational foreign policy to be good foreign policy; for only a rational foreign policy minimizes risks and maximizes benefits and, hence, complies both with the moral precept of prudence and the political requirement of success. Political realism wants the photographic picture of the political world to resemble as much as possible its painted portrait. Aware of the inevitable gap between good—that is, rational—foreign policy and foreign policy as it actually is, political realism maintains not only that theory must focus upon the rational elements of political reality, but also that foreign policy ought to be rational in view of its own moral and practical purposes.

Hence, it is no argument against the theory here presented that actual foreign policy does not or cannot live up to it. That argument misunderstands the intention of this book, which is to present not an indiscriminate description of political reality, but a rational theory of international politics. Far from being invalidated by the fact that, for instance, a perfect balance of power policy will scarcely be found in reality, it assumes that reality, being deficient in this respect, must be understood and evaluated as an approximation to an ideal system of balance of power.

3. Realism does not endow its key concept of interest defined as power with a meaning that is fixed once and for all. The idea of interest is indeed of the essence of politics and is unaffected by the circumstances of time and place. Thucydides' statement, born of the experiences of ancient Greece, that "identity of interests is the surest of bonds whether between states or individuals" was taken up in the nineteenth century by Lord Salisbury's remark that "the only bond of union that endures" among nations is "the absence of all clashing interests." It was erected into a general principle of government by George Washington:

> A small knowledge of human nature will convince us, that, with far the greatest part of mankind, interest is the governing principle; and that almost every man is more or less, under its influence. Motives of public virtue may for a time, or in particular instances, actuate men to the observance of a conduct purely disinterested; but they are not of themselves sufficient to produce persevering conformity to the refined dictates and obligations of social duty. Few men are capable of making a continual sacrifice of all views of private interest, or advantage, to the common good. It is vain to exclaim against the depravity of human nature on this account; the fact is so, the experience of every age and nation has proved it and we must in a great measure, change the constitution of man, before we can make it otherwise. No institution, not built on the presumptive truth of these maxims can succeed.[1]

It was echoed and enlarged upon in our century by Max Weber's observation:

> Interests (material and ideal), not ideas, dominate directly the actions of men. Yet the "images of the world" created by these ideas have very often served as switches determining the tracks on which the dynamism of interests kept actions moving.[2]

Yet the kind of interest determining political action in a particular period of history depends upon the political and cultural context within which foreign policy is formulated. The goals that might be pursued by nations in their foreign policy can run the whole gamut of objectives any nation has ever pursued or might possibly pursue.

The same observations apply to the concept of power. Its content and the manner of its use are determined by the political and cultural environment. Power may comprise anything that establishes and maintains the control of man over man. Thus power covers all social relationships which serve that end, from physical violence to the most subtle psychological ties by which one mind controls another. Power covers the domination of man by man, both when it is disciplined by moral ends and controlled by constitutional safeguards, as in Western democracies, and when it is that untamed and barbaric force which finds its laws in nothing but its own strength and its sole justification in its aggrandizement.

Political realism does not assume that the contemporary conditions under which foreign policy operates, with their extreme instability and the ever present threat of large-scale violence, cannot be changed. The balance of power, for instance, is indeed a perennial element of all pluralistic societies, as the authors of *The Federalist* papers well knew; yet it is capable of operating, as it does in the United States, under the conditions of relative stability and peaceful conflict. If the factors that have given rise to these conditions can be duplicated on the international scene, similar conditions of stability and peace will then prevail there, as they have over long stretches of history among certain nations.

What is true of the general character of international relations is also true of the nation state as the ultimate point of reference of contemporary foreign policy. While the realist indeed believes that interest is the perennial standard by which political action must be judged and directed, the contemporary connection between interest and the national state is a product of history, and is therefore bound to disappear in the course of history. Nothing in the realist position militates against the assumption that the present division of the political world into nation states will be replaced by larger units of a quite different character, more in keeping with the technical potentialities and the moral requirements of the contemporary world.

The realist parts company with other schools of thought before the all-important question of how the comtemporary world is to be transformed. The realist is persuaded that this transformation can be achieved only through the workmanlike manipulation of the perennial forces that have shaped the past as they will the future. The realist cannot be persuaded that we can bring about that transformation by confronting a political reality that has its own laws with an abstract ideal that refuses to take those laws into account.

4. Political realism is aware of the moral significance of political action. It is also aware of the ineluctable tension between the moral command and the requirements of successful political action. And it is unwilling to gloss over and obliterate that tension and thus to obfuscate both the moral and the political issue by making it appear as though the stark facts of politics were morally more satisfying than they actually are, and the moral law less exacting than it actually is.

Realism maintains that universal moral principles cannot be applied to the actions of states in their abstract universal formulation, but that they must be filtered through the concrete circumstances of time and place. The individual may say for himself: "*Fiat justitia, pereat mundus* (Let justice be done, even if the world perish)," but the state has no right to say so in the name of those who are in its care. Both individual and state must judge political action by universal moral principles, such as that of liberty. Yet while the individual has a moral right to sacrifice himself in defense of such a moral principle, the state has no right to let its moral disapprobation of the infringement of liberty get in the way of successful political action, itself inspired by the moral principle of national survival. There can be no political morality without prudence; that is, without consideration of the political consequences of seemingly moral action. Realism, then, considers prudence—the weighing of the consequences of alternative political actions—to be the supreme virtue in politics. Ethics in the abstract judges action by its conformity with the moral law; political ethics judges action by its political consequences. Classical and medieval philosophy knew this, and so did Lincoln when he said:

> I do the very best I know how, the very best I can, and I mean to keep doing so until the end. If the end brings me out all right, what is said against me won't amount to anything. If the end brings me out wrong, ten angels swearing I was right would make no difference.

5. Political realism refuses to identify the moral aspirations of a particular nation with the moral laws that govern the universe. As it distinguishes between truth and opinion, so it distinguishes between truth and idolatry. All nations are tempted—and few have been able to resist the temptation for long—to clothe their own particular aspirations and actions in the moral purposes of the universe. To know that nations are subject to the moral law is one thing, while to pretend to know with certainty what is good and evil in the relations among nations is quite another. There is a world of difference between the belief that all nations stand under the judgment of God,

inscrutable to the human mind, and the blasphemous conviction that God is always on one's side and that what one wills oneself cannot fail to be willed by God also.

The lighthearted equation between a particular nationalism and the counsels of Providence is morally indefensible, for it is that very sin of pride against which the Greek tragedians and the Biblical prophets have warned rulers and ruled. That equation is also politically pernicious, for it is liable to engender the distortion in judgment which, in the blindness of crusading frenzy, destroys nations and civilizations—in the name of moral principle, ideal, or God himself.

On the other hand, it is exactly the concept of interest defined in terms of power that saves us from both that moral excess and that political folly. For if we look at all nations, our own included, as political entities pursuing their respective interests defined in terms of power, we are able to do justice to all of them. And we are able to do justice to all of them in a dual sense: We are able to judge other nations as we judge our own and, having judged them in this fashion, we are then capable of pursuing policies that respect the interests of other nations, while protecting and promoting those of our own. Moderation in policy cannot fail to reflect the moderation of moral judgment.

6. The difference, then, between political realism and other schools of thought is real, and it is profound. However much the theory of political realism may have been misunderstood and misinterpreted, there is no gainsaying its distinctive intellectual and moral attitude to matters political.

Intellectually, the political realist maintains the autonomy of the political sphere, as the economist, the lawyer, the moralist maintain theirs. He thinks in terms of interest defined as power, as the economist thinks in terms of interest defined as wealth; the lawyer, of the conformity of action with legal rules; the moralist, of the conformity of action with moral principles. The economist asks: "How does this policy affect the wealth of society, or a segment of it?" The lawyer asks: "Is this policy in accord with the rules of law?" The moralist asks: "Is this policy in accord with moral principles?" And the political realist asks: "How does this policy affect the power of the nation?" (Or of the federal government, of Congress, of the party, of agriculture, as the case may be.)

The political realist is not unaware of the existence and relevance of standards of thought other than political ones. As political realist, he cannot but subordinate these other standards to those of politics. And he parts company with other schools when they impose standards of thought appropriate to other spheres upon the political sphere. It is here that political realism takes issue with the "legalistic-moralistic approach" to international politics. That this issue is not, as has been contended, a mere figment of the imagination, but goes to the very core of the controversy, can be shown from many historical examples. Three will suffice to make the point.[3]

In 1939 the Soviet Union attacked Finland. This action confronted France and Great Britain with two issues, one legal, the other political. Did that action violate the Covenant of the League of Nations and, if it did, what countermeasures should France and Great Britain take? The legal question could easily be answered in the affirmative, for obviously the Soviet Union had done what was prohibited by the Covenant. The answer to the political question depended, first, upon the manner in which the Russian action affected the interests of France and Great Britain; second, upon the existing distribution of power between France and Great Britain, on the one hand, and the Soviet Union and other potentially hostile nations, especially Germany, on the other; and, third, upon the influence that the countermeasures were likely to have upon the interests of France and Great Britain and the future distribution of power. France and Great Britain, as the leading members of the League of Nations, saw to it that the Soviet Union was expelled from the League, and they were prevented from joining Finland in the war against the Soviet Union only by Sweden's refusal to allow their troops to pass through Swedish territory on their way to Finland. If this refusal by Sweden had not saved them, France and Great Britain would shortly have found themselves at war with the Soviet Union and Germany at the same time.

The policy of France and Great Britain was a classic example of legalism in that they allowed the answer to the legal question, legitimate within its sphere, to determine their political actions. Instead of asking both questions, that of law and that of power, they asked only the question of law; and the answer they received could have no bearing on the issue that their very existence might have depended upon.

The second example illustrates the "moralistic approach" to international politics. It concerns the international status of the Communist government of China. The rise of that government confronted the Western world with two issues, one moral, the other political. Were the nature and policies of that government in accord with the moral principles of the Western world? Should the Western world deal with such a government? The answer to the first question could not fail to be in the negative. Yet it did not follow with necessity that the answer to the second question should also be in the negative. The standard of thought applied to the first—the moral—question was simply to test the nature and the policies of the Communist government of China by the principles of Western morality. On the other hand, the second—the political—question had to be subjected to the complicated test of the interests involved and the power available on either side, and of the bearing of one or the other course of action upon these interests and power. The application of this test could well have led to the conclusion that it would be wiser not to deal with the Communist government of China. To arrive at this conclusion by neglecting this test altogether and answering the political question in terms of the moral issue was indeed a classic example of the "moralistic approach" to international politics.

The third case illustrates strikingly the contrast between realism and the legalistic-moralistic approach to foreign policy. Great Britain, as one of the guarantors of the neutrality of Belgium, went to war with Germany in August 1914 because Germany had violated the neutrality of Belgium. The British action could he justified either in realistic or legalistic-moralistic terms. That is to say, one could argue realistically that for centuries it had been axiomatic for British foreign policy to prevent the control of the Low Countries by a hostile power. It was then not so much the violation of Belgium's neutrality per se as the hostile intentions of the violator which provided the rationale for British intervention. If the violator had been another nation but Germany, Great Britain might well have refrained from intervening. This is the position taken by Sir Edward Grey, British Foreign Secretary during that period. Under Secretary for Foreign Affairs Hardinge remarked to him in 1908: "If France violated Belgian neutrality in a war against Germany, it is doubtful whether England or Russia would move a finger to maintain Belgian neutrality, while if the neutrality of Belgium was violated by Germany, it is probable that the converse would be the case." Whereupon Sir Edward Grey replied: "This is to the point." Yet one could also take the legalistic and moralistic position that the violation of Belgium's neutrality per se, because of its legal and moral defects and regardless of the interests at stake and of the identity of the violator, justified British and, for that matter, American intervention. This was the position which Theodore Roosevelt took in his letter to Sir Edward Grey of January 22, 1915:

> To me the crux of the situation has been Belgium. If England or France had acted toward Belgium as Germany has acted I should have opposed them, exactly as I now oppose Germany. I have emphatically approved your action as a model for what should be done by those who believe that treaties should be observed in good faith and that there is such a thing as international morality. I take this position as an American who is no more an Englishman than he is a German, who endeavors loyally to serve the interests of his own country, but who also endeavors to do what he can for justice and decency as regards mankind at large, and who therefore feels obliged to judge all other nations by their conduct on any given occasion.

This realist defense of the autonomy of the political sphere against its subversion by other modes of thought does not imply disregard for the existence and importance of these other modes of thought. It rather implies that each should be assigned its proper sphere and function. Political realism is based upon a pluralistic conception of human nature. Real man is a composite of "economic man," "political man," "moral man," "religious man," etc. A man who was nothing but "political man" would be a beast, for he would be completely lacking in moral restraints. A man who was nothing but "moral man" would be a fool, for he would be completely lacking in prudence. A man who was nothing but "religious man" would be a saint, for he would be completely lacking in worldly desires.

Recognizing that these different facets of human nature exist, political realism also recognizes that in order to understand one of them one has to deal with it on its own terms. That is to say, if I want to understand "religious man," I must for the time being abstract from the other aspects of human nature and deal with its religious aspect as if it were the only one. Furthermore, I must apply to the religious sphere the standards of thought appropriate to it, always remaining aware of the existence of other standards and their actual influence upon the religious qualities of man. What is true of this facet of human nature is true of all the others. No modern economist, for instance, would conceive of his science and its relations to other sciences of man in any other way. It is exactly through such a process of emancipation from other standards of thought, and the development of one appropriate to its subject matter, that economics has developed as an autonomous theory of the economic activities of man. To contribute to a similar development in the field of politics is indeed the purpose of political realism.

It is in the nature of things that a theory of politics which is based upon such principles will not meet with unanimous approval—nor does, for that matter, such a foreign policy. For theory and policy alike run counter to two trends in our culture which are not able to reconcile themselves to the assumptions and results of a rational, objective theory of politics. One of these trends disparages the role of power in society on grounds that stem from the experience and philosophy of the nineteenth century; we shall address ourselves to this tendency later in greater detail.[4] The other trend, opposed to the realist theory and practice of politics, stems from the very relationship that exists, and must exist, between the human mind and the political sphere. For reasons that we shall discuss later[5] the human mind in its day-by-day operations cannot bear to look the truth of politics straight in the face. It must disguise, distort, belittle, and embellish the truth—the more so, the more the individual is actively involved in the processes of politics, and particularly in those of international politics. For only by deceiving himself about the nature of politics and the role he plays on the political scene is man able to live contentedly as a political animal with himself and his fellow men.

Thus it is inevitable that a theory which tries to understand international politics as it actually is and as it ought to be in view of its intrinsic nature, rather than as people would like to see it, must overcome a psychological resistance that most other branches of learning need not face. A book devoted to the theoretical understanding of international politics therefore requires a special explanation and justification.

Notes

1. *The Writings of George Washington*, edited by John C. Fitzpatrick (Washington: United States Printing Office, 1931–44), Vol. X, p. 363.
2. Marianne Weber, *Max Weber* (Tuebingen: J. C. B. Mohr, 1926), pp. 347–8.
3. See the other examples discussed in Hans J. Morgenthau, "Another 'Great Debate': The National Interest of the United States," *The American Political Science Review*, XLVI (December 1952), pp. 979 ff. See also Hans J. Morgenthau, *Politics in the 20th Century*, Vol. I, *The Decline of Democractic Politics* (Chicago: University of Chicago Press, 1962), pp. 70 ff.
4. See pages 29 ff.
5. See pages xxx ff.

Liberalism and World Politics

MICHAEL W. DOYLE

Although not responding directly to *Politics Among Nations*, the following extract from the *American Political Science Review* addresses the primary points of the Realist perspective that Morgenthau has come to epitomize. Doyle's analysis is state-centric like the Realist lens, but reaches different conclusions. What, according to Doyle, makes liberal democratic states peaceful? What is it about the internal institutions of a liberal democratic state that encourages this behavior?

Promoting freedom will produce peace, we have often been told. In a speech before the British Parliament in June of 1982, President Reagan proclaimed that governments founded on a respect for individual liberty exercise "restraint" and "peaceful intentions" in their foreign policy. He then announced a "crusade for freedom" and a "campaign for democratic development" (Reagan, June 9, 1982).

In making these claims the president joined a long list of liberal theorists (and propagandists) and echoed an old argument: the aggressive instincts of authoritarian leaders and totalitarian ruling parties make for war. Liberal states, founded on such individual rights as equality before the law, free speech and other civil liberties, private property, and elected representation are fundamentally against war this argument asserts. When the citizens who bear the burdens of war elect their governments, wars become impossible. Furthermore, citizens appreciate that the benefits of trade can be enjoyed only under conditions of peace. Thus the very existence of liberal states, such as the U.S., Japan, and our European allies, makes for peace.

Despite the contradictions of liberal pacifism and liberal imperialism, I find, with Kant and other liberal republicans, that liberalism does leave a coherent legacy on foreign affairs. Liberal states are different. They are indeed peaceful, yet they are also prone to make war, as the U.S. and our "freedom fighters" are now doing, not so covertly, against Nicaragua. Liberal states have created a separate peace, as Kant argued they would, and have also discovered liberal reasons for aggression, as he feared they might. I conclude by arguing that the differences among liberal pacifism, liberal imperialism, and Kant's liberal internationalism are not arbitrary but rooted in differing conceptions of the citizen and the state.

Liberal Pacifism

There is no canonical description of liberalism. What we tend to call *liberal* resembles a family portrait of principles and institutions, recognizable

Michael W. Doyle, "Liberalism and World Politics." *American Political Science Review*, Vol. 80, No. 4 (Dec. 1986).

by certain characteristics—for example, individual freedom, political participation, private property, and equality of opportunity—that most liberal states share, although none has perfected them all.

Democratic capitalism leads to peace. As evidence, Schumpeter claims that throughout the capitalist world an opposition has arisen to "war, expansion, cabinet diplomacy"; that contemporary capitalism is associated with peace parties; and that the industrial worker of capitalism is "vigorously anti-imperialist." In addition, he points out that the capitalist world has developed means of preventing war, such as the Hague Court and that the least feudal, most capitalist society—the United States—has demonstrated the least imperialistic tendencies (Schumpeter, 1955, pp. 95–96). An example of the lack of imperialistic tendencies in the U.S., Schumpeter thought, was our leaving over half of Mexico unconquered in the war of 1846–48.

Schumpeter's explanation for liberal pacifism is quite simple: Only war profiteers and military aristocrats gain from wars. No democracy would pursue a minority interest and tolerate the high costs of imperialism. When free trade prevails, "no class" gains from forcible expansion because

> foreign raw materials and food stuffs are as accessible to each nation as though they were in its own territory. Where the cultural backwardness of a region makes normal economic intercourse dependent on colonization it does not matter, assuming free trade, which of the "civilized" nations undertakes the task of colonization. (Schumpeter, 1955, pp. 75–76)

The discrepancy between the warlike history of liberal states and Schumpeter's pacifistic expectations highlights three extreme assumptions. First, his "materialistic monism" leaves little room for noneconomic objectives, whether espoused by states or individuals. Neither glory, nor prestige, nor ideological justification, nor the pure power of ruling shapes policy. These nonmaterial goals leave little room for positive-sum gains, such as the comparative advantages of trade. Second, and relatedly, the same is true for his states. The political life of individuals seems to have been homogenized at the same time as the individuals were "rationalized, individualized, and democratized." Citizens—capitalists and workers, rural and urban—seek material welfare. Schumpeter seems to presume that ruling makes no difference. He also presumes that no one is prepared to take those measures (such as stirring up foreign quarrels to preserve a domestic ruling coalition) that enhance one's political power, despite deterimental effects on mass welfare. Third, like domestic politics, world politics are homogenized. Materially monistic and democratically capitalist, all states evolve toward free trade and liberty together. Countries differently constituted seem to disappear from Schumpeter's analysis. "Civilized" nations govern "culturally backward" *regions*. These assumptions are not shared by Machiavelli's theory of liberalism.

Liberal Imperialism

Machiavelli argues, not only that republics are not pacifistic, but that they are the best form of state for imperial expansion. Establishing a republic fit for imperial expansion is, moreover, the best way to guarantee the survival of a state.

Machiavelli's republic is a classical mixed republic. It is not a democracy—which he thought would quickly degenerate into a tyranny—but is characterized by social equality, popular liberty, and political participation (Machiavelli, 1950, bk. 1, chap. 2, p. 112; see also Huliung, 1983, chap. 2; Mansfield, 1970; Pocock, 1975, pp. 198–99; Skinner, 1981, chap. 3). The consuls serve as "kings," the senate as an aristocracy managing the state, and the people in the assembly as the source of strength.

Liberty results from "disunion"—the competition and necessity for compromise required by the division of powers among senate, consuls, and tribunes (the last representing the common people). Liberty also results from the popular veto. The powerful few threaten the rest with tyranny, Machiavelli says, because they seek to dominate. The mass demands not to be dominated, and their veto thus preserves the liberties of the state (Machiavelli, 1950, bk. 1, chap. 5, p. 122). However, since the people and the rulers have different social characters, the people need to be "managed" by the few to avoid having their recklessness overturn or their fecklessness undermine the ability of the state to expand (Machiavelli, 1950, bk. 1, chap. 53, pp. 249–50). Thus the senate and the consuls plan expansion, consult oracles, and employ religion to manage the resources that the energy of the people supplies.

Strength, and then imperial expansion, results from the way liberty encourages increased population and property, which grow when the citizens know their lives and goods are secure from arbitrary seizure. Free citizens equip large armies and provide soldiers who fight for public glory and the common good because these are, in fact, their own (Machiavelli, 1950, bk. 2, chap. 2, pp. 287–90). If you seek the honor of having your state expand, Machiavelli advises, you should organize it as a free and popular republic like Rome, rather than as an aristocratic republic like Sparta or Venice. Expansion thus calls for a free republic.

"Necessity"—political survival—calls for expansion. If a stable aristocratic republic is forced by foreign conflict "to extend her territory, in such a case we shall see her foundations give way and herself quickly brought to ruin"; if, on the other hand, domestic security prevails, "the continued tranquility would enervate her, or provoke internal disensions, which together, or either of them seperately, will apt to prove her ruin" (Machiavelli, 1950, bk. 1, chap. 6, p. 129). Machiavelli therefore believes it is necessary to take the constitution of Rome, rather than that of Sparta or Venice, as our model.

Hence, this belief leads to liberal imperialism. We are lovers of glory, Machiavelli announces. We seek to rule or, at least, to avoid being oppressed. In either case, we want more for ourselves and our states than just material welfare (materialistic monism). Because other states with similar aims thereby threaten us, we prepare ourselves for expansion. Because our fellow citizens threaten us if we do not allow them either to satisfy their ambition or to release their political energies through imperial expansion, we expand.

There is considerable historical evidence for liberal imperialism. Machiavelli's (Polybius's) Rome and Thucydides' Athens both were imperial republics in the Machiavellian sense (Thucydides, 1954, bk. 6). The historical record of numerous U.S. interventions in the postwar period supports Machiavelli's argument (Aron, 1973, chaps. 3–4; Barnet, 1968, chap. 11), but the current record of liberal pacifism, weak as it is, calls some of his insights into question. To the extent that the modern populace actually controls (and thus unbalances) the mixed republic, its diffidence may out-weigh elite ("senatorial") aggressiveness.

We can conclude either that (1) liberal pacifism has at least taken over with the further development of capitalist democracy, as Schumpeter predicted it would or that (2) the mixed record of liberalism—pacifism and imperialism—indicates that some liberal states are Schumpeterian democracies while others are Machiavellian republics. Before we accept either conclusion, however, we must consider a third apparent regularity of modern world politics.

Liberal Internationalism

Modern liberalism carries with it two legacies. They do not affect liberal states separately, according to whether they are pacifistic or imperialistic, but simultaneously.

The first of these legacies is the pacification of foreign relations among liberal states,[1] During the nineteenth century, the United States and Great Britain engaged in nearly continual strife; however, after the Reform Act of 1832 defined actual representation as the formal source of the sovereignty of the British parliament, Britain and the United States negotiated their disputes. They negotiated despite, for example, British grievances during the Civil War against the North's blockade of the South, with which Britain had close economic ties. Despite severe Anglo-French colonial rivalry, liberal France and liberal Britain formed an entente against illiberal Germany before World War I. And from 1914 to 1915, Italy, the liberal member of the Triple Alliance with Germany and Austria, chose not to fulfill its obligations under that treaty to support its allies. Instead, Italy joined in an alliance with Britain and France, which prevented it from having to fight other liberal states and then declared war on Germany and Austria. Despite generations of Anglo-American tension and Britain's wartime restrictions on American trade with Germany, the United States leaned toward Britain and France from 1914 to 1917 before entering World War I on their side.

Beginning in the eighteenth century and slowly growing since then, a zone of peace, which Kant called the "pacific federation" or "pacific union," has begun to be established among liberal societies. More than 40 liberal states currently make up the union. Most are in Europe and North America, but they can be found on every continent, as Appendix 1 indicates.

Here the predictions of liberal pacifists (and President Reagan) are borne out: liberal states do exercise peaceful restraint, and a separate peace exists among them. This separate peace provides a solid foundation for the United States' crucial alliances with the liberal powers, e.g., the North Atlantic Treaty Organization and our Japanese alliance. This foundation appears to be impervious to the quarrels with our allies that bedeviled the Carter and Reagan administrations. It also offers the promise of a continuing peace among liberal states, and as the number of liberal states increases, it announces the possibility of global peace this side of the grave or world conquest.

Of course, the probability of the outbreak of war in any given year between any two given states is low. The occurrence of a war between any two adjacent states, considered over a long period of time, would be more probable. The apparent absence of war between liberal states, whether adjacent or not, for almost 200 years thus may have significance. Similar claims cannot be made for feudal, fascist, communist, authoritarian, or totalitarian forms of rule (Doyle, 1983a, pp. 222), nor for pluralistic or merely similar societies. More significant perhaps is that when states are forced to decide on which side of an impending world war they will fight, liberal states all wind up on the same side despite the complexity of the paths that take them there. These characteristics do not prove that the peace among liberals is statistically significant nor that liberalism is the sole valid explanation for the peace.[2] They do suggest that we consider the possibility that liberals have indeed established a separate peace—but only among themselves.

Liberalism also carries with it a second legacy: international "imprudence" (Hume, 1963, pp. 346–47). Peaceful restraint only seems to work in liberals' relations with other liberals. Liberal states have fought numerous wars with nonliberal states. (For a list of international wars since 1816 see Appendix 2.)

Many of these wars have been defensive and thus prudent by necessity. Liberal states have been attacked and threatened by nonliberal states that do not exercise any special restraint in their dealings with the liberal states. Authoritarian rulers both stimulate and respond to an international political environment in which conflicts of prestige, interest, and pure fear of what other states might do all lead states toward war. War and conquest have thus characterized the careers of many authoritarian rulers and ruling parties, from Louis XIV and Napoleon to Mussolini's fascists, Hitler's Nazis, and Stalin's communists.

Yet we cannot simply blame warfare on the authoritarians or totalitarians, as many of our more enthusiastic politicians would have us do.[3] Most wars arise out of calculations and miscalculations of interest, misunderstandings, and mutual suspicions, such as those that characterized the origins of World War I. However, aggression by the liberal state has also characterized a large number of wars. Both France and Britain fought expansionist colonial wars throughout the nineteenth century. The United States fought a similar war with Mexico from 1846 to 1848, waged a war of annihilation against the American Indians, and intervened militarily against sovereign states many times before and after World War II. Liberal states invade weak nonliberal states and display striking distrust in dealings with powerful nonliberal states (Doyle, 1983b).

Neither realist (statist) nor Marxist theory accounts well for these two legacies. While they can account for aspects of certain periods of international stability (Aron, 1968, pp. 151–54; Russett, 1985), neither the logic of the balance of power nor the logic of international hegemony explains the separate peace maintained for more than 150 years among states sharing one particular form of governance—liberal principles and institutions. Balance-of-power theory expects—indeed is premised upon—flexible arrangements of geostrategic rivalry that include preventive war. Hegemonies wax and wane, but the liberal peace holds. Marxist "ultra-imperialists" expect a form of peaceful rivalry among capitalists, but only liberal capitalists maintain peace. Leninists expect liberal capitalists to be aggressive toward nonliberal states, but they also (and especially) expect them to be imperialistic toward fellow liberal capitalists.

Kant's theory of liberal internationalism helps us understand these two legacies. The importance of Immanuel Kant as a theorist of international ethics has been well appreciated (Armstrong, 1931; Friedrich, 1948; Gallie, 1978, chap. 1; Galston, 1975; Hassner, 1972; Hinsley, 1967, chap. 4; Hoffmann, 1965; Waltz, 1962; Williams, 1983), but Kant also has an important analytical theory of international politics. *Perpetual Peace*, written in 1795 (Kant, 1970, pp. 93–130), helps us understand the interactive nature of international relations. Kant tries to teach us methodologically that we can study neither the systemic relations of states nor the varieties of state behavior in isolation from each other. Substantively, he anticipates for us the ever-widening pacification of a liberal pacific union, explains this pacification, and at the same time suggests why liberal states are not pacific in their relations with nonliberal states. Kant argues that perpetual peace will be guaranteed by the ever-widening acceptance of three "definitive articles" of peace. When all nations have accepted the definitive articles in a metaphorical "treaty" of perpetual peace he asks them to sign, perpetual peace will have been established.

Conclusion

Kant's liberal internationalism, Machiavelli's liberal imperialism, and Schumpeter's liberal pacifism rest on fundamentally different views of the nature of the human being, the state and international relations.[4] Schumpeter's humans are rationalized, individualized, and democratized. They are also homogenized, pursuing material interests "monistically." Because their material interests lie in peaceful trade, they and the democratic state that these fellow citizens control are pacifistic. Machiavelli's citizens are splendidly diverse in their goals but fundamentally unequal in them as well, seeking to rule or fearing being dominated. Extending the rule of the dominant elite or avoiding the political collapse of their state, each calls for imperial expansion.

Kant's citizens, too, are diverse in their goals and individualized and rationalized, but most importantly, they are capable of appreciating the moral equality of all individuals and of treating other individuals as ends rather than as means. The Kantian state thus is governed publicly according to law, as a republic. Kant's is the state that solves the problem of governing individualized equals, whether they are the "rational devils" he says we often find ourselves to be or the ethical agents we can and should become. Republics tell us that

> In order to organize a group of rational beings who together require universal laws for their survival, but of whom each separate individual is secretly inclined to exempt himself from them, the constitution must be so designed so that, although the citizens are opposed to one another in their private attitudes, these opposing views may inhibit one another in such a way that the public conduct of the citizens will be the same as if they did not have such evil attitudes. (Kant, *PP*, p. 113)

Unlike Machiavelli's republics, Kant's republics are capable of achieving peace among themselves because they exercise democratic caution and are capable of appreciating the international rights of foreign republics. These international rights of republics derive from the representation of foreign individuals, who are our moral equals. Unlike Schumpeter's capitalist democracies, Kant's republics—including our own—remain in a state of war with nonrepublics. Liberal republics see themselves as threatened by aggression from nonrepublics that are not constrained by representation. Even though wars often cost more than the economic return they generate, liberal republics also are prepared to protect and promote—sometimes forcibly—democracy, private property, and the rights of individuals overseas against nonrepublics, which, because they do not authentically represent the rights of individuals, have no rights to noninterference. These wars may liberate oppressed individuals overseas; they also can generate enormous suffering.

Preserving the legacy of the liberal peace without succumbing to the legacy of liberal imprudence is both a moral and a strategic challenge. The bipolar stability of the international system, and the near certainty of mutual devastation resulting from a nuclear war between the superpowers, have created a "crystal ball effect" that has helped to constrain the tendency toward miscalculation present at the outbreak of so many wars in the past (Carnesale, Doty, Hoffmann, Huntington, Nye, and Sagan, 1983, p. 44; Waltz, 1964). However, this "nuclear peace" appears to be limited to the superpowers. It has not curbed military interventions in the Third World. Moreover, it is subject to a desperate technological race designed to overcome its constraints and to crises that have pushed even the superpowers to the brink of war. We must still reckon with the war fevers and moods of appeasement that have almost alternately swept liberal democracies.

Yet restraining liberal imprudence, whether aggressive or passive, may not be possible without threatening liberal pacification. Improving the strategic acumen of our foreign policy calls for introducing steadier strategic calculations of the national interest in the long run and more flexible responses to changes in the international political environment. Constraining the indiscriminate meddling of our foreign interventions calls for a deeper appreciation of the "particularism of history, culture, and membership" (Walzer, 1983, p. 5), but both the improvement in strategy and the constraint on intervention seem, in turn, to require an executive freed from the restraints of a representative legislature in the management of foreign policy and a political culture indifferent to the universal rights of individuals. These conditions, in their turn, could break the chain of constitutional guarantees, the respect for representative government, and the web of transnational contact that have sustained the pacific union of liberal states.

Perpetual peace, Kant says, is the end point of the hard journey his republics will take. The promise of perpetual peace, the violent lessons of war, and the experience of a partial peace are proof of the need for and the possibility of world peace. They are also the grounds for moral citizens and statesmen to assume the duty of striving for peace.

Notes

I would like to thank Marshall Cohen, Amy Gutmann, Ferdinand Hermens, Bonnie Honig, Paschalis Kitromilides, Klaus Knorr, Diana Meyers, Kenneth Oye, Jerome Schneewind, and Richard Ullman for their helpful suggestions. One version of this paper was presented at the American Section of the International Society for Social and Legal Philosophy, Notre Dame, Indiana, November 2–4, 1984, and will appear in *Realism and Morality,* edited by Kenneth Kipnis and Diana Meyers. Another version was presented on March 19, 1986, to the Avoiding Nuclear War Project, Center for Science and International Affairs, The John F. Kennedy School of Government, Harvard University. This essay draws on research assisted by a MacArthur Fellowship in International Security awarded by the Social Science Research Council.

1. Clarence Streit (1938, pp. 88, 90–92) seems to have been the first to point out (in contemporary foreign relations) the empirical tendency of democracies to maintain peace among themselves, and he made this the foundation of his proposal for a (non-Kantian) federal union of the 15 leading democracies of the 1930s. In a very interesting book, Ferdinand Hermens (1944) explored some of the policy implications of Streit's analysis. D. V. Babst (1972, pp. 55–58) performed a quantitative study of this phenomenon of "democratic peace," and R. J. Rummel (1983) did a similar study of "libertarianism" (in the sense of laissez faire) focusing on the postwar period that drew on an unpublished study (Project No. 48) noted in Appendix 1 of his *Understanding Conflict and War* (1979, p. 386). I use the term *liberal* in a wider, Kantian sense in my discussion of this issue (Doyle, 1983a). In that essay, I survey the period from 1790 to the present and find no war among liberal states.
2. Babst (1972) did make a preliminary test of the significance of the distribution of alliance partners in World War I. He found that the possibility that the actual distribution of alliance partners could have occurred by chance was less than 1% (Babst, 1972, p. 56). However, this assumes that there was an equal possibility that any two nations could have gone to war with each other, and this is a strong assumption. Rummel (1983) has a further discussion of the

issue of statistical significance as it applies to his libertarian thesis.

3. There are serious studies showing that Marxist regimes have higher military spending per capita than non-Marxist regimes (Payne, n.d.), but this should not be interpreted as a sign of the inherent aggressiveness of authoritarian or totalitarian governments or of the inherent and global peacefulness of liberal regimes. Marxist regimes, in particular, represent a minority in the current international system; they are strategically encircled, and due to their lack of domestic legitimacy, they might be said to "suffer" the twin burden of needing defenses against both external and internal enemies. Andreski (1980), moreover, argues that (purely) military dictatorships, due to their domestic fragility, have little incentive to engage in foreign military adventures. According to Walter Clemens (1982, pp. 117–18), the United States intervened in the Third World more than twice as often during the period 1946–1976 as the Soviet Union did in 1946–79. Relatedly, Posen and VanEvera (1980, p. 105; 1983, pp. 86–89) found that the United States devoted one quarter and the Soviet Union one tenth of their defense budgets to forces designed for Third World interventions (where responding to perceived threats would presumably have a less than purely defensive character).
4. For a comparative discussion of the political foundations of Kant's ideas, see Shklar (1984, pp. 232–38).

References

Andreski, Stanislav. 1980. On the Peaceful Disposition of Military Dictatorships. *Journal of Strategic Studies*, 3:3–10.

Armstrong, A. C. 1931. Kant's Philosophy of Peace and War. *The Journal of Philosophy*, 28:197–204.

Aron, Raymond. 1966. *Peace and War: A Theory of International Relations*. Richard Howard and Annette Baker Fox, trans. Garden City, NY: Doubleday.

Aron, Raymond. 1974. *The Imperial Republic*. Frank Jellinek, trans. Englewood Cliffs, NJ: Prentice Hall.

Babst, Dean V. 1972. A Force for Peace. *Industrial Research*. 14 (April): 55–58.

Banks, Arthur, and William Overstreet, eds. 1983. *A Political Handbook of the World; 1982–1983*. New York: McGraw Hill.

Barnet, Richard. 1968. *Intervention and Revolution*. Cleveland: World Publishing Co.

Brzezinski, Zbigniew, and Samuel Huntington. 1963. *Political Power: USA/USSR*. New York: Viking Press.

Carnesale, Albert, Paul Doty, Stanley Hoffmann, Samuel Huntington, Joseph Nye, and Scott Sagan. 1983. *Living With Nuclear Weapons*. New York. Bantam.

Chan, Steve. 1984. Mirror, Mirror on the Wall...: Are Freer Countries More Pacific? *Journal of Conflict Resolution*, 28:617–48.

Clemens, Walter C. 1982. The Superpowers and the Third World. In Charles Kegley and Pat McGowan, eds., *Foreign Policy; USA/USSR*. Beverly Hills: Sage. pp. 111–35

Doyle, Michael W. 1983a. Kant, Liberal Legacies, and Foreign Affairs: Part 1. *Philosophy and Public Affairs*, 12:205–35.

Doyle, Michael W. 1983b. Kant, Liberal Legacies, and Foreign Affairs: Part 2. *Philosophy and Public Affairs*, 12:323–53.

Doyle, Michael W. 1986. *Empires*. Ithaca: Cornell University Press.

The Europa Yearbook for 1985. 1985. 2 vols. London. Europa Publications.

Friedrich, Karl. 1948. *Inevitable Peace*. Cambridge, MA: Harvard University Press.

Gallie, W. B. 1978. *Philosophers of Peace and War*. Cambridge: Cambridge University Press.

Galston, William. 1975. *Kant and the Problem of History*. Chicago: Chicago University Press.

Gastil, Raymond. 1985. The Comparative Survey of Freedom 1985. *Freedom at Issue*, 82:3–16.

Haas, Michael. 1974. *International Conflict*. New York: Bobbs-Merrill.

Hassner, Pierre. 1972. Immanuel Kant. In Leo Strauss and Joseph Cropsey, eds., *History of Political Philosophy*. Chicago: Rand McNally. pp. 554–93.

Hermens, Ferdinand A. 1944. *The Tyrants' War and the People's Peace*. Chicago: University of Chicago Press.

Hinsley, F. H. 1967. *Power and the Pursuit of Peace.* Cambridge: Cambridge University Press.

Hoffmann, Stanley. 1965. Rousseau on War and Peace. In Stanley Hoffmann, ed. *The State of War.* New York: Praeger. pp. 45–87.

Holmes, Stephen. 1979. Aristippus in and out of Athens. *American Political Science Review*, 73:113–28.

Huliung, Mark. 1983. *Citizen Machiavelli*, Princeton: Princeton University Press.

Hume, David. 1963. Of the Balance of Power. *Essays: Moral, Political, and Literary.* Oxford: Oxford University Press.

Kant, Immanuel. 1970. *Kant's Political Writings.* Hans Reiss, ed. H. B. Nisbet, trans. Cambridge: Cambridge University Press.

Kelly, George A. 1969. *Idealism, Politics, and History.* Cambridge: Cambridge University Press.

Keohane, Robert, and Joseph Nye. 1977. *Power and Interdependence.* Boston: Little Brown.

Langer, William L., ed. 1968. *The Encylopedia of World History.* Boston: Houghton Mifflin.

Machiavelli, Niccolo. 1950. *The Prince and the Discourses.* Max Lerner, ed. Luigi Ricci and Christian Detmold, trans. New York: Modern Library.

Mansfield, Harvey C. 1970. Machiavelli's New Regime. *Italian Quarterly*, 13:63–95.

Montesquieu, Charles de. 1949 *Spirit of the Laws.* New York: Hafner. (Originally published in 1748.)

Murphy, Jeffrie. 1970. *Kant: The Philosophy of Right.* New York: St. Martins.

Neustadt, Richard. 1970. *Alliance Politics.* New York: Columbia University Press.

Payne, James L. n.d. Marxism and Militarism. *Polity.* Forthcoming.

Pocock, J. G. A. 1975. *The Machiavellian Moment.* Princeton: Princeton University Press.

Polanyi, Karl. 1944. *The Great Transformation.* Boston: Beacon Press.

Posen, Barry, and Stephen VanEvera. 1980. Overarming and Underwhelming. *Foreign Policy*, 40:99–118.

Posen, Barry, and Stephen VanEvera. 1983. Reagan Administration Defense Policy. In Kenneth Oye, Robert Lieber, and Donald Rothchild, eds., *Eagle Defiant.* Boston: Little Brown. pp. 67–104.

Powell, G. Bingham. 1982. *Contemporary Democracies.* Cambridge, MA: Harvard University Press.

Reagan, Ronald. June 9, 1982. Address to Parliament. *New York Times.*

Riley, Patrick. 1983. *Kant's Political Philosophy.* Totowa, NJ: Rowman and Littlefield.

Rummel, Rudolph J. 1979. *Understanding Conflict and War*, 5 vols. Beverly Hills: Sage Publications.

Rummel, Rudolph J. 1983. Libertarianism and International Violence. *Journal of Conflict Resolution*, 27:27–71.

Russett, Bruce. 1985. The Mysterious Case of Vanishing Hegemony. *International Organization*, 39:207–31.

Schumpeter, Joseph. 1950. *Capitalism, Socialism, and Democracy.* New York: Harper Torchbooks.

Schumpeter, Joseph. 1955. The Sociology of Imperialism. In *Imperialism and Social Classes.* Cleveland: World Publishing Co. (Essay originally published in 1919.)

Schwarz, Wolfgang. 1962. Kant's Philosophy of Law and International Peace. *Philosophy and Phenomenonological Research*, 23:71–80.

Shell, Susan. 1980. *The Rights of Reason.* Toronto: University of Toronto Press.

Shklar, Judith. 1984. *Ordinary Vices.* Cambridge, MA: Harvard University Press.

Skinner, Quentin. 1981. *Machiavelli*, New York: Hill and Wang.

Small, Melvin, and J. David Singer. 1976. The War-Proneness of Democratic Regimes. *The Jerusalem Journal of International Relations*, 1(4):50–69.

Small, Melvin, and J. David Singer. 1982. *Resort to Arms.* Beverly Hills: Sage Publications.

Streit, Clarence. 1938. *Union Now: A Proposal for a Federal Union of the Leading Democracies.* New York: Harpers.

Thucydides. 1954. *The Peloponnesian War.* Rex Warner, ed. and trans. Baltimore: Penguin.

U.K. Foreign and Commonwealth Office. 1980. *A Yearbook of the Commonwealth 1980.* London: HMSO.

U.S. Congress. Senate. Select Committee to Study Governmental Operations with Respect to Intelligence Activities. 1975. *Covert Action in*

Chile, 1963–74. 94th Cong., 1st sess., Washington, D.C.: U.S. Government Printing Office.

U.S. Department of State. 1981. *Country Reports on Human Rights Practices*. Washington, D.C.: U.S. Government Printing Office.

Waltz, Kenneth. 1962. Kant, Liberalism, and War. *American Political Science Review*, 56:331–40.

Waltz, Kenneth. 1964. The Stability of a Bipolar World. *Daedalus*, 93:881–909.

Walzer, Michael. 1983. *Spheres of Justice*. New York: Basic Books.

Weede, Erich. 1984. Democracy and War Involvement. *Journal of Conflict Resolution*, 28:649–64.

Wilkenfeld, Jonathan. 1968. Domestic and Foreign Conflict Behavior of Nations. *Journal of Peace Research*, 5:56–69.

Williams, Howard. 1983. *Kant's Political Philosophy*. Oxford: Basil Blackwell.

Wright, Quincy. 1942. *A Study of History*. Chicago: Chicago University Press.

Yovel, Yirmiahu. 1980. *Kant and the Philosophy of History*. Princeton: Princeton University Press.

Structural Realism after the Cold War

KENNETH N. WALTZ

Professor Waltz is often cited as the founder of structural realism. As noted above, the notion of an anarchic international system of states forms the central premise of this perspective. In this except written prior to the September 11, 2001, attacks, Waltz addresses critics of structural realism like Doyle who assert that, in effect, "peace has broken out" and therefore a "democratic peace" along the lines that Doyle predicted will develop in the international system. What does Waltz say to those critics? Why does it matter that he calls the Doyle perspective the "democratic peace thesis"? Can you develop a democratic peace advocate reply to Waltz?

Some students of international politics believe that realism is obsolete.[1] They argue that, although realism's concepts of anarchy, self-help, and power balancing may have been appropriate to a bygone era, they have been displaced by changed conditions and eclipsed by better ideas. New times call for new thinking. Changing conditions require revised theories or entirely different ones.

True, if the conditions that a theory contemplated have changed, the theory no longer applies. But what sorts of changes would alter the international political system so profoundly that old ways of thinking would no longer be relevant? Changes *of* the system would do it; changes *in* the system would not. Within-system changes take place all the time, some important, some not. Big changes in the means of transportation, communication, and war fighting, for example, strongly affect how states and other agents interact. Such changes occur at the unit level. In modern history, or perhaps in all of history, the introduction of nuclear weaponry was the greatest of such changes. Yet in the nuclear era, international politics remains a self-help arena. Nuclear weapons decisively change how some states provide for their own and possibly for others' security; but nuclear weapons have not altered the anarchic structure of the international political system.

Changes in the structure of the system are distinct from changes at the unit level. Thus, changes in polarity also affect how states provide for their security. Significant changes take place when the number of great powers reduces to two or one. With more than two, states rely for their security both on their own internal efforts and on alliances they may make with others. Competition in multipolar systems is more complicated than competition in bipolar ones because uncertainties about the comparative capabilities of states multiply as numbers grow, and because estimates of the cohesiveness and strength of coalitions are hard to make.

Both changes of weaponry and changes of polarity were big ones with ramifications that spread through the system, yet they did not transform it. If the system were transformed, international politics would no longer be international politics, and the past would no longer serve as a guide to the future. We would begin to call international politics by another name, as some do. The terms "world politics" or "global politics," for example, suggest that politics among self-interested states concerned with their security has been replaced by some other kind of politics or perhaps by no politics at all.

What changes, one may wonder, would turn international politics into something distinctly different? The answer commonly given is that international politics is being transformed and realism is being rendered obsolete as democracy extends its sway, as interdependence tightens its grip, and as institutions smooth the way to peace. I consider these points in successive sections. A fourth section explains why realist theory retains its explanatory power after the Cold War.

Democracy and Peace

The end of the Cold War coincided with what many took to be a new democratic wave. The trend toward democracy combined with Michael Doyle's rediscovery of the peaceful behavior of liberal democratic states *inter se* contributes strongly to the belief that war is obsolescent, if not obsolete, among the advanced industrial states of the world.[2]

The democratic peace thesis holds that democracies do not fight democracies. Notice that I say "thesis," not "theory." The belief that democracies constitute a zone of peace rests on a perceived high correlation between governmental form and international outcome. Francis Fukuyama thinks that the correlation is perfect: Never once has a democracy fought another democracy. Jack Levy says that it is "the closest thing we have to an empirical law in the study of international relations."[3] But, if it is true that democracies rest reliably at peace among themselves, we have not a theory but a purported fact begging for an explanation, as facts do. The explanation given generally runs this way: Democracies of the right kind (i.e., liberal ones) are peaceful in relation to one another. This was Immanuel Kant's point. The term he used was *Rechtsstaat* or republic, and his definition of a republic was so restrictive that it was hard to believe that even one of them could come into existence, let alone two or more.[4] And if they did, who can say that they would continue to be of the right sort or continue to be democracies at all? The short and sad life of the Weimar Republic is a reminder. And how does one define what the right sort of democracy is? Some American scholars thought that Wilhelmine Germany was the very model of a modern democratic state with a wide suffrage, honest elections, a legislature that controlled the purse, competitive parties, a free press, and a highly competent bureaucracy.[5] But in the French, British, and American view after August of 1914, Germany turned out not to be a democracy of the right kind. John

Owen tried to finesse the problem of definition by arguing that democracies that perceive one another to be liberal democracies will not fight.[6] That rather gives the game away. Liberal democracies have at times prepared for wars against other liberal democracies and have sometimes come close to fighting them. Christopher Layne shows that some wars between democracies were averted not because of the reluctance of democracies to fight each other but for fear of a third party—a good realist reason. How, for example, could Britain and France fight each other over Fashoda in 1898 when Germany lurked in the background? In emphasizing the international political reasons for democracies not fighting each other, Layne gets to the heart of the matter.[7] Conformity of countries to a prescribed political form may eliminate some of the causes of war; it cannot eliminate all of them. The democratic peace thesis will hold only if all of the causes of war lie inside of states.

The causes of war

To explain war is easier than to understand the conditions of peace. If one asks what may cause war, the simple answer is "anything." That is Kant's answer: The natural state is the state of war. Under the conditions of international politics, war recurs; the sure way to abolish war, then, is to abolish international politics.

Over the centuries, liberals have shown a strong desire to get the politics out of politics. The ideal of nineteenth-century liberals was the police state, that is, the state that would confine its activities to catching criminals and enforcing contracts. The ideal of the laissez-faire state finds many counterparts among students of international politics with their yen to get the power out of power politics, the national out of international politics, the dependence out of interdependence, the relative out of relative gains, the politics out of international politics, and the structure out of structural theory.

Proponents of the democratic peace thesis write as though the spread of democracy will negate the effects of anarchy. No causes of conflict and war will any longer be found at the structural level. Francis Fukuyama finds it "perfectly possible to imagine anarchic state systems that are nonetheless peaceful." He sees no reason to associate anarchy with war. Bruce Russett believes that, with enough democracies in the world, it "may be possible in part to supersede the 'realist' principles (anarchy, the security dilemma of states) that have dominated practice... since at least the seventeenth century."[8] Thus the structure is removed from structural theory. Democratic states would be so confident of the peace-preserving effects of democracy that they would no longer fear that another state, so long as it remained democratic, would do it wrong. The guarantee of the state's proper external behavior would derive from its admirable internal qualities.

This is a conclusion that Kant would not sustain. German historians at the turn of the nineteenth century wondered whether peacefully inclined states could be planted and expected to grow where dangers from outside pressed daily upon them.[9] Kant a century earlier entertained the same worry. The seventh proposition of his "Principles of the Political Order" avers that establishment of the proper constitution internally requires the proper ordering of the external relations of states. The first duty of the state is to defend itself, and outside of a juridical order none but the state itself can define the actions required. "Lesion of a less powerful country," Kant writes, "may be involved merely in the condition of a more powerful neighbor prior to any action at all; and in the State of Nature an attack under such circumstances would be warrantable."[10] In the state of nature, there is no such thing as an unjust war.

Every student of international politics is aware of the statistical data supporting the democratic peace thesis. Everyone has also known at least since David Hume that we have no reason to believe that the association of events provides a basis for inferring the presence of a causal relation. John Mueller properly speculates that it is not democracy that causes peace but that other conditions cause both democracy and peace.[11] Some of the major democracies—Britain in the nineteenth century and the United States in the twentieth century—have been among the most powerful states of their eras. Powerful states often gain their ends by peaceful means where weaker states either fail or have to resort to war.[12] Thus, the American government deemed the democratically elected Juan Bosch of the Dominican Republic too weak to bring order to his country. The United States toppled his government by sending 23,000 troops within a week, troops whose mere presence made fighting a war unnecessary. Salvador Allende, democratically elected ruler of Chile, was systematically and effectively undermined by the United States, without the open use of force, because its leaders thought that his government was taking a wrong turn. As Henry Kissinger put it: "I don't see why we need to stand by and watch a country go Communist due to the irresponsibility of its own people."[13] That is the way it is with democracies—their people may show bad judgment. "Wayward" democracies are especially tempting objects of intervention by other democracies that wish to save them. American policy may have been wise in both cases, but its actions surely cast doubt on the democratic peace thesis. So do the instances when a democracy did fight another democracy.[14] So do the instances in which democratically elected legislatures have clamored for war, as has happened for example in Pakistan and Jordan.

One can of course say, yes, but the Dominican Republic and Chile were not liberal democracies nor perceived as such by the United States. Once one begins to go down that road, there is no place to stop. The problem is heightened because liberal democracies, as they prepare for a war they may fear, begin to look less liberal and will look less liberal still if they begin to fight one. I am tempted to say that the democratic peace thesis in the form in which its proponents cast it is irrefutable. A liberal democracy at war with another country is unlikely to call it a liberal democracy.

Democracies may live at peace with democracies, but even if all states became democratic, the structure of international politics would remain anarchic. The structure of international politics is not transformed by changes internal to states, however widespread the changes may be. In the absence of an external authority, a state cannot be sure that today's friend will not be tomorrow's enemy. Indeed, democracies have at times behaved as though today's democracy is today's enemy and a present threat to them. In Federalist Paper number six, Alexander Hamilton asked whether the thirteen states of the Confederacy might live peacefully with one another as freely constituted republics. He answered that there have been "almost as many popular as royal wars." He cited the many wars fought by republican Sparta, Athens, Rome, Carthage, Venice, Holland, and Britain. John Quincy Adams, in response to James Monroe's contrary claim, averred "that the government of a Republic was as capable of intriguing with the leaders of a free people as neighboring monarchs."[15] In the latter half of the nineteenth century, as the United States and Britain became more democratic, bitterness grew between them, and the possibility of war was at times seriously entertained on both sides of the Atlantic. France and Britain were among the principal adversaries in the great power politics of the nineteenth century, as they were earlier. Their becoming democracies did not change their behavior toward each other. In 1914, democratic England and France fought democratic Germany, and doubts about the latter's democratic standing merely illustrate the problem of definition. Indeed, the democratic pluralism of Germany was an underlying cause of the war. In response to domestic interests, Germany followed policies bound to frighten both Britain and Russia. And today if a war that a few have feared were fought by the United States and Japan, many Americans would say that Japan was not a democracy after all, but merely a one-party state.

What can we conclude? Democracies rarely fight democracies, we might say, and then add as a word of essential caution that the internal excellence of states is a brittle basis of peace.

Democratic wars

Democracies coexist with undemocratic states. Although democracies seldom fight democracies, they do, as Michael Doyle has noted, fight at least their share of wars against others.[16] Citizens of democratic states tend to think of their countries as good, aside from what they do, simply because they are democratic. Thus former Secretary of State Warren Christopher claimed that "democratic nations rarely start wars or threaten their neighbors."[17] One might suggest that he try his proposition out in Central or South America. Citizens of democratic states also tend to think of undemocratic states as bad, aside from what they do, simply because they are undemocratic. Democracies promote war because they at times decide that the way to preserve peace is to defeat nondemocratic states and make them democratic.

During World War I, Walter Hines Page, American ambassador to England, claimed that there "is no security in any part of the world where people cannot think of a government without a king and never will be." During the Vietnam War, Secretary of State Dean Rusk claimed that the "United States cannot be secure until the total international environment is ideologically safe."[18] Policies aside, the very existence of undemocratic states is a danger to others. American political and intellectual leaders have often taken this view. Liberal interventionism is again on the march. President Bill Clinton and his national security adviser, Anthony Lake, urged the United States to take measures to enhance democracy around the world. The task, one fears, will be taken up by the American military with some enthusiasm. Former Army Chief of Staff General Gordon Sullivan, for example, favored a new military "model," replacing the negative aim of containment with a positive one: "To promote democracy, regional stability, and economic prosperity."[19] Other voices urge us to enter into a "struggle to ensure that people are governed well." Having apparently solved the problem of justice at home, "the struggle for liberal government becomes a struggle not simply for justice but for survival."[20] As R.H. Tawney said: "Either war is a crusade, or it is a crime."[21] Crusades are frightening because crusaders go to war for righteous causes, which they define for themselves and try to impose on others. One might have hoped that Americans would have learned that they are not very good at causing democracy abroad. But, alas, if the world can be made safe for democracy only by making it democratic, then all means are permitted and to use them becomes a duty. The war fervor of people and their representatives is at times hard to contain. Thus Hans Morgenthau believed that "the democratic selection and responsibility of government officials destroyed international morality as an effective system of restraint."[22]

Since, as Kant believed, war among self-directed states will occasionally break out, peace has to be contrived. For any government, doing so is a difficult task, and all states are at times deficient in accomplishing it, even if they wish to. Democratic leaders may respond to the fervor for war that their citizens sometimes display, or even try to arouse it, and governments are sometimes constrained by electoral calculations to defer preventive measures. Thus British Prime Minister Stanley Baldwin said that if he had called in 1935 for British rearmament against the German threat, his party would have lost the next election.[23] Democratic governments may respond to internal political imperatives when they should be responding to external ones. All governments have their faults, democracies no doubt fewer than others, but that is not good enough to sustain the democratic peace thesis.

That peace may prevail among democratic states is a comforting thought. The obverse of the proposition—that democracy may promote war against undemocratic states—is disturbing. If the latter holds, we cannot even say for sure that the spread of democracy will bring a net decrease in the amount of war in the world.

With a republic established in a strong state, Kant hoped the republican form would gradually take hold in the world. In 1795, America provided the hope. Two hundred years later, remarkably, it still does. Ever since liberals first expressed their views, they have been divided. Some have urged liberal states to work to uplift benighted peoples and bring the benefits of liberty, justice, and prosperity to them. John Stuart Mill, Giuseppe Mazzini, Woodrow Wilson, and Bill Clinton are all interventionist liberals. Other liberals, Kant and Richard Cobden, for example, while agreeing on the benefits that democracy can bring to the world, have emphasized the difficulties and the dangers of actively seeking its propagation.

If the world is now safe for democracy, one has to wonder whether democracy is safe for the world. When democracy is ascendant, a condition that in the twentieth century attended the winning of hot wars and cold ones, the interventionist spirit flourishes. The effect is heightened when one democratic state becomes dominant, as the United States is now. Peace is the noblest cause of war. If the conditions of peace are lacking, then the country with a capability of creating them may be tempted to do so, whether or not by force. The end is noble, but as a matter of *right,* Kant insists, no state can intervene in the internal arrangements of another. As a matter of *fact,* one may notice that intervention, even for worthy ends, often brings more harm than good. The vice to which great powers easily succumb in a multipolar world is inattention; in a bipolar world, overreaction; in a unipolar world, overextention.

Peace is maintained by a delicate balance of internal and external restraints. States having a surplus of power are tempted to use it, and weaker states fear their doing so. The laws of voluntary federations, to use Kant's language, are disregarded at the whim of the stronger, as the United States demonstrated a decade ago by mining Nicaraguan waters and by invading Panama. In both cases, the United States blatantly violated international law. In the first, it denied the jurisdiction of the International Court of Justice, which it had previously accepted. In the second, it flaunted the law embodied in the Charter of the Organization of American States, of which it was a principal sponsor.

If the democratic peace thesis is right, structural realist theory is wrong. One may believe, with Kant, that republics are by and large good states *and* that unbalanced power is a danger no matter who wields it. Inside of, as well as outside of, the circle of democratic states, peace depends on a precarious balance of forces. The causes of war lie not simply in states or in the state system; they are found in both. Kant understood this. Devotees of the democratic peace thesis overlook it.

Conclusion

Every time peace breaks out, people pop up to proclaim that realism is dead. That is another way of saying that international politics has been transformed. The world, however, has not been transformed; the structure of international politics has simply been remade by the disappearance of the Soviet Union, and for a time we will live with unipolarity. Moreover, international politics was not remade by the forces and factors that some believe are creating a new world order. Those who set the Soviet Union on the path of reform were old Soviet apparatchiks trying to right the Soviet economy in order to preserve its position in the world. The revolution in Soviet affairs and the end of the Cold War were not brought by democracy, interdependence, or international institutions. Instead the Cold War ended exactly as structural realism led one to expect. As I wrote some years ago, the Cold War "is firmly rooted in the structure of postwar international politics and will last as long as that structure endures."[24] So it did, and the Cold War ended only when the bipolar structure of the world disappeared.

Structural change affects the behavior of states and the outcomes their interactions produce. It does not break the essential continuity of international politics. The transformation of international politics alone could do that. Transformation, however, awaits the day when the international system is no longer populated by states that have to help themselves. If the day were here, one would be able to say who could be relied on to help the disadvantaged or endangered. Instead, the ominous shadow of the future continues to cast its pall over interacting states. States' perennial uncertainty about their fates presses governments to prefer relative over absolute gains. Without the shadow, the leaders of states would no longer have to ask themselves how they will get along tomorrow as well as today. States could combine their efforts cheerfully and work to maximize collective gain without worrying about how each might fare in comparison to others.

Occasionally, one finds the statement that governments in their natural, anarchic condition act myopically—that is, on calculations of immediate interest—while hoping that the future will take care of itself. Realists are said to suffer from this optical defect.[25] Political leaders may be astigmatic, but responsible ones who behave realistically do not suffer from myopia. Robert Axelrod and Robert Keohane believe that World War I might have been averted if certain states had been able to see how long the future's shadow was.[26] Yet, as their own discussion shows, the future was what the major states were obsessively worried about. The war was prompted less by considerations of present security and more by worries about how the balance might change later. The problems of governments do not arise from their short time horizons. They see the long shadow of the future, but they have trouble reading its contours, perhaps because they try to look too far ahead and see imaginary dangers. In 1914, Germany feared Russia's rapid industrial and population growth. France and Britain suffered from the same fear about Germany, and in addition Britain worried about the rapid growth of Germany's navy. In an important sense, World War I was a preventive war all around. Future fears dominated hopes for short-term gains. States do not live in the happiest of conditions that Horace in one of his odes imagined for man:

> Happy the man, and happy he alone, who can say,
> Tomorrow do thy worst, for I have lived today.[27]

Robert Axelrod has shown that the "tit-for-tat" tactic, and no other, maximizes collective gain over time. The one condition for success is that the game be played under the shadow of the future.[28] Because states coexist in a self-help system, they may, however, have to concern themselves not with maximizing collective gain but with lessening, preserving, or widening the gap in welfare and strength between themselves and others. The contours of the future's shadow look different in hierarchic and anarchic systems. The shadow may facilitate cooperation in the former; it works against it in the latter. Worries about the future do not make cooperation and institution building among nations impossible; they do strongly condition their operation and limit their accomplishment. Liberal institutionalists were right to start their investigations with structural realism. Until and unless a transformation occurs, it remains the basic theory of international politics.

Notes

1. For example, Richard Ned Lebow, "The Long Peace, the End of the Cold War, and the Failure of Realism," *International Organization*, Vol. 48, No. 2 (Spring 1994), pp. 249–277; Jeffrey W. Legro and Andrew Moravcsik, "Is Anybody Still a Realist?" *International Security*, Vol. 24, No. 2 (Fall 1999), pp. 5–55; Bruce Russett, *Grasping the Democratic Peace: Principles for a Post–Cold War Peace* (Princeton, N.J.: Princeton University Press, 1993); Paul Schroeder, "Historical Reality vs. Neorealist Theory," *International Security*, Vol. 19, No. 1 (Summer 1994), pp. 108–148; and John A. Vasquez, "The Realist Paradigm and Degenerative vs. Progressive Research Programs: An Appraisal of Neotraditional Research on Waltz's Balancing Proposition," *American Political Science Review*, Vol. 91, No. 4 (December 1997), pp. 899–912.
2. Michael W. Doyle, "Kant, Liberal Legacies, and Foreign Affairs, Parts 1 and 2," *Philosophy and Public Affairs*, Vol. 12, Nos. 3 and 4 (Summer and Fall 1983); and Doyle, "Kant: Liberalism and World Politics," *American Political Science Review*. Vol. 80, No. 4 (December 1986), pp. 1151–1169.
3. Francis Fukuyama, "Liberal Democracy as a Global Phenomenon," *Political Science and Politics*, Vol. 24, No. 4 (1991), p. 662. Jack S. Levy, "Domestic Politics and War," in Robert I. Rotberg and Theodore K. Rabb, eds., *The Origin and Prevention of Major Wars* (Cambridge: Cambridge University Press, 1989), p. 88.
4. Kenneth N. Waltz, "Kant, Liberalism, and War," *American Political Science Review*, Vol. 56, No. 2 (June 1962). Subsequent Kant references are found in this work.
5. Ido Oren, "The Subjectivity of the 'Democratic' Peace: Changing U.S. Perceptions of Imperial Germany," *International Security*, Vol. 20, No. 2 (Fall 1995), pp. 157ff.; Christopher Layne, in the second half of Layne and Sean M. Lynn-Jones, *Should America Spread Democracy? A Debate* (Cambridge, Mass.: MIT Press, forthcoming), argues convincingly that Germany's democratic control of foreign and military policy was no weaker than France's or Britain's.
6. John M. Owen, "How Liberalism Produces Democratic Peace," *International Security*, Vol. 19, No. 2 (Fall 1994), pp. 87–125. Cf. his *Liberal Peace, Liberal War: American Politics and International Security* (Ithaca, N.Y.: Cornell University Press, 1997).
7. Christopher Layne, "Kant or Cant: The Myth of the Democratic Peace," *International Security*, Vol. 19, No. 2 (Fall 1994), pp. 5–49.

8. Francis Fukuyama, *The End of History and the Last Man* (New York: Free Press, 1992), pp. 254–256. Russett, *Grasping the Democratic Peace,* p. 24.
9. For example, Leopold von Ranke, Gerhard Ritter, and Otto Hintze. The American William Graham Sumner and many others shared their doubts.
10. Immanuel Kant, *The Philosophy of Law,* trans. W. Hastie (Edinburgh: T. and T. Clark, 1887), p. 218.
11. John Mueller, "Is War Still Becoming Obsolete?" paper presented at the annual meeting of the American Political Science Association, Washington, D.C., August-September 1991, pp. 55ff; cf. his *Quiet Cataclysm: Reflections on the Recent Transformation of World Politics* (New York: HarperCollins, 1995).
12. Edward Hallett Carr, *Twenty Years' Crisis: An Introduction to the Study of International Relations,* 2d ed. (New York: Harper and Row, 1946), pp. 129–132.
13. Quoted in Anthony Lewis, "The Kissinger Doctrine," *New York Times,* February 27, 1975, p. 35; and see Henry Kissinger, *The White House Years* (Boston: Little, Brown, 1979), chap. 17.
14. See, for example, Kenneth N. Waltz, "America as Model for the World? A Foreign Policy Perspective," *PS: Political Science and Politics,* Vol. 24, No. 4 (December 1991); and Mueller, "Is War Still Becoming Obsolete?" p. 5.
15. Quoted in Walter A. McDougall, *Promised Land, Crusader State* (Boston: Houghton Mifflin, 1997), p. 28 and n. 36.
16. Doyle, "Kant, Liberal Legacies, and Foreign Affairs, Part 2," p. 337.
17. Warren Christopher, "The U.S.-Japan Relationship: The Responsibility to Change," address to the Japan Association of Corporate Executives, Tokyo, Japan, March 11, 1994 (U.S. Department of State, Bureau of Public Affairs, Office of Public Communication), p. 3.
18. Page quoted in Waltz, *Man, the State, and War: A Theoretical Analysis* (New York: Columbia University Press, 1959), p. 121. Rusk quoted in Layne, "Kant or Cant," p. 46.
19. Quoted in Clemson G. Turregano and Ricky Lynn Wad dell, "From Paradigm to Paradigm Shift: The Military and Operations Other than War," *Journal of Political Science,* Vol. 22 (1994), p. 15.
20. Peter Beinart, "The Return of the Bomb," *New Republic,* August 3, 1998, p. 27.
21. Quoted in Michael Straight, *Make This the Last War* (New York: G.P. Putnam's Sons, 1945), p. 1.
22. Hans J. Morgenthau, *Politics among Nations: The Struggle for Power and Peace,* 5th ed. (New York: Knopf, 1973), p. 248.
23. Gordon Craig and Alexander George, *Force and Statecraft: Diplomatic Problems of Our Time,* 2d ed. (New York: Oxford University Press, 1990), p. 64.
24. Kenneth N. Waltz, "The Origins of War in Neorealist Theory," *Journal of Interdisciplinary History,* Vol. 18, No. 4 (Spring 1988), p. 628.
25. The point is made by Robert O. Keohane, *After Hegemony: Cooperation and Discord in the World Political Economy* (Princeton, N.J.: Princeton University Press, 1984), pp. 99, 103, 108.
26. Robert Axelrod and Robert O. Keohane, "Achieving Cooperation under Anarchy: Strategies and Institutions," in David Baldwin, ed., *Neorealism and Neoliberalism: The Contemporary Debate* (New York: Columbia University Press, 1993). For German leaders, they say, "the shadow of the future seemed so small" (p. 92). Robert Powell shows that "a longer shadow... leads to greater military allocations." See Powell, "Guns, Butter, and Anarchy," *American Political Science Review,* Vol. 87, No. 1 (March 1993), p. 116; see also p. 117 on the question of the compatibility of liberal institutionalism and structural realism.
27. My revision.
28. Robert Axelrod, *The Evolution of Cooperation* (New York: Basic Books, 1984).

Imperialist Expansion: Accident and Design

HARRY MAGDOFF

Harry Magdoff was many things during in his life: an official in the U.S. Commerce Department during the Roosevelt and Truman administrations; prolific writer and critic of U.S. foreign economic policy; long-time editor of the socialist journal *Monthly Review*; college professor; and when he was blacklisted during the McCarthy era in the United States, Magdoff even sold insurance. In this excerpt written in the late 1960s Magdoff attacks the idea, popular at the time, that the foreign economic policies of both the United Kingdom and the United States happened by chance, not the result of deliberate decisions by government officials. Can you find some ways in which a Marxist perspective influences Magdoff's views? How does Magdoff use statistics to bolster his argument? Thinking about foreign economic policy today, how have things changed since the 1960s?

Toward the end of the nineteenth century the British Empire was celebrated in a popular history, *The Expansion of England* by J. R. Seeley. While this book is generally ignored by modern scholars, its epigrammatic summation lives on: "We seem, as it were, to have conquered and peopled half the world in a fit of absence of mind."[1] This theme, along with its corollary that the British were reluctant imperialists, has penetrated the literature of empire, providing the kernel of more sophisticated formulations. Not as a witticism but as a summary of sober historical analysis, a modern British specialist puts it this way: "In short, the modern empires lacked rationality and purpose: they were the chance products of complex historical forces operating over several centuries, and more particularly during the period after 1815."[2]

Now that U.S. scholars and publicists are beginning to acknowledge the reality of an American Empire, they too seem to find comfort, or significance, in the elements of chance and reluctance that pervade history. Thus two diplomatic correspondents who have recently published a book tracing, quite superficially, the roots of U.S. interest in Asia back to 1784 entitle their opening chapter, with no hint of satire, "The Reluctant Imperialists."[3] In a more scholarly and penetrating study, *Pax Americana*, Ronald Steel recites the extensive U.S. military involvement around the globe and recalls James Reston's words that these are "commitments the like of which no sovereign nation ever took on in the history of the world." But Steel is quick to point out: "These entanglements happened more by accident than by design.... We had no intention of virtually annexing Okinawa, of occupying South Korea, of preventing the return of Taiwan to China, of fighting in Indochina, or of remaining in Western Europe. If someone had said in 1947 that twenty years later there would be 225,000 soldiers in Germany, 50,000 in Korea, and a half million Americans fighting in Vietnam, he would have been considered mad."[4]

Both accident and reluctance are, of course, ever present in empire-building. Hitler, and Kaiser Wilhelm before him, must surely have experienced some reluctance: it would have been safer and more efficient to obtain Germany's long-standing goals of empire without the costs and risks of war. And it is equally probable that the U.S. decision-makers are reluctantly bombing Vietnam: they would most likely prefer to exert their will in Southeast Asia without ruining the people and land of Vietnam and without war-induced domestic social and economic problems. As for the influence of chance, it should be obvious that in the absence of omniscience and omnipotence all of history in one sense consists of a series of accidents. Or as Trotsky, a firm believer in the existence of laws in history, observed, "The entire historical process is a refraction of historical law through the accidental." Faced with the reality of empire-building, as with any other recurring phenomenon in history, the analyst needs to discover, or try to understand, why, through the very operations of accident, history moves in one direction rather than another. One might even ask why some countries or social organisms are more accident-prone than others or why at certain times rather than at other times.

While it should go without saying that, given the shortcomings of astrology and the flaws in crytal balls, no one in 1947 could have foreseen the specific future configuration of U.S. global involvement, it is nevertheless essential to recognize that the polices and pressures that produced the U.S. drive to global hegemony were far from accidental and were in evidence long before 1947. In fact, the mainsprings of U.S. global strategy during the past quarter century had already taken shape well before World War II was over.[5] But even more important, the striving for empire stretches back to the earliest days of the republic, and even into colonial times.

"Man's character is his fate," said Heraclitus, the ancient Greek philosopher. The same may be said of nations. And the key to the character of the U.S. social organism which had determined its destiny—modified and adapted to be sure, in reaction to chance events and to complex historical forces—has been its persistent urge to expand. Taking the long view, Professor Van Alstyne in *The Rising American Empire* sees this urge as one of "direction and unbroken continuity in the history of the United States":

> The early colonies were no sooner established in the seventeenth century than expansionist impulses began to register in each of them. Imperial patterns took shape, and before the middle of the eighteenth century the concept of an empire that would take in the whole continent was fully formed. A drive south into the Spanish Caribbean was also in progress, with the ultimate goal in view of converting the Caribbean into an American lake. In the Revolution the spirit of conquest was a powerful force, and it took about a century thereafter to satisfy the territorial ambitions of the United States. Except for the internal dissension which was a constant factor during the first half of the nineteenth century, and which finally exploded into a civil war of vast proportions, it seems probable that these ambitions would have been pursued more persistently and energetically, that indeed they would have been pushed to the limit. But by the time of the Mexican War, the controversy between the North and South developed into an obsession; and further conquests became for the time being impossible. On the North American continent American expansion reached its maximum limits by 1867, the process of advance having been delayed long enough to enable the Canadians to develop the necessary counter-moves. The two related drives, south into the Caribbean and westward to China via Cape Horn, continued to the end of the century, when a burst of energy finished off the process in a war against Spain.[6]

While the focus of attention in U.S. history books is on continental expansion, the conquest of the Indians, and the acquisition of Mexican territory, they often overlook the fact that the so-called frontier was not only on land but on the seas as well, and that the absorption of the Far West was considerably influenced by desire to control the Pacific Ocean and thus to widen trading opportunities in Asia. The early United States was not only an agricultural but also a mercantile and seafaring society. This was especially so of the New England states, where a relative poverty of natural resources meant the lack of suitable agricultural or mineral export products that could be exchanged for European manufactures. The road to prosperity was found in commerce, bringing with it the dominance of a merchant class that spread its interests around the globe: not only in the rum-molasses trade with the West Indies, the marketing of African slaves, and the coastal traffic, but also in whaling, sealing, and trade (including opium) in the Pacific. To facilitate and expand this commerce, U.S. business firms spread to Asia during the earliest days of the Republic: "In the Pacific, Americans established themselves in the Sandwich Islands, 1787; Nootka Sound, 1788; Marquesas, 1791; Fanning, 1797; and Fiji, 1800. American interest in the North Pacific was in whale fisheries, which encouraged the start of an American settlement in Honolulu. The consul to Canton, Major Samuel Shaw, started the firm of Shaw & Randall in that city in 1786, only two years after the Chinese port had been opened to American trade."[7]

These commercial stakes in Asia may seem puny by today's standards, but not if judged in the perspective of the world economy in the eighteenth and early nineteenth centuries. For this spread into the Pacific, in addition to the Caribbean and the slave trade, spurred the emergence of a competitive merchant marine, a supportive navy, and the sort of trade that brought not only wealth to the merchant classes in North Atlantic ports but also nurtured the roots of eventual economic as well as political independence of the nation as a whole.

At the heart of the current economic underdevelopment of most Asian countries, as well as former colonies and semicolonies throughout the world, are the enormous economic and social distortions imposed by Western nations: the transfer of the traditional international trade of these countries into European bands and their eventual adaptation to serve as raw materials and food suppliers for the industrializing nations and as markets for their manufactured products. And it is in this respect that the history of the United States differs so strikingly from that of other colonial or ex-colonial territories. For, instead of becoming a victim of the colonial system, this country emerged at an early stage as an active participant and rival in seeking a share of the profits from the growing world commerce and the forcible opening up of new business opportunities in the non-Western world.

An important ingredient of U.S. ability to compete in the ever-widening sphere of imperialist influence was the attainment, for a variety of reasons, of a high degree of independence as a shipbuilder, trader, and shipper. This was the very opposite of the situation in the colonial areas which, at that time as well as in the future, were transformed into adjuncts of militarily superior powers, an outstanding characteristic of colonial and semicolonial countries being the concentration of import and export shipping in foreign hands. It is noteworthy that the ability of American merchants and shippers to compete with those of the mother country contributed significantly to the tensions and resulting struggle leading up to the final separation. In 1790, U.S.-owned ships already handled 59 percent of its foreign trade. By 1807 this proportion rose to 92 percent. The forward push to economic as well as political independence provided by the American Revolution was strengthened by the opportunities arising from the subsequent wars between European powers. Thus a large part of the shipping business at the end of the eighteenth century fell to U.S. entrepreneurs during the war years: "...several new routes, on which the profits were very high, developed during the war years. These were the trade in the Dutch East Indies, which first assumed significent proportions in 1797, and the China trade, frequently in conjunction with the fur trade of the American Northwest. The latter route was initiated in 1784, but expanded in the 1790s, when the United States became the major shipper of tea to Europe during the war."[8]

Trade, fishing, and shipping were only the initial nuclei of expansion. Traders became investors; missionaries discovered untold numbers of pagans; and the U.S. navy found steadily increasing duties as the protector of businessmen and missionaries in foreign lands, as explorer of new trade routes, and as opener of additional doors for commerce. (The U.S. Navy Pacific Squadron was organized in 1821, the East India Squadron in 1835. These were in addition to the Mediterranean, West India, and Brazil, or South Atlantic Squadrons during the early nineteenth century.)

There were thus two strands of empire-building: a maritime domain in addition to the better-known acquisition of land across the continent. These were often complementary and mutually supporting, rather than conflicting, movements. Such a complementary relationship manifested itself especially in the struggle for control of the Pacific coast. Jefferson and Adams both saw the Pacific Northwest "as the American window on the Pacific, the corridor across the continent which would give the United States the advantage of a direct route to the great trade routes of Asia."[9] As commercial relations with China grew and rivalry with Britain, Russia, and France for control of Pacific ports and trade routes mounted, ownership of the coastal ports (stretching down to San Francisco, Los Angeles, and San Diego) became an ever more urgent consideration in determining the boundaries the United States sought with Mexico and Canada.[10] Annexation of the coastal ports, however, did not mark the end of western expansion. They became, instead, safe harbors for the growing trade on the long and arduous route around Cape Horn to Asia, and home ports for the U.S. navy operating in the Pacific.

The road to empire in Asia was not built in a continuous and methodical fashion. It proceeded in fits and starts, tempered by competing demands on limited resources (e.g., for the Indian, Mexican, and Civil wars) and by constraints imposed by rival empire-seekers, most especially the British with their dominant navy during the nineteenth century and, beginning at the turn of the twentieth century, the expanding naval power of Japan. Still, the United States didn't miss too many opportunities—for example: taking advantage of Britain's breakthroughs (via the Opium Wars) to obtain treaty ports and extraterritorial rights in China; sending Commodore Perry to force open ports in Japan; pushing for special position in Korea; helping to put down the Boxer Rebellion; stretching U.S. frontiers northward to Alaska and the Aleutians, and westward to Hawaii, Midway, Samoa, Wake, Guam, and the Philippines; imposing the Open Door Policy, and continuing to enforce this policy with the use of the U.S. marines and by patrolling nearly 2,000 miles of the Yangtze River with gunboats.

Seen in this historical context, U.S. imperialist activities in Asia since World War II appear less as the result of a combination of accidents and more as the fruition under favorable circumstances of its long-standing imperial strivings. With Japan, the main Pacific rival, utterly defeated, with Russia, a potential rival, severely weakened, and with Great Britain lacking the resources to create the air force and aircraft carriers needed under modern conditions to dominate the Pacific, it was perfect weather for the United States to spread its sails. Obviously, the contraction of the world imperialist system due to the emergence of socialist systems and the threat of further contraction arising from spreading national liberation movements spurred U.S. interest and active involvement in Asia and other areas of the underdeveloped world. But there is no denying the continuous path of empire-building in Asia and elsewhere throughout U.S. history, independent of the "red menace."

It is important to understand that this expansionism is not the result of some mystical force inherent in the character of the American people. On the contrary, expansion was central to the evolving social system and its remarkable productivity and wealth. Expansion played a major role at each historical stage and helped to mold the resulting economic structure and the cultural environment—both of which reinforced the drive for further expansion. Enterprising capitalists, supported by an energetic state, kept pushing forward in the search for more opportunities for profit; in turn, each new frontier fired the ambition of restless businessmen and spurred the imagination of political leaders dreaming of national wealth and glory.

In interpreting this process of dynamic expansion it is important to recognize that the opportunities for capital formation and accumulation do not make their appearance in the smooth self-generating manner implicitly assumed in the neat mathematical models which economic theorists like to design. While such models may be useful in exploring the mechanisms of coordination which must be present in an anarchic economic system, they overlook certain crucial facts: (1) that such progress as actually does take place is never continuous and orderly, and (2) that unbalanced development is an integral, one might even say necessary, part of capitalist growth.

The most obvious feature of this spasmodic development is the alternating cycle of prosperity and depression. But perhaps more important for understanding the process of expansion are the longer waves in which periods of rapid growth are followed by slow and sluggish growth. Based on evidence for the United States since the 1830s, Professor Moses Abramovitz summarizes this phenomenon as follows:

> The economic growth of the United States has taken place in a series of surges during which growth was especially rapid, followed by relapses when growth proceeded much more slowly. In periods of rapid growth, output has increased at rates two, and often three, times as fast as in periods of slow growth.... The long waves in the rate of growth reflect similar waves in the rate of growth of resources, both labor and capital; in the rates of growth of productivity; and in the intensity with which resources are utilized.[11]

Underlying these phenomena—both the ordinary boombust cycle and the longer swings of alternating galloping and crawling growth—are certain essential characteristics of capitalist development: (1) The speed of growth and even the presence or absence of growth depend in the final analysis on the aggregate investment decisions of businessmen. (2) Capitalist enterprise inevitably entails taking risks, even risks that might end in total loss of invested capital. These risks are generally not incurred unless the odds are right, that is, unless the profit prospects are so encouraging that they far outweigh the danger of loss.

It should go without saying that capitalist societies thrive best when stimulated by exceptionally good profit opportunities, and especially so during waves of speculative fervor and "reasonable" inflation. But these favorable circumstances are not always present. They appear in clusters and are due to various causes, as, for example, a major technological innovation, an upsurge in urbanization, sudden access to new domestic and/or foreign markets, an arms buildup, or war and its aftermath. The impact of any one or a combination of these stimulants can propel the economy forward at a feverish pace. But the factors that induce accelerated growth have an inherent tendency to peter out. It is true that new opportunities for capital investment tend to have a cumulative effect, for they spur related lines of business activity and prolong boom times. But these stimulants are self-limiting. The main canals and railroad lines get completed; areas of settlement are occupied; competing nations encroach on new trade routes; the more independent foreign nations erect tariff walls. And running like a red thread through all the ups and downs of capitalist development is the fundamental paradox: the very process of capital accumulation (the primary engine of growth) generates an imbalance between consumer demand and the output resulting from capital investment; if profits are to be high enough to warrant the risks of enterprise, the flow of income to the mass of consumers must be limited.

So far it has been stressed that capitalist development is characterized both by "normal" business cycles and by longer waves of speedup and slowdown in the rate of growth. But these two kinds of fluctuations are not unrelated. During the longer upswings booms are strong and depressions weak, while the reverse is true during the long downswings. The latter are therefore periods of more or less continuous stagnation which threaten not only the economy but the health of the society as a whole. It is hence not surprising that it is precisely in these periods of stagnation (or slow growth) that new stimuli are sought, and that business and political leaders should be especially receptive to whatever opportunities for foreign expansion may present themselves—or may be created by those with the necessary imagination and daring. This is by no means the exclusive component of the expansionary urge. Other pressures keep coming up, ranging over the centuries—from land speculators promoting acquisition and settlement of new territory; to merchants, farmers, and manufacturers seeking new markets; to monopoly firms desiring control over their sources of raw materials and privileged market conditions. The cause is advanced, and sometimes initiated, by daring, farsighted political and ambitious military chiefs who foster expansion for the sake of their own "personal politics," their notions of patriotism, or their vision of what is needed to increase the power and wealth of their country.

But with all this, it is still important to recognize that these policies are arrived at in a capitalist environment that time and again is faced with the need for stimulants to rev up the engine. The stimulants pounced upon are not always effective; they frequently fail to produce all the hoped-for results. Moreover, domestic political strife may emerge over the choice of strategy and tactics concerning the mode, pace, and geographic concentration of expansion as well as over the preferred method of exercising influence and control—differences that may reflect variations in judgment and/or interpretation of self-interest. But in light of the limited alternatives available for stimulating growth in a profit-oriented society, and the pressure to cope with competing nations also confined to similar limited alternatives and hence pursuing analogous policies, the road to empire becomes well trodden.

It is not uncommon for traditional historians and economists to ridicule the notion that the foreign policies of capitalist powers are strongly influenced by stagnation or the threat of stagnation. Thus, in dealing with the burst of U.S. imperialist expansion at the end of the nineteenth century, they point to the great internal growth of the United States during the twentieth century as proof that there had been plenty of outlets for domestic savings in the last quarter of the nineteenth century. The weakness of this approach is that it interprets history unhistorically. The capitalists and politicians of the 1890s may have dreamed about their country's great and glorious future, but their urgent task was to deal with the present. They may even have made stimulating commencement-day addresses about the country's youth and potential for development, but what faced them the day after commencement was the threat of business failure against the backdrop of repetitive depressions. One of the longest depressions in U.S. business history lasted from October 1873 to March 1879. Indeed, about half the years in the last quarter of the nineteenth century were years of depression.

The point is that theoretical economists and historians do not make decisions about how the nation's savings are to be disposed of. Such decisions are made by practical business people who are very alert to the profit-and-loss potential of opportunities actually available to them. Furthermore, the professorial hindsight that can now identify the enormous investment outlets which materialized in the twentieth century has a way of overlooking the extent to which the Spanish-American War and the subsequent two world wars contributed to the creation of these enlarged domestic investment opportunities.

Just as many economic and other historians are still perplexed by what seems to them the narrow-mindedness and lack of vision of those who masterminded the burst of U.S. imperialist activity in Latin American and Asia at the close of the nineteenth century, so there are now many who have little appreciation of the impact of the depression of the 1930s on the decision-makers before, during, and after World War II. Once again hindsight calls attention to the very substantial growth of the postwar period and casts doubt on the judgment of those in the thirties and forties who had so little faith. It may therefore be worthwhile to review the dimensions of the dilemma of those years. Just to get a sense of what was at stake, let us look at the fluctuations in the production of steel—an indispensable input for the construction, machinery, autos, and other consumer goods, and armaments industries.

Steel Ingots and Castings Produced (millions of long tons)

Year		Year	
1929	56.4	1944	80.0
1932	13.7	1946	59.5
1937	50.7	1948	79.1
1938	28.3	1949	69.6
1939	47.1	1950	86.5
1941	74.0		

Source: *Historical Statistics of the United States: Colonial Times to 1957* (Washington, D.C.: U.S. Bureau of the Census, 1960), p. 416.

The most striking change, of course, is the drastic drop from 1929 to 1932, with production in 1932 less than one-fourth the previous high. This decline reflects the extent of the crisis in the users of steel. Not all production went down so precipitously, but this kind of contraction was typical of the machinery and construction industries. Thus, residential construction, measured in 1947–1949 prices, slid from $11.6 billion in its peak year of 1926 to $1.7 billion in 1932. Despite the efforts of the New Deal, the recovery reached in 1937 still did not create a demand for steel as high as that of 1929. And this recovery, as can be seen in the figure for 1938, was at best a shaky one. Ten years of depression, during which population and labor productivity kept increasing, left steel production still considerably below 1929. The so-called domestic outlets for savings were surely there, but only on paper. As far as the business community was concerned, there was no point in speculating on the profitability of these theoretical domestic outlets. It was only in 1941 that steel output shot ahead—in response to the war needs of Europe and the heavy armaments program undertaken by the United States in view of the probability that it would soon participate in World War II.

There is no intention here to draw the inference that the United States went to war, or encouraged others to go to war, as a crisis-remedy; the issues are much more complex. But what is important and too often neglected is that the depth and persistence of depression, the apparent inability of the system to snap out of its illness either through a so-called normal recovery or acceptable government measures, dominated all policy-making in those years.

Opinions differed strongly on the proper road to eventual full recovery, but the range of policy recommendations was necessarily limited, since the choice had to remain within the conditions imposed by capitalist economics. For example, only when mobilization for war, and more especially the war itself, imposed its priorities on the system did the American people get fed more or less properly and the agricultural surpluses disappear. Surplus food and the potential for producing even more food were both present throughout the depression. But it took the mobilization of twelve million men and women into the armed forces, led by the government, and full employment of the remaining civilian population, made possible by a war-directed economy, to generate the income flows and effective demand that wiped out plaguing agricultural surpluses. Short of war, the policy alternatives had been limited to methods of restimulating market demand. But, since domestic markets proved time and again to be too sluggish either to feed the population or to stimulate business enterprise growth, the capture of foreign markets (including the issue of how to handle the closing down of market opportunities by aggressive rival powers) necessarily rose on the list of policy priorities.

Despite the lift to the U.S. economy given by the war, the experience of the depression and fear of recurrence of stagnation weighed heavily on postwar policy-making. It was clear at the end of the war that the economy was ripe for a new and significant upturn. This optimism was, however, moderated by uncertainty over how long the recovery would last, along with grave doubts about the ability of the private economy to generate enough jobs for the vast number of returning servicemen. The way the war had been financed created large reserves of cash throughout the economy; workers, perhaps for the first time in history, had substantial savings accounts, and veterans' benefits added additional temporary stimuli. At the same time, the backlog of consumer demand was extraordinary, piled up after a long drought of housing construction and some five years of almost no new civilian passenger-car production. Yet, despite the omens of a new wave of prosperity, the economy began to turn down only three years after the war. As can be seen in the above table, steel production in 1949 fell back to below the 1941 prewar high. While the first postwar decline was short lived, and the recovery reinforced on the way up by the Korean War and a new wave of military spending, the experience nevertheless reconfirmed the dangers of stagnation.

It was against the still vivid background of a prolonged depression and an accompanying breakdown of world financial and commercial markets that the United States sought to reconstitute a postwar world order. To reap the potential profits made possible by the war-created deferred demand, industrialists would need to invest vast sums to quickly create new capacity. The temptations (and the competitive pressure) for such expansion were great, but so was the fear, supported by the recollection of the recent 1930s, that the mouth-watering profit prospects might be transformed into devastating losses just as soon as the effects of the proposed demand wore off. Added assurance of long-term growth was needed to justify the risk of spiraling new investment. This was in the cards if the potential foreign markets could also be tapped. But in order to convert the potential into effective and sustained demand it was necessary to restore the health of traditional trading partners, to overcome the limitations imposed by the dollar and gold shortage outside the United States, and to replace the complex national trade, exchange, and investment barriers that had been erected in self-defense during the depression. The methods adopted to solve these problems fitted in admirably with the long-run striving for hegemony in the capitalist world, reaching fruition as the U.S. dollar became the key currency in foreign trade and New York the hub of world banking and the international money market. The components of the new capitalist world order, built on the ruins of war and the disruption of the preceding protracted economic crisis, fell into place like the pieces of a jigsaw puzzle, influenced by the long history of U.S. empire-building, the ever-present threat of stagnation, the U.S. emergence from the war as the unquestioned dominant military and economic power, and the revolutionary upsurge in the colonial world.

The postwar world economic, financial, and political system erected after World War II is under special stress these days as the United States, its designer and leader, exposes its feet of clay. The inability to suppress the revolution in South Vietnam, the quaking of the world financial system, originally based on the inviolability of the dollar, and the thrust of rival powers, notably Japan and Germany, to attain more competitive and independent positions vis-à-vis the United States—these are all signs of a transition to a new stage. These changes, however, do not as yet portend an alteration of fundamentals: both the struggle for hegemony in Asia and the basic social problems of the underdeveloped countries are still with us and will continue to be for the visible future.

To understand developments in the American Empire and, looming on the horizon, the Japanese Empire in Asia, one must comprehend the basic contradictions in the opportunities for development of the subordinate countries, whether or not they formerly had the status of colonies. Neither the transfer of advanced technology nor injections of foreign aid has succeeded in shaking them out of the morass of poverty, persistent mass unemployment, and misery. They are stuck on the capitalist road, but the options that had been available to the successful capitalist countries in past centuries—options which helped pull them out of impending, recurrent periods of stagnation—are out of the question. Conquest of territory, providing new surges of investment, is impossible. Nor is there, as in the past, the opportunity to dispose, in new areas of settlement, of surplus populations generated by the agricultural and industrial revolutions. At the same time, the economic and financial structure shaped by a long and continuing history of dependence on the more advanced capitalisms, imposes additional limits on the possibility of bootstrap-lifting via the route of profit-seeking capital investment.

It is hard to avoid the conclusion that, more and more, the only real alternative facing these peoples is whether to accept their lot of misery and its accompanying wastage of human lives or to revolutionize their societies so that labor can be fully utilized to begin to meet the real needs of the people.

Notes

This was originally written as an Introduction to Mark Selden, ed., *Remaking Asia: Essays on the American Uses of Power* (New York: Pantheon, 1974). It also appeared in the January 1974 issue of *Monthly Review.*

1. J. R. Seeley, *The Expansion of England* (London: Macmillan, 1883), p. 8.
2. D. K. Fieldhouse, *The Colonial Empires: A Comparative Survey, from the Eighteenth Century* (London: Weidenfeld & Nicolson, 1966), p. 239.
3. Marvin Kalb and Elie Abel, *Roots of Involvement: The U.S. in Asia 1784–1971* (New York: W. W. Norton,

1971). The theme of reluctance is one of the most pervasive explanations found in histories of colonialism. A characteristic example, in this case referring to South Africa, is the following:

> The border... remained too thinly settled to provide real protection; the area instead became an irresistible attraction to Bantu cattle rustlers with grievances against the newcomers. Settlers and tribesmen could not be kept apart; both moved to and fro across the boundary. Governments then tried to enforce security by more advanced lines of demarcation, but each new boundary further compressed the territory of the indigenous tribes and ultimately led to further conflicts, with the result that the imperial power, regardless of its original intentions, reluctantly kept adding to its commitments.

(L. H. Gann and Peter Duignan, *Burden of Empire: An Appraisal of Western Colonialism in Africa South of the Sahara* [New York: Praeger, 1967], p. 19)

4. Ronald Steel, *Pax Americana* (New York: Viking Press, 1968), pp. 10–11.
5. This theme is thoroughly explored in two valuable studies: Gabriel Kolko, *The Politics of War: The World and United States Foreign Policy, 1943–1945* (New York: Random House, 1969), and Joyce and Gabriel Kolko, *The Limits of Power: The World and United States Foreign Policy, 1945–1954* (New York: Harper & Row, 1972).
6. R. W. Van Alstyne, *The Rising American Empire* (Chicago: Quadrangle Books, 1965), p. v.
7. Mira Wilkins, *The Emergence of Multinational Enterprise: American Business Abroad from the Colonial Era to 1914* (Cambridge, Mass.: Harvard University Press, 1970), p. 7.
8. The quotation as well as the preceding percentages are from Douglas C. North, *The Economic Growth of the United States, 1790–1860* (Englewood Cliffs, New Jersey: Prentice-Hall, 1961), pp. 41–42.
9. Van Alstyne, *The Rising American Empire*, p. 93.
10. Professor Graebner puts the case forcefully:

> What [the] traditional approaches overlook is the essential fact that the expansion of the United States was a unified, purposeful, precise movement that was ever limited to specific maritime objectives. It was the Pacific Ocean that determined the territorial goals of all American presidents from John Quiney Adams to Polk. From the beginning, travelers, traders, and officials who concerned themselves with the coastal regions had their eyes trained on ports. The goal of American policy was to control the great harbors of San Francisco, San Diego, and Juan de Fuca Strait.... But mercantile interests in the Pacific proved more than a contributing motive to American expansionism. They determined the course of empire. Maritime calculations first defined the objectives of American statesmen on the distant shore. Next, they augmented the strong inclination of British and American officials to seek a peaceful solution to the Oregon controversy. And, finally, they fused Oregon and California into one irreducible issue and created a vision of empire that encompassed both regions. The sea made the settlement of the Oregon question contingent upon the acquisition of California in the fulfillment of the American purpose.

(Norman A. Graebner, *Empire on the Pacific: A Study in American Continental Expansion* [New York: Ronald Press, 1955], p. vi)

11. *Hearings before the Joint Economic Committee, Congress of the United States, Employment, Growth and Price Levels*, Part 2, April 7–10, 1959 (Washington, D.C.: Government Printing Office, 1959), p. 412.

Anarchy Is What States Make of It: The Social Construction of Power Politics

ALEXANDER WENDT

Like Hans Morgenthau for Realism, Alexander Wendt is often the first name that IR scholars mention when they discuss the Constructivist perspective on the study of the field. Wendt's argument is deceptively simple: how we perceive global politics is often the result of what words we use to describe events. How does Wendt structure his argument? What examples does he use to illustrate his assertions? Can you think of counter-arguments to the Constructivist lens? For instance, is the notion of "power" a constant in global politics?

Anarchy and Power Politics

Classical realists such as Thomas Hobbes, Reinhold Niebuhr, and Hans Morgenthau attributed egoism and power politics primarily to human nature, whereas structural realists or neorealists emphasize anarchy. The difference stems in part from different interpretations of anarchy's causal powers. Kenneth Waltz's work is important for both. In *Man, the State, and War,* he defines anarchy as a condition of possibility for or "permissive" cause of war, arguing that "wars occur because there is nothing to prevent them."[1] It is the human nature or domestic politics of predator states, however, that provide the initial impetus or "efficient" cause of conflict which forces other states to respond in kind.[2] Waltz is not entirely consistent about this, since he slips without justification from the permissive causal claim that in anarchy war is always possible to the active causal claim that "war may at any moment occur."[3] But despite Waltz's concluding call for third-image theory, the efficient causes that initialize anarchic systems are from the first and second images. This is reversed in Waltz's *Theory of International Politics,* in which first- and second-image theories are spurned as "reductionist," and the logic of anarchy seems by itself to constitute self-help and power politics as necessary features of world politics.[4]

This is unfortunate, since whatever one may think of first- and second-image theories, they have the virtue of implying that practices determine the character of anarchy. In the permissive view, only if human or domestic factors cause A to attack B will B have to defend itself. Anarchies may contain dynamics that lead to competitive power politics, but they also may not, and we can argue about when particular structures of identity and interest will emerge. In neorealism, however, the role of

Alexander Wendt, "Anarchy is What States Make of It: The Social Construction of Power Politics," *International Organization*, 46:2 (Spring, 1992), pp. 391–425.

practice in shaping the character of anarchy is substantially reduced, and so there is less about which to argue: self-help and competitive power politics are simply given exogenously by the structure of the state system.

Anarchy, self-help, and intersubjective knowledge

Waltz defines political structure on three dimensions: ordering principles (in this case, anarchy), principles of differentiation (which here drop out), and the distribution of capabilities.[5] By itself, this definition predicts little about state behavior. It does not predict whether two states will be friends or foes, will recognize each other's sovereignty, will have dynastic ties, will be revisionist or status quo powers, and so on. These factors, which are fundamentally intersubjective, affect states' security interests and thus the character of their interaction under anarchy. Self-help is one such intersubjective structure and, as such, does the decisive explanatory work in the theory. The question is whether self-help is a logical or contingent feature of anarchy.

A fundamental principle of constructivist social theory is that people act toward objects, including other actors, on the basis of the meanings that the objects have for them.[6] States act differently toward enemies than they do toward friends because enemies are threatening and friends are not. Anarchy and the distribution of power are insufficient to tell us which is which. U.S. military power has a different significance for Canada than for Cuba, despite their similar "structural" positions, just as British missiles have a different significance for the United States than do Soviet missiles. The distribution of power may always affect states' calculations, but how it does so depends on the intersubjective understandings and expectations, on the "distribution of knowledge," that constitute their conceptions of self and other.[7] If society "forgets" what a university is, the powers and practices of professor and student cease to exist; if the United States and Soviet Union decide that they are no longer enemies, "the cold war is over." It is collective meanings that constitute the structures which organize our actions.

Actors acquire identities—relatively stable, role-specific understandings and expectations about self—by participating in such collective meanings.[8] Identities are inherently relational: "Identity, with its appropriate attachments of psychological reality, is always identity within a specific, socially constructed world," Peter Berger argues.[9] Each person has many identities linked to institutional roles, such as brother, son, teacher, and citizen. Similarly, a state may have multiple identities as "sovereign," "leader of the free world," "imperial power," and so on.[10] The commitment to and the salience of particular identities vary, but each identity is an inherently social definition of the actor grounded in the theories which actors collectively hold about themselves and one another and which constitute the structure of the social world.

Identities are the basis of interests. Actors do not have a "portfolio" of interests that they carry around independent of social context; instead, they define their interests in the process of defining situations.[11] More often they have routine qualities in which we assign meanings on the basis of institutionally defined roles. When we say that professors have an "interest" in teaching, research, or going on leave, we are saying that to function in the role identity of "professor," they have to define certain situations as calling for certain actions. This does not mean that they will necessarily do so (expectations and competence do not equal performance), but if they do not, they will not get tenure. The absence or failure of roles makes defining situations and interests more difficult, and identity confusion may result. This seems to be happening today in the United States and the former Soviet Union: without the cold war's mutual attributions of threat and hostility to define their identities, these states seem unsure of what their "interests" should be.

An institution is a relatively stable set or "structure" of identities and interests. Such structures are often codified in formal rules and norms, but these have motivational force only in virtue of actors' socialization to and participation in collective knowledge. Institutions are fundamentally cognitive entities that do not exist apart from actors' ideas about how the world works.[12] This does not mean that institutions are not real or objective, that they are "nothing but" beliefs. As collective knowledge, they are experienced as having an existence "over and above the individuals who happen to embody them at the moment."[13] In this way, institutions come to confront individuals as more or less coercive social facts, but they are still a function of what actors collectively "know." Identities and such collective cognitions do not exist apart from each other; they are "mutually constitutive."[14] On this view, institutionalization is a process of internalizing new identities and interests, not something occurring outside them and affecting only behavior; socialization is a cognitive process, not just a behavioral one. Conceived in this way, institutions may be cooperative or conflictual, a point sometimes lost in scholarship on international regimes, which tends to equate institutions with cooperation. There are important differences between conflictual and cooperative institutions to be sure, but all relatively stable self-other relations—even those of "enemies"—are defined intersubjectively.

Self-help is an institution, one of various structures of identity and interest that may exist under anarchy. Processes of identity-formation under anarchy are concerned first and foremost with preservation or "security" of the self. Concepts of security therefore differ in the extent to which and the manner in which the self is identified cognitively with the other,[15] and, I want to suggest, it is upon this cognitive variation that the meaning of anarchy and the distribution of power depends. Let me illustrate with a standard continuum of security systems.[16]

At one end is the "competitive" security system, in which states identify negatively with each other's security so that ego's gain is seen as alter's loss. Negative identification under anarchy constitutes systems of "realist" power politics: risk-averse actors that infer intentions from capabilities and worry about relative gains and losses. At the limit—in the Hobbesian war of all against all—collective action is nearly impossible in such a system because each actor must constantly fear being stabbed in the back.

In the middle is the "individualistic" security system, in which states are indifferent to the relationship between their own and others' security. This constitutes "neoliberal" systems: states are still self-regarding about their security but are concerned primarily with absolute gains rather than relative gains. One's position in the distribution of power is less important, and collective action is more possible (though still subject to free riding because states continue to be "egoists").

Competitive and individualistic systems are both "self-help" forms of anarchy in the sense that states do not positively identify the security of self with that of others but instead treat security as the individual responsibility of each. Given the lack of a positive cognitive identification on the basis of which to build security regimes, power politics within such systems will necessarily consist of efforts to manipulate others to satisfy self-regarding interests.

This contrasts with the "cooperative" security system, in which states identify positively with one another so that the security of each is perceived as the responsibility of all. This is not self-help in any interesting sense, since the "self" in terms of which interests are defined is the community; national interests are international interests.[17] In practice, of course, the extent to which states' identification with the community varies, from the limited form found in "concerts" to the full-blown form seen in "collective security" arrangements.[18] Depending on how well developed the collective self is, it will produce security practices that are in varying degrees altruistic or prosocial. This makes collective action less dependent on the presence of active threats and less prone to free riding.[19] Moreover, it restructures efforts to advance one's objectives, or "power politics," in terms of shared norms rather than relative power.[20]

On this view, the tendency in international relations scholarship to view power and institutions as two opposing explanations of foreign policy is therefore misleading, since anarchy and the distribution of power only have meaning for state action in virtue of the understandings and expectations that constitute institutional identities and interests. Self-help is one such institution, constituting one kind of anarchy but not the only kind. Waltz's three-part definition of structure therefore seems underspecified. In order to go from structure to action, we need to add a fourth: the intersubjectively constituted structure of identities and interests in the system.

This has an important implication for the way in which we conceive of states in the state of nature before their first encounter with each other. Because states do not have conceptions of self and other, and thus security interests, apart from or prior to interaction, we assume too much about the state of nature if we concur with Waltz that, in virtue of anarchy, "international political systems, like economic markets, are formed by the coaction of self-regarding units."[21] We also assume too much if we argue that, in virtue of anarchy, states in the state of nature necessarily face a "stag hunt" or "security dilemma."[22] These claims presuppose a history of interaction in which actors have acquired "selfish" identities and interests; before interaction (and still in abstraction from first- and second-image factors) they would have no experience upon which to base such definitions of self and other. To assume otherwise is to attribute to states in the state of nature qualities that they can only possess in society.[23] Self-help is an institution, not a constitutive feature of anarchy.

What, then, *is* a constitutive feature of the state of nature before interaction? Two things are left if we strip away those properties of the self which presuppose interaction with others. The first is the material substrate of agency, including its intrinsic capabilities. For human beings, this is the body; for states, it is an organizational apparatus of governance. In effect, I am suggesting for rhetorical purposes that the raw material out of which members of the state system are constituted is created by domestic society before states enter the constitutive process of international society,[24] although this process implies neither stable territoriality nor sovereignty, which are internationally negotiated terms of individuality (as discussed further below). The second is a desire to preserve this material substrate, to survive. This does not entail "self-regardingness," however, since actors do not have a self prior to interaction with an other; how they view the meaning and requirements of this survival therefore depends on the processes by which conceptions of self evolve.

This may all seem very arcane, but there is an important issue at stake: are the foreign policy identities and interests of states exogenous or endogenous to the state system? The former is the answer of an individualistic or undersocialized systemic theory for which rationalism is appropriate; the latter is the answer of a fully socialized systemic theory. Waltz seems to offer the latter and proposes two mechanisms, competition and socialization, by which structure conditions state action.[25] The content of his argument about this conditioning, however, presupposes a self-help system that is not itself a constitutive feature of anarchy.

Anarchy and the social construction of power politics

If self-help is not a constitutive feature of anarchy, it must emerge causally from processes in which anarchy plays only a permissive role.[26] This reflects a second principle of constructivism: that the meanings in terms of which action is organized arise out of interaction.[27] This being said, however, the situation facing states as they encounter one another for the first time may be such that only self-regarding conceptions of identity can survive; if so, even if these conceptions are socially constructed, neorealists may be right in holding identities and interests constant and thus in privileging one particular meaning of anarchic structure over process.

Consider two actors—ego and alter—encountering each other for the first time.[28] Each wants to survive and has certain material capabilities, but neither actor has biological or domestic imperatives for power, glory, or conquest, and there is no history of security or insecurity between the two. What should they do? Realists would probably argue that each should act on the basis of worst-case assumptions about the other's intentions, justifying such an attitude as prudent in view of the possibility of death from making a mistake. Such a possibility always exists, even in civil society; however, society would be impossible if people made decisions purely on the basis of worst-case possibilities. Instead, most decisions are and should be made on the basis of probabilities, and these are produced by interaction, by what actors *do*.

In the beginning is ego's gesture, which may consist, for example, of an advance, a retreat, a brandishing of arms, a laying down of arms, or an attack.[29] For ego, this gesture represents the basis on which it is prepared to respond to alter. This basis is unknown to alter, however, and so it must make an inference or "attribution" about ego's intentions and, in particular, given that this is anarchy, about whether ego is a threat.[30] The content of this inference will largely depend on two considerations. The first is the gesture's and ego's physical qualities, which are in part contrived by ego and which include the direction of movement, noise, numbers, and immediate consequences of the gesture.[31] The second consideration concerns what alter would intend by such qualities were it to make such a gesture itself. Alter may make an attributional "error" in its inference about ego's intent, but there is also no reason for it to assume a priori—before the gesture—that ego is threatening, since it is only through a process of signaling and interpreting that the costs and probabilities of being wrong can be determined.[32] Social threats are constructed, not natural.

Consider an example. Would we assume, a priori, that we were about to be attacked if we are ever contacted by members of an alien civilization? I think not. We would be highly alert, of course, but whether we placed our military forces on alert or launched an attack would depend on how we interpreted the import of their first gesture for our security—if only to avoid making an immediate enemy out of what may be a dangerous adversary. The possibility of error, in other words, does not force us to act on the assumption that the aliens are threatening: action depends on the probabilities we assign, and these are in key part a function of what the aliens do; prior to their gesture, we have no systemic basis for assigning probabilities. If their first gesture is to appear with a thousand spaceships and destroy New York, we will define the situation as threatening and respond accordingly. But if they appear with one spaceship, saying what seems to be "we come in peace," we will feel "reassured" and will probably respond with a gesture intended to reassure them, even if this gesture is not necessarily interpreted by them as such.[33]

This process of signaling, interpreting, and responding completes a "social act" and begins the process of creating intersubjective meanings. It advances the same way. The first social act creates expectations on both sides about each other's future behavior: potentially mistaken and certainly tentative, but expectations nonetheless. Based on this tentative knowledge, ego makes a new gesture, again signifying the basis on which it will respond to alter, and again alter responds, adding to the pool of knowledge each has about the other, and so on over time. The mechanism here is reinforcement; interaction rewards actors for holding certain ideas about each other and discourages them from holding others. If repeated long enough, these "reciprocal typifications" will create relatively stable concepts of self and other regarding the issue at stake in the interaction.[34]

The simple overall model of identity- and interest-formation proposed in Figure 1 applies to competitive institutions no less than to cooperative ones. Self-help security systems evolve from cycles of interaction in which each party acts in ways that the other feels are threatening to the self, creating expectations that the other is not to be trusted. Competitive or egoistic identities are caused by such insecurity; if the other is threatening, the self is forced to "mirror" such behavior in its conception of the self's relationship to that other.[35] Being treated as an object for the gratification of others precludes the positive identification with others necessary for collective security; conversely, being treated by others in ways that are empathic with respect to the security of the self permits such identification.[36]

Competitive systems of interaction are prone to security "dilemmas," in which the efforts of actors to enhance their security unilaterally threatens the security of the others, perpetuating distrust and alienation. The forms of identity and interest that constitute such dilemmas, however, are themselves ongoing effects of, not exogenous to, the interaction; identities are produced in and through "situated activity."[37] We do not *begin* our relationship with the aliens in a security dilemma; security dilemmas are not given by anarchy or nature. Of course, once institutionalized such a dilemma may be hard to change (I return to this below), but the point remains: identities and interests are constituted by collective meanings that are always in process. If states find themselves in a self-help system,

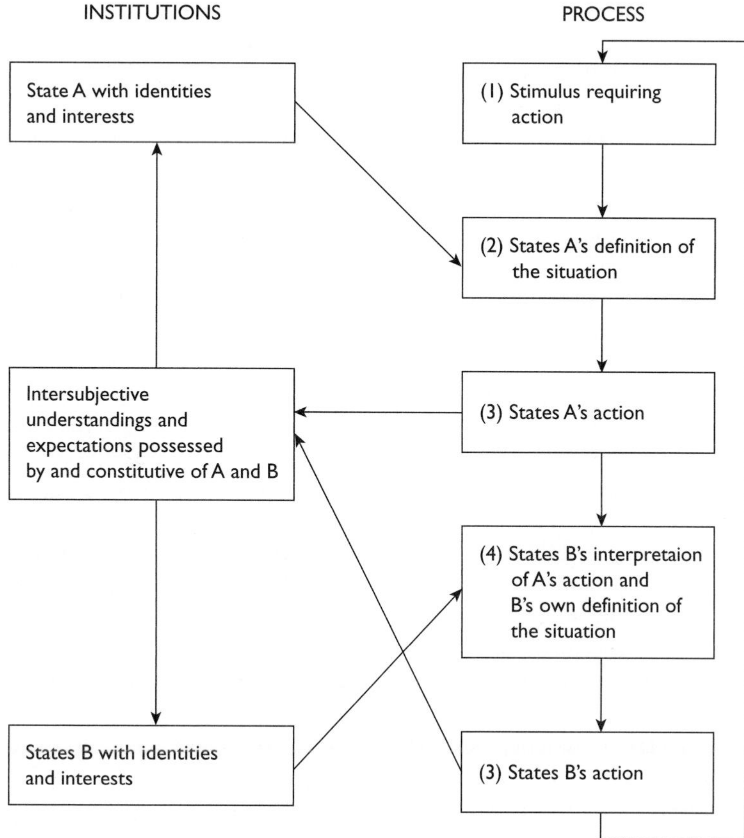

Figure 1. The Codetermination of Institutions and Process

this is because their practices made it that way. Changing the practices will change the intersubjective knowledge that constitutes the system.

Predator states and anarchy as permissive cause

The mirror theory of identity-formation is a crude account of how the process of creating identities and interests might work, but it does not tell us why a system of states—such as, arguably, our own—would have ended up with self-regarding and not collective identities. In this section, I examine an efficient cause, predation, which, in conjunction with anarchy as a permissive cause, may generate a self-help system. In so doing, however, I show the key role that the structure of identities and interests plays in mediating anarchy's explanatory role.

The predator argument is straightforward and compelling. For whatever reasons—biology, domestic politics, or systemic victimization—some states may become predisposed toward aggression. The aggressive behavior of these predators or "bad apples" forces other states to engage in competitive power politics, to meet fire with fire, since failure to do so may degrade or destroy them. One predator will best a hundred pacifists because anarchy provides no guarantees. This argument is powerful in part because it is so weak: rather than making the strong assumption that all states are inherently power-seeking (a purely reductionist theory of power politics), it assumes that just one is power-seeking and that the others have to follow suit because anarchy permits the one to exploit them.

In making this argument, it is important to reiterate that the possibility of predation does not in itself force states to anticipate it a priori with competitive power politics of their own. The possibility of predation does not mean that "war may at any moment occur"; it may in fact be extremely unlikely. Once a predator emerges, however, it may condition identity- and interest-formation in the following manner.

In an anarchy of two, if ego is predatory, alter must either define its security in self-help terms or pay the price. If predation occurs right after the first encounter in the state of nature, it will force others with whom it comes in contact to defend themselves, first individually and then collectively *if* they come to perceive a common threat. The emergence of such a defensive alliance will be seriously inhibited if the structure of identities and interests has already evolved into a Hobbesian world of maximum insecurity, since potential allies will strongly distrust each other and face intense collective action problems; such insecure allies are also more likely to fall out amongst themselves once the predator is removed. If collective security identity is high, however, the emergence of a predator may do much less damage. If the predator attacks any member of the collective, the latter will come to the victim's defense on the principle of "all for one, one for all," even if the predator is not presently a threat to other members of the collective. If the predator is not strong enough to withstand the collective, it will be defeated and collective security will obtain. But if it is strong enough, the logic of the two-actor case (now predator and collective) will activate, and balance-of-power politics will reestablish itself.

The timing of the emergence of predation relative to the history of identity-formation in the community is therefore crucial to anarchy's explanatory role as a permissive cause. Predation will always lead victims to defend themselves, but whether defense will be collective or not depends on the history of interaction within the potential collective as much as on the ambitions of the predator. Identities and interests are relationship-specific, not intrinsic attributes of a "portfolio"; states may be competitive in some relationships and solidary in others. "Mature" anarchies are less likely than "immature" ones to be reduced by predation to a Hobbesian condition, and maturity, which is a proxy for structures of identity and interest, is a function of process.[38]

The source of predation also matters. If it stems from unit-level causes that are immune to systemic impacts (causes such as human nature or domestic politics taken in isolation), then it functions in a manner analogous to a "genetic trait" in the constructed world of the state system. Even if successful, this trait does not select for other predators in an evolutionary sense so much as it teaches other states to respond in kind, but since traits cannot be unlearned, the other states will continue competitive behavior until the predator is either destroyed or transformed from within. However, in the more likely event that predation stems at least in part from prior systemic interaction—perhaps as a result of being victimized in the past (one thinks here of Nazi Germany or the Soviet Union)—then it is more a response to a learned identity and, as such, might be transformed by future social interaction in the form of appeasement, reassurances that security needs will be met, systemic effects on domestic politics, and so on. In this case, in other words, there is more hope that process can transform a bad apple into a good one.

The role of predation in generating a self-help system, then, is consistent with a systematic focus on process. Even if the source of predation is entirely exogenous to the system, it is what states *do* that determines the quality of their interactions under anarchy. In this respect, it is not surprising that it is classical realists rather than structural realists who emphasize this sort of argument. The former's emphasis on unit-level causes of power politics leads more easily to a permissive view of anarchy's explanatory role (and therefore to a processual view of international relations) than does the latter's emphasis on anarchy as a "structural cause";[39] neorealists do not need predation because the system is given as self-help.

Notes

1. Kenneth Waltz, *Man, the State, and War* (New York: Columbia University Press, 1959), p. 232.
2. Ibid., pp. 169–70.
3. Ibid., p. 232. This point is made by Hidemi Suganami in "Bringing Order to the Causes of War Debates," *Millennium* 19 (Spring 1990), p. 34, fn. 11.

4. Kenneth Waltz, *Theory of International Politics* (Boston: Addison-Wesley, 1979).
5. Waltz, *Theory of International Politics*, pp. 79–101.
6. See, for example, Herbert Blumer, "The Methodological Position of Symbolic Interactionism," in his *Symbolic Interactionism: Perspective and Method* (Englewood Cliffs, N.J.: Prentice-Hall, 1969), p. 2 Throughout this article, I assume that a theoretically productive analogy can be made between individuals and states. There are at least two justifications for this anthropomorphism. Rhetorically, the analogy is an accepted practice in mainstream international relations discourse, and since this article is an immanent rather than external critique, it should follow the practice. Substantively, states are collectivities of individuals that through their practices constitute each other as "persons" having interests, fears, and so on. A full theory of state identity-and interest-formation would nevertheless need to draw insights from the social psychology of groups and organizational theory, and for that reason my anthropomorphism is merely suggestive.
7. The phrase "distribution of knowledge" is Barry Barnes's, as discussed in his work *The Nature of Power* (Cambridge: Polity Press, 1988); see also Peter Berger and Thomas Luckmann, *The Social Construction of Reality* (New York: Anchor Books, 1966). The concern of recent international relations scholarship on "epistemic communities" with the cause-and-effect understandings of the world held by scientists, experts, and policymakers is an important aspect of the role of knowledge in world politics; see Peter Haas, "Do Regimes Matter? Epistemic Communities and Mediterranean Pollution Control," *International Organization* 43 (Summer 1989), pp. 377–404; and Ernst Haas, *When Knowledge Is Power.* My constructivist approach would merely add to this an equal emphasis on how such knowledge also *constitutes* the structures and subjects of social life.
8. For an excellent short statement of how collective meanings constitute identities, see Peter Berger, "Identity as a Problem in the Sociology of Knowledge," *European Journal of Sociology*, vol. 7, no. 1, 1966, pp. 32–40. See also David Morgan and Michael Schwalbe, "Mind and Self in Society: Linking Social Structure and Social Cognition," *Social Psychology Quarterly* 53 (June 1990), pp. 148–64. In my discussion, I draw on the following interactionist texts: George Herbert Mead, *Mind, Self, and Society* (Chicago: University of Chicago Press, 1934); Berger and Luckmann, *The Social Construction of Reality;* Sheldon Stryker, *Symbolic Interactionism: A Social Structural Version* (Menlo Park, Calif.: Benjamin/Cummings, 1980); R. S. Perinbanayagam, *Signifying Acts: Structure and Meaning in Everyday Life* (Carbondale: Southern Illinois University Press, 1985); John Hewitt, *Self and Society: A Symbolic Interactionist Social Psychology* (Boston: Allyn & Bacon, 1988); and Turner, *A Theory of Social Interaction.* Despite some differences, much the same points are made by structurationists such as Bhaskar and Giddens. See Roy Bhaskar, *The Possibility of Naturalism* (Atlantic Highlands, N.J.: Humanities Press, 1979); and Anthony Giddens, *Central Problems in Social Theory* (Berkeley: University of California Press, 1979).
9. Berger, "Identity as a Problem in the Sociology of Knowledge," p. 111.
10. While not normally cast in such terms, foreign policy scholarship on national role conceptions could be adapted to such identity language. See Kal Holsti, "National Role Conceptions in the Study of Foreign Policy," *International Studies Quarterly* 14 (September 1970), pp. 233–309; and Stephen Walker, ed., *Role Theory and Foreign Policy Analysis* (Durham, N.C.: Duke University Press, 1987). For an important effort to do so, see Stephen Walker, "Symbolic Interactionism and International Politics: Role Theory's Contribution to International Organization," in C. Shih and Martha Cottam, eds., *Contending Dramas: A Cognitive Approach to Post-War International Organizational Processes* (New York: Praeger, forthcoming).
11. On the "portfolio" conception of interests, see Barry Hindess, *Political Choice and Social Structure* (Aldershot, U.K.: Edward Elgar, 1989), pp. 2–3. The "definition of the situation" is a central concept in interactionist theory.
12. In neo-Durkheimian parlance, institutions are "social representations." See Serge Moscovici, "The Phenomenon of Social Representations," in Rob Farr and Serge Moscovici, eds., *Social Representations* (Cambridge: Cambridge University Press, 1984), pp. 3–69. See also Barnes, *The Nature of Power.* Note that this is a considerably more socialized cognitivism than that found in much of the recent scholarship on the role of "ideas" in world politics, which tends to treat ideas as commodities that are held by individuals and intervene between the distribution of power and outcomes. For a form of cognitivism

closer to my own, see Emanuel Adler, "Cognitive Evolution: A Dynamic Approach for the Study of International Relations and Their Progress," in Emanuel Adler and Beverly Crawford, eds., *Progress in Postwar International Relations* (New York: Columbia University Press, 1991), pp. 43–88.

13. Berger and Luckmann, *The Social Construction of Reality,* p. 58.
14. See Giddens, *Central Problems in Social Theory;* and Alexander Wendt and Raymond Duvall, "Institutions and International Order," in Ernst-Otto Czempiel and James Rosenau, eds., *Global Changes and Theoretical Challenges* (Lexington, Mass.: Lexington Books, 1989), pp. 51–74.
15. Proponents of choice theory might put this in terms of "interdependent utilities." For a useful overview of relevant choice-theoretic discourse, most of which has focused on the specific case of altruism, see Harold Hochman and Shmuel Nitzan, "Concepts of Extended Preference," *Journal of Economic Behavior and Organization* 6 (June 1985), pp. 161–76. The literature on choice theory usually does not link behavior to issues of identity. For an exception, see Amartya Sen, "Goals, Commitment, and Identity," *Journal of Law, Economics, and Organization* 1 (Fall 1985), pp. 341–55; and Robert Higgs, "Identity and Cooperation: A Comment on Sen's Alternative Program," *Journal of Law, Economics, and Organization* 3 (Spring 1987), pp. 140–42.
16. Security systems might also vary in the extent to which there is a functional differentiation or a hierarchical relationship between patron and client, with the patron playing a hegemonic role within its sphere of influence in defining the security interests of its clients. I do not examine this dimension here; for preliminary discussion, see Alexander Wendt, "The States System and Global Militarization," Ph.D. diss., University of Minnesota, Minneapolis, 1989; and Alexander Wendt and Michael Barnett, "The International System and Third World Militarization," unpublished manuscript, 1991.
17. This amounts to an "internationalization of the state." For a discussion of this subject, see Raymond Duvall and Alexander Wendt, "The International Capital Regime and the Internationalization of the State," unpublished manuscript, 1987. See also R. B. J. Walker, "Sovereignty, Identity, Community: Reflections on the Horizons of Contemporary Political Practice," in R. B. J. Walker and Saul Mendlovitz, eds., *Contending Sovereignties* (Boulder, Colo.: Lynne Rienner, 1990), pp. 159–85.
18. On the spectrum of cooperative security arrangements, see Charles Kupchan and Clifford Kupchan, "Concerts, Collective Security, and the Future of Europe," *International Security* 16 (Summer 1991), pp. 114–61; and Richard Smoke, "A Theory of Mutual Security," in Richard Smoke and Andrei Kortunov, eds., *Mutual Security* (New York: St. Martin's Press, 1991), pp. 59–111. These may be usefully set alongside Christopher Jencks' "Varieties of Altruism," in Jane Mansbridge, ed., *Beyond Self-Interest* (Chicago: University of Chicago Press, 1990), pp. 53–67.
19. On the role of collective identity in reducing collective action problems, see Bruce Fireman and William Gamson, "Utilitarian Logic in the Resource Mobilization Perspective," in Mayer Zald and John McCarthy, eds., *The Dynamics of Social Movements* (Cambridge, Mass.: Winthrop, 1979), pp. 8–44; Robyn Dawes et al., "Cooperation for the Benefit of Us—Not Me, or My Conscience," in Mansbridge, *Beyond Self-Interest,* pp. 97–110; and Craig Calboun, "The Problem of Identity in Collective Action," in Joan Huber, ed., *Macro-Micro Linkages in Sociology* (Beverly Hills, Calif.: Sage, 1991), pp. 51–75.
20. See Thomas Risse-Kappen, "Are Democratic Alliances Special?" unpublished manuscript, Yale University, New Haven, Conn., 1991. This line of argument could be expanded usefully in feminist terms. For a useful overview of the relational nature of feminist conceptions of self, see Paula England and Barbara Stanek Kilbourne, "Feminist Critiques of the Separative Model of Self: Implications for Rational Choice Theory," *Rationality and Society* 2 (April 1990), pp. 156–71. On feminist conceptualizations of power, see Ann Tickner, "Hans Morgenthau's Principles of Political Realism: A Feminist Reformulation," *Millennium* 17 (Winter 1988), pp. 429–40; and Thomas Wartenberg, "The Concept of Power in Feminist Theory," *Praxis International* 8 (October 1988), pp. 301–16.
21. Waltz, *Theory of International Politics,* p. 91.
22. See Waltz, *Man, the State, and War;* and Robert Jervis, "Cooperation Under the Security Dilemma," *World Politics* 30 (January 1978), pp. 167–214.
23. My argument here parallels Rousseau's critique of Hobbes. For an excellent critique of realist appropriations of Rousseau, see Michael Williams, "Rousseau, Realism, and Realpolitik," *Millennium* 18 (Summer

1989), pp. 188–204. Williams argues that far from being a fundamental starting point in the state of nature, for Rousseau the stag hunt represented a stage in man's fall. On p. 190, Williams cites Rousseau's description of man prior to leaving the state of nature: "Man only knows himself; he does not see his own well-being to be identified with or contrary to that of anyone else; he neither hates anything nor loves anything; but limited to no more than physical instinct, he is no one, he is an animal." For another critique of Hobbes on the state of nature that parallels my constructivist reading of anarchy, see Charles Landesman, "Reflections on Hobbes: Anarchy and Human Nature," in Peter Caws, ed., *The Causes of Quarrel* (Boston: Beacon, 1989), pp. 139–48.

24. Empirically, this suggestion is problematic, since the process of decolonization and the subsequent support of many Third World states by international society point to ways in which even the raw material of "empirical statehood" is constituted by the society of states. See Robert Jackson and Carl Rosberg, "Why Africa's Weak States Persist: The Empirical and the Juridical in Statehood," *World Politics* 35 (October 1982), pp. 1–24.

25. Waltz, *Theory of International Politics*, pp. 74–77.

26. The importance of the distinction between constitutive and causal explanations is not sufficiently appreciated in constructivist discourse. See Wendt, "The Agent-Structure Problem in International Relations Theory," pp. 362–65; Wendt, "The States System and Global Militarization," pp. 110–13; and Wendt, "Bridging the Theory/Meta-Theory Gap in International Relations," *Review of International Studies* 17 (October 1991), p. 390.

27. See Blumer, "The Methodological Position of Symbolic Interactionism," pp. 2–4.

28. This situation is not entirely metaphorical in world politics, since throughout history states have "discovered" each other, generating an instant anarchy as it were. A systematic empirical study of first contacts would be interesting.

29. Mead's analysis of gestures remains definitive. See Mead's *Mind, Self, and Society.* See also the discussion of the role of signaling in the "mechanics of interaction" in Turner's *A Theory of Social Interaction*, pp. 74–79 and 92–115.

30. On the role of attribution processes in the interactionist account of identity-formation, see Sheldon Stryker and Avi Gottlieb, "Attribution Theory and Symbolic Interactionism," in John Harvey et al., eds., *New Directions in Attribution Research*, vol. 3 (Hillsdale, N.J.: Lawrence Erlbaum, 1981), pp. 425–58; and Kathleen Crittenden. "Sociological Aspects of Attribution," *Annual Review of Sociology*, vol. 9, 1983 pp. 425–46. On attributional processes in international relations, see Shawn Rosenberg and Gary Wolfsfeld, "International Conflict and the Problem of Attribution," *Journal of Conflict Resolution* 21 (March 1977), pp. 75–103.

31. On the "stagecraft" involved in "presentations of self," see Erving Goffman, *The Presentation of Self in Everyday Life* (New York: Doubleday, 1959). On the role of appearance in definitions of the situation, see Gregory Stone, "Appearance and the Self," in Arnold Rose, ed., *Human Behavior and Social Processes* (Boston: Houghton Mifflin, 1962), pp. 86–118.

32. This discussion of the role of possibilities and probabilities in threat perception owes much to Stewart Johnson's comments on an earlier draft of my article.

33. On the role of "reassurance" in threat situations, see Richard Ned Lebow and Janice Gross Stein, "Beyond Deterrence," *Journal of Social Issues*, vol. 43, no. 4, 1987, pp. 5–72.

34. On "reciprocal typifications," see Berger and Luckmann, *The Social Construction of Reality*, pp. 54–58.

35. The following articles by Noel Kaplowitz have made an important contribution to such thinking in international relations: "Psychopolitical Dimensions of International Relations: The Reciprocal Effects of Conflict Strategies," *International Studies Quarterly* 28 (December 1984), pp. 373–406; and "National Self-Images, Perception of Enemies, and Conflict Strategies: Psychopolitical Dimensions of International Relations," *Political Psychology* 11 (March 1990), pp. 39–82.

36. These arguments are common in theories of narcissism and altruism. See Heinz Kohut, *Self-Psychology and the Humanities* (New York: Norton, 1985); and Martin Hoffmann, "Empathy, Its Limitations, and Its Role in a Comprehensive Moral Theory," in William Kurtines and Jacob Gewirtz, eds., *Morality, Moral Behavior, and Moral Development* (New York: Wiley, 1984), pp. 283–302.

37. See C. Norman Alexander and Mary Glenn Wiley, "Situated Activity and Identity Formation," in Morris Rosenberg and Ralph Turner, eds., *Social Psychology: Sociological Perspectives* (New York: Basic Books, 1981), pp. 269–89.

38. On the "maturity" of anarchies, see Barry Buzan, *People, States, and Fear* (Chapel Hill: University of North Carolina Press, 1983).
39. A similar intuition may lie behind Ashley's effort to reappropriate classical realist discourse for critical international relations theory. See Richard Ashley, "Political Realism and Human Interests," *International Studies Quarterly* 38 (June 1981), pp. 204–36.

Man, the State, and War: Gendered Perspectives on National Security

J. ANN TICKNER

The title of this chapter—"Man, the State, and War"—is Tickner's explicit challenge to the dominance of Realism in the study of IR. It refers directly to the work of Kenneth Waltz, whose book *Man, the State and War* makes only one reference to "women." Although her argument in this extract challenges the Realist perspective, some of Tickner's criticisms apply to what many feminist writers believe are the shortcomings of the Liberal lens, too. Can you find examples of this? Describe some of what Tickner calls the gender biases of Realism. What might be a Realist counter-argument? How does the Feminist perspective differ from the Constructivist lens?

In the face of what is generally perceived as a dangerous international environment, states have ranked national security high in terms of their policy priorities. According to international relations scholar Kenneth Waltz, the state conducts its affairs in the "brooding shadow of violence," and therefore war could break out at any time.[1] In the name of national security, states have justified large defense budgets, which take priority over domestic spending, military conscription of their young adult male population, foreign invasions, and the curtailment of civil liberties. The security of the state is perceived as a core value that is generally supported unquestioningly by most citizens, particularly in time of war. While the role of the state in the twentieth century has expanded to include the provision of domestic social programs, national security often takes precedence over the social security of individuals.

When we think about the provision of national security we enter into what has been, and continues to be, an almost exclusively male domain. While most women support what they take to be legitimate calls for state action in the interests of international security, the task of defining, defending, and advancing the security interests of the state is a man's affair, a task that, through its association with war, has been especially valorized and rewarded in many cultures throughout history. As Simone de Beauvoir's explanation for male superiority suggests, giving one's life for one's country has been considered the highest form of patriotism, but it is an act from which women have been virtually excluded. While men have been associated with defending the state and advancing its international interests as soldiers and diplomats, women have typically been engaged in the "ordering" and "comforting" roles both in the domestic sphere, as mothers and basic needs providers, and in the caring professions, as teachers, nurses, and social workers.[2] The role of women with respect to national security has been ambiguous: defined as those whom the state and its men are protecting, women have had little control over the conditions of their protection.

For realists, security is tied to the military security of the state. Given their pessimistic assumptions about the likely behavior of states in an "anarchic" international environment, most realists are skeptical about the possibility of states ever achieving perfect security. In an imperfect world, where many states have national security interests that go beyond self-preservation and where there is no international government to curb their ambitions, realists tell us that war could break out at any time because nothing can prevent it. Consequently, they advise, states must rely on their own power capabilities to achieve security. The best contribution the discipline of international relations can make to national security is to investigate the causes of war and thereby help to design "realistic" policies that can prolong intervals of peace. Realists counsel that morality is usually ineffective in a dangerous world: a "realistic" understanding of amoral and instrumental behavior, characteristic of international politics, is necessary if states are not to fall prey to others' ambitions.

In looking for explanations for the causes of war, realists, as well as scholars in other approaches to international relations, have distinguished among three levels of analysis: the individual, the state, and the international system. While realists claim that their theories are "objective" and of universal validity, the assumptions they use when analyzing states and explaining their behavior in the international system are heavily dependent on characteristics that we, in the West, have come to associate with masculinity. The way in which realists describe the individual, the state, and the international system are profoundly gendered; each is constructed in terms of the idealized or hegemonic masculinity described in chapter 1. In the name of universality, realists have constructed a worldview based on the experiences of certain men: it is therefore a worldview that offers us only a partial view of reality.

Realism's prescriptions for national security, described above, rest on the claims of its scholars that they are presenting a rational, objective assessment of the international system and the behavior of the states that constitute it. Labeling those who believe in the possibility of eliminating war through international law, international cooperation, or disarmament "idealists," realists claim that only through this "realistic" understanding of the nature of the international system can states undertake policies that will be successful in preserving their national security. Realists believe that explanations of states' behavior can be described in terms of laws that are objective, universal, and timeless. Politics, Morgenthau tells us, is governed by objective laws that have their roots in human nature; therefore it is possible to discover a rational theory that reflects these objective laws. Political realism, which for Morgenthau is the concept of interest defined in terms of power, stresses the rational, objective, and unemotional. Morgenthau claims that, in order to develop an autonomous theory of political behavior, "political man" must be abstracted from other aspects of human behavior. Political man is amoral; a failure to understand this drive to power, which is at the root of the behavior of both individuals and states, can be the pitfall of well-meaning statesmen whose attempts to act morally in the conduct of foreign relations can jeopardize the security of their own people.[3]

Since Morgenthau wrote the first edition of *Politics Among Nations* in 1948, the search for an objective, rational science of international politics based on models imported from economics and the natural sciences has been an important goal of the realist agenda. Neorealists, who have attempted to construct a positivist "science" of international relations, have used game theoretic and rational choice models in an effort to insert more scientific rigor into the field. Realists, as well as some of their critics, have also introduced the concept of "levels of analysis" to explore the causes of international wars more systematically. In international relations scholarship, causal explanations for war are conventionally situated at the levels of the individual, the state, or the international system.[4]

While most international relations literature concentrates on the second and third levels, neorealists, who are attempting to build more parsimonious and "scientific" approaches to the discipline, favor system-level explanations. Rejecting what he terms reductionist theories, Waltz claims that only at the level of the international system can we discover laws that can help us to understand the international behavior of states and the propensity for conflict.

A Gendered Perspective on National Security

Morgenthau, Waltz, and other realists claim that it is possible to develop a rational, objective theory of international politics based on universal laws that operate across time and space. In her feminist critique of the natural sciences, Evelyn Fox Keller points out that most scientific communities share the "assumption that the universe they study is directly accessible, represented by concepts shaped not by language but only by the demands of logic and experiment." The laws of nature, according to this view of science, are beyond the relativity of language.[5] Like most contemporary feminists, Keller rejects this positivist view of science that, she asserts, imposes a coercive, hierarchical, and conformist pattern on scientific inquiry. Since most contemporary feminist scholars believe that knowledge is socially constructed, they are skeptical of finding an unmediated foundation for knowledge that realists claim is possible. Since they believe that it is language that transmits knowledge, many feminists suggest that the scholarly claims about the neutral uses of language and about objectivity must continually be questioned.[6]

"Political man"

In his *Politics Among Nations*, a text rich in historical detail, Morgenthau has constructed a world almost entirely without women. Morgenthau claims that individuals are engaged in a struggle for power whenever they come into contact with one another, for the tendency to dominate exists at all levels of human life: the family, the polity, and the international system; it is modified only by the conditions under which the struggle takes place.[7] Since women rarely occupy positions of power in any of these arenas, we can assume that, when Morgenthau talks about domination, he is talking primarily about men, although not all men.[8] His "political man" is a social construct based on a partial representation of human nature abstracted from the behavior of men in positions of public power.[9] Morgenthau goes on to suggest that, while society condemns the violent behavior that can result from this struggle for power within the polity, it encourages it in the international system in the form of war.

While Morgenthau's "political man" has been criticized by other international relations scholars for its essentializing view of human nature, the social construction of hegemonic masculinity and its opposition to a devalued femininity have been central to the way in which the discourse of international politics has been constructed more generally. In Western political theory from the Greeks to Machiavelli, traditions upon which contemporary realism relies heavily for its analysis, this socially constructed type of masculinity has been projected onto the international behavior of states. The violence with which it is associated has been legitimated through the glorification of war.

The militarized version of citizenship, can be traced back to the ancient Greek city-states on whose history realists frequently draw in constructing their analysis. For the Greeks, the most honored way to achieve recognition as a citizen was through heroic performance and sacrifice in war. The real test of manly virtue or "arete," a militarized notion of greatness, was victory in battle.[10] The Greek city-state was a community of warriors. Women and slaves involved in the realm of "necessity" in the household or the economy were not included as citizens for they would pollute the higher realm of politics.[11]

For feminists, warrior-citizenship is neither a negative, unavoidable characterization of human nature, nor a desirable possibility; it is a revisable, gendered construction of personality and citizenship. Feminist political theorist Wendy Brown suggests that Machiavelli's representation of the political world and its citizenry is profoundly gendered; it is dependent on an image of true manliness that demands qualities that are superior to those that naturally inhere in men.[12] True manliness, demanded of the ideal citizen-warrior, is encompassed in the concept "virtu," which means, in its literal sense, manly activity. For Machiavelli, virtu is insight, energetic activity, effectiveness, and courage: it demands overcoming a man's self-indulgence and laziness.[13]

In Machiavelli's writings this feminine other is "fortuna," originally a Roman goddess associated with capriciousness and unpredictability. Hannah Pitkin claims that in Machiavelli's writings fortuna is presented as the feminine power in men themselves against which they must continually struggle to maintain their autonomy.[14] In the public world, Machiavelli depicts fortuna as chance, situations that could not have been foreseen or that men fail to control. The capriciousness of fortuna cannot be prevented, but it can be prepared against and overcome through the cultivation of manly virtues. According to Brown, fortuna and virtu are in permanent combat: both are supremely gendered constructions that involve a notion of manliness that is tied to the conquest of women.[15] In Machiavelli's own words, "Fortune is a woman, and it is necessary if you wish to master her, to conquer her by force."[16]

While contemporary international relations does not employ this explicitly misogynist discourse, the contemporary understanding of citizenship still remains bound up with the Greeks' and Machiavelli's depictions of the citizen-warrior. The most noble sacrifice a citizen can make is to give his life for his country. When the National Organization for Women decided to support the drafting of women into the United States military, it argued its case on the grounds that, if women were barred from participation in the armed forces on an equal footing with men, they would remain second-class citizens denied the unique political responsibility of risking one's life for the state.[17] But in spite of women's increasing numbers in noncombat roles in the armed forces of certain states, the relationship between soldiering, masculinity, and citizenship remains very strong in most societies today.

To be a soldier is to be a man, not a woman; more than any other social institution, the military separates men from women. Soldiering is a role into which boys are socialized in school and on the playing fields. A soldier must be a protector; he must show courage, strength, and responsibility and repress feelings of fear, vulnerability, and compassion. Such feelings are womanly traits, which are liabilities in time of war.[18] War demands manliness; it is an event in which boys become men, for combat is the ultimate test of masculinity. When women become soldiers, this gender identity is called into question; for Americans, this questioning became real during the Persian Gulf war of 1991, the first time that women soldiers were sent into a war zone in large numbers.[19]

To understand the citizen-warrior as a social construction allows us to question the essentialist connection between war and men's natural aggressiveness. Considerable evidence suggests that most men would prefer not to fight; many refuse to do so even when they are put in positions that make it difficult not to. One study shows that in World War II, on the average, only 15 percent of soldiers actually fired their weapons in battle, even when threatened by enemy soldiers.[20] Because military recruiters cannot rely on violent qualities in men, they appeal to manliness and patriotic duty. Judith Stiehm avers that military trainers resort to manipulation of men's anxiety about their sexual identity in order to increase soldiers' willingness to fight. In basic training the term of utmost derision is to be called a girl or a lady.[21] The association between men and violence therefore depends not on men's innate aggressiveness, but on the construction of a gendered identity that places heavy pressure on soldiers to prove themselves as men.

To be a first-class citizen therefore, one must be a warrior. It is an important qualification for the politics of national security for it is to such men that the state entrusts its most vital interests. Characteristics associated with femininity are considered a liability when dealing with the realities of international politics. When realists write about national security, they often do so in abstract and depersonalized terms, yet they are constructing a discourse shaped out of these gendered identities. This notion of manhood, crucial for upholding the interests of the state, is an image that is frequently extended to the way in which we personify the behavior of the state itself.

The masculine state

"'To Saddam,' Mr. Cheney wrote on the 2,000 pound bomb destined for an Iraqi target. 'With appreciation, Dick Cheney.'"[22] In times of war, the state itself becomes a citizen-warrior: military commanders refer to the enemy as a singular "he." The 1991 Persian Gulf war was frequently depicted as a personal contest between Saddam Hussein and George Bush and described in the appropriate locker-room or football language.[23] When realists describe the international behavior of states more generally, they present us with similarly masculine images of stag hunts or "games nations play."[24] Hans Morgenthau described the Soviet-American rivalry of the early Cold War period as "the primitive spectacle of two giants eying each other with watchful suspicion.... Both prepare to strike the first decisive blow, for if one does not strike it the other might."[25]

More recently, however, neorealism has depicted states rather differently, as abstract unitary actors whose actions are explained through laws that can be universalized across time and place and whose internal characteristics are irrelevant to the operation of these laws. States appear to act according to some higher rationality that is presented as independent of human agency. Nowhere in the rational power-balancing behavior of states can we find the patriot willing to go to war to defend his women and children in the name of national security. As poststructuralist international relations theorist Richard Ashley suggests, the "rationalization of global politics" has led to an antihumanism whereby states, posited unproblematically as unitary actors, act independently of human interests.[26] It is a world in which, as Jean Elshtain observes, "No children are ever born, and nobody ever dies.... There are states, and they are what is."[27]

Behind this reification of state practices hide social institutions that are made and remade by individual actions. In reality, the neorealist depiction of the state as a unitary actor is grounded in the historical practices of the Western state system: neorealist characterizations of state behavior, in terms of self-help, autonomy, and power seeking, privilege characteristics associated with the Western construction of masculinity. Since the beginning of the state system, the national security functions of states have been deeded to us through gendered images that privilege masculinity.

The Western state system began in seventeenth-century Europe. As described by Charles Tilly, the modern state was born through war; leaders of nascent states consolidated their power through the coercive extraction of resources and the conquest of ever-larger territories. Success in war continued to be imperative for state survival and the building of state apparatus.[28] Throughout the period of state building in the West, nationalist movements have used gendered imagery that exhorts masculine heroes to fight for the establishment and defense of the mother country. The collective identity of citizens in most states depends heavily on telling stories about, and celebration of, wars of independence or national liberation and other great victories in battle. National anthems are frequently war songs, just as holidays are celebrated with military parades and uniforms that recall great feats in past conflicts. These collective historical memories are very important for the way in which individuals define themselves as citizens as well as for the way in which states command support for their policies, particularly foreign policy. Rarely, however, do they include experiences of women or female heroes.

The international system: the war of everyman against everyman

According to Richard Ashley, realists have privileged a higher reality called "the sovereign state" against which they have posited anarchy understood in a negative way as difference, ambiguity, and contingency—as a space that is external and dangerous.[29] All these characteristics have also been attributed to women. Anarchy is an actual or potential site of war. The most common metaphor that realists employ to describe the anarchical international system is that of the seventeenth-century English philosopher Thomas Hobbes's depiction of the state of nature. Although Hobbes did not write much about international politics, realists have applied his description of individuals' behavior in a hypothetical precontractual state of nature, which Hobbes termed the war of everyman against everyman, to the behavior of states in the international system.[30]

As a model of human behavior, Hobbes's depiction of individuals in the state of nature is partial at best; certain feminists have argued that such behavior could be applicable only to adult males, for if life was to go on for more than one generation in the state of nature, women must have been involved in activities such as reproduction and child rearing rather than in warfare. Reproductive activities require an environment that can provide for the survival of infants and behavior that is interactive and nurturing.

Just as the image of waging war against an exterior other figured centrally in Machiavelli's writings, war is central to the way we learn about international relations. Our historical memories of international politics are deeded to us through wars as we mark off time periods in terms of intervals between conflicts. We learn that dramatic changes take place in the international system after major wars when the relative power of states changes. Wars are fought for many reasons; yet, frequently, the rationale for fighting wars is presented in gendered terms such as the necessity of standing up to aggression rather then being pushed around or appearing to be a sissy or a wimp. Support for wars is often garnered through the appeal to masculine characteristics.

As Jean Elshtain points out, war is an experience to which women are exterior; men have inhabited the world of war in a way that women have not.[31] The history of international politics is therefore a history from which women are, for the most part, absent. Little material can be found on women's roles in wars; generally they are seen as victims, rarely as agents. While war can be a time of advancement for women as they step in to do men's jobs, the battlefront takes precedence, so the hierarchy remains and women are urged to step aside once peace is restored. When women themselves engage in violence, it is often portrayed as a mob or a food riot that is out of control.[32] Movements for peace, which are also part of our history, have not been central to the conventional way in which the evolution of the Western state system has been presented to us. International relations scholars of the early twentieth century, who wrote positively about the possibilities of international law and the collective security system of the League of Nations, were labeled "idealists" and not taken seriously by the more powerful realist tradition.

Metaphors, such as Hobbes's state of nature are primarily concerned with representing conflictual relations between great powers. The images used to describe nineteenth-century imperialist projects and contemporary great power relations with former colonial states are somewhat different. Historically, colonial people were often described in terms that drew on characteristics associated with women in order to place them lower in a hierarchy that put their white male colonizers on top. As the European state system expanded outward to conquer much of the world in the nineteenth century, its "civilizing" mission was frequently described in stereotypically gendered terms. Colonized peoples were often described as being effeminate, masculinity was an attribute of the white man, and colonial order depended on Victorian standards of manliness. Cynthia Enloe suggests that the concept of "ladylike behavior" was one of the mainstays of imperialist civilization. Like sanitation and Christianity, feminine respectability was meant to convince colonizers and colonized alike that foreign conquest was right and necessary. Masculinity denoted protection of the respectable lady; she stood for the civilizing mission that justified the colonization of benighted peoples.[33] Whereas the feminine stood for danger and disorder for Machiavelli, the European female, in contrast to her colonial counterpart, came to represent a stable, civilized order in nineteenth-century representations of British imperialism.

Feminist perspectives on national security take us beyond realism's statist representations. They allow us to see that the realist view of national security is constructed out of a masculinized discourse that, while it is only a partial view of reality, is taken as universal. Women's definitions of security are multilevel and multidimensional. Women have defined security as the absence of violence whether it be military, economic, or sexual. Not until the hierarchical social relations, including gender relations, that have been hidden by realism's frequently depersonalized discourse are brought to light can we begin to construct a language of national security that speaks out of the multiple experiences of both women and men. As I have argued, feminist theory sees all these types of violence as interrelated. I shall turn next to the economic dimension of this multidimensional perspective on security.

Note

I owe the title of this chapter to Kenneth Waltz's book *Man, the State, and War.*

References

Addams, Jane, Emily G. Balch, and Alice Hamilton. *Women at The Hague: The International Congress of Women and Its Results.* New York: Macmillan, 1916.

Arendt, Hannah. *On Violence.* New York: Harcourt, Brace and World, 1969.

Aron, Raymond. *Peace and War: A Theory of International Relations.* Garden City, N.Y.: Doubleday, 1966.

Ashley, Richard K. "Untying the Sovereign State: A Double Reading of the Anarchy Problematique." *Millennium: Journal of International Studies* 17(2) (1988): 227–262.

Beauvoir, Simone de. *The Second Sex.* New York: Knopf, 1952.

Beitz, Charles. *Political Theory and International Relations.* Princeton: Princeton University Press, 1979.

Brock-Utne, Birgit. *Educating for Peace: A Feminist Perspective.* New York: Pergamon Press, 1985.

Brock-Utne, Birgit. *Feminist Perspectives on Peace and Peace Education.* New York: Pergamon Press, 1989.

Brock-Utne, Birgit. "Gender and Cooperation in the Laboratory." *Journal of Peace Research* 26(1) (1989): 47–56.

Brown, Sarah. "Feminism, International Theory, and International Relations of Gender Inequality." *Millennium: Journal of International Studies* 17(3) (1988): 461–475.

Brown, Wendy. *Manhood and Politics: A Feminist Reading in Political Theory.* Totowa, N.J.: Rowman and Littlefield, 1988.

Choucri, Nazli and Robert C. North. *Nations in Conflict: National Growth and International Violence.* San Francisco: W. H. Freeman, 1975.

Cohn, Carol. "Sex and Death in the Rational World of Defense Intellectuals." *Signs: Journal of Women in Culture and Society* 12(4) (1987): 687–718.

Common Security: A Blueprint for Survival. New York: Simon and Schuster, 1982.

Eisler, Riane. *The Chalice and the Blade: Our History, Our Future.* San Francisco: Harper & Row, 1988.

Elshtain, Jean Bethke. *Public Man, Private Woman: Women in Social and Political Thought.* Oxford: Martin Robertson, 1981.

Elshtain, Jean Bethke. "Reflections on War and Political Discourse: Realism, Just War, and Feminism in the Nuclear Age." *Political Theory* 13(1) (February 1985): 39–57.

Elshtain, Jean Bethke. *Women and War.* New York: Basic Books, 1987.

Elshtain, Jean Bethke and Sheila Tobias, eds. *Women, Militarism, and War.* Savage, Md.: Rowman and Littlefield, 1990.

Enloe, Cynthia. *Bananas, Beaches, and Bases: Making Feminist Sense of International Politics.* Berkeley: University of California Press, 1990.

Enloe, Cynthia. *Does Khaki Become You?* Boston: South End Press, 1983.

Falk, Richard A. "Contending Approaches to World Order." *Journal of International Affairs* 31(2) (Fall/Winter 1977): 171–198.

Falk, Richard A., Samuel S. Kim, and Saul H. Mendolvitz, eds. *Toward a Just World Order.* Boulder: Westview, 1980.

Gerzon, Mark. *A Choice of Heroes: The Changing Face of American Manhood.* Boston: Houghton Mifflin, 1984.

Haraway, Donna. *Primate Visions: Gender, Race, and Nature in the World of Modern Science.* New York: Routledge, 1989.

Jackson, Robert H. and Carl G. Rosberg. "Why Africa's Weak States Persist: The Empirical and the Juridical in Statehood." *World Politics* 35(1) (October 1982): 1–24.

Jaggar, Alison. *Feminist Politics and Human Nature.* Totowa, N.J.: Rowman and Allanheld, 1983.

Keller, Evelyn Fox. *A Feeling for the Organism: The Life and Work of Barbara McClintock.* New York: W. H. Freeman, 1983.

Keller, Evelyn Fox. *Reflections on Gender and Science.* New Haven: Yale University Press, 1985.

Keohane, Robert O. *After Hegemony: Cooperation and Discord in the World Political Economy.* Princeton: Princeton University Press, 1984.

Keohane, Robert O., ed., *Neorealism and Its Critics.* New York: Columbia University Press, 1986.

Mies, Maria. *Patriarchy and Accumulation on a World Scale: Women in the International Division of Labour.* London: Zed Books, 1986.

Millennium: Journal of International Studies, Special Issue: Women and International Relations, 17(3) (Winter 1988).

Morgenthau, Hans J. *Politics Among Nations: The Struggle for Power and Peace,* 5th ed. New York: Knopf, 1973.

Pietilä, Hilkka and Jeanne Vickers. *Making Women Matter: The Role of the United Nations.* London: Zed Books, 1990.

Pitkin, Hanna F. *Fortune Is a Woman: Gender and Politics in the Thought of Niccolo Machiavelli.* Berkeley: University of California Press, 1984.

Peterson, V. Spike, ed. *Gendered States: Feminist (Re) visions of International Relations Theory.* Boulder: Lynne Rienner, 1992.

Reardon, Betty A. *Sexism and the War System.* New York: Teachers College Press, 1985.

Renner, Michael. *National Security: The Economic and Environmental Dimensions.* Washington, D.C.: Worldwatch Institute, 1989.

Ruddick, Sara. *Maternal Thinking: Toward a Politics of Peace.* New York: Ballantine Books, 1989.

Runyan, Anne Sisson. "Feminism, Peace, and International Politics: An Examination of Women Organizing Internationally for Peace and Security." Ph.D. diss., American University, 1988.

Runyan, Anne Sisson and V. Spike Peterson. "The Radical Future of Realism: Feminist Subversions of IR Theory." *Alternatives* 16(1) (1991): 67–106.

Schelling, Thomas C. *The Strategy of Conflict.* Cambridge, Mass.: Harvard University Press, 1960.

Segal, Lynne. *Is The Future Female? Troubled Thoughts on Contemporary Feminism.* New York: Peter Bedrick, 1988.

Stiehm, Judith Hicks. *Arms and the Enlisted Woman.* Philadelphia: Temple University Press, 1989.

Stiehm, Judith Hicks. *Women and Men's Wars.* Oxford: Pergamon Press, 1983.

Stiehm, Judith Hicks. *Women's Views of the Political World of Men.* Dobbs Ferry, N.Y.: Transnational Publishers, 1984.

Stockholm International Peace Research Institute (SIPRI). *Policies for Common Security.* London and Philadelphia: Taylor and Francis, 1985.

Sylvester, Christine. "Some Dangers in Merging Feminist and Peace Projects." *Alternatives* 12(4) (October 1987): 493–509.

Tannen, Deborah. *You Just Don't Understand: Women and Men in Conversation.* New York: Morrow, 1990.

Tickner, J. Ann. "Hans Morgenthau's Principles of Political Realism: A Feminist Reformulation." *Millennium* 17(3) (Winter 1988): 429–440.

Tickner, J. Ann. *Self-Reliance Versus Power Politics: The American and Indian Experiences in Building Nation States.* New York: Columbia University.

Waltz, Kenneth N. *Man, the State, and War.* New York: Columbia University Press, 1959.

Waltz, Kenneth N. *Theory of International Politics.* Boston: Addison-Wesley, 1979.

Waring, Marilyn. *If Women Counted: A New Feminist Economics.* San Francisco: Harper & Row, 1988.

White, Lynn. "The Historical Roots of Our Ecological Crisis." *Science,* March 10, 1987.

Williams, Michael C. "Rousseau, Realism, and *Realpolitik.*" *Millennium: Journal of International Studies* 18(2) 185–203.

Wilson, G. Kenneth and Peter Wallensteen. *Major Armed Conflicts in 1987.* Uppsala, Sweden: Department of Peace and Conflict Research, Uppsala University, 1988.

Internations of Feminism and International Relations

CHRISTINE SYLVESTER

In a nontraditional (for an academic) essay, Sylvester takes the student on a global excursion, asking us to imagine how scholars of various IR perspectives might be as traveling companions. Which scholar would you like to travel with? Why that one? When you travel, do you bring along many pairs of sunglasses, or do you rely upon just one? Why? What might a scholar from the Realist, Liberal, or Marxist tradition say about this reading?

"Internations" characterizes the fulcrum/impasse/fulcrum of IR and feminism and suggests literary ways to world-travel in and around it. Ann Tickner (1997:611–612) claims that "[w]hile feminist scholars, as well as a few IR theorists, have called for conversations and dialogue across paradigms . . . few conversations or debates have occurred." To her, good communication stumbles around the different ontologies and epistemologies driving the two fields and mires around gaps in the power to set dominant discourse. This concluding essay offers another spin on the issue: the two fields talk past each other because they are so very similar, and powerfully so.

IR and feminism, it can be said, are variants of the imagined nations that Benedict Anderson (1991) describes. They are nations of knowledge, identity, and practice that endeavor to incorporate a great deal of territory and to embrace all eligible members. Each "nation," however, fails to persuade some constituencies that they are part of the enterprise and should throw in their lot with it. Feminism can be off-putting to Third World women (and postcolonial analysts such as Ien Ang (1995)), who suspect that their issues and identities will always languish in a nation that is western at its core. IR is supposedly about the vast international and its many relations but tends to leave a fair bit of both out of its nation, including feminists, all those "bottom-rung" types of whom Enloe speaks, and relations of the international that do not center on Great Power concerns.

Feminism is eager to offer all women in the world a home, eager to be accepted as well as part of the home-spaces of IR. IR is reluctant, standoffish, snobbish, and exclusionary in general, despite its encompassing portfolio. One "nation" overreaches and the other puts up walls, but both are ambitious and prone to immodesty. Can they interact with each other productively without manifesting national perspectives that are at once ambitious and self-limited? Can each avoid invading or colonizing the other in order to appreciate – indeed thrive on – creative elements of their internations?

A "nation" problematic gave rise to IR and feminism to begin with. Both camp followers had experienced a certain homelessness or invisibility in fields that made universalizing claims but had, in fact, left them out. The swallowing-up entities around incipient IR were the fields of political science and diplomatic history. Feminist-minded scholars felt eviscerated within every academic story that used "he" or "mankind" to embrace the world. Today, the nation problematic continues, with postcolonial studies and feminism accusing IR of neglecting a range of global relations and gay and lesbian studies (as well as postcolonial scholars) needling feminism about problems with difference. Yet internations appear at points where aspects of IR nation cannot help but be part of cacophonous feminist nation and vice versa.

Having cited the heuristic potential of visual method in chapter 13, I return here in spirit to the third chapter of this volume ("Handmaids' Tales") and present a literary method to travel feminist/IR internations. That is to say, an unfinished journey continues by entering realms of difference that we in IR and we in feminism have trouble seeing when we stick to the usual data preferred by each field. Of course, feminism already incorporates literary approaches in its canons – so this exercise can be seen as yet another way of bringing IR questions onto feminist turf. Yet, judging by the arguments of postcolonial feminists, feminism has a great deal of reading left to do before it can cite the diversity of the world convincingly. Leaning on the literary assists both fields to develop in-sights and siting skills needed to cite the salient people, activities, movements, and odd relations of the world without commanding, ordering, appropriating, clashing with, or subsuming "them."

Three feminists go on a journey. One selects unfamiliar sites and wanders quietly, so as to avoid disturbing local culture. She talks to those around her but not about difficult or sensitive topics. Back home she decides against writing up what she has learned because to do so could distort and perhaps orientalize the "other." A second feminist visits places of difference too and does not keep a low profile once arriving. She seeks to bring international feminist standpoints to bear on what she sees, hears, and does – all as part of the effort to help disadvantaged women and their nations. She talks to locals but is also a bit remote, set apart – albeit being eager to record and report injustices. A third feminist monitors herself as both similar to and different than those she encounters through her various travels. Seeking out conversations, she asks others questions, lets herself be queried by locals, and queries herself – all in a context of slowly increasing comfort with situations that defy her control.

Three IR theorists are *en voyage.* One travels uneasily, preoccupied with water-borne diseases and the possible theft of personal items. Everything looms as a difference, and in that difference is a potential threat or conflict. This traveler is so distracted that he does not take much notice of feminists – or anyone else – he meets along the way. The second IR traveler is having a ball "out there." Wherever he goes he sees similarity: parents worry about their kids and heads of state bustle off to international meetings. It's like home, albeit colors, styles, and foods signal elseness. The feminists he runs into are proof to him that common norms can be found everywhere these days. For the third traveler from IR, the world is what he makes of it, as he analyzes how different countries respond to globalization's homogenizing cum difference-creating forces. He runs into the first feminist, talks with her for a while, finds many of her observations intriguing, and notes ways he can strengthen his own constructions by inserting some of her concerns into his frameworks.

We find at that location the feminist and IR travelers noted above serendipitously converged at the edge of a rural town. Disengaging from backpacks, trunks lowered to the ground, each sits in his or her own space and reads in silence. Time passes; they are still there, first ignoring one another and then reading passages to fellow travelers and local passers-by, laughing, arguing, showing books around, telling and listening to stories. The travelers forget IR (Bleiker, 1997), and feminisms, and themselves as local *griots* and *n'angas* provide more tales to contemplate. Having become sociable, the travelers find themselves unpreoccupied with the next place to go, the self, the professional mission, the "strange other." Books and minds and national experiences open in the internations on view.

"Nations" of Feminism and International Relations

The three feminist travelers seem different to each other. The first avoids speaking for "the other," knowing that her western-subject-centered "I" may block the sounds of another speaking (Spivak, 1988). The development feminist is willing to represent the other in order to help her (Parpart, 1995; Sylvester, 2000a). The third feminist listens and engages; she finds one or two nodes of common identity across difference and builds a learning experience around them with those she meets.

Different approaches, yes? In fact, Jen Ang (1995) argues, feminism is one nation that expands to incorporate as many women as possible. That nation is not marked by a common lingua franca, demarcated territory, or clear ethnic boundaries (although there may be some body boundaries). It is not a homogeneous nation either, but, rather, constructs its far-flung members in a spirit of contention and contingency. None the less, Ang (p. 57) thinks feminism is a western-identified effort to pose a "'natural' political destination for all women, no matter how multicultural." It is the motherlode, the culture point where differences compress into a tolerance-oriented, culturally white, western, feminist world. The amalgamation occurs – despite recognition that "women" is an unstable category cross-cut by statuses of class, race, ethnicity, nationality, age, and so on, despite travels that prove difference is indeed diverse. That two of the three feminist travelers strike out into the world from western locations would probably not surprise Aug. She thinks feminist nation pledges allegiance to western feminist interest in dialoging with difference in order, ultimately, to overcome it, as the second feminist traveler does (the first is immobilized by her sense of immutable identities and cannot engage at all). Put differently, difference is to be respectfully inserted into a firmly established prior tradition that absorbs the ambiguity of such sentiments as: "I'm a feminist but..."

Ang overstates her case as a way of relaying postmodern skepticism about modernist confidence in multicultural dialog. Her sense of the nation of feminism, though, teases us metaphorically and serves as a cautionary tale in which women are meant to inhabit two sites of the world with empowering ease – a material living place and a special place of women's politics and dreams. Terry Eagleton (cited in Wallace, 2000:39) suggests the downside of this vision by asserting that people like to situate themselves and that so many cannot help but do so: "It's OK for high-flying (literally) intellectuals to talk about mixing and mingling identities [in a global world]; they can do it. Most people have to live where they are. People live in a particular place in time. Most of them can't afford to travel at all" (p. 39).

Arguably, a parallel nation of global reach orbits near feminist nation. This is the academically imagined "nation" of International Relations (IR), the community that takes the relations of the world as its unique professional portfolio, its oyster. Through at least eighty years a small and elite nation has imagined the international and cited its imaginings as real: international relations have become what an IR clique makes them. The world it has imagined has been potentially vast – everywhere; but in fact the field narrowed early to something called, in cartoon language, Great Powers and their (important) relations. IR's small nation of like-minded thinkers (and their states) then took up places, often conflictually, under a shared umbrella; the majority of potential members (and their states) were on the outside getting wet. Instead of opening to all locations of international relations over time, IR persists in preferring those who can converse about impersonal, power-seeking, and functionally equivalent nation-states, an international society of states bound by common (mostly western) norms, patterns of international political economy emanating from or concerning the West (such as globalization), and decision-makers who enjoy playing games. With the western "I" stretched across only some parts of the planet, yet determining the international to be studied and the ways to do so, IR developed its own universality illusion. Whereas feminist nation has wanted every woman to feel comfortable within it, IR nation mostly wants to avoid uncomfortable journeys "out there" and associate more with its own kind. Thus, the first IR traveler is uneasy with difference and the second is ebullient because he sees himself wherever he goes.

Dissidents in IR fuss about this strange land, just as do dissidents from/in feminism; indeed, some feminists are inter-nationally positioned.[1] There is also sparring within the mainstream of the field, which gives the impression that IR nation welcomes controversy (now constructivists and rationalists are having their day). Yet dissidents find that the controversies they generate can be ignored or summarily dismissed by other national members;[2] or their ideas can be appropriated with the political guts removed first, *à la* IR's third traveler (Weber, 1999). As for feminist dissidents in IR, they tell of eerie spaces of masculinity they slide into when crossing from places where women are in the majority of feminist nation to homeless statuses in IR (Elshtain, 1987; Sylvester, 1994a; Tickner, 1992). Historically always men secretaries-general of the UN have the "good offices" in international relations while unnoted secretaries keep their dinners warm. Wars emulate those violent software games (Shapiro, 1990) that are also known to target women. And diplomacy, in James Der Derian's (1987:199) words, is "the mediation of men estranged from an infinite yet abstracted power which they themselves have constructed." Periodically left out of even the good critiques, or included through arch representations by men (Ashley and Walker, 1990a), feminists crossing over to IR often sit apart reading each other's stories, like the IR dissidents do.

There is a nation of IR, imply critics of the field, which erects walls and evacuates many places, texts, people, and concerns from the small land of mainstream significance – all while proclaiming itself portfolio holder for the international and its relations. There is a nation of feminism, suggest dissident feminists, which shows the opposite tendency to immodest inclusiveness.

Boundaries and "Nations"

But wait. Can IR construct feminism as an alien nation? Can women who are assigned feminist nation be forced into homelessness in IR (Sylvester, 1998b) – "stuck," so to speak, inside feminist nation looking out at the rest of the world? Although analysts have taken up questions related to the exclusion or marginalization of feminism within IR (e.g., Stancich, 1998; Tickner, 1997), I wish to scrutinize the boundaries and ask whether feminism and IR *can* be universal in claims, memberships, and representations. Are there feminist places in nonfeminist IR and IR places in the proclaimed feminist homeplace of only-women? Are there internations of feminism and IR? In tackling these questions, I draw on an article by Etienne Balibar that has become a classic of left-leaning globalization literature.

Balibar (1995) addresses several universalizing tendencies and the ways they fail to capture the ambiguities of the time. He refers to nations as instances of fictitious universalism. Their sweep can be achieved only by deconstructing particularistic, primary identities of would-be members in order to reconstruct a common representation of "'what it means to be a person,' to 'be oneself,' or to be a 'subject'" (p. 56). IR and feminism fill this category if we bear in mind Anderson's argument that a national community need be no less false for being imagined. Feminism, for Ang (1995:73), represents the subjects "women," wherever they live and whether or not, as she puts it, other "identifications are sometimes more important and politically pressing than, or even incompatible with, those related to their being women." IR has deconstructed generations of student identifications in order to reconstruct canonical parameters for "what it means to be a person" who "does" IR. There is an obvious constructivist ring to fictive nation. "Material resources," to use Alexander Wendt's (1995:73) words, "only acquire meaning for human action through the structure of shared knowledge in which they are embedded." Or as Richard Price and Christian Reus-Smit (1998:266) put it, "institutionalized meaning systems are thought to define the social identities of actors, and…social identities are said to constitute actors' interests and shape their actions."

And yet "nation" is not fully entrapping either, because nations are not power points of consensus. Within imagined communities are those who resist institutionally accepted ways "of being a person" and attend to contradictions in the rules of personhood. Balibar (1995:62) maintains that "[t]o confront the hegemonic structure by denouncing the gap or contradiction between its official values and the actual practice – with greater or lesser success – is the most effective way to enforce its universality." For Ang to struggle against feminist encompassings of all women, for critics in IR to denounce a field that does not account for all of the international nor study many relations, can be a badge of membership in the imagined communities of feminism and IR. Fighting words enforce the universalist claims of nations by keeping attention on the importance of normal community debates about "what it means to be a subject." One might say then that challengers *escape* aspects of national fictions when they reveal the social processes that construct the usual norms; but at the same time, they *maintain* national myths by drawing attention to the gap between national aspirations and the current moment of national reality. Ang is a feminist but…she both argues with feminism, beseeching the nation to countenance partiality, and reveals the flawed logic of the normal in feminism (that only seemingly universal category "women"). The effects are intensive: "more aspects of the life of the constitutive units are dependent on what other units have been doing in the past, or are currently doing" (p. 49).

Minorities proliferate in an era of mass global communications and so do real possibilities for contact across minority identities. In some cases, the contactenables prior conflict to diminish. In other cases, "global communication networks provide every individual with a distorted image or a stereotype of all the others, either as 'kin' or as 'aliens,' thus raising gigantic obstacles before any dialogue" (p. 56). Far from bringing global community together in a way that ends particularistic conflicts, real universality "coincides with a generalized pattern of conflicts, hierarchies, and exclusion…'[i]dentities' are less isolated *and* more compatible, less univocal *and* more antagonistic" (p. 56). And the prospect for a global social contract, which would end these Hobbesian wars or conflicts of difference, seems utterly utopian.

Caught in the ambiguous outcomes of intersecting universalizing tendencies, feminist and IR nations may seem to loom large before our eyes but, in fact, they cannot convincingly determine "what it means to be a person, a subject." National membership is increasingly porous and open, despite our best efforts to hold on to old membership rituals. Ang's warning about a nation of feminism at odds with the views of some it seeks to bring home illustrates this dynamic. Her concerns reflect the communication with/in western feminism that elements of real universality make possible. At the same time, those forces open feminist nation to contradictions of difference it cannot contain. Mainstream IR, wherever located, finds itself unable to stage a "debate" these days that it can absolutely win against all the minorities undermining national control. Internations of feminism and IR are not just possible, it is an era of internations. Nations exceed their moorings in a world instantaneously bombarded by interdependencies, disjunctures, assimilations and insurgencies, virtualities, fictions and more fictions.

"Nations" of IR and Feminism Struggle to Be

Events suggest that IR cannot wrap up the world in the bosom of Great Power concerns and consign everything else – small states, working-class people, women, children, wives of diplomats, Zimbabwean co-operatives, Tongan chiefs, novels, and art museums – to near oblivion. Feminism cannot easily assimilate the challenges of minorities either, because the very existence of minorities disperses and diversifies the majority. The national ambitions of both – one to keep interlopers out and the other to assimilate all conceivable members – are impossible to realize. Events rapidly exceed national discourses of control.

IR exceeded

IR's world is exceeded by the world that complicates it – the world of simultaneous homogenizing forces around market capitalism, information technology, and global consumerism, and the world that begs the question Bruce Robbins (1995:167) asks: is "there... a single system... or perhaps only the *appearance* of a single system?" What of eastern Europe, where ethnic nations seeking states cause disintegrations around themselves and the build-up of particularistic nationalisms too? What of Africa's general expulsion from high-technology globalization, and other uneven, perhaps Satanic, geographies (Smith, 1997)? What of the Taliban wars on all ideas, practices, and art deemed non-Islamic? Balibar's discussion of the equivocity of universality supports the sense that we can be connected globally while, at the same time, connections spawn fictions, conflicts, and dis/connections.

IR is connected to feminism through the minority problematic that infiltrates it. Yet the field has not connected well with feminist scholarship in the sense of examining the gender concerns its own work raises. IR has not studied gender relations as relations of international power. It has never studied power as the ability of nations and professional academic fields to block "women" and their internationally relevant activities from scholarly significance (Enloe, 1989). IR is exceeded, therefore, by a dissident minority that its masculine performing "nation" has either tried to pull into normality (ignoring feminist queries about "what it means to be a person" in IR), ignored, or failed to capture or to quiet. It is exceeded by el(l)e-phants who paint the landscapes of IR differently, or who paint abstract shadowlands of gender that defy the normal outlines of a field.[3]

Feminism exceeded

Feminism simultaneously is one of the minority groups created by the real universality of international relations and is itself beset by minorities everywhere and conflicts within. Its early association with a women's movement gave feminism the cast of what Balibar calls an ideal universality as insurrection against the many institutions of fictitious universality that excluded people called women. Balibar (1995:64) writes of insurgents "who collectively rebel against domination in the name of freedom and equality." Their very existence reflects "history as a general process of emancipation, a realization of the idea of man (or the human essence, or the classless society, etc.)" (p. 65). In the case of feminism, ideal universality is the realization of the idea of woman, but... Ang and other dissidents charge that the white, western, heterosexual woman became the model for all. This is not what Balibar (p. 72) means when he speaks of ideal universality as transindividual and, multiple "in the sense of being always already beyond any simple or 'absolute' unity, therefore a source of conflicts forever."

Herein is the feminist rub. In order to make the claim that feminism is a difference-tolerant univocality, dissidents to feminism have to make the assumption that white western culture is immune from periphery to center international migrations and conflicts – just as endists do in IR. Yet the minority position that dissidents to feminist nation believe they occupy in feminism (or at the edges of it) coexists with so much cross-migration – (just through UN conferences alone) that feminism is now, arguably, an ensemble of "minorities without stable or unquestionable majorities." It is not seen this way by those who believe that feminism continues to have the majoritarian components that were amply visible during days of debate between liberal, Marxist, radical, and socialist wings.[4] Although written and practiced earnestly, with good intentions and some good results, these feminisms had a certain disregard for countervailing experiences.

In the end, the feminist/women's movement fragmented into the various postmodern and postcolonial elements we see today. We should bear in mind, though, that mainstream feminism was always made up of contentious minorities, who disallowed one another from reaching hegemony or from writing what Jean Elshtain (1993) calls "a" narrative of closure. That is to say, the nation of feminist truth was always exceeded.

World Traveling the Universals

IR has not found a method to accommodate the contradictions around it. It simply breaks into schools of thought and shouts across divides. Some feminism has success with IR when it speaks the language of that nation and takes on recognizable and delimited IR puzzles. It has less success when it brings IR to the language and concerns of minoritarian feminism, to the IR questions there. Recently, however, some feminists have considered ways to move across centers and peripheries instead of encouraging one-way travel to a (fictitiously) fixed nation of identity, from whence one tries to overcome difference (Gwin, 1996; Sylvester, 1994a, 1995a). We can therefore consider how to be in the world without reinforcing or instantiating nations of belief.

Notes

1. The term "dissident" is used by Ashley and Walker (1990a).
2. Fred Halliday (1994:40) describes work from the poststructuralist-postmodern wing of dissidence as "pretentious, derivative and vacuous, an Anglo-Saxon mimesis of what was already in its Parisian form, a confused and second-rate debate."
3. For a discussion of elephants who paint, and thereby turn topsy our notion of what elephant is, and el(l)ephants who similarly step out of IR's shadows to paint relations international (where no such phantoms were supposed to exist), see Sylvester (1994a).
4. Liberal feminism sought to make liberal western rights of men applicable to women without querying what the men had built and bequeathed and would still manage for women as a group. The feminist development approach WID (women in development) is its descendant. Marxist feminist theorizing put biological women where social relations of production would activate a worker consciousness, without dealing with patriarchy in the workplace and women (and men) who, for various reasons, work at home. Radical feminism lambasted patriarchy and then reified its notions of women by lumping all such biologically determined people together as keepers of mysterious submerged wisdom or culture. WAD (women and development) has no pretensions toward mysticism, but does advocate a separatist work position for biological women in Third World societies. Socialist feminism sought to assault capitalism and patriarchy through progressive cross-cultural alliances; but, as with radical feminism, says Judith Grant (1993: 45), "a universal female experience was necessary in order to ground [it]."

References

Anderson, Benedict (1991), *Imagined Communities: Reflections on the Origins and Spread of Nationalism* (London: Verso)

Ang, Ien (1995), "'I'm a Feminist But...' Other Women and Postnational Feminism," in Barbara Caine and Rosemary Pringle, eds., *Transitions: New Australian Feminism* (Sydney: Allen & Unwin):57–73

Balibar, Etienne (1995), "Ambiguous Universality," *Differences: Journal of Feminist Cultural Studies*, 7, 1:48–74

Bleiker, Roland (1997), "Forget IR Theory," *Alternatives: Social Transformation and Humane Governance*, 22,257–85

Elshtain, Jean Bethke (1987) *Women and War* (New York: Basic Books)

Price, Richard and Christian Reus-Smit (1998), "Dangerous Liaisons? Critical International Theory and Constructivism," *European Journal of International Relations*, 4, 3:259–294

Robbins, Bruce (1995), "The Weird Heights: On Cosmopolitanism, Feeling, and Power," *Difference: A Journal of Feminist Cultural Studies*, 7, 1:165–187

Smith, Neil (1997), "The Satanic Geographies of Globalization: Uneven Development in the 1990s," *Public Culture*, 10, 1:169–189

Sylvester, Christine (1998b), "Homeless in International Relations? 'Women's Place in Canonical Texts and in Feminist Reimaginings," in Anne Phillips, ed., *Feminism and Politics* (New York: Oxford University Press): 44–66

Sylvester, Christine, (1999a), "(Sur)Real Internationalism: Emigres, Native Sons and Ethical War Creations, *Alternatives: Social Transformation and Human and Governance*, 24, 2:219–247

Tickner, J. Anne, (1992), *Gender in International Relations: Feminist Perspectives on Achieving Global Security* (New York: Columbia University Press)

Wendt, Alexander (1992) Anarchy is what States Make of it: The Social Construction of Power Politics *International Organization*, Vol. 46, No. 2 (Spring, 1992), pp. 391–425

Re-Imagining IR in India

NAVNITA CHADHA BEHERA

A significant criticism that scholars aim at the academic study of IR is that the discipline seeks to explain events, trends, and phenomena that are primarily those of the developed world. This extract takes that criticism and applies it to the status of IR theorizing in India. What is the author's central argument? What explains how IR is taught in India? Is there a uniquely "India" perspective in IR theory? Why or why not?

Re-imagining IR in India is *not* about creating an Indian school of IR but redefining IR itself. This problematizes the basic formulation and idiom of our query: why there is no non-Western IR theory in India by highlighting its implicit binary character, which is not merely descriptive but hierarchical: the 'dominant' West and the 'dominated' non-West. From this standpoint, even if scholars were to succeed in creating an Indian school of IR, it would at best cam a small, compartmentalized space *within* the master narrative of IR (read Western IR[1]). The challenge, therefore, is not to discover or produce non-Western IR theory in India but for the Indian IR community to work towards fashioning a post-Western IR.

When India became independent in 1947, its ruling elite believed India was destined to play a major role in Asian and world affairs commensurate with its geographical placement, historical experiences and power potential. Such self-conscious aspirations should have helped the growth of an IR discipline but nearly six decades later, it has yet to earn the status of a separate discipline. There are no undergraduate programmes and only four universities offer a Masters programme though it is home to probably the world's single largest school of international studies – the School of International Studies (SIS) at Jawaharlal Nehru University. Although India's 'social science research capacity' has been in a state of 'crisis' due to several economic, political and demographic factors (Abraham 2004: Chatterjee *et al.* 2002), a detailed analysis of IR's poor state points to a different direction.

IR's relationship with the parent disciplines of political science and area studies has tremendously stilted its growth. The Indian conception of IR, known as 'International Studies', is a peculiar product of conceptual conflation of area studies and disciplinary-oriented IR (Rana and Misra 2004: 74). Area studies is multidisciplinary and IR is only one of the disciplines they embrace but they were wrongly equated with the latter based on a somewhat simplistic assumption that the areas being studied were 'foreign'. Funding for IR within the rubric of area studies was a fundamental mistake as the latter 'had, in fact, "emasculated" IR instead of advancing it' (ibid.).

IR's disciplinary location in political science departments also caused its severe marginalization. Even in the large and better reputed departments, 'the academic space available to this area of scholarship... has relatively shrunk... alarmingly so' (ibid.: 76). Unlike political science that is more deeply rooted in political theory, the theoretical component of Indian IR remains thin. Most syllabi consist of an amalgam of diplomatic histories of major powers (read Europe) during World War I and World War II followed by the Cold War and India's foreign relations with little attention devoted to fundamental concepts and theoretical debates in IR. The subfields of IR, including security studies, peace and conflict studies and international political economy, mostly remain confined to optional courses at the Masters level and others such as ecology, globalization and gender studies are rarely taught. This has resulted in a very narrow intellectual base of the discipline.

There is no well-knit community of Indian IR scholars. Though they interact they don't seem to have cumulatively tried 'to build a coherent edifice of work in well defined areas, related to key IR disciplinary concerns and problems in some kind of a dialectical correlation' (Rana and Misra 2004: 111). Seminars are held on topical issues but collaborative work on disciplinary themes, even within a department, is rare. The academic culture of peer review is conspicuous by its absence and lack of mutual acknowledgement is most evident in the footnoting protocols of the discipline.

The Practice of International Relations

For nearly two decades after independence, Nehru completely dominated policy-making as well as intellectual analyses of foreign affairs. His extensive knowledge of international issues resulted in the expertise in IR being concentrated largely in the Ministry of External Affairs. This has begun to change recently with the constitution of a National Security Advisory Board having a separate and functional secretariat though the thick walls of suspicion between academia and government officials persist.

The lack of a discipline-oriented growth of Indian IR has been exposed in vigorous state-of-the-field critiques (Rana 1988a, 1988b, 1989; Rajan 1997). Theorizing has also run aground due to an overwhelming insistence that social science must be relevant though this is not unique to IR or to India. Social sciences in India, including IR, have also contended with the dominance of Western theoretical frameworks (Misra and Beal 1980; Bajpai and Shukul 1995; Ray 2004).

Two schools of thought seek to explain the lack of state-of-the-art theorizing in Indian IR. Simply put, the first argues: '*we* don't theorize', and the problem does not lie with the Western frameworks *per se*, while the second proffers: 'we *do* theorize' but it is not recognized 'as theory' by the predominantly Western IR community. It is important not to view either argument in absolute terms as the two overlap at critical junctures.

Jawaharlal Nehru is widely regarded as the founding father of non-alignment. He was joined by other Third World leaders including Josip Broz Tito of Yugoslavia and Gamal Abdel Nasser of Egypt. The non-aligned movement created a coalition of more than 100 states from Asia. Africa. Europe, the Arab world. Latin America and the Carihbean that supported the decolonization process, literally changing the world's geopolitical landscape. Whether conceptualizations of non-alignment qualify as 'systemic.' IR theory would however, depend upon the criteria being used. If the first criteria 'it be substantially acknowledged by others in the IR academic community as being theory' is used, it will fail the test. Theoretical writings on non-alignment rarely figured in the core IR journals published in North America and Europe throughout the 1950s to the 1970s. On the contrary, most dismissed it as 'variants of neutrality' (Armstrong 1956–7). Disparaging references to these countries as 'uncommitted' or 'neutral' questioned non-alignment's political legitimacy (Debrah 1961; Dinh 1975). Indian scholars had little choice but to write books on non-alignment distributed by Indian publishers (Khan 1981; Jaipal 1983: Bajpai 1985). Despite offering an alternative world view of how the global state system should function, non-alignment was never accorded the status or recognition as a 'systemic' IR theory because it did not suit the interests of powers that be.

Likewise, neither Nehru's idea of non-exclusionary regionalism, the concept of *panchsheel* nor the mandala theory of regionalism got recognition in the core literature in IR. Exceptions figure only in the case of Indian scholars based at US or European universities or whose texts have been published and distributed by Western publishers. Ayoob's work on the state-making processes in the Third World and their security predicament is a case in point (1995) though this, too, got recognition largely in the context of the Third World. It is clearly not easy to move from the domain of 'particular' to 'universal.' Unlike Europe, where 'Western local patterns being turned into [general] IRT concepts is common practice.'

The real story lies in the Indian IR's uncritical acceptance of the state being a 'benevolent protector' rather than an 'oppressor' in the domestic/international domain. A subconscious albeit *complete* internalization of the tenets, philosophical ethos and legitimacy of political realism in its mental structures has tremendously stifled the scope of its intellectual inquiries. Together these characterize what was earlier termed us traditional IR.

So, IR is mainly concerned with power struggles among states. These are underpinned by two critical unstated assumptions: theorizing in IR *means* producing scientific knowledge and 'Europe [later America] remains the covering, theoretical subject of all histories [read IR]. including the ones we call "Indian," "Chinese," "Korean," and so on' (Chakrabarty 2000; 1491). With its constitutive ideas and practices rooted in the Eurocentric experiences and an abiding faith in the 'liberating power of reason (*logos*) as it threw off the shackles of traditions (*mythos*)' (Davetak 1995: 31), the domain of IR was bounded in a manner that India's various 'traditional pasts' got de-legitimized as a possible source of knowledge creation in IR. A positivist enterprise precluded a debate about what issues of inquiry could be included in IR and how its key concepts of nation-state, nationalism, sovereignty and territoriality could acquire *different meanings.* This may be briefly explained with reference to nationalism.

Thus, nation 'controls the life of the individual insofar as the needs of the State or Nation make it necessary' (cited in Fenn Jr 1929: 321). Gandhi too forewarned that 'modern state does indeed swallow up individual persons, even as it is, ironically celebrating their autonomy, and that it has also destroyed the intimate ties of traditional community life' (cited in Gier 1996: 263).

The impoverishment of traditional IR's political thought becomes further evident on its chosen ground political realism – that does not recognize or *own* Indian political philosopher, Kautilya, as 'the father of realpolitik.' Kautilya is not taught in any 'principal IR theory courses' and though *Arthashastra* (Indian science of politics dating from the fourth century BC) has much to offer for theorizing IR, the broader applicability of his ideas is not acknowledged – almost universally. Kautilya's theory of mandala (sphere or circle of influence, interest and ambitions) stipulates that every king or *vijigeesoo* (aspirant to conquest) is to regard his realm as located at the centre of a concentric circle of kingdoms or mandalas (rings), which represented alternately his natural enemies and possible allies. Each kingdom's similar aspirations spur a struggle for existence, self-assertion and world domination among *vijigeesoos* resulting into *matsya-nyaya* (the logic of the fish), that is, should there be no ruler to wield punishment on earth the stronger would devour the weak like fishes in the water. The mandala theory assumes and is prepared for a world of eternally warring states by stressing 'perpetual preparedness' or the doctrine of *danda* (punishment, sanction) (Sarkar 1919: 402: 1921: 83–9). International relations conceived in this political tradition derive from a purely secular theory of state with power as its sole basis permitting no ethical or moral considerations.

To recapitulate, bound by its fundamental *'givens'*, traditional IR has truly been 'boxed in' – metaphorically and substantively. It is not our intention or purpose to dismiss the entire genre of Indian IR literature that remains grounded in the realist paradigm, but it is important to understand that the structural reason why traditional IR in India has not, indeed, *could not* produce a non-Western IR theory is because it has fought that intellectual battle on a turf chosen by the West, with tools designed and provided by the West and rules-of-game set by the West enforced, as they were, not just by its political and military might but more important, its all-pervasive discursive power. That is why Indian scholarship of traditional IR has remained on the margins of the larger discipline. And yet, it may be argued that the situation looks bleak only as long as traditional IR stays within the stifling confines of those concentric circles. What is needed then is to create alternative sites of knowledge construction by stepping out of this box.

Re-imagining IR

Re-imagining IR is primarily about rethinking foundational knowledge of what constitutes IR. It calls for creating alternative sites of knowledge construction with an alternative set of tools and resources. Before suggesting such an alternative roadmap for the Indian IR, three generic issues need to be addressed.

The first pertains to the disciplinary boundaries of IR which 'are fundamental in determining who its legitimate speakers are, what rules of the game it condones, and what authoritative disciplinary practice consists of' (Bourdieu cited in Tickner 2005: 8). In critiquing the kind of knowledge Indian IR has produced thus far and urging its scholarly community to transgress its disciplinary boundaries by inviting in the 'outsiders' – postcolonial and development theorists, feminists and cultural critics – we may be accused of committing hara-kiri. These propositions, critics will argue, may sound the death knell of this discipline rather than infuse a new life into it.

The second issue refers to privileging of 'expertise', invariably at the cost of devaluing 'everyday life experiences', in the practices of knowledge-building.

The third issue involves the indigenization of academic discourses in IR. Having discussed the genetic ethnocentrism of this discipline, it is important to clarify that the intellectual endeavour of re-imagining IR does not advocate 'mimicking the west' (Bhabha 1987) or 'catching up' with the West but to work towards making IR turn post-Western. If Indian IR were to follow the trajectory laid down by the West, it can *never* catch up and will remain stuck 'in the transition narrative that will always remain grievously incomplete'.

The idea is to create spaces for alternative thinking on IR, which cannot be accomplished without a critical self-awareness *and* questioning of the a priori assumptions, procedures and values embedded in the positivist enterprise. It means that 'the question of what we keep and what we discard from the heritage of modernity needs explicit and ongoing discussion' (Inayatullah and Blaney 2004: 201). Indigenizing also does not seek to reject everything modern (or Western) or eulogize the premodern (or Indian) world. According to ancient Indian wisdom, every *yuga* or age has its own distinctive problems and needs to come to terms with them in its own way. The past can be a resource or a great source of inspiration and self-confidence, but it can never become a model or blueprint for the present. Therefore, the scholarly community that may shape the contours of new IR cannot take the *dharma* of another age as its own.

The enterprise of re-imagining IR needs to generate an alternative set of resources. Two lines of inquiry are suggested to begin with: more, we hope, will emerge along the way. The first, already noted above, explores the role of everyday experience in theory-building by examining 'the relationship between lived experience, understanding and knowledge' to show how 'lived world is fundamental for understanding how knowledge of the world is constructed'.

A second line of inquiry calls for IR scholars to undertake a thorough re-reading of the Indian history and analyse the political thought of various Indian philosophers and political thinkers including Manu, Valmiki, Buddha, Iqbal, Aurobindo Ghosh, Dadabhai Naroji and Tagore and political leaders such as Gandhi, Nehru, Sardar Patel and Maulana Azad among others. In view of our analysis of Kautilya's *Arthshastra*, the issue of 'how to' read history is of critical importance. There is much to learn from subaltern studies and postcolonial traditions. It is important to be aware and eschew modernist practices of imposing Western concepts and categories into the distant pasts of diverse non-Western societies because they 'recreate only those structures which they want to see: intellectual projects become guided tours [and] we see only what we have been trained and told to recognize' (Nagaraj 1998: 8). A scholarly understanding of the past must be undertaken with a healthy dose of sociological and geo-cultural reflexivity.

Notes

1. Admittedly, the term 'Western IR' is problematic for its essentialist overtones. As used in this paper, it mainly points to the shared epistemological foundations of IR rooted in Anglo-American traditions – the birth place of IR – in a historical sense. In its subsequent evolution, it has predominantly been referred to as 'an American social science' (Hoffman 1977: 41–60, Crawford and Jarvis 2000). Waever recounts the growing differentiation between 'continental and American traditions in international thought' (1999: 80–3), and for a larger debate between the 'core and periphery', see Aydlini and Mathews 2000: 298–303.

References

Abraham, Itty (1998) *The Making of the Indian Atom Bomb: Science, Secrecy and the Post-Colonial State,* Zed Books, London.

—— (2004), 'The Changing Institutional-Intellectual Ecology of Knowledge-Production in South Asia', paper presented at the UNESCO Forum on Higher Education, Knowledge and Research, Paris, 1–3 December.

Ahmed, Imtiaz (1993), *State and Foreign Policy in India,* Vikas Publishing House. New Delhi.

Alatas, Syed Farid (1993), 'On the Indigenisation of Academic Discourse', *Alternatives,* vol. 18, no. 3, pp. 307–38.

Ali, Mahmud S. (1993), *The Fearful State: Power, People and Internal War in South Asia,* Zed Books, London.

Appadurai, Arjun (1996), *Modernity at Large: Cultural Dimensions of Globalization,* University of Minnesota Press, Minnesota.

Armstrong, H. F. (1956–7), 'Neutrality: Varying Tunes', *Foreign Affairs,* 35, pp. 57–83.

Aydlini, Ersel and Julie Matthews (2000) 'Are the Core and Periphery Irreconcilable? The Curious World of Publishing in Contemporary International Relations', *International Studies Perspectives,* vol. 1, no. 3, pp. 289–303.

Ayoob, Mohammed (1995), *The Third World Security Predicament: State Making, Regional Conflict and International System,* Lynne Rienner, Boulder, CO.

Bajpai, Kanti (2003), 'Indian Conceptions of Order and Justice: Nehruvian, Gandhian, Hindutva and Neo-Liberal', in Rosemary Foot, John Lewis Gaddis and Andrew Hurrell (eds), *Order and Justice in International Relations.* Oxford University Press, New York, pp. 236–61.

—— and Siddharth Mallavarapu (eds) (2004), *International Relations in India: Bringing Theory Back Home,* Orient Longman, New Delhi.

——and Harish Shukul (eds) (1995), *Interpreting World Politics,* Sage Publications, New Delhi.

Bajpai, U. S. (1985), *Non-Alignment: Perspectives and Prospects,* New Delhi: Humanities Press Int. Inc.

Basrur, Rajesh (2005), *Minimum Deterrence and India's Security,* Stanford University Press, Stanford.

Behera, Navnita Chadha (2000), *State, Identity and Violence: Jammu, Kashmir and Ladakh,* Manohar, New Delhi.

—— (2003), 'Engaging Tomorrow: Ford Foundation. Regional Security, Peace and Cooperation in South Asia', a report, unpublished.

——(2004), 'Meta Narratives and Subaltern Voices: Role of the Ford Foundation in South Asia', paper presented at 45th Annual Convention of International Studies Association, Montreal, March.

—— (2005), 'India and the International Order: From Norms to Realpolitik', occasional paper. Department of Political Science, University of Delhi, New Delhi.

——(ed.) (2006), *Gender, Conflict and Migration.* Sage Publications, New Delhi.

Bergsten, C. Fred in association with John A. Mathieson (1973). 'The International Economic World Order', report to the Ford Foundation, New York.

Bhaba, Homi (1994), *The Location of Culture*, Routledge, London.

Bhargava K. K., H. Bongartz and F. Sobhan (eds) (1995), *Shaping South Asia's Future: Role of Regional Cooperation,* Vikas Publishing House. New Delhi.

Butalia, Urvashi (ed.) (2002), *Speaking Peace: Women's Voices from Kashmir,* Kali for Women, New Delhi.

Chakrabarty, Dipesh (2000). 'Postcoloniality and the Artifice of History: Who Speaks for "Indian" Pasts?', in Diana Brydon (ed.), *Postcolonialism: Critical Concepts in Literary and Cultural Studies,* vol. 4, Routledge, London, pp. 1491–518.

Chatterjee, P. (1985), *Nationalist Thought and Colonial World: A Derivative Discourse,* Zed Books. London.

Chatterjee, Partha in collaboration with Nirmala Banerjee, Apurba K. Baruah, Satish Deshpande, Peter Ronald de Souza, Krishna Hachhethu, B.K. Jahangir, M.S.S. Pandian, Nira Wickramasinghe, S. Akbar Zaidi and Itty Abraham (2002), *Social Science Capacity in India: A Report,* SSRC Working Paper Series, vol. 6, SSRC, New York.

Chenoy. Anuradha M. (2002), *Militarism and Women in South Asia*, Kali for Women, New Delhi.

Chimni, B. S. (1993), *International Law and World Order: A Critique of Contemporary Approaches*, Sage Publications, New Delhi.

Cox, Robert (1986), 'Social Forces, States and World Orders: Beyond International Relations Theory', in Robert O. Keohane (ed.), *Neo-Realism and its Critics*, Columbia University Press, New York, pp. 204–54.

Crawford, Robert A. and Darryl S. L. Jarvis (eds) (2001), *International Relations – Still an American Social Science?: Towards Diversity in International Thought*, State University of New York Press, New York.

Dallmayr, Fred (1996), 'Global Development? Alternative Voices From Delhi', *Alternatives,* vol. 21. no. 2, pp. 259–82.

Darby, Phillip (2003), 'Reconfiguring "the International": Knowledge Machines, Boundaries, and Exclusions', *Alternatives,* vol. 28, no. 1, pp. 141–66.

Davetak, Richard (1995), 'The Project of Modernity and International Relations Theory', *Millennium,* vol. 24, no. 1, pp. 27–51.

Debrah, E. M. (1961), 'Will Uncommitted Countries Remain Uncommitted', *Annals of the American Academy of Political and Social Science,* 331, July, pp. 83–93.

Dinh, Tran Van (1975), 'Non-aligned but Committed to the Hilt', *Pacific Community,* vol. 7, no. 1, October, pp. 118–31.

Dutt, Sri Kant (1984), *India and the Third World: Altruism or Hegemony?*, Zed Books, London.

Fay, Brian (1975), *Social Theory and Political Practice,* George Allen and Unwin, London.

Fenn Jr, Percy Thomas (1929), 'An Indian Poet Looks at the West', *International Journal* of Ethics, vol. 39, no. 3, pp. 313–23.

Gier, Nicholas F. (1996), 'Gandhi: Pre-Modern, Modern or Post-Modern?', *Gandhi Marg.* October–December, pp. 261–81.

Gowen, Herbert H. (1929), 'The Indian Machiavelli or Political Theory in India Two Thousand Years Ago', *Political Science Quarterly,* vol. 44, no. 2, June.

Gupta, Sisir (1964), *India and Regional Integration in Asia,* Asia Publishing House, Bombay.

Gyawali, Dipak (2002), 'Defining Environmental Conflict: A Cultural Theory Perspective', in Navnita Chadha Behera (ed.), *State, People and Security: The South Asian Context,* Har Anand, New Delhi.

Harshe, Rajen (1997), *Twentieth Century Imperialism: Shifting Contours and Changing Perceptions,* Sage Publications, New Delhi.

——(ed.) (2004), *Interpreting Globalisation: Perspectives in International Relations,* ICSSR and Rawat Publications, New Delhi.

Hoffman, Stanley (1977), 'An American Social Science: International Relations', *Daedalus,* vol. 106, no. 3 (Summer), pp. 41–60.

Hussain, Neelam, Samiya Mumtaz and Rubina Saigol (eds) (1997), *Engendering the Nation-State,*

Volume I & II, Simorgh Women's Resource & Publication Centre, Lahore.

Inayatullah, Naeem and David L. Blancy (2004), *International Relations and the Problem of Difference,* Routledge, New York.

Jaipal, Rikhi (1983), *Non-Alignment: Origins, Growth and Potential for World Peace,* South Asia Books, New Delhi.

Karnad, Bharat (2002), *Nuclear Weapons and Indian Security: The Realist Foundations of Strategy,* Macmillan, New Delhi.

Kaviraj, Sudipto (1991), 'On State, Society and Discourse in India', in James Manor (ed.), *Rethinking Third World Politics,* Longman, London.

——(1995), 'Crisis of the Nation-State in India', in John Dunn (ed.), *Contemporary Crisis of the Nation-State,* Blackwell. Oxford.

Khan, Rasheeduddin (ed.) (1981), *Perspectives on Non-Alignment,* Kalamkar Prakashan, New Delhi.

Kothari, Rajni (1978–9), 'Disarmament, Development and a Just World Order', *Alternatives,* vol. 4, no. 1, pp. 1–10.

—— (1979–80) 'Towards a Just World', *Alternatives,* vol. 5, no. 1, June, pp. 1–42.

Lal, Vinay (ed.) (2000), *Dissenting Knowledges. Open Futures: The Multiple Selves and Strange Destinations of Ashis Nandy,* Oxford University Press, New Delhi.

Manchanda, Rita (ed.) (2001), *Women, War and Peace in South Asia: Beyond Victimhood to Agency,* Sage Publications, New Delhi.

McCaughey, Robert A. (1979), 'The Permanent Revolution: An Assessment of the Current State of International Studies in American Universities', report to the International Division of the Ford Foundation.

Menon, Ritu and Kamla Bhasin (1998), *Borders and Boundaries: Women in India's Partition,* Kali for Women, New Delhi.

Misra, K. P. and R. C. Beal (eds) (1980), *International Relations Theory: Western and Non-Western Perspectives,* Vikas Publishing House, New Delhi.

Muni, S. D. and Anuradha Muni (1984), *Regional Cooperation in South Asia,* National Publishing House, New Delhi.

Nagaraj, R. (1998), 'Introduction', in *Exiled at Home: Ashis Nandy,* Oxford University Press, New Delhi.

Nandy, Ashis (1987), *Traditions, Tyranny and Utopia,* Oxford University Press, New Delhi.

—— (1998), 'The Savage Freud', reprinted in *Nandy: Return From Exile,* Oxford University Press, New Delhi.

Nehru, Jawaharlal (1950), *Independence and After: A Collection of Speeches, 1946–1949,* Ayer Co, New York.

—— (2004), *The Discovery of Indio,* Penguin Books, New Delhi.

—— (2004a), *An Autobiography,* Penguin Books, New Delhi.

Osborne, Peter (1992), 'Modernity is a Qualitative, Not a Chronological, Category', *New Left Review,* 192, pp. 65–84.

Parajuli, Pramod (1991), 'Power and Knowledge in Development Discourse: New Social Movements and the State in India', *International Social Science Journal,* 127, pp. 173–90.

Phadnis, Urmila (1989), *Ethnicity and Nation Building in South Asia,* Sage Publications, New Delhi.

Rajagopalan, Swarna and Farah Faizal (eds) (2005), *Women, Security, South Asia: A Clearing in the Thicket,* Sage Publications, New Delhi.

Rana, A. P. (1988a), *Reconstructing International Relations as a Field of Study in India: A Program for the Disciplinary Development of International Relations Studies,* Studying International Relations, The Baroda Perspective, Occasional Review-I, The Maharaja Sayajirao University, Baroda.

—— (1988b), *The International Relations Study of the Political Universe: A Note on Supplementary Strategies for the Explorotion of the Political Science-International Relations-Area Studies Continuum,* Studying International Relations, The Baroda Perspective, Occasional Review-II, The Maharaja Sayajirao University, Baroda.

—— (1989), *The Study of International Relations in India: State of the Field Conference and Colloquia Reports,* Studying International Relations, The Baroda Perspective, Occasional Review-III, The Maharaja Sayajirao University, Baroda.

—— and K. P. Misra (2004), 'Communicative Discourse and Community in International Relations Studies in India: A Critique', in Kanti Bajpai and Siddharth Mallavarapu (eds), *International Relations in India: Bringing Theory*

Back Home, Orient Longman, New Delhi, pp. 71–122.

Ray, Ashwini (2004), *Western Realism and International Relations: A Non-Western View*, Foundation Books, New Delhi.

Ross, Dorothy (1992) *The Origins of American Social Science*, Cambridge University Press, Cambridge, MA.

Said, Edward W. (1994), *Representations of the Intellectual*, Vintage Books, New York.

Sardar, Ziauddin (1998), 'Introduction: The A, B, C, D (and E) of Ashis Nandy', in *Return from Exile: Ashis Nandy*, Oxford University Press, New Delhi.

Sarkar, Benoy Kumar (1919), 'Hindu Theory of International Relations', *The American Political Science Review*, vol. 13, no. 3, August, pp. 400–14.

—— (1921), 'The Hindu Theory of the State', *Political Science Quarterly*, vol. 36, no. 1, March, pp. 79–90.

Samaddar, R. and Helmut Reifeld (eds) (2001), *Peace as Process: Reconciliation and Conflict Resolution in South Asia*, Manohar, New Delhi.

Savarkar, V. D. (1969), *Hindutva: Who is a Hindu?* S. S. Savarkar, Bombay.

Sheth, D. L. (1983), 'Grass Roots Stirrings and the Future of Politics', *Alternatives*, vol. 9, no. 1, pp. 1–24.

Singh, Jasjit (1998), 'A Nuclear Strategy for India', in Jasjit Singh (ed.), *Nuclear India*, Knowledge World, New Delhi.

Singh, Karan (1967), *Prophet of Indian Nationalism: A Study of the Political Thought of Sri Aurobindo Ghosh, 1893–1910*, Bhartiya Vidya Bhavan, New Delhi.

Singh, K. Suresh (1994), *People of India: An Introduction, National Series, Volume I*, Anthropological Survey of India, Calcutta.

Smith, Steve (1990), 'The Discipline of International Relations: Still an American Social Science?', *British Journal of Politics and International Relations*, vol. 2, no. 3, pp. 374–402.

——(2001), 'Reflectivist and Constructivist Approaches to International Relations Theory', in John Baylis and Steve Smith (eds), *The Globalization of World Politics: An Introduction to International Relations*, 2nd edn, Oxford University Press, Oxford.

Spivak, Gayatri Chakravorty (2000), 'Can the Subaltern Speak?', in Diana Brydon (ed.), *Postcolonialism: Critical Concepts in Literary and Cultural Studies, Volume IV*, Routledge, London, pp. 1427–77.

Subrahmanyam, K. (1994). 'Nuclear Force Design and Minimum Deterrence Strategy for India', in Bharat Kamad (ed.), *Future Imperilled: India's Security in the 1990s and Beyond*, Penguin Viking, New Delhi.

Sylvester, Christine (1996), 'The Contributions of Feminist Theory to International Relations', in Steve Smith, Ken Booth and Marysia Zalewski (eds), *International Theory, Positivism and Beyond*, Cambridge University Press, Cambridge, pp. 254–78.

Tagore, Rabindranath (2002), *Nationalism*, Rupa & Co, New Delhi.

Tellis, Ashley (2001), *India's Emerging Nuclear Posture: Between Recessed Deterrence and Ready Arsenal*, Rand, Santa Monica.

Tickner, Arlene B. (2003), 'Seeing IR Differently: Notes from the Third World', *Millennium*, vol. 32, no. 2, pp. 295–324.

——(2005), 'Everyday Experience as IR Theory', paper presented at the ISA Annual Meeting, Honolulu, Hawaii, 2–5 March.

Vanaik, Achin (2004), 'Globalization and International Relations', in Achin Vanaik (ed.), *Globalization and South Asia: Multidimensional Perspectives*, Manohar, New Delhi.

Wæver, Ole (1999), 'The Sociology of a Not So International Discipline: American and European Developments in International Relations', in Peter J. Katzenstein, Stephen D. Krasner and Robert O. Keohane (eds), *Exploration and Contestation in the Study of World Politics*, MIT Press, Cambridge, pp. 47–87.

Walker, R. B. J. (1984), 'East Wind, West Wind: Civilisations, Hegemonies, and World Orders', in R. B. J. Walker (ed.), *Culture, Ideology and World Order*, Westview, Boulder, CO.

——(1993), *Inside/Outside: International Relations as Political Theory*, Cambridge University Press, Cambridge.

——(1994), 'Social Movements/World Politics', *Millennium*, vol. 23, no. 3, pp. 669–700.

Wignaraja, Ponna and Akmal Hussain (eds) (1989), *The Challenge in South Asia: Development, Democracy and Regional Cooperation*, Sage Publications, New Delhi.

Social Evolution of International Politics: From Mearsheimer to Jervis

SHIPING TANG

Combining elements of Constructivist thought with Charles Darwin's notions of scientific evolution, Professor Tang offers a simple resolution to the debates between the various strands of Realism: in place of a static offensive realist, or defensive realist worldview, we should think of the international structure as an evolving structure. Tang believes this social evolutionary approach will account for the dynamic nature of world politics. How does he use history to support this argument? How might Kenneth Waltz respond to this notion of an evolving structure, with its focus on longer-term historical trends?

To Charles Darwin, on the 150th anniversary of his *Origin of Species* 'Give Darwin his Due'
(Philip Kitcher, 2003)

Introduction

In the past century, debates between major grand theories of international politics (e.g. realism, neoliberalism) have, to a very large extent, shaped the development of study of international politics as a science. From these inter-paradigmatic debates, two important themes have emerged.

First, except for a few notable voices (e.g. Mearsheimer, 2001: 2; Waltz, 1979: 66), most scholars would agree that the international system has experienced some kind of fundamental transformation, although they may disagree on what had caused the transformation (e.g. Ruggie, 1983; Schroeder, 1994: xiii; Wendt, 1992, 1999). Second, some fundamental differences divide the different grand theories, and these differences often are derived from some hidden assumptions, not from deductive logic.

These two themes, I argue, are inherently connected and can only be adequately understood together. This article advances an explanation for the systemic transformation of international politics and offers a neat resolution of one of the debates through a social evolution paradigm.

I underscore that an offensive realism world (Mearsheimer's world) is a self-destructive system and it will *inevitably and irreversibly* self-transform into a defensive realism world (Jervis's world) over time exactly because of the imperative of an offensive realism world for state behavior. In an offensive realism world, a state must either conquer or be conquered. This central mechanism of seeking security through conquest, together with three

---

Shiping Tang, "Social evolution of international politics: From Mearsheimer to Jervis," *European Journal of International Relations* March 2010 vol. 16 no. 1; pp. 32–34, 37–47,

other auxiliary mechanisms, will eventually transform an offensive realism world into a defensive realism world. Due to this transformation of the international system, offensive realism and defensive realism apply to two different worlds rather than a single world. In other words, each of these two theories explains a period of human history, but not the whole. Different grand theories of international politics are for different periods of international politics, and different epochs of international politics actually need different grand theories of international politics.

Before I proceed further, three caveats are in order.

First, although I focus on the evolution from Mearsheimer's world to Jervis's world and the debate between offensive realism and defensive realism, my exercise is *not* another effort to restate the realism case. My central goal, to repeat, is to advance a social evolution paradigm, or, more precisely, a social evolution paradigm toward international politics. I am *not* endorsing offensive realism or defensive realism, in the theoretical sense. Rather, I am interested in offering a neat resolution of the debate between the two realisms.

Second, despite focusing on the evolution from Mearsheimer's world to Jervis's world, I am *not* suggesting that the evolution of international politics starts from Mearsheimer's world and stops at Jervis's world. I focus on the evolution from Mearsheimer's world to Jervis's world and the debate between offensive realism and defensive realism because it is a more convenient launch pad for my thesis. Most students of international politics are familiar with the historical evidence of this evolutionary phase but are less familiar with the empirical evidence for the making of Mearsheimer's world because the evidence will be mostly anthropological and archeological (e.g. Cioffi-Revilla, 1996; Snyder J, 2002; Thayer, 2004). The same social evolution paradigm, however, can explain the making of Mearsheimer's world and can offer important insights into—although not predict—the future of international politics.

Finally, just because international politics has evolved from an offensive realism world to a defensive realism world does not mean that offensive realist states cannot exist in a defensive realism world (think of Iraq under Saddam Hussein). It merely means that the system has been fundamentally transformed and it will not go backwards.

The rest of the article is structured as follows. Section 1 briefly introduces the social evolution paradigm. Section 2 recalls the debate between offensive realism and defensive realism, making it explicit that an implicit assumption that the fundamental nature of international politics has remained pretty much the same has been the critical cause why this debate could not be resolved. Sections 3 and 4 together present the case that international politics had evolved from an offensive realism world to a defensive realism world. Section 3 identifies 'to conquer or be conquered'—the imperative for state behavior in an offensive realism world—as the fundamental mechanism behind the transformation. Section 4 underscores selection against offensive realist states, negative learning that conquest is difficult, and the rise and spreading of sovereignty and nationalism as the three auxiliary mechanisms behind the transformation. Section 5 explores the implications of a social evolution paradigm for theorizing international politics and managing states' security. A brief conclusion follows.

The Social Evolution Paradigm Toward Social Changes

A systematic statement on the social evolution paradigm can only be offered elsewhere. This section briefly introduces the social evolution paradigm, focusing on the aspects that are most relevant for the discussion below.

Evolution and the evolutionary approach

The evolutionary approach deals with systems populated by living creatures. These systems inevitably undergo changes through time. The process of change proceeds in three distinctive stages: variation (i.e. mutation), selection (i.e. eliminating and retaining some phenotypes/genotypes), and inheritance (i.e. replication and spreading of some genotypes/phenotypes). The process runs infinitely so long as the system exists.

Two distinctive characteristics of the evolutionary approach are most relevant for the discussion below.

First, the evolutionary approach neither completely proves nor predicts specific evolutionary outcomes because evolution allows accidents (e.g. the earth hit by an asteroid) and mutations are randomly generated. The strength of the evolutionary approach lies in that it provides a *coherent and complete* explanation for the wonders of life, whereas non-evolutionary or partially evolutionary approaches cannot. The evolutionary approach is elegant—all it needs is the single mechanism of variation–selection–inheritance. The evolutionary approach also subsumes all other micro- or middle-level mechanisms (e.g. punctuated equilibrium): the evolutionary approach, as Daniel Dennett (1995: 62) put it, is 'a universal acid' that dissolves everything.

Second, the evolutionary approach is *not* directional. Evolution may look directional (in hindsight), but the 'directionality' is caused by the random mechanism of variation–selection–inheritance. Moreover, the seemingly directional nature of changes may come as the unintended consequences of micro-level forces interacting with accidents.

Natural (biotic) evolution versus social evolution

Two systems—the biotic world and human society—are the natural domain of the evolutionary approach: these two systems can only be adequately understood with an evolutionary approach. While the evolution of the biotic world and the evolution of human society share some fundamental similarities, they also harbor fundamental differences, and the fundamental differences between the two systems can be traced to the emergence of a new force at play in social evolution. Unlike biological evolution where only material forces are at play, social evolution has a whole new force—the ideational force—at play. The presence of ideational force in social evolution gives social evolution all the fundamental new characteristics that biological evolution does not possess.

Most prominently, while objective reality in the biotic world is all material, objective reality in human society is more than material: the objective world of human society consists of not only material but also ideational parts, and some social realities (e.g. professors) cannot exist without a contribution from ideational forces. Of course—and this must be emphasized unequivocally—*no* social realities can exist without contribution from material forces: ideational forces alone cannot create social reality. As such, a social evolution paradigm toward social change must be both materialistic and ideationalistic, although it must give material forces the ontological priority (Searle, 1995: 55–6). Moreover, a social evolution paradigm brings material forces and ideational forces into an *organic* synthesis: material forces and ideational forces interact with each other, rather than function independently, to drive social changes.

Hence, a social evolution paradigm rejects a purely materialistic approach or a purely ideationalistic approach for understanding human society. A purely materialistic approach is obviously untenable because human beings invent ideas. A purely ideationalistic approach will not do either, because even if one insists that an idea matters—and ideas do matter—one still needs to explain how that idea comes to exist, spread, and matter. Unless one is prepared to accept infinite regression, one has to look at the material world for explaining how and why an idea comes to exist, spread, and matter. The social evolution paradigm thus triumphs over not only purely materialistic or purely ideationalistic approaches, but also approaches that do not synthesize the two types of forces organically.

Bringing material forces and ideational forces into an organic synthesis also means rejecting the urge to assign precise or even rough weight to material forces and ideational forces in shaping our history, an urge that has been implicitly or explicitly demanded in the heated debate between constructivism and realism. Although the social evolution paradigm gives material forces the ontological priority over ideational forces—that is, material forces came before ideational forces—it does not imply that ideational forces have played a less significant role than material forces in the whole human history or that material forces trump ideational forces all the time. The approach merely stresses that material forces came before ideational forces and that ideational forces cannot operate totally independently from material forces.

The presence of both material forces and ideational forces also means that social evolution is Lamarckian nested in Darwinism (Hodgson, 2001). Specifically, in the ideational dimension within social evolution, inheritance of acquired characteristics or Lamarckian inheritance—in the form of (learned) ideas or behaviors—not only becomes possible but also becomes a critical force in driving social changes.

The social evolution paradigm explains a system's transformation as well as its relative stability, again with a single mechanism. A social system generally depends on endogenous forces at the micro-level to drive changes at the macro-level. As a result, for most of the time, a system is relatively stable unless it encounters a powerful external shock (e.g. an asteroid hits the earth). Because micro-level changes accumulate within a system, however, the system can be transformed when micro-level changes accumulate to a threshold level. The social evolution paradigm thus endogenizes a system's transformation by grounding it upon forces at the micro-level: actions and interactions among units (agents) within the system can lead to the system's transformation.

Finally, just as Darwinian evolution is 'the universal acid' for understanding biotic evolution, the social evolution paradigm is also 'the universal acid' for understanding social evolution. For instance, some of the mechanisms singled out below have been recognized as major causes of systemic transformation of international politics separately, but the social evolution paradigm integrates these mechanisms into a unified framework. The social evolution paradigm also subsumes and integrates other micro- and middle-level mechanisms that have been uncovered for understanding international politics such as the struggle for survival, strategic behavior, selection, learning, socialization, and so on (see below).

Ancient China (1046/4 BC to 1759 AD)

Ancient Chinese history (recorded) has the unique feature of going through cycles of fragmentation to unification, and each episode of state death can be conveniently demarcated as the period between fragmentation and (re)unification. Ancient China thus experienced five major episodes of state death (Table 1).

The first episode lasted from 1046/4 to 221 BC. Between 1046 and 1044 BC, the Zhou tribe, which was a major tribe within the Shang Kingdom, initiated the attack against Shang by commanding an alliance of more than 800 tribes (Sima, 1997 [~91–87 BC]: 82). In 221 BC, the state of Qin eliminated all other states in the system and founded the first unified empire in Chinese history. In this episode of 825 years, more than 800 independent political entities were eliminated, and the rate of state death was more than 97 state deaths per century.

The Qin dynasty lasted barely 20 years and was replaced by the Han dynasty. The (Eastern) Han dynasty went into an implosion in 184 AD. In 190 AD, a major war between two rival factions of warlords erupted and China entered its second episode of state death. At the beginning of this episode, there were about 25 major warlords (Luo, 1999 [~1330–1440]). In 280 AD, the state of Jin, which replaced the state of Wei with a coup, eliminated the last remaining rival state Wu in the system. In this episode of 91 years, about 24 states were eliminated, and the rate of state death was about 26.7 state deaths per century.

In 316 AD, (Western) Jin was attacked by the Huns and the Chinese core plunged into fragmentation again, and it was not until 589 AD that the Sui dynasty was able to unify the Chinese core again. The Sui dynasty was again short-lived (lasting from 581 to 618 AD), and a stable unification was not achieved until 668 AD under the Tang dynasty. In this episode of 353 years, 28 states were eliminated, and the rate of state death had decreased to 7.9 state deaths per century.

Table 1. Pattern of state deaths in Ancient China, 1045 BC to 1759 AD[a]

Period	Western Zhou to Han Qin	Post-Eastern Han to Western Jin	Eastern (Dong) Jin to Tang	Post-Tang to Yuan	Post-Yuan to Qing
Timeframe	1045 to 221 BC	190 to 280 AD	316 to 668 AD	907 to 1276 AD	1583 to 1759 AD
Number of states at the beginning	>800	>25	29	21	8
Total territory controlled by all the states at the beginning (million km^2)	~1	~5	~6.5	~7.5	~11
Years of the period (years to eliminate all other states in the system)	825	91	353	370	177
Rate of state death (states eliminated per century)	>97	>26.7	7.9	5.4	3.9
Average time (years) needed to eliminate a state	~1.03	~3.79	~12.6	~18.5	~25.3

[a]The details of the calculations are available upon request from the author. The data presented in Tables 1 and 2 can be manipulated to obtain other results (e.g. the percentage of states eliminated in different periods), but those results do not jeopardize the central conclusion that the rate of state death had steadily decreased.

The Tang dynasty imploded from 875 to 884 AD and finally collapsed in 907 AD, and China entered its fourth episode of state death. This episode of state death would last until 1276 AD when Genghis Khan's Mongol army finally conquered China. In this episode of 370 years, 20 states were eliminated and the rate of state death had decreased to 5.4 state deaths per century.

The Mongol Yuan dynasty was replaced by the Ming dynasty in 1368. In 1583, the Manchus, which would eventually found the Qing dynasty, began its long drive toward the conquest of China and finally eliminated all the other states in the system in 1759. In this episode of 177 years, seven states were eliminated and the rate of state death had decreased to 3.9 state deaths per century.

Post-Holy Roman Empire Europe, 1450–1995 AD

For convenience, I focus on Continental Europe and exclude the littoral states (e.g. the British Isles). Thus, the European international system denotes the area between the British Channel in the west and the Urals in the east, and between the Iberian Peninsula in the south and Norway in the north. Excluding the littoral states has minimal influence on the results due to the overwhelming weight of the remaining Continental states.

I chose 1450 AD as the starting point of my inquiry for two reasons. First, the Holy Roman Empire became highly fragmented in the 15th century and its domain began to resemble a genuine anarchy. Second, states in the modern Weberian/IR sense began to emerge around the mid-15th century and state deaths caused by war began to play a prominent role in shaping European politics.

The whole time span from 1450 to 1995 is divided into five major phases: 1450–1648, 1648–1815, 1815–1919, 1919–45, and 1945–95. Except for the last phase, each phase contained at least one major war that had caused many state deaths (Table 2).

The first episode of state death in post-Roman Empire Europe lasted from 1450 to 1648. At the beginning of this episode, there were more than 581 independent political entities. Major causes of state death in this episode included the unification of France and the Netherlands, the expansion of Sweden and the Austria-Habsburg Empire, the expansion of the Ottoman Empire into Southeast Europe, and the Thirty Years War. By the end of the Thirty Years War (1648), the number of states in the system was reduced to about 260. In this episode of 199 years, more than 321 states were eliminated, and the rate of state death was about 161 state deaths per century.

The second episode lasted from 1648 to 1815. Major causes of state death in this episode included the Napoleonic Wars, the expansion of Prussia, and the expansion of Austria. In this episode of 168 years, the number of states in the system was reduced from about 260 to 63, and the rate of state death was about 117 state deaths per century.

The third episode lasted from 1815 to 1919. Major causes of state death in this episode included the unification of Italy and Germany and World War I. In this episode of 105 years, the number of states in the system was reduced from 63 to 30, and the rate of state death was about 31 state deaths per century.

The fourth episode lasted from 1919 to 1945. In this episode, the major cause of state death was the Soviet Union's annexation of East European states after World War II. In this episode of 27 years, the number of states in the system was reduced from 30 to 25, and the rate of state death was about 19 state deaths per century.

The final episode lasted from 1945 to 1995. Major causes of state death in this episode included the (re) unification of Germany, the collapse of the former Soviet Union, and the disintegration of the former Yugoslavia Federation and the former Czechoslovakia Republic. Other than the case of German unification, however, state deaths in this episode actually led to the (re)birth of many states. Moreover, none of the four state deaths was caused by wars of conquest and expansion. As a result, the number of states in the system actually increased from 25 to 35.

Summary: state death and the evolution of the international system

Although the two international systems examined above had evolved in different space and time, they had gone through a similar evolutionary path. In both systems, the number of states had decreased greatly and the average size of states had increased significantly, precisely because states in the two systems had been operating according to the logic of offensive realism (i.e. security through conquest and expansion). As a result, both systems eventually reached the same outcome that conquest had become increasingly difficult (although conquest

Table 2. Pattern of state deaths in post-Roman Empire Europe, 1450–1995 AD

Period	1450–1648	1648–1815	1815–1919	1919–45	1945–95
Number of states at the beginning of each period	~581	~260	~63	30	25
Number of states at the end of each period	~260	~63	30	25	35
Years of the period	199	168	105	27	51
Number of states eliminated in the period	~321	~197	33	5	4[a]
Rate of state death (states eliminated per century)	~161	~117	~31	~19	ND
Average time (years) needed to eliminate a state	~0.62	~0.85	~3.18	5.4	ND

[a] These state deaths have actually led to an increase in the number of states in the system. As such, it is not really meaningful to calculate rate of state death for this period.

did succeed from time to time), reflected in the steadily decreasing rate of state death.

The conclusion is also supported by evidence from more recent history. After Westphalia, no major attempts at empire-building on the European Continent had ever succeeded. Napoleon and Hitler came really close, but a powerful counter-alliance eventually overwhelmed them. Indeed, in the Great Power Era, only one attempt toward achieving regional hegemony through conquest—the continental expansion by the United States—had actually succeeded. Arguably, the success of the United States was largely due to its unique geographical environment: there was no crippling counter-alliance to counter the United States even though it behaved aggressively (Elman, 2004).

The evidence strongly suggests that as states in an offensive realism world operate according to the imperatives of an offensive realism system, they will also make the logic of offensive realism increasingly inoperable. The offensive realism world is a self-destructive system: precisely because states act according to the logic of an offensive realism world, the world will be transformed. The inherent dynamics of the offensive realism system eventually leads to the system's own demise.

From Mearsheimer to Jervis: Three Auxiliary Mechanisms

The last section highlights states' pursuit of conquest and expansion according to the logic of the offensive realism system as the fundamental mechanism behind the transformation of an offensive realism system into a defensive realism system. This section focuses on three auxiliary mechanisms—all of them depend on and build upon the outcome engineered by the fundamental mechanism—that will further cement the world into a defensive realism system.

Selection against offensive realist states

At the beginning of an offensive realism world, there may be other types of states (e.g. defensive realist states) in the system. Yet, as the system evolves, only offensive realist states that have attempted and succeeded in conquest could have survived in the system, and other types of states will either be quickly eliminated or socialized into offensive realist states. Thus, for much of the time of an offensive realism world, only one type of state—the offensive realism type—can exist in the system.

By the time that the offensive realism system reaches its late stage—that is, after the number of states has been greatly reduced and the average size of each state has greatly increased—some states would have accumulated sufficient defensive power against a potential aggressor. As a result, these states can survive mostly on defensive strategies, *if they choose to*. And if some of these states do choose to survive mostly on defensive strategies, then a new type of state—the defensive realism type—emerges in the offensive realism system. Once the system becomes populated by two types of states—an offensive realism type and a defensive realism type—a new selection dynamics becomes possible within the system.

In this late stage of an offensive realism world in which most states have accumulated more power to defend themselves either alone or by forming alliances, conquest becomes more difficult. Moreover, if a state pursues expansion but fails, it will be severely punished by the victors. As a result, more likely than not, offensive realist states will be punished—sometimes severely.

In contrast, while defensive realist states may have to fend off aggression from time to time, they will more often end up in a better position than aggressors, not only because they are more likely to defend themselves successfully but also because they do not have to endure the punishment for losing a war of conquest.

Hence, as the offensive realism systems evolves to its late stage, selection within the system will increasingly go against offensive realist states and favor of defensive realist states. The foundation of this shifting of selection pressure is the increased size of states through the elimination of states.

The negative spreading of ideas: Conquest is getting difficult

If states are strategic actors, then they must also be learning actors: states will learn and adopt ideas that are deemed to be good for their interests and reject those that are deemed to be bad for their interests, *in the long run.*

When conquest has become quite difficult in the late stage of the offensive realism world, a state that pursues conquest is more likely to be severely punished than to be rewarded. If so, one can expect that this state (and other states) will gradually learn the hard lesson that conquest is getting more difficult and rarely pays from its own and other states' experiences of having failed in pursuing conquest. Coupled with the selection pressure against offensive realist states, one can expect a majority of the states to eventually learn the lesson that conquest is getting more difficult at some point, even if the learning process may be slow and non-linear.

As a result, the system of states will gradually become a system populated mostly by states that have largely given up the option of conquest as a means toward security because they have learned the lesson that conquest is difficult and no longer pays. Such a world does not preclude the possibility that some states may remain offensive realist states and some new offensive realist states may still pop up from time to time. Because even these offensive realist states will more often than not be severely punished, however, one should expect that most of them too will eventually learn the lesson.

Further, after a period of time of spreading via negative learning, the idea that conquest is no longer easy can then spread via positive learning. The net result of this whole learning process is a change of belief among states—from one that conquest is easy and profitable to another that conquest is no longer easy and profitable.

Finally, after the idea that conquest is no longer easy and profitable is generally accepted among states, the notion that security via defensive strategies is superior to security via offensive strategies logically becomes the next idea to spread among states. This positive spreading of the idea that security via defensive strategies is superior to security via offensive strategies reinforces the change of beliefs among states—from a belief that conquest is easy and profitable and offensive strategy is a better way toward security to a new belief that conquest is no longer easy and profitable and defensive strategy is a better way toward security.

This rise and spread of ideas, first through negative and then positive learning, is *not* a purely ideational process. Instead, it has a firm foundation in *objective* social reality, and this objective foundation was provided by the repeated failures of conquest and the selection against offensive realist states, which was in turn underpinned by the decreased number of states and increased average size of state.

Only with more and more objective cases of unsuccessful conquest will states gradually learn that conquest has indeed become more difficult and it hardly pays in a world of bigger and harder targets. Only after the idea that conquest is easy has been largely disproved (or the idea that conquest is difficult has been proved) can the idea that conquest is difficult spread via positive learning.

The rise and spread of sovereignty and nationalism

The third auxiliary mechanism behind the transformation from Mearsheimer's world to Jervis's world has been the rise and spread of sovereignty and nationalism, the twin ideational pillars of the defensive realism world.

Many have argued that the gradual rise and spread of sovereignty after the medieval period has played a critical role in transforming the offensive realism world into a more benign defensive realism world (e.g. Ruggie, 1983: 273–81; Spruyt, 2006; Wendt, 1992: 412–15). Yet, none of them has explained why sovereignty rose and then spread after the medieval period, but not before.

Sovereignty is essentially a judicial recognition of the norm of coexistence within the state system (Barkin and Cronin, 1994: 111). Hence, acceptance of coexistence as a norm is the first step toward sovereignty. Acceptance of co existence as a norm, however, critically depends on coexistence as a reality, and this reality can only be provided by the increasing difficulty of conquest and expansion. In a world in which conquest is easy, it will be impossible for the norm of coexistence to rise and then spread. As such, sovereignty can only rise after many states recognize the futility of conquest. Counterfactually, why would states respect each other's sovereignty if they can easily conquer each other? Indeed, before World War I, the norm in international politics was the 'right to conquest.' The 'right to conquest' became de-legitimatized only after World War II, with respecting other states' sovereignty gradually becoming the new norm concurrently (Fazal, 2007: Ch. 7; Korman, 1996).

The rise of sovereignty provides the objective foundation for nationalism to rise and then spread because nationalism critically depends on the occupation of a core territory. The rise and spread of nationalism further cements the system of states into a defensive realism system.

First, consistent with prospect theory (Levy, 1997), a population that takes the state as its own cherished property will be more willing and determined to defend the state (than to grab somebody else's territory). Nationalism thus makes conquest less likely to succeed initially. Moreover, even if the conquest succeeded initially, occupation would be more difficult because a more nationalistic population will be less willing to obey the new master. The net result is to make the whole enterprise of conquest more difficult and thus less rewarding (Edelstein, 2004), in spite of the fact that nationalism might have indeed contributed to the outbreak of many wars (Van Evera, 1994).

Second, because offensive alliances that are geared for conquest and expansion usually cannot form and sustain themselves if parties in the alliance cannot first agree how to divide the potential spoils of conquest, and yet nationalism makes dividing and trading territory more difficult (Jervis, 1978: 205), nationalism makes offensive alliances more difficult to form and sustain. Because an offensive realist state will be less likely to initiate conquest without allies, the net result from this interaction between nationalism and the dynamics of offensive alliances makes offensive alliances more difficult to form, thus again making conquest more difficult and less likely to be pursued in the first place.

Summary

The three auxiliary mechanisms, by building upon the outcome engineered by the fundamental mechanism outlined in the last section, have all played indispensable although auxiliary roles in transforming an offensive realism world into a defensive realism world. Together with the fundamental mechanism, they have gradually but firmly transformed an offensive realism world into a defensive realism world. This conclusion is also supported by more recent developments.

After World War II, violent state death virtually ceased: a phenomenon that had no historical precedence (Fazal, 2007; Zacher, 2001). After World War II, the number of states in the international system has not decreased, but has actually increased. Most evidently, many weak states and small buffer states that would have very little chance of survival in an offensive realism world (e.g. Bhutan, Luxemburg, Singapore) survive today (Fazal, 2007). After World War II, once a country gained *de jure* independence and was recognized by the international community, respect for that country's territorial integrity is the norm and to annex that country—or even part of it—will not be accepted by the international community (Zacher, 2001). Conquest has become not only more difficult, but also increasingly, if not fully, illegitimate in the international system.

For much of human history, most wars were wars of conquest. By eliminating conquest as a principal cause of war, the evolution from an offensive realism world into a defensive realism world has also eliminated many wars. To paraphrase John Mueller (1989), war of conquest and expansion has been becoming or already is obsolete. All these developments suggest that international politics has firmly evolved from Mearsheimer's world into Jervis's world. Our world today is really a much less dangerous world for states' survival than it used to be.

Theoretical and Policy Implications

I have offered a social evolutionary account for the transformation from an offensive realism world to a defensive realism world.

I reject those theses that cannot imagine transformations in international politics and believe that international politics will be permanently stuck in the offensive realism world. International politics has always been an evolutionary system and the fundamental nature of the system can be transformed even if some features of the system (e.g. anarchy) remain the same.

My thesis improves upon those theses that seek to understand the making of the offensive realism world but say nothing about the possibility of its evolution into a different world (e.g. Mercer, 1995; Thayer, 2004). It also betters those theses that identify different types of anarchies but do not fully explain how one type of anarchy has been transformed to another type of anarchy (e.g. Wendt, 1992, 1999).

Finally, my thesis improves upon those that offer only a partial explanation of the transformation from one type of anarchy to another type of anarchy. Many have emphasized the prominence of norms and ideas in governing international politics without explaining how those ideational forces originate and come to dominate international politics in the first place (e.g. Kratochwil, 1989; Mueller, 1989; Spruyt, 2006). Others do say something about how those ideational forces arise and spread, but either do not include the objective/material world in their historical narrative or do not ground those ideational forces upon the objective/material world, and thus do not offer an endogenous explanation for the origin and spread of ideas (e.g. Adler, 2005; Buzan, 1993: 340–3; Crawford, 2002; Onuf, 1989; Ruggie, 1983; Wendt, 1992: 419, 1999: Chs 6 and 7).

For instance, Wendt argues that the three anarchies can only be sustained by self-reinforcing behaviors, and thus can only be transformed by exogenous changes in ideas and practices: the cause of transformation was purely ideational, according to Wendt (1999: Ch. 6). For Wendt (1992: 418–22), a specific precondition for the transformation from the Hobbesian world to a Lockeian world is that 'there must be *a reason* to think of oneself in novel terms' (419; emphasis added), yet he never explains why states would want to change their ideas and practices, other than heeding exogenous (i.e. Wendt's) preaching.

In contrast, in the social evolutionary framework, states will change their ideas and practices without having to heed exogenous teaching: the transformation of ideas and practices is endogenously driven. Rather than merely emphasizing the impact of ideas behind the transformation, I provide an objective foundation for the rise and spread of the ideas. I show that the gradual reduction in the number of states and increase in the average size of states provides the objective foundation for the rise and spread of several powerful ideas and that the rise and spread of those ideas in turn cement the transformation of the system from an offensive realism world into a defensive realism world.

If my social evolutionary interpretation of the transformation of international politics is sound, then it should have important implications for understanding international politics (and social changes in general). Below, I shall merely emphasize the approach's two immediate implications for international politics, leaving its wider implications for understanding social changes to be dealt with elsewhere.

An evolutionary resolution of the debates among grand theories

If international politics has been an evolutionary system and the system has undergone fundamental changes, then systemic theories—no matter how sophisticated—are inherently incapable of understanding the whole history of international politics. Systemic theories are adequate only for understanding a particular system within a specific time frame. This, I contend, has been the ultimate cause why past debates on the three major grand theories of international politics—offensive realism, defensive realism, and neoliberalism—cannot be resolved.

All three grand theories are systemic theories, but not evolutionary theories. More importantly, in these debates, proponents of these three major grand theories all strive to prove that their favored theory is the better, if not the best, theory for understanding international politics, thus implicitly striving toward the goal of explaining the whole history of international politics with a single grand theory. This belief in a better or best grand theory of international politics for the whole history of international politics is underpinned by the (implicit) assumption that the fundamental nature of international politics has remained roughly the same. As such, these debates have been implicitly trying to impose non-evolutionary theories upon an evolutionary system.

This assumption that the fundamental nature of international politics has remained roughly the same is wrong. International politics has always been an evolutionary system, and its fundamental nature has undergone transformational changes despite the fact that some of its properties (e.g. anarchy) persist. As such, to impose a single grand theory on the whole history of international politics cannot be but doomed from the start.

Once we grasp the ultimate cause why the debates among the three grand theories have not been resolved, a resolution becomes evident: *different epochs of international politics may require different grand theories of international politics*. In other words, the three different grand theories may be for three different epochs of international politics.

To begin with, offensive realism does not seem to fit well with the history of the Great Power Era. Offensive realism predicts that every great power will seek expansion and conquest until achieving regional hegemony because expansion and conquest is conducive to security. Yet, as Mearsheimer himself admitted, all but one major attempt of expansion in the Great Power Era failed and their perpetrators were severely punished. If so, then to predict (and recommend) that great powers will continue to pursue expansion is to demand that great powers strive toward the impossible and act against their own interests, thus violating realism's assumption that states are strategic actors. Indeed, offensive realist states among great powers have become increasingly rare since the late 19th century (Schweller, 2006: 104).

In contrast, defensive realism seems to fit with the history of the Great Power Era much better. Defensive realism predicts that conquests will be difficult and empires will not last, and much of the history of the Great Power Era seems to show that this has indeed been the case (Kupchan, 1994; Snyder, 1991; Walt, 1987).

From the preceding discussion it becomes clear that the reason why defensive realism fits better with the history of the Great Power Era than offensive realism is simply that international politics had begun to evolve toward a defensive realism world by the time of the Great Power Era. By then, the number of states had decreased significantly and the average size of states had increased significantly. Thus, defensive realists have been looking at the right period of history for their theory by focusing on the Great Power Era. In contrast, because international politics had begun to evolve out of the offensive realism world and toward a defensive realism world by the time of the Great Power Era, offensive realists have been looking at the wrong period of history for their theory by focusing on the Great Power Era.

If so, then while both offensive realists and defensive realists have strived to draw from and explain the history of the Great Power Era, they should actually look at two different historical periods for supporting evidence. Offensive realists should look at the pre-Great Power Era, whereas defensive realists should look at the Great Power Era. Consequently, while the two realisms can be unified *methodologically*, they should not be unified because they are *ontologically incompatible*: they are from (and for) two different historical periods.

The relationship between neoliberalism and defensive realism is a bit more complex. Robert Jervis (1999: 45, 47) rightly pointed out that 'the disagreements between neoliberalism and [defensive] realism have not only been exaggerated, but they have also been misunderstood...and their differences have been at least partly due to their tendency to focus on two different domains: Neoliberalism tends to focus on issues of international political economy and environment, whereas realism is more interested in international security.'

Jervis, however, failed to notice an even more outstanding contrast between neoliberalism and defensive realism. Whereas defensive realism has tried to examine a long period of history of international politics (from Westphalia or 1495 to today) and realism in general has claimed to apply to an even longer stretch of history (from ancient China and Greece to today), neoliberalism has rarely ventured into the terrain of international politics before World War II: almost all of the empirical cases that neoliberalists claim to support their theory have been from the post-World War II period.

Neoliberalism's self-consciously imposed temporal restriction is fundamental—it speaks of something critical about neoliberalism loud and clear. Although neoliberals have also implicitly tried to prove that neoliberalism is valid across the entire history of international politics, they have long conceded the temporal limit of neoliberalism: neoliberals have known all along that while their theory is useful for understanding the post-World War II world, it is largely irrelevant for understanding the pre-World War II period.

Neoliberals are right to concede the temporal limit of their theory. A neoliberalism world can only evolve from a defensive realism world, but cannot possibly evolve directly from an offensive realism world. In an offensive realism world in which the logic is 'to kill or be killed', attempts to pursue cooperation will be generally suicidal, and there will be no repeated cooperative interactions.

Only in a defensive realism world, in which the logic is 'to live and let live', would cooperation finally become a viable means of self-help. Moreover, only in a defensive realism world can ideas and norms that emerged from repeated cooperative interactions have a chance of being solidified into institutions. Repeated or institutionalized cooperation as self-help requires an objective foundation, and that foundation could only be provided by the transformation of the offensive realism world into the defensive realism world. Because the transformation was not firmly completed until after World War II, it is no wonder that neoliberals have self-consciously restricted their inquiries to the post-World War II era.

International politics has always been an evolutionary system and the nature of the system has undergone fundamental changes. As such, different epochs of international politics really do need different grand theories of international politics.

Consequently, the increasingly unproductive enterprise of proving that one grand theory is a 'scientifically' superior theory than another should give way to the more productive enterprise of refining individual grand theories within different historical eras. Indeed, it is impossible to know which grand theory is a scientifically superior theory without first specifying the specific historical epoch that the theory claims to explain. Theories of international politics are not timeless.

References

Adler E. (2005) *Communitarian International Relations: The Epistemic Foundations of International Relations*. London: Routledge.

Anderson B. (1983) *Imagined Communities: Reflections on the Origins and Spread of Nationalism*. London: Verso.

Barkin JS, Bruce C. (1994) The state and the nation: Changing norms and the rules of sovereignty in international relations. *International Organization* 48(1): 107–130.

Barraclough G. (ed.) (1978) *The Times Atlas of World History*. London: Times Books Limited.

Braubach M. et al. (1978) *Gebhardt Handbuch der Deutschen Geschichte (Gebhardt Handbook of German History, GHGH)*. Stuttgart: Gebhardt.

Brooks SG. (1997) Dueling realisms. *International Organization* 51(3): 445–477.

Buzan B. (1993) From international system to international society: Structural realism and regime theory meet the English School. *International Organization* 47(3): 327–352.

Carnerio R. (1978) *Political expansion as an expression of the principle of competitive exclusion*. In: Cohen R and Service E (eds) *Origins of the State*. Philadelphia, PA: Institute for the Study of Human Issues, 203–223.

Cioffi-Revilla C. (1996) Origins and evolutions of war and politics. *International Studies Quarterly* 40(1): 1–22.

Cioffi-Revilla C, David L. (1995) War and politics in Ancient China, 2700 BC to 722 BC. *Journal of Conflict Resolution* 39(3): 467–494.

Crawford NC. (2002) *Argument and Change in World Politics: Ethics, Decolonization, and Humanitarian Intervention*. Cambridge: Cambridge University Press.

Dennett DC. (1995) *Darwin's Dangerous Ideas: Evolution and the Meaning of Life*. New York: Simon & Schuster.

Diamond J. (1997) *Guns, Germs, and Steel*. New York: Norton.

Edelstein D. (2004) Occupation hazards: Why military occupations succeed or fail? *International Security* 29(1): 49–91.

Elman C. (2004) Extending offensive realism: The Louisiana purchase and America's rise to regional hegemony. *American Political Science Review* 98(4): 563–576.

Fazal TM. (2007) *State Death: The Politics and Geography of Conquest, Occupation, and Annexation*. Princeton, NJ: Princeton University Press.

Gellner E. (1983) *Nations and Nationalism*. Ithaca, NY: Cornell University Press.

Glaser C. (1994/5) Realists as optimists: Cooperation as self-help. *International Security* 19(3): 50–90.

Hodgson G. (2001) *Is social evolution Lamarckian or Darwinian?* In: Laurent J and Nightingale J (eds) *Darwinism and Evolutionary Economics*. Cheltenham: Edward Elgar, 87–120.

Hui VT. (2005) *War and State Formation in Ancient China and Early* Modern Europe. Cambridge: Cambridge University Press.

Jervis R. (1978) Cooperation under the security dilemma. *World Politics* 30(2): 167–214.

Jervis R. (1997) *System Effects: Complexity in Political and Social Life*. Princeton, NJ: Princeton University Press.

Jervis R. (1999) Realism, neoliberalism, and cooperation: Understanding the debate. *International Security* 24(1): 42–63.

Kahler M. (1999) *Evolution, choice, and international change*. In: Lake DA and Powell R (eds) *Strategic Choices and International Relations*. Princeton, NJ: Princeton University Press, 165–196.

Kang D. (2005) Hierarchy in Asian international relations: 1300–1900. *Asian Security* 1(1): 53–79.

Keegan J. (1993) *A History of Warfare*. New York: Vintage Books.

Keohane RO. (2000) Ideas part-way down', *Review of International Studies* 26(1): 125–130.

Kitcher P. (2003) *Give Darwin his due. Unpublished manuscript*, Columbia University, New York.

Korman S. (1996) *The Right of Conquest: The Acquisition of Territory by Force in International Law and Practice*. Oxford: Clarendon Press.

Kratochwil FV. (1989) *Rules, Norms, and Decisions: On the Conditions of Practical and Legal Reasoning in International Relations and Domestic Affairs*. Cambridge: Cambridge University Press.

Kremer M. (1993) Population growth and technological change: One million BC to 1990. *Quarterly Journal of Economics* 108(3): 681–716.

Kupchan CA. (1994) *The Vulnerability of Empire*. Ithaca, NY: Cornell University Press.

Levy JS. (1982) *War in the Modern Great Power System, 1495–1975*. Lexington, KY: The University Press of Kentucky.

Levy JS. (1994) Learning and foreign policy: Sweeping a conceptual minefield. *International Organization* 48(2): 279–312.

Levy JS. (1997) Prospect theory, rational choice, and international relations. *International Studies Quarterly* 41(1): 87–112.

Luo G. (1999 *[~1330–1440])* *Sanguo Yangyi* (Romance of the Three Kingdoms) trans. Roberts M. Berkeley, CA: University of California Press.

Mearsheimer JJ. (1990) Back to the future: Instability in Europe after the Cold War. *International Security* 15(1): 5–56.

Mearsheimer JJ. (2001) *The Tragedy of Great Power Politics*. New York: Norton.

Mearsheimer JJ. (2006) Interview. *International Affairs* 20(1 & 2): 105–23, 231–243.

Mercer J. (1995) Anarchy and identity. *International Organization* 49(2): 229–252.

Mueller J. (1989) *Retreat from Doomsday: The Obsolescence of Major War*. New York: Basic Books.

Muller HJ. (1959) One hundred years without Darwinism are enough. *School Science and Mathematics* 59(2): 304–316.

Onuf NG. (1989) *World of Our Making: Rules and Rule in Social Theory and International Relations*. Los Angeles, CA: University of South Carolina Press.

Palan R. (2000) A world of their making: An evaluation of the constuctivist critique in international relations. *Review of International Studies* 26(4): 575–598.

Popper K. (1979) *Objective Knowledge: An Evolutionary Approach*. Oxford: Claredon Press.

Powell R. (1994) Anarchy in international relations theory: The neorealist-neoliberal debate. *International Organization* 48(2): 313–344.

Ruggie JG. (1983) Continuity and transformation in the world polity: Toward a neorealist synthesis. *World Politics* 25(2): 261–285.

Schroeder P. (1994) *The Transformation of Europe Politics 1763–1848*. Oxford: Clarendon Press.

Schweller RL. (2006) *Unanswered Threats: Political Constraints on the Balance of Power*. Princeton, NJ: Princeton University Press.

Searle J. (1995) *The Construction of Social Reality*. New York: Free Press.

Sima Q. (1997 *[~91–87 BC]*) *Shi-ji (History)*. Shanghai: Shanghai Guji Chubanshe.

Smith A. (1986) *The Ethnic Origins of Nations*. Oxford: Basil Blackwell.

Snyder GH. (2002) Mearsheimer's world: Offensive realism and the struggle for security. *International Security* 27(1): 149–173.

Snyder J. (1991) *Myth of Empire: Domestic Politics and International Ambition*. Ithaca, NY: Cornell University Press.

Snyder J. (2002) Anarchy and culture: Insights from the anthropology of war. *International Organization* 56(1): 7–45.

Spruyt H. (1994) *The Sovereign State and its Competitors: An Analysis of Systems Changes*. Princeton, NJ: Princeton University Press.

Spruyt H. (2006) *Normative transformations in international relations and the waning of major War*. In: Vayrynen R (ed.) *The Waning of Major War*. London: Routledge, 185–205.

Sterling-Folker J. (2001) *Evolutionary tendencies in realist and liberal theory*. In: Thompson WR (ed.) *Evolutionary Interpretations of World Politics*. London: Routledge, 62–109.

Taliaferro JW. (2000/1) Security seeking under anarchy: Defensive realism revisited. *International Security* 25(3): 128–161.

Tan Q. (ed.) (1991) *Zhongguo Lishi Ditu Ji (Concise Historical Atlas of China)*. Beijing: Sinomaps Press (Zhongguo ditu chubanshe).

Tang S. (2008a) Fear in international politics: Two positions. *International Studies Review* 10(3): 451–471.

Tang S. (2008b) *From offensive to defensive realism: A social evolutionary interpretation of China's security strategy*. In Ross R and Feng Z (eds) *China's Ascent: Power, Security, and the Future of International Politics*. Ithaca, NY: Cornell University Press, 141–162.

Tang S. (2010a) *A Theory of Security Strategy for Our Time: Defensive Realism*. New York: Palgrave Macmillan.

Tang S. (2010b) Offense-defense theory: Toward a definitive understanding. *Chinese Journal of International Politics*, forthcoming.

Thayer BA. (2004) *Darwin and International Relations: On the Evolutionary Origins of War and Ethnic Conflict*. Lexington, KT: University of Kentucky Press.

Tilly C. (1990) *Coercion, Capital, and European States, AD 990–1992*. Malden, MA: Blackwell.

Van Evera S. (1990) Primed for peace: Europe after the Cold War. *International Security* 15(3): 5–57.

Van Evera S. (1994) Hypotheses on nationalism and war. *International Security* 18(4): 5–39.

Vayrynen R. (ed.) (2006) *The Waning of Major War*. London: Routledge.

Walt SM. (1987) *The Origins of Alliance*. Ithaca, NY: Cornell University Press.

Waltz KN. (1979) *Theory of International Politics*. Reading, MA: Addision-Wesley.

Wendt A. (1992) Anarchy is what states makes of it. *International Organization* 46(2): 391–425.

Wendt A. (1999) *Social Theories of International Politics*. Cambridge: Cambridge University Press.

Wendt A. (2003) Why a world state is inevitable. *European Journal of International Relations* 9(4): 491–542.

Wohlforth WC, Little R., Kaufman SJ, et al. (2007) Testing balance-of-power theory in world history. *European Journal of International Relations* 13(2): 155–185.

Zacher MW. (2001) The territorial integrity norm: International boundaries and the use of force. *International Organization* 55(2): 215–250.

Increasing the Incentives for International Cooperation

MANCUR OLSON

Many Realist and Liberal IR scholars depend upon what they call the "rational choice model" as the basis for their analyses. This article examines one aspect of this rational behavior: the inducements for cooperation. Central to Olson's analysis is the notion of collective security as a "public good." How is this public good different from others that Olson discusses? What is unique about war? How do traditional ideas of international politics as the "Prisoner's Dilemma" game shape Olson's argument? How might an adherent of the Constructivist perspective respond to this article?

II

International cooperation sometimes takes place through what might loosely be called "independent contributions." In this case cooperating or member states agree in principle to cooperate for some specified purpose or purposes and then individually determine the extent of that cooperation. In the real world this type of arrangement is usually combined with the other polar type of arrangement, to be discussed shortly, so most of the real examples that come to mind are not completely clear or altogether apt. Perhaps military alliances (and most conspicuously NATO) provide the best examples. The potential allies usually agree to form an alliance to protect each other in case one is attacked or to join in an offensive against some other power or powers. Then, once the alliance is created, the member states independently make decisions about how much military force to provide. That is, each ally decides on its own how much military force it will raise and thus contribute to the strength of the alliance. In reality these decisions may not be entirely independent because a continuous bargaining process may go on between the member states. There may also be some alliance activities which are not handled in this way at all, as in the case of NATO "infrastructure" in which, roughly speaking, each ally pays some specified share of the costs of a given facility and there is something like a joint decision about how much to spend on the facility. Nonetheless, the polar case of independent contributions is very often relevant, and not only in military alliances.

The example of support of pure research should also be emphasized here given the interesting regression results that Russett and Sullivan provide on this subject. In agreeing, however tacitly, to share pure scientific advances (if they have no currently foreseeable military or commercial value) with other states through open scientific publications the scientifically advanced countries have in effect agreed to share the benefits of their

Olson, Mancur. "Increasing the Incentives for International Cooperation." Originally published in *International Organization* 25.4 (Autumn 1971): 866–874.

expenditures on basic research. But they have not agreed, even tacitly, on how much each country is to spend on pure research. Thus the contribution each state makes to the world's cooperative search for basic laws of nature is determined independently.

In the case of the United Nations the regular financial contributions are not independently determined, at least in theory, because each state is supposed to pay a certain assessment which is (or was) collectively determined. Yet sacrifices of other kinds, including the forgoing of freedom to choose preferred national policies (e.g., trade with Rhodesia) which go against announced goals of the UN, are in large part determined independently.

Can an organization supported through independent contributions provide an optimal supply of the collective goods for which it is expected to be responsible? We can get some insight into this question from figure 1. The vertical axis measures benefits and costs in a common metric such as dollars. The logic of the argument holds whether these benefits and costs are sums of money or whether they are advantages or disadvantages of any kind that may be perceived and treated as commensurable by the states concerned. To simplify the analysis, however, the model does not include what in economics are called "income effects." These effects are usually small, and in any event the model is robust enough for the main qualitative conclusion to hold whatever the income effects may be. The horizontal axis of the figure measures the quantity of whatever collective good the international cooperation provides, e.g., the degree of pollution control, the size of an international police force, the level of defense alliance strength. The "C" curve denotes the *total* costs of each level of provision of the collective good. The "V_g" curve gives the aggregate value to all active participants of each level of provision of the collective good while the curves marked "V_i" give the value of each level to an individual state. V_i^l denotes the value of the collective good to the state that values it more highly, and V_i^s gives the same information for the state that puts the lower absolute value on the collective good. These are absolute values, so generally the larger state will have the higher curve. We could here conveniently assume that state "l" and state "s" were democracies composed of people with identical wants and incomes but that l had exactly twice the population of s so that V_i^l was exactly two-thirds as great, and V_i^s one-third as great, as V_g. This assumption and the fact that a two-member international organization is depicted are not, of course, necessary to the conclusions.

If the two member states in this example independently determine what contribution they will make to their international organization, what will each do? The only equilibrium consistent with independent determination is for country l, the large state, to provide quantity X of the collective good and for country s to provide none at all. Clearly country l finds that it maximizes the excess of benefits over costs—the distance between the V_i^l and C curves—by choosing to provide X of the collective good. Since the good is collective, it follows that if the large state provides X, that amount is also available to the small state. But when country s already has the benefit of X amount of the collective good, the value to it of an additional unit of the good is given by the slope of the V_i^s line above point X. The gain it would get from an extra unit of the collective good is less than the cost of a unit of the good so it provides none at all.

This argument has been set out in a fuller and more general way in *The Logic of Collective Action* and in the articles on alliances written by Richard Zeckhauser and myself.[1] The main point that most readers have drawn from those writings has been what I have called "the exploitation of the great by

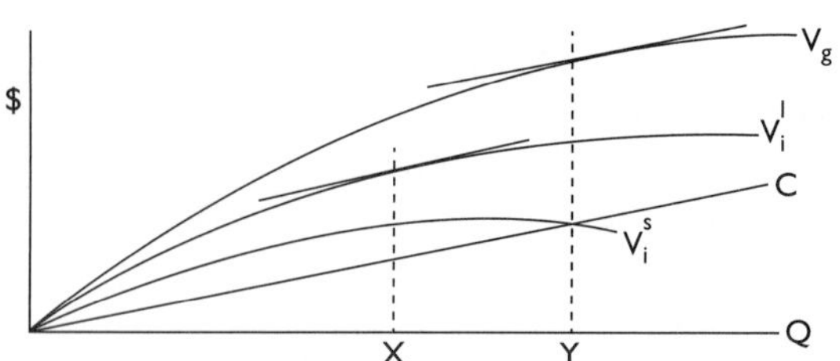

Figure 1. Support of International Organization through Independent Contributions.

the small"—a disproportionality in burden sharing that works against the big countries, as the United States government argues occurs in NATO.[2] Russett and Sullivan also emphasize this point.

For present purposes, however, the important point is quite different. It is that a much less than optimal amount of the collective good is provided. The efficient or "Pareto-optimal" level of provision of the collective good—the level at which no state could be made better off without making the other worse off—is level Y. At this point the excess of total gain over total cost is greatest so that at least one arrangement for sharing costs and benefits exists that would leave both parties as well off as, or better off than, they would be at any other level of output. If there are, as in the hypothetical example, only two members of the international organization, there is a real chance that they would bargain with each other about contributions and levels of provision until they approximated level Y. They would, in any event, have some reason to continue bargaining with each other until that result occurred. But, for the reasons pointed out in *The Logic of Collective Action,* the likelihood that bargaining will lead to an optimal solution falls off strikingly as the number of members increases and will ultimately be out of the question if there is rational, self-interested behavior. Such bargaining about contributions would, moreover, not be consistent with the polar case of "independent contributions" that we have been discussing.

III

The other polar case is that of "marginal cost sharing." This is defined as a system whereby the members of an international organization share the sacrifices needed to provide at least marginal units of a collective good in the same proportion in which they share the benefits of the additional units while simultaneously working out the level of provision and each member's contribution. The way such a system works can be illustrated by imagining that the extra cost of an additional unit of the collective good at point X in figure 1 was shared in such a way that country l paid two-thirds of the cost of that unit and country s one-third. In that case each state would have an interest in agreeing that an additional unit should be provided. They would, indeed, continue to agree to provide more, if this ideal marginal cost sharing existed, until they reached level of provision Y which is Pareto-optimal.

Simply stated, the point is this: The collective goods that international organizations provide in most cases inevitably go to all of the states in a group and in some cases probably even to all states in the world. If the arrangement for providing the collective good is such that all countries determine independently how much to contribute, they will have an interest in ceasing to contribute when their share of the total gain from another unit of the collective good (i.e., their gain from that unit) equals the cost to them of that contribution. If a state is small in relation to other members of the organization or if it is only one among a great many countries, the share of the total benefits it gets may well be, say, but a tenth or a hundredth of the total. It therefore neglects, if rational and self-interested, to make contributions that would have been worth ten or 100 times as much to the members of the organization as a whole as they cost. The level of activity of international organizations in such cases accordingly falls very far short of the desired level.

If, on the other hand, the members of the organization agree to share costs and gains at the margin in the same proportion so that the country that gets, for example, a tenth of the benefit of an additional unit of the collective good pays a tenth of the marginal cost, then that state will have an incentive to contribute more until it reaches the point at which, from the perspective of the membership as a whole, the benefits of additional activity by the international organization just equal their costs. When every member state pays just that share of the marginal cost that is equal to its share of the marginal benefit, they will also all agree on how much of the collective good to provide. If the number of members of an organization reaches the thousands or millions, such a completely voluntary marginal-cost-sharing arrangement becomes unworkable, but it may be practically feasible when the number of members is limited as it always is for organizations of nation-states.

To some degree the marginal-cost-sharing approach is already being used in international organizations. The case of infrastructure expenditures for NATO has already been mentioned, and the regressions Zeckhauser and I have reported indicate that outcomes for infrastructure appear to be greatly different from those for other NATO activities. To some extent the United Nations and a variety of other international organizations also have a faint approximation of the marginal-cost-sharing arrangement in their present policies for sharing dues or assessments. For two distinct reasons these arrangements tend to be only very faint approximations of what is set out here.

First, many dues or cost assessment schemes presumably fail to share marginal costs in the same proportion as benefits are shared even when costs of marginal units are shared in some way. Apart from other problems assessments may be arbitrary or out of date. Even when the marginal costs of an international organization are, on the average, shared in exactly the same proportion as benefits, these proportions may not hold true for each of the organization's activities considered separately. Some members of the United Nations have been more reluctant to pay a special assessment arising out of particular actions than they have been to pay assessments for regular activities, presumably because the benefits of the special activities are shared in a different way than the benefits of the regular activities. If differences in the evaluation of a collective good are so great that an activity desired by some members is deemed to be positively harmful by others, then some negative contributions, or claims to subsidies, may be needed to attain general agreement; this no doubt sometimes happens implicitly through bargaining on diverse sets of issues. There is much to be said for having separate cost-sharing arrangements for activities of different types with different configurations of benefits. (There is, by the way, no incompatibility between the idea of sharing marginal costs in the same proportion as benefits at the margin and efforts to make those states with high income pay disproportionate shares of the total cost in the interest of a more equal distribution of income. The cost of intramarginal units can be shared in any way that is desired without preventing the attainment of an optimal level of provision of the collective good, and side payments can of course also be used for redistribution).

Second, many existing dues or assessment schemes are different from the polar case set forth here in that votes on whether a given activity should be undertaken are separated from decisions about what, if anything, particular members will do or pay to support that activity. Once a given activity has been decided on, a small state in an organization the size of the United Nations knows that the level of that activity will be only triflingly affected by its own contribution. If, however, there is simultaneous decisionmaking about whether an activity should be increased or not and which state will pay how much of the additional cost, then it is at least possible that member states can, out of rational self-interest alone, agree to make the sacrifices needed to carry on an international activity to an optimal degree. As the number of members increases, even this becomes more difficult. But, since I have already discussed the reasons for this at some length in *The Logic of Collective Action,* I will write no more about them here.

Though it is presumably utopian to expect anything like an exact identity of each member's shares of marginal costs and benefits (and any deviation from this ideal leads, as I have shown elsewhere,[3] to a less than optimal level of provision), it will often be feasible to align marginal cost and benefit shares more closely than they have been aligned in the past if there is a conscious effort to do so. In those cases in which there have been simply independent contributions mutually advantageous improvements should often be easy to work out. Even changes of agenda designed to make the member states bargain more about each other's contributions—at the time that they make decisions about whether to carry on or increase particular activities—could often lead to mutually advantageous arrangements to increase the level of provision of international public goods. If what has been said about the polar case of marginal cost sharing is taken to be merely a guide about the direction in which it is best to move, however slightly at first, then it is clear that this exposition can have practical significance.

The problem which I have treated, and which also was a major concern of Russett's and Sullivan's article, is that of getting a more nearly optimal level of provision of international collective goods when optimal is defined in terms of the existing beliefs and desires of the relevant states. The desire for peace, for the other goods that could be obtained with the resources now devoted to deterrence, for orderly financial arrangements for multilateral trade, for the advance of basic knowledge, and for an ecologically viable planet are now virtually universal, yet these collective goods are only episodically or scantily supplied. Thus it would seem that the individual states of the world do not have incentives to act to obtain the collective goods they want. Taken individually, the states of the world are more often than not rational; taken together, they constitute an international system that is usually irrational. They conform, in other words, to the central insight of the theory of collective goods: With these goods, unlike others, rational individual behavior normally does not spontaneously lead to a rational collective outcome. Only arrangements designed to give individual states an incentive to act in their common interest can bring a collectively sane result. It is not in general politically naïve to propose such arrangements; since an increased provision of collective goods that are in less than optimal supply could, with an appropriate sharing of the costs of the increased supply, leave all of the participants better off in terms of their own values, there is reason to hope they can often be persuaded to accept schemes that would give each of them incentives to undertake the collectively desired behavior. Collective goods, then, are of the essence of the problem of international order. When we appreciate this, moreover, we can sometimes see politically feasible ways to increase the incentives for collectively rational behavior. Given this view, even someone with a vested interest in the collective goods approach to international organization may be forgiven for urging other students of international relations to join in the type of inquiry that Russett and Sullivan have here so insightfully moved ahead.

Notes

1. Mancur Olson, Jr., and Richard Zeckhauser, "An Economic Theory of Alliances," *Review of Economics and Statistics,* August 1966 (Vol. 48, No. 3), pp. 266–279; and by the same authors, "Collective Goods, Comparative Advantage, and Alliance Efficiency," in *Issues in Defense Economics,* ed. Roland N. McKean (National Bureau of Economic Research, Universities-National Bureau Conference Series, No. 20) (New York: National Bureau of Economic Research, 1967), pp. 25–48.
2. Quote is from Olson, *The Logic of Collective Action,* p. 29.
3. Ibid., pp. 30–31.

Collective Action and the Evolution of Social Norms

ELINOR OSTROM

Does personality matter in decision-making? Professor Ostrom, a winner of the Nobel Prize in Economics, contends that it does. In what some IR theorists, like Waltz, might dismiss as a first image analysis, Ostrom asserts that to understand the outcomes of collective action, we must consider the effects of individual psychology. How does this approach differ from that of Olson in the previous excerpt? How would Morgenthau or Waltz respond to Ostrom's findings?

With the publication of *The Logic of Collective Action* in 1965, Mancur Olson challenged a cherished foundation of modern democratic thought that groups would tend to form and take collective action whenever members jointly benefitted. Instead, Olson (1965, p. 2) offered the provocative assertion that no self-interested person would contribute to the production of a public good: "[U]nless the number of individuals in a group is quite small, or unless there is coercion or some other special device to make individuals act in their common interest, *rational, self-interested individuals will not act to achieve their common or group interests.*" This argument soon became known as the "zero contribution thesis."

The idea that rational agents were not likely to cooperate in certain settings, even when such cooperation would be to their mutual benefit, was also soon shown to have the structure of an n-person prisoner's dilemma game (Hardin 1971, 1982). Indeed, the prisoner's dilemma game, along with other social dilemmas, has come to be viewed as the canonical representation of collective action problems (Lichbach, 1996). The zero contribution thesis underpins the presumption in policy textbooks (and many contemporary public policies) that individuals cannot overcome collective action problems and need to have externally enforced rules to achieve their own long-term self-interest.

The zero contribution thesis, however, contradicts observations of everyday life. After all, many people vote, do not cheat on their taxes, and contribute effort to voluntary associations. Extensive fieldwork has by now established that individuals in all walks of life and all parts of the world voluntarily organize themselves so as to gain the benefits of trade, to provide mutual protection against risk, and to create and enforce rules that protect natural resources.[1] Solid empirical evidence is mounting that governmental policy can frustrate, rather than facilitate, the private provision of public goods (Montgomery and Bean, 1999). Field research also confirms that the temptation to free ride on the provision of collective benefits is a universal problem. In all known self-organized resource governance regimes that have survived for multiple generations, participants invest resources in monitoring and sanctioning the actions of each other so as to reduce the probability of free riding (Ostrom, 1990).

While these empirical studies have posed a severe challenge to the zero contribution theory, these findings have not yet been well integrated into an accepted, revised theory of collective action. A substantial gap exists between the theoretical prediction that self-interested individuals will have extreme difficulty in coordinating collective action and the reality that such cooperative behavior is widespread, although far from inevitable.

Both theorists and empirical researchers are trying to bridge this gap. Recent work in game theory—often in a symbiotic relationship with evidence from experimental studies—has set out to provide an alternative micro theory of individual behavior that begins to explain anomalous findings (McCabe, Rassenti and Smith, 1996; Rabin, 1993; Fehr and Schmidt, 1999; Selten, 1991; Bowles, 1998). On the empirical side, considerable effort has gone into trying to identify the key factors that affect the likelihood of successful collective action (Feeny *et al.*, 1990; Baland and Platteau, 1996; Ostrom, forthcoming).

This paper will describe both avenues of research on the underpinnings of collective action, first focusing on the experimental evidence and potential theoretical explanations, and then on the real-world empirical evidence. This two-pronged approach to the problem has been a vibrant area of research that is yielding many insights. A central finding is that the world contains multiple types of individuals, some more willing than others to initiate reciprocity to achieve the benefits of collective action. Thus, a core question is how potential cooperators signal one another and design institutions that reinforce rather than destroy conditional cooperation. While no full-blown theory of collective action yet exists, evolutionary theories appear most able to explain the diverse findings from the lab and the field and to carry the nucleus of an overarching theory.

The Evolution of Rules and Norms in the Field

Field studies of collective action problems are extensive and generally find that cooperation levels vary from extremely high to extremely low across different settings. (As discussed above, the seventh core finding from experimental research is that contextual factors affect the rate of contribution to public goods.) An immense number of contextual variables are also identified by field researchers as conducive or detrimental to endogenous collective action. Among those proposed are: the type of production and allocation functions; the predictability of resource flows; the relative scarcity of the good; the size of the group involved; the heterogeneity of the group; the dependence of the group on the good; common understanding of the group; the size of the total collective benefit; the marginal contribution by one person to the collective good; the size of the temptation to free ride; the loss to cooperators when others do not cooperate; having a choice of participating or not; the presence of leadership; past experience and level of social capital; the autonomy to make binding rules; and a wide diversity of rules that are used to change the structure of the situation (see literature cited in Ostrom, forthcoming).

Some consistent findings are emerging from empirical field research. A frequent finding is that when the users of a common-pool resource organize themselves to devise and enforce some of their own basic rules, they tend to manage local resources more sustainably than when rules are externally imposed on them (for example, Tang, 1992; Blomquist, 1992; Baland and Platteau, 1996; Wade, 1994). Common-pool resources are natural or humanly created systems that generate a finite flow of benefits where it is costly to exclude beneficiaries and one person's consumption subtracts from the amount of benefits available to others (Ostrom, Gardner and Walker, 1994). The users of a common-pool resource face a first-level dilemma that each individual would prefer that others control their use of the resource while each is able to use the resource freely. An effort to change these rules is a second-level dilemma, since the new rules that they share are a public good. Thus, users face a collective action problem, similar in many respects to the experiments discussed above, of how to cooperate when their immediate best-response strategies lead to suboptimal outcomes for all. A key question now is: How does evolutionary theory help us understand the well-established finding that many groups of individuals overcome both dilemmas? Further, how can we understand how self-organized resource regimes, that rarely rely on external third-party enforcement, frequently outperform government-owned resource regimes that rely on externally enforced, formal rules?

The emergence of self-organized collective action

From evolutionary theory, we should expect some individuals to have an initial propensity to follow a norm of reciprocity and to be willing to restrict their own use of a common pool resource so long as almost everyone reciprocates. If a small core group of users identify each other, they can begin a process of cooperation without having to devise a full-blown organization with all of the rules that they might eventually need to sustain cooperation over time. The presence of a leader or entrepreneur, who articulates different ways of organizing to improve joint outcomes, is frequently an important initial stimulus (Frohlich, Oppenheimer and Young, 1971; Varughese, 1999).[2]

If a group of users can determine its own membership—including those who agree to use the resource according to their agreed-upon rules and excluding those who do not agree to these rules—the group has made an important first step toward the development of greater trust and reciprocity. Group boundaries are frequently marked by well-understood criteria, like everyone who lives in a particular community or has joined a specific local cooperative. Membership may also be marked by symbolic boundaries and involve complex rituals and beliefs that help solidify individual beliefs about the trustworthiness of others.

Design principles of long-surviving, self-organized resource regimes

Successful self-organized resource regimes can initially draw upon locally evolved norms of reciprocity and trustworthiness and the likely presence of local leaders in most community settings. More important, however, for explaining their long-term survival and comparative effectiveness, resource regimes that have flourished over multiple generations tend to be characterized by a set of design principles. These design principles are extensively discussed in Ostrom (1990) and have been subjected to extensive empirical testing.[3] Evolutionary theory helps to explain how these design principles work to help groups sustain and build their cooperation over long periods of time.

We have already discussed the first design principle—the presence of clear boundary rules. Using this principle enables participants to know who is in and who is out of a defined set of relationships and thus with whom to cooperate. The second design principle is that the local rules-in-use restrict the amount, timing, and technology of harvesting the resource; allocate benefits proportional to required inputs; and are crafted to take local conditions into account. If a group of users is going to harvest from a resource over the long run, they must devise rules related to how much, when, and how different products are to be harvested, and they need to assess the costs on users of operating a system. Well-tailored rules help to account for the perseverance of the resource itself. How to relate user inputs to the benefits they obtain is a crucial element of establishing a fair system (Trawick, 1999). If some users get all the benefits and pay few of the costs, others become unwilling to follow rules over time.

In long-surviving irrigation systems, for example, subtly different rules are used in each system for assessing water fees used to pay for maintenance activities, but water tends to be allocated proportional to fees or other required inputs (Bardhan, 1999). Sometimes water and responsibilities for resource inputs are distributed on a share basis, sometimes on the order in which water is taken, and sometimes strictly on the amount of land irrigated. No single set of rules defined for all irrigation systems in a region would satisfy the particular problems in managing each of these broadly similar, but distinctly different, systems (Tang, 1992; Lam, 1998).

The third design principle is that most of the individuals affected by a resource regime can participate in making and modifying their rules. Resource regimes that use this principle are both able to tailor better rules to local circumstances and to devise rules that are considered fair by participants. The Chisasibi Cree, for example, have devised a complex set of entry and authority rules related to the fish stocks of James Bay as well as the beaver stock located in their defined hunting territory. Berkes (1987, p. 87) explains that these resource systems and the rules used to regulate them have survived and prospered for so long because effective "social mechanisms ensure adherence to rules which exist by virtue of mutual consent within the community. People who violate these rules suffer not only a loss of favor from the animals (important in the Cree ideology of hunting) but also social disgrace." Fair rules of distribution help to build trusting relationships, since more individuals are willing to abide by these rules because they participated in their design and also because they meet shared concepts of fairness (Bowles, 1998).

In a study of 48 irrigation systems in India, Bardhan (1999) finds that the quality of maintenance of irrigation canals is significantly lower on those systems where farmers perceive the rules to be made by a local elite. On the other hand, those farmers (of the 480 interviewed) who responded that the rules have been crafted by most of the farmers, as contrasted to the elite or the government, have a more positive attitude about the water allocation rules and the rule compliance of other farmers. Further, in all of the villages where a government agency decides how water is to be allocated and distributed, frequent rule violations are reported and farmers tend to contribute less to the local village fund. Consistent with this is the finding by Ray and Williams (1999) that the deadweight loss from upstream farmers stealing water on government-owned irrigation systems in Maharashtra, India, approaches one-fourth of the revenues that could be earned in an efficient water allocation and pricing regime.

Few long-surviving resource regimes rely only on endogenous levels of trust and reciprocity. The fourth design principle is that most long-surviving resource regimes select their own monitors, who are accountable to the users or are users themselves and who keep an eye on resource conditions as well as on user behavior. Further, the fifth design principle points out that these resource regimes use *graduated sanctions* that depend on the seriousness and context of the offense. By creating official positions for local monitors, a resource regime does not have to rely only on willing punishers to impose personal costs on those who break a rule. The community legitimates a position. In some systems, users rotate into this position so everyone has a chance to be a participant as well as a monitor. In other systems, all participants contribute resources and they hire monitors jointly. With local monitors, conditional cooperators are assured that someone is generally checking on the conformance of others to local rules. Thus, they can continue their own cooperation without constant fear that others are taking advantage of them.

On the other hand, the initial sanctions that are imposed are often so low as to have no impact on an expected benefit-cost ratio of breaking local rules (given the substantial temptations frequently involved). Rather, the initial sanction needs to be considered more as information both to the person who is "caught" and to others in the community. Everyone can make an error or can face difficult problems leading them to break a rule. Rule infractions, however, can generate a downward cascade of cooperation in a group that relies only on conditional cooperation and has no capacity to sanction (for example, Kikuchi et al., 1998). In a regime that uses graduated punishments, however, a person who purposely or by error breaks a rule is notified that others notice the infraction (thereby increasing the individual's confidence that others would also be caught). Further, the individual learns that others basically continue to extend their trust and want only a small token to convey a recognition that the mishap occurred. Self-organized regimes rely more on what Margaret Levi calls "quasi-voluntary" cooperation than either strictly voluntary or coerced cooperation (Levi, 1988). A real threat to the continuance of self-organized regimes occurs, however, if some participants break rules repeatedly. The capability to escalate sanctions enables such a regime to warn members that if they do not conform they will have to pay ever-higher sanctions and may eventually be forced to leave the community.

Threats to sustained collective action

All economic and political organizations are vulnerable to threats, and self-organized resource-governance regimes are no exception. Both exogenous and endogenous factors challenge their long-term viability. Here we will concentrate on those factors that affect the distribution of types of participants within a regime and the strength of the norms of trust and reciprocity held by participants. Major migration (out of or into an area) is always a threat that may or may not be countered effectively. Out-migration may change the economic viability of a regime due to loss of those who contribute needed resources. In-migration may bring new participants who do not trust others and do not rapidly learn social norms that have been established over a long period of time. Since collective action is largely based on mutual trust, some self-organized resource regimes that are in areas of rapid settlement have disintegrated within relatively short times (Baland and Platteau, 1996).

In addition to rapid shifts in population due to market changes or land distribution policies, several more exogenous and endogenous threats have been identified in the empirical literature (Sengupta, 1991; Bates, 1987; and literature cited in Ostrom, 1998b; Britt, 2000). These include: 1) efforts by national governments to impose a single set of rules on all governance units in a region; 2) rapid changes in technology, in factor availability, and in reliance on monetary transactions; 3) transmission failures from one generation to the next of the operational principles on which self-organized governance is based; 4) turning to external sources of help too frequently; 5) international aid that does not take account of indigenous knowledge and institutions; 6) growth of corruption and other forms of opportunistic behavior; and 7) a lack of large-scale institutional arrangements that provide fair and low-cost resolution mechanisms for conflicts that arise among local regimes, educational and extension facilities, and insurance mechanisms to help when natural disasters strike at a local level.

Contextual variables are thus essential for understanding the initial growth and sustainability of collective action as well as the challenges that long-surviving, self-organized regimes must try to overcome. Simply saying that context matters is not, however, a satisfactory theoretical approach. Adopting an evolutionary approach is the first step toward a more general theoretical synthesis that addresses the question of how context matters. In particular, we need to address how context affects the presence or absence of conditional cooperators and willing punishers and the likelihood that the norms held by these participants are adopted and strengthened by others in a relevant population.

Conclusion

Both laboratory experiments and field studies confirm that a substantial number of collective action situations are resolved successfully, at least in part. The old-style notion, pre-Mancur Olson, that groups would find ways to act in their own collective interest was not entirely misguided. Indeed, recent developments in evolutionary theory—including the study of cultural evolution—have begun to provide genetic and adaptive underpinnings for the propensity to cooperate based on the development and growth of social norms. Given the frequency and diversity of collective action situations in all modern economies, this represents a more optimistic view than the zero contribution hypothesis. Instead of pure pessimism or pure optimism, however, the picture requires further work to explain why some contextual variables enhance cooperation while others discourage it.

Empirical and theoretical work in the future needs to ask how a large array of contextual variables affects the processes of teaching and evoking social norms; of informing participants about the behavior of others and their adherence to social norms; and of rewarding those who use social norms, such as reciprocity, trust, and fairness. We need to understand how institutional, cultural, and biophysical contexts affect the types of individuals who are recruited into and leave particular types of collective action situations, the kind of information that is made available about past actions, and how individuals can themselves change structural variables so as to enhance the probabilities of norm-using types being involved and growing in strength over time.

Further developments along these lines are essential for the development of public policies that enhance socially beneficial, cooperative behavior based in part on social norms. It is possible that past policy initiatives to encourage collective action that were based primarily on externally changing payoff structures for rational egoists may have been misdirected—and perhaps even crowded out the formation of social norms that might have enhanced cooperative behavior in their own way. Increasing the authority of individuals to devise their own rules may well result in processes that allow social norms to evolve and thereby increase the probability of individuals better solving collective action problems.

Notes

1. See Milgrom, North and Weingast (1990) and Bromley et al. (1992). An extensive bibliography by Hess (1999) on diverse institutions for dealing with common pool resources can be searched on the web at (http://www.indiana.edu/—workshop/wsl/wsl.html) or obtained on a CD-ROM disk.
2. Empirical studies of civil rights movements, where contributions can be very costly, find that organizers search for ways to assure potential participants of the importance of shared internal norms and that many others will also participate (Chong, 1991). Membership in churches and other groups that jointly commit themselves to protests and other forms of collective action is also an important factor (Opp, Voss and Gem, 1995).
3. The design principles that characterize long-standing common-pool resource regimes have now been subject to considerable further empirical studies since they were first articulated (Ostrom, 1990). While minor modifications have been offered to express the design principles somewhat differently, no empirical study has challenged their validity, to my knowledge (Morrow and Hull, 1996; Asquith, 1999; Bardhan, 1999; Lam, 1998).

References

Acheson, James M. 1988. *The Lobster Gangs of Maine*. Hanover, NH: University Press of New England.

Agrawal, Arun. 1999. *Greener Pastures: Politics, Markets, and Community among a Migrant Pastoral People*. Durham, NC: Duke University Press.

Ahn, Toh-Kyeong, Elinor Ostrom, David Schmidt and James Walker. 1999. "Dilemma Games: Game Parameters and Matching Protocols." Bloomington: Indiana University, Workshop in Political Theory and Policy Analysis, Working paper.

Ahn, Toh-Kyeong, Elinor Ostrom and James Walker. 1998. "Trust and Reciprocity: Experimental Evidence from PD Games." Bloomington: Indiana University, Workshop in Political Theory and Policy Analysis, Working paper.

Asquith, Nigel M. 1999. *How Should the World Bank Encourage Private Sector Investment in Biodiversity Conservation?* A Report Prepared for Kathy MacKinnon, Biodiversity Specialist, The World Bank, Washington, D.C. Durham, North Carolina: Sanford Institute of Public Policy, Duke University.

Axelrod, Robert. 1986. "An Evolutionary Approach to Norms." *American Political Science Review*. December 80:4, pp. 1095–1111.

Baland, Jean-Marie and Jean-Philippe Platteau. 1996. *Halting Degradation of Natural Resources: Is There a Role for Rural Communities?* Oxford: Clarendon Press.

Bardhan, Pranab. 1999. "Water Community: An Empirical Analysis of Cooperation on Irrigation in South India." Berkeley: University of California, Department of Economics, Working paper.

Barkow, Jerome H., Leda Cosmides and John Tooby, eds. 1992. *The Adapted Mind: Evolutionary Psychology and the Generation of Culture*. Oxford: Oxford University Press.

Bates, Robert H. 1987. *Essays on the Political Economy of Rural Africa*. Berkeley: University of California Press.

Berkes, Fikret. 1987. "Common Property Resource Management and Cree Indian Fisheries in Subarctic Canada," in *The Question of the Commons: The Culture and Ecology of Communal*

Resources. Bonnie J. McCay and James Acheson, eds. Tucson: University of Arizona Press, pp. 66–91.

Blomquist, William. 1992. *Dividing the Waters: Governing Groundwater in Southern California*. San Francisco, CA: ICS Press.

Bohnet, Iris and Bruno S. Frey. 1999. "The Sound of Silence in Prisoner's Dilemma and Dictator Games." *Journal of Economic Behavior and Organization*. January, 38:1, pp. 43–58.

Bohnet, Iris, Bruno S. Frey and Steffen Huck. 1999. "More Order with Less Law: On Contract Enforcement, Trust, and Crowding." Cambridge, MA: Harvard University, Working paper.

Börgers, Tilman and Rajiv Sarin. 1997. "Learning Through Reinforcement and Replicator Dynamics." *Journal of Economic Theory*. 77, pp. 1–14.

Bowles, Samuel. 1998. "Endogenous Preferences: The Cultural Consequences of Markets and Other Economic Institutions." *Journal of Economic Literature*. March, 36, pp. 75–111.

Boyd, Robert and Peter J. Richerson. 1985. *Culture and the Evolutionary Process*. Chicago: University of Chicago Press.

Britt, Charla. 2000. "Forestry and Forest Policies." Bloomington: Indiana University, Workshop in Political Theory and Policy Analysis, Working paper.

Bromley, Daniel W. et al., eds. 1992. *Making the Commons Work: Theory, Practice, and Policy*. San Francisco, CA: ICS Press.

Cain, Michael. 1998. "An Experimental Investigation of Motives and Information in the Prisoner's Dilemma Game." *Advances in Group Processes*. 15, pp. 133–60.

Cameron, Lisa. 1995. "Raising the Stakes in the Ultimatum Game: Experimental Evidence from Indonesia." Princeton, NJ: Princeton University, Discussion paper.

Cardenas, Juan-Camilo, John K. Stranlund and Cleve E. Willis. 2000. "Local Environmental Control and Institutional Crowding-Out." *World Development*. Autumn, forthcoming.

Chong, Dennis. 1991. *Collective Action and the Civil Rights Movement*. Chicago: University of Chicago Press.

Clark, Andy and Annette Karmiloff-Smith. 1991. "The Cognizer's Innards: A Psychological and Philosophical Perspective on the Development of Thought." *Mind and Language*. Winter, 8:4, pp. 487–519.

Crawford, Sue E. S. and Elinor Ostrom. 1995. "A Grammar of Institutions." *American Political Science Review*. September, 89:3, pp. 582–600.

Cummins, Denise D. 1996. "Evidence of Deontic Reasoning in 3- and 4-Year-Olds." *Memory and Cognition*. 24, pp. 823–29.

Davis, Douglas D. and Charles A. Holt. 1993. *Experimental Economics*. Princeton, NJ: Princeton University Press.

Dawes, Robyn M., Jeanne McTavish and Harriet Shaklee. 1977. "Behavior, Communication, and Assumptions about Other People's Behavior in a Commons Dilemma Situation." *Journal of Personality and Social Psychology*. 35:1, pp. 1–11.

Epstein, Joshua M. and Robert Axtell. 1996. *Growing Artificial Societies: Social Science from the Bottom Up*. Cambridge, MA: MIT Press.

Eshel, Ilan, Larry Samuelson and Avner Shaked. 1998. "Altruists, Egoists, and Hooligans in a Local Interaction Model." *American Economic Review*. March, 88:1, pp. 157–79.

Feeny, David, Fikret Berkes, Bonnie J. McCay and James M. Acheson. 1990. "The Tragedy of the Commons: Twenty-Two Years Later." *Human Ecology*. 18:1, pp. 1–19.

Fehr, Ernst and Simon Gächter. Forthcoming. "Cooperation and Punishment in Public Goods Experiments." *American Economic Review*. 90:1.

Fehr, Ernst and Klaus Schmidt. 1999. "A Theory of Fairness, Competition, and Cooperation." *Quarterly Journal of Economics*. 114:3, pp. 817–68.

Frank, Robert H., Thomas Gilovich and Dennis T. Regan. 1993. "The Evolution of One-Shot Cooperation: An Experiment." *Ethology and Sociobiology*. July, 14, pp. 247–56.

Frey, Bruno S. 1994. "How Intrinsic Motivation is Crowded Out and In." *Rationality and Society*. 6, pp. 334–52.

Frohlich, Norman and Joe A. Oppenheimer. 1996. "Experiencing Impartiality to Invoke Fairness in the N-PD: Some Experimental Results." *Public Choice*. 86, pp. 117–35.

Frohlich, Norman, Joe A. Oppenheimer and Oran Young. 1971. *Political Leadership and Collective Goods*. Princeton, NJ: Princeton University Press.

Ghate, Rucha. 2000. "The Role of Autonomy in Self-Organizing Process: A Case Study of Local Forest Management in India." Bloomington: Indiana University, Workshop in Political Theory and Policy Analysis, Working paper.

Güth, Werner. 1995. "An Evolutionary Approach to Explaining Cooperative Behavior by Reciprocal Incentives." *International Journal of Game Theory*. 24, pp. 323–44.

Güth, Werner and Hartmut Kliemt. 1998. "The Indirect Evolutionary Approach: Bridging the Gap between Rationality and Adaptation." *Rationality and Society*. August, 10:3, pp. 377–99.

Güth, Werner and Menahem Yaari. 1992. "An Evolutionary Approach to Explaining Reciprocal Behavior in a Simple Strategic Game," in *Explaining Process and Change. Approaches to Evolutionary Economics*. Ulrich Witt, ed. Ann Arbor: University of Michigan Press, pp. 23–34.

Hardin, Russell. 1971. "Collective Action as an Agreeable n-Prisoners' Dilemma." *Science*. September-October, 16, pp. 472–81.

Hardin, Russell. 1982. *Collective Action*. Baltimore, MD: Johns Hopkins University Press.

Hess, Charlotte. 1999. *A Comprehensive Bibliography of Common Pool Resources*. CD-ROM. Bloomington: Indiana University, Workshop in Political Theory and Policy Analysis.

Isaac, R. Mark, James Walker and Arlington W. Williams. 1994. "Group Size and the Voluntary Provision of Public Goods: Experimental Evidence Utilizing Large Groups." *Journal of Public Economics*. May, 54:1, pp. 1–36.

Johnson, Ronald N. and Gary D. Libecap. 1982. "Contracting Problems and Regulation: The Case of the Fishery." *American Economic Review*. December, 27:5, pp. 1005–1023.

Kagel, John and Alvin Roth, eds. 1995. *The Handbook of Experimental Economics*. Princeton, NJ: Princeton University Press.

Kikuchi, Masao, Yoriko Watanabe and Toshio Yamagishi. 1996. "Accuracy in the Prediction of Others' Trustworthiness and General Trust: An Experimental Study." *Japanese Journal of Experimental Social Psychology*. 37:1, pp. 23–36.

Kikuchi, Masao, Masako Fujita, Esther Marciano and Yujiro Hayami. 1998. "State and Community in the Deterioration of a National Irrigation System." Paper presented at the World Bank-EDI Conference on "Norms and Evolution in the Grassroots of Asia," Stanford University, February 6–7.

Kreps, David M., Paul Milgrom, John Roberts and Robert Wilson. 1982. "Rational Cooperation in the Finitely Repeated Prisoner's Dilemma." *Journal of Economic Theory*. 27, pp. 245–52.

Lam, Wai Fung. 1998. *Governing Irrigation Systems in Nepal: Institutions, Infrastructure, and Collective Action*. Oakland, CA: ICS Press.

Ledyard, John. 1995. "Public Goods: A Survey of Experimental Research," in *The Handbook of Experimental Economics*. John Kagel and Alvin Roth, eds. Princeton, NJ: Princeton University Press, pp. 111–94.

Levi, Margaret. 1988. *Of Rule and Revenue*. Berkeley: University of California Press.

Lichbach, Mark Irving. 1996. *The Cooperator's Dilemma*. Ann Arbor: University of Michigan Press.

Manktelow, Ken I. and David E. Over. 1991. "Social Roles and Utilities in Reasoning with Deontic Conditionals." *Cognition*. 39, pp. 85–105.

McCabe, Kevin A., Stephen J. Rassenti and Vernon L. Smith. 1996. "Game Theory and Reciprocity in Some Extensive Form Experimental Games." *Proceedings of the National Academy of Sciences*. November, 93, 13, 421–13, 428.

McCabe, Kevin A. and Vernon L. Smith. 1999. "Strategic Analysis by Players in Games: What Information Do They Use." Tucson: University of Arizona, Economic Research Laboratory, Working paper.

Milgrom, Paul R., Douglass C. North and Barry R. Weingast. 1990. "The Role of Institutions in the Revival of Trade: The Law Merchant, Private Judges, and the Champagne Fairs." *Economics and Politics*. March, 2:1, pp. 1–23.

Montgomery, Michael R. and Richard Bean. 1999. "Market Failure, Government Failure, and the Private Supply of Public Goods: The Case of Climate-Controlled Walkway Networks." *Public Choice*. June, 99:3/4, pp. 403–37.

Morrow, Christopher E. and Rebecca Watts Hull. 1996. "Donor-Initiated Common Pool Resource Institutions: The Case of the Yanesha Forestry Cooperative." *World Development*. 24:10, pp. 1641–1657.

Nowak, Martin A. and Karl Sigmund. 1998. "Evolution of Indirect Reciprocity by Image Scoring." *Nature*. 393:6685, pp. 573–77.

Oaksford, Mike and Nick Chater. 1994. "A Rational Analysis of the Selection Task as Optimal Data Selection." *Psychological Review*. 101:4, pp. 608–31.

Offerman, Theo. 1997. *Beliefs and Decision Rules in Public Goods Games: Theory and Experiments*. Dordrecht, the Netherlands: Kluwer Academic Publishers.

Olson, Mancur. 1965. *The Logic of Collective Action: Public Goods and the Theory of Groups*. Cambridge, MA: Harvard University Press.

Opp, Karl-Dieter, Peter Voss and Christiana Gern. 1995. *Origins of Spontaneous Revolution*. Ann Arbor: University of Michigan Press.

Ostrom, Elinor. 1990. *Governing the Commons: The Evolution of Institutions for Collective Action*. New York: Cambridge University Press.

Ostrom, Elinor. 1998a. "A Behavioral Approach to the Rational Choice Theory of Collective Action." *American Political Science Review*. March, 92:1, pp. 1–22.

Ostrom, Elinor. 1998b. "Institutional Analysis, Design Principles, and Threats to Sustainable Community Governance and Management of Commons," in *Law and the Governance of Renewable Resources: Studies from Northern Europe and Africa*. Erling Berge and Nils Christian Stenseth, eds. Oakland, CA: ICS Press, pp. 27–53.

Ostrom, Elinor. Forthcoming. "Reformulating the Commons," in *The Commons Revisited: An Americas Perspective*. Joanna Burger, Richard Norgaard, Elinor Ostrom, David Policansky, and Bernard Goldstein, eds. Washington, DC: Island Press.

Ostrom, Elinor, Roy Gardner and James Walker. 1994. *Rules, Games, and Common-Pool Resources*. Ann Arbor: University of Michigan Press.

Ostrom, Elinor and James Walker. 1997. "Neither Markets Nor States: Linking Transformation Processes in Collective Action Arenas," in *Perspectives on Public Choice: A Handbook*. Dennis C. Mueller, ed. Cambridge: Cambridge University Press, pp. 35–72.

Pinker, Steven. 1994. *The Language Instinct*. New York: W. Morrow.

Posner, Richard A. and Eric B. Rasmusen. 1999. "Creating and Enforcing Norms, with Special Reference to Sanctions." *International Review of Law and Economics*. September, 19:3, pp. 369–82.

Rabin, Matthew. 1993. "Incorporating Fairness into Game Theory and Economics." *American Economic Review*. 83, pp. 1281–1302.

Ray, Ishar and Jeffrey Williams. 1999. "Evaluation of Price Policy in the Presence of Water Theft." *American Journal of Agricultural Economics*. November, 81, pp. 928–41.

Schlager, Edella. 1994. "Fishers' Institutional Responses to Common-Pool Resource Dilemmas," in *Rules, Games, and Common-Pool Resources*. Elinor Ostrom, Roy Gardner, and James Walker, eds. Ann Arbor: University of Michigan Press, pp. 247–65.

Selten, Reinhard. 1991. "Evolution, Learning, and Economic Behavior." *Games and Economic Behavior*. February, 3:1, pp. 3–24.

Sengupta, Nirmal. 1991. *Managing Common Property: Irrigation in India and the Philippines*. New Delhi: Sage.

Sethi, Rajiv and Eswaran Somanathan. 1996. "The Evolution of Social Norms in Common Property Resource Use." *American Economic Review*. September, 86:4, pp. 766–88.

Tang, Shui Yan. 1992. *Institutions and Collective Action: Self Governance in Irrigation*. San Francisco, CA: ICS Press.

Trawick, Paul. 1999. "The Moral Economy of Water: 'Comedy' and 'Tragedy' in the Andean Commons." Lexington: University of Kentucky, Department of Anthropology, Working paper.

Varughese, George. 1999. "Villagers, Bureaucrats, and Forests in Nepal: Designing Governance for a Complex Resource." Ph.D. dissertation, Indiana University.

Wade, Robert. 1994. *Village Republics: Economic Conditions for Collective Action in South India*. San Francisco, CA: ICS Press.

Yoder, Robert D. 1992. *Performance of the Chhattis Mauja Irrigation System, a Thirty-five Hundred Hectare System Built and Managed by Farmers in Nepal*. Colombo, Sri Lanka: International Irrigation Management Institute.

Useful Internet Resources

These four sources of primary texts of philosophy will be useful to students for outside reading assignments:

Internet Classics Archive, http://classics.mit.edu/index.html

Online Library of Liberty, http://oll.libertyfund.org/

Perseus Digital Library, http://www.perseus.tufts.edu/hopper/

Project Gutenberg, http://promo.net/pg/

Marxists Internet Encyclopedia, www.marxists.org, the source for anything to do with the past, present, and future of Marx and his followers. Includes biographical sketches, texts, and letters. The latter includes letters from Jenny Marx to Engels and others.

United Nations Women Watch: Women, Peace and Security, http://www.un.org/womenwatch/feature/wps/. The UN site for information of on all aspects of women in international politics.

Stanford Encyclopedia of Philosophy, http://plato.stanford.edu/. An excellent peer-reviewed free encyclopedia that features articles on all schools of thought.

Discussion Questions and Activities

1. Which of the perspectives presented in this part best fits with your worldview? Why? Give examples of recent events to support your reasoning.
2. Did any of the reading extracts in this part change the way that you perceive global events? In what ways did your personal perspective change?
3. Can human nature—and state behavior, as Morgenthau argues—be reduced to a set of rules? Explain your answer.
4. What helps to explain the dominance of Realism in the academic study of IR?
5. In January 2011, U.S. President Barack Obama hosted a state visit by Chinese President Hu Jintao. In preparation for this meeting, you, as assistant to the National Security Advisor, are asked to create a briefing paper of the key areas of interaction between the two countries. From which of the academic perspectives presented in this part would you argue? Why? How would an advocate of another academic theory presented here respond to your briefing paper?

Foreign Policy Actors: States, IOs, NGOs

Having safely navigated the mysterious waters of IR theory, we turn now to an overview of the major actors of our discipline. As we learned in the previous part, proponents of the five main schools of thought give different weight in their work to each of these actors. If you need to refresh your memory, look back to Table 2.1. But remember this: as with other concepts and terms, there are disagreements both between and within each IR theory perspective about this topic as well.

We do not need an in-depth analysis of the intellectual origins of these disagreements at this point. If you take other IR classes, you will no doubt learn more about this. Right now we need to know only that the disputes relating to terminology and definitions stem from the ways in which experts in the discipline conduct their research. Many members of the discipline follow the positivist method of political science. Using that method, political scientists look for answers to questions by isolating dependent and independent variables as they seek to establish what we call "causal connections" between events. Therefore, just like biologists, chemists, and others in the natural or physical sciences, IR specialists need to be able to isolate and compare similar items. For example, a biologist would probably not conduct research that compared the flight characteristics of fruit flies with those of bowling balls. In the same manner, our research should compare the same kinds of actors: states to states; or the influence of various transnational corporations (TNCs) on trade policy among a certain category of states. We have said enough for now. Let's turn to a discussion of the kinds of actors that specialists study in the discipline of IR.

The State

As we saw in the Part Two, since 1648 the state has been recognized as the sole sovereign and legitimate authority in the modern international system. But what do we mean by "the state"? For students in the United States, this can be confusing for an obvious reason: fifty states make up the union. For IR specialists the term has a different meaning. The state can also mean "the government;" the two are often used interchangeably as synonyms. Some scholars often expand the definition of the state to include any domestic actor or organization that helps to give legitimacy to the state. This can include the news media, schools, religious institutions, and labor unions. Even the music we listen to or the movies we watch might help to build support for the state if it encourages us to behave and follow orders. Compare, for example, the message of the 1960s war movie "The Green Berets" with that of the "Jason Bourne" series. This is not a new idea: in *The Republic* Socrates describes the correct kind of music that Guardians-in-training should be permitted to hear.

The state is the highest-order structure in domestic politics, the major actor of that political system that engages with the outside world. As a result of this psychological location on the frontier, we as citizens tend to give the state certain prerogatives: for example, national governments conduct legitimate and authoritative foreign policy actions as opposed to cities or counties. States interact with other states in the development of international law. States also go to war with other states.

Recently this idea that the state is the sole legitimate actor has become the subject of debate between some IR specialists. These attacks come from two directions: from advocates of the enhanced role of "supranational organizations" that we discuss next and from those who assert an important role for non-governmental organizations, the topic of a subsequent section.

International Organizations (IOs)

Like the name suggests, international organizations are institutions composed of states. IOs are often called "supranational organizations" because they exist at a level above that of the nation-states. A subfield of international relations examines IOs and international cooperation. The field has a well-developed theory base that helps to explain why and when states will cooperate.

The amount of authority and legitimacy an IO has is a direct result of how much of its own authority and legitimacy member-states are willing to give to that institution. For example, all member-states of the United Nations are expected to pay their membership assessment (dues) on time. Yet, during the 1980s the United States—the prime mover in the creation of the UN—refused to pay its assessment because of a dispute about the way a UN specialized agency, UNESCO, did its business. This is ironic because in the 1950s and 1960s the USSR and its allies often criticized the UN for being a tool of U.S. foreign policy. On a more mundane level, the UN General Assembly passes "resolutions," not "laws." These resolutions are not binding on the behavior of member-states but provide agreed-upon "suggestions" as to how states should act or behave. We see this with human rights resolutions discussed below. Many member-states solemnly promise at UN General Assembly sessions to respect specific kinds of human rights, and then carry on with repression as usual at home.

These negative examples aside, there is one very successful supranational organization: the European Union. Beginning as the six-member European Economic Community, the EU now has twenty-seven member-states, with others seeking to join. The EU has a parliament that enacts binding legislation, a legal system, and most importantly a single currency, the Euro, which sixteen of its members use. Recently the global recession that began in 2008 has shaken the financial health of the EU, but the organization seems able to cope with the challenge.

Non-Governmental Organizations (NGOs)

Non-governmental organizations (NGOs) are part of what some scholars call "global civil society" that is composed of non-state and private groups. There are many kinds of NGOs, including TNCs, trade unions, religious groups, and environmental groups. Table 3.1 summarizes some of the kinds of groups that are active today. Because they transcend state borders, NGOs represent a challenge to the state-centric model of IR that the Realist perspective champions. For example, a TNC conducts its operations in several nation-states at once: the corporate offices might be in London, the design staff might be in Philadelphia, and the production facilities might be in Vietnam, Hong Kong, and Sri Lanka. With a global reach like this, the corporation is able to take advantage of regulatory loopholes to maximize profits and in many cases avoid taxation.

Table 3.1 Some Non-State Actors in Global Civil Society

	Approximate Global Total	Activities	Examples
Transnational corporations	77,200+ parent firms, with 800,000+ foreign affiliates	Production, marketing, sales of goods and services	Adidas, Nike, Volkswagen, Starbucks, IKEA, Accenture, RIM/BlackBerry
Transnational advocacy networks (TANs), transnational social movements (TSMOs)	Single-country NGOs: 100,000+ International NGOs: 29,000+; 1,700+ in direct association with the UN	Working for change on a range of social, economic, political causes	Global Witness; Human Rights Watch; Amnesty International; Friends of the Earth; World Federalist Movement
Criminal organizations	Unknown	Production and sale of illegal or contraband items	Medellín cartel
Revolutionary movements	Unknown	Seeking political or social change	Taliban; Al Qaeda; Red Army Faction

(Source: Lamy et al, *Introduction to Global Politics*, First Edition)

An advocacy network is a kind of NGO that strives to push public policy on an issue in a direction that the group favors. Like the Alternative Globalization Movement and the anti-landmine coalition discussed in the readings below, the global environmental movement is an example of an advocacy network. Although groups like Friends of the Earth and Greenpeace International have a transnational reach, regional and national groups like Sierra Club, the Appalachian Mountain Club, Réseau Action Climat France, Amazon Watch, and the Nepali National Trust for Nature Conservation can join the network. As you will see in the readings, advocacy networks often share e-mail addresses, organize joint meetings, and stage media events to attract attention to their causes.

We turn now to the reading excerpts.

READING SELECTIONS

On the Political Relevance of Global Civil Society

RICHARD FALK

Professor Richard Falk confronts in this reading the state-centric approach favored by the realist perspective. Noted for his advocacy of the radical liberal World Order Models Project (WOMP), Falk shows us how globalized capitalism created its own opposing force. According to Falk, the emerging global civil society can help to create capitalism with a human face. How did the end of the Cold War alter the relationship between states, corporations, and civil society? Does Falk believe that states and corporations have an obligation to engage with members of civil society? Why? Why not? What role should normative considerations have in creating public goods in global society? What proof does Falk offer for his assertion that civil society is "regrouping"?

12.1 Engaging the Project

The pursuit of a responsible global capitalism needs to be understood, above all, as both a political project and an evolving process. By this is meant that there must be given some attention to what political scientists call the problem of agency, the actors, and social forces that are committed to the desired course of change. Such a view is sceptical about reliance on patterns of voluntary adjustment, whether as a result of moral sentiments, the benevolence of those in the private sector whose behaviour is under critical scrutiny, or as a pragmatic response to social pressures. Ideas do matter, and voluntary adjustments can be significant under certain circumstances, but the history of social change confirms the view that very little of lasting significance occurs without threats posed to the established order by those advocates of change sufficiently engaged to mount a struggle, take risks, make sacrifices, and in the end, generate incentives for elites to strike bargains of accommodation. Crudely put, the humanization of industrial capitalism since the mid-nineteenth century must be understood predominantly as an outcome of struggle, centring upon the emergence in civil society of a robust labour movement increasingly influenced by radical thought, especially by the Marxist critique of capitalist exploitation combined with revolutionary optimism about the socialist future of humanity.

When the forces seeking change become 'dangerous classes' then elites move beyond gestures of compromise to seek negotiated settlements that aim to institutionalize a regulatory regime that is reflective of a new societal consensus giving rise to an equilibrium between civil society and the private business sector. The great triumph of capitalism was its willingness to give ground in relation to successive phases of this challenge during the latter part of the nineteenth and until last decade of the twentieth century. In so doing, it gradually

MAKING GLOBALIZATION GOOD edited by Dunning (2004) 2200w from Chp. "On the Political Relevance of Global Civil Society" pp. 280–291, 296, 298 incorporated into its operations a sufficient degree of moral sensitivity to overcome the challenges posed by Marxist ideas and labour radicalism, a challenge made also geopolitically formidable after the First World War. Again moral adjustments were mainly achieved as a result of pressures, both from within and without, and a sense in the private sector, that unless social reforms were accepted, the capitalist system could not survive, and especially could not be combined with political liberalism, which here meant moderation of governmental authority as assured by the rule of law reinforced by constitutionalism. Economists, especially Keynes, gave intellectual respectability to a new, and more socially responsible capitalism, that pledged full employment, and accorded organized labour an important seat at the tables of government and policy formation.

But the long period of the Cold War, with its priorities of national security, the changing nature of capitalist enterprise, and the public dislike of the governmental bureaucracy that administered the huge programmes of social democracy, created a climate of opinion that over time became anti-government and anti-labour. Such a climate gave rise in the 1980s to the Thatcher/Reagan reorientation of capitalism around a more economistic approach that weakened the weight of moral factors, especially the compassionate elements of welfare capitalism, and substituted in their place an increased reliance on efficiency and the profit motive. When the Cold War wound down, inducing the collapse of the Soviet Union, the ideological endorsement of neo-liberalism by the governments and rapidly constituted business elites of the successor states was immediate and abrupt. The Chinese embrace of capitalism, coupled with its spectacular rate of economic growth, provided further testimony that the way to go was through reliance on capital-guided market factors. Also influential was the impressive records of sustained economic growth by Japan and the emerging markets, especially in Asia. This ideological consensus was further promoted by the growing influence of international financial institutions, the efforts of the World Economic Forum at its annual meetings at Davos, and the actions taken at the Group of Seven annual economic summits of industrial countries. Moreover, it was being increasingly accepted even by left-leaning political leaders in the third world. In this 'end of history' atmosphere, it seemed as if the global future belonged to this interplay of banks and corporations, helped along by the dominance of neo-liberal ideas as promoted by leading governments, by the Internet, and by the waning national and global influence of labour.

It is not surprising that, in such a political environment, global capitalism abandoned its moral pretensions, and reverted to its virtually unregulated form of the early industrial revolution. There no longer existed, domestically or internationally, a credible socialist alternative, and it was socialism with its explicit focus on human well-being that all along gave capitalists the practical incentive to achieve moral credibility in the eyes of the public, even at the cost of narrowing profit margins.

In the face of these developments, there are abundant reasons to be concerned about the overall effects of economic globalization. In the 1980s and early 1990s, the income gaps between rich and poor within and between societies were widening at an exponential rate, while poverty afflicted half of the world's population that was earning less than $2 per day, not to mention the hundreds of millions without safe drinking water, health facilities, and educational opportunities. Whole regions, especially sub-Saharan Africa and the Caribbean/Central America, were virtually excluded from the benefits of global economic growth. There were resentments associated with the way in which the IMF and World Bank seemed to be following the lead of Wall Street and Davos, without regard to their social effects or moral implications, especially in relation to the more economically disadvantaged countries and the poor generally. It became clear that these global managers of fiscal discipline were often precluding third world governments from devoting scarce resources to social priorities and rapid development.

Despite these signs of distress there was little adverse reaction to globalization until the two shocks of the late 1990s. First, the Asian Economic Crisis, which started in 1997 with volatile currency markets and banking scandals in South Asia, not only cancelled overnight the gains of the poorest half of the population in countries such as Indonesia, Thailand, and Malaysia, but burst the bubble of globalization. These regional adversities, in a variety of forms, soon spread to Japan, Russia, Turkey, and elsewhere in succeeding years. Second, there was the dramatic birth of the anti-globalization movement at Seattle during the WTO ministerial meetings at the end of 1999, which generated a series of demonstrations around the world whenever and wherever the policymakers of globalization gathered. The movement reached its climax at Genoa, where turbulent and large Genoa anti-globalization manifestations took place, which were timed to coincide with the meetings of the G-7 (now G-8, with the inclusion of Russia).

As with earlier efforts of capitalism to achieve wider societal acceptance, these developments posed new threats to the global capitalist order: functional threats associated with the absence of appropriate regulation and normative threats arising from the spreading grassroots perception of globalization as both immoral and anti-democratic. More to the point, these challenges helped to shape a double political project: first, the transformation of globalization by civil society; and, second, the legitimation of globalization by business elites and their allies in government. The problem of agency was far from solved, but, at the very least, the combination of chaotic markets and massive street protests shook the champions of globalization out of their mood of complacency.

The common ground was the need for *normative* (moral, legal, and regulative) adjustment in the actual and perceived workings of the world economy, so that economic growth was seen as contributing a greater share of the returns on investment and trade revenue to *public goods* (domestically, regionally, and globally); and by so doing, to insulate fragile economies from sharp declines. As with the backlash against the abuses of early industrial capitalism almost two centuries ago, it became clear that unbridled market forces lead to corruption, exploitation, and zones of severe deprivation. The humanizing of capitalism is not a self-generating force, but must be achieved by the constant exertion of pressure. These include both challenges from those that allege victimization and responses by those that control economic policy.

Such an evolving set of circumstances was seriously dislocated by the events of 11 September, and its aftermath, especially the military campaign in Afghanistan. All at once, the United States was at war—not in a conventional sense of a struggle carried on against another state, but in the form of an undertaking to crush terrorism on a worldwide basis. Such a war, new in the annals of warfare, knows no boundaries of time or space, and its perpetrators—on both sides—pick their targets without any show of deference to the territorial rights of sovereign states. With the United States as the chief target of the al Qaeda network, as well as the leader of the response, the preoccupations of the moment have shifted away from transnational economic issues, back in the direction of traditional strategic geopolitics with its focus of global security and the war/peace agenda. The world economy persists, evolves, and its positive and negative effects are felt in a variety of settings, but at this point it is no longer the focal point of political and media attention. Indeed, it is now unclear whether we are experiencing a temporary diversion in the emergent era of globalization or we are at the early stages of a second Cold War fought along civilizational lines.

The transnational forces of civil society are also in the process of regrouping. To some extent, their attention has also shifted in the direction of war/peace issues and the adoption of priorities associated with the resistance to what is seen as American empire-building. True, the World Social Forum (modeled as a counterpart to the World Economic Forum) in 2002 held successful meetings in Porto Allegro, Brazil, but the momentum for global economic reform and regulation seems to have slowed to a virtual halt. There are some minor countertrends that could in time, alter this assessment, such as the acknowledgement that mass impoverishment may act as breeding grounds for terrorists, leading to some attention being devoted to economically deprived states by the United States and other governments.

12.2 The Politics of Language

The emphasis of this chapter is upon social forces and moral pressures that are responding in politically significant ways to the patterns of behaviour associated with the current phase of global capitalism. As a consequence, it seems preferable to frame such activity by reference to 'global civil society' rather than to 'transnational civil society'. Even so, the word 'society' is definitely problematic at this stage of global social and political evolution, due to the increasing porosity of natural boundaries and the persisting weakness of social bonds transcending nation, race, and gender. Such a difficulty exists whether the reference is to 'transnational civil society' or to 'global civil society'. But the transnational referent tends to root the identity of the actors in the subsoil of national consciousness, and in so doing, tends to neglect the degree to which the orientation is not one of crossing borders, but of inhabiting and constructing a polity appropriate for the globalizing social order. Such a nascent global polity is already partly extant, yet remains mostly emergent (Wapner 1996).

A similar issue arises with respect to the selection of appropriate terminology to rely upon when identifying the actors. It seems convenient to retain the term non-governmental organizations (NGOs) to designate those actors associated with global civil society, because it is accurate and convenient, widely used, and thus easily recognizable. But it is also somewhat misleading in relation to the fundamental hypothesis of a diminishing ordering capability by the sovereign state and states system. To contrast the actors and action of global civil society with the governments of states, as is done by calling them NGOs, is to confer a derivative and subordinate status, and to imply the persistence of a superordinate Westphalian world of sovereign states as the principal constituents of the contemporary world order. Until recently, this hierarchical dualism was justifiable because the pre-eminence of the state was an empirical reality, and the absence of any other significant international actors capable of autonomous action.

There is by now a wide and growing literature on 'global civil society,' especially as related to environmental politics on a global level (Wapner 1996; Lipschutz 1996; *Global Civil Society Yearbook* 2001). For our purposes, global civil society refers to the field of action and thought occupied by individual and collective citizen initiatives of a voluntary, non-profit character both within states and transnationally. These initiatives proceed from a global orientation, and are responses, in part at least, to certain globalizing tendencies that are perceived to be partially or totally adverse. At present, most of the global provocation is associated directly or indirectly with market forces and the discipline of regional and global capital. As will be made clear, such a critical stance towards economic globalization does not entail an overall repudiation, but it does seek to identify the ways in which its adverse effects correct social injustices, and reconcile the management of the world economy with aspirations for global democracy.

To further focus our inquiry, I also propose to rely upon a distinction that I have used previously, although always with some misgivings: that is, between global market forces identified as *globalization-from-above* and a set of oppositional responses of transnational social activism and global civil society that are identified as *globalization-from-below* (Falk 1993, 1995). This distinction may seem unduly polarizing and hierarchical, and to construct a dualistic world of good and evil. My intention is neither hierarchical nor moralistic, and there is no illusion that the social forces emanating from global civil society are inherently benevolent, while those from the corporate/statist collaboration are necessarily malevolent. Far from it. One of the contentions of the chapter is that there are dangerous chauvinistic and extremist societal energies being released by one series of ultra-nationalist responses to *globalization-from-above* that are threatening the achievements of the modern secular world that had been based on the normative side of the evolution of an anarchic society of states in the cumulative direction of humane governance (Bull 1977). It is no less important to acknowledge that there are strong positive effects and potentialities arising from the various aspects of *globalization-from-above* (Hirst and Thompson 1996; Held and McGrew 1999). At the same time, the historic role of *globalization-from-below* is to challenge, resist, and transform the negative features of *globalization-from-above*, both by providing alternative ideological and political space to that currently occupied by market-oriented and statist outlooks and by offering opposition to the excesses and distortions that can be properly attributed to globalization in its current phase. That is, *globalization-from-below* is not dogmatically opposed to *globalization-from-above*, but addresses itself to the avoidance of its adverse effects, and to providing an overall counterweight to the essentially unchecked influence currently exerted by business and finance on the process of decision at the level of the state and beyond.

12.3 Responding to Economic Globalization

There have been varied failed responses to economic globalization, conceived of as the capitalist portion of the world economy. Without entering into an assessment of these failures, it is worth noticing that the efforts of both Soviet-style socialism and Maoism, especially during the period of the Cultural Revolution in China, to avoid the perceived deforming effects of global capitalism, were dramatic and drastic, and ended in disaster. By contrast, despite the difficulties, the subsequent embrace of the market by China under the rubric of 'modernization', and even by Russia (and the former members of the Soviet empire), in the form of the capitalist path have been generally successful. The same is true for many third world countries that have forged a middle path between socialism and capitalism, and in doing so have relied on the state as a major player in the economy, particularly with respect to market facilitating support services, public utilities, and energy. For most of these countries, as well, the change from a defensive hostility toward the world market to a position of enthusiastic accommodation has been generally treated by domestic elites as a blessing.

In the last two decades, the learning experience at the level of the state has been largely one of submission to the discipline of global capitalism as it pertains to the specific conditions of each country. Fashionable ideas of 'de-linking' and 'self-reliance' are in a shambles, as is perhaps best illustrated by the inability of North Korea, the greatest of all champions of a stand alone anti-capitalist economics, to feed its population. In contrast, its capitalist rival sibling, South Korea, has often been observed scaling the peaks of affluence, as well as moving ahead with democratization. Looked at differently, it is the geopolitical managers of the world economy who use such policies of exclusion and denial as a punishment for supposedly deviant and hostile states seeking to legitimize such a coercive diplomacy under the rubric of 'sanctions', a policy often widely criticized in this period because of its cruel effects on the civilian population of the target society.

Another response to the hegemonic influence global capitalism has taken the negative form of extreme backlash politics. Such a response looks for inspiration either backwards towards some pre-modern traditional framework deemed viable and virtuous (as with religious extremists of varying identity, or of indigenous peoples), or forwards by ultra-territorialists who want to construct an economic and political system around the archaic model of protectionism, keeping capital at home and excluding foreigners to the extent possible. These responses, aside from those of indigenous peoples, have a rightist flavour because of their intense affirmation of a religious or nationalist community that is at war with the evil 'other' or the infidel, being identified as secularist or outsider, and more graphically, as Western, Christian, Crusader, American. The most menacing form of such backlash politics is now associated with the al Qaida efforts to launch an inter-civilizational war on 11 September. To the extent that these movements have gained control of states, as in Iran since the Islamic Revolution, or even threatened to do so, as in Algeria since 1992, the results have been dismal: economic deterioration, political repression, widespread civil strife, exclusion from world markets. Even more serious, however, is its recourse to mega-terrorism that has unleashed a global war against terrorism being conducted under US leadership on a broad basis that poses its own dangers (Falk 2002).

Specific causes of these backlash phenomena are related to the perceived political and economic failures of global capitalism, and its secularist and materialist outlook as an example of post-colonial Western or American hegemony. However, the correctives proposed have yet to exhibit a capacity to generate an alternative that is capable of either successful economic performance or able to win genuine democratic consent from relevant political communities. At the same time, at least prior to 11 September, the anti-glohalization movement was coming of age. One aspect of its growing maturity was its tighter internal discipline and intellectual coherence. Another was its entry into dialogue in prime-time arenas of global capitalism such as the World Economic Forum and the World Bank; and, perhaps most impressive of all, its capacity to work in collaboration with governments to promote global reforms.

Local grassroots politics has been another type of response directed at the siting of a nuclear power reactor or large dam, mobilizing residents of the area facing displacement and loss of traditional livelihood, and sometimes involving others from the society and beyond, who identify with the poor, the displaced, and with nature. These struggles have had some notable successes. But these are reactions to symptomatic disorders associated with the choice of developmental shortcuts, either motivated by glory-seeking national leaders, by greedy investors, by international financial institutions thinking mainly of aggregate economic growth, and most often some combination of these factors. Such local forms of resistance can be effective, and over the years, have led the World Bank, and more generally the investment community, to be more sensitive to the human, environmental, and health effects of large-scale development projects.

Closely related to the above issues have been a variety of activist attempts by elements of global civil society to protect the global commons against the more predatory dimensions of globalization (Shiva 1987; Rich 1994; Keck and Sikkuk 1998). Here Greenpeace has had a pioneering and distinguished record of activist successes. For instance, by exhibiting an imaginative and courageous willingness to challenge entrenched military and commercial forces by direct action it has had a dramatic impact on public consciousness, and has helped to reshape market behaviour in the process. Examples include its campaigns to outlaw commercial whaling, to oppose the plan of Shell Oil to dispose of the oil rig Brent Spar in the North Sea, to mobilize global support for a fifty year moratorium on mineral development in Antarctica, and, perhaps most significantly of all—though focused on the behaviour of governments rather than market forces—its resistance for many years to nuclear testing in the Pacific (Prins and Sellwood 1998). Rachel Carson's lyrical environmentalism and Jacques Cousteau's extraordinarily intense dedication to saving the oceans suggest the extent to which even single, gifted individuals can exert powerful counter-tendencies to the most destructive sides of an insufficiently regulated market or of governments that put military activities ahead of all other concerns. But these efforts, although plugging some of the holes in the dikes, are not based on a coherent critique or alternative ideology. As a consequence, they can only operate at the level of the symptom and in particular situations, while neglecting the disorders embedded in the dynamics of globalization. There is no effort to build a movement that focuses a large portion of its energies on monitoring or reshaping the outlook and operational ethos of global capitalism.

A better connected and more recent effort to address overall global issues was attempted by the Commission on Global Governance—an initiative inspired by Willy Brandt and the earlier work of the Brandt Commissions on North/South relations, as expressed in its main report, *Our Neighborhood*

(Global Governance, 1995). This venture, claiming authority and credibility on the basis of the eminence of its membership drawn from the leading ranks of society—including past and present government ministers—seemed too farsighted for existing power structures and yet too timid to engage the imagination of the more activist and militant actors in civil society. The Commission's report failed to arouse any wide-spread or sustained interest despite the comprehensiveness and thoughtfulness of its proposals. As an intellectual tool, it was also disappointing. It failed, for example, to clarify the challenge of globalization that existed in the early 1990s. It ignored the then especially troublesome character of Bretton Woods approaches to world economic policy, and it exempted the operations of global capitalism from critical scrutiny. As a result, the Commission's efforts to anchor an argument for global reform around an argument for 'global governance' seemed more likely to consolidate *globalization-from-above* than to promote a creative equilibrium based on struggle that was beginning to be associated with the still disparate activities grouped beneath the rubric of *globalization-from-below*.

What is being argued, then, is that the various challenges arising from global capitalism in its post-industrial phase have not, as yet, engendered a sufficient response in two respects. First, there is an absence of an ideological alternative to what is offered by the various renditions of neoliberalism, and which could provide the social forces associated with *globalization-from-below* with a common analytical framework, political language, and programme. Second, there is need for a clear expression of a critique of *globalization-from-above* that seeks to meet the basic challenges associated with poverty, social marginalization, and environmental decay, while preserving the economic benefits derived from capitalism in its present form. The political imperatives of *globalization-from-below* are thus at once *both* drastic and reformist. While accepting the global capitalist framing of economic choice, they believe that ethical and ecological factors should be brought to bear more systematically. In short, they favour an abandonment of neoliberalism in the search for a more socially and politically regulated framework for this latest phase of global capitalism.

Different versions of neoliberal ideology have exerted a defining influence upon the orientation of political elites governing sovereign states. Of course, there are many variations reflecting conditions and personalities in each particular state and region, but the generalization holds without important exception (Sakamoto 1994; Falk 1997). Even China, despite adherence to its ideology of state socialism, has implemented by state decree, and with impressive results, an extreme market-oriented approach to economic policy. This suggests that the state can remain authoritarian in relation to its citizenry without necessarily jeopardizing its economic performance—and indeed advancing its competitiveness—so long as it adheres, more or less, to the discipline of global capitalism. In these respects, neoliberalism as a *global* ideology is purely economistic in character, and does not imply a commitment to democratic governance in even the minimal sense of periodic fair elections. Order and stability plus a high degree of receptivity to foreign investment and trade are all that is currently *necessary* to be a global economic player, as evidenced by China's admission to the World Trade Organization in 2001. Of course, where geopolitics intrudes, exclusions without an economic rationale may take place, as, for example, when the United States takes the lead in sanctioning a wide variety of governments it deems hostile to its interests. Sometimes, as with the case of Cuba, the exclusion is mainly justified by reference to deficiencies of human rights, but such an argument is mounted so selectively as to appear arbitrary.

Globalization-from-below, in addition to a multitude of local struggles, is also a vehicle for the transnational promotion of substantive democracy, an ideological counterweight to neoliberalism, and as a partial programme for a responsible global capitalism. It provides an alternative, or series of convergent alternatives, that has not yet been posited as a coherent body of theory and practice, but nevertheless offers the tacit common ground of an emergent global civil society. Normative democracy, unlike backlash politics or the coercive diplomacy of sanctions that closes off borders and hardens identities, seeks to promote a politics of reconciliation that maintains much of the openness and dynamism associated with *globalization-from-above,* but counters its pressures to privatize and marketize the production of public goods.

The popularity of codes of conduct and other voluntary programmes are suggestive of an eagerness on the part of the managers of global capitalism to improve their image as ethically sensitive and humanly constructive players in the world economy (Broad 2002). It is also helpful to remember that such an unanticipated convergence of previously opposed social forces led to the sort of consensus that produced 'social democracy' and 'the welfare state' at the level of the state over the course of the nineteenth and twentieth centuries. There is no evident reason to preclude such comparable convergences on regional and global levels as a way of resolving some of the tensions being caused by the manner in which globalization is *currently* being enacted.

Even 11 September gives rise to some moves in these directions, as well as its major diversionary impact. The 2002 odd couple journey of U-2 singer Bono touring Africa with the US Secretary of the Treasury, Paul O'Neill, on the theme of enhancing the role of foreign economic assistance and reducing the debt burden could not have occurred without the growing realization that 'failed states' are dangerous to the rich and powerful. Such a climate of awareness may yet push global capitalism to seek legitimacy by affirming a stakeholder ethos that includes the poor, workers, future generations, and environmental protection. As described by Hans Küng in Chapter 6 and Robert Davies in Chapter 13, the UN Secretary General has been encouraging such a voluntary process of engagement on the part of the business sector, by creating within the UN System of a 'global compact' that formalizes in a public way corporate commitments to these goals, which certainly moves away from the spirit and substance of neoliberal and irresponsible global capitalism. Whether such initiatives are more than gestures will depend on whether the vigilance of global civil society assumes a potent form.

Note

Portions of this chapter were drawn from a previous article published in *Oxford Development Studies* (Falk 1998).

References

Archibugi, D., and Held, D. (eds.) (1995), *Cosmopolitan Democracy: An Agenda for a New World Order* (Cambridge: Polity Press).

Bello, W. (1997), 'Alternate Security Systems in the Asia-Pacific', Bangkok Conference of Focus Asia, 27–30 March.

Broad, R. (2002), *Global Backlash: Citizen Initiatives for a Just World Economy* (Lanham, Md.: Rowman & Littlefield).

Bull, H. (1977), *The Anarchical Society: A Study of Order in World Politics* (New York: Columbia University Press).

Clark, I. (1997), *Globalization and Fragmentation: International Relations in the Twentieth Century* (Oxford: Oxford University Press).

Dubash, N. K., Dupar, M., Kothari, S., and Lissu, T. (2001), *A Watershed in Global Governance? An Independent Assessment of the World Commission on Dams* (Lokayan, India: World Resources Institute).

Falk, R. (1972), *This Endangered Planet: Proposals and Prospects for Human Survival* (New York: Random House).

——(1993), 'The Making of Global Citizenship.' In J. Brecher, J. B. Childs, and J. Cutler (eds.), *Global Visions: Beyond the New World Order* (Boston, Mass.: South End Press).

——(1995), *On Humane Global Governance: Toward a New Global Politics* (Cambridge: Polity Press).

——(1997), 'State of Siege: will globalization win out?' *International Affairs* 73: 123–36.

——(1998), 'Global Civil Society: Perspectives, Initiatives, and Movements', *Oxford Development Studies* 26(1): 99–110.

——(2001), *Religion and Humane Global Governance* (New York: Palgrave).

——(2002), *Winning (and Losing) the War Against Global Terror* (Northampton, Mass.: Interlink).

Fukuyama, F. (1992), *The End of History and the Last Man* (New York: Free Press).

Global Civil Society Yearbook (2001) (Oxford: Oxford University Press).

Global Governance, Commission on (1995) (Oxford: Oxford University Press).

Goldsmith, E., et al. (1972), *Blueprint for Survival* (Boston, Mass.: Houghton Mifflin).

Held, D. (1995), *Democracy and the Global Order: From the Modern State to Cosmopolitan Governance* (Cambridge: Cambridge University Press, 1995).

——and McGrew, A., et al. (1999), *Global Transformations* (Cambridge: Polity Press).

Hirst, P., and Thompson, G. (1996), *Globalization in Question* (Cambridge: Polity Press), 1–17, 170–94.

Keck, M., and Sikkink, K. (1998), *Activists Beyond Borders: Advocacy Networks Beyond Borders* (Ithaca, NY: Cornell University Press).

Lipschutz, R. D. (1996), *Global Civil Society and Global Environmental Governance* (Albany, NY: State University of New York).

Meadows, D., and Associates (1972), *The Limits to Growth* (New York: Free Press).

Mendlovitz, S. H. (1975), *On the Creation of a Just World Order* (New York: Free Press).

Nerfin, M. (1986), 'Neither Prince nor Merchant: Citizen—an Introduction to the Third System,' *IFDA Dossier* 56: 3–29.

Prins, G., and Sellwood, E. (1998), 'Global Security Problems and the Challenge to Democratic Process,' in D. Archibugi, D. Held, and M. Kohler (eds.), *Re-imagining Political Community: Studies in Cosmopoliton Democracy* (Cambridge: Polity Press), 252–72.

Rich, B. (1994), *Mortgaging the Earth: The World Bank, Environmental Impoverishment, and the Crisis of Development* (Boston, Mass.: Beacon Press).

Rosenau, J. N. (1990), *Turbulence in World Politics: A Theory of Change and Continuity* (Princeton: Princeton University Press).

Roy, A. (2001), *Power Politics* (Boston, Mass.: South End Press).

Shiva, V. (1987), 'People's Ecology: The Chipko Movement.' In R. B. J. Walker and Mendlovitz (eds.), *Towards a Just World Peace: Perspectives from Social Movements* (London: Butterworths), 253–70.

Soros, G. (2002), *On Globalization* (Oxford: Public Affairs).

Wapner, P. (1996), 'The Social Construction of Global Governance,' paper presented at Annual Meeting, American Political Science Association, 28–31 Aug. 1996.

International Public Goods without International Government

CHARLES P. KINDLEBERGER

An enduring tenet of international cooperation holds that institutions that structure global politics reflect the goals of the hegemonic state in that system. Professor Kindelberger, in his 1985 presidential address to the American Economic Association, asks what happens when the hegemon begins to lose control over the system. What does Kindelberger think about the concept of "international regime" that is favored by some Liberal institutionalist scholars? What roles does leadership play in his perspective?

I

That sharp and sometimes angry theorist, Frank Graham (1948), thought it a mistake to think of trade between nations. Trade took place between firms, he insisted. The fact that they were in different states was irrelevant so long as economic policy was appropriately minimal, consisting perhaps of free trade, annually balanced budgets, and the gold standard. But states may differentiate between firms, through such measures as tariffs, embargos, monetary, fiscal, and exchange rate policy which affect all firms within a given space, and this adds a political dimension (see my 1978 study). The essence may go deeper. In an early graduate quiz, I asked for the difference between domestic and international trade, expecting a Ricardian answer on factor mobility. One paper, however, held that domestic trade was among "us," whereas international trade was between "us" and "them." The student who wrote this (now escaped from economics and teaching international law at a leading university) had come from Cambridge University and a course with Harry Johnson. We go beyond this simple statement today in saying that nations are groups of people with common tastes in public goods (Richard Cooper, 1977). Geography discriminates between countries, as a hypothetical customs union between Iceland and New Zealand would demonstrate, and so do governments. Behind and alongside of governments, people discriminate.

Public goods, let me remind you, are that class of goods like public works where exclusion of consumers may be impossible, but in any event consumption of the good by one consuming unit—short of some level approaching congestion—does not exhaust its availability for others. They are typically underproduced—not, I believe, for the Galbraithian reason that private goods are advertized and public goods are not—but because the consumer who has access to the good anyhow has little reason to vote the taxes, or pay his or her appropriate share. Unless the consumer is a highly moral person, following the Kantian Categorical Imperative of acting in ways which can be generalized, he or she is apt to be a "free rider." The tendency for public goods to be underproduced is serious enough within a nation bound by some sort of social contract, and directed in public matters by a government with the power to impose and collect taxes. It is, I propose to argue in due course, a more serious problem in international political and economic relations in the absence of international government.

Adam Smith's list of public goods was limited to national defense, law and order, and public works that it would not pay individuals to produce for themselves. Most economists are prepared now to extend the list to include stabilization, regulation, and income redistribution (Cooper, 1977), even nationalism (Albert Breton, 1964), and standards that reduce transaction costs, including weights and measures, language, and money. Public goods were popular a decade ago. There is something of a tendency today, at least in political science, to draw back and claim that such institutions as open world markets are not public goods because countries can be excluded from them by discrimination. One monetarist goes so far as to maintain that money is not a public good, arguing, I believe, from the store-of-value function where possession by one individual denies possession by others, rather than from the unit-of-account function in which exclusion is impossible and exhaustion does not hold (Roland Vaubel, 1984).

IV

But I want to move on to the geopolitical unit that produces public goods. It is a cliche that these have increased in size as costs of transport and communication have declined. Under the eighteenth-century Poor Law in England, the parish resisted immigration from neighboring parishes because of reluctance to share with outsiders. Fernand Braudel (1982) and Sir John Hicks (1969) have each expatiated on the rise of the size of the economic unit from the city-state to the nation-state. National and international markets for goods and money grew slowly, with entrepot centers that intermediated between buyers and sellers surviving in money—cheap to move in space—and largely disappearing for goods where costs of transport were high and could be saved by direct selling, rather than relaying goods through fairs in the Middle Ages and later through cities such as Amsterdam, Hamburg, Frankfurt, and London. The hub-and-spoke system recently discovered in airplane travel and still in place for money has long been superceded in goods. Caroline Isard and Walter Isard's (1945) point that the most pervasive changes in the economy came from innovations in transport and communications remains valid: contemplate the rudder (in place of the steering oar), fore-and-aft sails; the turnpike; canal; railroad (despite Robert Fogel, 1964); the steamship; iron-clad ship; telegraph; telephone; refrigerator ship; radio; airplane; bulk carrier; jet airplane; satellite television. The numbers of people brought into face-to-face contact across continents and hemispheres has increased exponentially. It is true, to be sure, as was said about a well-known governor and presidential candidate, that it was impossible to dislike him until one got to know him, and increases in mobility and communications have been accompanied by separatism: of the Walloons from the Flemish in Belgium, of Scotland and Wales in the United Kingdom (to pass over the troubled Irish question), and of the *Québecois* in Canada.[1] But it is easier than in Adam Smith's day to imagine ourselves in the circumstances of the Chinese, the inhabitants of the Sahelian desert in Africa, or the tornado-struck islands of Bangladesh as we see them nightly on our television screens via satellite. Do wider communication and transport change the production and distribution of public goods?

Conflicts between economics and political science abound, and many arise from the fact that goods, money, corporations, and people are mobile, whereas the state is fixed. The increase in mobility produced by innovations in transport and communication during and after World War II led some of us to conclude that the nation-state was in difficulty. A reaction occurred in the 1970's. It is significant that Raymond Vernon's influential book *Sovereignty at Bay* (1971), showing the multinational corporation ascendant over the state, was followed by his *Storm over Multinationals* (1977) in which the position is reversed. Cooper's *The Economics of Interdependence* (1968) was followed by an upsurge of interest in national autonomy, decoupling, and pluralism among political scientists, most of whom approve the nation-state and have as heroes, if they will forgive me, not Adam Smith and Woodrow Wilson, but Otto von Bismarck and perhaps even Charles de Gaulle. The tension remains, however. Mobility limits the state's capacity to enforce its writ in taxation, in foreign policy, in standards on such matters as antitrust, pure food and drugs, insider trading in securities, and the like. Mobility undermines social cohesion through the easy intrusion of different nationalities, races, religions, and traditions into the body politic.

V

I come at long last to international public goods. The primary one is peace. Economists are poorly qualified to discuss how, after war, peace is restored and maintained. Most of us reject the Marxian view that war grows directly out of capitalism, and as ordinary citizens and amateur students of history are prepared to agree that peace may be provided by a dominant world power—Pax Romana or Pax Britannica—or by balance-of-power maneuvering, although that seems accident prone. Among the more audacious economists producing an economic theory or set of theories on war is Walt Rostow (1960, pp. 108 ff.). There are views that ascribe war to population pressure, to ambitious rulers aggressively seeking power, and to complex miscalculation. How these are to be avoided or contained is a question primarily for political science.

In the economic sphere, various international public goods have been identified: an open trading system, including freedom of the seas, well-defined property rights, standards of weights and measures that may include international money, or fixed exchange rates, and the like. Those that have interested me especially in a study of the 1929 depression and other financial and economic crises have been trading systems, international money, capital flows, consistent macroeconomic policies in periods of tranquility, and a source of crisis management when needed. By the last I mean the maintenance of open markets in glut and a source of supplies in acute shortage, plus a lender of last resort in acute financial crisis (see my 1973 book, revised 1986, forthcoming).

Public goods are produced domestically by government, unless the governmental agenda is blocked in stalemate among competing distributional coalitions as described by Mancur Olson (1982). Voluntary provision of public goods is plagued by the free rider. In the international sphere where there is no world government, the question remains how public goods are produced. Ralph Bryant is one of the few economists who has discussed the public good element in international cooperation. His vocabulary is different from that of the political scientists: their "regimes" are his "supranational traffic regulations" (1980, p. 470), and he expects leadership in cooperation in monetary and fiscal policy from supranational institutions such as the International Monetary Fund (p. 481). I find this doubtful on the basis of the interwar record of such institutions as the League of Nations.

Political science in this field has produced two schools: the realists who hold to a national-interest theory of international politics, and the moralists, whom Robert Keohane prefers to call "institutionalists" (1984, p. 7). Realists maintain that international public goods are produced, if at all, by the leading power, a so-called "hegemon," that is willing to bear an undue part of the short-run costs of these goods, either because it regards itself as gaining in the long run, because it is paid in a different coin such as prestige, glory, immortality, or some combination of the two. Institutionalists recognize that hegemonic leaders emerge from time to time in the world economy and typically set in motion habits of international cooperation, called "regimes," which consist of "principles, norms, rules and decision-making procedures around which the expectations of international actors converge in given issue areas" (Stephen Krasner, 1983, p. 1). Under British hegemony, the regimes of free trade and the gold standard developed more or less unconsciously. With subsequent American hegemony, a more purposeful process of institution making was undertaken, with agreements at Bretton Woods, on tariffs and trade, the Organization for Economic Cooperation and Development, and the like. Political scientists recognize that regimes are more readily maintained than established since marginal costs are below average costs; as hegemonic periods come to an end with the waning of the leading country's economic vitality, new regimes needed to meet new problems are difficult to create. Cooper (1985) has written of the eighty years it took to create and get functioning the World Health Organization despite the clear benefits to all countries from controlling the spread of disease. And it takes work to maintain regimes; in the absence of infusions of attention and money, they tend in the long run to decay.

I originally suggested that the 1929 depression was allowed to run unchecked because there was no leading country able and willing to take responsibility for crisis management, halting beggar-thy-neighbor policies from 1930, and especially acting as a lender of last resort to prevent the serious run on the Creditanstalt in May 1931 spreading, as it did, to Germany, Britain, Japan, the United States, and ultimately to the gold bloc. Britain, the leading economic power of the nineteenth century, was unable to halt the run; the United States, which might have had the ability, possibly assisted by France, was unwilling. This view has been rejected by one economic historian who holds that the troubles of the interwar period were more deep-seated, and that what was needed was more fundamental therapy than maintaining open markets and providing a lender of last resort, something, that is, akin to the heroic public good after World War II, the Marshall Plan (D. E. Moggridge, 1982). That may have been true, though there is no way I see that the issue can be settled. Leadership at an earlier stage in the 1920's, presumably furnished by the United States with some cost in foregone receipts on war-debt account, might have resolved the war-debt-reparations-commercial-debt tangle that proved so destabilizing after the 1929 stock market crash. I conclude that the existence of an international lender of last resort made the financial crises of 1825, 1836, 1847, 1866, and 1907 more or less ephemeral, like summer storms, whereas its absence in 1873, 1890, and 1929 produced deep depressions—shortened in the 1890 case by the *deus ex machina* of gold production from the Rand. Again there is room for disagreement.

The point of all this is that after about 1971, the United States, like Britain from about 1890, has shrunk in economic might relative to the world as a whole, and more importantly, has lost the appetite for providing international economic public goods—open markets in times of glut, supplies in times of acute shortage, steady flows of capital to developing countries, international money, coordination of macroeconomic policy and last-resort lending. The contraction of concern from the world to the nation is general, and applies to economists as well as to politicians and the public. In reading recent books on macroeconomic policy by leading governmental economists under both Democratic and Republican administrations, the late Arthur Okun (1981) and Herbert Stein (1984), I have been struck by how little attention the authors paid to international repercussions. The same observation has been made by Ralph Bryant (1980, p. *xviii*) and by the British economist R. C. O. Matthews, reviewing Arjo Klamer's *Conversations with Economists*... (1985, p. 621). There has been a recent upsurge of interest in the international dimension because of the connections among the federal deficit, the exchange rate for the dollar, and the balance-of-payments deficit, but the focus of this interest is almost exclusively on what the connections mean for U.S. interest rates, industrial policy, growth, and wealth. The international impact is largely ignored, bearing out the truth in former German Chancellor Helmut Schmidt's statement that "the United States seems completely unconscious of the economic efforts of its policies on the Alliance" (1984, p. 27).

Some of the discussion of international regimes by political scientists verges on what my teacher, Wesley Clair Mitchell, used to call "implicit theorizing," that is, convenient *ad hoc* theoretical explanations to fit given facts that lack generality. Charles Lipson (1985), for example, suggested that the slippage in U.S. hegemony in the 1970's resulted in a loss of the international public good of secure property rights and therefore in the widespread nationalization of foreign direct investment. He went on to say that the reason less developed countries (*LDCs*) did not default on their debts to bank syndicates was that bank lending was "better institutionalized," "a smaller group," "better protected by legal remedies" (pp. 136, 158, 170). He was surprised that the decline of British hegemony in the interwar period did not result in more *LDC* aggression against foreign property (p. 191), but failed to observe the widespread default on foreign bonds in the 1930's, despite the organization of international finance. In my judgement Keohane exaggerates the efficacy and importance of the international regime in oil that was formed after the first OPEC oil shock of 1973 (see his ch. 10). The crisis caused by the Yom Kippur embargo of the Netherlands was to my mind shockingly mishandled by governments, and the public good of crisis management was left to the private multinational oil companies. The formation of the International Energy Agency was a classic operation in locking the barn door after the horse had been stolen.

Between national self-interest and the provision of international public goods, there is an intermediate position: indifference to both. An interesting contrast has been observed in the 1930's between Britain which forced Argentina into a bilateral payments agreement (the Roca-Runciman Agreement of 1933) in order to take advantage of its monopsony position, and the United States that had a similar opportunity vis-à-vis Brazil but ignored it (Marcelo de Paiva Abreu, 1984).

It is fairly clear from the historical record that economic hegemony runs down in decay—in the British case after 1913 and the United States about 1971—leading Felix Rohatyn (1984) to say that the American century lasted only twenty years. The Nixon shock of 1973 in cutting off soya bean exports to Japan—a significant harm to an ally for a small gain to this country—was the act of a bad Samaritan. The import surcharge of the same year may have been required to move the dollar out from the position of the *n*th currency when only *n*–1 countries are free to fix their exchange rates, but it would have been possible to start with the later attempt at cooperation that resulted in the Smithsonian agreement. This is especially true when so much of the case against the 1971 exchange rate was the result of the easy-money policy of the Federal Reserve System under Chairman Arthur Burns, at a time when the Bundesbank was tightening its money market/go-it-alone policies of both banks that flooded the world with dollars.

The present U.S. administration claims to be working for open trade and does fairly well in resisting appeals for protection. The positive push for a Reagan round of trade liberalization in services and agriculture, however, is in pursuit of a national and not an international public good. The regime in capital movements—the World Bank, the regional development banks and that in-last-resort lending orchestrated by the IMF—seems to be working, with bridging loans and an *ad hoc* purchase of oil from Mexico for the U.S. stockpile in 1982 when the IMF finds itself unable to move fast enough. But there are signs of dissension that may spell trouble. The June 1985 bridging loan for Argentina was declined by Germany and Switzerland on the grounds that Argentina had not been sufficiently austere and that its problems were not a threat to the world financial system (*New York Times*, June 15, 1985, p. 1). The Japanese contribution, moreover, was said to have been small, although no figures were given.

What I worry about mostly is exchange policy and macroeconomic coordination. The U.S. Treasury under Donald Regan was committed to the policy of neglect, presumably benign, but in any event ideological. And the commitment to consultative macro-economic policies in annual summit meetings of seven heads of state has become a shadow play, a dog-and-pony show, a series of photo opportunities—whatever you choose to call them—with ceremony substituted for substance. The 1950's and 1960's, when serious discussions were held at the lowly level of Working Party No. 3 of the O.E.C.D., were superior because the United States and other countries took them seriously.

I am a realist when it comes to regimes. It seems to me that the momentum set in motion by a hegemonic power—if we must use that expression,

I prefer to think of leadership or responsibility—runs down pretty quickly unless it is sustained by powerful commitment. The IMF and World Bank were agreed at Bretton Woods largely as a result of the U.S. Treasury: the forms were international, the substance was dictated by a single country (Armand van Dormel, 1978). In the early days of the IMF, Frank Southard told me, if the United States made no proposal, nothing happened. Today the same is true of the European Economic Community: unless Germany and France see eye to eye, which is infrequent, nothing happens. Proposals of great technical appeal from individuals or small countries are not welcomed as the preparatory phases of the World Economic Conference of 1933 demonstrated (see my 1973 book, pp. 210–14). There needs to be positive leadership, backed by resources and a readiness to make some sacrifice in the international interest.

The leadership role is not applauded. When the United States accused the rest of the world of being free riders, Andrew Shonfield countercharged the United States of being a "hard rider," "hustling and bullying the Europeans," "kicking over chairs when it did not get its way" (1976, pp. 86, 88, 102). Furnishing the dollar to the world as international money has brought the United States an accusation of extracting seignorage, although the facts that the dollar is not a monopoly currency and that foreign holdings earn market rates of interest deflect that criticism in sophisticated quarters.

Neglect can verge on sabotage. When the European central banks collaborated to hold the dollar down at the end of February 1985, the conspicuous failure of the United States to participate on a significant scale encouraged speculators not to cover long positions. A former trader for the Federal Reserve Bank of New York has expressed concern that the habits of central bank cooperation and U.S. official intimacy with the workings of the foreign-exchange market that have been built up over thirty years are being squandered for ideological reasons (Scott Pardee, 1964, p. 2).

Regimes are clearly more attractive in political terms than hegemony, or even than leadership with its overtones of the German *Führerprinzip* or of Italy's *Il Duce*, if not necessarily more so than responsibility. Polycentralism, pluralism, cooperation, equality, partnership, decoupling, self-reliance, and autonomy all have resonance. But it is hard to accept the view, so appealing to the political right, that the path to achieve cooperation is a tit-for-tat strategy, applied in a repetitive game, that teaches the other player or players to cooperate (Robert Axelrod, 1984). As Tibor Scitovsky demonstrated years ago (1937), this path can readily end by wiping out trade altogether. Hierarchical arrangements are being examined by economic theorists studying the organization of firms, but for less cosmic purposes than would be served by political and economic organization of the production of international public goods (Raj Sah and Joseph Stiglitz, 1985).

Minding one's own business—operating in the robust zone of indifference—is a sound rule on trend when macroeconomic variables are more or less stable. To the economist it means reliance on the market to the extent that the conditions for a Pareto optimum solution are broadly met. But the fallacy of composition remains a threat, and one cannot count on the Categorical Imperative. Markets work most of the time, as a positivesum game in which the gain for one does not imply a loss for another. Experience teaches, however, that crises may arise. When they do, the rule changes from government and public indifference to the production of public goods by leadership or by a standby regime.

Leadership or responsibility limited to crises encounters another problem: how to keep the machinery for handling crises from obsolescence. In crisis one needs forceful and intelligent people, capable of making decisions with speed under pressure. It is sometimes said that the Japanese practice of decision by consensus with ideas coming up from below, makes it hard for that country to discharge in timely fashion the responsibilities of world leadership. In Marcus Goodrich's *Delilah* (1941), the amiable practice of fraternization between a watch officer and enlisted men on the bridge of the destroyer proved dangerous in a typhoon since the men had fallen into the habit of discussing the officer's orders. The paradox is that the attributes needed in crisis tend to atrophy in quiet times; for example in the control room of a Three Mile Island nuclear power plant.

Let me conclude by emphasizing once again my concern that politicians, economists, and political scientists may come to believe that the system should be run at all times by rules, including regimes, not people. Rules are desirable on trend. In crisis the need is for decision. I quote once more the letter of Sir Robert Peel of June 1844 a propos of the Bank Charter Act of that year:

> My Confidence is unshaken that we have taken all the Precautions which Legislation can prudently take against the Recurrence of a pecuniary Crisis. It may occur in spite of our Precautions; and if it be necessary to assume a grave Responsibility, I dare say Men will be found willing to assume such a Responsibility.
>
> [*Parliamentary Papers*, 1857, 1969, p. *xxix*]

Notes

1. Tastes in public goods can of course differ within countries. A striking comparison is furnished in E. Digby Baltzell's *Puritan Boston and Quaker Philadelphia* (1979). Boston is characterized as intolerant, extremely homogenous, ascetic, philanthropic, and devoted to social and political responsibility. Philadelphia, on the other hand, was an ethnic and religious melting pot, materialistic, believing in money making, and shunning power and responsibility. Boston produced four presidents of the United States, including one non-Puritan affected by the values of the city. Philadelphia none. Social scientists are wary of ascribing social responses to national (or urban) character. There may nonetheless be occasions when it is inescapable.

References

Arrow, Kenneth, J., "Gifts and Exchanges," in Edmund S. Phelps, ed., *Altruism, Morality and Economic Theory*, New York: Russell Sage Foundation, 1975.

Axelrod, Robert, *The Evolution of Cooperation*, New York: Basic Books, 1984.

Baltzell, E. Digby, *Puritan Boston and Quaker Philadelphia: Two Protestant Ethics and the Spirit of Class Authority and Leadership*, New York: Free Press, 1979.

Becker, Gary, *A Treatise on the Family*, Cambridge: Harvard University Press, 1981.

Berry, Brian J. L., "City-Size Distribution and Economic Development," *Economic Development and Cultural Change*, July 1961, 9, 573–88.

Braudel, Fernand, *Civilization and Capitalism* (15th-18th Century), Vol. 2, *The Wheels of Commerce*, translated from the French by Sian Reynolds, New York: Harper and Row, 1982.

Breton, Albert, "The Economics of Nationalism" *Journal of Political Economy*, August 1964, *72*, 376–86.

Bryant, Ralph C., *Money and Monetary Policy in Independent Nations*, Washington: The Brookings Institution, 1980.

Calabrese, Guido and Bobbitt, Philip, *Tragic Choices*, New York: W. W. Norton, 1978.

Cooper, Richard N., *The Economic of Interdependence: Economic Policy in the Atlantic Community*, New York: McGraw-Hill, 1968.

——, "World-Wide vs Regional Integration: Is There an Optimal Size of the Integrated Area?," in Fritz Machlup, ed., *Economic Integration: Worldwide, Regional, Sectoral*, New York: Halstead, 1977.

——, "International Economic Cooperation: Is it Desirable? Is it Likely?," *Bulletin*, American Academy of Arts and Sciences, November 1985, 39, 11–35.

de Paiva Abreu, Marcelo, "Argentina and Brazil During the 1930s: The Impact of British and American Economic Policies," in Rosemary Thorp, ed., *Latin America in the 1930s: The Role of the Periphery in World Crisis*, London: Macmillan, 1984.

Fishkin, James S., *The Limits of Obligation*, New Haven: Yale University Press, 1982.

Fogel, Robert W., *Railroads and American Economic Growth: Essays in Econometric History*, Baltimore: Johns Hopkins Press, 1964.

Goodrich, Marcus, *Delilah*, New York: Farrar & Rinehart, 1941.

Graham, Frank D., *The Theory of International Values*, Princeton: Princeton University Press, 1948.

Harris, Seymour E., *The Economics of New England: Case Study of an Older Area*, Cambridge: Harvard University Press, 1965.

Hicks, John R., *A Theory of Economic History,* London: Oxford University Press, 1969.

Hirschman, Albert O., *Exit, Voice and Loyalty*, Cambridge: Harvard University Press, 1970.

Isard, Caroline and Isard, Walter, "Economic Implications of Aircraft," *Quarterly Journal of Economics*, February 1945, *59*, 145–69.

Johnson, Harry G., "An 'Internationalist' Model," in Walter Adams, ed., *The Brain Drain*, New York: Macmillan, 1968.

Keohane, Robert O., *After Hegemony: Cooperation and Discord in the World Political Economy*, Princeton: Princeton University Press, 1984.

Kindleberger, Charles P., *The World in Depression, 1929–1939*, Berkeley: University of California Press, 1973.

——, "Internationalist and Nationalist Models in the Analysis of the Brain Drain: Progress and Unsolved Problems," *Minerva*, Winter 1977, *15*, 553–61.

——, "Government and International Trade," *Essays in International Finance,* No. 129, International Finance Section, Princeton University, 1978.

——, *Multinational Excursions*, Cambridge, MIT Press, 1984.

——, "Des biens public internationaux en l'absence d'un gouvernment international," in *Croissance, échange et monnaie en économie international, Mélange en l'honneur de Monsieur le Professeur Jean Weiller*, Paris: Economica, 1985.

Knight, Frank H., *The Ethics of Competition and Other Essays*, London: George Allen & Unwin, 1936.

—— and Merriam, Thornton W., *The Economic Order and Religion*, London: Kegan Paul, Trend, Trubner, 1947.

Krasner, Stephen D., *International Regimes,* Ithaca: Cornell University Press, 1983.

Labasse, Jean, *L'espace financier: analyze geographique*, Paris: Colin, 1974.

Lichtenberg, Judith, "National Boundaries and Moral Boundaries," in Peter G. Brown and Henry Shue, eds., *Boundaries: National Autonomy and Its Limits*, Totowa: Rowman and Littlefield, 1981.

Lipson, Charles, *Standing Guard: Protecting Foreign Capital in the Nineteenth and Twentieth Centuries*, Berkeley: University of California Press, 1985.

McCloskey, Donald N., "The Rhetoric of Economics," *Journal of Economic Literature,* June 1983, *21*, 481–517.

McKinnon, Ronald I., "Optimum Currency Areas," *American Economic Review*, September 1963, *53*, 717–25.

Matthews, R. C. O., Review of Arjo Klamer, *Conversations with Economists…*, 1983, *Journal of Economic Literature*, June 1985, *23*, 621–22.

Meade, James E., *The Theory of International Economic Policy*, Vol. II, *Trade and Welfare*, New York: Oxford University Press, 1955.

Moggridge, D. E., "Policy in the Crises of 1920 and 1929," in C. P. Kindleberger and J.-P. Laffargue, eds., *Financial Crises: Theory, History and Policy*, Cambridge: Cambridge University Press, 1982.

Mundell, Robert A., "A Theory of Optimum Currency Areas," *American Economic Review*, September 1961, *51*, 657–65.

Nozick, Robert, *Anarchy, State and Utopia,* New York: Basic Books, 1974.

Ohlin, Bertil, *Interregional and International Trade*, Cambridge: Harvard University Press, 1933.

Okun, Arthur M., *Prices and Quantities,* Washington: Brookings Institution, 1981.

Olson, Mancur, *The Rise and Decline of Nations: Economic Growth, Stagflation and Social Rigidities*, New Haven: Yale University Press, 1982.

Pardee, Scott, "The Dollar," address before the Georgetown University Bankers Forum, Washington, D.C., September 22, 1964.

Patinkin, Don, "A 'Nationalist' Model," in Walter Adams, ed., *The Brain Drain*, New York: Macmillan, 1968.

Robertson, Sir Dennis, "What Do Economists Economize?," in R. Leckachman, ed., *National Policy for Economic Welfare at Home and Abroad*, New York: Doubleday, 1955.

Rohatyn, Felix G., *The Twenty-Year Century: Essays on Economics and Public Finance,* New York: Random House, 1984.

Rostow, Walt W., *The Stages of Economic Growth: A Non-Communist Manifesto,* Cambridge: Cambridge University Press, 1960.

Sah, Raaj Kumar and Stiglitz, Joseph E., "Human Fallibility and Economic Organization," *American Economic Review Proceedings*, May 1985, *75*, 292–97.

Scitovsky, Tibor, "A Reconsideration of the Theory of Tariffs," reprinted in AEA *Readings in the Theory of International Trade,* Homewood: Richard D. Irwin, 1949.

Shonfield, Andrew, *International Economic Relations of the Western World,* Vol. I, *Politics and Trade,* New York: Oxford University Press, 1976.

Singer, Peter, "Famine, Affluence and Morality," *Philosophy and Public Affairs,* Spring 1972, *1*, 229–43.

Smith, Adam, *The Theory of Moral Sentiments, or An Essay Toward an Analysis of the Principles by which Men Naturally Judge Concerning the Conduct and Character First of the Neighbours and then of Themselves,* 11th ed., Edinburgh: Bell and Bradfute, 1759; 1808.

——, *An Inquiry into the Nature and Causes of the Wealth of Nations,* Canaan ed., New York: Modern Library, 1776; 1937.

Schmidt, Helmut, "Saving Western Europe," *New York Review of Books,* May 31, 1984, *31*, 25–27.

Stigler, George J., "Economics—The Imperial Science?," mimeo., 1984.

Stein, Herbert, *Presidential Economics: The Making of Economic Policy from Roosevelt to Reagan and Beyond,* New York: Simon and Schuster, 1984.

Van Dormel, Armand, *Bretton Woods: Birth of a Monetary System,* New York: Holmes and Meier, 1978.

Vaubel, Roland, "The Government's Money Monopoly: Externalities or Natural Monopoly?," *Kyklos,* 1984, *27*, 27–57.

Vernon, Raymond, *Sovereignty at Bay,* Cambridge: Harvard University Press, 1971.

——, *Storm Over Multinationals,* Cambridge: Harvard University Press, 1977.

Walzer, Michael, "The Distribution of Membership," in Peter G. Brown and Henry Shue, eds., *Boundaries: National Autonomy and Its Limits,* Totowa: Rowman and Littlefield, 1981.

——, *Spheres of Justice,* New York: Basic Books, 1983.

Parliamentary Papers: Monetary Policy, Commercial Distress, Shannon: Irish University Press, 1957, 1969.

Resisting Globalization: The Alternative Globalization Movement

CHAMSY EL-OJEILI AND PATRICK HAYDEN

While Falk argues that globalization is a fact that civil society must address, el-Ojeili and Hayden argue that the Alternative Globalization Movement (AGM) can mitigate its economic and social changes impacts. How do el-Ojeili and Hayden use social science theory to explain the AGM? What evidence do the authors select to support their claims? What is the connection between the World Bank's policies and the emergence of the Zapatista movement during the 1990s? What do el-Ojeili and Hayden mean by a "postmodern political movement"? How is that different from earlier movements? What kinds of Adbuster-style advertisements can you create for some of your personal possessions?

Social Movements

Social movements are vital features in social change. Buechler (2000: 213) defines social movements as 'intentional, collective efforts to transform the social order. Social movements were not discussed explicitly in the social sciences until the 1960s, in the face of the rise of the civil rights, feminist, and other so-called 'new social movements'. Until this point, what we now view as social movements were analyzed by reference to explanations of collective behaviour (Scott, 2001). These explanations tended to gather social movements together with very different types of collective action such as panics and crowds (Buechler, 2000). This collective behaviour tended to be read as shapeless, as a reaction to stress, as psychological and individualistic, and as irrational and menacing (Buechler, 2000). After the 1960s, there was a shift in the Interpretation of these movements, away from collective behaviour theory and towards understandings that focussed on social movements as enduring, patterned, rational, and political (Buechler, 2000).

The most significant early interpretation of social movements was resource mobilization theory (RMT). Social movements were treated by RMT as comparable to other sorts of organizations, interacting with other social movements and with the state (Scott, 2001). RMT asked crucial questions about the resources available to movements, about the organizational features of the movement, about the influence of the state on a movement, and about the possible outcomes of movement mobilization (Mueller, 1992). This orientation is interpreted by Meyer (2002) as an 'outside in' approach, because it analyzed social movements in terms of factors external to the movements themselves.

A prominent theorist of the RMT paradigm is Charles Tilly. Tilly (2004) contends that three elements, in particular, are essential in defining and analyzing social movements. Social movements involve:

1. sustained, co-ordinated public efforts that make collective claims – a combination of identity, programme, and standing (similarities to and differences from other actors) – on target authorities;
2. an array of claim-making performances, such as rallies, petitions, marches, sit-ins, and so forth;
3. and sustained public representations around notions of worthiness, unity, numbers, and commitment.

For Tilly (2004), such social movements are distinctly a product of modernity, emerging in the late eighteenth century in England (in particular) and the US. Central in the emergence of social movements were the following: the 'nationalization of politics, a greatly increased role of special-purpose associations, a decline in the importance of communities as the loci of shared interests, a growing importance of organized capital and organized labour as participants in the power struggle' (in Scott, 2001: 130).

The so-called 'cultural turn' in social theorizing after the 1960s, the rise and evident importance of the 'new social movements', and challenges to Marxism's relegation of these movements to the status of the 'merely cultural' (Butler, 1998) saw social movement theory moving towards an 'Inside out' approach, focussing increasingly on the importance of symbols, meanings, discourse, and identity (Meyer, 2002). Thus, the social constructionist paradigm of the 1980s onwards studied social movements in terms of 'framing', exploring the significance of the making of meaning in collective action – the voicing of grievances, the assignation of blame, the development of solutions, and the engagement with tactical and strategic questions (Buechler, 2000) – in contrast to the widely perceived neglect of questions of grievances, ideologies, and collective identity in RMT (Mueller, 1992).

It might also be argued that the events of September 11 have altered the terrain significantly, with the AGM connected by opponents to terrorism and anti-Americanism, resulting in a 'chilling effect' that is deepened by the post-9/11 enhancement of security and surveillance measures by states leading to what is arguably the 'criminalization of politics' (Panitch, 2002: 24). Some might feel that the movement faces dangers of absorption or incorporation into mainstream decision making institutions (Veltmeyer, 2004). There are, furthermore, a range of potential impacts that the movement might have – for instance, innovations in values (perhaps a general animus towards MNCs), organizational influences on other social movements, further challenges to the power of nation-states, the generation of a 'thicker' global consciousness around a range of issues such as Southern debt, environmental degradation, or pressure towards greater democratization and accountability within transnational institutions. On this last issue, for example, it might be argued that already the AGM has altered the agenda of institutions such as the World Bank and the WTO, who must now at least pay lip-service to issues such as poverty, the environment, and labour rights. This is a mere taste of the kinds of analytical implications social movement theory has for the AGM, and we will take up some of these issues in more detail below.

The Emergence and Eclipse of the Socialist Movement

A common emphasis for both enthusiasts and detractors of the AGM is the connection of the movement to socialism. Thus, in the words of Malcolm Wallop, a former US Senator from Wyoming, 'It's necessary to look at the endgame of these anti-globalist groups – a utopian, pollution-free, socialist world – and decide whether to fight for your business or let the radicals destroy it, issue by issue'. In a more positive vein, Bygrave (2002) asks, 'So is "global justice" [the aim of the alternative globalization movement] the socialism that dare not speak its name?' Because of the widespread sense of the resonances between the

AGM and the socialist movement, we will in this section discuss, very schematically, the emergence and subsequent decline of socialism as a movement for social change, and in a later section we will analyze continuities and ruptures between these two movements.

The Emergence of the Alternative Globalization Movement

The alternative globalization movement has been given many names: the global movement for social justice, the anti-corporate movement, the civil society movement, the global justice movement, the citizens' movement for world democracy, the anti-neoliberal movement, the anti-capitalist movement, and, most prominently, the anti-globalization movement. In particularly, this last label, 'anti-globalization', has been the one that has stuck. We think, however, that 'anti-globalization' is a misleading description, as many within the movement do not oppose globalization *per se*, but the particular version of globalization that currently dominates. Here, many participants would distinguish current 'globalization from above' from a possible and perhaps emerging 'globalization from below'. For this reason, the name 'alternative-globalization' seems a much more accurate and promising starting point.

Although the AGM became clearly visible as an important collective actor in the late 1990s, most spectacularly after the 'battle of Seattle' of 1999, its roots can be traced to a much earlier period. According to Katsiaficas (2004), for instance, the AGM has important origins in the resistance within the developing world to free market structural adjustment policies pushed by the World Bank and the International Monetary Fund since the 1980s. Since 1976, there have been at least 100 protests globally against IMF and World Bank policies (Znet. nd). The origins of the AGM are also often tied to the environmental movement from the 1980s, which drew attention to the way in which the aspirations to economic growth and profitability were casting an increasing shadow over the viability of life on the planet. And environmentalists were widely mobilized in the mid-1990s by prominent WTO rulings against environmental protection measures. Importantly, too, after a long period in which labour organizations were widely viewed as nationalized (functioning as integral features of nation-states), as capital became more internationalized after the 1970s a new labour internationalism grew (Munck, 2002). Thus, organized labour increasingly concerned itself with global issues such as the campaign against apartheid; and during the 1990s, for instance, American organizations the National Labour Committee and Global Exchange coordinated prominent and successful campaigns against corporations such as Gap who were subcontracting to manufacturers in the third world charged with union busting, providing unsafe work environments, and utilizing child and forced labour (Munck, 2002; Anderson *et al.*, 2000).

For Alex Callinicos (2003), the more recent coalescence of the AGM can be traced most centrally to a number of important events and struggles: the North American Free Trade Agreement, NAFTA, beginning in January 1994; the Zapatista rebellion of 1994, sparked, among other things, by NAFTA; the spread of NGOs through the 1990s, many of them contesting the effects of neoliberal restructuring; mobilization around the issue of third world debt; the East Asian crisis of 1997; and instances of large-scale resistance to neoliberalism – for example, the French public sector strikes of 1995, in response to plans for a widespread reform of the welfare system. We will now examine some of these central moments, in the process citing certain organizations and thinkers as a way of drawing out some of the key emphases of the AGM.

The Zapatista movement in Mexico is frequently taken to be an exemplary in terms of the AGM, and has been viewed, in terms of its values, goals, and strategies, as a 'postmodern' political movement (Burbach, 1994). The Zapatista rebellion began on January 1, 1994, the first day of the North American Free Trade Agreement (NAFTA), when 3,000 members of the Zapatista National

Army (the EZLN), took control of a number of municipalities in the Southern Mexican state of Chiapas (Castells, 2000). The Mexican army soon forced the Zapatistas to withdraw into the forest, a ceasefire was declared and a process of negotiation initiated, and since this time there has been a long running stand-off in the region (Cleaver, 1994; Collier and Collier, 2003). This stand-off has left the Zapatistas in control over large areas (autonomous zones), where local life has been organized according to the principle of self-management, and the rebellion has had significant impacts across Mexico – electoral reform, greater recognition of indigenous rights, the invigoration of Mexican civil society, and the decline in the hegemony of the Institutional Revolutionary Party (PRI) (Collier and Collier, 2003).

Most of the Zapatistas are Indian peasants (10 per cent of the Mexican population), and their rebellion has been presented as part of a 500 year struggle against colonization and the marginalization of the indigenous population (Castells, 2000). The more recent roots of the movement are to be found in transformations that have taken place in the region over the past 30 years. Chiapas is a wealthy state, with hydroelectric power production, petroleum exploitation, and corn and coffee production, but about three-quarters of its peoples are malnourished (Burbach, 1994). From the 1970s, there has been an intensification of social polarization in the region, with the growth of the cattle industry, the monopolization of land, the displacement of traditional crops through an increasing orientation of agriculture towards export, and the uprooting of peasants through the building of dams and the search for petroleum (Burbach, 1994). These processes resulted in resistance and violent state responses. For many of these peasants, NAFTA – and the threat of a reduction of subsidies for corn production and the elimination of price protection on coffee – and neoliberal policies in general spelled a 'death sentence' for their livelihoods (Castells, 2000). In Zapatista communiqués neoliberalism is clearly the adversary, with the Zapatistas initiating in 1996 the First Encounter for Humanity and Against Neoliberalism (Marcos, 1996; Seoane and Taddei, 2002). And while the EZLN is fighting for recognition of Indian and peasant rights, there is more than an echo of socialism in their communiqués.

The Zapatistas have proved to be not only popular in Mexico but extraordinarily successful and influential globally. Key here is their communication strategy – Castells (2000), for instance, describes this strategy as the first informational guerrilla movement. When commercial media refused to transmit Zapatista communiqués, dispatches went to Usenet groups around the world (Russell, 2001). There are today over 45,000 Zapatista-related websites in 26 countries, and the writings of the Zapatista's nominal leader, Subcomandante Marcos, are available in at least 14 languages. The Zapatistas were, in this way, able to attract a great deal of attention and bring international journalists and members of NGOs into the region, making it hard for the Mexican government to engage in repressive measures, and bringing into focus issues of political corruption and social exclusion, forcing the government to negotiate (Castells, 2000). In this way the Zapatistas have been able to bring a local struggle to global attention, to reach the centre with their 'peripheral vision' (Russell, 2001). They have very skilfully connected their struggle to those taking place elsewhere, in sentiments such as Marcos's slogan 'we are you': 'Marcos is gay in San Francisco, black in South Africa, an Asian in Europe, an anarchist in Spain, a Palestinian in Israel, a Jew in Germany, a gypsy in Poland, a Mohawk in Quebec, a single woman on the metro at 10 p.m., a peasant without land, an unemployed worker and, of course, a Zapatista in the mountains'. Collier and Collier (2003) conclude that the Zapatistas, despite their meagre resources, have managed to win the media battle.

Despite the importance of the romantic mystique around the persona of Subcomandante Marcos, the Zapatistas are also seen as exemplary in breaking from older socialist emphases on leaders, parties, and socialist organization. A middle class urban intellectual committed to Marxism, Marcos (2001) insists that he was soon forced to abandon his plans to lead the peasants in the region and to abandon the vanguardist ideology of Marxist orthodoxy. Marcos thus denies that he is the leader of the movement, with the EZLN instead taking their orders from the Clandestine Revolutionary Indigenous Committee, which is made up of delegates from the local communities (Irish Mexico Group, 2001). The following quote gives some sense of the radically democratic and decentralizing organizational practice of the Zapatistas – a key matter to which we will return.

The Brazilian Landless Workers Movement, the MST, also deserves mention here. Sader (2005) notes that because of the extremity of restructuring since the 1980s and ensuing crises in the continent, Latin America has been the main focus for resistance to neoliberalism, with the emergence of Leftist governments and the flowering of social movements. Since the movement began in 1985, the MST have helped over 350,000 families to win titles to over 15 million acres of land, following MST occupations of unused land (MST, 2003; Stedile, 2002). In addition, the MST has helped create literacy programmes, over 60 food co-operatives, and a number of small agricultural industries (MST, 2003). The extreme polarization of wealth in Brazil is a central issue for the MST, and the organization views itself as promoting democracy and protecting the food sovereignty of ordinary people – in their opposition to GM seeds and in their commitment to redistribution – against the neoliberal programme and the interests of international capital (Stedile, 2002).

We have seen, thus far, that contestation of neoliberalism and concern over the effects of an overriding emphasis on free trade are crucial nodes in AGM discourse. These concerns have since 1999 issued in a number of very significant protests against institutions such as the WTO, the IMF and World Bank, the G8, the World Economic Forum, and against free trade agreements and regional bodies seen as promoting a free trade agenda. As mentioned, a key juncture in the crystallization of the AGM was the 1999 'battle of Seattle', the confrontations that erupted during the WTO's Third Ministerial Conference. During this conference a significantly international and highly variegated protest of between 40,000–50,000 protestors representing over 700 groups forced an early close to the meetings (Steger, 2002). On the first day of the conference, protestors sought to use non-violent direct action to shut down the meeting (Steger, 2002). Police moved in, using tear gas, batons, and rubber bullets, and soon a civil emergency was declared and a curfew imposed. Matters then became more extreme and National Guard units were called in, with over 600 arrests in all (Steger, 2002). Since Seattle, a number of similarly large and sometimes violent contestations have taken place across the world.

Many of these protests centred on the activities of the WTO, the IMF, and the World Bank. These Institutions are seen as pushing the free trade and neoliberal agenda, often viewed as working primarily in the interests of investors and MNCs in the North. Focus on the Global South is a Bangkok-based research, analysis, and advocacy programme focussed on North-South Issues (Steger, 2005). Walden Bello is a central figure within this organization, opposing corporate-driven globalization, which he views as increasing poverty and inequality, and oppressive economic and political institutions (Focus, 2005). Much of Bello's analysis of globalization has been focussed on international organizations such as the IMF, World Bank, and WTO. For instance, Bello (2004b: 59) sees the WTO as 'an opaque, unrepresentative and undemocratic organization driven by a free-trade Ideology which…has generated only greater poverty and inequality… [T]he WTO is not an Independent body but a representative of American state and corporate Interests'. Bello (2004a) seeks what he calls 'deglobalization', a process of both deconstruction – a drastic reduction of the power of MNCs, the political and military hegemony of states that protect them, the Bretton Woods Institutions and the WTO, and greater control of capital movements – and reconstruction – re-empowerment of the local and national, with ordinary people as active participants, within the framework of an alternative system of global governance.

It is already clear that for the large part of those within the movement, current globalization favours financial and commercial elites, at the expense of the mass of people (especially in the South). Implicit here is a critique of the present unaccountable power and practices of MNCs. Not only are these MNCs, as mentioned in Chapter 3, seen as wielding power without accompanying social responsibility – resulting in environmental destruction and violation of labour rights, for instance – but AGM activists also frequently draw attention to issues of privatization and commodification. One of the most prominent alternative globalization writers is Naomi Klein, whose book *No Logo* (2000) became something of an alternative globalization manifesto. In *No Logo*, Klein argues that today, the brand – Coke, McDonald's, Gap, Microsoft, Starbucks – has overtaken the product itself and become emblematic of an entire way of life. That is, Nike, for example, is not simply about sportswear, but is connected to a life-style, to dreams, and to fantasy. Klein sees this tendency as a manifestation of spreading commodification, a process in which a price is put on everything. Beneath the images and fantasies contained in brands are the realities of unaccountable corporate power. For Klein (2002), the corporate-led globalization of the present is associated with the image of the fence: 'barrters created by privatization that separate people from public resources like land and water, and restricting them from crossing borders and voicing dissent'. Meanwhile, globalization means that vital fences – for example, keeping advertising out of schools – are under attack by corporate forces. According to Klein (2002), 'Every protected public space has been cracked open, only to be re-enclosed by the market', so that the 'fences that protect the public interest seem to be fast disappearing, while the ones that restrict our liberty keep multiplying'. Klein sees the possibility, though, of a reversal of this process in a growing movement of people around the world to 'reclaim the commons'.

Representations of the AGM have frequently portrayed participants as deluded, marginal, and primitivist. Bhagwati (2002: 2), for instance, argues that The opposition [to globalization] stems more from nostalgia and sterile theory than from economic realities'. Along these lines, protesters are often described, for example, as 'causists [sic] and all-purpose agitators', 'the terminally aggrieved', a 'travelling circus' of anarchists, selfish protectionists indifferent to the fate of the world's poor (Bygrave, 2002; Klein, 2002), or, in Thomas Friedman's words, 'a Noah's ark of flat-earth advocates, protectionist trade unions and yuppies looking for the 1960s fix' (in Steger, 2002). More disturbing are recent attempts to link the AGM to anti-Americanism and/or terrorism – for instance, the following from Canada's *National Post:* 'Like terrorists, the anti-globalization movement is disdainful of democratic institutions.... Terrorism, if not so heinous as what we witnessed last week, has always been part of the protesters' game plan' (In Panitch, 2002: 13). The preceding survey and the discussion that follows should dispel these simplified and highly politicized representations.

Alternative Globalization as Postmodern Socialism?

We have already noted that no exhaustive map of the AGM is feasible. As we have said, the period of 'happy globalization', during which a dominant Imaginary posited the final death of socialism, gave way to the clear rise of the AGM and, in our opinion, the emergence of what might be described as a 'postmodern socialism' (Beilharz, 1994, 2005). We will then, at this point, note some of the resonances between socialism broadly and the AGM. We will also consider some central dilemmas within the movement, and, finally, we will comment upon two issues that appear to differentiate this form of socialism from the older socialist orthodoxy.

For a start, a glance at the key concerns of the AGM listed above indicates clear affinities between the AGM and socialism broadly understood. These include: a common cosmopolitanism or at least internationalism: a common opposition to the prioritization and autonomization of the economic; a common concern with the effects of spreading commodification; a common commitment to participation, justice, equality, and democracy; a common concern with imperialism and militarism; and, within sections of both movements, a common emphasis on notions of national or local autonomy and self-determination. Having noted these affinities, there are immediately key nodes of differentiation between the two movements as well. We could, schematically, say that while socialism's adversary is capitalism and it speaks on behalf of those exploited and/or dominated by capitalism – first and foremost, the working class – In the case of the AGM, the principal adversary is, above all, neoliberal globalization, and it speaks on behalf of a plurality of social groups suffering at the hands of this form of globalization.

Concluding Comments and Reflections on Utopia: 'Another World Is Possible'

There are a number of important issues raised by this rather brief survey of the AGM. In terms of the direction of the movement, we believe that the 'horizontal' mode is encouraging and important, reflecting significant contestation around the meaning of democracy, and providing a different modality of politics for a transformed world. Nevertheless, this does not mean that there are not strategic questions to be asked towards increasing the effectiveness of the movement. Wallerstein (2003), for instance, contends that to become a genuinely anti-systemic alternative, the AGM needs to address four issues. First, a process of open debate and dialogue is needed around the transition the movement is seeking. Second, the movement cannot Ignore short-term defensive action, including electoral action, in contrast to an older revolutionary tradition that rigidly separated itself from official political involvement in the present in favour of hopes for a total revolution in the future. Third, the movement needs somehow to establish middle-range goals as well. Here, Wallerstein suggests progressive decommodification (with performance and survival rather than profits as goals) against neoliberal attempts to commodity everything. Fourth, the movement needs to develop the substantive meaning of its long-term emphases.

Wallerstein's fourth emphasis is intended to accent the revival of a critical utopian dimension, what he calls 'utopistics'. In our view, this last suggestion must be given the kind of serious consideration that the other issues tend to receive. In this regard, while the openness of and excitement generated by the World Social Forum's insistence that 'another world is possible' may be viewed as enough. It is still perhaps seen as less pressing than some other dimensions of the AGM. This insistence in itself, though, is an important utopian moment. We believe that one of the most unfortunate aspects of the period of 'happy globalization' or 'the end of history' was the apparent evacuation from the popular imaginary of any sort of utopian dimension. For some, the demise of utopia was an extremely positive thing because utopias, in this view, are in essence religious and irrational, projecting the possibility of perfect future harmony, transparency, and order, thereby fleeing dangerously from the complex realities of modern life and modern people. The inevitable failure of such unrealistic aims, it is often argued, leads Inexorably first to disillusionment then to coercion and totalitarianism. From this perspective, the apparent triumph of liberal modesty about what we can know and do would be viewed as an important victory.

For others, the loss of the utopian dimension would be a tragedy, meaning an end to thinking deeply about what makes politics meaningful in human life and a closing down of democracy's potential. Thus, Perry Anderson (2004) laments the general suspension of utopia since the mid-1970s, which has produced a 'remorseless closure of space'. Similarly, Bourdleu (1998) spoke of the spread of a 'banker's fatalism' across the world, and Castoriadis (1997a, 1997b, 2004) was concerned that the postmodern present was threatening to fall back into what he called 'heteronomy'. Castoriadis's argument was that *autonomy*, the radical political move away from tradition, wherein the social order was viewed as established outside of the activities and imaginations of human beings acting collectively, had appeared twice in history – first with Greek Antiquity and then again in the modern period. This autonomy signified the realization that human beings were collectively responsible for the institutions they had created, with the radical accompanying thought that, therefore, we could collectively take up and transform these institutions again. For this reason autonomy requires the ability to think both in and through the present, to imagine a better future – what Camus (1991: 121) called a 'relative utopia' – that can be realistically constructed from the contradictory conditions of the current global system. Here the utopian impulse remains strong, although shorn of any messianism (found in both Marxist and capitalist ideologies) bent on perfecting the world in an absolute sense, that is, according to a single and final 'blueprint', and thereby ushering in the supposedly inevitable 'end' of history.

In both pro- and anti-globalization arguments, there is frequently a desperate sense that the system is moving all by itself, that we can do nothing to alter its inexorahle unfolding. Thus, Thomas Friedman (1999) contends that no one is to blame for globalization and its failures, no one can control its dynamic, and therefore we need to submit to its dictates and learn to love it. From a very different Ideological pole, Bauman (1999a) notes the widespread sense of globalization's unstoppabillty, likening our contemporary experience to that of passengers in a plane who discover that the pilot's cabin is empty. Such senses of globalization's self-propelling dynamic are, to our minds, the very opposite of the autonomy Castoriadis speaks of. It means a closing down of the utopian imagination, and this in turn is devastating to democracy, which surely should be precisely about the sort of unlimited and unending critique and questioning that Castoriadis points to as a central modern achievement. This reinvigoration of the utopian dimension means a return to one of the crucial dimensions of critical theory – 'thinking beyond' the politics of the present while acutely aware of the demands and limits that the present places upon us – and the message we wish this book to send: that the utopian heartbeat can and must still be detected In our globalizing world.

References

Agence France-Presse 'French Anti-Globalization Leader José Bové Jailed' (www.commondreams.org/headlines03/0622-02.htm, 22 June 2003).

Anderson, P. 'Internationalism: A Breviary', *New Left Review*, 14 (2002) 5–25.

Anderson, P. 'The River of Time', *New Left Review*, 26 (2004) 67–77.

Anderson, S. and Cavanagh, J. 'Top 200: The Rise of Global Corporate Power' (wwwglobalpolicy.org/socecon/tncs/top200.htm, 2000).

Anderson, S., Cavanagh, J., and Lee, T. *Field Guide to the Global Economy* (New York: The New Press, 2000).

Annan, K. *In Larger Freedom: Towards Development, Security, and Human Rights for All*, A/59/2005, 21 March 2005.

Appadurai, A. 'Disjuncture and Difference in the Global Cultural Economy', in M. Featherstone (ed.), *Global Culture: Nationalism, Globalization and Modernity* (London: Sage, 1990).

Archibugi, D. 'Demos and Cosmopolis', *New Left Review*, 13 (2002) 24–38.

Archibugi, D. 'Cosmopolitical Democracy', in D. Archibugi (ed.), *Debating Cosmopolitics* (London: Verso, 2003).

ATTAC 'Platform of the International Movement ATTAC' (www.attac.org/contact/indexpfen.htm, nd).

ATTAC 'Trade is a Women's Issue' (www.globalpolicy.org/socecon/inequal/labor/2003/0220women.htm, 2003).

Balakrishnan, G. 'Hardt and Negri's Empire', *New Left Review*, 5 (2000) 142–48.

Barber, B. R. *Jihad Versus McWorld: How Globalism and Tribalism are Reshaping the World* (New York Ballantine Books, 1996).

Beilharz, P. '*Postmodern Socialism: Romanticism, City and State* (Melbourne: Melbourne University Press, 1994).

Beilharz, P. 'Postmodern Socialism Revisited', in P. Hayden and C. el-Ojelli (eds), *Confronting Globalization: Humanity, Justice and the Renewal of Politics* (London: Palgrave Macmillan, 200S).

Beilharz, P. *et al.* The Globalization of Nothing: A Review Symposium of George Ritzer, *The Globalization of Nothing*', *Thesis Eleven*, 76 (2004) 103–14. York: Basic Books, 1999).

Bello, W., Bullard, N., and Malhotra, K. *Global Finance: New Thinking on Regulating Speculative Capital Markets* (London: Zed, 2000).

Bello, W. *Deglobalization: Ideas for a New World Economy* (London: Zed, 2004a).

Bello, W. 'The Global South', in T. Mertes (ed.), *A Movement of Movements: Is Another World Really Possible?* (London: Zed, 2004b).

Bhagwati, J. 'Coping With Antiglobalization: A Trilogy of Discontents', *Foreign Affairs*, 81 (2002) 2–7.

Boggs, C. *The Socialist Tradition: From Crisis to Decline* (London: Routledge, 1995).

Bové, J. 'A Farmers' International?', *New Left Review*, 12 (2001) 89–101.

Buechler, S. M. *Social Movements in Advanced Capitalism: The Political Economy and Cultural Construction of Social Activism* (Oxford: Oxford University Press, 2000).

Burbach, R. 'Roots of the Postmodern Rebellion in Chiapas', *New Left Review*, 205 (1994) 113–24.

Bygrave, M. 'Where Did all the Protesters Go?', *The Observer* (www.observer.co.uk comment/ story/0,6903.754862.00.html, 2002)

Callinicos, A. and Harman, C. *The Changing Working Class: Essays on Class Structure Today* (London: Bookmarks, 1987).

Callinicos, A. *Against Postmodernism* (Cambridge: Polity, 1989).

Callinicos, A. *An Anti-Capitalist Manifesto* (Cambridge: Polity, 2003).

Castells, M. *The Information Age: Economy, Society and Culture – The Power of Identity* (Oxford: Blackwell, 2000).

Cleaver, H. 'Introduction' (http://lanic.utexas.edu/project/Zapatistas/INTRO.TXT, 1994).

Cleaver, T. *Understanding the World Economy*, 2nd edn (London: Routledge, 2002).

Collier, G. A. and Collier, J. F. 'The Zapatista Rebellion in the Context of Globalization', in J. Foran (ed.), *The Future of Revolutions: Rethinking Radical Change in the Age of Globalization* (London: Zed, 2003).

Commission on Global Governance. *Our Global Neighbourhood: The Report of the Commission on Global Governance* (Oxford: Oxford University Press, 1995).

de Goede, M. 'Carnival of Money: Politics of Dissent in an Era of Globalizing Finance', in L. Amoore (ed.), *The Global Resistance Reader* (London: Routledge, 2005).

Deleuze, G. and Guattari, F. *A Thousand Plateaus: Capitalism and Schizophrenia* (Minneapolis: University of Minnesota Press, 1987).

Friedman, T. *The Lexus and the Olive Tree* (London: HarperCollins, 1999).

Friedman, T. 'It's a Flat World, After All', *The New York Times*, 3 April 2005.

Fukuyama, F. *The End of History and the Last Man* (London: Penguin, 1992).

Giddens, A. *The Consequences of Modernity* (Palo Alto: Stanford University Press, 1990).

Giddens, A. *Modernity and Self-Identity* (Palo Alto: Stanford University Press, 1991).

Giddens, A. *Runaway World* (London: Profile Books, 1999).

Giddens, A. *The Third Way* (Cambridge: Polity: 2000).

Giddens, A. 'An Interview With Anthony Giddens', *Journal of Consumer Culture*, 3 (2003a) 387–99.

Giddens, A. (ed.) *The Progressive Manifesto* (Cambridge: Polity: 2003b).

Giddens, A. 'French Headscarf Ban Against Interests of Women', *Global Viewpoint* (www.dlgitalnpq.org/global_services/global9620viewpoint/01-05-04.html, 2004).

Giddens, A. 'Giddens and the "G" Word: An Interview With Anthony Giddens', *Global Media and Communication* 1 (2005) 63–77.

Gorz, A. *Capitalism, Socialism and Ecology* (London: Verso, 1994).

Graeber, D. 'The New Anarchists', *New Left Review*, 13 (2002), pp. 61–73.

Gross, F. *The Revolutionary Party: Essays in the Politics of Socialism* (London: Greenwood Press, 1974).

Hardt, M. 'Porto Alegre: Today's Bundung?', *New Left Review*, 14 (2002) 112–19.

Hardt, M. and Negri, A. *Labour of Dionysus: Critique of the State-Form* (Minneapolis: University of Minnesota Press, 1994).

Hardt, M. and Negri, A. *Empire* (Cambridge, MA: Harvard University Press, 2000).

Held, D. *Democracy and the Global Order* (Cambridge: Polity, 1995).

Held, D. 'Realism Versus Cosmopolitanism: A Debate Between Barry Buzan and David Held' (www.polity.co.uk/global/realism.htm, 1996).

Held, D. (ed.) *A Globalising World? Culture, Economics, Politics* (London: Routledge, 2000).

Held, D. 'Global Social Democracy', in A. Giddens (ed.), *The Progressive Manifesto* (Cambridge: Polity, 2003).

Held, D. 'Introduction to Critical Theory', in D. Rasmussen and J. Swindal (eds), *Critical Theory: Volume I – Historical Perspectives* (London: Sage, 2004a).

Held, D. *Global Covenant: The Social Democratic Alternative to the Washington Consensus* (Cambridge: Polity, 2004b).

Held, D. and McGrew, A. *Globalization/Anti-Globalization* (Cambridge: Polity, 2002).

Held, D., McGrew, A., Goldblatt, D., and Perraton, J. *Global Transformations: Politics, Economics and Culture* (Cambridge: Polity, 1999).

Indymedia 'Frequently Asked Questions' (www.docs.indymedia.org/view/ Global/ FrequentlyAskedQuestionsEn, 2004).

Irish Mexico Group 'Chiapas Revealed' (http://flag.blackened.net/revolt/mexico/ pdf/revealed1.html, 2001).

Kidd, D. 'Indymedia.org: A New Communications Commons', in M. McCaughey and M. Ayers (eds), *Cyberactivism: Online Activism In Theory and Practice* (New York: Routledge, 2003).

Klein, N. *No Logo* (New York: HarperCollins, 2000).

Klein, N. 'The Unknown Icon'. *The Guardian* (www.gaurdian.co.uk/Columnists/Column/0,5673,446977,00.html, 3 March 2001).

Klein, N. *Fences and Windows: Dispatches From the Front Lines of the Globalization Debate* (London: Flamingo, 2002).

Klein, N. 'Culture Jamming: Ads Under Attack', in L. Amoore (ed.), *The Global Resistance Reader* (London: Routledge, 2005).

Lane, D. *The Rise and Fall of State Socialism: Industrial Society and the Socialist State* (Cambridge: Polity, 1996).

Lewandowski, J. D. 'Disembedded Democracy? Globalization and the "Third Way" ', *European Journal of Social Theory*, 6 (2003) 115–31.

Marcos, Subcommandante 'Closing Words of the EZLN at the Intercontinental Encounter – Second Declaration of La Realidad' (www.struggle.ws/mexico/ezin/1996/ccri_encount_aug.html, 1996).

Marcos, Subcomandante 'The Punch Card and the Hour Glass', *New Left Review*, 9 (2001) 69–79.

Meyer, D. S., Whittier, N., and Bobnett, B. (eds) *Social Movements: Identity, Culture, and the State* (Oxford: Oxford University Press, 2002).

Mueller, C. M. 'Building Social Movement Theory', in A. D. Morris and C. M. Mueller (eds), *Frontiers in Social Movement Theory* (New Haven: Yale University Press, 1992).

Munck, R. *Globalisation and Labour: The New 'Great Transformation'* (London: Zed Books, 2002).

Panitch, L. 'Violence as a Tool of Order and Change: The War on Terrorism and the Antiglobalization Movement', *Monthly Review*, 54 (2002) 12–32.

Platon, S. and Dueze, M. 'Indymedia Journalism: A Radical Way of Making, Selecting and Sharing News?', *Journalism*, 4 (2003) 336–55.

Russell, A. 'The Zapatistas Online: Shifting the Discourse of Globalization', *Gazette*, 63 (2001) 399–413.

Sader, E. 'Beyond Civil Society: The Left After Porto Alegre', *New Left Review*, 17 (2002) 87–99.

Sader, E. 'Taking Lula's Measure', *New Left Review*, 33 (2005) 58–80.

Scott, A. 'Political Culture and Social Movements', In J. Allen, P. Braham, and P. Lewis (eds), *Political and Economic Forms of Modernity* (Cambridge: Polity, 2001).

Sellers, J. 'Raising a Ruckus', *New Left Review*, 10 (2001) 71–85.

Seoane, J. and Taddei, E. 'From Seattle to Porto Alegre: The Anti-Neoliberal Globalization Movement', *Current Sociology*, 50 (2002) 99–122.

Stedile, J. P. 'Landless Battalions: The Sem Terra Movement of Brazil', *New Left Review*, 15 (2002) 76–104.

Steger, M. *Globalism: The New Market Ideology* (Lanham: Rowman and Littlefield, 2002).

Steger, M. *Globalization: A Very Short Introduction* (Oxford: Oxford University Press, 2003).

Steger, M. *Globalism: Market Ideology Meets Terrorism*, 2nd edn (Lanham: Rowman and Littlefield, 2005).

Tilly, C. *Social Movements, 1768–2004* (Boulder: Paradigm, 2004).

Tormey, S. 'Against "Representation": Deleuze, Zapatismo and the Search for the Post-Political Subject' (http://homepage.ntlworld.com/simon.tormey/articles/representation.pdf. 2003).

Tormey, S. *Anti-Capitalism: A Beginner's Guide* (Oxford: Oneworld, 2004).

Veltmeyer, H. (ed.) Globalization and Antiglobalization: Dynamics of Change in the New World Order (Aldershot: Ashgate, 2004).

Wallerstein, I. 'New Revolts Against the System', *New Left Review*, 18 (2002) 29–39.

Whittaker, D. J. *United Nations in the Contemporary World* (London: Routledge, 1997).

The Rise of the Region State

KENICHI OHMAE

Is the nation-state obsolete? Ohmae, an international business consultant, asserts globalization has eliminated the need for certain state functions. Written early in 1993 before NAFTA, before the late 1990s Asian financial collapse, and long before the 2008 global recession, in this article Ohmae predicts a process that will result in geographic regions taking precedence over the states that they comprise. What developments will cause this change? Will states retain any functions? If yes, which ones? Has this "region-state" developed? Does Ohmae base his analysis on any particular academic perspective of IR?

The Nation State Is Dysfunctional

The nation state has become an unnatural, even dysfunctional, unit for organizing human activity and managing economic endeavor in a borderless world. It represents no genuine, shared community of economic interests; it defines no meaningful flows of economic activity. In fact, it overlooks the true linkages and synergies that exist among often disparate populations by combining important measures of human activity at the wrong level of analysis.

For example, to think of Italy as a single economic entity ignores the reality of an industrial north and a rural south, each vastly different in its ability to contribute and in its need to receive. Treating Italy as a single economic unit forces one—as a private sector manager or a public sector official—to operate on the basis of false, implausible and nonexistent averages. Italy is a country with great disparities in industry and income across regions.

On the global economic map the lines that now matter are those defining what may be called "region states." The boundaries of the region state are not imposed by political fiat. They are drawn by the deft but invisible hand of the global market for goods and services. They follow, rather than precede, real flows of human activity, creating nothing new but ratifying existing patterns manifest in countless individual decisions. They represent no threat to the political borders of any nation, and they have no call on any taxpayer's money to finance military forces to defend such borders.

Region states are natural economic zones. They may or may not fall within the geographic limits of a particular nation—whether they do is an accident of history. Sometimes these distinct economic units are formed by parts of states, such as those in northern Italy, Wales, Catalonia, Alsace-Lorraine or Baden-Württemberg. At other times they may be formed by economic patterns that overlap existing national boundaries, such as those between San Diego and Tijuana, Hong Kong and southern China, or the "growth triangle" of Singapore and its neighboring Indonesian islands.

Kenichi Ohmae, "The Rise of the Region State," *Foreign Affairs*, Vol. 72, No. 2 (Spring, 1993), pp. 78–87.

In today's borderless world these are natural economic zones and what matters is that each possesses, in one or another combination, the key ingredients for successful participation in the global economy.

Look, for example, at what is happening in Southeast Asia. The Hong Kong economy has gradually extended its influence throughout the Pearl River Delta. The radiating effect of these linkages has made Hong Kong, where gnp per capita is $12,000, the driving force of economic life in Shenzhen, boosting the per capita gnp of that city's residents to $5,695, as compared to $317 for China as a whole. These links extend to Zhuhai, Amoy and Guangzhou as well. By the year 2000 this cross-border region state will have raised the living standard of more than 11 million people over the $5,000 level. Meanwhile, Guangdong province, with a population of more than 65 million and its capital at Hong Kong, will emerge as a newly industrialized economy in its own right, even though China's per capita gnp may still hover at about $1,000. Unlike in Eastern Europe, where nations try to convert entire socialist economies over to the market, the Asian model is first to convert limited economic zones—the region states—into free enterprise havens. So far the results have been reassuring.

These developments and others like them are coming just in time for Asia. As Europe perfects its single market and as the United States, Canada and Mexico begin to explore the benefits of the North American Free Trade Agreement (NAFTA), the combined economies of Asia and Japan lag behind those of the other parts of the globe's economic triad by about $2 trillion—roughly the aggregate size of some 20 additional region states. In other words, for Asia to keep pace existing regions must continue to grow at current rates throughout the next decade, giving birth to 20 additional Singapores.

Many of these new region states are already beginning to emerge. China has expanded to 14 other areas—many of them inland—the special economic zones that have worked so well for Shenzhen and Shanghai. One such project at Yunnan will become a cross-border economic zone encompassing parts of Laos and Vietnam. In Vietnam itself Ho Chi Minh City (Saigon) has launched a similar "sepzone" to attract foreign capital. Inspired in part by Singapore's "growth triangle," the governments of Indonesia, Malaysia and Thailand in 1992 unveiled a larger triangle across the Strait of Malacca to link Medan, Penang and Phuket. These developments are not, of course, limited to the developing economies in Asia. In economic terms the United States has never been a single nation. It is a collection of region states: northern and southern California, the "power corridor" along the East Coast between Boston and Washington, the Northeast, the Midwest, the Sun Belt, and so on.

What Makes a Region State

The primary linkages of region states tend to be with the global economy and not with their host nations. Region states make such effective points of entry into the global economy because the very characteristics that define them are shaped by the demands of that economy. Region states tend to have between five million and 20 million people. The range is broad, but the extremes are clear: not half a million, not 50 or 100 million. A region state must be small enough for its citizens to share certain economic and consumer interests but of adequate size to justify the infrastructure—communication and transportation links and quality professional services—necessary to participate economically on a global scale.

It must, for example, have at least one international airport and, more than likely, one good harbor with international-class freight-handling facilities. A region state must also be large enough to provide an attractive market for the brand development of leading consumer products. In other words, region states are not defined by their economies of scale in production (which, after all, can be leveraged from a base of any size through exports to the rest of the world) but rather by their having reached efficient economies of scale in their consumption, infrastructure and professional services.

For example, as the reach of television networks expands, advertising becomes more efficient.

Although trying to introduce a consumer brand throughout all of Japan or Indonesia may still prove prohibitively expensive, establishing it firmly in the Osaka or Jakarta region is far more affordable—and far more likely to generate handsome returns. Much the same is true with sales and service networks, customer satisfaction programs, market surveys and management information systems: efficient scale is at the regional, not national, level. This fact matters because, on balance, modern marketing techniques and technologies shape the economies of region states.

Where true economies of service exist, religious, ethnic and racial distinctions are not important—or, at least, only as important as human nature requires. Singapore is 70 percent ethnic Chinese, but its 30 percent minority is not much of a problem because commercial prosperity creates sufficient affluence for all. Nor are ethnic differences a source of concern for potential investors looking for consumers.

Indonesia—an archipelago with 500 or so different tribal groups, 18,000 islands and 170 million people—would logically seem to defy effective organization within a single mode of political government. Yet Jakarta has traditionally attempted to impose just such a central control by applying fictional averages to the entire nation. They do not work. If, however, economies of service allowed two or three Singapore-sized region states to be created within Indonesia, they could be managed. And they would ameliorate, rather than exacerbate, the country's internal social divisions. This holds as well for India and Brazil.

The New Multinational Corporation

When viewing the globe through the lens of the region state, senior corporate managers think differently about the geographical expansion of their businesses. In the past the primary aspiration of multinational corporations was to create, in effect, clones of the parent organization in each of the dozens of countries in which they operated. The goal of this system was to stick yet another pin in the global map to mark an increasing number of subsidiaries around the world.

More recently, however, when Nestlé and Procter & Gamble wanted to expand their business in Japan from an already strong position, they did not view the effort as just another pin-sticking exercise. Nor did they treat the country as a single coherent market to be gained at once, or try as most Western companies do to establish a foothold first in the Tokyo area, Japan's most tumultuous and overcrowded market. Instead, they wisely focused on the Kansai region around Osaka and Kobe, whose 22 million residents are nearly as affluent as those in Tokyo but where competition is far less intense. Once they had on-the-ground experience on how best to reach the Japanese consumer, they branched out into other regions of the country.

Much of the difficulty Western companies face in trying to enter Japan stems directly from trying to shoulder their way in through Tokyo. This instinct often proves difficult and costly. Even if it works, it may also prove a trap; it is hard to "see" Japan once one is bottled up in the particular dynamics of the Tokyo marketplace. Moreover, entering the country through a different regional doorway has great economic appeal. Measured by aggregate gnp the Kansai region is the seventh-largest economy in the world, just behind the United Kingdom.

Given the variations among local markets and the value of learning through real-world experimentation, an incremental region-based approach to market entry makes excellent sense. And not just in Japan. Building an effective presence across a landmass the size of China is of course a daunting prospect. Serving the people in and around Nagoya City, however, is not.

If one wants a presence in Thailand, why start by building a network over the entire extended landmass? Instead focus, at least initially, on the region around Bangkok, which represents the lion's share of the total potential market. The same strategy applies to the United States. To introduce a new top-of-the-line car into the U.S. market, why replicate up front an exhaustive coast-to-coast dealership network? Of the country's 3,000 statistical metropolitan areas, 80 percent of luxury car buyers can be reached by establishing a presence in only 125 of these.

The Challenges for Government

Traditional issues of foreign policy, security and defense remain the province of nation states. So, too, are macroeconomic and monetary policies—the taxation and public investment needed to provide the necessary infra-structure and incentives for region-based activities. The government will also remain responsible for the broad requirements of educating and training citizens so that they can participate fully in the global economy.

Governments are likely to resist giving up the power to intervene in the economic realm or to relinquish their impulses for protectionism. The illusion of control is soothing. Yet hard evidence proves the contrary. No manipulation of exchange rates by central bankers or political appointees has ever "corrected" the trade imbalances between the United States and Japan. Nor has any trade talk between the two governments. Whatever cosmetic actions these negotiations may have prompted, they rescued no industry and revived no economic sector. Textiles, semiconductors, autos, consumer electronics—the competitive situation in these industries did not develop according to the whims of policymakers but only in response to the deeper logic of the competitive marketplace. If U.S. market share has dwindled, it is not because government policy failed but because individual consumers decided to buy elsewhere. If U.S. capacity has migrated to Mexico or Asia, it is only because individual managers made decisions about cost and efficiency.

The implications of region states are not welcome news to established seats of political power, be they politicians or lobbyists. Nation states by definition require a domestic political focus, while region states are ensconced in the global economy. Region states that sit within the frontiers of a particular nation share its political goals and aspirations. However, region states welcome foreign investment and ownership—whatever allows them to employ people productively or to improve the quality of life. They want their people to have access to the best and cheapest products. And they want whatever surplus accrues from these activities to ratchet up the local quality of life still further and not to support distant regions or to prop up distressed industries elsewhere in the name of national interest or sovereignty.

When a region prospers, that prosperity spills over into the adjacent regions within the same political confederation. Industry in the area immediately in and around Bangkok has prompted investors to explore options elsewhere in Thailand. Much the same is true of Kuala Lumpur in Malaysia, Jakarta in Indonesia, or Singapore, which is rapidly becoming the unofficial capital of the Association of Southeast Asian Nations. São Paulo, too, could well emerge as a genuine region state, someday entering the ranks of the Organization of Economic Cooperation and Development. Yet if Brazil's central government does not allow the São Paulo region state finally to enter the global economy, the country as a whole may soon fall off the roster of the newly industrialized economies.

Unlike those at the political center, the leaders of region states—interested chief executive officers, heads of local unions, politicians at city and state levels—often welcome and encourage foreign capital investment. They do not go abroad to attract new plants and factories only to appear back home on television vowing to protect local companies at any cost. These leaders tend to possess an international outlook that can help defuse many of the usual kinds of social tensions arising over issues of "foreign" versus "domestic" inputs to production.

In the United States, for example, the Japanese have already established about 120 "transplant" auto factories throughout the Mississippi Valley. More are on the way. As their share of the U.S. auto industry's production grows, people in that region who look to these plants for their livelihoods and for the tax revenues needed to support local communities will stop caring whether the plants belong to U.S.- or Japanese-based companies. All they will care about are the regional economic benefits of having them there. In effect, as members of the Mississippi Valley region state, they will have leveraged the contribution of these plants to help their region become an active participant in the global economy.

Region states need not be the enemies of central governments. Handled gently, region states can provide the opportunity for eventual prosperity for all areas within a nation's traditional political control. When political and industrial leaders accept and act on these realities, they help build prosperity. When they do not—falling back under the spell of the nationalist economic illusion—they may actually destroy it.

Consider the fate of Silicon Valley, that great early engine of much of America's microelectronics industry. In the beginning it was an extremely open and entrepreneurial environment. Of late, however, it has become notably protectionist—creating industry associations, establishing a polished lobbying presence in Washington and turning to "competitiveness" studies as a way to get more federal funding for research and development. It has also begun to discourage, and even to bar, foreign investment, let alone foreign takeovers. The result is that Boise and Denver now prosper in electronics; Japan is developing a Silicon Island on Kyushu; Taiwan is trying to create a Silicon Island of its own; and Korea is nurturing a Silicon Peninsula. This is the worst of all possible worlds: no new money in California and a host of newly energized and well-funded competitors.

Elsewhere in California, not far from Silicon Valley, the story is quite different. When Hollywood recognized that it faced a severe capital shortage, it did not throw up protectionist barriers against foreign money. Instead, it invited Rupert Murdoch into 20th Century Fox, C. Itoh and Toshiba into Time-Warner, Sony into Columbia, and Matsushita into MCA. The result: a $10 billion infusion of new capital and, equally important, $10 billion less for Japan or anyone else to set up a new Hollywood of their own.

Political leaders, however reluctantly, must adjust to the reality of economic regional entities if they are to nurture real economic flows. Resistant governments will be left to reign over traditional political territories as all meaningful participation in the global economy migrates beyond their well-preserved frontiers.

Canada, as an example, is wrongly focusing on Quebec and national language tensions as its core economic and even political issue. It does so to the point of still wrestling with the teaching of French and English in British Columbia, when that province's economic future is tied to Asia. Furthermore, as NAFTA takes shape the "vertical" relationships between Canadian and U.S. regions—Vancouver and Seattle (the Pacific Northwest region state); Toronto, Detroit and Cleveland (the Great Lakes region state)—will become increasingly important. How Canadian leaders deal with these new entities will be critical to the continuance of Canada as a political nation.

In developing economies, history suggests that when gnp per capita reaches about $5,000, discretionary income crosses an invisible threshold. Above that level people begin wondering whether they have reasonable access to the best and cheapest available products and whether they have an adequate quality of life. More troubling for those in political control, citizens also begin to consider whether their government is doing as well by them as it might.

Such a performance review is likely to be unpleasant. When governments control information—and in large measure because they do—it is all too easy for them to believe that they "own" their people. Governments begin restricting access to certain kinds of goods or services or pricing them far higher than pure economic logic would dictate. If market-driven levels of consumption conflict with a government's pet policy or general desire for control, the obvious response is to restrict consumption. So what if the people would choose otherwise if given the opportunity? Not only does the government withhold that opportunity but it also does not even let the people know that it is being withheld.

Regimes that exercise strong central control either fall on hard times or begin to decompose. In a borderless world the deck is stacked against them. The irony, of course, is that in the name of safeguarding the integrity and identity of the center, they often prove unwilling or unable to give up the illusion of power in order to seek a better quality of life for their people. There is at the center an understandable fear of letting go and losing control. As a result, the center often ends up protecting weak and unproductive industries and then passing along the high costs to its people—precisely the opposite of what a government should do.

The Goal Is to Raise Living Standards

The Clinton administration faces a stark choice as it organizes itself to address the country's economic issues. It can develop policy within the framework of the badly dated assumption that success in the global economy means pitting one nation's industries against another's. Or it can define policy with the awareness that the economic dynamics of a borderless world do not flow from such contrived head-to-head confrontations, but rather from the participation of specific regions in a global nexus of information, skill, trade and investment.

If the goal is to raise living standards by promoting regional participation in the borderless economy, then the less Washington constrains these regions, the better off they will be. By contrast, the more Washington intervenes, the more citizens will pay for automobiles, steel, semiconductors, white wine, textiles or consumer electronics—all in the name of "protecting" America. Aggregating economic policy at the national level—or worse, at the continent-wide level as in Europe—inevitably results in special interest groups and vote-conscious governments putting their own interests first.

The less Washington interacts with specific regions, however, the less it perceives itself as "representing" them. It does not feel right. When learning to ski, one of the toughest and most counterintuitive principles to accept is that one gains better control by leaning down toward the valley, not back against the hill. Letting go is difficult. For governments region-based participation in the borderless economy is fine, except where it threatens current jobs, industries or interests. In Japan, a nation with plenty of farmers, food is far more expensive than in Hong Kong or Singapore, where there are no farmers. That is because Hong Kong and Singapore are open to what Australia and China can produce far more cheaply than they could themselves. They have opened themselves to the global economy, thrown their weight forward, as it were, and their people have reaped the benefits.

For the Clinton administration, the irony is that Washington today finds itself in the same relation to those region states that lie entirely or partially within its borders as was London with its North American colonies centuries ago. Neither central power could genuinely understand the shape or magnitude of the new flows of information, people and economic activity in the regions nominally under its control. Nor could it understand how counterproductive it would be to try to arrest or distort these flows in the service of nation-defined interests. Now as then, only relaxed central control can allow the flexibility needed to maintain the links to regions gripped by an inexorable drive for prosperity.

Human Rights Advocacy Networks in Latin America

MARGARET E. KECK AND KATHRYN SIKKINK

What has been the role of individuals in promoting the transnational human rights advocacy network? During the Cold War, how did state sovereignty slow the spread of the Liberal internationalist norms of human rights? What are the ways in which the growth of the human rights advocacy network displays aspects of the Realist, Liberal, and Constructivist perspectives?

We can trace the idea that states should protect the human rights of their citizens back to the French Revolution and the U.S. Bill of Rights, but the idea that human rights should be an integral part of foreign policy and international relations is new. As recently as 1970, the idea that the human rights of citizens of any country are legitimately the concern of people and governments everywhere was considered radical. Transnational advocacy networks played a key role in placing human rights on foreign policy agendas.

The doctrine of internationally protected human rights offers a powerful critique of traditional notions of sovereignty, and current legal and foreign policy practices regarding human rights show how understandings of the scope of sovereignty have shifted. As sovereignty is one of the central organizing principles of the international system, transnational advocacy networks that contribute to transforming sovereignty will be a significant source of change in international politics.

After the Second World War the transnational human rights advocacy network helped to create regional and international human rights regimes, and later contributed to the implementation and enforcement of human rights norms and policy.

Emergence of the Human Rights Idea and the Network

The history of the emergence of the human rights network is the story of the founding, growth, and linking of the organizations in the network. The values that bind the actors together are embodied in international human rights law, especially in the 1948 Universal Declaration of Human Rights. This body of law justifies actions and provides a common language to make arguments and sets of procedures to advance claims. How these international human rights norms and regimes emerged in the UN has been discussed at length elsewhere and does not need to be repeated here.[1] What is often missed, however, is how nongovernmental organizations helped spur state action at each stage in the process.[2]

The entities that make up the current transnational human rights advocacy network include the following: (1) parts of intergovernmental organizations, at both the international and regional level; (2) international NGOs; (3) domestic NGOs; (4) private foundations; and (5) parts of some governments. The most important organizations for human rights in Latin America include the UN Commission on Human Rights, the UN Committee on Human Rights, the Inter-American Commission on Human Rights (IACHR), Amnesty International, Americas Watch, the Washington Office on Latin America, domestic NGOs like the Mothers of the Plaza de Mayo in Argentina and the Academy of Human Rights in Mexico, and the Ford Foundation as well as the European foundations that fund international and domestic human rights NGOs.

Before 1945 none of these organizations existed. In 1961, when Amnesty International was founded, most still either did not exist, or, in the case of the foundations, had not yet begun to pay attention to human rights. But even before the modern networks emerged, key individuals and NGOs advanced the idea that human rights should be an international concern.

Inspired by liberal internationalism, Woodrow Wilson articulated some human rights concerns in his campaign for global democracy and the rights of national self-determination during 1917–20. But the Convention of the League of Nations contained no mention of human rights, although it does mention "fair and humane conditions of labor" and "just treatment" of native inhabitants of dependent territories.[3]

Lawyer-diplomats first introduced and promoted the idea of internationally recognized human rights in the interwar period, and lawyers have continued to play a central role (in contrast with precursor campaigns where religious leaders predominated). Chilean jurist Alejandro Alvarez, Russian jurist and diplomat André Mandelstam, and Greek jurist and diplomat Antoine Frangulis first drafted and publicized declarations on international rights of man as part of their work with non-governmental legal organizations—the American Institute of International Law, the International Law Institute, and the International Diplomatic Academy.[4]

At the same time, a Jewish lawyer from Poland named Raphael Lemkin began a personal struggle to develop international law against racial massacres. Until Lemkin came up with the word "genocide" after the Second World War, there was no word for the phenomenon in any language. Influenced as a boy by the massacre of Armenians in Turkey, he became convinced that the Nazis would carry out parallel outrages against Jews.[5] In 1933, at a conference sponsored by the League of Nations in Madrid, Spain, Lemkin proposed that an international treaty should be negotiated making "destruction of national, religious, and ethnic groups" an international crime akin to piracy, slavery, and drug smuggling.[6] "Lemkin's proposal met with howls of derision in which the delegates of Nazi Germany took the lead."[7]

An alternative source of internationalism in the early twentieth century was the tradition of solidarity that developed in trade union and socialist movements. These movements began by denying the relevance of the nation-state for workers, espousing a simple cosmopolitanism that fell before the decisions by most socialist parties to support their governments in the First World War. Despite this setback, the idea of international working-class solidarity remained a core value of the left throughout most of the twentieth century. It inspired thousands of young Communists and a considerable number of others to risk (and lose) their lives in Spain in the 1930s.[8] The Spanish Civil War also inspired liberal intellectuals who were stunned by the collapse of democratic ideals and institutions in the face of the fascist advance.

In 1939, recognizing that war was coming. Wells wrote that "if many of us are to die for democracy we better know what we mean by the word."[9] He launched a spirited public debate and effort to draft a new declaration of the rights of man that would clarify the war aims of the Allies by expressing "the broad principles on which our public and social life is based."[10] Wells sent the declaration to many people, including President Roosevelt, Gandhi, and Nehru (all of whom sent him reactions), and Jan Christiaan Smuts, prime minister of South Africa, who later drafted the preamble of the UN Charter.

Franklin Roosevelt incorporated this concern with human rights as part of the postwar order into his "Four Freedoms" State of the Union speech in January 1941.[11] The concept of a world founded upon essential freedoms—freedom of speech and expression, freedom of worship, freedom from want, and freedom from fear—was in part an outgrowth of his New Deal beliefs. Yet Roosevelt's concern for the international dimension of human rights was stimulated by the war and by a need to articulate war and peace aims that would set the Allies apart from Nazi Germany and the Axis powers.[12] Roosevelt was a friend of H. G. Wells, and was a member of the International Diplomatic Academy, which had actively studied and promoted the cause of international human rights under the leadership of Frangulis and Mandelstam.[13] It is likely that these were among the sources he turned to as he formulated his "Four Freedoms" speech.

An explosion of intellectual, governmental, and nongovernmental activity followed upon the Wells campaign and Roosevelt's speech. This was a crucial moment of collaboration in creating a new postwar order, one of the pillars of which was to be the international protection of human rights. The U.S. domestic campaign for postwar international organization and the intense cooperation between the State Department and citizens' groups in this period can only be understood in the light of the administration's fear of a repeat of the U.S. failure to ratify the Versailles Treaty. For this reason, congressional and nongovernmental leaders were well represented in the official U.S. delegation to the 1945 conference in San Francisco that established the United Nations, and in addition the U.S. government invited 42 nongovernmental organizations to serve as consultants to the U.S. delegation in San Francisco.

The Inter-American Tradition of Support for International Human Rights

In Latin America there was a strong tradition of support for international law as a means by which weaker countries might contest the interventions of the more powerful, especially the United States. But while legalism had primarily been used to support concepts of sovereignty and nonintervention, international law also supported the promotion of human rights and democracy, which involved recognizing limits to the doctrine of absolute sovereignty and nonintervention. Until the Second World War this tension was resolved in favor of nonintervention. Nevertheless, support for the idea of protecting human rights through international or regional mechanisms has a long history in the region.[14] After the First World War most Latin American states joined the League of Nations and accepted the jurisdiction of the International Court of Justice. The regional legalist tradition found expression in the American Institute of International Law, founded in 1915 by Alejandro Alvarez with the sponsorship and financial support of the Carnegie Endowment for International Peace. Although the institute's main goals were codification of existing international law and promotion of principles of nonintervention, its members did not see a contradiction between nonintervention and the protection of individual liberties.[15]

Although after the Second World War Latin American states increasingly made commitments and paid lip service to human rights, nonintervention was still the "touchstone" of the inter-American system.[16] Nevertheless, this legal tradition led Latin American states to support human rights language in the UN Charter, and to draft and pass the American Declaration on the Rights and Duties of Man at the Bogotá Conference in 1948, months before the UN passed the Universal Declaration of Human Rights. The Latin American countries attended the San Francisco conference and became charter members of the new United Nations Organization. They participated in drafting the human rights language that became the normative underpinning of all future network activities. These normative commitments, however, did not lead to regional efforts to promote human rights until the 1970s, when the regional and international human rights network emerged.

The UN Charter and Beyond

At the San Francisco conference, NGOs played a pivotal role in securing the inclusion of human rights language in the final UN charter. NGOs representing churches, trade unions, ethnic groups, and peace movements, aided by the delegations of some of the smaller countries, "conducted a lobby in favor of human rights for which there is no parallel in the history of international relations, and which was largely responsible for the human rights provisions of the Charter."[17]

NGOs found allies for their efforts in a number of Latin American nations, especially Uruguay, Panama, and Mexico.[18] The Mexican delegation, known for its spirited defense of nonintervention, nevertheless argued that the Dumbarton Oaks proposals "contain a serious hiatus in regard to the International Rights and Duties of Man, respect for which constitutes one of the essential objectives of the present war."[19] What is striking about the legislative history of the human rights language in the UN charter and in the inter-American system is how much the key Latin American delegations participated in, embraced, and furthered the human rights cause.[20] This contribution later undermined Latin American dictators' claims that human rights policies and pressures were an intolerable intervention in their internal affairs.

The charter itself testifies to the success of efforts by NGO lobbyists and Latin American delegations. The original Dumbarton Oaks proposal had only one reference to human rights; the final UN Charter has seven, including the key amendments proposed by the NGO consultants and Latin American states. It lists promotion of human rights among the basic purposes of the organization and calls upon the Economic and Social Council (ECOSOC) to set up a human rights commission, the only commission specifically mandated in the charter.

The U.S. record at San Francisco on human rights issues was mixed. It supported the effort to include human rights language in the charter, but opposed references to economic human rights. Together with the two other key governmental actors, the USSR and the United Kingdom, the United States also wanted to limit possible infringement on domestic jurisdiction.[21] Although the human rights provisions had no teeth at this early stage, states were wary of their sovereignty implications.

As a result, the charter mandate on human rights is weaker than many NGOs desired, calling only for promoting and encouraging respect for human rights, rather than assuring or protecting them.[22] Though NGO consultants and a handful of Latin American states spoke eloquently at San Francisco for a more far-reaching vision of international human rights, that alternative vision, which called upon the UN to actively protect rights and provide the institutional machinery to do so, would have to wait another forty years to materialize. Still, by assigning institutional responsibility for human rights to the General Assembly and ECOSOC and by specifically recommending the creation of a human rights commission, the charter paved the way for all subsequent human rights actions within the UN system.

The very first human rights treaty adopted by the UN was the Convention on the Prevention and Punishment of the Crime of Genocide, passed on 9 December 1948, one day before the UN approved the comprehensive Universal Declaration of Human Rights. As with some later human rights treaties, the genocide convention owed a special debt to the work of one individual, Raphael Lemkin. Lemkin came as a refugee to the United States in 1941, carrying with him documentary evidence of the policies of racial massacre the Nazis were inflicting on the Jews. In 1944 he published a book in which he coined the word "genocide" by combining the Greek word for race or tribe with the Latin word for killing.[23] Lemkin later served on the staff on the chief American prosecutor at the Nuremberg war crimes tribunal, where he introduced the new word and helped conduct seminars for the staff on the principles and background of the Nazi party and the administration of the German government under the Nazis.[24] The authors of the indictment incorporated the new word into their document as part of their discussion of crimes against humanity, and it was used repeatedly during the trial.[25] Although the word was not included in the court's judgment and sentence, it had already begun to gain wide currency. On 20 October 1946, a week after the Allies executed ten high Nazi officials and generals, a *New York Times* story carried the headline "Genocide is the New Name for the Crime Fastened on the Nazi Leaders." The *Times* gave Lemkin full credit for coining and popularizing the term.[26]

The Senate's failure to ratify the genocide treaty was a signal of troubled times ahead for human rights in U.S. foreign policy. In the United States liberal internationalism had peaked in the immediate postwar period, giving way to a generation of liberal realists who saw only the hope of balancing clashing interests.[27] International human rights norms were subordinated to anticommunism during the Cold War.

International Nongovernmental Organizations (INGOs)

The nongovernmental actors that promoted the idea of internationally protected human rights in the 1940s did not constitute a transnational advocacy network. Few organizations specialized in human rights, and those that did lacked the dense and constant information flows that characterize modern networks. Although some organizations are much older,[28] in the 1970s and 1980s human rights NGOs proliferated and diversified (see Table 1 in Chapter 1). Human rights organizations also formed coalitions and communication networks.[29] They developed strong links to domestic organizations in countries experiencing human rights violations. As these actors consciously developed linkages with each other, the human rights advocacy network emerged.

The network grew in the south as well. In the 1970s and 1980s domestic human rights organizations appeared throughout Latin America, increasing from 220 to 550 between 1981 and 1990.[30] Chilean organizations that were formed to confront government repression, especially the Catholic church's human rights office, the Vicaria de Solidaridad, became models for human rights groups throughout Latin America and sources of information and inspiration for human rights activists in the United States and Europe. A handful of visionary leaders within the human rights movement—such as Pepe Zalaquette; the exiled Chilean lawyer who later became the chairman of the International Executive Committee of Amnesty International, and Aryeh Neier, the strategist and fundraiser behind the phenomenal growth of the Watch committees—sensed its potential, conceived strategies, and attracted a generation of exceptional young leaders to the network. The work of these "political entrepreneurs" was fundamental to the emergence and growth of the network in the early years.

Domestic NGOs

Unlike the international NGOs that work on human rights violations in other countries, domestic NGOs focus on violations in their home countries. The number and capability of such domestic organizations vary enormously by country and by region. Latin America has more domestic human rights NGOs than do other parts of the third world. A 1981 directory of organizations in the developing world concerned with human rights and social justice listed 220 such organizations in Latin America, compared to 145 in Asia and 123 in Africa and the Middle East. A 1990 directory lists over 550 human rights groups in Latin America; some countries have as many as sixty.[31] An international "demonstration effect" was at work in Latin America during the decade of the 1980s, as the activities and successes of early human rights organizations inspired others to follow their example.

Foundations and Funders

A handful of private and public foundations have provided funding for human rights organizations. Foundations may be the most autonomous of all the actors in the network. Intergovernmental actors depend on the consensus of their governmental members, and most NGOs are financially dependent upon membership and foundations. Foundations, however, have independent incomes, and are formally accountable only to self-perpetuating boards of trustees. Peter Bell has argued that the Ford Foundation acted as an "entrepreneur of ideas."[32] Nonetheless, foundations cannot implement their own ideas, but must seek and support other organizations that can.

The most important United States foundation for human rights issues in Latin America has been the Ford Foundation,[33] but a number of European funders have also played key roles, especially European church foundations. In addition, official development assistance agencies and semipublic foundations in Canada, Scandinavia, the Netherlands, and the United States have also funded human rights NGOs.

Networks and Governments

Most governments' human rights policies have emerged as a response to pressure from organizations in the human rights network, and have depended fundamentally on network information. For this reason it is hard to separate the independent influences of government policy and network pressures. Networks often have their greatest impact by working through governments and other powerful actors. In the United States the earliest governmental group to work actively on human rights was the House Subcommittee on International Organizations under the chairmanship of Donald Fraser (D-Minn.).[34] Beginning in 1973 this subcommittee held a series of hearings on human rights abuses around the world.[35] The main witnesses providing human rights information in these hearings were representatives of human rights NGOs. Although human rights policy began to form in the U.S. Congress three years before Jimmy Carter was elected president,[36] Carter administration officials gave it a higher profile, and, by lending the weight of the United States to that of progressive European countries in the UN, spurred action in international forums. Under Carter the U.S. State Department's Bureau of Human Rights and Humanitarian Affairs sought contacts with and information from NGOs, which continued to influence executive policy making even during the Reagan and Bush administrations.

Conclusions

Although the cases of Argentina and Mexico are not sufficient to confirm this argument, the contrast between them provides substantiation for it and suggests it is worth further study.[37] The international human rights network has not always been effective in changing understandings or practices about human rights. In Latin America, for example, network activities failed to stem massive violations in Guatemala in the 1970s and 1980s, and endemic abuses in Colombia in the 1990s; elsewhere we might point to China and Cambodia. The central question then becomes, under what conditions can the international human rights network be effective?

A network's existence and its decision to focus on abuses in a particular country is a necessary but not sufficient condition for changing human rights practices. Many argue that human rights pressures would not be effective against strong states that can impose significant costs on the states that pressure them. Network activists admit that they have been less effective against states that superpowers consider important to their national security interests: countries such as Saudi Arabia, Israel, Turkey, China, and Pakistan.[38] The vulnerability of the target state is thus a key factor in network effectiveness.

One aspect of target vulnerability is the availability of leverage. The United States and European countries provided Mexico and Argentina substantial amounts of military and economic assistance and trade credits. In the case of Mexico, in addition, the United States and Canada were negotiating a free trade agreement that the Mexican government believed was necessary for further economic development. This gave the network many avenues for leverage, which it used quite skillfully, lobbying its several governments to limit, condition, or cut aid, and arguing against trade credits or agreements until human rights goals were met.

Notes

1. Jack Donnelly, *Universal Human Rights in Theory and Practice* (Ithaca: Cornell University Press, 1989). See esp. table on pp. 224–25.
2. But see David Forsythe, *Human Rights and World Politics*, 2d ed. (Lincoln: University of Nebraska Press, 1989), pp. 83–101, 127–59; and Lars Schoultz. *Human Rights and United States Policy toward Latin*

America (Princeton: Princeton University Press, 1981), pp. 74–93, 104–8, 373–74.

3. Jan Herman Burgers, "The Road to San Francisco: The Revival of the Human Rights Idea in the Twentieth Century," *Human Rights Quarterly* 14 (1992): 449.
4. Mandelstam drafted a text of a "Declaration of the International Rights of Man" which the plenary session of the International Law Institute adopted in October of 1929. He later published articles and a book on the subject and taught human rights courses in Geneva and the Hague. Two networks of NGOs, the International Federation of Leagues for the Defense of the Rights of Man and of the Citizen, and the International Union of Associations for the League of Nations, endorsed the principles of the declaration in 1931 and 1933. Frangulis introduced an international human rights resolution in the League of Nations in 1933, but it received scant support from countries already in the midst of the crisis leading to German withdrawal from the League. This section draws heavily on Burgers, "The Road to San Francisco," pp. 450–59, as well as on an interview with Burgers in the Hague, Netherlands, 13 November 1993.
5. William Korey, "Raphael Lemkin: The Unofficial Man," *Midstream* (June/July 1989): 45–46.
6. The Fifth International Conference for the Unification of Penal Law, held in cooperation with the Fifth Committee of the League of Nations. Raphael Lemkin, *Axis Rule in Occupied Europe: Laws of Occupation, Analysis of Government, Proposals for Redress* (Washington, D.C.: Carnegie Endowment, 1944), p. xiii.
7. Korey, "Raphael Lemkin," p. 46.
8. See Peter N. Carroll, *The Odyssey of the Abraham Lincoln Brigade: Americans in the Spanish Civil War* (Stanford: Stanford University Press, 1994).
9. Ibid., p. 428.
10. H. G. Wells, *The Times*, 23 October 1939, as cited in Burgers. "The Road to San Francisco," p. 464.
11. Samuel I. Rosenman, *Working with Roosevelt* (New York: Harper, 1952), pp. 262–64.
12. M. Glen Johnson, "The Contributions of Eleanor and Franklin Roosevelt to the Development of International Protection for Human Rights," *Human Rights Quarterly* 9 (1987): 21–23.
13. Interview with Jan Herman Burgers, the Hague, Netherlands, 13 November 1993.
14. Larman Curtis Wilson, "The Principle of Non-intervention in Recent Inter-American Relations: The Challenge of Anti-Democratic Regimes," Ph.D. diss., University of Maryland, 1964, pp. 85–89; G. Pope Atkins, *Latin America in the International Political System*, 2d ed. (Boulder: Westview Press, 1989), p. 228.
15. See Alejandro Alvarez, "Declaración sobre Las Bases Fundamentales y los Grandes Principios del Derecho International Moderno," in *La Reconstrucción del Derecho de Gentes* (Santiago de Chile: Editorial Nascimento, 1943), pp. 89–91; and Alejandro Alvarez, *International Law and Related Subjects from the Point of View of the American Continent* (Washington, D.C.: Carnegie Endowment, 1922), pp. 27, 37.
16. Wilson, "The Principle of Non-intervention," p. 374.
17. John P. Humphrey, *Human Rights and the United Nations: A Great Adventure* (Dobbs Ferry, N.Y.: Transnational Publishers, 1984), p. 13. Also see U.S. Department of State. *The United Nations Conference on International Organization, San Francisco, California, 25 April to 26 June 1945: Selected Documents* (Washington: U.S. Government Printing Office, 1946).
18. *Documents of the United Nations Conference on International Organization, San Francisco 1945*, vol. III: *Dumbarton Oaks Proposals, Comments, and Proposed Amendments* (New York: UN Information Organizations, 1945), p. 34: "New Uruguayan Proposals on the Dumbarton Oaks Proposals," 5 May 1945.
19. "Opinion of the Department of Foreign Relations of Mexico Concerning the Dumbarton Oaks Proposals for the Creation of a General International Organization," 23 April 1945, *United Nations Conference on International Organization*, pp. 63, 71–73.
20. Ibid, pp. 71–73.
21. Johnson, "Contributions of Eleanor and Franklin Roosevelt," p. 24.
22. Report of Rapporteur, Subcommittee I/1/A (Farid Zeineddine, Syria), to Committee I/1, 1 June 1945, *Documents of the United Nations Conference on International Organization*, p. 705.
23. Lemkin, *Axis Rule*, p. 79.
24. Robert Storey, *The Final Judgment? Pearl Harbor to Nuremberg* (San Antonio: Naylor, 1968), p. 96.

25. Victor H. Bernstein, *Final Judgment: The Story of Nuremberg* (New York: Boni and Gaer, 1947), p. 136.
26. *New York Times*, 20 October 1946, section 4, p. 13.
27. David Steigerwald, *Wilsonian Idealism in America* (Ithaca: Cornell University Press, 1994), pp. 138–50, 169–71.
28. David Weissbrodt, "The Contribution of International Nongovernmental Organizations to the Protection of Human Rights," in *Human Rights in International Law: Legal and Policy Issues*, ed. Theodor Meron (Oxford: Clarendon Press, 1984), pp. 403–38.
29. Laurie S. Wiseberg and Harry M. Scoble, "Monitoring Human Rights Violations: The Role of Nongovernmental Organizations," in *Human Rights and American Foreign Policy*, ed. Donald P. Kommers and Gilbert D. Loescher (Notre Dame: University of Notre Dame Press, 1979), pp. 183–84. In interviews, directors and staff of nine key human rights INGOs also stressed these links.
30. Human Rights Internet, *Human Rights Directory: Latin America, Africa, and Asia*, ed. by Laurie S. Wiseberg and Harry M. Scoble (Washington, D.C., 1981); "Human Rights Directory: Latin American and the Caribbean." *Human Rights Internet Reporter* 13: 2–3 (January 1990).
31. Human Rights Internet, *Human Rights Directory: Latin America, Africa, and Asia;* "Human Rights Directory: Latin American and the Caribbean," *Human Rights Internet Reporter* 13: 2–3. The definition used by these directories is broader than that of many human rights groups in Latin America; still, comparing the 1981 and 1990 figures give an idea of the dramatic growth in the Latin American network.
32. Peter Bell, "The Ford Foundation as an International Actor" *International Organization* 25 (Summer 1971): 472.
33. Ibid., pp. 465–78; Jeffrey M. Puryear, "Higher Education, Development Assistance, and Repressive Regimes," *Studies in Comparative International Development* 17 (Summer 1982): 3–35.
34. Later renamed the Subcommittee on Human Rights and International Organizations.
35. Interview with John Salzberg, Washington, D.C., April 1991.
36. See Schoultz, *Human Rights*, pp. 74–88; Forsythe, *Human Rights and World Politics*, pp. 127–59.
37. Cases similar to Argentina might include Uruguay and Chile. Mexico is unique, both for the lack of attention it received on human rights issues initially and for the rapidity of its subsequent response. Other cases of semidemocratic governments where international pressures have led to change include the Dominican Republic during the 1978 elections and, more recently, Paraguay.
38. Interview with Michael Posner, New York City, 19 March 1992.

Danger—Landmines! NGO–Government Collaboration in the Ottawa Process

MATTHEW J.O. SCOTT

The end of the Cold War brought wide-ranging arms control efforts. In this reading Scott describes how states and individuals exercised soft power in the case of the International Campaign to Ban Landmines (ICBL). Should national security decisions be a state prerogative, as scholars in the Realist IR tradition argue? What are the ways in which this case shows the limits of soft power in changing states' behavior? How did certain states use anti-landmine NGOs to enhance the state's own international prestige? Which IR theory perspective best explains the ICBL drafting process?

A Treaty with Few Precedents

The Convention on the Prohibition of the Use, Stockpiling, Production, and Transfer of Anti-Personnel Mines and on Their Destruction is a landmark in international humanitarian law. This convention was drafted, negotiated, signed, and ratified wholly outside the UN Conference on Disarmament, the traditional international arena for such agreements. By the time it was signed by 122 states in Ottawa on December 3, 1997, the convention had received wider assent in less time than any other UN agreement. Less than three years passed between the first major international landmine conference in Cambodia in early 1995 and the Convention's signature. At a follow-up conference to Cambodia in Ottawa in 1996, Canada's foreign minister, Lloyd Axworthy, surprised diplomats and activists alike when he challenged all like-minded states to agree on a treaty within a year. In the fourteen months following Axworthy's challenge, the main players of the "new multilateralism," with Austria, Norway, South Africa, New Zealand, and Canada prominent among them, carried the treaty through a host of international conferences and demonstrated the efficacy of determined and like-minded middle powers in reforming international relations. In the same period. NGOs displayed diplomatic, analytical, and political skills that challenged the stereotype of NGOs as naïve do-gooders. One NGO representative in particular, Jody Williams, became an exemplar of an increasingly connected global civil society able to mobilize powerful public constituencies with great speed. The joint efforts of the middle-power governments and the coalition of NGOs known as the International Campaign to Ban Landmines (ICBL) mobilized a worldwide effort that culminated in 122 signatures on the first day of the Ottawa conference. Immediately following its signature, the UN Secretary-General reintroduced the treaty to the UN through the General

Assembly, and it has since been ratified by ninety-four states.[1]

The Ottawa treaty is rare in successfully combining humanitarian law and disarmament practice in a single convention. Other civil society campaigns, notably the nuclear nonproliferation movement in the late 1980s, that have attempted to marry these two fields have not seen the same speedy progress as the landmines campaign. Much scholarship has already been devoted to the significance of its detour around, and re-entry into, UN processes, but that is not the focus of this chapter. The goal here is to explain how two traditionally disparate streams of civil society and government came together to exchange ideas and hold each other accountable for different outcomes.

The Ottawa process also blurred the traditional distinctions between diplomacy and humanitarian action in ways that merit further examination particularly as other NGO-government campaigns, on topics from small arms to child soldiers, are incubating. These campaigns have tried to build on the invigorating speed and energy of the landmines campaign and have studied the Ottawa process in considerable detail. Civil society around the world sees the success of the convention as a precedent, paving the way for similar campaigns to ban small arms, child soldiers, child labor, and a variety of other global problems. Does this soft-power model hold genuine promise for a future era of foreign policy cooperation between governments and NGOs, or is it the exception that proves the rule, never to be repeated?[2]

The convention's success was facilitated by a variety of factors: personal relationships, the innovative use of technology, raw perseverance, and, most importantly, the specific and finite nature of the task of banning one class of highly destructive weapons. Whether or not these factors rule out successor campaigns remains to be seen. In one sense, the fate of the Ottawa process seems to have been predestined; by their own unanimous admission, everyone involved was astonished by the speed and scope of its success. Over the course of the last years since the treaty's signature, however, internal tensions have surfaced and subsided within the coalitions that drove the campaign. Relations between civil society and government have strained and threatened the campaign's steady progress toward its goal of a total ban with no exceptions, loopholes, or reservations.

Because the campaign prominently and graphically portrayed the horrific injuries inflicted by landmines, it has been described by many as an obvious approach. Who, after all, would publicly defend a weapon that terrorizes millions of innocent civilians? Although the landmine campaign was complex and intricate, most of the campaigns being proposed as sequels to the Ottawa process focus on issues that are even more diffuse.[3] Most important, these other campaigns face far more determined, vocal, and sustained opposition, overshadowing the lack of support shown by the United States during the Ottawa process.[4] However, it is important not to be defeatist. Early in the campaign, Canadian government representatives were discouraged by their peers in their efforts to pursue the landmines ban. Mark Gwozdecky, a key Canadian diplomat during the landmine campaign, was warned early in his tenure about the prospects of a global ban: "Nobody here is interested in this file, and nobody else in the world will let it go anywhere" (Tomlin 1998).

Issues of Focus: Reparation and Regulation

As with any successful movement, criticism of the ICBL has come from both within and outside. When it had the opportunity to expand its reach to broader issues, the campaign remained narrowly focused on achieving a ban on antipersonnel landmines only. In doing so, critics claimed that the campaign had sacrificed the opportunity to ride a rising wave of support for "global human security," passing up an important chance to highlight poverty in the developing world. Others had more practical fears that the ICBL had an excessively narrow focus. For example, mine-clearance experts working to make a Cambodian village safe will clear any and all dangers they detect—whether they be unexploded ordnance, antitank mines, or antipersonnel mines. All of these remnants of war pose great dangers to local inhabitants, but the Ottawa treaty only addresses the last of the three. Most of the operational NGOs that became involved in the campaign did so out of a desire to effect substantive change for those affected by landmines on the ground. Generally more reluctant to be seen as political, the operational NGOs were more concerned with removing mines than with fostering a paradigm shift in global governance.

Others criticized the campaign as being excessively broad in its humanitarian mandate, thus distracting from the main political goal of achieving a ban that might actually be implemented. These more activist elements within the campaign cited the lack of substantive Russian, American, Chinese, and Indian participation in the process as a sign of diluted effectiveness. They contended that real, sustained change would only result by shaming the major powers into signing the UN convention. Such critics contended that broadening the campaign to include assistance to landmine victims and mine clearance allowed offender states such as the United States to divert attention away from the ban. By pledging millions of dollars in humanitarian assistance for these areas while openly opposing the ban, states that still deployed landmines threatened to subvert the goals of the Ottawa process. From the perspective of many activist NGOs, the most important achievement of the campaign was its contribution to the democratization of foreign policy, with a ban on landmines as an important precedent and sustained international political will to work with NGOs as a primary goal. Other factors, like attention, public support, and resources for humanitarian action, would follow later.

This dual concern with regulation and reparation is the result of the blurring of the campaign's two streams—humanitarian praxis and disarmament law. But while intriguing, this synergy remains too poorly understood to be successfully replicated. Many have described it as a victory for NGO policy analysts and the advocates of foreign policy democratization, yet—although many academics have speculated on the question—few NGOs have asked themselves what it really means to "democratize foreign policy" (Cameron 1998). Bringing government and nongovernmental actors together like this challenges the way each goes about its business.

New Ways of Working: Campaigning in Cyberspace

One of the keys to the landmines campaign was the technological mastery shown by the ICBL. Even after a global ban had been achieved, the ICBL is still able to execute an agile strategy of countering opponents and critics and persuading would-be allies in government, the media, or other NGOs. The impressive abilities of this global network of humanitarians have been described elsewhere in almost mythological terms (Williams and Goose 1998). A highly diverse set of organizations within the ICBL were tightly connected to each other by electronic mail and fax, often enlisted at very short notice to lobby a particular government or international forum. As NGO campaigners took to the Internet in droves in the mid-1990s, many governments also experienced a simultaneous shift toward e-mail as a primary means of communication. On balance, the shift towards e-mail seems to have benefited NGOs more than governments, at least for the landmine campaign. In particular, NGOs in the South gained inexpensive access to a powerful mass communications medium in a very short period and, in the process, a direct megaphone to opinion-shapers and decisionmakers in the North.[5] As Beier and Crosby (1998) note, "The new communications technologies facilitate the identification of civil society expertise in specific issue areas, and the organization of that expertise into networks of knowledge-based relations amongst the world's peoples."

The personal tenacity and energy of Jody Williams, cofounder and former coordinator of the ICBL, was well suited to this form of network-based specialized advocacy. Under Williams's leadership, subgroups on victim assistance, mine clearance, and nonstate actors interacted electronically on a regular basis and continue to do so, long after the treaty's signature. In 1998–1999 this network of networks became the Landmine Monitor, facilitating the ongoing work of monitoring the implementation of the Ottawa treaty. The Landmine Monitor network published the first global survey of landmine infestation, activity, and legislation, which was presented at the First Meeting of States Parties in Mozambique in mid-1999. The Landmine

Monitor's ongoing stability well after the treaty's signature demonstrates the potential of civil society data-gathering networks for other campaigns. Indeed, the entire landmine network still stands on the communications infrastructure that Williams and other activists pieced together, involving over one thousand different organizations across forty countries (Beier and Crosby 1998).

Action alerts sent out to this network by the ICBL executive office were crucial in using late-breaking information to urge domestic advocacy by campaign members across the globe. For example, when the U.S. delegation delayed proceedings at the Oslo treaty-text negotiations in 1997, the ICBL viewed this as an attempt to divide and rule, a tactic designed to intimidate other countries into softening the language of the proposed treaty. In a news flash posted to the conference website, the ICBL urged the following action among members in typically informal Internet style (capital letters denote shouting in Internet etiquette): "alert: U.S. of COURSE still high alert, and they are still getting support from australia, poland and japan . . . CAMPAIGNERS KEEP UP THE ALERT FROM YESTERDAY, spain as well, thank you spanish campaign for your fast response but PLEASE KEEP IT UP, and JAPAN get to work!!"[6]

Internet-based collaboration and campaigning benefits from high levels of flexibility and dynamism, along with very short iterative cycles. However, it has the concomitant weakness of being susceptible to paralysis, and occasionally fraudulent behavior. In the case of the ICBL landmine campaign, the ability to act quickly and multilaterally on time-sensitive information exhausted campaigners, who waded through hundreds of e-mails on the same topic from the vast network of NGO and government contacts. So far, the ICBL has largely been free of campaign espionage, but future campaigns may face more concerted opposition. Recently an aggressive gun-lobby activist posed as an "interested researcher" in order to join an e-mail discussion list on restricting trade in small arms and used the information gathered from that discussion to foment opposition to the campaign to ban small arms. The capacity of electronically based campaigns to unite activists through virtually instantaneous information exchange is considerable, but there are substantial liabilities in relying solely on electronic means of communication. Without strong personal relationships to hold these virtual networks together, the campaign would have been severely handicapped. Its success has undoubtedly paved the way for a new phase of more sophisticated electronic civil-society networking, particularly as the campaign moves toward treaty verification and monitoring.

Personalities and Relationships

"Will you marry me?" was Jody Williams's very public and good-humored proposal to then Canadian Landmine Ambassador Jill Sinclair in 1998. Sinclair had just delivered the keynote address at an NGO-government meeting hosted by Canada to commemorate the first anniversary of the treaty signing. Such relational facility among diplomats and humanitarian activists has been a hallmark of the Ottawa process and has characterized conference protocol and correspondence between the two sectors. This interpersonal chemistry, combined with the charisma of some of the campaign's more prominent personalities, gave it a life and vigor all of its own. Internationally, Princess Diana's popular appeal added unprecedented levels of public support to the campaign's efforts. After two highly publicized visits to mine-affected regions during 1997 (Angola and Bosnia), she raised the campaign's profile from that of just another group of disarmament activists haranguing the UN to a humanitarian cause célèbre. Although the Canadian arm of the campaign had enlisted celebrity spokespersons to educate Canadians on the landmines problem, Princess Diana's photogenic Angolan visit catapulted the issue onto millions of television screens and forward to international prominence. This came as a welcome gift to the international campaign, which had struggled to find an internationally recognizable spokesperson to speak compassionately on behalf of the 26,000 casualties of landmines every year. Ironically, Diana's untimely death served to raise the profile of mine victims even further, coming only days before the international meeting in Oslo at which the text of the UN Mine Ban was drafted.

Paradigm Shift or Co-optation?

One of the most hotly debated issues among participants in, and analysts of, the landmines campaign remains the question of causality. A substantial change in diplomatic style took place from one set of meetings to another in preparation for the first Ottawa conference, prompting some commentators to ask "whether elements of an emergent global civil society acted as agents of that change or served as a conduit through which broader military, political, and economic forces could find new ways to realize old interests" (Beier and Crosby 1998).[7] While unprecedented levels of coordination and information sharing within and among NGOs and governments put to rest much of the skepticism about false motives on both sides, the suspicion that NGOs were being coopted by the process never entirely dissipated, despite Lloyd Axworthy's assurances (Axworthy 1998b). Some skeptics contended that the campaign simply served as another vehicle through which NGOs tried to gain international legitimacy at the negotiating table.

There were certainly examples of campaign manipulation for political purposes. In May of 1998 for example, Valerie Warmington (then chair of the Canadian campaign) was invited to Taiwan to observe the island's efforts to join the international consensus on landmines. Warmington's visit was packed with meetings with the prime minister, high-ranking generals, the diplomatic corps, and the media. Tours of abandoned stockpiles of mines and declarations of Taiwan's mine-free status were carried out to convince the world that Taiwan—in stark contrast to China—was ready to join the campaign. Given Taiwan's international political goals, however, some would be justified in seeing the visit as a thinly veiled exercise in self-interest. Similar skepticism faced the Afghan Campaign to Ban Landmines, which succeeded in gaining a landmark public statement from the fundamentalist Taliban regime in 1998. Citing verses from the Qur'an, the official declaration denounced the use of landmines as "un-Islamic" and urged other Islamic states to join the Taliban in ceasing the use and production of antipersonnel landmines on grounds of faith.[8] Although a major achievement, this was largely unreported by the international press and viewed skeptically by most countries.[9]

Some of the NGOs in the ICBL may have had just cause for feeling coopted. The 1997 Ottawa Treaty—Signing Conference coincided perfectly with Canada's intense campaign to fill one of the vacant seats on the UN Security Council. Skeptics might have viewed the entire Ottawa process as a chest-beating affair to demonstrate the value of Canada's soft power assets in the global human security arena (Axworthy 1998a). A less sinister view among campaigners regarded the two events—Canada's campaign for a Security Council seat and its leadership of the landmines ban—as complementary at best, slightly disingenuous at worst. Naturally, the government players, headed by Axworthy, are quick to rule out any notion of coopting NGOs or of government being prey to special interest groups: "Our diplomats did not compromise Canada's position through cooperation, nor did NGOs become coopted by the state. We worked together to achieve common ends" (Axworthy 1998b).

In part, the campaign may have been a victim of its own success. Governments saw the NGO contribution chiefly in terms of motivating public support for the Ottawa process, which they did very successfully. Perhaps because many of the bureaucrats and activists involved shared a history of campaigning against nuclear proliferation, there may have been a perception that building public support was the *only* NGO role, at least in Canada. But most of the large operational NGOs saw their involvement in the campaign not only in terms of public engagement or lobbying but also as an extension of their field-based work in mine clearance and victim assistance. World Vision, the Mines Advisory Group, the Red Cross, CARE, and many others joined the ICBL because they saw the chance to address the landmine issue at a systemic level, not just at the level of removing the mines and patching up the victims.

Conclusions

Global civil society campaigning can learn much from the landmines example. The importance of strong government-NGO relationships, charismatic campaign personalities, and effective electronic constituency management cannot be overemphasized. Some of the other attributes that contributed to the success of the Ottawa process are less tangible, and in some ways contradictory. Clearly, as the other contributors to this volume demonstrate, citizen action is inherently complex and multicausal. But the question of causality remains important for humanitarian agencies with lofty ideals and limited budgets. Whether or not there is a clear answer, operational NGOs in particular want to know. So what worked? These NGOs have a mandate to make the donor dollar stretch further, which forces them to ponder the causality question before investing in new research, lobbying, and public constituency building. Whatever the prioritizing of its various causes, the campaign's success was fueled by the zealous idealism of activist NGOs, tempered by the cool pragmatism of the operational NGOs. This combination yielded a treaty that made few concessions but remained focused on what was realistic and achievable. Although the campaign does illustrate the possibilities of the new multilateralism, it also suggests some limitations: Activists engrossed in the short-term outcome—banning an entire class of weapons—may have lost sight of the longer-term process of ensuring that the ban is implemented.

In the long-term, malaria, malnutrition, and HIV/AIDS will kill far more people annually than landmines ever will. Though landmines and the havoc they wreak deserve our attention, the continuing campaign to ban landmines and repair their damage must locate itself in a broader context of poverty alleviation and disaster relief. An ancient Hebrew proverb says, "For everything there is a season." While the past century has witnessed seasons of famine, war, and poverty, perhaps the current one will see that season's death. In the meantime, civil society has the opportunity to trigger the kind of courageous multilateralism that can ban an entire class of weapons, protect children from war, and—over the very long haul—turn swords into ploughshares.

Notes

1. This was true according to Mines Action Canada as of April 10, 2000. See the Mines Action Canada website at http://www.minesactioncanada.com.
2. "Soft power is 'the art of disseminating information in such a way that desirable outcomes are achieved through persuasion rather than coercion' " (Axworthy 1998b).
3. The International Conference on War-Affected Children, convened by the Canadian government in September 2000 in Winnipeg, for instance, has broad aims to reduce the impact of armed conflict on children. It is not clear, however, what would constitute success in the case of this campaign, apart from a complete end to the involvement of children in war.
4. The U.S. National Rifle Association (NRA) and other gun lobby groups have already set their sights on opposing any international effort to control small arms. The NRA and other similar groups have secured NGO consultative status with the UN and have publicly stated their intent to expand their horizons to the international arena.
5. "The South" is used here as a blanket term for developing countries.
6. This landmine ban treaty newsflash was the second such alert to be posted on the Vietnam Veterans of America Foundation website, http://www.vvaf.org/landmine/1997/news9_3b.htm, on September 4, 1997.
7. Until the establishment of the Ottawa process, the Geneva-based Convention on Certain Conventional Weapons (CCW) had been the primary arena of NGO advocacy against antipersonnel landmines. At best, the CCW could only accomplish weak restrictions on mine use. The convention's failure to achieve any substantial progress against mines largely motivated the Canadian-led initiative.
8. See the Taliban's statement to the Non-State Actors Working Group of the ICBC at http://www.icbi.org/wg/nsa/library/nsadeclarations.htm/.
9. Despite the Taliban regime's military rule, clearance efforts in Afghanistan have proceeded at a rapid pace, thanks to the Afghan-based Mine Clearance Planning Agency (MCPA), highly regarded within

the campaign for the safety, speed, and cost-efficiency of their mine clearance.

References

Axworthy, L. (1998a) "Towards a New Multilateralism," in M. Cameron et al. (eds.) *To Walk Without Fear: The Global Movement to Ban Landmines.* Toronto: Oxford University Press.

Axworthy, L. (1998b) "Lessons from the Ottawa Process," *Canadian Foreign Policy* 33): 1–2. Bankwatch (1999) *Activities and Workplans. <http:// www.bankwatch.org/*

Beier, J. M., and A. Denholm Crosby (1998) "Harnessing Change for Continuity: The Play of Political and Economic Forces Behind the Ottawa Process." *Canadian Foreign Policy* 5(3): 85- 104.

Cameron, M. (1998) "Democratization of Foreign Policy: The Ottawa Process as a Model," *Canadian Foreign Policy* 5(3): 147–1 63.

Cameron, M. A, R. J. Lawson, and B. W. Tomlin (eds.) (1998) *To Walk Without Fear: The Global Movement to Ban Landmines.* Toronto: Oxford University Press.

Tomlin, Brian. (1998) "On a Fast Track to a Ban: The Canadian Policy Process," in M. A. Cameron et al. (eds.) *To Walk Without Fear: The Global Movement to Ban Landmines.* Toronto: Oxford University Press.

Governing Intimacy in the World Bank

KATE BEDFORD

Global governance is a major subfield within the larger discipline of IR. Scholars who study global governance examine the structures that institutions provide to public activities of people around the world. In this excerpt Bedford applies some of the pieces of the subfield to a study of gender-related decisions within the World Bank. What methods does the World Bank use to push women into paid work activities? How do traditional notions about correct gender roles shape those methods? What is "social reproduction work"? Does the World Bank encourage or undermine that kind of work?

Introduction

This chapter charts the policymaking efforts of gender staff in the World Bank – the world's largest and most influential development institution.[1] It attempts to analyse those efforts through the lens of governance, a process that draws on four particularly important insights:

(1) That governance, as "a system of rules for public life," involves multiple sites and

actors employing heterogeneous strategies oriented to numerous – and sometimes conflicting – ends (Waylen and Rai, this book; Rose 1999: 21; Mosse and Lewis 2005). The state is only one actor among many here, and multilateral institutions have become increasingly central players in global governance debates (Larner and Walters 2004a).

(2) That the deployment of expertise is a key mechanism of governance (Valverde 1998; Terry 1999).

(3) That there are crucial links between micro and macro governance projects. Using Nikolas Rose's formulation, government refers to the processes through which individuals are urged and educated to bridle their own passions and control their own instincts (Valverde 1998; Rose 1999: 3). The governance perspective thus presupposes the freedom of the governed (Rose 1999: 4), but it considers how apparent exercises of free will are connected, in complex and uneven ways, to larger social, economic, and political processes (Cruikshank 1999). For example the family has often been a target of state management efforts, and many attempts to achieve national and imperial prosperity have relied on expert interventions into individual lives, using notions of hygiene, education, health, and so on (Rose 1999: 6; Levine 2003). This insight provides space to consider how multilateral institutions oriented to economic development, trade, and finance, are involved in governance of micro level concerns.

(4) That analysis of governance involves tracking the common-sense nature, or normativity, of discourses entrenched as self-evident (Rai, Chapter 1, this book). Specifically, the governance lens requires a disturbance of what forms the "groundwork of the present," to make the given seem strange and to question what is taken as natural (Rose 1999: 58).

The World Bank, Gender, and Governance Debates: The Social Reproduction Dilemma Revisited

A focus on the Bank is particularly important for feminists interested in global governance. It remains the "flagship" (Yunus 1994: ix) and "pacesetter" (Hancock 1989: 57) of international development policy, employing nearly 10,000 people and lending more money to more countries than any other development body – the Board approved US$22.3 billion in loans and grants for 278 projects in FY2005 (World Bank 2006). The institution's growing research role also ensures that its staff remain entrenched as *the* development experts. As Arturo Escobar puts it the prevailing wisdom in the policy field is that "if 'the Bank' does not have clear answers, nobody else does" (1995: 160; see also Birdsall and Kapur 2005: 4).

This primacy is of particular relevance to feminists due to the Bank's recent shift in mission to embrace social concerns. During the 1980s the Bank was a key advocate of the neo-liberal Washington Consensus, aiming to cut back the state, open trade, reduce social spending, deregulate, and privatize. However, the institution was transformed after the appointment of James Wolfensohn as President in 1995 (Fox and Brown 1998; Gilbert and Vines 2000; O'Brien *et al.* 2000; Pincus and Winters 2002; Mallaby 2004). Wolfensohn met with Bank critics, he launched partnership initiatives with civil society groups, and he spoke of holistic development frameworks that re-centered poverty. He also made gender more central to Bank lending. He led the Bank's delegation to the UN's 1995 Beijing Conference on Women, for example, and between 1995 and 2001 the proportion of projects that included some consideration of gender issues in their design almost doubled, to nearly 40 per cent (Long 2003: 7). By 2001 the Bank was positioning itself as the disseminator of "good practice" on gender in the development community (World Bank 2001: 273).

I am interested in the impact of this mission-shift on the Bank's response to a key dilemma outlined by feminist political economists regarding tensions between paid and unpaid work.

Overall, the Bank has prioritized efforts to get women into paid work as the "cure all" for gender inequality.[2] Yet this prioritization of employment leaves the Bank with a remaining policy problem, since it must deal with the work women already do – the unpaid labours of caring, socialization, and human needs fulfilment known in feminist literature as social reproduction work. This includes childcare, housework, subsistence agriculture, cooking, voluntary work to sustain community organizations, and so on – activities that are rarely counted in official statistics as work because they are seen as non-productive. Feminists have long argued that dominant models of growth overlook the economic value of these activities, disproportionately done by women (Waring 1988; Folbre 1994; Elson 1996; Peterson 2003; Benería and Feldman 1992). Many have criticized the Bank specifically for assuming what I call an exhaustion solution to the social reproduction dilemma, wherein it does nothing to resolve tensions between renumerated employment and unpaid caring labour such that women are overburdened when they are forced, through economic necessity, to enter paid work (O'Brien *et al.* 2000; Long 2003; Wood 2003; Zuckerman and Qing 2003; Kuiper and Barker 2006). To reiterate, however, the Bank has changed. Space now exists for feminist policy entrepreneurs to seize hold of the Bank's discovery of the "social," to argue that markets are socially embedded institutions to which gendered processes are central (Rai, Chapter 1, this book). How is the social reproduction dilemma being resolved in this space, and how are feminist interventions reshaping the governance of development?

To explore these issues I focused on World Bank gender activities undertaken in Ecuador since Wolfensohn took over as President in 1995. Using interviews with Gender And Development (GAD) staff and consultants conducted in 2003 and 2004, analysis of relevant documents put out by the Bank's resident mission in Quito, and fieldwork on Bank gender lending, I considered how Bank GAD policy entrepreneurs were attempting to resolve the social reproduction dilemma. Ecuador is an excellent site for research into Bank gender policy. The Latin American and Caribbean region is regarded as having the most advanced gender unit in the Bank (Hafner-Burton and Pollack 2002: 368; Long 2003: 9; Zuckerman and Qing 2003: 27). In turn the Bank's resident mission in Quito put out one of the most comprehensive gender reviews of all countries in the region, mentioned in a recent worldwide Bank report on gender progress within the institution (World Bank 2000a: 27). Bank gender staff in Ecuador also have close links to domestic feminists,[3] funding national events for women's day, and collaborating with academic institutions, the state's women council (CONAMU), and Afro-Ecuadorian and indigenous women's groups. Finally, the Bank has put out several important documents on gender in Ecuador, including most notably Caroline Moser's research into gender and household coping strategies under structural adjustment (1993, 1996, 1997; World Bank 1996). Moser is particularly well known for a pioneering study in the 1980s on gender and poverty in a low-income housing settlement in Guayaquil (Ecuador's largest city). This was subsequently extended into a larger project on household vulnerability to economic change, funded and published by the Bank as *Confronting Crisis.* More recently, the Bank funded an important study on gender and time use focused on the Ecuadorian flower industry (Newman 2001), used to inform the aforementioned *Ecuador Gender Review.* In short Ecuador is a good site for investigating Bank gender policy because feminists are active policy entrepreneurs in this resident mission, attempting to intervene in the governance of the global economy to promote gender equity. Exploring their experiences is thus helpful in ascertaining how they grapple (if at all) with the social reproduction problem.

Feminist Recognition of the Social Reproduction Dilemma

Getting women into paid employment was a clear priority for Bank gender staff in Ecuador, expressed in both interviews and policy documents. Work was framed as a way to increase productivity and growth, to achieve poverty reduction, and to empower women.[4] Policy success was thus identified based on work-related criteria. For example the abstract of the *Ecuador Gender Review* used women's increased labour force participation as proof that "Ecuador has made considerable strides in addressing gender issues" (Correia 2000: v). Moreover work was marked as a continued policy priority, given remaining problems of unequal wages, unequal training opportunities, higher female unemployment, and occupational segregation. This led to a persistent emphasis on work-related solutions to gender concerns. For example the gender chapter of a 2002a Bank report on dollarization in Ecuador identified getting women into work as part of a broader empowerment initiative, concluding that increasing women's labour force participation "enhanc(es) their economic independence and reduc(es) their vulnerability" (Correia 2002: 205). Increased employment was also framed as part of an effort to "break the culture of dependency" (206) affecting poor communities, whereby women were targeted as potential employees in order to increase self-reliance and thereby achieve empowerment.

That said, however, gender policymakers were also fully aware of the social reproduction dilemma. Gender staff on one loan frequently expressed concern about women being overburdened through projects that failed to take into account their multiple responsibilities, for example, and one consultant told me that most people considered un- or underemployed by the Bank were wrongly classified since they were engaged in productive subsistence activities. Similarly when teaching staff and organizations how to "do" gender in Bank-funded projects attention was devoted to Caroline Moser's triple role framework, a planning tool that highlights the importance of non-market activities (see P.R.O.D.E.P.I.N.E. 2001: n.p.). Time use surveys, which record social reproduction labour as work, were also used in case studies of gender and ethnicity conducted for a prominent rural development loan (see Bedford 2005b for a more in-depth discussion).

Bank gender texts on Ecuador replicated this recognition of unpaid labour. For example Moser's *Confronting Crisis* study repeatedly noted the blurred boundaries between productive and unproductive work, and it urged the Bank to value women's reproductive and community managing roles as crucial to household and community survival. The first line to the section on "balancing productive work with domestic responsibilities" argued that "although labor is understood to be the poor's most valuable asset, the invisibility of domestic labour means that demands on women to perform unpaid domestic labour remain unrecognized" (Moser 1997: 68). Women's need to take on extra work to pick up the slack of economic restructuring was also seen to have generated unmet care needs for children and the sick (Moser 1996: 68; 1997: 12), and to have caused depression, anxiety, and burn-out (Moser in World Bank 1996: 129). Likewise, recognition of social reproduction concerns was evident in the *Ecuador Gender Review*, the Bank's flagship gender document on the country. The report asserted unambiguously that women's employment opportunities were restricted because they "continue to bear the burden of care giving and domestic tasks" (Correia 2000: 35), and it noted that increased female labour force participation caused by macro-economic crisis could lead to "greater pressures on (women's) time" (50). Thus one of the "lessons learnt" from a recent attempt to integrate gender into a rural development loan was "the need to address women's reproductive and domestic time constraints in conjunction with supporting their productive activities" (76). Similar arguments were made in the gender chapter of the Bank's 2002a report on Ecuador's dollarization (Correia 2002: 178).

Crucially, awareness of the social reproduction dilemma also made its way into more mainstream Bank discussions. For example the 1996 *Ecuador Poverty Report* contained several references to the issue, outside of Moser's chapter on gender which repeated the claims made above. The introduction noted that household and childcare duties "are the major reason why women do not participate in the workforce, and these are more pressing the poorer they are" (World Bank 1996: 39). The Bank's 2003 report on *Ecuador: An Economic and Social Agenda in the New Millennium* also included multiple references to social reproduction. These were particularly evident in Alexandra Ortiz's chapter on urban development, which used Moser's research to argue that during economic crisis "mothers are forced to increase their participation in the working world and decrease the amount of time they spend taking care of their children" (Ortiz 2003: 259). The prioritization of these findings reflected an awareness that unpaid work was important, and that "trade offs" between market and non-market labour could overburden women.

In short, then, gender staff at the Bank in Ecuador recognized that unpaid caring labour must be dealt with in policy if efforts to get women into work were to be effective – they expressed this in interviews and gender texts, and were relatively successful at getting the recognition into the Bank's mainstream documents. Staff did not endorse an exhaustion solution to the social reproduction dilemma, and they did not assume women's time to be "infinitely elastic" (Elson 1996: 71). It remains to examine the solutions designed in response, and to explore how they relate to governance concerns.

Governing Intimacy to Resolve the Social Reproduction Dilemma

The most prominent policy solution[5] endorsed by Bank gender staff to the tension between paid work and social reproduction was the restructuring of normative heterosexuality to encourage a two-partner model of love and labour, wherein women work more and men care better. This sharing approach attempted to (re)privatize responsibility for social reproduction by adjusting the way in which love was expressed in the family. It stemmed from the Bank's framing of gender policy as involving complementary attention to men and women, and from the promotion of loving partnerships as empowering. Indeed Bank gender efforts hinge on assumptions about the normative desirability of complementary relations between men and women at the personal level.[6] In its formally cleared, D.C.-level documents the Bank has defined gender policy as requiring male inclusion, and thus attention to men and to encouraging men and women to share development benefits and responsibilities is a key contemporary characteristic of GAD work. Policies and projects that are seen to ignore men are designated failures, and pressure is put on gender staff at the country level to include men in their activities.

This approach to gender was clearly evident in Ecuador. As defined by one consultant, the official policy was that "we don't believe that there should be projects for women and projects for men; there should be projects with a focus on equity for men and women." Likewise, in policy texts attention to men and organizing in mixed groups were identified as key elements distinguishing an "ideological women in development approach over a true gender perspective" (Correia 2000: 76). Gender analysis itself was thus defined as involving complementary attention to men and women. Hence the *Ecuador Gender Review* criticized Ecuador's state feminist organization CONAMU for failing to include men in its gender work, and it recommended the inclusion of men and the organizing of men's groups as one of the "lessons learnt" from a failed rural development loan (Correia 2000: 80). Similarly the chapter on gender in the Bank's 2002a report on Ecuador's dollarization lamented that literature on gender and macroeconomic crisis "focuses almost solely on women to the exclusion of men" (Correia 2002: 178).

Given that the Bank's gender efforts required inclusion of men and rested on a celebratory approach to sharing couplehood, the solutions to the social reproduction dilemma that were preferred by staff focused on keeping men around and making them more reliable partners. Specifically, the Bank's gender specialists sought to teach poor Ecuadorian men how to be responsible family members, particularly in order that they could help pick up the slack of unmet care needs as their wives moved into paid employment. Getting poor women into work and getting poor men into parenting classes were thus considered complementary strategies, persistently framed as mutually supportive and equally necessary priorities, and as empowering to both parties. Consider, for example, the priority areas mentioned by the *Ecuador Gender Review*:

> First, both female and male gender issues need to be considered when designing and implementing social safety nets and emergency assistance programs, so that, inter alia, programs strengthen the role of fathers and provide income generating opportunities for women
>
> (Correia 2000: xii).[7]

Specific suggested interventions included "programs to promote men as fathers" which although "still very new in the Region and elsewhere . . . could be piloted in Ecuador" given models that exist elsewhere (xi). For example the *Gender Review* mentioned the need for reproductive health programs that include men "to develop services for men in line with their needs, and to promote more active male participation in childcare and parenthood" (54). It also noted approvingly that "increasingly adolescent men are the targets of safe sex, family planning and responsible parenthood programs" (16). Later the report recommended teaching parenting skills to boys and girls as part of its health sector reform (57). Elsewhere, in a discussion of how to help female farmers overcome obstacles to participation in rural development, the report mentioned "working with male farmers so that they understand that supporting women's participation does not mean they are "mandarinas" (wimps/softies/unmanly) *and training men to share domestic chores and childcare*" (59 emphasis added). Another report recommended using the United States as a guide:

> "one possible model is that of Family Resource Centers that have been established in poor latino communities in the United States to target mothers, fathers, adolescent boys, and adolescent girls in dealing with issues such as responsible fathering, male alcoholism, women's economic opportunities and empowerment, pregnancy among teenage girls, and gang violence and drug abuse among male adolescents. *In particular, these centers have played an important role for men by broadening their roles as fathers*" (Correia 2002: 206 emphasis added).

In some respects these policies were understood to empower all people, since "broadening male gender roles could benefit men as well as women and their families, given that substance abuse, violence and depression among men have been linked to gender roles and the limited ways men have to affirm their identity" (Correia 2000: xi). That said, however, the effort to liberate men from restrictive masculinity did not apply equally. It was intended to "promote men's roles as fathers and caregivers, *particularly among unemployed men*" (xi, emphasis added), because:

> "Men are often underemployed or off work during economic downturns and therefore could share the burden of household responsibilities. In contrast, women often enter the workforce to compensate for household income losses during periods of economic crisis and have less time to engage in domestic chores" (xiv).

Global economic shifts were hereby understood to have generated an abundance of poor men sitting around with time on their hands, the perfect candidates for an apparently easy and universally empowering resolution of tensions between unpaid care and renumerated labour.

Gender Expertise and Policy Formulation

Knowledge from gender experts was crucial in these initiatives. Indeed this policy preference is a nice case study of the ways in which epistemic authority gets deployed in debates about gender, to enhance what Rai (Chapter 1, this book) calls the "knowledge-based managerialism" of multilateral institutions in reference to the social reproduction dilemma. The expert voices privileged in such a process were those advocating a privatized solution to tensions between paid and unpaid work resting on re-distribution of caring labour within loving couples. For example, asserting that the "the problem of the gender division of labour in the household is universal and is not limited to Latin America or to Ecuador" (Correia 2000: 36), the *Ecuador Gender Review* discussed the research of US social psychologist Francine

Deutsch, claiming that her findings would be relevant to the country.[8] Arguing that "equality in parenting is achieved in the details of everyday life" (Deutsch 1999: 3), Deutsch's research sought out "equal sharers…ordinary people simply inventing and reinventing solutions to the dilemmas of modern family life" (11). Her policy advice centred on encouraging complementary sharing among mothers and fathers such that they could "buffer each other" (228) and better serve their children's needs. This is precisely the solution to the domestic labour burden being advocated by the Bank. Thus the *Ecuador Gender Review* closed a discussion headed "domestic work and childcare" with the following policy argument:

> "According to Deutsch's seminal research on how shared parenting works in the United States, three conditions need to be in place if gender equality in the household is to be achieved: (a) men need to learn new skills; (b) women need to give up the control they have had over the household; and (c) men and women need to have flexible work schedules. Short-term efforts in Ecuador should focus on the first two conditions, which can be promoted by civil society organizations working at the local level, for example, through youth programs, community water programs, adult education programs etc. The last condition – which involves the reorganization of work – would be a long-term objective given the pressing nature of unemployment in Ecuador today"
>
> (Correia 2000: 58/9).

There was no mention of childcare provision whatsoever in this section; the issue of "domestic work and childcare" was framed as one about shared parenting, men learning caring skills, and women giving up caring monopolies. Thus the Bank's own gender policymakers ended up endorsing a completely privatizing solution to the social reproduction dilemma and erasing childcare provision as a priority, using U.S. gender experts advocating similar policies.

Questioning the Mainstreamed Common Sense About Sexuality

As noted above, a key insight of the governance perspective is that power can operate very effectively when deployed in arguments about common sense and "the natural order of things," allowing the production of alliances based on shared worldviews that do not seem, to their advocates, to involve explicit political claims. In addition to tracing the deployment of expertise evident in this policy site, then, it is also helpful to explore the common sense assumptions at work, particularly as they relate to sexuality. As Foucault notes, "[S] exuality is not the most intractable element in power relations, but rather one of those endowed with the greatest instrumentality, useful for the greatest number of manoeuvres and capable of serving as a point of support, as a linchpin, for the most varied

Conclusion: Tools and Languages of Governing

Through a focus on the Bank, this chapter has attempted to show how macroeconomic concerns are being linked to expressions of intimacy, and to elucidate the assumptions about sexuality and masculinity upon which the Bank's current GAD approach rests. The tensions embedded in this approach warrant further examination, if only to enable better identification of the spaces within which we can critically intervene. The policies to which I draw attention are sites for struggle within the Bank – they should at the very least be subjects for debate among feminist development scholars.

To close with this issue in mind, it is helpful to revisit an enduring question about feminist policymaking and its relationship to global governance institutions posed by Kathleen Staudt. In a recent essay on feminist policymaking, she asked "to 'speak truth to power' has long been the goal of policy analysts, but just how similar must the speech be to the master's language?" (2002: 52). Contesting Audre Lorde's claim that activists cannot use the master's tools to, dismantle the master's house, Staudt insists that "master-free houses are few and far between" (2002: 57), and hence that "engagement in the master's house is one among many valid political strategies in contemporary development enterprises" (58). On this basis effective engagement rests, at least in part, on knowing when the languages we are using should not be ours. As I have argued elsewhere, this is relatively straightforward when feminists are discussing Bank efficiency rhetoric, grounded in claims that integration of gender concerns will increase productivity and growth (Bedford 2007). Feminists both inside and outside the Bank have been relatively confident in their ability to distinguish "the master's language" from "ours" here, especially given that economics-based efficiency talk sounds foreign to many of us.

However since 1995 the Bank has opened up to other languages, including those that sound far less foreign to feminist policymakers. The distinction between "them" and "us" is far harder to draw when we talk about empowerment as balanced complementary sharing, when we use promises of happy loving couples to get support, when we frame certain men as pathologically violent and irresponsible and seek to include them through domestication. To know how to fully answer Staudt's question, then, we must first know what the master's language is, in order that we can know what concessions we are making; how "his" language influences "our" policymaking, and when "we" are actually generating that language ourselves. In this sense I suggest that the Bank's current solution to the social reproduction dilemma relies on, and reinforces, common sense languages about sexuality and masculinity that should not be ours. If we are to help generate policies that promise an alternative vision of empowering freedom, and that forge different, more politically progressive connections between macroeconomic tensions and individual subjectivities, we might start by revisiting our policy languages and the common sense assumptions on which they are based.

Notes

1. The "World Bank Group" includes five organizations. It is customary to refer to the two most prominent agencies – the International Bank for Reconstruction and Development and the International Development Association – as "the Bank."
2. I trace the emergence of this policy preference, and the institutional factors that explain it, in Bedford 2005a.
3. See Lind 2004; Herrera 2001; Prieto 2005 for an introduction to the Ecuadorian women's movement.
4. These arguments are also central to the Bank's prioritization of women's employment outside of Ecuador; I trace this process in the Bank's broader D.C.-produced, formally cleared gender policy texts in Bedford 2005a.
5. It was not the only response – infrastructural provision was also an important priority. See Bedford 2005a.
6. I explore this in far greater detail, and connect it to sexuality studies literature on functional heteronormativity in Bedford 2005a and 2005b.
7. This "priority" to make women into workers and men into responsible loving family members was repeated word for word in the summary to the report (53). Institutionally sensitive reading methods should direct particular attention to opening and closing pages of Bank documents, given that they are often the only parts of a text read by busy staff – see Bedford 2005a for more on reading methodology as it relates to Bank texts.
8. Interestingly Deutsch expresses doubt about whether her findings are broadly applicable in the US; her sample was 96 per cent white and 100 per cent English speaking, and in half of her couples both husbands and wives had graduate degrees (1999: 240).
9. See for example Cohen 1997; Smith 2001; Cooper 1995; Carabine 2000; Ingraham 2005. For exceptions to the tendency of sexuality studies to focus on state actors, see Alexander 1994; Wilson 2004; Adams and Prigg 2005.
10. I recognize that the emphasis accorded poor men's misbehaviour in this publication stems from the complaints of women in the sample. Yet this raises methodological issues of crucial importance to feminist development researchers. Given the difficulty of ascertaining causality when discussing macroeconomic issues, and given the tendency to blame proximate factors for one's own life crises, how does one develop analyses that remain attentive to people's lived experiences when informants persistently blame poor men, migrants, sex workers, and so on for their own poverty?

References

Beneria, L. and Feldman, S. (eds) (1992) Unequal Burden: Economic Crises, Persistent Poverty, and Women's Work. Boulder, CO: Westview Press.

Birdsall, N. and Kapur, D. (2005) The Hardest Job in the World: Five Crucial Tasks for the New President of the World Bank. An Agenda for the Next World Bank President. Washington, DC: Center for Global Development.

Correia, M. (2000) Ecuador Gender Review: Issues and Recommendations. A World Bank Country Study. Washington DC: World Bank.

Correia, M. (2002) 'Gender Dimensions of Vulnerability to Exogenous Shocks: The Case of Ecuador'. In P. Beckerman and A. Solimano (eds) Crisis and Dollarization in Ecuador: Stability, Growth, and Social Equity. Washington DC: World Bank, pp. 177–215.

Cruikshank, B. (1999) The Will to Empower. Democratic Citizens and Other Subjects. Ithaca, NY: London.

Deutsch, F. (1999) Halving It All: How Equally Shared Parenting Works. Cambridge: Harvard UP.

Eguiguren, A., Maldonado A. and Marchin, M. (2002) Seis Estudios De Caso Sobre Identidades Y Roles De Género En Las Nacionalidades Y Pueblos Del Ecuador: Estudio De Caso Sobre El Pueblo Chachi—Fecche, Norte De Esmeraldas. Quito: P.R.O.D.E.P.I.N.E.

Elson, D. (1996) 'Gender-Aware Analysis and Development Economics'. In Flobre, N. (1994) Who Pays for the Kids? Gender and the Structures of Constraint. New York: Routledge.

Fox, J. and Brown, D. (1998) The Struggle for Accountability: The World Bank, NGOs, and Grassroots Movements. Cambridge: MIT Press.

Gilbert, C. and Vines, D. (eds) (2000) The World Bank: Structure and Policies. New York: Cambridge University Press.

Giugale MM, Fretes-Cibils V, Lopez Calix JR (eds) Ecuador: An Economic and Social Agenda in the New Millennium. Washington, DC: World Bank, pp. 251–264.

Hancock, G. (1989) Lords of Poverty: The Power, Prestige, and Corruption of the International Aid Business. New York: Atlantic Monthly Press.

K. P. Jameson and C. K. Wilber (eds) The Political EconomyofDevelopmentandUnderdevelopment. New York: McGraw Hill.

Kuiper, E. and Barker, D. (eds) (2006) Feminist Economics and the World Bank: History, Theory and Policy. New York: Routledge.

Long, C. (2003) The Advocate's Guide to Promoting Gender Equality at the World Bank. Washington DC: Women's Edge.

Long, C. (2006) 'An Assessment of Efforts to Promote Gender Equality at the World Bank'. In E. Kuiper and D. Barker (eds) Feminist Economics and the World Bank: History, Theory and Policy. London: Routledge.

Mallaby, S. (2004) The World's Banker: A Story of Failed States, Financial Crises, and the Wealth and Poverty of Nations. New York: Penguin Press.

Moser, C. (1993) Gender Planning and Development: Theory, Practice and Training. New York: Routledge.

Moser, C. (1996) Confronting Crisis: A Summary of Household Responses to Poverty and Vulnerability in Four Poor Urban Communities. Washington DC: Environmentally Sustainable Development Studies and Monographs Series No. 7, World Bank.

Moser, C. (1997) Household Responses to Poverty and Vulnerability Volume 1: Confronting Crisis in Cisne Dos, Guayaquil, Ecuador. Urban Management Program Policy Paper 21. Washington DC: World Bank.

Moser, C. (2005) 'Has Gender Mainstreaming Failed?' International Feminist Journal of Politics 7(4): 576–590.

Mosse, D. and Lewis, D. (eds) (2005) The Aid Effect: Giving and Governing in International Development. Ann Arbor, MI: Pluto Press.

Newman, C. (2001) Gender, Time Use, and Change: Impacts of Agricultural Export Employment in Ecuador. Washington, DC: World Bank.

O'Brien, R., Goetz, A. M., Scholtle, J. A. and Williams, M. (eds) (2000) Contesting Global Governance: Multilateral Economic Institutions and Global Social Movements. Cambridge: Cambridge University Press.

Ortiz, A. (2003) 'Urban Development'. In V. Fretes-Cibils, M. M. Giugale and P.R.O.D.E.P.I.N.E.

(2001) Documento Básico Y Orientador Sobre El Tema de Género Quito: P.R.O.D.E.P.I.N.E.

P.R.O.D.E.P.I.N.E. (n.d.) Sistematizaci—n del Primer Congreso de Las Mujeres de la OSG COCIP: Tema: Género y Equidad. Quito: P.R.O.D.E.P.I.N.E.

Peterson, V. S. (2003) A Critical Rewriting of Global Political economy: Integrating Reproductive, Productive and Virtual Economies. New York: Routledge.

Pincus, J. R. and Winters, J. (eds) (2002) Reinventing the World Bank. Ithaca: Cornell UP.

Pollack, M. A. and Hafner-Burton, E. (2002) 'Mainstreaming Gender in Global Governance'. European Journal of International Relations 8(3): 339–373.

Rai, Shirin (2008) Analysing Global Governance, in Global Governance: feminist perspectives / edited by Shirin M. Rai and Georgina Waylen. Basingstoke: Palgrave Macmillan, 2008.

Rose, N. (1999) Powers of Freedom: Reframing Political Thought. New York: Cambridge University Press.

Staudt, K. (2002) 'Dismantling the Master's House with the Master's Tools? Gender Work in and with Powerful Bureaucracies'. In K. Saunders (ed.) Feminist Post Development Thought: Rethinking Modernity, Post Colonialism and Representation. London: Zed Press, pp. 57–68.

Valverde, M. (1998) Diseases of the Will: Alcohol and the Dilemmas of Freedom. New York: Cambridge University Press.

Waring, M. (1988). If Women Counted: A New Feminist Economics. San Francisco: Harper and Row.

World Bank (1992) Governance and Development. Washington, DC: World Bank.

World Bank (1994) Enhancing Women's Participation in Economic Development: A World Bank Policy Paper. Washington, DC: World Bank.

World Bank (1996) Ecuador Poverty Report: A World Bank Country Study. Washington, DC: World Bank.

World Bank (2000a) Advancing Gender Equality: World Bank Action since Beijing. Washington, DC: World Bank.

World Bank (2000b) Precis: Evaluating Gender and Development at the World Bank. Operations Evaluation Department. Washington, DC: World Bank.

World Bank (2001) Engendering Development through Gender Equality in Rights, Resources, and Voice. Washington, DC: World Bank/Oxford University Press.

World Bank (2002a) 'Building Institutions for Markets'. http://econ.worldbank. org/wdr/WDR2002.

World Bank (2002b) Integrating Gender into the World Bank's Work: A Strategy for Action. Washington, DC: World Bank.

World Bank (2006a) World Bank Group: Working Toward a World Free of Poverty. Washington, DC: World Bank.

World Bank (2006b) 'Gender Equality as Smart Economics, World Bank Gender Action Plan, Sept'. http://siteresources.worldbank.org/INTGENDER/Resources/GAPNov2.pdf.

Yunus, M. (1994) 'Preface: Redefining Development'. In K. Danaher (ed.) 50 Years Is Enough. Boston: South End Press.

Zuckerman, E. and Qing, W. (2003) Reforming the World Bank: Will the New Gender Strategy Make a Difference? A Study With China Case Examples. Washington, DC: Heinrich Boll Foundation/Gender Action.

Zuckerman, E. and Qing, W. (2005) Reforming the World Bank? Will the Gender Strategy Make a Difference A Study With Chinese Examples, 2nd edition. Washington, DC: Heinrich Boll Foundation/Gender Action.

Press extracts:
Applying European Values to Foreign Policy

THE EUROPEAN UNION

Obama (or Netanyahu) as Modern Moses!

MARWAN BISHARA

UN Expert Says Security Council Counterterrorism Measures Anti-Human Rights

NOKOLA KRASTEV

The following three extracts show us some of the ways in which the academic and foreign policy-making worlds intersect. These intersections can produce analyses that combine two or more academic perspectives so that we can better understand the world. The first piece is an advertisement the European Union placed in Foreign Policy, an opinion-shaping journal published in the United States. Are you surprised by the ad's assertion that there is a shared set of "European values"? Which of the IR theory perspectives best describes this set of values?

Marwan Bishara, a former university professor of IR, is more obvious in his discussion of IR perspectives, describing U.S. Middle East policy as "hardcore" realism and "neo-conservatism." Some U.S.-based foreign policy specialists might disagree with this assertion and stress the Obama administration's commitment to multilateralism, a key component of the liberal IR lens. What reasons does Bishara give for his conclusions? What would be an effective counter-argument that defends the U.S. position?

A university professor is the focus of the final press extract in Part Three. In addition to his position at the European University Institute in Florence, Italy, Martin Scheinin is the Special Rapporteur on the Promotion and Protection of Human Rights and Fundamental Freedoms. As the job title suggests, Scheinin is responsible for conducting research into the status of human rights globally. Special Rapporteurs often submit reports that are unpopular because the documents can present unfavorable or embarrassing information about the behaviors of governments. In this instance Professor Scheinin criticized the counterterrorism actions of some UN member-states. What were Scheinin's conclusions? How would advocates of the five IR perspectives presented in this book analyze Scheinin's findings?

Applying European Values to Foreign Policy

THE EUROPEAN UNION

> Effective multilateralism – The development of a stronger international society, with well-functioning international institutions and a rule-based international order.

The EU's core values are the foundation of its relations with the rest of the world. The EU does recognize that values are a subject on which societies can legitimately differ, for instance, by placing varying degrees of emphasis on the role of science, labor, and environmental standards in the formulation of policy. The EU regards negotiation as the way to resolve differences and offers credible leadership by example.

The EU is committed to reaching its foreign policy goals through diplomacy – that is, by the force of its arguments and ideas. Economic sanctions and military operations are considered only as a last resort, to be used when diplomacy has been exhausted.

Multilateralism is at the core of EU foreign policy. The Union maintains that many of today's challenges can be addressed only by countries and international institutions working together. For this reason, the EU seeks to project a united view and push for multilateral dialogue and solutions on issues such as peace, security, development, trade, terrorism, and the environment.

The EU has helped to foster and advance the network of international treaties and agreements that make up international law. The EU has been an active supporter of instruments such as the Vienna Conventions; governing economic and trade relations through rules-based organizations such as the World Trade Organization (WTO); and more broadly, using cooperative approaches through the United Nations system to address global problems.

The EU's advocacy of the multilateral system is grounded in its own 20th century history. Following the carnage of World War II, European political leaders assessed the damage and set about to make war among European nations inconceivable. The 1950 "Schuman Declaration" called for "the first concrete foundation of a European federation indispensable to the preservation of peace," and set in motion the process that ultimately led to the formation of the European Coal and Steel Community, forerunner to the modern European Union. Thus was born a new system of governance – the sharing of sovereignty – which was nurtured and expanded over subsequent decades. Today, 25 European states are members of this community, linked together by a foundation of shared values.

The EU believes that what has worked so successfully in Europe – bringing a half-century of peace, stability, and prosperity – can be applied to the broader world in many policy areas.

- **In support of democracy,** the EU provides direct assistance to countries making the transition from authoritarian to democratic governments.

The Union helps emerging democracies develop good governance procedures, supports the strengthening of civil society, and works to ensure open and fair elections.

- **To foster global economic growth and integration,** the EU is a leader in advancing trade liberalization under the WTO. It seeks a global economy in which competition reigns in open markets, and liberalization and integration benefit all nations. Hence, in the current Doha Development Round of global trade talks, the EU aims to generate, among other things, benefits for developing countries, most notably poverty reduction.
- **To advance human rights** around the world, the EU makes respect for human rights a condition in all its trade and cooperation agreements, most of which provide aid and preferential trade access to the Union, as well as regular political dialogue and conflict resolution. Failure to comply can result in a suspension of EU aid or preferential market access.
- **In promoting sustainable development,** the EU's ability to rally the world around a consensus of sound action rests first on its ability to implement sustainable policies at home. The EU is, for example, strictly implementing its obligations under the Kyoto agreement.

Europe, with its mosaic of geographic, ethnic, cultural, religious, and language diversity, is a microcosm of the world community. Its half-century of experience sharing sovereignty to pursue common interests while respecting differences provides a sound basis for using the tools of diplomacy and negotiation in dealing with the international community.

Obama (or Netanyahu) as Modern Moses!

MARWAN BISHARA

Secretary of State Hillary Clinton has delivered another "The US and I personally are in love with Israel" speech to America's pro-Israeli lobby – with a twist.

Her three-part speech at the annual policy conference of the American Israel Public Affairs Committee (Aipac) on Monday underlined Washington's unshaken strategic and moral commitment to Israel "for ever" and, in the second part, threatened Iran with tougher sanctions and warned it will never allow it to develop nuclear weapons.

In the third, and much awaited part, of the speech, Clinton delineated a hardcore realist approach to the Arab-Israeli conflict in the context of US security in the Middle East that envisions a freeze on settlement paving the way for direct talks that culminate in two states.

Like Moses, Obama – an unflinching supporter of Israel who has its interest and security at heart – will take it and the region to the promised land.

[Supporters of John McCain, the Republican candidate in the 2008 US presidential election, also depicted Obama, albeit sarcastically, as the "One" – that is, Moses – during the campaign.]

If you doubt it, Clinton said, look at what we've done yesterday, meaning the healthcare bill.

Realists vs Neoconservatives

Two decades and seven transitional agreements since the peace process started, the US and Israel can't seem to agree between themselves, let alone with the Palestinians, on the necessary condition to resolve the Palestinian question.

US realists including the Obama administration (and the Israeli Labor Party) believe that a two-state solution is good for Israel as a "democratic Jewish state". Clinton made it as clear in her speech to Aipac today.

Otherwise, continued Jewish settlement will exacerbate Israel's security and lead to apartheid state, to quote Israel Defence Minister and Labor leader Ehud Barak.

Likewise, a Palestinian state is consistent with US national security as it would help boost the "moderate" anti Iranian, anti-Islamic fundamentalist movements, Clinton pleaded with her audience.

Escalation in Palestine would endanger US lives in Middle East war zones, according to General David Petreaus, the head of US Central Command.

On the other hand, US nneoconservatives, like the previous Bush administration and by extension the Israeli Likud party, reckon that US support for the "Jewish state" – a strategic ally and "moral soulmate" – must be unconditional.

It's up to Israel alone to define the outcome of any negotiations with the Palestinians according to its security imperatives.

Israel's approach to Palestine, they argue, must be seen in the context of the US war on terror and against violent extremists in the region from Hamas in Gaza to the Taliban in Afghanistan/Pakistan.

Marwan Bishara, "Obama (or Netanyahu) as Modern Moses!" March 22, 2010. Al Jazeera English. http://blogs.aljazeera.net/imperium/2010/03/22/obama-or-netanyahu-modern-moses.

Two Decades of More-of-the-Same

For two decades, progress and regress in the peace process was measured by balancing out the two approaches. When the gap is substantial as it has been over the last year, paralysis or a fallout can be expected.

In 1991, the Bush administration refused to back down, and its confrontation with Israel – over the same settlement issue – paved the way for convening the Madrid International peace conference.

The urgency is far higher today. Unlike Bush Sr, who presided over a US victorious in the Cold War and the war against Iraq, President Obama presides over major foreign-policy crises as he tries to finish a war in Iraq and escalate another in Afghanistan/Pakistan.

Moreover, the deterioration in the occupied territories is creating a credibility problem for the Obama administration as it tries to rally Arab support against Tehran and radical fundamentalist groups.

However, as long as Likud and Labor are governing together and in coalition with the two most radical Israeli parties, Shas and Yisrael Beiteinu, US pressure will fail to lead to concrete concessions.

As in 1992, US will save face only when a new less extremist Israeli government comes into being. But would that resolve the Palestinian questions?

Palestine, Nuance or Nuisance

Meanwhile, the Palestinian and Arab leaderships are watching Hillary Clinton from the sidelines, hoping that the US present the Netanyahu government with ultimatum will be disappointed.

But even if the Obama administration forces the Israeli government to accept its approach, the result could hardly meet the minimum requirement of the Palestinians.

A Palestinian state as a compromise between the US and Israel, might enjoy the trappings of sovereignty, but in reality it would be no more than a Bantustan.

Palestinian leaders who still need Israeli passes to move around and out of occupied Palestine, already welcome foreign dignitaries in front of a guard of honour as they did when they welcomed UN Secretary-General Ban Ki-moon over the weekend.

However, as Clinton warned, the Israeli civilian and military occupation will soon reach the point of no return, rendering separation into two sovereign and viable states impossible.

In fact, the borders problem will soon be insolvable without major ethnic cleansing – which means war – or apartheid, leading to de facto one-state solution.

The Disagreement Goes On…

Ultimately it was in the latter part of her speech that Clinton revealed the administration's three-part explanation why Israel must accept a Palestinians state.

Israel faces three main challenges – demography, technology and ideology – that work against its security and against the security of the US.

Although she promised that the US will augment its military and diplomatic support for Israel, she arged that rockets from Gaza and Lebanon have no military solutions.

Furthermore, Palestinian population growth, coupled with expanding Israeli settlements, renders separation (as we said above) impossible.

Likewise, Israel's policies in Palestine is feeding Middle Eastern and other "extremists" with much ammunition, that a peaceful solution will deny them.

Needless to say, the Netanyahu government and the US neocons have answered to all of the three challenges: a bilateral commitment to combat terrorism and extremism, not give in or reward the extremists.

As Netanyahu will tell you, Islamist extremists don't need reasons for actions. They are terrorists because they are. Or, in his words, the reason for religious extremism and terrorism is the terrorists and the fundamentalists.

Obama can play Moses all he wants, but Netanyahu seeks King David persona!

UN Expert Says Security Council Counterterrorism Measures Anti-Human Rights

NIKOLA KRASTEV

UNITED NATIONS – An independent scholar hired by the United Nations to report on the promotion and protection of human rights says the UN Security Council's counterterrorism regime is operating outside the scope of its power.

Martin Scheinin, a Finnish expert on international law and the UN special rapporteur on counter-terrorism and human rights, presented his findings in his annual report on October 26.

At a news conference at UN headquarters in New York, Scheinin said his main concern was that the arbitrary application of counterterrorism measures by the Security Council jeopardizes one of the UN's fundamental goals: the protection of human rights.

For his report, he analyzed the consequences of two landmark Security Council counterterrorism resolutions.

Resolution 1373 was adopted unanimously by the Security Council in the aftermath of the September 11, 2001 terrorist attacks on the United States. The resolution is notable because it took the council only three minutes to pass, and there is no record of the meeting. Resolution 1373 imposes barriers on the movement, organization, and fund-raising activities of terrorist groups.

Scheinin also analyzed resolution 1267 adopted in 1999. Resolution 1267 imposed a regime of sanctions on Taliban and al-Qaeda individuals and entities, including an asset freeze, travel ban and arms embargo.

Currently, there are more than 400 names and entities on the sanctions list, even though dozens of politicians and diplomats have protested their seemingly arbitrary inclusion. Questions have been raised about the fairness of the inclusion of some individuals and the lack of recourse they have to protest their listing.

The government of Afghanistan, for one, has been lobbying for years to invalidate 1267 or at least to remove a number of influential names and entities with alleged or suspected Taliban connections. Without their removal, Kabul argues, the process of national reconciliation will not move forward.

Scheinin said 1373 – the post-9/11 resolution – "continues to pose risks to the protection of human rights and international rule of law."

He recommended the Security Council abandon the practice of creating official blacklists altogether, though he said he understood that such an extreme measure would likely meet with resistance from the Security Council.

Member States Disagree

The United States and Russia, two of the Council's five permanent members, strongly disagreed with Scheinin's findings. Both countries consider themselves at high risk for terrorist attacks, having been

Krastev, Nikola. "UN Expert Says Security Council Counterterrorism Measures Anti-Human Rights." October 27, 2010 (http://www.rferl.org/content/UN_Expert_Says_Security_Council_Counterterrorism_Measures_Anti Human_Rights/2202525.html).

targets of major terrorist attacks in recent years, and have implemented a raft of anti-terrorism measures.

Scheinin said that it's wrong to impose binding permanent obligations for acts of terrorism that have not yet taken place, since there is no universally accepted definition of terrorism.

When the Security Council adopts counterterrorism measures, it does so under the authority granted to it by Chapter Seven of the UN Charter, which gives the council the power to maintain world peace.

However, Scheinin argued that measures taken by the Security Council under the authority of Chapter Seven would be better meted out through international treaties.

"Whatever we now have under Chapter Seven powers is not going to last eternally and there has to be willingness on the side of the members of the Security Council to rethink sooner or later," Scheinin said.

The Security Council has taken some steps to reform how it includes and removes suspected terrorists from its sanctions list, and Scheinin acknowledged as much.

But he said people are still being denied due process and stressed that it was "essential that listed individuals and entities have access to the courts to challenge sanctions that are result of political decisions taken by diplomats."

At present, listed individuals and entities do not have any such option.

There is a better solution to the council's desire to be proactive by adopting counterterrorism measures, Scheinin says. Replacing the existing resolutions with a single resolution, which would not have the legal weight of the UN's Charters Chapter 7, but would contain human rights protections, would prove a better solution, according to Scheinin.

Useful Internet Resources

Amnesty International, http://www.amnesty.org/
Foundation for Sustainable Development, http://www.fsdinternational.org/
International Committee of the Red Cross, http://www.icrc.org/
International Court of Justice, http://www.icj-cij.org/
International Criminal Court, http://www.icc-cpi.int/
Multinational Monitor, http://multinationalmonitor.org/monitor.html
United Nations Department of Public Information NGO Directory, http://www.un.org/dpi/ngosection/dpingo-directory.asp
United Nations Department of Public Information NGO Section, http://www.un.org/dpi/ngosection/index.asp
United Nations High Commissioner for Refugees, http://www.unhcr.org/cgi-bin/texis/vtx/home
United Nations High Commissioner of Human Rights, http://www.ohchr.org/EN/Pages/WelcomePage.aspx
United Nations internet portal, www.un.org
United Nations Office of Peacekeeping Operations, http://www.un.org/Depts/dpko/dpko/dpko.shtml
United States Central Intelligence Agency World Factbook, http://odci.gov/cia/publications/factbook/index.html
World Federalist Society, http://www.wfm-igp.org/site/

Discussion Questions and Activities

1. Do NGOs have a valuable role in global politics? Answer this question from each of the academic perspectives presented in this book.
2. In Part Two the writers were very clear about which academic theory each believes best explains global politics. This is somewhat less clear in the reading extracts in Part Three. Find examples from each text that give indications of the authors' theoretical perspective.
3. If, as Realists assert, military security is a state prerogative, why did states let NGOs take the lead on the Convention to Ban Landmines? What does this say about the value of Realism as an analytical tool? Do other perspectives provide an insight into the negotiations leading to the Convention to Ban Landmines?
4. Using the official websites of several countries, research the extent to which the countries you select work together with NGOs on global issues such as security, human rights, development, and the environment.
5. Using the official websites of several countries, try to determine what foreign policy role or foreign policy style the country's leaders see for their state.

PART

IV

Global Issues

In this final part of the book, we will investigate a range of issues that have a global reach: security, including terrorism, nuclear weapons proliferation, and human rights; political economy, covering trade and finance; and the environment, with essays on resource depletion, climate change, food supply, and becoming "green." As in previous parts of the book, the readings come from the five major perspectives on international relations and examine the roles of states, IOs, NGOs, and individuals. Curiously, although the writers come to their studies from a variety of academic traditions, all share one belief: the problems that leaders confront today in security, political economy and the environment are truly global. Solutions to these challenges require multilateral, regional, and global action.

Security

Two events changed our current understanding of international security: the end of the Cold War in 1991 and the Al-Qaeda attacks on the United States on September 11, 2001. The former brought the promise of a world of Liberal Institutionalist cooperation; the latter seemed to justify the Realist anarchic worldview. Or, to put it another way: on the one hand Adam Smith, on the other Thomas Hobbes. These occurrences affected several aspects of security affairs the reading selections in this section discuss: the "global war on terror"; nuclear proliferation in the developing world; human rights and security; children and war; and peace-building activities.

From an academic perspective, the September 11 attacks perhaps signaled the more significant shift: a non-state actor, Al-Qaeda, was able to outwit the intelligence collection and counter-terrorism agencies of the hegemon of the international system, the United States. This blow to the prestige—"soft power" as Joseph Nye called it—of a state actor would have far-reaching practical consequences. It led many analysts to suggest that the power of the United States to control world events was in decline. Some saw this as a positive trend, for it meant that global civil society, perhaps in the shape of a reformed and more active United Nations, would lead to a more peaceful world. This was the Kantian dream of world federalism found in the often-cited essay "Perpetual Peace."

But what if the ability of the United States to control world events were in decline? What would be the long-term ramifications? A Realist answer might refer us to concepts like the balance of power, or Thucydides' Melian dialogue and the need for the strong to act forcefully, otherwise anarchy would result. A Constructivist might indicate that little had really changed for the United States, for the country still had the ability to project its military power globally. Like Wendt's analysis of the concept of international anarchy we studied in Part Two, "prestige" and "power" are themselves suffused with meanings that change with time.

Certainly the reaction of the Bush Administration to the September 11 attacks was indeed the strong response that Thucydides might have admired. The assaults on Afghanistan in October 2001 and Iraq in March 2003 sent clear signals that the leaders of the United States would not shy away from employing military power. However, international reaction to these campaigns varied. The United States' NATO allies all supported the invasion of Afghanistan and the subsequent removal of the ruling Taliban from Kabul and other major cities. The Iraq operation, on the other hand, divided those same allies. The German and French governments refused to join the U.S.-led attack, while the United Kingdom sent troops that were part of the invading army.

In time, however, as word spread of the "enhanced interrogation" methods that U.S. personnel used to obtain information from suspected Al-Qaeda members, a vigorous debate arose about the most effective means to fight transnational extremist groups that use terrorist methods. Several readings in this section examine this disagreement. On one side were people who argued that countries were at war against non-state actors like Al-Qaeda and its affiliates. Therefore, since these groups did not adhere to longstanding norms of international law states—especially the United States, argued the Bush Administration officials—should use any means to stop future attacks. This meant pre-emptive attacks—often with remote-controlled aircraft—that targeted the extremist groups and sent a signal of U.S. dissatisfaction to the states that harbored those groups. Another component of the new U.S. "get tough" policy was the notorious technique known as "water boarding" that caused a prisoner to believe he was drowning. The other side in this debate insisted that liberal democracies must not forsake the rule of law, even in the face of potential terrorist attacks. They argued that these "enhanced"—and illegal under international and U.S. domestic law—interrogations destroyed longstanding Western traditions of civil liberties and human rights. In effect, the terrorists had "won" because the West had destroyed its own system of values. Several of the readings in this part discuss these matters.

While this debate about methods to fight the global war on terror continued, other threats to international security remained. One of these is the problem of nuclear weapons proliferation. During the Cold War, the focus had been on the vertical proliferation of these weapons and the so-called five declared nuclear weapon states (USSR, USA, UK, France, and China), primarily the weapons in the arsenals of the Soviet Union and the United States. Horizontal proliferation, the spread of nuclear weapons technology to other countries, was considered to be less of a threat to global security. For example, Israel and India had nuclear weapon programs, but many analysts viewed these programs as stabilizing regional security. The argument went like this: the Arab states that border Israel would exercise caution in a crisis in the face of potential Israeli nuclear retaliation. Similarly, the fact that India had—or could potentially have—nuclear weapons would help stabilize the conflict with Pakistan.

This publicly sanguine Western view of controlling nuclear proliferation ignored actual events. The justification for the 2003 U.S. invasion of Iraq was, among other reasons, to find and eliminate the alleged weapons of mass destruction program of that state. North Korea and Pakistan both have had active nuclear weapons programs at least since the 1970s. What distinguishes these programs is that the former remains technically at war with South Korea and the United States, while the latter is ostensibly a U.S. ally in the fight against Muslim fundamentalists who use terror. Iran, citing its legitimate right of self-defense, has an active nuclear weapons research program that may produce its first bomb in as little as two years, according to some estimates.

Whether these Asian nuclear weapons programs pose a threat to global security is the subject of debate in policy-making circles. It is the subject of the Alagappa essay. Some experts assert that nuclear-armed Asian states will be at least as responsible with the technology as the United States and the Soviet Union were during the Cold War. A few analysts and government officials in this camp occasionally suggest that it is racist to contend that Asian states will be irresponsible with their nuclear weapons. Other experts highlight the unstable domestic political structures of North Korea and Pakistan as a reason to try to encourage disarmament in Asia. In the case of North Korea, analysts remind us that the dynastic change from Kim Jong-Il to Kim Jong-On may not be a smooth one, that rivals might challenge this transfer of political rule from father to son. Political instability, the argument goes, could lead to an attack on South Korea or potentially other countries, such as Japan.

The Pakistani case is perhaps even more complicated. As the U.S. diplomatic cables that the Wikileaks organization released in late November and early December 2010 indicate, U.S. officials were quite concerned both about the commitment of the Pakistani government to fight the Taliban and about the safety of Pakistani nuclear weapons, as many as thirty bombs according to some estimates. The irony in both cases is that although the states have active—and expensive—nuclear weapons programs, economic conditions in North Korea and Pakistan are not good. For example, press reports about the former often contain stories of widespread starvation. From a Realist academic perspective this might be seen as the high politics/low politics dichotomy at work: national security and prestige are more important than adequate food supplies.

Observers of Middle East politics can find little to like about a nuclear-armed Iran. The government leadership makes frequent threats to, among other things, destroy Israel and choke much of the world's oil supply by interdicting shipping lanes through the Straits of Hormuz. Whether a nuclear-armed Ahmadinejad government would follow through with such threats remains unclear. Certainly the government of Saudi Arabia is not happy about the weapons program of its neighbor to the north. News items citing the U.S. diplomatic cables report that King Abdullah repeatedly urged the United States to launch a pre-emptive strike that would "cut the head off the snake" (cited in http://www.guardian.co.uk/world/2010/nov/28/us-embassy-cables-saudis-iran, accessed Dec. 15, 2010).

The last three readings on international security concern aspects of human security, a relatively new concept in the discipline. This most un-Realist idea encompasses human rights and peace-building and is meant to convey the idea that if people *within* states feel unsafe, security *between* states is nearly meaningless. Since member-states of the United Nations adopted the Universal Declaration of Human Rights in 1947, the topic of human security has been on the international agenda. Like many such non-binding international declarations, it is largely unenforceable, leaving the matter to individual United Nations member-states. One method to encourage states that violate human rights to behave is through a combination of diplomatic carrots and sticks. In exchange for acceptable conduct, a state will receive a benefit. The Hafner-Burton essay examines the effect of international trade agreements on human rights protection and promotion. Although her conclusion is that there is a positive correlation between trade agreements and respect for human rights, ultimately the contemporary human rights records of many states remain deplorable.

In many regions of the developing world, human security is at risk because of internal conflict. In far too many of these conflicts, children under the age of sixteen are soldiers. Brocklehurst shows us the many ways in which children are forced or seduced into this role. Sometimes adults, usually male, take advantage of the seemingly natural fascination that children, again often male, have with machines of all kinds. Sadly, the machine in this case is often an automatic rifle or grenade launcher. Once "hooked" on this conveyor belt of violence, the children are socialized into believing that murder and atrocities are proper behavior.

Is there a way to end this route of violence? Anderlini contends there is, involving a mélange of Feminist and Constructivist perspectives on human security. She argues that there are numerous examples of women building networks of nonviolent social organizations that break the cycle of death and destruction in war-torn societies. At least in the short term these organizations have changed what had become the norm; we must wait to see the long-term results. For unless people have jobs and education, the violence might return. Therefore, the political-economic situation must improve.

Political Economy: Trade, Finance, Equality

As noted earlier, the end of the Cold War promised a world of Liberal Institutional cooperation. This was to be the era of Economic Globalization, the rising tide that would lift all ships that Adam Smith predicted so long ago. Time has demonstrated this to be a largely hollow promise for millions of people around the world. Many commentators blame the 2008 global economic collapse on the same 1980s and early 1990s neo-liberal policies that advocated trade and market reforms, an end to government subsidies for basic commodities such as foodstuffs, and the free flow of investment capital. They assert that the rush to wealth was largely free of government regulation and oversight, which are indeed central tenets of liberal and neo-liberal economic thought. However, the global economic collapse of 2008; the Madoff Ponzi scheme; and the implosion of the Spanish, Greek, and Irish economies in 2010 all highlight the downside of deregulation. The readings in this section discuss three central topics in the debate about the advantages and disadvantages of economic globalization: trade, finance, and development.

For many people economics is what Thomas Carlyle satirically called "the dismal science." Nobel Prize winner Paul Krugman has a solution. One of the few voices warning of the impending perils of unregulated capitalism, Professor Krugman has long been known for his ability to make complex ideas appear simple. As you have perhaps have already learned in your class, international trade is an exceedingly complex topic. Unlike international security, in which the major actors are states, international trade has a plethora of actors, including—to name a few—states, individuals, multinational corporations, transnational corporations, transnational trade association lobbying groups, international governmental organizations, and regional free trade associations. Krugman debunks the seemingly limitless praise for globalization, providing us with the essentials of international trade.

While it is true that economic globalization generated profits for shareholders and jobs for many people, there are clear negative effects of the trend. The 2008–2010 global recession demonstrated that the wealth a stock certificate represents is ultimately only a piece of paper. Moreover, globalized production of material goods created pockets of industrialization and wealth in places like China, Vietnam, Mexico, and Indonesia that are surrounded by abject poverty. Even those lucky people with jobs were not always satisfied. For example, in the summer of 2010 a wave of suicides occurred among workers at plants in China that made parts for iPhones and other "must-have" technology items destined for markets in Europe and the United States. The workers took their own lives to call attention to the living conditions and low pay at the factory compounds. (See http://www.bbc.co.uk/news/10316621, accessed Dec. 18, 2010.)

Women are often harmed the most in economic hard times, facing social, economic, and political effects. Economic hardship in societies often revives seemingly dormant cultural norms, for instance that a "woman's place" is in the home, not taking scarce industrial jobs from men. Also, in developing societies many women work at jobs such as child care, firewood gathering, or growing food for household consumption that do not appear in GDP statistics and therefore are not counted. As a result, International Monetary Funding or World Bank accounting methods do not record the full impacts for women of events like the 2008 global recession. Finally, as the Gray, Kittilson, and Sandholtz reading demonstrates, globalization has produced widely different political results for women.

After seeing these consequences, many analysts challenged the actual worth of the globalization experience. These criticisms include questioning the neo-liberal bias of the phenomenon. Perhaps, they argue, the problem is not globalization and its promise of widespread benefits, but its geographic point of origin: the United States. Writers such as Samir Amin, Lim Wonhyuk, and Ahn Choong Yong contend that there is a fundamental flaw in what many see believe is the greed-driven profit motive of U.S.-based investors and corporations. Critics assert there is no sense of social responsibility in the profit-at-all-costs model. This profit-driven worldview has negative effects for the global environment, the subject of the last set of readings.

Environment

For many years the discipline of IR tended to treat the environment as "low politics" best left to ecologists and others in the natural sciences and to domestic politics specialists. After all, since the 1700s, major diplomatic summits addressed the matters of national security that Realists focus on in their research: alliances, boundary disputes, arms control, and other topics in the traditional security issue area. The names of the diplomats who wrote the terms of the 1918 Migratory Bird Treaty Act or created the European Commission of the Danube River in 1856 are in many cases lost to history. We remember Talleyrand, Metternich, Palmerston, and Balfour, not Cunningham and Prokesch-Osten.

The state-centric perspective on global politics reinforced this high politics/low politics dichotomy. Where international law did apply to environmental matters, it was states that sued on behalf of their citizens, and enforcement was left to the states themselves. We see this with Trail Smelter Case of the late 1930s, in which the U.S. government sued the Canadian government to stop the owners of an ore smelter from creating atmospheric pollution that wafted into the United States. The low politics model also relied on what can be called the domestic analogy. For example, the Hardin essay in this section is often cited as an illustration of a likely result of unfettered national use of resources found in the world's oceans.

Several factors account for the recognition that global environmental problems merit serious attention by IR specialists. First, there was growing awareness that scarce resources might cause wars, since human-caused environmental problems do not respect international borders. For example, in the arid regions disputes over access to water for drinking and agriculture might be a cause of conflict. With the end of European and American control over oil fields around the world, analysts thought wars over access to oil supplies, the lifeblood of modern industries, could occur. Certainly the Iraq–Iran war (1980–1988) drove this fear. Disputes over potential oil fields also push tensions in other regions: the Spratly Islands in the South China Sea, for instance. China, Taiwan, Vietnam, the Philippines, and Brunei claim all or some of the tiny islands, which have a total land mass of less than 2 square miles. For the five states the key, of course, is the oil that is in the underwater sedimentary rock that holds the promise of oil wealth. If one of the five could gain exclusive control over the reefs, international law of the sea permits it to extend a 200-mile Economic Exclusion Zone that would prohibit access for the other four.

These gloomy predictions of war for water or war for oil aside, a second, more pressing factor propelled IR specialists into the environmental issue area. Basing their conclusions on decades of empirically based research, climate scientists discovered that atmospheric temperatures had increased globally. This powered the growing awareness that many environmental problems transcend international borders, even if the pollution itself comes from a specific location, what experts call a "point source." The research suggested, among other things, that even a 3 degrees Fahrenheit increase of atmospheric temperatures could cause species extinctions. Such an increase could also melt the North and South polar ice caps, which could in turn inundate small island states in the Caribbean and Pacific, like Nauru. Even if these dire predictions do not materialize at once, in the short term, climate change has already altered rainfall patterns and extended the geographic range of species, including pests like mosquitoes and pine borer beetles (http://www.metoffice.gov.uk/climatechange/guide/downloads/quick_guide_emag/#/1/).

Because the state remains the sole actor with the legitimate right to allocate scarce resources, both domestically and internationally, states must take action, as they did at the December 2010 Cancun, Mexico, Climate Summit. IR specialists had a hand in shaping the academic and legal discourse of the summit. The key concept here is that of the "epistemic community," the name given to cross-cutting coalitions—both within states and between states—of political leaders, international organizations, NGOs, scientists, and individual activists. However, as in other fields of IR, the academics arrived in the environment issue area with their theoretical perspectives in hand. For example, a Realist might see competition in anarchy and the likelihood of war; a Liberal Institutionalist the potential for cooperation; a Constructivist the evolution of definitions; a Feminist the masculinist notion of dominating "Mother Nature"; a Marxist capitalist exploitation. Certainly the course and outcome of the Cancun negotiations contained elements for each of these five academic worldviews to discover.

MILITARY SECURITY, HUMAN SECURITY, HUMAN RIGHTS: READING SELECTIONS

A World Without Power

NIALL FERGUSON

Niall Ferguson, a professor of economic history at Harvard University, asks the reader to consider what the world would be like if no one state were the global hegemon. What would that world look like? What would be the "rules of the game" if no actor could "call the shots"? The essay is meant to be a rebuttal to certain academic perspectives. Can you find examples of this?

We tend to assume that power, like nature, abhors a vacuum. In the history of world politics, it seems, someone is always the hegemon, or bidding to become it. Today, it is the United States; a century ago, it was the United Kingdom. Before that, it was France, Spain, and so on. The famed 19th-century German historian Leopold von Ranke, doyen of the study of statecraft, portrayed modern European history as an incessant struggle for mastery, in which a balance of power was possible only through recurrent conflict.

The influence of economics on the study of diplomacy only seems to confirm the notion that history is a competition between rival powers. In his bestselling 1987 work, *The Rise and Fall of the Great Powers: Economic Change and Military Conflict from 1500 to 2000*, Yale University historian Paul Kennedy concluded that, like all past empires, the U.S. and Russian superpowers would inevitably succumb to overstretch. But their place would soon be usurped, Kennedy argued, by the rising powers of China and Japan, both still unencumbered by the dead weight of imperial military commitments.

In his 2001 book, *The Tragedy of Great Power Politics*, University of Chicago political scientist John J. Mearsheimer updates Kennedy's account. Having failed to succumb to overstretch, and after surviving the German and Japanese challenges, he argues, the United States must now brace for the ascent of new rivals. "[A] rising China is the most dangerous potential threat to the United States in the early twenty-first century," contends Mearsheimer. "[T]he United States has a profound interest in seeing Chinese economic growth slow considerably in the years ahead." China is not the only threat Mearsheimer foresees. The European Union (EU) too has the potential to become "a formidable rival."

Power, in other words, is not a natural monopoly; the struggle for mastery is both perennial and universal. The "unipolarity" identified by some commentators following the Soviet collapse cannot last much longer, for the simple reason that history hates a hyperpower. Sooner or later, challengers will emerge, and back we must go to a multipolar, multipower world.

But what if these esteemed theorists are all wrong? What if the world is actually heading for a period when there is no hegemon? What if, instead of a balance of power, there is an absence of power?

Such a situation is not unknown in history. Although the chroniclers of the past have long been preoccupied with the achievements of great powers—whether civilizations, empires, or nation-states—they have not wholly overlooked eras when power receded. Unfortunately, the world's experience with power vacuums (eras of "apolarity," if you will) is hardly encouraging. Anyone who dislikes U.S. hegemony should bear in mind that, rather than a multipolar world of competing great powers, a world with no hegemon at all may be the real alternative to U.S. primacy. Apolarity could turn out to mean an anarchic new Dark Age: an era of waning empires and religious fanaticism; of endemic plunder and pillage in the world's forgotten regions; of economic stagnation and civilization's retreat into a few fortified enclaves.

Pretenders to the Throne

Why might a power vacuum arise early in the 21st century? The reasons are not especially hard to imagine.

The clay feet of the U.S. colossus

Powerful though it may seem—in terms of economic output, military might, and "soft" cultural power—the United States suffers from at least three structural deficits that will limit the effectiveness and duration of its quasi-imperial role in the world. The first factor is the nation's growing dependence on foreign capital to finance excessive private and public consumption. It is difficult to recall any past empire that long endured after becoming so dependent on lending from abroad. The second deficit relates to troop levels: The United States is a net importer of people and cannot, therefore, underpin its hegemonic aspirations with true colonization. At the same time, its relatively small volunteer army is already spread very thin as a result of major and ongoing military interventions in Afghanistan and Iraq. Finally, and most critically, the United States suffers from what is best called an attention deficit. Its republican institutions and political traditions make it difficult to establish a consensus for long-term nation-building projects. With a few exceptions, most U.S. interventions in the past century have been relatively short lived. U.S. troops have stayed in West Germany, Japan, and South Korea for more than 50 years; they did not linger so long in the Philippines, the Dominican Republic, Haiti, or Vietnam, to say nothing of Lebanon and Somalia. Recent trends in public opinion suggest that the U.S. electorate is even less ready to sacrifice blood and treasure in foreign fields than it was during the Vietnam War.

"Old Europe" grows older

Those who dream the EU might become a counterweight to the U.S. hyperpower should continue slumbering. Impressive though the EU's enlargement this year has been—not to mention the achievement of 12-country monetary union—the reality is that demography likely condemns the EU to decline in international influence and importance. With fertility rates dropping and life expectancies rising, West European societies may, within fewer than 50 years, display median ages in the upper 40s. Europe's "dependency ratio" (the number of non-working-age citizens for every working-age citizen) is set to become cripplingly high. Indeed, Old Europe will soon be truly old. By 2050, one in every three Italians, Spaniards, and Greeks is expected to be 65 or older, even allowing for ongoing immigration. Europeans therefore face an agonizing choice between Americanizing their economies, i.e., opening their borders to much more immigration, with the cultural changes that would entail, or transforming their union into a fortified retirement community. Meanwhile, the EU's stalled institutional reforms mean that individual European nation-states will continue exercising considerable autonomy outside the economic sphere, particularly in foreign and security policy.

China's coming economic crisis

Optimistic observers of China insist the economic miracle of the past decade will endure, with growth continuing at such a sizzling pace that within 30 or 40 years China's gross domestic product will surpass that of the United States. Yet it is far from clear that the normal rules for emerging markets are suspended for Beijing's benefit. First, a fundamental incompatibility exists between the free-market economy, based inevitably on private property and the rule of law, and the Communist monopoly on power, which breeds corruption and impedes the creation of transparent fiscal, monetary, and regulatory institutions. As is common in "Asian tiger" economies, production is running far ahead of domestic consumption—thus making the economy heavily dependent on exports—and far ahead of domestic financial development. Indeed, no one knows the full extent of the problems in the Chinese domestic banking sector. Those Western banks that are buying up bad debts to establish themselves in China must remember that this strategy was tried once before: a century ago, in the era of the Open Door policy, when U.S. and European firms rushed into China only to see their investments vanish amid the turmoil of war and revolution.

Then, as now, hopes for China's development ran euphorically high, especially in the United States. But those hopes were dashed, and could be disappointed again. A Chinese currency or banking crisis could have earth-shaking ramifications, especially when foreign investors realize the difficulty of repatriating assets held in China. Remember, when foreigners invest directly in factories rather than through intermediaries such as bond markets, there is no need for domestic capital controls. After all, how does one repatriate a steel mill?

The fragmentation of Islamic civilization

With birthrates in Muslim societies more than double the European average, the Islamic countries of Northern Africa and the Middle East are bound to put pressure on Europe and the United States in the years ahead. If, for example, the population of Yemen will exceed that of Russia by 2050 (as the United Nations forecasts, assuming constant fertility), there must either be dramatic improvements in the Middle East's economic performance or substantial emigration from the Arab world to aging Europe. Yet the subtle Muslim colonization of Europe's cities—most striking in places like Marseille, France, where North Africans populate whole suburbs—may not necessarily portend the advent of a new and menacing "Eurabia." In fact, the Muslim world is as divided as ever, and not merely along the traditional fissure between Sunnis and Shiites. It is also split between those Muslims seeking a peaceful modus vivendi with the West (an impulse embodied in the Turkish government's desire to join the EU) and those drawn to the revolutionary Islamic Bolshevism of renegades like al Qaeda leader Osama bin Laden. Opinion polls from Morocco to Pakistan suggest high levels of anti-American sentiment, but not unanimity. In Europe, only a minority expresses overt sympathy for terrorist organizations; most young Muslims in England clearly prefer assimilation to jihad. We are a long way from a bipolar clash of civilizations, much less the rise of a new caliphate that might pose a geopolitical threat to the United States and its allies.

In short, each of the potential hegemons of the 21st century—the United States, Europe, and China—seems to contain within it the seeds of decline; and Islam remains a diffuse force in world politics, lacking the resources of a superpower.

Dark and Disconnected

Suppose, in a worst-case scenario, that U.S. neoconservative hubris is humbled in Iraq and that the Bush administration's project to democratize the Middle East at gunpoint ends in ignominious withdrawal, going from empire to decolonization in less than two years. Suppose also that no aspiring rival power shows interest in filling the resulting vacuums—not only in coping with Iraq but conceivably also Afghanistan, the Balkans, and Haiti. What would an apolar future look like?

The answer is not easy, as there have been very few periods in world history with no contenders for the role of global, or at least regional, hegemon. The nearest approximation in modern times could be the 1920s, when the United States walked away from President Woodrow Wilson's project of global democracy and collective security centered on the League of Nations. There was certainly a power vacuum in Central and Eastern Europe after the collapse of the Romanov, Habsburg, Hohenzollern, and Ottoman empires, but it did not last long. The old West European empires were quick to snap up the choice leftovers of Ottoman rule in the Middle East. The Bolsheviks had reassembled the czarist empire by 1922. And by 1936, German *revanche* was already far advanced.

One must go back much further in history to find a period of true and enduring apolarity; as far back, in fact, as the ninth and 10th centuries.

In this era, the remains of the Roman Empire—Rome and Byzantium—receded from the height of their power. The leadership of the West was divided between the pope, who led Christendom, and the heirs of Charlemagne, who divided up his short-lived empire under the Treaty of Verdun in 843. No credible claimant to the title of emperor emerged until Otto was crowned in 962, and even he was merely a German prince with pretensions (never realized) to rule Italy. Byzantium, meanwhile, was dealing with the Bulgar rebellion to the north.

By 900, the Abbasid caliphate initially established by Abu al-Abbas in 750 had passed its peak; it was in steep decline by the middle of the 10th century. In China, too, imperial power was in a dip between the T'ang and Sung dynasties. Both these empires had splendid capitals—Baghdad and Ch'ang-an—but neither had serious aspirations of territorial expansion.

The weakness of the old empires allowed new and smaller entities to flourish. When the Khazar tribe converted to Judaism in 740, their khanate occupied a Eurasian power vacuum between the Black Sea and the Caspian Sea. In Kiev, far from the reach of Byzantium, the regent Olga laid the foundation for the future Russian Empire in 957 when she converted to the Orthodox Church. The Seljuks—forebears of the Ottoman Turks—carved the Sultanate of Rum as the Abbasid caliphate lost its grip over Asia Minor. Africa had its mini-empire in Ghana; Central America had its Mayan civilization. Connections between these entities were minimal or nonexistent. This condition was the antithesis of globalization. It was a world broken up into disconnected, introverted civilizations.

One feature of the age was that, in the absence of strong secular polities, religious questions often produced serious convulsions. Indeed, religious institutions often set the political agenda. In the eighth and ninth centuries, Byzantium was racked by controversy over the proper role of icons in worship. By the 11th century, the pope felt confident enough to humble Holy Roman Emperor Henry IV during the battle over which of them should have the right to appoint bishops. The new monastic orders amassed considerable power in Christendom, particularly the Cluniacs, the first order to centralize monastic authority. In the Muslim world, it was the ulema (clerics) who truly ruled. This atmosphere helps explain why the period ended with the extraordinary holy wars known as the Crusades, the first of which was launched by European Christians in 1095.

Yet, this apparent clash of civilizations was in many ways just another example of the apolar world's susceptibility to long-distance military raids directed at urban centers by more backward peoples. The Vikings repeatedly attacked West European towns in the ninth century—Nantes in 842, Seville in 844, to name just two. One Frankish chronicler lamented "the endless flood of Vikings" sweeping southward. Byzantium, too, was sacked in 860 by raiders from Rus, the kernel of the future Russia. This "fierce and savage tribe" showed "no mercy," lamented the Byzantine patriarch. It was like "the roaring sea... destroying everything, sparing nothing." Such were the conditions of an anarchic age.

Small wonder that the future seemed to lie in creating small, defensible, political units: the Venetian republic—the quintessential city-state, which was conducting its own foreign policy by 840—or Alfred the Great's England, arguably the first thing resembling a nation-state in European history, created in 886.

Superpower Failure

Could an apolar world today produce an era reminiscent of the age of Alfred? It could, though with some important and troubling differences.

Certainly, one can imagine the world's established powers—the United States, Europe, and China—retreating into their own regional spheres of influence. But what of the growing pretensions to autonomy of the supranational bodies created under U.S. leadership after the Second World War? The United Nations, the International Monetary Fund, the World Bank, and the World Trade Organization (formerly the General Agreement on Tariffs and Trade) each considers itself in some way representative of the "international community." Surely their aspirations to global governance are fundamentally different from the spirit of the Dark Ages?

Yet universal claims were also an integral part of the rhetoric of that era. All the empires claimed to rule the world; some, unaware of the existence of other civilizations, maybe even believed that they did. The reality, however, was not a global Christendom, nor an all-embracing Empire of Heaven. The reality was political fragmentation. And that is also true today. The defining characteristic of our age is not a shift of power upward to supranational institutions, but downward. With the end of states' monopoly on the means of violence and the collapse of their control over channels of communication, humanity has entered an era characterized as much by disintegration as integration.

If free flows of information and of means of production empower multinational corporations and nongovernmental organizations (as well as evangelistic religious cults of all denominations), the free flow of destructive technology empowers both criminal organizations and terrorist cells. These groups can operate, it seems, wherever they choose, from Hamburg to Gaza. By contrast, the writ of the international community is not global at all. It is, in fact, increasingly confined to a few strategic cities such as Kabul and Pristina. In short, it is the nonstate actors who truly wield global power—including both the monks and the Vikings of our time.

So what is left? Waning empires. Religious revivals. Incipient anarchy. A coming retreat into fortified cities. These are the Dark Age experiences that a world without a hyperpower might quickly find itself reliving. The trouble is, of course, that this Dark Age would be an altogether more dangerous one than the Dark Age of the ninth century. For the world is much more populous—roughly 20 times more—so friction between the world's disparate "tribes" is bound to be more frequent. Technology has transformed production; now human societies depend not merely on freshwater and the harvest but also on supplies of fossil fuels that are known to be finite. Technology has upgraded destruction, too, so it is now possible not just to sack a city but to obliterate it.

For more than two decades, globalization—the integration of world markets for commodities, labor, and capital—has raised living standards throughout the world, except where countries have shut themselves off from the process through tyranny or civil war. The reversal of globalization—which a new Dark Age would produce—would certainly lead to economic stagnation and even depression. As the United States sought to protect itself after a second September 11 devastates, say, Houston or Chicago, it would inevitably become a less open society, less hospitable for foreigners seeking to work, visit, or do business. Meanwhile, as Europe's Muslim enclaves grew, Islamist extremists' infiltration of the EU would become irreversible, increasing trans-Atlantic tensions over the Middle East to the breaking point. An economic meltdown in China would plunge the Communist system into crisis, unleashing the centrifugal forces that undermined previous Chinese empires. Western investors would lose out and conclude that lower returns at home are preferable to the risks of default abroad.

The worst effects of the new Dark Age would be felt on the edges of the waning great powers. The wealthiest ports of the global economy—from New York to Rotterdam to Shanghai—would become the targets of plunderers and pirates. With ease, terrorists could disrupt the freedom of the seas, targeting oil tankers, aircraft carriers, and cruise liners, while Western nations frantically concentrated on making their airports secure. Meanwhile, limited nuclear wars could devastate numerous regions, beginning in the Korean peninsula and Kashmir, perhaps ending catastrophically in the Middle East. In Latin America, wretchedly poor citizens would seek solace in Evangelical Christianity imported by U.S. religious orders. In Africa, the great plagues of aids and malaria would continue their deadly work. The few remaining solvent airlines would simply suspend services to many cities in these continents; who would wish to leave their privately guarded safe havens to go there?

For all these reasons, the prospect of an apolar world should frighten us today a great deal more than it frightened the heirs of Charlemagne. If the United States retreats from global hegemony—its fragile self-image dented by minor setbacks on the imperial frontier—its critics at home and abroad must not pretend that they are ushering in a new era of multipolar harmony, or even a return to the good old balance of power.

Be careful what you wish for. The alternative to unipolarity would not be multipolarity at all. It would be apolarity—a global vacuum of power. And far more dangerous forces than rival great powers would benefit from such a nor-so-new world disorder.

The Clash of Civilizations?

SAMUEL P. HUNTINGTON

This article caused quite a stir in both academic and policy-making realms when it was published in the highly influential journal *Foreign Affairs* in the summer of 1993. As you will read, Professor Huntington claimed to have captured the essence of future international tensions after the end of the Cold War. Have subsequent events proved or refuted Huntington's thesis? Has globalization generally prevailed over this clash of civilizations? Has a global economic culture emerged that lessened some of the tensions that Huntington asserted would cause global strife?

The Next Pattern of Conflict

WORLD POLITICS IS entering a new phase, and intellectuals have not hesitated to proliferate visions of what it will be—the end of history, the return of traditional rivalries between nation states, and the decline of the nation state from the conflicting pulls of tribalism and globalism, among others. Each of these visions catches aspects of the emerging reality. Yet they all miss a crucial, indeed a central, aspect of what global politics is likely to be in the coming years.

It is my hypothesis that the fundamental source of conflict in this new world will not be primarily ideological or primarily economic. The great divisions among humankind and the dominating source of conflict will be cultural. Nation states will remain the most powerful actors in world affairs, but the principal conflicts of global politics will occur between nations and groups of different civilizations. The clash of civilizations will dominate global politics. The fault lines between civilizations will be the battle lines of the future.

Conflict between civilizations will be the latest phase in the evolution of conflict in the modern world. For a century and a half after the emergence of the modern international system with the Peace of Westphalia, the conflicts of the Western world were largely among princes—emperors, absolute monarchs and constitutional monarchs attempting to expand their bureaucracies, their armies, their mercantilist economic strength and, most important, the territory they ruled. In the process they created nation states, and beginning with the French Revolution the principal lines of conflict were between nations rather than princes. In 1793, as R. R. Palmer put it, "The wars of kings were over; the wars of peoples had begun." This nineteenth-century pattern lasted until the end of World War I. Then, as a result of the Russian Revolution and the reaction against it, the conflict of nations yielded to the conflict of ideologies, first among communism, fascism-Nazism and liberal democracy, and then between communism and liberal democracy. During the Cold War, this latter conflict became embodied in the struggle between the two superpowers, neither of which was a nation state in the classical European sense and each of which defined its identity in terms of its ideology.

These conflicts between princes, nation states and ideologies were primarily conflicts within Western civilization, "Western civil wars," as William Lind has labeled them. This was as true of the Cold War as it was of the world wars and the earlier wars of the seventeenth, eighteenth and nineteenth centuries. With the end of the Cold War, international politics moves out of its Western phase, and its centerpiece becomes the interaction between the West and non-Western civilizations and among non-Western civilizations. In the politics of civilizations, the peoples and governments of non-Western civilizations no longer remain the objects of history as targets of Western colonialism but join the West as movers and shapers of history.

The Nature of Civilizations

During the Cold War the world was divided into the First, Second and Third Worlds. Those divisions are no longer relevant. It is far more meaningful now to group countries not in terms of their political or economic systems or in terms of their level of economic development but rather in terms of their culture and civilization.

What do we mean when we talk of a civilization? A civilization is a cultural entity. Villages, regions, ethnic groups, nationalities, religious groups, all have distinct cultures at different levels of cultural heterogeneity. The culture of a village in southern Italy may be different from that of a village in northern Italy, but both will share in a common Italian culture that distinguishes them from German villages. European communities, in turn, will share cultural features that distinguish them from Arab or Chinese communities. Arabs, Chinese and Westerners, however, are not part of any broader cultural entity. They constitute civilizations. A civilization is thus the highest cultural grouping of people and the broadest level of cultural identity people have short of that which distinguishes humans from other species. It is defined both by common objective elements, such as language, history, religion, customs, institutions, and by the subjective self-identification of people. People have levels of identity: a resident of Rome may define himself with varying degrees of intensity as a Roman, an Italian, a Catholic, a Christian, a European, a Westerner. The civilization to which he belongs is the broadest level of identification with which he intensely identifies. People can and do redefine their identities and, as a result, the composition and boundaries of civilizations change.

Civilizations may involve a large number of people, as with China ("a civilization pretending to be a state," as Lucian Pye put it), or a very small number of people, such as the Anglophone Caribbean. A civilization may include several nation states, as is the case with Western, Latin American and Arab civilizations, or only one, as is the case with Japanese civilization. Civilizations obviously blend and overlap, and may include subcivilizations. Western civilization has two major variants, European and North American, and Islam has its Arab, Turkic and Malay subdivisions. Civilizations are nonetheless meaningful entities, and while the lines between them are seldom sharp, they are real. Civilizations are dynamic; they rise and fall; they divide and merge. And, as any student of history knows, civilizations disappear and are buried in the sands of time.

Westerners tend to think of nation states as the principal actors in global affairs. They have been that, however, for only a few centuries. The broader reaches of human history have been the history of civilizations. In *A Study of History,* Arnold Toynbee identified 21 major civilizations; only six of them exist in the contemporary world.

Why Civilizations Will Clash

Civilization identity will be increasingly important in the future, and the world will be shaped in large measure by the interactions among seven or eight major civilizations. These include Western, Confucian, Japanese, Islamic, Hindu, Slavic-Orthodox, Latin American and possibly African civilization. The most important conflicts of the future will occur along the cultural fault lines separating these civilizations from one another.

Why will this be the case?

First, differences among civilizations are not only real; they are basic. Civilizations are differentiated from each other by history, language, culture, tradition and, most important, religion. The people of different civilizations have different views on the relations between God and man, the individual and the group, the citizen and the state, parents and children, husband and wife, as well as differing views of the relative importance of rights and responsibilities, liberty and authority, equality and hierarchy. These differences are the product of centuries. They will not soon disappear. They are far more fundamental than differences among political ideologies and political regimes. Differences do not necessarily mean conflict, and conflict does not necessarily mean violence. Over the centuries, however, differences among civilizations have generated the most prolonged and the most violent conflicts.

Second, the world is becoming a smaller place. The interactions between peoples of different civilizations are increasing; these increasing interactions intensify civilization consciousness and awareness of differences between civilizations and commonalities within civilizations. North African immigration to France generates hostility among Frenchmen and at the same time increased receptivity to immigration by "good" European Catholic Poles. Americans react far more negatively to Japanese investment than to larger investments from Canada and European countries. Similarly, as Donald Horowitz has pointed out, "An Ibo may be...an Owerri Ibo or an Onitsha Ibo in what was the Eastern region of Nigeria. In Lagos, he is simply an Ibo. In London, he is a Nigerian. In New York, he is an African." The interactions among peoples of different civilizations enhance the civilization-consciousness of people that, in turn, invigorates differences and animosities stretching or thought to stretch back deep into history.

Third, the processes of economic modernization and social change throughout the world are separating people from longstanding local identities. They also weaken the nation state as a source of identity. In much of the world religion has moved in to fill this gap, often in the form of movements that are labeled "fundamentalist." Such movements are found in Western Christianity, Judaism, Buddhism and Hinduism, as well as in Islam. In most countries and most religions the people active in fundamentalist movements are young, college-educated, middle-class technicians, professionals and business persons. The "unsecularization of the world," George Weigel has remarked, "is one of the dominant social facts of life in the late twentieth century." The revival of religion, "la revanche de Dieu," as Gilles Kepel labeled it, provides a basis for identity and commitment that transcends national boundaries and unites civilizations.

Fourth, the growth of civilization-consciousness is enhanced by the dual role of the West. On the one hand, the West is at a peak of power. At the same time, however, and perhaps as a result, a return to the roots phenomenon is occurring among non-Western civilizations. Increasingly one hears references to trends toward a turning inward and "Asianization" in Japan, the end of the Nehru legacy and the "Hinduization" of India, the failure of Western ideas of socialism and nationalism and hence "re-Islamization" of the Middle East, and now a debate over Westernization versus Russianization in Boris Yeltsin's country. A West at the peak of its power confronts non-Wests that increasingly have the desire, the will and the resources to shape the world in non-Western ways.

In the past, the elites of non-Western societies were usually the people who were most involved with the West, had been educated at Oxford, the

Sorbonne or Sandhurst, and had absorbed Western attitudes and values. At the same time, the populace in non-Western countries often remained deeply imbued with the indigenous culture. Now, however, these relationships are being reversed. A de-Westernization and indigenization of elites is occurring in many non-Western countries at the same time that Western, usually American, cultures, styles and habits become more popular among the mass of the people.

Fifth, cultural characteristics and differences are less mutable and hence less easily compromised and resolved than political and economic ones. In the former Soviet Union, communists can become democrats, the rich can become poor and the poor rich, but Russians cannot become Estonians and Azeris cannot become Armenians. In class and ideological conflicts, the key question was "Which side are you on?" and people could and did choose sides and change sides. In conflicts between civilizations, the question is "What are you?" That is a given that cannot be changed. And as we know, from Bosnia to the Caucasus to the Sudan, the wrong answer to that question can mean a bullet in the head. Even more than ethnicity, religion discriminates sharply and exclusively among people. A person can be half-French and half-Arab and simultaneously even a citizen of two countries. It is more difficult to be half-Catholic and half-Muslim.

Finally, economic regionalism is increasing. The proportions of total trade that were intraregional rose between 1980 and 1989 from 51 percent to 59 percent in Europe, 33 percent to 37 percent in East Asia, and 32 percent to 36 percent in North America. The importance of regional economic blocs is likely to continue to increase in the future. On the one hand, successful economic regionalism will reinforce civilization-consciousness. On the other hand, economic regionalism may succeed only when it is rooted in a common civilization. The European Community rests on the shared foundation of European culture and Western Christianity. The success of the North American Free Trade Area depends on the convergence now underway of Mexican, Canadian and American cultures. Japan, in contrast, faces difficulties in creating a comparable economic entity in East Asia because Japan is a society and civilization unique to itself. However strong the trade and investment links Japan may develop with other East Asian countries, its cultural differences with those countries inhibit and perhaps preclude its promoting regional economic integration like that in Europe and North America.

Common culture, in contrast, is clearly facilitating the rapid expansion of the economic relations between the People's Republic of China and Hong Kong, Taiwan, Singapore and the overseas Chinese communities in other Asian countries. With the Cold War over, cultural commonalities increasingly overcome ideological differences, and mainland China and Taiwan move closer together. If cultural commonality is a prerequisite for economic integration, the principal East Asian economic bloc of the future is likely to be centered on China. This bloc is, in fact, already coming into existence. As Murray Weidenbaum has observed,

> Despite the current Japanese dominance of the region, the Chinese-based economy of Asia is rapidly emerging as a new epicenter for industry, commerce and finance. This strategic area contains substantial amounts of technology and manufacturing capability (Taiwan), outstanding entrepreneurial, marketing and services acumen (Hong Kong), a fine communications network (Singapore), a tremendous pool of financial capital (all three), and very large endowments of land, resources and labor (mainland China).... From Guangzhou to Singapore, from Kuala Lumpur to Manila, this influential network—often based on extensions of the traditional clans—has been described as the backbone of the East Asian economy.[1]

Culture and religion also form the basis of the Economic Cooperation Organization, which brings together ten non-Arab Muslim countries: Iran, Pakistan, Turkey, Azerbaijan, Kazakhstan, Kyrgyzstan, Turkmenistan, Tadjikistan, Uzbekistan and Afghanistan. One impetus to the revival and expansion of this organization, founded originally in the 1960s by Turkey, Pakistan and Iran, is the realization by the leaders of several of these countries that they had no chance of admission to the European Community. Similarly, Caricom, the Central American Common Market and Mercosur rest on common cultural foundations. Efforts to build a broader Caribbean-Central American economic entity bridging the Anglo-Latin divide, however, have to date failed.

As people define their identity in ethnic and religious terms, they are likely to see an "us" versus "them" relation existing between themselves and people of different ethnicity or religion. The end of ideologically defined states in Eastern Europe and the former Soviet Union permits traditional ethnic identities and animosities to come to the fore. Differences in culture and religion create differences over policy issues, ranging from human rights to immigration to trade and commerce to the environment. Geographical propinquity gives rise to conflicting territorial claims from Bosnia to Mindanao. Most important, the efforts of the West to promote its values of democracy and liberalism as universal values, to maintain its military predominance and to advance its economic interests engender countering responses from other civilizations. Decreasingly able to mobilize support and form coalitions on the basis of ideology, governments and groups will increasingly attempt to mobilize support by appealing to common religion and civilization identity.

The clash of civilizations thus occurs at two levels. At the micro-level, adjacent groups along the fault lines between civilizations struggle, often violently, over the control of territory and each other. At the macro-level, states from different civilizations compete for relative military and economic power, struggle over the control of international institutions and third parties, and competitively promote their particular political and religious values.

The West versus the Rest

The West is now at an extraordinary peak of power in relation to other civilizations. Its superpower opponent has disappeared from the map. Military conflict among Western states is unthinkable, and Western military power is unrivaled. Apart from Japan, the West faces no economic challenge. It dominates international political and security institutions and with Japan international economic institutions. Global political and security issues are effectively settled by a directorate of the United States, Britain and France, world economic issues by a directorate of the United States, Germany and Japan, all of which maintain extraordinarily close relations with each other to the exclusion of lesser and largely non-Western countries. Decisions made at the U.N. Security Council or in the International Monetary Fund that reflect the interests of the West are presented to the world as reflecting the desires of the world community. The very phrase "the world community" has become the euphemistic collective noun (replacing "the Free World") to give global legitimacy to actions reflecting the interests of the United States and other Western powers.[2] Through the IMF and other international economic institutions, the West promotes its economic interests and imposes on other nations the economic policies it thinks appropriate. In any poll of non-Western peoples, the imf undoubtedly would win the support of finance ministers and a few others, but get an overwhelmingly unfavorable rating from just about everyone else, who would agree with Georgy Arbatov's characterization of IMF officials as "neo-Bolsheviks who love expropriating other people's money, imposing undemocratic and alien rules of economic and political conduct and stifling economic freedom."

Western domination of the U.N. Security Council and its decisions, tempered only by occasional abstention by China, produced U.N. legitimation of the West's use of force to drive Iraq out of Kuwait and its elimination of Iraq's sophisticated weapons and capacity to produce such weapons. It also produced the quite unprecedented action by the United States, Britain and France in getting the Security Council to demand that Libya hand over the Pan Am 103 bombing suspects and then to impose sanctions when Libya refused. After defeating the largest Arab army, the West did not hesitate to throw its weight around in the

Arab world. The West in effect is using international institutions, military power and economic resources to run the world in ways that will maintain Western pre-dominance, protect Western interests and promote Western political and economic values.

That at least is the way in which non-Westerners see the new world, and there is a significant element of truth in their view. Differences in power and struggles for military, economic and institutional power are thus one source of conflict between the West and other civilizations. Differences in culture, that is basic values and beliefs, are a second source of conflict. V. S. Naipaul has argued that Western civilization is the "universal civilization" that "fits all men." At a superficial level much of Western culture has indeed permeated the rest of the world. At a more basic level, however, Western concepts differ fundamentally from those prevalent in other civilizations. Western ideas of individualism, liberalism, constitutionalism, human rights, equality, liberty, the rule of law, democracy, free markets, the separation of church and state, often have little resonance in Islamic, Confucian, Japanese, Hindu, Buddhist or Orthodox cultures. Western efforts to propagate such ideas produce instead a reaction against "human rights imperialism" and a reaffirmation of indigenous values, as can be seen in the support for religious fundamentalism by the younger generation in non-Western cultures. The very notion that there could be a "universal civilization" is a Western idea, directly at odds with the particularism of most Asian societies and their emphasis on what distinguishes one people from another. Indeed, the author of a review of 100 comparative studies of values in different societies concluded that "the values that are most important in the West are least important worldwide."[3] In the political realm, of course, these differences are most manifest in the efforts of the United States and other Western powers to induce other peoples to adopt Western ideas concerning democracy and human rights. Modern democratic government originated in the West. When it has developed in non-Western societies it has usually been the product of Western colonialism or imposition.

The central axis of world politics in the future is likely to be, in Kishore Mahbubani's phrase, the conflict between "the West and the Rest" and the responses of non-Western civilizations to Western power and values.[4] Those responses generally take one or a combination of three forms. At one extreme, non-Western states can, like Burma and North Korea, attempt to pursue a course of isolation, to insulate their societies from penetration or "corruption" by the West, and, in effect, to opt out of participation in the Western-dominated global community. The costs of this course, however, are high, and few states have pursued it exclusively. A second alternative, the equivalent of "band-wagoning" in international relations theory, is to attempt to join the West and accept its values and institutions. The third alternative is to attempt to "balance" the West by developing economic and military power and cooperating with other non-Western societies against the West, while preserving indigenous values and institutions; in short, to modernize but not to Westernize.

Notes

1. Murray Weidenbaum, *Greater China: The Next Economic Superpower?*, St. Louis: Washington University Center for the Study of American Business, Contemporary Issues, Series 57, February 1993, pp. 2–3.
2. Almost invariably Western leaders claim they are acting on behalf of "the world community." One minor lapse occurred during the run-up to the Gulf War. In an interview on "Good Morning America," Dec. 21, 1990, British Prime Minister John Major referred to the actions "the West" was taking against Saddam Hussein. He quickly corrected himself and subsequently referred to "the world community." He was, however, right when he erred.
3. Harry C. Triandis, *The New York Times*, Dec. 25, 1990, p. 41, and "Cross-Cultural Studies of Individualism and Collectivism," Nebraska Symposium on Motivation, vol. 37, 1989, pp. 41–133.
4. Kishore Mahbubani, "The West and the Rest," *The National Interest*, Summer 1992, pp. 3–13.

The Triad: America, Europe, and Japan—United or Fragmented?

SAMIR AMIN

If globalization theorists are correct, the trend could eventually erode the dominance of states in world affairs and the hegemony of the United States specifically. Samir Amin, a noted Marxist scholar, considers this assertion. Will the United States be able to maintain its control over international politics? Since 1990, for what reasons has the United States waged wars? If you did not know that Amin is a Marxist writer, how could you surmise this from the extract? What clues do his writing style and language usage offer?

The phase of the global deployment of capitalism, which began in 1945 but was impeded until the collapse of the post-war social orders (welfare state, Sovietism, national populism in the South), is characterized by the emergence of a collective imperialism. The 'triad' (that is, the United States plus its Canadian external province, Europe west of the Polish frontier, and Japan – to which we should add Australia and New Zealand) defines the area of this collective imperialism. It 'manages' the economic dimension of capitalist globalization through the institutions at its service (WTO, IMF, World Bank, OECD), and the political–military dimension through Nato, whose responsibilities have been redefined so that it can in effect substitute itself for the United Nations.

Yet the current moment in this phase is also characterized by a US offensive to impose its own leadership on the triad, involving a conception of 'military control of the planet' worked out by the George W. Bush administration. The question that immediately arises is whether this is a viable conception. Are the triad partners forced to accept US leadership, either in the stark forms unilaterally decided by Washington or with some 'concessions' that allow for a less unbalanced division of responsibilities and benefits? Or are we heading towards a radical, if gradual, challenge to Arlanticism (and the complementary asymmetrical alliance between the USA and Japan), and therefore towards the breaking up of the triad? In both cases, we need to be clear what the different developments would entail for North–South relations.

In the immediate term, the United States enjoys an evident strategic advantage: its project is the only one that is clearly and openly formulated and, by virtue of the initiatives taken by Washington, the only one that is actually in play. Up to now its partners in the international community – the triad allies and the rest – have done nothing more than respond to those initiatives, whether by falling into line, accepting with bad grace or seeking to limit some of the consequences they find most troubling to themselves. None has a really positive alternative to guide its strategy, and in a thoroughly

Samir Amin, *Beyond U.S. Hegemony?*. Zed Books, 2006.

disorganized manner each places the immediate emphasis on what it considers to be the defence of its own interests.

The question we posed does not admit of a simple answer, for the contemporary world has been undergoing a number of massive changes. Europe, now the largest trading power, has embarked on a common project of political construction that will probably rule out a return to the internecine wars of its past. Japan has become a major economic power, and a large part of Asia is heading along the road of accelerated development. The United States, for its part, has made a sensational comeback, while the disappearance of 'actually existing socialism' has helped to spread the idea that capitalism is the only possible future for all nations. In these conditions, the geometry of possible rapprochement among the different poles of power and wealth has become extremely complex.

To see our way more clearly, we may usefully start by analysing the project of the US ruling class and identifying its strengths and weaknesses. Then we shall consider how Europe – or the different Europes – and Japan are responding to the challenge, and which conditions need to be fulfilled if the various options of the triad partners are to take effect. This analysis will allow us to clarify the nature of possible conflicts within the triad, and to identify the terrain on which they might occur. It will also enable us to begin discussion on what the various scenarios would entail for North-South relations.

The Project of the American Ruling Class: Extension of the Monroe Doctrine to the Rest of the World

The project that the US ruling class has cherished since 1945 now has five objectives: (i) to neutralize and subjugate the other triad partners (Europe and Japan) and to minimize their capacity to act outside the American fold; (ii) to establish military control over Nato and to 'Latin Americanize' the former parts of the Soviet world; (iii) to assert undivided control over the Middle East and its oil resources; (iv) to break up China, to ensure the subordination of the other major states (India, Brazil), and to prevent the constitution of any regional blocs that might renegotiate the terms of globalization; and (v) to marginalize regions in the South that are of no strategic interest.

The project, which was devised after Potsdam and grounded on the American nuclear monopoly, has always assigned a key role to its military dimension. In a very short time the United States put in place a global military strategy, divided the globe into a number of regions, and created several 'Military Commands' to take responsibility for each. The aim was not only to encircle the USSR (and China) but also to make Washington the worldwide master of last resort: in other words, to extend to the whole planet the Monroe doctrine that had already staked its claim to run the New World in accordance with its own 'national interests'.

The main instrument in the current US drive for hegemony is therefore military. Such hegemony would in turn guarantee that of the triad over the global system, but the allies of the United States would have to accept their subaltern status, as Britain and Japan already do, and to recognize its necessity without feeling even any 'cultural' qualms. This means, however, that the talk of economic strength with which European politicians regale their local constituencies would lose all purchase on reality. If Europe places itself entirely on the ground of mercantile disputes, without advancing any project of its own, it will have been defeated in advance. People in Washington are well aware of that.

The project implies that the 'sovereign national interests of the United States' should hold sway over all other principles defining what is regarded as legitimate political behaviour; it leads to systematic distrust of all international law.

The ruling class of the United States freely proclaims that it will not 'tolerate' the reconstitution of any economic or military power capable of challenging its global domination. To this end, it has given itself the right to wage 'preventive wars', with three main potential adversaries in mind.

First, the dismemberment of the Russian Federation, following that of the USSR, is a major strategic objective for the United States. Until now the Russian ruling class does not appear to have understood this. It seemed convinced that, having lost the war, it could go on to win the peace – as Germany and Japan did before it. What it forgot was that Washington needed the recovery of its two wartime enemies, precisely in order to face down the Soviet challenge. The new conjuncture is different, as the United States no longer has a serious rival. Its option is therefore to destroy its defeated Russian adversary once and for all. Has Putin finally understood this? Is Russia beginning to shake off its illusions?

Second, the huge size and economic success of China are such that the United States is seriously worried, and here too has a strategic goal of dismembering the country.

Europe comes third in the list, as seen by the new lords of the earth. Up to now, however, the North American establishment does not appear to be so uneasy about its relations with Europe. The unconditional Atlanticism of some countries (Britain and the EU's new servile members in the East), the 'shifting sands' of Europeanism itself, the convergent interests of dominant capital within the triad's collective imperialism: all this is tending to roll back the European project, or to maintain it as the European 'section' of the US project. Washington's diplomatic efforts have managed to keep Germany in tow; the reunification and conquest of Eastern Europe have even appeared to strengthen the Atlantic alliance, as Germany has ostensibly been encouraged to resume its traditional *Drang nach Osten* (witness Berlin's role in breaking up Yugoslavia through the hasty recognition of Slovenian and Croatian independence) and otherwise asked to steer in the American wake. Is a change of course currently under way? The German political class appears hesitant, perhaps divided, in its choice of strategy.

The alternative to Atlanticist alignment calls instead for the strengthening of a Paris–Berlin–Moscow axis, which could become the backbone of a European system independent of Washington.

The prevailing opinion is that US military power is only the tip of the iceberg, prolonging its economic as well as political and cultural superiority. In my view, however, the United States has no decisive economic advantages within the system of collective imperialism; on the contrary, scarcely any of its sectors could be certain of seeing off competitors in the kind of truly open market imagined by liberal economists. Evidence of this is the fact that the US trade deficit keeps growing year after year, having soared from $100 billion in 1989 to $500 billion in 2002, and that this deficit involves practically every segment of the productive system. The competition between Ariane and Nasa space rockets, or between Airbus and Boeing, testifies to the vulnerability of the American advantage. Indeed, without extra-economic means that violate the 'liberal' principles imposed on its rivals, the United States would probably not be able to compete with Europe or Japan in high technology, with China, Korea and other industrial countries of Asia and Latin America in ordinary manufactured products, or with Europe and the Southern Cone of Latin America in agriculture.

The US economy lives as a parasite off its partners in the global system, with virtually no national savings of its own. The world produces while North America consumes. The advantage of the United States is that of a predator whose deficit is covered by what others agree, or are forced, to contribute. Washington uses various means to make up for its deficiencies: for example, repeated violations of the principles of liberalism, arms exports, and the hunting down of oil super-profits (which involves the periodic felling of producers: one of the real motives behind the wars in Central Asia and Iraq). But the fact is that the bulk of the American deficit is covered by capital inputs from Europe and Japan, China and the South, rich oil-producing countries and comprador classes from all regions, including the poorest, in the Third World – to which should be added the debt-service levy that is imposed on nearly every country in the periphery of the global system. The American superpower depends from day to day on the flow of capital that sustains the parasitism of its economy and society. The vulnerability of the United States therefore represents a serious danger for Washington's project.

The hegemonist strategy of the United States, which operates within the framework of the new collective imperialism, seeks nothing less than to establish Washington's military control over the entire planet. This is the means to ensure privileged access to all of the world's natural resources, and to compel subaltern allies, Russia, China and the whole third world to swallow their status as vassals. Military control of the planet is the means to impose, as a last resort, the draining of 'tribute' through political violence – as a substitute for the 'spontaneous' flow of capital that offsets the American deficit, the Achilles heel of US hegemony. The aim of this strategy is neither to ensure open markets for all (which exist only in the propaganda of neoliberal sycophants) nor, of course, to make democracy prevail throughout the world.

The neoliberal option for Europe, reinforced by a supposedly 'nonpolitical' management of its common currency (the euro), is a major handicap for any strategy to lift the continent clear of stagnation. This absurd monetary policy suits Washington down to the ground, since the US currency (the dollar) is managed in a quite different, thoroughly political manner that has nothing to do with neoliberal dogma. Combined with the possibility that Washington will gain exclusive control over the world's oil reserves, it ensures that what I call the oil/dollar standard will remain in the end the sole international monetary instrument, relegating the euro to the status of a subaltern regional currency.

The political conflict that might oppose Europe (or some major European countries) to the United States does not stem from fundamental disagreements expressing a clash of interests between dominant capitals. I would locate it, rather, within the conflict between different 'national intetests' and profoundly different political cultures. My answer to whether the triad is united or fragmented may therefore be summarized in a single sentence. The dominant economic tendency operates in favour of triad unity, whereas politics points towards the break-up of triad unity, because of the diversity of national interests and political cultures.

The Shifting Sands of the European Project

Up to now, all the governments of European countries have rallied to the theses of economic liberalism. This has meant nothing less than the eclipse of the European project, a dilution both economic (the advantages of the EU dissolved into globalization) and political (disappearing political and military autonomy). As things stand today, there is no European project. It has been replaced with a North Atlantic (or triad) project under American command.

Wars 'made in the USA' have certainly woken public opinion (especially in Europe against the latest war, in Iraq) and even some governments (especially the French, but also the German, Russian and Chinese). Yet these same governments have not reconsidered their loyal attachment to the requirements of 'liberalism'. This adds up to a major contradiction, which will have to be overcome in one way or the other: either by bowing to Washington's demands or by making a real break that puts an end to Atlanticism.

This shift has plunged European societies into a multidimensional crisis. First, there is simply the economic crisis built into the liberal option, a crisis deepened by Europe's alignment with the North American leader and its agreement to fund the US deficit at the expense of its own interests. Then there is the social crisis, which has grown sharper through the rise of popular resistance and class struggles against the baneful consequences of the neoliberal turn. Finally, there are the beginnings of a political crisis, visible in the refusal to fall unconditionally into line with the US perspective of endless war against the South.

How are the peoples and governments of Europe facing up to this threefold challenge? Those who are Europeanist by principle divide into three rather different groups:

- Those who support the neoliberal orientation and more or less unconditionally accept US leadership.
- Those who support the neoliberal orientation but would like to see a politically independent Europe break from its alignment with America.
- Those who would like to see (and who fight for) a 'social Europe' – that is, a capitalism tempered by a new Europe-wide social compromise between capital and labour – and a political Europe that

practises different (friendly, democratic and peaceful) relations with the South, Russia and China. Public opinion throughout Europe has expressed its sympathy for such a position on a number of occasions, at the European Social Forum (Florence 2002, Paris 2003 and London 2004) and in opposition to the war in Iraq.

The Clash of Political Cultures

With regard to the differences between 'Europeans' and 'North Americans', I should point out that since 1990 my analyses of the 'empire of chaos' have situated the main conflict between them at the level not of economic interests but of political cultures. When mention is made of 'economic interests', it would be useful to draw a clear distinction between the interests of the dominant segments of capital (the large transnational corporations and their financial vanguard tooted in neoliberal globalization) and what is meant by the vague term 'national (economic) interests'. If there is a collective imperialism, this is because the dominant segments of capital share common interests in running the globalized system. To be sure, each TNC competes with other TNCs, and each state (none more than the United States) actively supports its own TNCs in the competitive struggle. But the conflicts and alliances in question, which often take shape between transnational blocs of interests, involve variable geometries that should not be reduced to a narrowing or widening of the gap between states.

This brings us to the question of political cultures. The term 'political' here marks out my own theoretical position: I do not speak of 'cultures' in general, in the manner of the fashionable discourse of 'difference'; what I mean by political culture is a complex outcome of historical social struggles in the country in question, combined with the international conflicts that define the place of the nation in the global order.

Within this conceptual framework, I have defined the political culture or cultures of Europe (or of a large part of the continent) as the historical outcome of four elements: (i) the philosophy of the Enlightenment; (ii) the 'bourgeois revolutions' that ushered in modernity, especially the most radical of them, the French Revolution, which was at once a bourgeois revolution and a people's revolution; (iii) the early rise of the workers' movement (in all its 'reformist' and 'revolutionary' tendencies) that made its mark on the nineteenth and twentieth centuries; and (iv) the impact of the Russian Revolution and the resulting break between Communists and Social Democrats. The complex outcome of this itinerary shaped the left/right divide peculiar to Europe, as it shaped basic concepts of society that combined the conflicting values of liberty and equality and the practices of a secular democracy where the notion of citizenship occupied a central place.

The political culture of the United States produced a system of concepts very different from those found in Europe. Its concept of liberty places a distinctive emphasis on free enterprise, while also attaching a comparatively low value to equality. Unlike Europe – which has gone further in this sense – it has never understood the secular principle as anything more than tolerance of religious diversity.

This political culture serves wonderfully to ensure the undivided and internalized rule of capital, which in Europe often has to remain constantly on its guard. The US system is well-nigh perfect for this purpose: its presidency and 'single party' (split between Democrats and Republicans) succeed in warding off the potential danger contained elsewhere in the practice of electoral democracy.

Will the contrast between the political cultures of the United States and Europe withstand Americanization of the old continent? In this connection, the draft constitution for the European Union was highly disturbing: it set in stone both economic liberalism and the Nato functions underpinning Atlanticism, and its Article 51 enshrined the role of the churches in the life of society. Sounding the death knell of secularism, it called for adaptation to American-style conceptions of the place of religion in society, for the acceptance of sects and fundamentalist movements as an ordinary part of the landscape, and for the crystallization of communalist tendencies. This obscurantist breakthrough was a great success for Opus Dei: its reactionary ideology inspired the authors of the draft and, most especially, Giscard d'Estaing, whose aim is to erase the Enlightenment, the French Revolution and socialism from the European memory. Had it been accepted, the only remaining reason for conflict among the triad partners would be divergences of national interests, with no basis in a diversity of political cultures.

In my view, this is the ground on which the 'clash of civilizations' between the United States and Europe is situated. In Europe (and large parts of the rest of the world) it is the same as the conflict between capitalism and socialism – a conflict that does not exist in the United States.

And Japan?

Readers will remember the waves of enthusiasm which, twenty or so years ago, cast Japan as the rising hegemon that would eventually supplant the United States. Japan the inventor of new forms of labour ('Toyotism'), Japan in the forefront of research and development, Japan the great saver buying up American industry! Such ideas never made much impression on me, as they seemed to disregard the structural weaknesses of the Empire of the Rising Sun.

In the foreseeable future, then, it is hard to imagine that Japan will play an active role in reconstructing the global system. Most probably, it will be carried along by Washington's militarist project – unless the popular classes enter the arena and, through the intensification of their struggles, begin to develop a challenge to the system. Meanwhile Japanese capital can derive only modest profits from the alignment with the United States, and these might be further limited by concessions that Washington imposes on Tokyo with regard to the exploitation of Southeast Asia's natural resources and cheap labour.

In Terrorem: Before and After 9/11[1]

JAMES DER DERIAN

James Der Derian, a professor at Brown University, is renowned for his analyses of the language we use to describe international politics. In this extract he asks us to consider how the attacks of September 11, 2001, changed global interactions. What is his central argument? Have those attacks altered the foreign policy of the United States? In what ways? What does Der Derian mean by the concept of "virtuous war"? Is this different from other forms of war?

Before 9/11 and after 9/11: it is as if the history and future of international relations were disappeared by this temporal rift. Old rules of statecraft, diplomacy and warfare have been thrown out by terrorist and anti-terrorist alike, and in this interregnum – best described by Chris Patten, the last governor of Hong Kong and current European Union Commissioner for External Affairs, as one of 'unilateralist overdrive' – critical enquiry is threatened by a global *in terrorem*.[2]

Obviously, the sheer scale, scope and shock of the events themselves are partially to blame for the paucity as well as the poverty of the response by the field of International Relations. Perhaps we witness once again what happened at academic conferences after the fall of the Berlin Wall, when social scientists were reluctant to posit cause and effect from a single data point. Or perhaps something more is at work, a great deal more. After terrorist hijackers transformed three commercial jetliners into highly explosive kinetic weapons, toppled the Twin Towers of the World Trade Center, substantially damaged the Pentagon, killed over 3000 people and triggered a state of emergency – and before the dead are fully grieved, Osama bin Laden's head brought on a platter, justice perceived as done, and information no longer considered a subsidiary of war – there is very little about 9/11 that is *safe* to say. Unless one was firmly situated in a patriotic, ideological, or religious position (which at home and abroad drew uncomfortably close), it is intellectually difficult and even politically dangerous to assess the meaning of a conflict that phase-shifted with every news cycle, from 'Terror Attack' to 'America Fights Back'; from a 'crusade' to a 'counter-terror campaign'; from 'the first war of the twenty-first century' to a now familiar combination of humanitarian intervention and remote killing; from kinetic terror to bioterror; from the spectacle of war to a war of spectacles.

Under such conditions, I believe the task is to uncover what is *dangerous* to think and say. Or as Walter Benjamin put it best in an earlier interim of violence and uncertainty, 'in times of terror, when everyone is something of a conspirator, everybody will be in a situation where he has to play detective'.[3]

Detective work and some courage are needed because questions about the root causes or political intentions of the terrorist acts have been either silenced by charges of 'moral equivalency' or rendered moot by claims that the exceptional nature of the act placed it outside political discourse: explanation is identified as exoneration.[4] Reflecting the nature of the attacks, as well as the chaos and confusion which followed, the conventional boundaries of the infosphere expanded during the first week to include political, historical and ethical analysis by some voices not usually heard on primetime. However, as the flow of information became practically entropic, there was a willingness (as judged by the unholy trinity of polls, pols and programming) to accept as wisdom President Bush's early declaration that evil – which expanded from a person to a network to the now notorious 'axis of evil' – was to blame. From that moment, policy debate and political action downshifted to a simple declarative with an impossible performative: to eradicate evil. Binary narratives displaced any complex or critical analysis of what happened and why. Retribution required certainty, and certainty was produced as salve for the actually as well as symbolically injured.

More sophisticated analysts like Michael Ignatieff also downplayed the significance of social or political enquiry by declaiming the exceptionality of the act:

> What we are up against is apocalyptic nihilism. The nihilism of their means – the indifference to human costs – takes their actions not only out of the realm of politics, but even out of the realm of war itself. The apocalyptic nature of their goals makes it absurd to believe they are making political demands at all. They are seeking the violent transformation of an irremediably sinful and unjust world. Terror does not express a politics, but a metaphysics, a desire to give ultimate meaning to time and history through ever-escalating acts of violence which culminate in a final battle between good and evil.[5]

By funnelling the experience through the image of American exceptionalism, 9/11 quickly took on an *exceptional ahistoricity.* For the most part, history was only invoked – mainly in the sepia tones of the Second World War – to prepare the US for the sacrifice and suffering that lay ahead. The influential conservative George Will wrote that there were now only two time zones left for the United States:

> America, whose birth was mid-wived by a war and whose history has been punctuated by many more, is the bearer of great responsibilities and

the focus of myriad resentments. Which is why for America, there are only two kinds of years, the war years and the interwar years.[6]

Under such forced circumstances, of being beyond experience, outside of history and between wars, 9/11 does not easily yield to philosophical, political or social enquiry. The best one can do is to thickly describe, robustly interrogate and directly challenge the authorized truths and official actions of all parties who posit a world view of absolute differences in need of final solutions. I do so here by first challenging the now common assumption that 9/11 is an exceptional event beyond history and theory, especially those theories tainted, as Edward Rothstein claimed in the *New York Times*, by 'postmodernism' and 'post-colonialism'.[7] Second, I examine the representations, technologies and strategies of network wars that have eluded mainstream journalism and 'traditional' social science. I conclude by uncovering what I consider to be the main dangers that emerged from the counter/terror of 9/11.

An Exceptional Act?

On the question of exceptionalism, consider a few testimonials; the first from an editorial in the *New York Times:*

> If the attack against the World Trade Center proves anything it is that our offices, factories, transportation and communication networks and infrastructures are relatively vulnerable to skilled terrorists... Among the rewards for our attempts to provide the leadership needed in a fragmented, crisis-prone world will be as yet unimagined terrorists and other socio-paths determined to settle scores with us.[8]

Another from a cover story of *Newsweek:*

> The explosion shook more than the building: it rattled the smug illusion that Americans were immune, somehow, to the plague of terrorism that torments so many countries.[9]

And finally, one from the *Sunday Times:*

> He began the day as a clerk working for the Dean Witter brokerage on the 74th floor of the World Trade Center in New York and ended it as an extra in a real-life sequel to *Towering Inferno...*[10]

It might surprise some to learn that these are all quotes taken from 1993, the first and much less deadly terrorist attack on the World Trade Center. They are presented here as a caution, against reading terrorism only in the light – the often-blinding light – of the events of September 11. Obviously the two WTC events differ in the scale of the devastation as well as the nature of the attack. 9/11 defied the public imagination of the real – not to mention, as just about every public official and media authority is loath to admit, the official imagination and pre-emptive capacity of the intelligence community, federal law enforcement, airport security, military and other governmental agencies. Shock and surprise produced an immediate and nearly uniform reading of the event that was limited in official discourse to condemnation, retribution and counter-terror. But there is a professional as well as a public responsibility to place 9/11 in a historical context and interpretive field that reaches beyond the immediacy of personal tragedy and official injury. Otherwise 9/11 will be remembered not for the attack itself but for the increasing cycles of violence that follow.

If 9/11 is not wholly new, what is it? As we have seen too well, the official response was a struggle of evil against good – of which, given the rhetorical excess deemed necessary by our leaders to mobilize the public to action, there have been more than a few cases in American history. As an actual practice of warfare we again received a better picture of what 9/11 is not than what it is: from the President and Secretary of Defense and on down the food chain of the national security hierarchy, we heard that this would not be the Gulf War or Kosovo, and it most definitely would not be Vietnam or Mogadishu. And they were partially right – certainly more so than commentators from the kneejerk factions of both the right and left, who flooded the airwaves with sloppy historical analogies from the Second World War (Pearl Harbor and the Reichstag fire being most prominent) and convergent conspiracy theories (the Israeli Mossad and Big Oil pulling all the strings).

From my perspective, new and old forms of representation and violence synergized on 9/11. The neo-medieval rhetoric of holy war reverberated from the minaret to the television and, at an unprecedented level, to the internet. A hyper-modern war of simulation and surveillance was played out at flight schools, airports and in practically every nook, cranny and cave of Afghanistan. A remote aerial war was directed from Central Command in Tampa, Florida, 7750 miles away from targets that were surveyed by drone aircraft like the Predator and Global Hawk, and destroyed by smart GPS-guided JDAMs (Joint Direct Attack Munitions with a circular error probability of about 10 feet), CBU-87 and CBU-103 'cluster bombs' (Combined Effects Munitions containing over 200 bomblets that have anti-tank, anti-personnel as well as an incendiary capability), and dumb bombs, topped by the 15,000 pound 'Daisy-cutter' (BLU-82) that explodes 3 feet above the ground and incinerates anything within 600 yards. And in a dirty war of blood and bluff, special operations forces led an anti-Taliban coalition in a limited and, by early reports, highly successful land campaign.

This strange new hybrid of conflict fully qualifies, perverse as it might sound, as a *virtuous war.* Post-Vietnam, post-Cold War, post-modern, virtuous war emerged prior to 9/11, from the battlespace of the Gulf War and the aerial campaigns of Bosnia and Kosovo in which the killing was kept, as much as it was technologically and ethically possible, virtual and virtuous. Virtuous war relies on computer simulation, media manipulation, global surveillance and networked warfare to deter, discipline and, if need be, destroy potential enemies. It draws on just war doctrine (when possible) and holy war (when necessary). Post-9/11, virtuous war now looks to be the ultimate means by which the US intends to re-secure its borders, maintain its hegemony and bring a modicum of order if not justice back to international politics. The difference from pre-9/11 is that the virtual enemy – at least at home – now comes with a face (indeed, 22 faces; all of them displayed on the FBI's new website of most-wanted terrorists[11]).

In the name of the holy trinity of international order – global free markets, democratic sovereign states and limited humanitarian interventions – the US has led the way in a revolution in military affairs (RMA) which underlies virtuous war. At the heart as well as the muscle of this transformation is the technical capability and ethical imperative to threaten and, if necessary, actualize violence from a distance – but again, with minimal casualties when possible. commentators like Ignatieff or Rothstein. In official circles, there was a concerted effort to fence off the void: the critical use of language, imagination, even humour, was tightly delimited by moral sanctions and government warnings. This first strike against critical thought took the peculiar form of a semantic debate over the meaning of 'coward'. In the *New Yorker* and on *Politically Incorrect*, the question was raised of whether it is more cowardly to commandeer a commercial airliner and pilot it into the World Trade Center, to bomb Serbians from 15,000 feet, or to direct a cruise missile attack against bin Laden from several thousand miles away. The official response was swift, with advertisements yanked, talk show condemnations, and Ari Fleischer, White House Press Secretary, saying that people like Bill Maher of *Politically Incorrect* 'should watch what they say, watch what they do'.

Other protected zones of language began to take shape. When Reuters news agency questioned the abuse-into-meaningless of the term 'terrorism', George Will, on a Sunday morning news programme, retaliated by advocating a boycott of Reuters.[12] Irony and laughter were permitted in some places, not in others. At a Defense Department press conference Secretary of Defense Rumsfeld could ridicule, and effectively disarm, a reporter who dared to ask if anyone in the Department of Defense would be authorized to lie to the news media.[13] President Bush was given room to joke in a morale-boosting visit to the CIA, saying that he had been 'spending a lot of quality time lately' with George Tenet, the director of the CIA.[14] And then there was *New York Times* reporter Edward Rothstein, taking his opportunistic shot at postmodernists and post-colonialists, claiming that their irony and relativism was 'ethically perverse' and produced a 'guilty passivity'.[15] Some of us were left wondering where that view would place fervent truth-seekers and serious enemies of relativism and irony like Osama bin Laden: terrorist foe but epistemological ally?

The Mimetic War of Images

The air war started on October 7, 2001, with a split-screen war of images: in one box, a desolate Kabul seen through a nightscope camera lens, in grainy-green pixels except for the occasional white arc of anti-aircraft fire followed by the flash of an explosion; in the other, a rotating cast of characters, beginning with President Bush, followed over the course of that day and the next by Secretary of Defense Rumsfeld, Chairman of the Joint Chiefs General Meyers and Attorney-General John Ashcroft, then progressively down the media food chain of war reporters, beltway pundits and recently retired generals. On the one side we witnessed images of embodied resolve in high resolution; on the other, nighttime shadows with nobody in sight.

Strategic and narrative binaries cropped up in President Bush's war statement, incongruously delivered from the Treaty Room of the White House: 'as we strike military targets, we will also drop food'; the United States is 'a friend to the Afghan people' and 'an enemy of those who aid terrorists'; 'the only way to pursue peace is to pursue those who threaten it'. And once more, the ultimate either/or was issued: 'Every nation has a choice to make. In this conflict there is no neutral ground.'[16]

However, the war programming was interrupted by the media-savvy bin Laden. Shortly after the air strikes began, he appeared on Qatar's al-Jazeera television network ('the Arab world's CNN') in a pre-taped statement that was cannily delivered as a counter air-strike to the US. Kitted out in turban and battle fatigues, bin Laden presented his own bipolar view of the world: 'These events have divided the world into two camps, the camp of the faithful and the camp of infidels.' But if opposition constituted his world view, it was a historical mimic battle that sanctioned the counter-violence: 'America has been filled with horror from north to south and east to west, and thanks be to God what America is tasting now is only a copy of what we have tasted.'[17]

Without falling into the trap of 'moral equivalency', one can discern striking similarities. Secretary of Defense Rumsfeld and others have made much of the 'asymmetrical' war being waged by the terrorists. And it is indeed a canny and even diabolical use of asymmetrical tactics as well as strategies when terrorists commandeer commercial aircraft and transform them into kinetic weapons of indiscriminate violence – and then deploy commercial media to counter the military strikes that follow. Yet a fearful symmetry is also at work at an uneonscious, possibly pathological level; a war of escalating and competing and imitative oppositions, a *mimetic war of images*.

A mimetic war is a battle of imitation and representation, in which the relationship of who we are and who they are is played out along a wide spectrum of familiarity and friendliness, indifference and tolerance, estrangement and hostility. It can result in appreciation or denigration, accommodation or separation, assimilation or extermination. It draws physical boundaries between peoples, as well as metaphysical boundaries between life and the most radical other of life, death. It separates human from god. It builds the fence that makes good neighbours; it builds the wall that confines a whole people. And it sanctions just about every kind of violence. President Bush announces that Iran is now part of the 'axis of evil'; Iran complies by staging the first large-scale anti-American demonstration since the moderate Khatami regime came to power.

More than a rational calculation of interests takes us to war. People go to war because of how they see, perceive, picture, imagine and speak of others; that is, how they construct the difference of others as well as the sameness of themselves through representations. From Greek tragedy and Roman gladiatorial spectacles to futurist art and fascist rallies, the mimetic mix of image and violence has proven to be more powerful than the most rational discourse. Indeed, the medical definition of mimesis is 'the appearance, often caused by hysteria, of symptoms of a disease not actually present'. Before one can find a cure, one must study the symptoms – or, as it was once known in medical science, practise *semiology.*

Mime-net

It was not long before morbid symptoms began to surface from an array of terror and counter-terror networks. Al-Qaeda members reportedly used encrypted email to communicate; steganography to hide encoded messages in web images (including pornography); Kinko's and public library computers to send messages; underground banking networks called *hawala* to transfer untraceable funds; 24/7 cable networks like al-Jazeera and CNN to get the word out; and, in their preparations for 9/11, a host of other information technologies like rented cell phones, online travel agencies, and flight simulators.

In general, networks – from television primetime to internet real-time – delivered events with an alacrity and celerity that left not only viewers but also decision makers racing to keep up. With information as the life-blood and speed as the killer variable of networks, getting inside the decision making as well the image making loop of the opponent became the central strategy of network warfare. This was not lost on the American national security team as it struggled after the initial attack to get ahead of the network curve. Sluggish reactions were followed by quicker pre-emptive actions on multiple networks. Congress passed the 'Uniting and Strengthening America by Providing Appropriate Tools Required to Intercept and Obstruct Terrorism (USA PATRIOT) Act', which allowed for 'roving wiretaps' of multiple telephones, easier surveillance of email and internet traffic, more sharing between foreign and domestic intelligence, and the divulgence of grand jury and wiretap transcripts to intelligence agencies.[18] National Security adviser Condoleeza Rice made personal calls to heads of the television networks, asking them to pre-screen and to consider editing al-Qaeda videos for possible coded messages.[19] Information about the air campaign as well as the unfolding ground interventions was heavily filtered by the Pentagon, which set up an Office of Strategic Influence' to correct unfavourable news reports and, supposedly, to plant favourable ones in the foreign press. Open information flows slowed to a trickle from the White House and the Defense Department after tough restrictions were imposed against leaks. Psychological operations were piggy-backed on to humanitarian interventions by the dropping of propaganda leaflets and food packs. The Voice of America began broadcasting anti-Taliban messages in Pashto. After the 22 'Most Wanted Terrorists' were featured on the FBI's website, the popular TV programme *America's Most Wanted* ran an extended program on their individual cases. The infowar was on.

Counter/terror Dangers

Terror came to America on 9/11 not by rogue state or ballistic missile or high-tech biological, chemical and nuclear weapons of mass destruction – as presaged by the intelligence and national security experts – but by an unholy network, hijacked airliners and the terrorist's favourite 'force-multiplier', primetime, cable and internet weapons of mass distraction and disruption. Have we learned the right lessons since then? Or will the 'evil' regimes, missiles and high-tech create more blindspots from which new threats will emerge with devastating effects? What lies ahead?

My greatest concern is not so much the future as how past futures become reproduced; that is, how we seem unable to escape the feedback loops of bad intelligence, bureaucratic thinking and failed imagination. From my own experience, when confronted by the complexity and speed of networked conflicts, the fields of political science and international relations are too slow to respond when it matters most. This leaves another intellectual void into which policy makers, military planners and media pundits are always ready to rush. Currently the RMA-mantra among the techno-optimists in the Pentagon is to swiftly implement 'network-centric warfare'. As first formulated by Vice Admiral Arthur Cebrowski (formerly President of the Naval War College and hand-picked by Defense Secretary Rumsfeld to head the Pentagon's new Office of Force Transformation), network-centric war is fought by getting inside the decision making loop of the adversary's network and disrupting or destroying it before it can do the same to yours. The basic idea is that people make war as they make wealth, and, in the information age, networked technology has become the enabler of both (probably not a view currently shared by Enron stockholders). Information and speed are now the key variables in warfare: whoever has the fastest network wins.

The shift from state-centric to network-centric modes of deterring and defeating new threats makes sense within a rational framework. However, diminishing the role of human decisions, *especially* ones in which emotion plays such a significant part, might not be the best way to confront future threats of terrorism. Furthermore, after the Pentagon released the bin Laden home video in December, where dreams and theology mix with strategies of destruction and slaughter, there was little evidence of any kind of rational purchase for a network-centric deterrence to work.[20] And after witnessing that same day the revival of missile defence as the *deus ex machina* cure for American vulnerability, the consignment of 'lower levels of decision making' to networked technology seems practically (rather than as it had been in the past, mutually) suicidal.

It is clear that the allure of technological solutions reaches across cultures and often beyond rationality. Bandwidth as well as bombs might offer short-term fixes for the immediate threats posed by terrorism. But no matter how weak the flesh, neural networks, human spirit and political will are still needed to make the future safe again. In the rush to harden and to accelerate networks, all kinds of checks and balances are being left behind. There seems to be little concern for what organizational theorists see as the negative synergy operating in tightly coupled systems, in which unintended consequences produce cascading effects and normal accidents, in which the very complexity and supposed redundancy of the network produce unforeseen but built-in disasters. Think Three Mile Island in a pre-1914.

My second concern is as much political as it is theoretical: are the social sciences intrinsically unsuited for the kind of investigation demanded by the emergence of a military–industrial–media–entertainment network? President Eisenhower in his 1961 farewell address famously warned the US of the emergence of a 'military–industrial complex', and of what might happen should 'public policy be captured by a scientific and technological elite'. Now that Silicon Valley and Hollywood have been added to the mix, the dangers have morphed and multiplied. Think *Wag the Dog* meets *The Matrix*. Think of C. Wright Mills' power elite with much better gear to reproduce reality.

So, for the near future, virtuous war as played out by the military-industrial-media-entertainment network will be our daily bread and nightly circus. Some would see us staying there, suspended perpetually, in between wars of terror and counter-terror. How do we break out of the distractive, often self-prophesying circles? Are there theoretical approaches that can respond critically without falling into the trap of the interwar? One that can escape the nullity of thought which equates the desire to comprehend with a willingness to condone terrorism? The use of sloppy analogies of resistance as well as petty infighting among critics does not give one much hope. We need to acknowledge that the majority of Americans, whether out of patriotism, trauma, apathy or sheer reasonableness, think it best to leave matters in the hands of the experts. That will not change, the cycle will not be broken, until a public rather than expert assessment is made of what distinguishes new from old dangers, real from virtual effects, terror from counter-terror – and whether we are then ready to live with new levels of uncertainty about those very distinctions.

Otherwise, the last word might well come from the first words I heard of the last war the US fought. Circling ten years ago over Chicago O'Hare airport, the captain came on the PA to inform us that the bombing of Iraq had just begun. In the taxi on the way to my hotel, I heard the first radio reports of stealth aircraft, smart bombs and incredibly low casualty rates. But what stuck from that evening were the last and only words of my cab driver. In the thickest Russian accent, in a terribly war-weary voice, without the benefit of any context but the overexcitement of the radio reports, he said: 'They told us we would be in Afghanistan for ten weeks. We were there for ten years.'

Notes

1. This chapter draws from earlier postings at <www.infopeace.org>,<http://www.ssrc.org/sept11/essays/der_derian.htm>and<http://muse.jhu.edu/journals/theory_&_event>.
2. '*in terrorem*, as a warning, in order to terrify or deter others' (*Oxford English Dictionary*).
3. Walter Benjamin, *A Lyric Poet in the Era of High Capitalism* (London: Verso, 1997).
4. For an earlier discussion of the ideological, epistemological and ontological obstacles facing any enquiry into terrorism, see my 'The Terrorist Discourse: Signs, States, and Systems of Global Political Violence', *Antidiplomacy: Spies, Terror, Speed, and War* (Cambridge, MA, and Oxford: Blackwell, 1992), pp. 92–126.
5. Michael Ignatieff, 'It's War – But It Doesn't Have to Be Dirty', *Guardian*, October 1, 2001.
6. George Will, 'On the Health of the State', *Newsweek*, October 1, 2001, p. 70.
7. Edward Rothstein, 'Attacks on US Challenge the Perspectives of Postmodern True Believers', *New York Times*, September 22, 2001, p. A17.
8. Mark Edington, *New York Times*, March 2, 1993.
9. *Newsweek*, March 8, 1993, p. 22.
10. *Sunday Times*, February 28, 1993, p. 10.
11. See <http://www.fb.gov/mostwant/terrorists/fugitives.htm>.
12. *ABC Sunday News*, September 30, 2001.
13. See <http://www.defenselink.mil/news/Sep2001/to9252001_to925sd.html>.
14. See <http://www.washingtonpost.com/wp-srv/nation/specials/attacked/transcripts/bushtext-092601.html>.
15. See *New York Times*, September 22, 2001 (<http://query.nytimes.com/search/abstract? res=FA091FF6355FOC718EDDA00894D9404482>).
16. See <http://www.whitehouse.gov/news/releases/2001/10/20011007–8.html>.
17. See <http://www.cnn.com/2002/US/01/31/gen.binladen.interview/index.html>.
18. See<http://www.eff.org/Privacy/Survillance/Terrorism_militias/20011025_hr3162_usa_patriot_bill.html>.
19. In a videotape interview with the Arabic cable network, al-Jazeera (which they never aired but was partially seen on January 31 on CNN), bin Laden displayed his affinity for information technology while scoffing at the White House 'request' that American television networks not broadcast his statements: 'They made hilarious claims. They said that Osama's messages have codes in them to the terrorists. It's as if we were living in the time of mail by carrier pigeon, when there are no phones, no travelers, no Internet, no regular mail, no express mail and no electronic mail.'

    See <http://www.washingtonpost.com/wp-dyn/articles/A5371–2002Jan31.html>.
20. See <http://www.defenselink.mil/news/Dec2001/b12132001_bt630–01.html>.

Jihad in the Cause of Allah

SAYYID QUTB

Sayyid Qutb's writings provide the scholarly basis for the Muslim Brotherhood movement in Egypt. Like other members of the Muslim Brotherhood, Qutb suffered at the hands of Nassar's Arab nationalist government. He was executed in 1966. A trenchant critic of secular Egyptian society, Qutb's work was based on a careful reading of the Koran as the correct basis for society. This excerpt is taken from *Milestones*, which contained Qutb's recommendations for purifying the increasingly secular Muslim world. What are the ways in which Qutb believes modern society has lost its way?

The great scholar Ibn Qayyim, in his book *Zad al-Ma'ad,* has a chapter entitled "The Prophet's Treatment of the Unbelievers and the Hypocrites from the Beginning of his Messengership Until his Death." In this chapter, he sums up the nature of Islamic Jihad.

"The first revelation from Allah that came to the Prophet—peace be on him—was *'Iqra. bism Rabbika ladhi Khalaqa.'* ("Read, in the name of they Sustainer. Who created".).

This was the beginning of his Prophethood. Allah commanded the Prophet—peace he on him—to recite this in his heart. The commandment to preach had not yet come Then Allah revealed *Ya ayyuba al-Muddatbir, qum fandbir'* ("O you who are enwrapped in your mantle, arise and warn"). Thus, the revelation of "Iqra" was his appointment to Prophethood, while *'Ya ayyuba al muddatbir'* was his appointment to Messengership. Later Allah commanded the Prophet—peace be on him—to warn his near relatives, then his people, then the Arabs who were around them, then all of Arabia, and finally the whole world. Thus for thirteen years after the beginning of his Messengership, he called people to Allah through preaching, without fighting or *fizyab*, and was commanded to restrain himself and to practice patience and forhearance. Then he was commanded to migrate, and later permission was given to fight. Then he was commanded to fight those who fought him, and to restrain himself from those who did not make war against him. Later he was commanded to fight the polytheists until Allah's *din* was fully established. After the command for jibad came, the non-believers were divided into three categories: those with whom the Muslims had peace treaties; the people with whom the Muslims were at war: and the *abimmies.* The Prophet was commanded that as long as the non-believers with whom he had a peace treaty met their obligations, he should fulfil the articles of the treaty, but if they broke the treaty, then they should be given notice that he considered the treaty broken. Until then, no war should be declared. If they persisted, then he should fight them. When the *Surab Bara'ab* was revealed, the details of treatment concerning these three categories of non-believers were described.

Sayyid Qutb, *Milestones*, pages 43–48, 50, 58–59, 61–62. Reprinted with permission from Kazi Publications.

It was also explained that war should be declared only against those from among the 'People of the Book' who declare open enmity, until they agree to pay *jizyah* or accept Islam. Concerning the polytheists and the hypocrites, it was commanded in this surah that jihad be declared against them and that they he treated sternly. The Prophet—peace he on him—carried on jihad against the polytheists by fighting and against the hypocrites by preaching and argument. In the same surah, it was commanded that the treaties with the polytheists be terminated at the end of their agreed term. In this respect, the people with whom there were treaties were divided into three categories: first, those who broke the treaty and failed to keep its terms. He was ordered to fight against them and was victorious. Then there were those with whom the treaty was made for a stated term, and who had neither violated this treaty nor helped anyone against the Prophet, peace be on him. Regarding them, Allah commanded that these treaties be completed to their full term. The third category consisted of those with whom there was no treaty but they were not at war against the Prophet, peace be on him, or those with whom he had a treaty without any stated term of expiration. Concerning these, it was commanded that they he given four months' notice, at the end of which they should he considered open enemies and engaged in combat. Thus, those who broke the treaty were fought against, and those who did not have any treaty or had an indeterminate period of expiration were given four months' period of grace, and terms were kept with those whose treaty was due to expire. Those in the last category embraced Islam even before the term expired, and the non-Muslims paid *jizyah*. Thus, after the revelation of the *surab Bara'ah,* the unbelievers were of three kinds: adversaries in war, people with treaties, and *dbimmies.* The people with treaties eventually became Muslims, so there were only two kinds left: people at war and *dbimmies.* The people at war were always afraid of him. Now the people of the whole world were of three kinds: the Muslims who believed in him: those with whom he had peace; and the opponents who kept fighting against him. As far as the hypocrites were concerned, Allah commanded the Prophet, peace be on him, to accept their appearances and leave their intentions to Allah, and carry on jihad against them by argument and persuasion. He was commanded not to pray at their funerals nor at their graves, nor to ask forgiveness of Allah for them, because their affair was with Allah. So this was the practice of the Prophet, peace be on him, concerning his enemies among the non-believers and the hypocrites.

In this description we find a summary of the stages of Islamic jihad presented in an excellent manner. In it we also find all the distinctive characteristics of the dynamic movement of the true *din* or way of life. We should ponder over them seriously. Here, however, we will confine ourselves to a few explanatory remarks.

First, the method of this *din* is very practical. This Islamic movement treats people as they actually are and uses resources that are available in the best manner possible under the prevalent conditions. Since this movement comes into conflict with a *jabiliyyab* that prevails over ideas and beliefs, and which shapes and controls practically all life, and enjoys full support of political and economic powers, the Islamic movement had to come up with parallel means and resources to confront this *jabiliyyab.* This movement uses the methods of preaching and persuasion to reform ideas and beliefs. And it uses physical power and jihad to abolish the organizations and authorities of the *jabili* system which prevent people from reforming their ideas and beliefs, forces them to follow deviant ways, and make them serve other humans instead of their Almighty Lord. This movement does not confine itself to mere preaching to confront physical power, just as it also does not use compulsion to change the ideas of people. These two principles are equally important in the method of the Islamic *din.* Its purpose is to free those people who wish to be freed from enslavement to men so that they may serve Allah alone.

The second aspect of this *din* as a practical movement is its progression stage by stage, so that at every stage it provides resources to meet the practical needs of a particular situation while at the same time preparing the ground for the next one. It does not face practical problems with abstract theories, nor does it confront various stages with unchangeable means. Many who talk about jihad in Islam and quote Qur'anic verses do not take into account this aspect, nor do they understand the nature of the various stages through which this movement develops, or the relationship of the verses revealed at various occasions to each stage. Thus, when they speak about jihad, they may speak clumsily and mix up the various stages, distorting the whole concept of jihad in an effort to use the Qur'anic text to establish general principles and rules for which there exists no justification. This is because they regard every verse of the Qur'an as if it were the final principle of the *din*. This group of thinkers, which is a product of the sorry state of the present Muslim generation, has nothing but the label of Islam and has laid down its spiritual and rational arms in defeat. They say. "Islam has prescribed only defensive war" and think that they have done some good for their faith by divesting it of its method, which is to abolish all injustice from the earth, to bring people to the worship of Allah alone, and to bring them out of servitude to servants into the service of the Lord of servants. Islam does not force people to accept its belief, but it wants to provide a free environment in which they will have the choice to believe. What it wants to abolish is those oppressive political systems under which people are prevented from expressing their freedom to choose whatever beliefs they want, and after that it gives them complete freedom to decide whether to accept Islam or not.

A third aspect of this universal *din* is the compatibility of the new resources or methods which it used during its progressive movement with its fundamental principles and aims. From the very first day. whether the Prophet, peace be on him, addressed his near relatives, or the Quraish, or the Arabs, or the entire world, his call was one and the same. He called them to submit to One Lord and to reject the lordship of other men. On this principle there is no compromise nor any flexibility. To attain this purpose, it proceeds according to a plan, which has certain stages, and every stage has its own resources, as we have just described.

A fourth aspect of the Islamic movement is the legal basis it provides for the relationship of the Muslim community with other groups, as is clear from the quotation from *Zad al-Ma'ad*. This legal formulation is based on the principle that Islam—that is, submission to Allah—is a universal Message which the whole of mankind should either accept or accommodate. No political system or material power should put obstacles in the way of preaching Islam. Every government and nation should leave every individual free to accept or reject it. If someone wants to accept Islam, no one should prevent him or fight him. If someone does so, then it is the duty of Islam to fight him until he either is killed or declares his submission.

When writers with defeatist and apologetic mentalities write about "jihad in Islam," and try to remove this 'blot' from Islam, they mix up two things: first, this *din* forbids the imposition of its belief by force, as is clear from the verse: "There is no compulsion in religion." Secondly, it tries to annihilate all those political and material powers that stand between people and Islam, which forces some people to bow before other people and prevent them from accepting the sovereignty of Allah. These two principles are independent of each other, and there is no justification for mixing them up. These defeatists, however, mix the two aspects confining jihad to what today is called 'defensive war'. The Islamic jihad has no relationship to modern warfare, either in its causes or in the way in which it is conducted. The causes of Islamic jihad should be sought in the very nature of Islam and its role in the world, and in its high principles, assigned to it hy Allah and for the implementation of which Allah sent the Prophet, peace be on him, as His Messenger and declared him to be the last of all Prophets and Messengers.

This *din* is a universal declaration of the freedom of man from slavery to other men and to his own desires, which is also a form of human servitude. It is a declaration that the sovereignty belongs only to Allah, the Lord of all the worlds. It challenges all such systems based on the concept of the sovereignty of man, i.e., where man attempts to usurp the attribute of Divine sovereignty. Any system in which the final decisions are referred to human beings, and in which the source of all authority are men, deifies human beings by designating others than Allah as lords over men. This declaration means the usurped authority of Allah be returned to Him and the usurpers thrown out—those who by themselves devise laws for others, elevating themselves to the status of lords and reducing others to the status of slaves. In short, to proclaim the authority and sovereignty of Allah means to eliminate all human kingships and to announce the rule of the Sustainer of the universe over the entire earth. In the words of the Qur'an:

> He alone is God in heaven and on earth.[1]
> The command belongs to Allah alone. He commands you not to worship anyone except Him. This is the right way of life.[2]
> Say: O People of the Book come to what is common between us: that we will not worship anyone except Allah, and will not associate anything with Him, and will not take lords from among ourselves besides Allah: and if they turn away, then tell them to bear witness that we are those who have submitted to Allah.[3]

The way to establish the rule of Allah on earth is not to give some consecrated people—the priests—the authority to rule, as was the case with the rule of the Church, nor to appoint some spokesmen of Allah as rulers, as is the case in a 'theocracy'. To establish Allah's rule means to enforce His laws so the final decision in all affairs be according to these laws.

Preaching alone is not enough to establish the dominion of Allah on earth, to abolish the dominion of man, to take away sovereignty from the usurper and return it to Allah, and to bring about the enforcement of the Divine *shari'ah* and the abolition of man-made laws. Those who have usurped the authority of Allah and are oppressing Allah's creatures are not going to give up their power merely through preaching. If it had been so, the task of establishing the *din* of Allah in the world would have been very easy for the Prophets of Allah! This is contrary to the evidence from the history of the Prophets and from the struggle of uncounted generations.

This universal declaration of the freedom of man on earth from every authority except that of Allah, and the declaration that sovereignty belongs to Allah alone and that He is the Lord of the universe, is not merely a theoretical, philosophical, and passive proclamation. It is a positive, practical, and dynamic message with a view to bringing about the implementation of the *shari'ah* of Allah and actually freeing people from their servitude to other men in order to bring them into the service of Allah, the One without rivals. This cannot be attained unless both "preaching" and "the movement" are used. This is so because appropriate means are needed to meet any and every practical situation.

Anyone who understands this particular character of the *din* will also understand the purpose of *jihad bil saif* (striving by the sword), which is to clear the way for freedom to strive through preaching in support of the Islamic movement. He will understand that Islam is not a "defensive movement" in today's narrow technical sense of "defensive war." This narrow meaning is ascribed to it by those who are puzzled under the pressure of circumstances and are confused by the wily attacks of the Orientalists, who distort the concept of Islamic jihad. It is a movement to wipe out tyranny and to introduce true freedom to mankind, using resources practically available in a given human situation, and it had definite stages, for each of which it utilized new methods.

If we insist on calling Islamic jihad a defensive movement, then we must change the meaning of the word "defense" and mean by it "the defense of man" against all those forces that limit his freedom. These forces may take the form of beliefs and concepts, as well of political systems based on economic, racial, or class distinctions. At the advent of Islam the world was full of such systems just as the present-day *jahiliyyah* abounds in various systems.

When we take this broad meaning of the word "defense," we understand the true character of Islam, in that it proclaims the universal freedom of every person and community from servitude to any other individual or society, the end of man's arrogance and selfishness, the establishment of the sovereignty of Allah and His Lordship throughout the world, and the rule of the Divine *shari'ah* in human affairs.

Those superficial thinkers who interpret Islamic jihad in the narrow sense of defensive war, claim that the battles fought in Islamic jihad were all for the defense of the homeland of Islam—some of them considering the homeland of Islam to be just the Arabian peninsula—against the aggression of neighboring powers. These people fail to understand the nature of Islam and its primary aim.

The purpose of jihad in Islam is to secure complete freedom for every man throughout the world by releasing him from servitude to other human beings so that he may serve Allah. Who is One and who has no associates. This is what motivated the early Muslims to fight in the cause of Allah. If they had been asked, "Why are you fighting?" none would have answered. "My country is in danger; I am fighting for its defense," or "The Persians and the Romans have attacked us," or "We want to extend our dominion and want more spoils." They would have answered the same as Raba'i ibn Amer. Huzaifa ibn Muhsin and Mughira ibn Sh'uba answered when the persian general Rustum asked them one by one during three successive days before the battle of Qadisiyyah: "For what purpose have you come?" Their answer was the same: "Allah has sent us to bring anyone who wishes from servitude to men into the service of Allah alone, from the narrowness of this world into the vastness of the hereafter, and from the tyranny of religions into the justice of Islam. Allah raised a Messenger for this purpose to teach His creatures His way. If anyone accepts this way of life, we turn back and give his country back to him, and we fight with those who rebel until we are martyred or become victorious." These are the reasons inherent in the very nature of the universal *din*. Similarly, its proclamation of universal freedom, its practical way of combating actual human conditions with appropriate methods, its development of new resources at various stages, has also been inherent in its message from the very beginning, and not because of any threat of aggression against Islamic lands or against the Muslims residing in them. The reason for jihad lies in the nature of its message and in the actual conditions it finds in human societies, and not merely in the necessity for defense, which may be temporary and of limited extent. A Muslim fights with his wealth and his person "in the way of Allah" for the sake of these values in which for him neither personal gain nor greed is a motive.

Before a Muslim steps into the battlefield, he has already fought a great battle within himself against Satan, against his own desires and ambitions, his personal interests and inclinations, the interests of his family and of his nation: against anything that is not from Islam; against every obstacle that comes into the way of worshipping Allah and implementing the Divine authority on earth by returning this authority to Allah and taking it away from the rebellious usurpers.

Those who say that Islamic jihad was merely for the defense of the "homeland of Islam" diminish the greatness of the Islamic way of life and consider it less important than their "homeland." This is not the Islamic point of view; it is a creation of the modern age and is completely alien to Islamic consciousness. The soil of the homeland has, in itself, no value or weight. From the Islamic point of view, any homeland has value only to the extent that on it the rule of Allah is established and His guidance is followed, so that the homeland becomes a fortress for Islamic belief, a homeland for its way of life, and a center for the movement for the total freedom of man, so that one's homeland becomes a "homeland for Islam." In this case the defense of the "homeland of Islam" means the defense of Islamic beliefs, the Islamic way of life and the Islamic community. This, however, is not the ultimate objective of the Islamic movement of jihad but is a means to establish the Divine authority within making it the headquarters for the movement of Islam, which is then to be carried throughout the world to the whole of mankind, because the object of this *din* is all humanity and its sphere of action is the whole earth.

Indeed, Islam has the right to take the initiative. Islam is not a heritage of any particular race or country. This is Allah's *din* and it is for the whole world. It has the right to destroy all obstacles in the form of institutions and traditions that restrict man's freedom of choice. It does not attack individuals nor does it force them to accept its beliefs. It attacks institutions and traditions in order to release human beings from their pernicious influence, which distorts human nature and curtails human freedom.

Islam has the obligation and the right to release mankind from servitude to human beings so that they may serve Allah alone, and so give practical meaning to its declaration that Allah is the true

Lord of all and that all men are free under Him. According to the Islamic concept and in actuality. Allah's rule on earth can be established only through the Islamic system, as it is the only system ordained by Allah for all human beings, whether they be rulers or ruled, black or white, poor or rich, ignorant or learned, it has the same law for all, and all human beings are equally responsible within it. In all other systems, human beings obey other human beings and follow man-made laws. Legislation is a Divine attribute. Any person who concedes this right to any human claimant, whether he considers him Divine or not, in reality accepts him as Divine.

Islam organizes its followers in its own way which the hostile societies seldom tolerate; they seek to put obstructions In its path. This leaves no option for Islam but to fight against them in order to remove all obstacles from the path to universal human freedom. Only in this manner can life be wholly dedicated to Allah.

Notes

1 Qur'an 43.84
2 Qur'an 12:40
3 Qur'an 3:64

Text of Fatwah Urging Jihad Against Americans

OSAMA BIN LADEN

When this Fatwah (a statement of religious basis for action) appeared in 1998, few people outside of specialist government agencies noticed. However, after the attacks of September 11, 2001, Al-Qaeda and Osama Bin-Laden became household names, certainly in the United States, and perhaps globally. What are the three crimes the United States committed against Islam, according to this Fatwah? If the United States changes its behavior, what will result? What do you think the reference to "defeat[ing] factionalism" in the first paragraph means?

Statement signed by Sheikh Usamah Bin-Muhammad Bin-Ladin; Ayman al-Zawahiri, leader of the Jihad Group in Egypt; Abu- Yasir Rifa'i Ahmad Taha, a leader of the Islamic Group; Sheikh Mir Hamzah, secretary of the Jamiat-ul-Ulema-e-Pakistan; and Fazlul Rahman, leader of the Jihad Movement in Bangladesh

Praise be to God, who revealed the Book, controls the clouds, defeats factionalism, and says in His Book "But when the forbidden months are past, then fight and slay the pagans wherever ye find them, seize them, beleaguer them, and lie in wait for them in every stratagem (of war)"; and peace be upon our Prophet, Muhammad Bin-'Abdallah, who said "I have been sent with the sword between my hands to ensure that no one but God is worshipped, God who put my livelihood under the shadow of my spear and who inflicts humiliation and scorn on those who disobey my orders." The Arabian Peninsula has never—since God made it flat, created its desert, and encircled it with seas—been stormed by any forces like the crusader armies now spreading in it like locusts, consuming its riches and destroying its plantations. All this is happening at a time when nations are attacking Muslims like people fighting over a plate of food. In the light of the grave situation and the lack of support, we and you are obliged to discuss current events, and we should all agree on how to settle the matter.

No one argues today about three facts that are known to everyone; we will list them, in order to remind everyone:

First, for over seven years the United States has been occupying the lands of Islam in the holiest of places, the Arabian Peninsula, plundering its riches, dictating to its rulers, humiliating its people, terrorizing its neighbors, and turning its bases in the Peninsula into a spearhead through which to fight the neighboring Muslim peoples.

If some people have formerly debated the fact of the occupation, all the people of the Peninsula have now acknowledged it.

The best proof of this is the Americans' continuing aggression against the Iraqi people using the Peninsula as a staging post, even though all its rulers are against their territories being used to that end, still they are helpless. Second, despite the great devastation inflicted on the Iraqi people by the crusader-Zionist alliance, and despite the huge number of those killed, in excess of 1 million... despite all this, the Americans are once against trying to repeat the horrific massacres, as though they are not content with the protracted blockade imposed after the ferocious war or the fragmentation and devastation.

So now they come to annihilate what is left of this people and to humiliate their Muslim neighbors.

Third, if the Americans' aims behind these wars are religious and economic, the aim is also to serve the Jews' petty state and divert attention from its occupation of Jerusalem and murder of Muslims there.

The best proof of this is their eagerness to destroy Iraq, the strongest neighboring Arab state, and their endeavor to fragment all the states of the region such as Iraq, Saudi Arabia, Egypt, and Sudan into paper statelets and through their disunion and weakness to guarantee Israel's survival and the continuation of the brutal crusade occupation of the Peninsula.

All these crimes and sins committed by the Americans are a clear declaration of war on God, his messenger, and Muslims. And ulema have throughout Islamic history unanimously agreed that the jihad is an individual duty if the enemy destroys the Muslim countries. This was revealed by Imam Bin-Qadamah in "Al- Mughni," Imam al-Kisa'i in "Al- Bada'i," al-Qurtubi in his interpretation, and the shaykh of al-Islam in his books, where he said "As for the militant struggle, it is aimed at defending sanctity and religion, and it is a duty as agreed. Nothing is more sacred than belief except repulsing an enemy who is attacking religion and life."

On that basis, and in compliance with God's order, we issue the following fatwa to all Muslims

The ruling to kill the Americans and their allies—civilians and military—is an individual duty for every Muslim who can do it in any country in which it is possible to do it, in order to liberate the al-Aqsa Mosque and the holy mosque from their grip, and in order for their armies to move out of all the lands of Islam, defeated and unable to threaten any Muslim. This is in accordance with the words of Almighty God, "and fight the pagans all together as they fight you all together," and "fight them until there is no more tumult or oppression, and there prevail justice and faith in God."

This is in addition to the words of Almighty God "And why should ye not fight in the cause of God and of those who, being weak, are ill-treated and oppressed–women and children, whose cry is 'Our Lord, rescue us from this town, whose people are oppressors; and raise for us from thee one who will help!' "

We – with God's help – call on every Muslim who believes in God and wishes to be rewarded to comply with God's order to kill the Americans and plunder their money wherever and whenever they find it. We also call on Muslim ulema, leaders, youths, and soldiers to launch the raid on Satan's U.S. troops and the devil's supporters allying with them, and to displace those who are behind them so that they may learn a lesson.

Almighty God said "O ye who believe, give your response to God and His Apostle, when He calleth you to that which will give you life. And know that

God cometh between a man and his heart, and that it is He to whom ye shall all be gathered."

Almighty God also says "O ye who believe, what is the matter with you, that when ye are asked to go forth in the cause of God, ye cling so heavily to the earth! Do ye prefer the life of this world to the hereafter? But little is the comfort of this life, as compared with the hereafter. Unless ye go forth, He will punish you with a grievous penalty, and put others in your place; but Him ye would not harm in the least. For God hath power over all things."

Almighty God also says "So lose no heart, nor fall into despair. For ye must gain mastery if ye are true in faith."

Islam, the Middle East, and the Pan-Islamic Movement

SOHAIL H. HASHMI

In the previous piece we asked you to consider what Bin Laden meant by "defeat[ing] factionalism." This is a powerful idea that has caught hold of the public image of Islam that many non-Muslims have about the faith. This extract (from a longer work about the history of Pan-Islamism) debunks the simplistic idea that all Muslims believe and act the same way. Professor Hashmi shows the many levels of identity and loyalties that people—both Muslims and non-Muslims—can have in modern technological societies. What are the three "domains" within which Muslims might live? Is one more important than the others? In what kinds of "domains" do you live? Which is the most important to you?

The Middle East in Contemporary Pan-Islam

Pan-Islam in the form of ideologies and organisations finds manifold expressions today around the world and in all three do mains of international society. The following discussion focuses on those aspects that specifically pertain to the place of the Middle East in pan-Islamic organisations and ideologies.

The interstate domain

The Organisation of the Islamic Conference (OIC) is the formal embodiment of pan-Islam at the interstate level today. Its present membership stands at 57 (56 states and the Palestinian territories). All Muslim majority states, with the possible exception of Eritrea, are members (a total of 44), including the 14 states located in what is generally considered to be the Middle East. Two other states, Kazakhstan and Nigeria, with Muslim populations in excess of 40 per cent of their total population are members. Thus, in terms of *states,* the OIC can lay claim to be a nearly universal organisation of those with a predominantly Muslim population.

Barry Buzan and Ana Gonzalez-Pelaez, International Society and the Middle East, published 2009, PALGRAVE MACMILLAN, reproduced with permission of Palgrave Macmillan.

In terms of Muslim *peoples*, however, the OIC as presently constituted excludes from formal representation large and growing Muslim populations around the world. India, with more than 136 million Muslims, ranks third behind Indonesia and Pakistan for total Muslim population. Its application to join the OIC has been blocked since the 1970s by Pakistan, which contends that despite the large numbers of Muslims, they constitute only 12 to 13 per cent of the total population, and thus India is an overwhelmingly non-Muslim country. Yet, Pakistan did not object to membership by Uganda, Suriname and Togo, which have percentages of Muslims comparable to India. The real reason for Pakistan's objection to India's membership is, of course, the Kashmir conflict. India's interest in joining the OIC has also cooled following repeated OIC resolutions backing the Pakistani position in this dispute. Still, India's involvement in the organisation in some capacity remains a perennial concern, with several prominent members such as Egypt, Iran, Malaysia and Saudi Arabia proposing at least an observer status akin to the role the Russian Federation currently plays within the OIC (Ansari, 2006). Apart from India, Muslims in China and North America are also not represented formally in the organs of the OIC. The single European country to participate is Bosnia and Herzegovina, but only as an observer.

Geographically, the OIC remains centred in Saudi Arabia, which hosts its secretariat and a number of other subsidiary organs. But in other important ways the organisation has made efforts not to be identified with any particular country or region. Islamic summits have been hosted by a number of Muslim countries, including Senegal, Morocco, Pakistan and Malaysia, as have the annual and extraordinary meetings of the Islamic Conference of Foreign Ministers, the OIC's principal decision-making body. Similarly, the secretaries-general have been elected to ensure wide ethnic representation in the office. The first secretary-general was Tunku 'Abd al-Rahman of Malaysia and his eight successors have come from Egypt, Senegal, Tunisia, Pakistan, Niger, Morocco and Turkey.

In terms of its objectives, the original OIC Charter, adopted in 1972, reflected the central role played by the Palestinian issue in the organisation's founding. Article 5 stated that the OIC would 'coordinate efforts for the safeguarding of the Holy Places and support of the struggle of the people of Palestine, to help them regain their rights and liberate their land' (Charter of the Organisation of the Islamic Conference, 1972: Article 5). In deference to some members' demands that other Muslim causes be recognised as well, the charter added in Article 6 that the OIC would 'back the struggle of all Muslim people with a view to preserving their dignity, Independence and national rights' (Charter of the Organisation of the Islamic Conference, 1972: Article 6). Nevertheless, the Israeli–Palestinian conflict has dominated the OIC agenda with greater consistency, frequency and relative unity of purpose than other conflicts that have diverted its attention from time to time. The unity is relative to the deep-rooted divisions that have stymied the organisation from playing any effective role in other Middle Eastern crises, including the Iran–Iraq War, the Gulf War and the Iraq War (Hashmi, 1997: 74–9).

The Iran–Iraq War and the Iraq War exposed a level of ethno-sectarian hostilities in Middle East interstate politics that had not been seen since the Ottoman–Safavid wars. At their root was the conservative Arab states' fear of Khomeinism, an anti-monarchical, anti-Western revolutionary ideology, with appeal to Sunni and Shi'i radicals. The Islamic Republic of Iran adopted in 1979 a constitution that included the following directive: 'All Muslims form a single nation, and the government of the Islamic Republic of Iran has the duty of formulating its general policies with a view to cultivating the friendship and unity of all Muslim peoples, and it must constantly strive to bring about the political, economic and cultural unity of the Islamic world' (Article 11). It is unclear how and if Khomeini and the Islamic Republic intended to pursue these pan-Islamic ambitions. The Iran-Iraq War diverted Iran from pursuing such efforts in a concerted way, and Iran has generally pursued pragmatic, state-centric policies in the years since.

The Iraq War, however, revived fears of Iranian irredentism in the Middle East. Iran is undoubtedly exploiting regional instability to strengthen its dominant position in the Persian Gulf. But it is Arab leaders such as King 'Abdallah of Jordan, Husni Mubarak of Egypt and King 'Abdallah of Saudi Arabia who have injected sectarianism into regional politics by warning against the 'Shi'i crescent' that Iran is fostering now that the Sunni Iraqi bulwark has collapsed. In its essence, the thesis is nothing more than a rehashing of old anti-Shi'i polemics in combination with the Arab–Persian rivalry of the Shu'ubiyya controversy. It disregards the deep-rooted divisions; in terms of religious authority and political loyalties, that often divide Arab Shi'is from Iranian Shi'is. In fact, the 'Alawis of Syria have historically not been considered Shi'is at all, but as heretics by the majority Twelver Imamis (Moosa, 1988: 409–18). Moreover, the idea that Iran is fostering a pan-Shi'i alliance in the Middle East neglects its close support of the staunchly Sunni Palestinian Hamas. In short, there is little substance to the Shi'i crescent thesis, and it seems to have found little credence among ordinary Middle Easterners.

After years of debating the organisation's priorities and how to make it more effective, the OIC adopted a new charter on 14 March 2008, as the central component of a 'New Vision'. The document still contains a reference to 'the struggle of the Palestinian people' in its list of objectives, but higher on the list are the goals of promoting human rights and democracy within member states and of fostering 'noble Islamic values concerning moderation, tolerance, respect for diversity, preservation of Islamic symbols and common heritage and to defend the universality of Islamic religion'. The new charter also promises to eliminate one perennial cause of paralysis within the organisation: Instead of unanimous agreement, a simple majority will now suffice to approve new members. Clearly, the OIC's New Vision reflects increased concerns with the strain that terrorism has caused in relations between Muslim and Western states and the sharp increase in Islainophobia in countries around the world. The rhetoric of the new charter is aimed at reaffirming that Muslims fully subscribe to the governing norms and institutions of international society.

The transnational domain

The Muslim *umma* today is not only global in its dispersion, it is also increasingly transnational. The transnational domain is robust and rapidly expanding. Muslims have made full use of technological advances in travel and communication to nurture traditionally transnational institutions, such as scholarly networks and Sufi and other pietist communities, as well as to create new transnational linkages and institutions, including charities and other philanthropic organisations, sporting events, and widely scattered and loosely connected militant groups. These have been amply studied in a number of recent works, most prominently by Peter Mandaville (Mandaville, 2001; 2007) and Olivier Roy (Roy, 2004).

Mandaville aptly observes that as much as transnationalism creates the possibilities for greater Muslim interaction, it simultaneously demonstrates ever more clearly the diversity and political divisions of the *umma*. 'In this regard, a new "umma consciousness" does not in and of itself lead to greater Muslim unity' (Mandaville, 2007: 299). Muslims are well aware of the centrifugal aspects of globalisation. I will discuss here only briefly three cases of attempts, each in their own way, to combat these disintegrative trends.

The Muslim World League based in Mecca not only survives as a relic from a previous era of pan-Islamic organisation, it has flourished, thanks largely to the generous financial support of the Saudi government. It has developed into an NGO with numerous branches, active in publication and distribution of Islamic literature, supervision of mosques supported by its funds, and charitable relief of Muslims suffering from natural disaster. Through it, critics charge, the Saudi state is able to project its Wahhabi creed into Muslim communities around the world. This has had the effect of promoting a conservative and intolerant strain of pan-Islam, one averse to Muslim political and cultural assimilation in non-Muslim countries and to the improvement of women's status (Abou El Fadl, 2007: 73–4).

Undoubtedly, the most politically potent transnational Muslim actors today are terrorist groups. The war against Soviet occupation of Afghanistan from 1980 to 1989 proved decisive in fostering transnational linkages among Islamic militants, many of whom made their way to Afghanistan as part of a multinational *jihad* effort. Al Qaeda emerged out of this conflict, and once they had acquired a base for their activities in Taliban-controlled Afghanistan, they took their *jihad* to the global level.

Osama bin Laden and Ayman al-Zawahiri, the group's leaders and principal spokesmen, have on occasion invoked the *umma* and the caliphate when describing their goals. In an interview bin Laden gave to al Jazeera on 21 October 2001, he stated, for example: 'Our concern is that our *umma* unites either under the Words of the Book of God or His Prophet, and that this nation should establish the righteous caliphate' (Lawrence, 200S: 121). Yet unification of the entire Muslim *umma* and the resurrection of the caliphate are not issues on which bin Laden or Zawahiri dwell. Al Qaeda's pressing concerns are relatively more immediate, in both space and time. The issues that recur in its declarations, including the two best-known statements of its mission, the 'manifesto' of 1996 and the 1998 *fatwa* declaring war against all Americans, are the American and Zionist-led 'crusade' against Muslims, which includes military invasion and occupation of Muslim lands, as well as political, economic and cultural intervention in Muslim affairs. Pan-Islamic appeals seem in al Qaeda's strategy to be more a means than an end – at least not a short-term end, which is to repulse the 'crusaders' and bring down their Muslim stooges as the first step in creating genuinely Islamic states in such countries as Saudi Arabia, Egypt and Pakistan (Hashmi, 2006).

The contemporary Muslim group most closely associated with the goal of re-establishing the caliphate is Hizb al-Tahrir. It was founded in the early 1950s in Jerusalem and now has an organisational presence in some 40 countries, including many in the West. It has a particularly active following in the United Kingdom. Hizb al-Tahrir's overarching goal is *da'wa* or the call to Islamic faith, but unlike the vast majority of such groups today, it links this religious mission with the political ambition of creating a universal Islamic state led by a *khalifa*. The group's 'draft constitution' establishes that the caliph will be elected by universal franchise of Muslims, and, once in power, only he will have the authority to pass the 'final constitution' of the Islamic state.

Hizb al-Tahrir's literature (much of it conveniently available on the group's website www.khilafah.com) describes the process of realising the new *dar al-islam* as consisting of stages that replicate the Prophet Muhammad's actions in creating the Medinan state. Leaders of the group have repeatedly declared that they do not advocate violence to realise their ends, but their critics charge this is a pragmatic, not a principled, stand. Clearly, the pan-Islamic aspirations central to Hizb al-Tahrir's mission pose a threat to the regimes that would have to be overthrown in order to reconstitute *dar al-Islam*, and the group has been declared illegal and suppressed in a number of Muslim and non-Muslim states.

The interhuman domain

The same technological advances that have helped foster Muslim transnational organisations and movements have undeniably increased the degree to which Muslims know about and interact with other Muslims. At the same time, greater information and contact have not diminished intra-Muslim conflicts, within and across states and within and across the Sunni–Shi'i divide. In recent years, Iraq has become the arena where intrasectarian as well as intersectarian conflict has played out in full. Is there any basis then for assuming that the *umma* concept has any relevance among ordinary Muslims today?

Two surveys conducted by the Pew Research Center in 2005 and 2006 as part of its Global Attitudes Project provide some of the most specific data available to date (Pew Global Attitudes Project 2005; 2006). In May 2005, Muslim respondents in Indonesia, Jordan, Lebanon, Morocco, Pakistan and Turkey were asked: 'Do you think of yourself first as a (name of country's people, such as Jordanian, Moroccan or Indonesian) or first as a Muslim?' In April and May 2006, the same question was posed to Muslim respondents in Indonesia, Jordan and

Pakistan, as well as in Egypt, France, Germany, Nigeria, Spain and the United Kingdom. Table 8.1 consolidates the results for both years, with the Muslim-majority states listed first.

In six of the eight Muslim-majority states surveyed, self-identification with Islam was considerably greater than with the respondents' own country. The results were almost evenly divided only in Indonesia (In both 2005 and 2006) and in Lebanon (in 2005). The most surprising result comes perhaps from Turkey, where, in spite of some 80 years of education and socialisation in Kemalist secular nationalism, healthy majorities professed greater identification as Muslims than as Turks. The number identifying with Islam in fact increased markedly from 2005 to 2006.

The percentages of Muslims who identify with Islam more than their home country were also greater in the four European countries sampled. Only French Muslims expressed comparable levels of primary identification with their country, whereas in Germany, Spain and the United Kingdom, the numbers were sharply lower.

Table 8.1 Muslim versus national identity (2005/06, per cent of respondents).

	Country's people	Muslim	Both equally	Other	Don't know/ refused
Egypt	na/23	na/59	na/18	na/*	na/0
Indonesia	35/39	39/36	26/25	na/0	*/0
Lebanon	30/na	30/na	39/na	na/na	1/na
Jordan	23/21	63/67	13/12	na/0	*/0
Morocco	7/na	70/na	23/na	na/na	*/na
Nigeria	na/25	na/71	na/2	na/*	na/2
Pakistan	7/6	79/87	13/7	na/*	1/0
Turkey	29/19	43/51	27/30	na/*	1/*
France	na/42	na/46	na/10	na/*	na/2
Germany	na/3	na/66	na/9	na/8	na/3
Spain	na/3	na/69	na/25	na/2	na/*
UK	na/7	na/81	na/8	na/1	na/3

* = less than 1 per cent

These results from Muslim populations are even more striking when they are contrasted with the results of a seven-nation Pew survey from 2006 in which self-identified Christian respondents were asked if they identified with their country or their religion. As Table 8.2 shows, all the Western countries had majorities declaring greater identification with their country, large majorities in all but the United States. Only Nigerian Christians expressed greater affinity for their faith, but still in substantially fewer numbers than Nigerian Muslims. In India, the Pew survey found only 10 per cent of Hindus who identified first with Hinduism compared to 90 per cent who identified themselves first as Indians.

The Pew surveys reveal the continuing salience of Islamic identity among large numbers of ordinary Muslims around the world. This finding is confirmed by other surveys as well, including Gallup polls in several Muslim countries in 2001 and between 2005 and 2007, which found large majorities (often exceeding 90 per cent) indicating 'that religion is an important part of their daily lives' (Esposito and Mogahed, 2007: 5). The Pew data do not directly support, however, any claims about the presence or power of pan-Islamic loyalties among Muslims today. The surveys did not ask, for example, if the Muslim respondents felt part of a global Muslim *umma*, and if so, in what concrete ways such identification affected them spiritually,

Table 8.2 Christian versus national identity (2006, per cent of respondents).

	Country's people	Christian	Both equally	Other	Don't know/ refused
France	83	14	3	*	*
Germany	59	33	8	1	*
Nigeria	43	53	3	0	1
Russia	63	16	20	1	1
Spain	60	14	21	4	1
UK	59	24	8	7	2
US	48	42	7	1	2

* = less than 1 per cent

culturally or politically. So we must be careful not to infer that because a majority of respondents answered they identify with Islam more than their country they would be ready to act on such identities in support of Muslims in other countries or of 'Muslim causes' in international politics, especially when such support challenges their country's official policies. In other words, one should not confuse *identity* with *loyalty*.

Moreover, the Pew surveys do not rule out the possibility that other identities, regional or tribal, for example, supersede both islamic and national identities. This possibility is in fact supported by an eight-nation survey conducted by Zogby international in March and April 2002 (Zogby, 2002: 49–59). In each country, Arab respondents were asked to rank the following six identity markers in the order of importance to them personally: family, the city or region where they live, the country in which they live, their religion, being Arab, and the social background of their family. They were asked to respond first as if they were defining their identity to a fellow Arab and second as if they were doing so to an American. In both cases, the respondents ranked Arabness, country and religion as the tap three sources of their identity. The percentages choosing each of these three markers as their first choice in both questions are presented together in Table 8.3.

The Zogby surveys do not separate Muslim from Christian respondents, so especially in the cases of Egyptians and Lebanese, we cannot assume that figures for 'religion' reflect exclusively Islamic identity. In general, however, the large majority of respondents in all countries except Lebanon were presumably Muslim. National identities continue to rank lower than religious identities in most of the countries surveyed, but the gap between the two is large only in Israel and Morocco. Yet Arabness conspicuously trumps both religion and country in all countries except Israel and Morocco, where some degree of ambivalence is manifest.

This Zogby poll does not allow us to conclude that pan-Arabism as an ideology is still a vital force among Arabs or that it is more appealing to Arabs than pan-Islam. It, together with the Pew surveys, reveals at most that after more than a half-century of state-building efforts in Muslim-majority states, national identities still lag behind (sometimes far behind) ethnicity (In the case of Arabs) and religion as sources of identity. In sum, we may say that at the interhuman level, popular identities in the Arab world leave open the *possibility* of a regional international society supported by shared ethnic and religious affinities. In the broader Muslim world, the *potential* for pan-Islamic affinities and action exists on the basis of the strong religious self-identification of large numbers of Muslims.

Conclusion: pan-Islam and International Society in the Middle East and Beyond

The central question underlying this chapter has been whether Islam strengthens or undermines the prospects for a regional society in the Middle East. With every country in the region except Israel and Lebanon having predominantly Muslim populations, the immediate response might be to see in Islam an important, if not crucial, religious and cultural glue for regional society. Indeed, as we have seen, Islamic ethics places a great deal of emphasis on strengthening the bonds among Muslims at all levels, including the political. Politically, therefore, Islam should also provide an impetus towards the formation of a regional society in the Middle East.

Table 8.3 Identity markers among Arab populations (to an Arab/to an American) (2002, per cent of respondents).

Most important	Egypt	Israel	Lebanon	Jordan	Kuwait	Morocco	Saudi Arabia	UAE
Arab	31/40	29/34	32/30	24/30	31/42	36/26	42/59	46/58
Country	26/25	17/24	31/42	24/19	19/20	15/7	13/6	9/8
Religion	29/26	36/28	20/16	13/20	15/18	34/53	18/22	16/18

Yet, historically and today, Islam has proven insufficient and in some ways averse to the development of a regional society, in the Middle East or other regions. The reason has both an ethical/ideological as well as a practical component. On the ethical or ideological level, political Islam tends towards pan-Islamic ideals and institutions, and these pan-Islamic aspirations tend towards universalism. This is not to say that Islam has not been used to legitimate less than universal political arrangements. Indeed, throughout Islamic history, principalities and empires found many an ardent defender among Muslim scholars. Muslim nation-states today face far less opposition on Islamic grounds than 50 or 60 years ago, certainly not from mainstream Muslim scholars and activists, and not even from radical groups. Islamic fundamentalism has generally embraced the nation-state as having at least partial utility and legitimacy. Its goal is not to eliminate the nation-state, but to seize it for itself. The withering away of the state and the coming of a pan-Islamic utopia are historical stages only vaguely outlined in fundamentalist ideologies. Groups such as Hizb al-Tahrir that make establishment of a universal caliphate their central mission are treated as fringe elements even by other fundamentalist groups.

Still, pan-Islamic urges remain alive today. Perhaps they will exist as long as Muslims exist. The nation-state has acquired some measure of Islamic respectability, but it cannot be said that ethically or ideologically it has entirely supplanted larger, more universal Islamic units. Phrased differently, nationalism has gained in Islamic legitimacy, but it has not replaced Islamic identities or the ideal of the *umma*. As interstate and transnational forms of pan-Islam demonstrate, the ideal is expressed today primarily in pluralist rather than solidarist forms, but there are constant expressions of hope that more solidarist forms may evolve. Thus, in terms of Islamic values, regionalism could be seen as a state of limbo: Muslims should pause there only long enough to reach the more inclusive paradise.

On the practical level, pan-Islam has proven no more effective than pan-Arabism in mobilising elites and masses to create alternatives to the nation-state. It is one thing to imagine political communities, quite another to replace existing ones, especially those commanding the coercive machinery of the modern state. The modern Middle Eastern and Muslim nation-state, labouring though it might under multiple contradictions, has still proven remarkably adaptable and resilient. Unable to achieve a clear idea of what constitutes an Islamic alternative to the nation-state or how to bring it about, advocates of pan-Islam seem by and large reconciled for the time being to symbolic, pluralist manifestations.

Finally, a brief comment on the role of Islam and pan-Islam specifically in the global international society. Starting with the Iranian revolution and bolstered by the emergence of what some call the 'global jihadi network', a popular view has developed that Islam is irreconcitably opposed to an international society built on the peaceful coexistence and cooperation of sovereign states. Some Muslims undeniably share this view and act on it. But in a global population of 1.3 billion they are a conspicuous minority. Pan-Islam, in its myriad forms today, is focused on cultivating an international society of Muslims; the universal international society receives very little attention, except insofar as it threatens the development of an Islamic subsystem. The OIC's commitment to the principles of the United Nations Charter and international law found in its first charter and reaffirmed in its second is more than mere rhetoric.

Note

1. This essay was made possible in part by a grant from the Carnegie Corporation of New York. The statements made and views expressed are solely the responsibility of the author. In addition to my fellow contributors to this volume, I thank Peter Mandaville for his assistance.

References

Abou El Fadl, Khaled (2007) *The Great Theft: Wrestling Islam from the Extremists*, New York: HarperCollins.

Ansari, Hamid (2006) 'The OIC and India: Signals of a Re-Think', *The Hindu*, 30 January 2006, http://www.thehindu.com/2006/01/30/stories/2006013004291000.htm (date accessed: 18 April 2008).

Charter of the Arab League (1945) Cairo, 22 March 1945, the website of the League of Arab States, http://www.arableagueonline.org/las/english/details_en.jsp? art_id=134&level_id=40 (date accessed: 15 April 2008).

Charter of the Gulf Cooperation Council (1981) Abu Dhabi, 25 May 1981, the website of the Gulf Cooperation Council, http://www.gcc-sg.org/eng/ index.php?action=Sec-Show&ID=1 (date accessed: 15 April 2008).

Charter of the Organisation of the Islamic Conference (1972) Jeddah, 29 February–4 March 1972, the website of the Organisation of the Islamic Conference, http://www.oic-oci.org/oicnew/page_detail.asp?p_id=53 (date accessed: 15 April 2008).

Hashmi, Sohail H. (2006) '9/11 and the Jihad Tradition', in Daniel J. Sherman and Terry Nardin (eds) *Terror, Culture, Politics: Rethinking 9/11*, Bloomington: Indiana University Press, 149–64.

Hashmi, Sohail H. (2003) 'Political Boundaries and Moral Communities: Islamic Perspectives', in Allen Buchanan and Margaret Moore (eds) *States, Nations, and Borders: The Ethics of Making Boundaries*, Cambridge: Cambridge University Press, 181–213.

Hashmi, Sohail H. (1997) 'Sovereignty, Pan-Islamism, and International Organisation', in Sohail H. Hashmi (ed.) *State Sovereignty: Change and Persistence in International Relations*, University Park: Pennsylvania State University Press, 49–80.

Esposito, John L. and Dalia Mogahed (2007) *Who Speaks for Islam? What a Billion Muslims Really Think*, New York: Gallup Press.

Lawrence, Bruce (ed.) (2005) *Messages to the World: The Statements of Osama bin Laden*, London: Verso.

Mandaville, Peter (2007) *Global Political Islam*, London: Routledge.

Mandaville, Peter (2001) *Transnational Muslim Politics: Reimagining the Umma*, London: Routledge.

Moosa, Matti (1988) *Extremist Shiites: The Ghulat Sects*, Syracuse, NY: Syracuse University Press.

Pew Global Attitudes Project (2006) 'Muslims in Europe: Economic Worries Top Concerns about Religious and Cultural Identity', Washington: Pew Research Center, http://pewglobal.org/reports/pdf/254.pdf (date accessed: 6 June 2008).

Pew Global Attitudes Project (2005) 'Islamic Extremism: Common Concern for Muslim and Western Publics', Washington: Pew Research Center, http://pewglobal.org/reports/pdf/248.pdf (date accessed: 6 June 2008).

Roy, Olivier (2004) *Globalized Islam: The Search for a New Ummah*, New York: Columbia University Press.

Zogby, James J. (2002) *What Arabs Think: Values, Beliefs, and Concerns*, Washington: Zogby International/The Arab Thought Foundation.

Wielding Masculinity Inside Abu Ghraib and Guantánamo: The Globalized Dynamics

CYNTHIA ENLOE

Cynthia Enloe asks us to consider a simple question: where are the women? In this extract Enloe examines the perhaps infamous events surrounding people held in the U.S. military prisons in Iraq and the base at Guantánamo, Cuba. How did U.S. personnel exploit Islamic perceptions of "correct" gender behavior at the two prisons? How do you think the female and male U.S. personnel felt when they took part in those actions? Did those actions lead to useful information?

In June 2006, two years after the Abu Ghraib scandal broke and set off worldwide consternation, a short article appeared in the *New York Times* reporting that an American army dog handler had been found guilty by a military court-martial. He had been charged with having used his dog to intimidate Iraqi male prisoners being held by the U.S. military at Abu Ghraib (Associated Press 2006). Sergeant Santos A. Cardona was the eleventh American soldier serving in Iraq's infamous Abu Ghraib, a U.S. military jail and interrogation center, to have been convicted of violations of the U.S. military code of conduct. His defense lawyers had argued, unsuccessfully, that Sergeant Cardona was doing only what he had been trained to do and what his military superiors had commanded him to do.

Three of the eleven American soldiers convicted of committing abuses at Abu Ghraib were women, eight were men. All eleven soldiers who were court-martialed and convicted were enlisted personnel or noncommissioned officers. None were higher-ranking officers. None were Washington-based civilian policymakers (Hillman 2005).

The only senior officer to receive an official reprimand and demotion was a woman, General Janis Karpinski. She was the army reserve officer then in charge of the U.S. occupation authority's cobbled-together military prison system in Iraq. Her own telling of the Abu Ghraib story is full of descriptions of wartime unpreparedness, lack of senior command support, autonomous actions by military and CIA interrogators, and routine behaviors in what has become the military's institutional culture of sexism (Karpinski 2005).

On the same June day in 2006 that the *New York Times* reported Sergeant Cardona's conviction, the paper's editors included two other reports that one could read as possibly connected to the short article about Abu Ghraib. First, there was another brief report of the last of the U.S. Army's trials concerning abuses at a U.S. detention center at the Bagram military base in Afghanistan. The last soldier to be prosecuted for abuse and the deaths of prisoners held at

Bagram was Private First Class Damien M. Corsetti. He was one of more than a dozen U.S. soldiers—all men—charged with abusing and causing the deaths of Afghan prisoners at Bagram. The military jury acquitted Private Corsetti (Golden 2006).

The Geneva Conventions are international agreements negotiated by governments in the mid-twentieth century. The agreements are not designed so much to reverse militarization as they are intended to globalize the ethics that should guide governments' war-waging behavior. War waging can continue but should be conducted according to these agreed-upon rules. The U.S. government is a signatory to the Geneva Conventions. Prescriptions for the treatment of prisoners captured in wartime is one of the major elements of the Geneva Conventions. That is, a soldier may be in the enemy's forces, but he or she is still a human being and, as a human being, deserves to be treated humanely.

Avoiding these internationally agreed upon requirements to treat prisoners of war humanely was a strategy adopted by U.S. government officials in the name of

- "urgency," coupled with
- "national security," in order to wage
- "the global war on terror."

Those who devised the political rationales, legal interpretations, and bureaucratic strategies for this avoidance were overwhelmingly civilians. They were civilians posted inside the Defense Department, the Justice Department, the White House legal counsel's office, and the office of the vice president (Danner 2004; Mayer 2005a; Mayer 2005b; Mayer 2005c; Mayer 2006).

Witnesses for both the defense and the prosecution at the June 2006 Corsetti court-martial described how the pressures imposed on guards and interrogators at Bagram to get more information from their prisoners increased in late 2002. It was then two months into the U.S.-led military invasion of Afghanistan. President Bush had declared that prisoners captured in Afghanistan were not to be deemed eligible for the international protections guaranteed to enemy combatants under the Geneva Conventions. Many of those male prisoners first detained and questioned at Bagrain would soon be flown in large cargo planes—after they had been dressed in orange jump suits, shackled, and had burlap bags placed over their heads—to the detention center the U.S. had recently constructed at its naval base in Guantánamo, Cuba (Lipman forthcoming). The links between Bagram and Guantánamo were being forged.

A year later, those forged links would be extended to Abu Ghraib. Trying to make sense of what happened inside Abu Ghraib in the fall and winter of 2003 turns out to be nearly impossible if one treats Abu Ghraib as an island. It was not an island. It was a link in a globalized chain (Greenberg and Dratel 2005). Among the materials used to weld those chain links—Bagram to Guantánamo, Guantánamo to Abu Ghraib—were American ideas about *feminization.*

Feminization is a process of imposing allegedly feminine characteristics on a person—man or woman—or a group or a kind of activity. Often the goal of feminizing someone (or something) is to lower his (or its) status. Feminization provokes anxiety when particular forms of masculinity are culturally, academically, politically, or economically privileged (Carver 2003; Elias forthcoming). Stitching sneakers for the global market has been feminized in the corporate hope of lowering labor costs. Military nursing has become feminized in an effort to use women in the military without diluting the military's prized image as a masculinized institution. A male candidate running for election against another male candidate may try to gain an advantage with voters by feminizing his opponent—for instance, by portraying his rival as "weak on national security." A male prisoner is feminized when his captors force him to look or act in ways those captors think will make him feel feminine. The presumption motivating his taunters is that a man who is being feminized will become more cooperative out of his sense of shame and helplessness.

In a patriarchal culture—in rich countries and poor countries, in countries with diverse cultural traditions—any person, group, or activity that can be feminized risks losing his or her (or its) influence, authority, and even self-respect.

So long as any culture remains patriarchal, then, feminization can be wielded as an instrument of intimidation.

Using a feminist curiosity to make sense of what happened in Abu Ghraib means both investigating any efforts to wield feminization in imprisonment and interrogation and looking for the women in all their various roles. Those roles can be both obvious and obscure. Ann Wright served as an army officer for twenty-nine years and then as a U.S. diplomat before resigning in opposition to the administration's preemptive war. After resigning, Ann Wright decided to use her new independence to find out where all the women were on the broad canvas that became "Abu Ghraib." She found Major General Barbara Fast, chief of military intelligence, serving in the U.S. military command's headquarters in Baghdad. She found Captain Carolyn Wood, a military intelligence officer who had been the leader of the interrogation team in Bagram and then, with her unit, transferred to Abu Ghraib. Wright found two lower-ranking women interrogators deployed to Abu Ghraib, as well as two women employed as interpreters by a civilian contractor, the Titan Company, working with a military intelligence unit inside the prison. Ann Wright also found three Army linguists working in interrogation teams at Guantánamo during 2003 and 2004. She discovered that during these same crucial months at least three other Army women were conducting interrogations at Guantánamo. An unknown number of additional women were serving at Guantánamo at the same time as private contract interrogators. None of these women came forward to stop the abuses they witnessed. Several of them, according to firsthand accounts, helped devise some of the practices meant to humiliate the male prisoners (Wright 2006; Saar 2005).

Is it surprising that there were so many American women inside Bagram, Guantánamo, and Abu Ghraib who, in 2003 and 2004, were playing roles up and down the chain of command as guards, interpreters, and interrogators? Probably not. After all, over the past two decades, in devising gender strategies for recruiting women while still maintaining the military's masculinized core—combat—officials of the U.S. Defense Department had channeled women soldiers into not just nursing and administration but such seemingly noncontroversial jobs as military police, military interpreters, and intelligence. By 2004, women, who made up only 15 percent of total U.S. Army personnel, represented 22 percent of military police and 25 percent of military interrogators (Wright 2006).

Still, using a feminist curiosity to make sense of Abu Ghraib, Bagram, and Guantánamo allows one to do more than look for where the women are—as revealing as that exploration is. Using a feminist curiosity prompts one to also pursue the answer to a question that most commentators fail to ask: what are the causes and consequences of wielding ideas about masculinity and femininity?

Feminization has been used during the Afghanistan and Iraq wars mainly by American militarized men (civilian and military), hut with the complicity and sometimes the direct involvement of a handful of American militarized women. Evidence gathered thus far suggests that feminization was intended by its wartime wielders to humiliate and thereby gain information from foreign men, mostly men identified by their American captors as "Muslim," "dangerous," and "the enemy." As they were transported by U.S. officials from Washington to Bagram to Guantánamo to Abu Ghraib, these practices of coercive feminization might be thought of as being *globally militarized.*

Back at Private Corsetti's June 2006 barely reported court-martial, defense witnesses sought to undercut the prosecution's case against Corsetti by noting that there were almost-daily phone calls to interrogators at Bagram from their civilian Defense Department superiors in Washington. Their superiors were infused with a sense of urgency. They demanded quick results from the interrogations being conducted at the Bagram base. The witnesses recalled how this pressure from Washington officials served to increase the aggressiveness of the physical tactics that Bagram soldiers and interrogators used on prisoners deemed uncooperative (Golden 2006). The jury seemed convinced.

American military interrogators' and guards' adoption of both painful "stress positions" and feminization to intimidate captive men can be traded globally, just as rifles can be traded globally, just as ideas about national security and creating "cheap labor" can be traded globally.

American male and female soldiers serving during late 2003 and early 2004 as prison guards in Abu Ghraib became the best known actors in this fast-globalizing drama. As individuals, they seemed far from being global players. They appeared quite parochial and isolated. The photographs that showed them deliberately humiliating and torturing scores of Iraqi men held in detention and under interrogation were taken apparently for their own private amusement, not for prime-time television or headline stories. But their audience expanded beyond their wildest dreams—or nightmares. Between April and June 2004, millions of viewers were looking at these private photos: American soldiers smiling broadly as they appeared to be taking enormous pleasure in frightening and humiliating their wartime Iraqi charges.

Most people who saw these photographs can still describe the scenes. An American male soldier standing in a self-satisfied pose, facing his army colleague holding the camera with his arms crossed and wearing surgical blue rubber gloves, a sign that this abuse was occurring in the age of AIDS. In front of him, we, the globalized viewers of these photographs, could see an American woman soldier smiling at the camera as she leaned on top of a pile of naked Iraqi men who were being forced to contort themselves into a human pyramid.

Other pictures whizzed around the planet. An American woman soldier, again smiling, holding an Iraqi male prisoner on a leash. An American woman soldier pointing to a naked Iraqi man's genitals, apparently treating them as a joke. American male soldiers intimidating naked Iraqi male prisoners with snarling guard dogs. An Iraqi male prisoner standing alone on a box, his head covered with a hood and electrical wires attached to different parts of his body. An Iraqi male prisoner forced to wear women's underwear. Not pictured, but substantiated, were Iraqi men forced to masturbate and to simulate oral sex with each other, as well as an Iraqi woman prisoner coerced by several American male soldiers into kissing them (Hersh 2004).

Few of the U.S. government's official investigators or the mainstream news commentators used feminist insights to make sense of what went on in the prison (Strasser 2004; Danner 2004). The result, I think, is that we have not really gotten to the bottom of the Abu Ghraib story. This, in turn, could undercut our attempts to understand how militarization can lead to torture.

This omission of a feminist analysis in investigations of Abu Ghraib—and of abusive actions inside Bagram and Guantánamo, *as well as* the connections forged between these places—could also limit our attempts to implement those changes that can enforce globalized treaties and conventions intended to either roll back militarization or at least reduce its harmful effects.

One place to start employing a feminist set of tools is to explain why one American woman soldier in particular—not even a guard, just a low-ranking clerk visiting the cell block the night the photos were taken—captured the attention of so many media editors and ordinary viewers and readers: the then twenty-one-year-old enlisted army reservist Lynndie England, now a single mother serving a sentence in a military prison.

Why didn't the name of Charles Graner, the apparent cell-block ringleader of the photographed abuses become as well known? More important to ask: why didn't the name of General Geoffrey Miller become globally known? General Geoffrey Miller was the commander of Guantánamo and when he was sent to Iraq, became the carrier of Washington's message from Guantánamo to Abu Ghraib—a message that this was a time demanding a sense of urgency, an urgency that called for more aggressive techniques in interrogations of Iraqi prisoners held in Abu Ghraib (Hersh 2004). The fact that neither Graner's nor, especially, Miller's name did become as familiar reflects the gendering not just of the abuse but also of the political consciousnesses of Americans and news consumers around the world: women in presumably masculinized places, such as a military prison in a war zone, make a better "story."

Several things proved shocking to the millions of viewers of the clandestine prison photos. First, the Abu Ghraib scenes suggested there existed a gaping chasm between, on the one hand, the Bush administration's claim that its military invasion and overthrow of the brutal Saddam Hussein regime would bring a civilizing sort of "freedom" to the Iraqi people and, on the other hand, the seemingly barbaric treatment that American soldiers were willfully meting out to Iraqis held in captivity without trial. Second, it was shocking to witness such blatant abuse of imprisoned detainees by soldiers representing a government that had passed its own anti-torture laws and had signed both the international Geneva Conventions against mistreatment of wartime combatants and the UN Convention against Torture and Other Cruel, Inhuman or Degrading Treatment or Punishment (sometimes referred to simply as the "Convention Against Torture").

Yet there was a third source of shock that prompted scores of early media commentaries and intense conversations among ordinary viewers: seeing women engage in torture. Of the seven American soldiers initially court-martialed (and eleven soldiers eventually court-martialed), all low-ranking army reserve military police guards, three were women. Somehow, the American male soldier in the blue surgical gloves (Charles Graner) was not shocking to most viewers and so did not inspire much private consternation or a stream of op-ed columns. Women, by contrast, were conventionally expected by most editors and news watchers to appear in wartime as mothers and wives of soldiers, occasionally as military nurses and truck mechanics, and most often as victims of wartime violence. Women were not—according to the conventional presumption—supposed to be the wielders of violence and certainly not the perpetrators of torture. When those deeply gendered presumptions were turned upside down, many people felt a sense of shock. "This is awful: how could this have happened?"

Private First Class Lynndie England, the young female military clerk (not a guard) photographed holding the man on a leash, thus became the source of intense public curiosity. The news photographers could not restrain themselves two months later, in early August 2004, from showing England in her camouflaged army maternity uniform when she appeared at Fort Bragg for her pretrial hearing. She had become pregnant as a result of her sexual liaison with another enlisted reservist while on duty in Abu Ghraib. Her sexual partner was Charles Graner. Yet Charles Graner's name was scarcely mentioned. He apparently was doing what men are expected to do in wartime: have sex and wield violence. The public's curiosity and its lack of curiosity thus matched its pattern of shock. All three—curiosity, lack of curiosity, and shock—were conventionally gendered. Using a feminist investigatory approach, one should find this lack of public and media curiosity about Charles Graner just as revealing as the public's and media's fascination with Lynndie England.

Yet more than Charles Graner was pushed aside. The government policymaking that implicitly approved the use of torture was never put on trial. In fact, one reporter who, with a handful of her colleagues followed the Abu Ghraib trials for months, all the way through to the trial of Lynndie England (the last of the low-ranking Abu Ghraib soldiers to be tried) and heard Lynndie England's sentence pronounced in the court room at Fort Hood, Texas, in September 2005, noted how narrow the focus remained throughout all the trials. Bigger issues were deemed irrelevant (Wypijewski 2006). In fact, it was considered quite exceptional when General Geoffrey Miller, the Guantanamo commander who had brought the message to Iraq in the fall of 2003 that pressure on captured suspected insurgents needed to be increased, appeared briefly at just one of the many court sessions. No senior civilian officials from the Defense or Justice Department made any appearances. This legalistic narrowing of the focus served to normalize in the minds of many ordinary people those government interrogation policies and the resultant practice of inflicting physical pain and feminized humiliation that flowed from them.

Responding to the torrent of Abu Ghraib stories coming out of Iraq during the spring and summer of 2004. President George W. Bush and Secretary of Defense Donald Rumsfeld, the president's appointee, tried to reassure the public that the abusive behavior inside the prison was not representative of America, nor did it reflect the Bush administration's own foreign policies. Rather, the Abu Ghraib abuses were the work of "rogue" soldiers, a "few bad apples."

The "bad apple" explanation always goes like this: the institution is working fine, its values are appropriate, its internal dynamics are of a sort that sustain positive values, along with respectful, productive behavior. Thus, according to the "bad apple" explanation, nothing needs to be reassessed or reformed in the way the organization works; all that needs to happen to stop the abuse is to prosecute and remove those few individuals who refused to play by the established rules. Sometimes this may be true. Some listeners to the administration's "bad apple" explanation, however, weren't reassured. They wondered if the Abu Ghraib abuses were not produced by just a few bad apples found in a solid, reliable barrel but instead were produced by an essentially "bad barrel." They also wondered whether this "barrel" embraced not only the Abu Ghraib prison, but the larger U.S. military, intelligence, and civilian command structures (Hersh 2004; Human Rights Watch 2004).

What makes a "barrel" go bad? That is, what turns an organization, an institution, or a whole system into one that ignores, perhaps even fosters, abusive behavior by the individuals operating inside it? This question is relevant for every workplace, every political system, every international alliance. Here, too, feminists have been working hard over the past three decades to develop a curiosity and a set of analytical tools with which we can all answer this important question. So many of us today live much of our lives within complex organizations, large and small—workplaces, local and national governments, health care systems, criminal justice systems, international organizations. Feminist researchers have revealed that virtually all organizations are gendered; that is, all organizations are shaped by the ideas about, and daily practices of wielding, norms of masculinity and femininity (Bunster-Burotto 1985; Ehrenreich 2004; Enloe 2000; Whitworth 2004; Burke 2004). Ignoring the workings of gender, feminist investigators have found, makes it impossible for us to explain accurately what makes any organization "tick." That failure makes it impossible for us to hold an organization accountable.

Yet most of the long official reports on the Abu Ghraib abuse scandal were written by people who ignored these feminist organizational lessons. They acted as if the dynamics of masculinity and femininity among low-level police and high-level policymakers made no difference. That assumption is very risky.

A series of U.S. Senate hearings, along with a string of Defense Department investigations, tried to explain what went wrong in Abu Ghraib and why. The most authoritative of the Defense Department reports were the "Taguba Report," the "Fay/Jones Report" (both named after generals who headed these investigations), and the "Schlesinger Report" (named after a civilian former secretary of defense who chaired this investigatory team) (Human Rights Watch 2004; Jehi 2004; Lewis and Schmitt 2004; Schmitt 2004; Taguba 2004). In addition, the CIA conducted its own investigation, since its officials were deeply involved in interrogating—and often hiding in secret prisons—captured Afghans and Iraqis. Moreover, there were several human rights groups and journalists that published their own findings in 2004.

Using our teminist curiosity leads us to ask several questions that the U.S. government's investigators failed to ask:

- Did it matter who the women were inside the prison and up and down the larger American military and intelligence hierarchies—low-level police reservists, a captain in the military intelligence unit, a general advising the chief U.S. commander in Iraq? Investigators apparently didn't ask.
- Did the nature of the daily personal relationships between the military policemen, including Charles Graner, and their female colleagues—who were a minority at Abu Ghraib—matter? The official investigators didn't seem to think that asking this question would yield any insights.
- Was it significant that so many of the abuses perpetrated on the Iraqi male prisoners were deliberately sexualized, designed to feminize and thus humiliate the prisoners? Was hooding a male prisoner the same (in motivation and in result) as forcing him to simulate oral sex? No one seemed to judge these questions to be pertinent.

- Was it at all relevant that Charles Graner, the oldest and apparently most influential of the low-ranking guards charged, had been accused of physical intimidation by his former wife? No questions asked, no answers forthcoming.
- Was subtle pressure to appear "manly" in a time of war placed on the lawyers in the Defense and Justice departments and in the White House who were ordered to draft guidelines to permit U.S. officials to sidestep the Geneva Conventions outlawing torture? This question too seems to have been left on the investigative teams' shelves to gather dust.

All of the authors of the reports on Abu Ghraib talked about a climate," an "environment," or a "culture," having been created inside Abu Ghraib that fostered abusive acts. The conditions inside Abu Ghraib were portrayed as having been part of a climate of "confusion." of "chaos." It is important to note that it was feminists who gave us this innovative concept of organizational climate.

When trying to figure out why women employees in some organizations were subjected to sexist jokes, unwanted advances, and retribution for not going along with the jokes or not accepting those advances, feminist lawyers, advocates, and scholars began to look beyond the formal policies and the written rules. They explored something more amorphous but just as potent, and maybe even more so: the set of unofficial presumptions that shapes workplace interactions between men and men and between men and women. They followed the bread crumbs to the casual, informal interactions between people up and down the organization's ladder. They investigated who drinks with whom after work, who sends sexist jokes to whom over office e-mail, who pins up which sorts of pictures of women in their lockers or next to the coffee machine. And they looked into what those people in authority did not do. They discovered that *in*action is a form of action: "turning a blind eye" is itself a form of action. Inaction sends out signals to everyone in the organization about what is condoned. Feminists labeled these webs of presumptions, informal interactions, and deliberate inaction as an organization's "climate." As feminists argued successfully in court, it is not sufficient for a stockbrokerage or a college to include anti-sexual-harassment guidelines in its official handbook; employers have to take explicit steps to create a workplace climate in which women are treated with fairness and respect.

By 2004, this feminist explanatory concept—organizational "climate"—had become so accepted by so many analysts that their debt to feminists had been forgotten. Generals Taguba, Jones, and Fay, as well as former defense secretary Schlesinger, may never have taken a women's studies course, but when they were assigned the job of investigating Abu Ghraib they were drawing on the ideas and investigatory skills crafted for them by feminists.

However, more worrisome than the failure by such investigators to acknowledge their intellectual and political debts was their ignoring the feminist lessons that went hand in hand with the concept of "climate." The first lesson: to make sense of any organization, we always must dig deep into the group's dominant presumptions about femininity and masculinity. The second lesson: we need to take seriously the experiences of women as they try to adapt to, or sometimes resist, those dominant gendered presumptions—not because all women are angels, but because paying close attention to women's ideas and actions will shed light on why men with power act the way they do.

Then in September 1995, the rape of a local school girl by two American male marines and a sailor in Okinawa sparked public demonstrations, the formation of new Okinawan women's advocacy groups, and more congressional investigations in the United States. At the start of the twenty-first century, American media began to notice the patterns of international trafficking in Eastern European and Filipino women around American bases in South Korea, prompting official embarrassment in Washington (embarrassment that had not been demonstrated earlier when American base commanders turned a classic "blind eye" to a prostitution industry organized locally to service those commanders' own male soldiers, because it employed "just" local South Korean women). And in 2003, three new American military sexism scandals caught Washington policymakers' attention: four American male soldiers returning from combat missions in Afghanistan murdered their female partners at Fort Bragg, North Carolina; a pattern of sexual harassment and rape by male cadets of female cadets—and superiors' refusal to treat these acts seriously—was revealed at the U.S. Air Force Academy: and at least sixty American women soldiers returning from tours of duty in Kuwait and Iraq testified that they had been sexually assaulted by their male colleagues there—once again, with senior officers choosing inaction and advising the American women soldiers to "get over it" (Jargon 2003; Lutz and Elliston 2004; Miles Foundation 2004; Moffeit and Herder 2004).

So it should have come as no surprise to senior uniformed and civilian policymakers seeking to make sense of the abuses perpetrated in Abu Ghraib that a culture of sexism had come to permeate many sectors of U.S. military life.

Perhaps ultimately the investigators did not make use of the feminist lessons and tools because they imagined that the lessons of Tailhook, Aberdeen, Fort Bragg, Okinawa, South Korea, and the Air Force Academy were relevant only when all the perpetrators of sexual abuse are men and all the victims are women. Perhaps they ignored their knowledge of the sexualized hazing practices common in American military organizations (and in fraternities and sports teams at American colleges) because, after all, those could be dismissed as "boys being boys" and could be imagined as having no serious consequences on either the men being hazed or the women implicitly being denigrated.

The presence of Lynndie England and the other women in Abu Ghraib's military police unit, they might have assumed, made the feminist tools sharpened in those earlier gendered military scandals inappropriate for their current investigation. But the lesson of Tail-book and the other military scandals was *not* that the politics of masculinity and femininity matter only when men are the perpetrators and women are the victims. Instead, the deeper lesson of all those other military scandals is that we must always ask "has this organization (or this system of interlocking organizations) become masculinized in ways that privilege certain forms of masculinity, feminize its opposition, and trivialize most forms of femininity?"

What about the American women soldiers themselves? In the U.S. military of 2004, women constituted 15 percent of active duty personnel, 17 percent of all reserves and the National Guard, and a surprising 24 percent of the army reserves alone. From the very time these particular young women joined this military police unit, they, like their fellow male recruits, probably sought to fit into the group. If the unit's evolving culture—perhaps fostered by their superiors for the sake of "morale" and "unit cohesion"—was one that privileged a certain form of masculinized humor, racism, and bravado, each woman would have had to decide how to deal with that. At least some of the women reservists might have decided to join in, to play the roles assigned to them in order to gain the hoped-for reward of male acceptance. The fact that the Abu Ghraib prison was grossly understaffed during the fall of 2003 (too few guards for the spiraling numbers of Iraqi detainees), that it was isolated from other military operations, and that its residents endured daily and nightly mortar attacks would only serve to intensify the pressures on each soldier to gain acceptance from those unit members who seemed to represent the group's dominant masculinized culture. And what about the fact that Lynndie England entered into a sexual liaison with Charles Graner? We need to treat this as more than merely a "lack of discipline." Looking back on the masculinized and sexualized climate inside the both internally troubled and externally besieged prison, Janis Karpinski, the army reserve general in charge of the prison, recalled how, over the years of her career, she had seen so many young women soldiers "seek protection" from older, more senior male soldiers, usually with those men more than willing to serve as their female subordinates' "protectors" (Karpinski forthcoming). It would be more useful to ask about the cause and effect dynamics between these soldiers' sexual behaviors and their abuses of Iraqi prisoners (including the staged photographs). Feminists have taught us never to brush off sexual relations as if they have nothing to do with organizational and political practices.

Then there is the masculinization of the military interrogators' organizational culture, the masculinization of the CIA's field operatives, and the ideas about "manliness" shaping the entire U.S. political system. Many men and women—lawyers, generals, cabinet members, elected officials—knew full well that aggressive interrogation techniques violated both the spirit and the language of the Geneva Conventions, the UN Convention against Torture, and U.S. federal law against torture. Yet during the months of waging wars in Afghanistan and Iraq, most of these men and women kept silent. Feminists have taught us always to be curious about silence. Thus, we need to ask: did any of the American men involved in interrogations keep silent because they were afraid of being labeled "soft" or "weak," thereby jeopardizing their status as "manly" men? We need also to discover if any of the women who knew better kept silent because they were afraid that they would be labeled "feminine," thus risking being deemed by their colleagues to be untrustworthy outsiders.

We are not going to get to the bottom of the tortures perpetrated by Americans at Abu Ghraib unless we make use of a feminist curiosity and unless we revisit the feminist lessons derived from the scandals that have been revealed at the Tailhook convention, Fort Bragg, the U.S. Naval Academy, Okinawa, and the Air Force Academy. A feminist curiosity, combined with those lessons, might shed a harsh light on an entire American military institutional culture and maybe even the climate of contemporary American political life. That military culture and that political climate together have profound implications for both Americans and for all those citizens in countries where the U.S. military is being held up as a model to emulate as they modernize their own armed forces. Those citizens being encouraged to adopt the American military's culture and political climate—in Eastern Europe's newest members of NATO, as well as in South Korea, Japan, the Philippines, Afghanistan, and Iraq—might find it valuable to consider these feminist-informed lessons.

Abu Ghraib was globalized, first, in that it exposed actions by military personnel and their civilian superiors that were in blatant violation of internationally agreed-upon norms of state behavior—norms written into international law and ratified by the U.S. government. Many people around the globe for the first time read paragraphs of the UN Convention against Torture, and Other Cruel, Inhuman or Degrading Treatment or Punishment, even though it had been adopted in 1984 and signed by their governments in their name. While often referred to simply as the "Convention Against Torture," its full title makes clear its far broader prohibition. The U.S. government, on behalf of all U.S. citizens, signed the Convention. The impetus for its creation in the early 1980s was the international revulsion at the news of the use of torture by military regimes in Chile and Argentina—something that was not uncommon in dozens of other countries ruled by authoritarian and militarized governments, which claimed that enemies within and without could be dealt with only by extraordinary and, if necessary, violent state methods. An international consensus rejected this justification. The Convention against Torture was the product of that historic consensus (Sands 2005).

Second, Abu Ghraib became globalized in that it sparked a worldwide discussion—one that is still going on today—about the ethics of waging war, about the definitions of torture, about the accountability of intelligence services, about urgency, about fear. During the spring and summer of 2004, as the evidence of what had occurred in the cell blocks of Abu Ghraib almost a year earlier mounted, ordinary citizens found themselves talking with friends about "sexual humiliation," "sleep deprivation," "stress positions," and "psychological torture." Many listened to, or read for the first time, detailed discussions by legal and political experts about what counts as "torture," whether torture "works," how ordinary individuals could be desensitized (and by whom) to the point that they could become torturers, and how torture undermines democratic cultures and the rule of law. In the age of satellite television and around-the-clock Internet communication, this became a globalized conversation.

Third, what American personnel—military and militarized—had done inside Abu Ghraib was globalized in the sense that people from scores of countries began to see themselves as having a stake in understanding and critiquing the causes and actions that were gradually revealed. Not everyone agreed that such critical national self-reflection was necessary. In fact, there were people who argued that since the September 11, 2001, attacks, preventing terrorism justified all means of capture, detention, and interrogation. The stakes were too high, they contended, to allow the norms of legal conventions and formal treaties to get in the way of effective prevention. On the other side, often in the same country, there were people who felt that the stakes were too high to treat Abu Ghraib as merely a one-country story.

Thus, Lynndie England was never "the story." She is interesting. She deserves to be fully understood. But so too do Janis Karpinski, Charles Graner's former wife. General Barbara Fast, Captain Carolyn Wood, and the women who served as military and contract interrogators and interpreters in both Guantánamo and Abu Ghraib. Paying attention to diverse militarized women's actions, motivations, assumptions, and immediate as well as distant relationships to male senior commanders and male civilian policymakers can help us see how militarized feminization operates, who wields it, who is complicit in it and why, whom it serves, and what larger cultural goals it promotes.

Note

An earlier, quite different, version of this chapter was published as: "Wielding Masculinity Inside Abu Ghraib." *Asian Journal of Women's Studies* 10, no. 3 (September 2004): 235–243.

References

Associated Press. 2006. "Dog Handler Convicted in Abu Ghraih Abuse." New York Times, June 2.

Bowers, Simon. 2004. "Merrill Lynch Accused of 'Institutional Sexism.'" Guardian (London), June 12.

Bunster-Buroito, Ximena. 1985. "Surviving Beyond Fear: Women and Torture in Latin America." In Women and Change in Latin America, ed. June Nash and Helen Safa, 297-325. Smith Hadley MA: Bergin and Garvey.

Burke, Carol. 2004. Camp All-American, Hanoi June, and the high-and-tight. Boston: Beacon Press.

Carver, Terrell. 2003. "Gender/Feminism/IR." International Studies Review 5 (2): 288–290.

Cloud, David S. 2006. "Inquiry Suggests Marines Excised Files on Killings." New York Times, August 18.

Danner, Mark. ed. 2004. Torture and Truth; America, Abu Ghraib, and the War on Terror New York: New York Review of Books.

Elias, Juanita, ed. Forthcoming. "Hegemonic Masculinities in International Politics." Special issue, Men and Masculinities.

Enloe, Cynthia 1993. The Morning After: Sexual Politics at the End of the Cold War Berkeley: University of California Press.

Enloe, Cynthia 2000. Maneuvers: The International Politics of Militarizing Women' Lives. Berkeley: University of California Press.

Enloe, Cynthia 2004. The Curious Feminist: Searching for Women in New Age of Empire. Berkeley: University of California Press.

Enloe, Cynthia. 1980. Ethnic Soldiers: State Security in Divided Societies. London: Penguin.

Golden, Tim. 2006. "The Battle for Guantanamo." New Times Magazine, September 17, 60–71, 140–145.

Greenberg, Karen, and Joshua Dratel, eds. 2005. The Torture Papers: The Road to Abu Ghraib. New York: Cambridge University Press.

Hersh, Seymour M. 2004. Chain of Command: The Road to Abu Ghraib. New York: HarperCollins.

Hillman, Elizabeth Lutes. 2005. Defending America: Military Culture and the Cold War court-martial. Princeton: Princeton University Press.

Human Rights Watch. 2004. The Road to Abu Ghraib. New York: Human Rights Watch. Jargon, Julie. 2003. "The War Within." Westword, January 30. http^/www.westword.com/issues/2003-0 1-30/feature.html.

Jehl, Douglas. 2004. "Some Ahu Ghraib Abuses Are Traced to Afghanistan." New York Times, August 26.

Karpinski, Janis. 2005. One Woman's Army: The Commanding General of Abu Ghraib Tells Her Story. New York: Hyperion.

Kwon, Insook 2000. "Militarism in My Heart: Militarization of Women's Consciousnessand Culture in South Korea." PhD diss., MA, Clark University.

Kwon, Insook. 1998. " 'The New Women's Movement' in 1920s Korea: Rethinking the Relationship Between Imperialism and Women." In "Feminism and Internationalism," special issue. Gender and History 10 (3): 381–405.

Lewis, Neil A., and Eric Schmitt. 2004. "Lawyers Decided Bans on Torture Didn't Bind Bush." New York Times, June 8.

Lipman, Jana K. Forthcoming. "Guantanamo: Working Class History of Revolution and Empire, 1939–1979." PhD diss., Yale University.

Lutz, Catherine, and Jon Elliston. 2004. "Domestic Terror." In *Interventions: Activists' and Academics' Perspectives on Violence*, ed. Elizabeth Castelli and Janet Jackson. New York: Palgrave Macmillan.

Mayer, Jane. 2005. "The Experiment." New Yorker, July 11–18, 60–71.

Mayer, Jane. 2005b. "The Memo." New Yorker, February 27, 32–41.

Mayer, Jane. 2005a. "Outsourcing Torture." New Yorker, February 14–21, 106–123.

Mayer, Jane. 2006. "The Hidden Power." New Yorker, July 3, 44–55.

Miles Foundation. 2004. "Brownback/Fitz Amendment to S. 2400" e-mail message to Miles Foundation mailing list June 14.

Moffett, Miles, and Amy Herder. 2004. "Returning Female GIs Report Rapes, Poor Care." http:/Avww.sirnosir.com/theiiln~resistor84.html.

Murphy, Evelyn, with E. J. Graff. 2005. Getting Even: Why Women Don't Get Paid Like Men-and What to Do about It. New York: Simon & Schuster.

Office of the Inspector General, U.S. Department of Defense. 2003. The Tailhook Report. New York: St. Martin's.

Ogasawara, Yuko. 1998. Office Studies and Salaried Men; Power, Gender, and Work in Japanese Companies. Berkeley: University of California Press.

Oppel, Richard A. 2006. "Iraqi Accuses U.S. of 'Daily' Attacks against Civilians." New York Times, June 2.

Saar, Eric. 2005. Inside the Wire: A Military Intelligence Soldier's Eyewitness Account of Life at Guantanamo. New York: Penguin.

Sands, Philippe. 2005. *Lawless World: America and the Breaking of Global Rules.* London: Penguin.

Schmidt, Eric. 2004. "Abuse Panel Says Rules on Inmates Need Overhaul." New York Times, August 25.

Stockford, Marjorie A. 2004. The Bellwomen: The Story of the Landmark AT&T Sex Discrimination Case. New Brunswick, NJ: Rutgers University Press.

Strasser, Steven, ed. 2004. The Abu Ghraib Investigations. New 'fork: Public Affairs.

Taguba, Antonio. 2004. Investigation of the 800th Military Polite Brigade. Washington, DC: U.S. Department of Defense.

Whitworth, Sandra. 2004. Men, Militarism and UN Peacekeeping. Boulder, CO: Lynne Rienner.

Wright, Ann. 2006. "Women involved in Prisoner Abuse: Perpetrators, Enablers, and Victims." In Proceedings of the Conference Women in the Military Today, 19-20 May 200.5, ed. Lory Manning, 64–1 11. Washington, DC: Women's Research and Education Institute.

Wypijewski, JoAnn. 2006. "Judgement Days: Lessons from the Abu Ghraib Courts-Martial." Harper's, February, 39–50.

Political Action: The Problem of Dirty Hands

MICHAEL WALZER

Michael Walzer, a professor of politics and ethics, contends in this extract that it is difficult for political leaders to avoid moral dilemmas when they take action. This, Walzer argues, is especially difficult when policy debates involve questions of national security. What does Walzer propose as a solution? Do you agree with his conclusion?

I

Let me begin, then, with a piece of conventional wisdom to the effect that politicians are a good deal worse, morally worse, than the rest of us (it is the wisdom of the rest of us). Without either endorsing it or pretending to disbelieve it, I am going to expound this convention. For it suggests that the dilemma of dirty hands is a central feature of political life, that it arises not merely as an occasional crisis in the career of this or that unlucky politician but systematically and frequently....

...The politician has, or pretends to have, a kind of confidence in his own judgment that the rest of us know to be presumptuous in any man.

The presumption is especially great because the victorious politician uses violence and the threat of violence—not only against foreign nations in our defense but also against us, and again ostensibly for our greater good. This is a point emphasized and perhaps overemphasized by Max Weber in his essay "Politics as a Vocation."[1] It has not, so far as I can tell, played an overt or obvious part in the development of the convention I am examining. The stock figure is the lying, not the murderous, politician—though the murderer lurks in the background, appearing most often in the form of the revolutionary or terrorist, very rarely as an ordinary magistrate or official. Nevertheless, the sheer weight of official violence in human history does suggest the kind of power to which politicians aspire, the kind of power they want to wield, and it may point to the roots of our half-conscious dislike and unease. The men who act for us and in our name are often killers, or seem to become killers too quickly and too easily.

Knowing all this or most of it, good and decent people still enter political life, aiming at some specific reform or seeking a general reformation. They are then required to learn the lesson Machiavelli first set out to teach: "how not to be good."[2] Some of them are incapable of learning; many more profess to be incapable. But they will not succeed unless they learn, for they have joined the terrible competition for power and glory; they have chosen to work and struggle as Machiavelli says, among "so many who are not good." They can do no good themselves unless they win the struggle, which they are unlikely to do unless they are willing and able to use the necessary means. So we are suspicious even of the best of winners. It is not a sign of our perversity if we think them only more clever than the rest. They have not won, after all, because they were good, or not only because of that, but also because they were not good. No one succeeds in politics without getting his hands dirty. This is conventional wisdom again, and again I don't mean to insist that it is true without qualification. I repeat it only to disclose the moral dilemma inherent in the convention. For sometimes it is right to try to succeed, and then it must also be right to get one's hands dirty. But one's hands get dirty from doing what it is wrong to do. And how can it be wrong to do what is right? Or, how can we get our hands dirty by doing what we ought to do?

II

It will be best to turn quickly to some examples. I have chosen two, one relating to the struggle for power and one to its exercise.... Let us imagine a politician who wants to do good only by doing good, or at least he is certain that he can stop short of the most corrupting and brutal uses of political power. Very quickly that certainty is tested. What do we think of him then?

He wants to win the election, someone says, but he doesn't want to get his hands dirty. This is meant as a disparagement, even though it also means that the man being criticized is the sort of man who will not lie, cheat, bargain behind the backs of his supporters, shout absurdities at public meetings, or manipulate other men and women. Assuming that this particular election ought to be won, it is clear, I think, that the disparagement is justified. If the candidate didn't want to get his hands dirty, he should have stayed at home; if he can't stand the heat, he should get out of the kitchen, and so on. His decision to run was a commitment (to all of us who think the election important) to try to win, that is, to do within rational limits whatever is necessary to win. But the candidate is a moral man. He has principles and a history of adherence to those principles. That is why we are supporting him. Perhaps when he refuses to dirty his hands, he is simply insisting on being the sort of man he is. And isn't that the sort of man we want?

Let us look more closely at this case. In order to win the election the candidate must make a deal with a dishonest ward boss, involving the granting of contracts for school construction over the next four years. Should he make the deal?...

Because he has scruples... we know him to be a good man. But we view the campaign in a certain light, estimate its importance in a certain way, and hope that he will overcome his scruples and make the deal. It is important to stress that we don't want just *anyone* to make the deal; we want *him* to make it, precisely because he has scruples about it. We know he is doing right when he makes the deal because he knows he is doing wrong. I don't mean merely that he will feel badly or even very badly after he makes the deal. If he is the good man I am imagining him to be, he will feel guilty, that is, he will believe himself to be guilty. That is what it means to have dirty hands.

All this may become clearer if we look at a more dramatic example, for we are, perhaps, a little blasé about political deals and disinclined to worry much about the man who makes one. So consider a politician who has seized upon a national crisis—a prolonged colonial war—to reach for power. He and his friends win office pledged to decolonization and peace; they are honestly committed to both, though not without some sense of the advantages of the commitment. In any case, they have no responsibility for the war; they have steadfastly opposed it. Immediately, the politician goes off to the colonial capital to open negotiations with the rebels. But the capital is in the grip of a terrorist campaign, and the first decision the new leader faces is this: he is asked to authorize the torture of a captured rebel leader who knows or probably knows the location of a number of bombs hidden in apartment buildings around the city, set to go off within the next twenty-four hours. He orders the man tortured, convinced that he must do so for the sake of the people who might otherwise die in the explosions—even though he believes that torture is wrong, indeed abominable, not just sometimes, but always.[3] He had expressed this belief often and angrily during his own campaign; the rest of us took it as a sign of his goodness. How should we regard him now? (How should he regard himself?)

Once again, it does not seem enough to say that he should feel very badly. But why not? Why shouldn't he have feelings like those of St. Augustine's melancholy soldier, who understood both that his war was just and that killing, even in a just war, is a terrible thing to do?[4] The difference is that Augustine did not believe that it was wrong to kill in a just war; it was just sad, or the sort of thing a good man would be saddened by. But he might have thought it wrong to torture in a just war, and later Catholic theorists have certainly thought it wrong. Moreover, the politician I am imagining thinks it wrong, as do many of us who supported him. Surely we have a right to expect more than melancholy from him now. When he ordered the prisoner tortured, he committed a moral crime and he accepted a moral burden. Now he is a guilty man. His willingness to acknowledge and bear (and perhaps to repent and do penance for) his guilt is evidence, and it is the only evidence he can offer us, both that he is not too good for politics and that he is good enough. Here is the moral politician: it is by his dirty hands that we know him. If he were a moral man and nothing else, his hands would not be dirty; if he were a politician and nothing else, he would pretend that they were clean.

III

Machiavelli's argument about the need to learn how not to be good clearly implies that there are acts known to be bad quite apart from the immediate circumstances in which they are performed or not performed. He points to a distinct set of political methods and strategems which good men must study (by reading his books), not only because their use does not come naturally, but also because they are explicitly condemned by the moral teachings good men accept—and whose acceptance serves in turn to mark men as good. These methods maybe condemned because they are thought contrary to divine law or to the order of nature or to our moral sense, or because in prescribing the law to ourselves we have individually or collectively prohibited them. Machiavelli does not commit himself on such issues, and I shall not do so either if I can avoid it. The effects of these different views are, at least in one crucial sense, the same. They take out of our hands the constant business of attaching moral labels to such Machiavellian methods as deceit and betrayal. Such methods are simply bad. They are the sort of thing that good men avoid, at least until they have learned how not to be good.

When rules are overridden, we do not talk or act as if they had been set aside, canceled, or annulled. They still stand and have this much effect at least: that we know we have done something wrong even if what we have done was also the best thing to do on the whole in the circumstances. Or at least we feel that way, and this feeling is itself a crucial feature of our moral life. For the consequences might be very bad indeed if the rules were overridden every time the moral calculation seemed to go against them. It is probably best if most men do not calculate too nicely, but simply follow the rules; they are less likely to make mistakes that way, all in all. And so a good man (or at least an ordinary good man) will respect the rules rather more than he would if he thought them merely guidelines, and he will feel guilty when he overrides them. Indeed, if he did not feel guilty, "he would not be such a good man." It is by his feelings that we know him. Because of those feelings he will never be in a hurry to override the rules, but will wait until there is no choice, acting only to avoid consequences that are both imminent and almost certainly disastrous.

Once again I will take a latter-day and a lapsed representative of the tradition and consider Albert Camus' *The Just Assassins.* The heroes of this play are terrorists at work in nineteenth-century Russia. The dirt on their hands is human blood. And yet Camus' admiration for them, he tells us, is complete. We consent to being criminals, one of them says, but there is nothing with which anyone can reproach us. Here is the dilemina of dirty hands in a new form. The heroes are innocent criminals, just assassins, because, having killed, they are prepared to die—*and will die.* Only their execution, by the same despotic authorities they are attacking, will complete the action in which they are engaged: dying, they need make no excuses. That is the end of their guilt and pain. The execution is not so much punishment as self-punishment and expiation. On the scaffold they wash their hands clean and, unlike the suffering servant, they die happy.

Now the argument of the play when presented in so radically simplified a form may seem a little bizarre, and perhaps it is marred by the moral extremism of Camus' politics. "Political action has limits," he says in a preface to the volume containing *The Just Assassins*, "and there is no good and just action but what recognizes those limits and if it must go beyond them, at least accepts death."[5] I am less interested here in the violence of that "at least"—what else does he have in mind?—than in the sensible doctrine that it exaggerates. That doctrine might best be described by an analogy: just assassination, I want to suggest, is like civil disobedience. In both men violate a set of rules, go beyond a moral or legal limit, in order to do what they believe they should do. At the same time, they acknowledge their responsibility for the violation by accepting punishment or doing penance. But there is also a difference between the two, which has to do with the difference between law and morality. In most cases of civil disobedience the laws of the state are broken for moral reasons, and the state provides the punishment. In most cases of dirty hands moral rules are broken for reasons of state, and no one provides the punishment. There is rarely a Czarist executioner waiting in the wings for politicians with dirty hands, even the most deserving among them. Moral rules are not usually enforced against the sort of actor I am considering, largely because he acts in an official capacity. If they were enforced, dirty hands would be no problem. We would simply honor the man who did bad in order to do good, and at the same time we would punish him. We would honor him for the good he has done, and we would punish him for the bad he has done. We would punish him, that is, for the same reasons we punish anyone else; it is not my purpose here to defend any particular view of punishment. In any case, there seems no way to establish or enforce the punishment. Short of the priest and the confessional, there are no authorities to whom we might entrust the task.

Notes

1. In *From Max Weber: Essays in Sociology*, trans. and ed. Hans H. Gerth and C. Wright Mills (New York, 1946), 77–128.
2. See *The Prince*, chap. 15; and see *The Discourses*, bk. 1, chaps. 9 and 18. I quote from the Modern Library edition of the two works (New York: Random House, 1950), 57.
3. I leave aside the question of whether the prisoner is himself responsible for the terrorist campaign. Perhaps he opposed it in meetings of the rebel organization. In any case, whether he deserves to be punished or not, he does not deserve to be tortured.
4. Other writers argued that Christians must never kill, even in a just war: and there was also an intermediate position which suggests the origins of the idea of dirty hands. Thus Basil the Great (bishop of Caesarea in the fourth century a.d.): "Killing in war was differentiated by our fathers from murder...nevertheless, perhaps it would be well that those whose hands are unclean abstain from communion for three years." Here dirty hands are a kind of impurity or unworthiness, which is not the same as guilt, though closely related to it. For a general survey of these and other Christian views, see Roland H. Bainton, *Christian Attitudes toward War and Peace* (New York, 1960), esp. chaps. 5–7.
5. *Caligula and Three Other Plays* (New York, 1958), x. (The preface is translated by Justin O'Brian, the plays by Stuart Gilbert.)

Reflections on the Problem of "Dirty Hands"

JEAN BETHKE ELSHTAIN

In this essay Jean Bethke Elshtain, a professor of ethics at the University of Chicago, responds to Walzer's arguments about political action and "dirty hands." Elshtain's focus is on the former President G.W. Bush's decision to order torture of people suspected of planning attacks on the United States. What is her argument? Is Elshtain more convincing than Walzer? After reading the Walzer and Elshtain extracts, watch the documentary "Torturing Democracy" found at http://www.torturingdemocracy.org. Do military experts in interrogation agree with Walzer, Elshtain, or neither? Why?

Torture invariably appears on the "never" list of the "forbiddens" of human politics. Genocide tops that list but torture follows close behind. There are good reasons for this. Brutal regimes historically, like Stalin's Soviet Union and Hitler's Nazi Germany, used torture as a routine dimension of the state apparatus. Enemies or alleged enemies of those two evil regimes were often tortured for the sadistic pleasure of it—not to get useful information. For torture was used primarily against internal foes of the regime. Torture was also widespread in Argentina at the time of its so-called dirty war in the late 1970s—before the restoration of constitutionalism in 1982. In my discussions with the "Mothers of the Disappeared" who had lost children to the military juntas, torture was listed as the most horrible thing imaginable that their children had suffered prior to their outright killing. One mother of three "disappeared" told me that she couldn't bear the thought that her children's last memories on earth were of being tortured. That final image of another human being torturing you, and doing so with sadistic pleasure, prior to taking your last breath, was too much for her to bear. Her health broke, and she never recovered either her health or her faith in humanity.

Before the watershed event of September 11, 2001, I had not reflected critically on the theme of torture. I was one of those who listed it in the category of "never." It did not seem to me possible that the United States would face some of the dilemmas favored by moral theorists in their hypothetical musings on whether torture could ever be morally permitted. Too, reprehensible regimes tortured. End of question. Not so, as it turns out.

The usual dilemma proffered in order to debate torture went something like the following (and there are many variations on the theme). A bomb has been planted in an elementary school building. There are several hundred such buildings in the city in question. A known member of a terrorist criminal gang has been apprehended. The authorities are as close to 100 percent certain as human beings can be in such circumstances that the man apprehended has specific knowledge of which school contains the deadly bomb, due to go off within the hour. He refuses to divulge the information as to which school, and officials know they cannot evacuate all of the schools, thereby guaranteeing the safety of thousands of school children. It follows that some four hundred children will soon die unless the bomb is disarmed. Are you permitted to torture a suspect in order to gain the information that might spare the lives of so many innocents? The circumstances are desperate. The villain is thoroughly villainous. The probability that he knows where the bomb is planted is as close to a certainty as human beings can be in such situations. It is also undeniably the case that, were police to see this man attempting to run into the school, bomb in hand, he would be shot outright. Is it not, therefore, acceptable in this rare instance to torture him to gain the information?

What usually followed the presentation of this, or some other, vivid example was a discussion of options within the framework of the two dominant and competing moral philosophies of modernity: deontology and utilitarianism. The deontologist says "never"—one is never permitted to use another human being as a means rather than an end in himself. The utilitarian says that the greatest good for the greatest number will be served by torturing the creep and saving the school children.[1] So—where do you stand? With Kant or with Bentham?

Most often I found myself standing with neither. I didn't realize it at the time but this "neither...nor" surely reflected my ethical formation within the Christian theological tradition, which is not primarily a deontological ethic (despite attempts by some Christian philosophers to assimilate Christianity to deontology). Instead, what is called up and called upon within Christianity is the concrete responsibility of neighbor-love and neighbor-regard. Where would one's responsibility lie in this circumstance? With the innocent or with the guilty? With school-children who cannot defend themselves or with a prisoner who cannot defend himself either? These are the sorts of considerations that are the stock-in-trade of the moral casuist. It is the tradition of casuistry—a discredited tradition in many quarters—that I will bring to bear in this discussion.[2]

Let me leave this particular dilemma for a moment in order to explore my "neither...nor" in greater detail. The burden of my argument is that, while deontology makes something called "torture" impossible, utilitarianism makes it too easy and too tempting. There is another problem, and that lies in the word itself. Is a shouted insult a form of torture? A slap in the face? Sleep deprivation? A beating to within an inch of one's life? Electric prods on the male genitals, inside a woman's vagina, or in a person's anus? Pulling out fingernails? Cutting off an ear or a breast? All of us, surely, would place every violation on this list beginning with the beating and ending with severing a body part as forms of torture and thus forbidden. No argument there. But let's turn to sleep deprivation and a slap in the face. Do these belong in the same torture category as bodily amputations and sexual assaults? There are even those who would add the shouted insult to the category of torture. But, surely, this makes mincemeat of the category. If everything from a shout to the severing of a body part is "torture," the category is so indiscriminate as to not permit of those distinctions on which the law and moral philosophy rest. If we include all forms of coercion or manipulation within "torture," we move in the direction of indiscriminate moralism and legalism—a kind of deontology run amok. At the same time, we deprive law enforcement, domestic and international, of some of its necessary tools in an often violent and dangerous world.

In the context of domestic life, we tend to place a *verbal insult*—at least we used to—in the realm of manners and basic human decency. A person who insults another is to be chastised, rebuked, even shunned. So we teach children not to insult others: "Don't be rude," we say. Nowadays, of course, because we tend to moralize and to criminalize nearly everything, shouted insults can become the occasion for lawsuits or charges of hate speech and harassment. That said, a verbal insult is rather far down on the scale of awful things that can happen to people. We think worse of a *slap in the face.* Slapping a child can lead to charges of child abuse and, whether the child is physically harmed or not, slapping demeans. If one spouse consistently slaps another, spousal abuse charges may result. A slap is meant to frighten and to demean, to remind someone of who is in the driver's seat. If a slap enters the realm of criminality and turns into a beating, we distinguish it from a *verbal insult*, for it has crossed that barrier that separates the symbolic—speech—from the corporeal—an affront to the body. A third case, *a beating with the butt of a gun*, is the most serious of all in this list of three. Such beatings are the occasion for charges of felonious assault and battery. If a policeman has beaten a person he has arrested, who is handcuffed and subdued, he, too, may be charged: his badge is no protection. Just as we discriminate between accidental death, manslaughter, and capital murder—for a dead body isn't just a dead body; we want to know how it got there—so we make distinctions when it comes to various 'assaults' on persons.

Just War Rules and Restraints

Now let's move to the realm of interrogation of prisoners in the context of a deadly and dangerous war against enemies who know no limits. We have seen these persons in action. We know that they torture, demean, and assault those they have apprehended and then exult when they have beheaded an unarmed man. (Here the murder of Daniel Pearl, a civilian, hence a noncombatant.) In warfare, the rules of *jus ad bellum* and *jus in bello* have no meaning to them. The whole point of terror is the purposeful, random killing of innocents, defined as those in no position to defend themselves. In actual war-fighting, it is often the case nowadays that some, like the United States military, take seriously those ethical restraints on war-fighting derived from the just or justified war tradition and encoded in various international conventions and agreements. Others may ignore these restraints. Nevertheless, those restraints—most importantly *noncombatant immunity*—are central to the way the United States makes war. Soldiers abide by rules of engagement that limit what they can do, and to whom. Terrorists simply unleash violence. Indeed, their favorite targets are "soft targets"—persons working or dining or going to school and who are not prepared, and have no means to, defend themselves.

There are hard-bitten *Realpolitikers* who claim that restraint in war-fighting amounts to "fighting with one hand tied behind your back" and gives the enemy unfair advantage. But the rules of war-making are clear and accepted as normative by the United States. Victory alone is not the singular goal. How one achieves victory is also important. There is, of course, no pristine way to make war. You cannot make war, any more than you can govern, without getting your hands dirty. Thirty years ago, Michael Walzer plumbed the question of "dirty hands" in what has become a standard essay on the subject. Those who take responsibility for the polity and for the wars fought by a polity will, at some point, incur moral guilt—not because they have intentionally committed crimes but, rather, because the courses of action to which they have committed the polity often result in unintended harm to innocents.

Michael Walzer's "Dirty Hands"

In his important essay, Walzer references St. Augustine's "melancholy soldier, who understood both that his war was just and that killing, even in a just war, is a terrible thing to do."[3] If the war is just, and if the person killed is, like the soldier who does the killing, a combatant, we do not burden the soldier with the burden of having murdered. That would be an act of injustice. But it is appropriate that he feel the burden of it all the same. Walzer pursues the issue further by nothing that Augustine "might have thought it wrong to torture in a just war, and later Catholic theorists have certainly thought it wrong. Moreover, the politician I am imagining thinks it wrong, as do many of us who supported him. Surely we have a right to expect more than melancholy from him now." (Walzer is here hypothesizing that the political leader has ordered a man tortured in order to protect civilians who might otherwise die in apartment buildings that have been booby-trapped.) "When he ordered the prisoner tortured, he committed a moral crime and he accepted a moral burden. Now he is a guilty man. His willingness to acknowledge and bear . . . his guilt is evidence, and it is the only evidence he can offer us, both that he is not too good for politics and that he is good enough."[4] He is good enough to do what is wrong but necessary in order to provide for the common defense—to protect the citizens he has a particular responsibility to protect—and he is guilty, as he should be, and as any decent person would be, at what he felt compelled to do, given his vocation of statecraft.

This imagined response of the political leader eschews the exculpatory stratagems of utilitarianism that would enable the leader to torture but to keep his hands clean at the same time. Nor is Walzer's leader a strict deontologist who must do the right thing even if thousands of innocents die. rather like the person Kant imagines who is forbidden, under Kantian deontology, to tell a lie even if it means turning a friend hidden about his house over to a murderer who comes inquiring as to his whereabouts.[5] As I noted earlier, there is an alternative. Although Walzer himself doesn't "name" it, he describes it. One begins with a rule-governed activity. Such rules are moral guidelines. The just war tradition is such a rule-governed activity. There may be situations that were not anticipated and that are so serious, so dire in their potential consequences, they may require overriding the rule. The rule in question is not thereby "set aside, canceled, or annulled."[6] One is obliged to acknowledge violation of the rule and to offer reasons for why, in this circumstance, the rule was temporarily overridden. This overriding of a rule should not be easy: it should, in fact, be *in extremis*, or close to it. And one overrides the rule in recognition that a moral wrong does not make a "right" but it might bring about a "less bad" or "more just" outcome.

In his essay, Walzer associates this form of prudential reasoning with the Catholic tradition. Interestingly, his example of such Catholic reasoning is that of Albert Camus, a lapsed Catholic who was, nonetheless, in dialogue with believers throughout his life. Camus reiterated over and over again the limits that must pertain in political action. If a situation requires the breaking of a moral rule, the person who violates the rule or goes beyond it must "acknowledge their responsibility" and, in many situations, accept punishment or do penance. This way of thinking differs from what Walzer characterizes as the "Protestant tradition" in which the rule-breaker is construed as a kind of tragic hero who has violated his own conscience. For Walzer, the latter sanctions a personal melodrama and directs our attention away from where it rightly belongs: with a system of moral rules and restraints and whether, and under what circumstances, overriding a rule may be the least bad thing to do.

Torture remains a horror and, in general, a tactic that is forbidden. But there are moments when this rule may be overridden. The refusal to legalize and to sanction something as extreme as torture is vitally important. It follows that Alan Dershowitz's suggestion that there may be instances of "legitimate torture" and those about to undertake it should be obliged to gain a "torture warrant" to sanction the activity is a stunningly bad idea. Sanctioning torture through torture warrants partakes of the same moralistic-legalism as the statesperson who values his pure conscience above all else and who will not violate a moral norm under any circumstances. We cannot—and should not—insulate political and military leaders from the often harsh demands of necessity by up-ending the moral universe: that which is rightly taboo now becomes just another piece in the armamentarium of the state.

Redefining Torture: Torture and Severe Coercion

The observant reader will have noted that I have not, as yet, defined what torture is. I have suggested, or hinted, that it is not any and all forms of physical restraint or coercion. Let's turn to another hypothetical. Suppose you had Terry Nichols in custody before the Oklahoma City bombing. You know enough to know that (1) a public building is going to be bombed, and (2) Terry Nichols knows *who, where, and when.* How do you think about torture in such a circumstance? The position I have developed pushes in the following direction: there is no absolute prohibition to what some call torture. Once again, torture is not sufficiently disaggregated. Recall the possibilities: pulling out fingernails; grinding the teeth down or pulling teeth as does a sadistic Laurence Olivier to Dustin Hoffman in the film *Marathon Man:* raping men or women; burning breasts, genitalia; hanging for hours from the arms; crucifying; torturing the spouse or children. There should be—and are—prohibitions against such practices. In an exceptional and truly extreme circumstance, would it be defendable to do any of these things? Everything in me says no and tells me that when we think of torture it is these sorts of extreme forms of physical torment we are thinking of. If torture is the inflicting of severe and devastating pain, as the dictionary defines it, the horrors I have listed are certainly torture.

But there are other options that also come under condemnation as torture. In a striking piece. "The Dark Art of Interrogation," Mark Bowden details some of these.[7] They are called "torture lite," and, Bowden tells us, some argue that such methods are not properly torture at all. This list includes

> sleep deprivation, exposure to heat or cold, the use of drugs to cause confusion, rough treatment (slapping, shoving or shaking), forcing a prisoner to stand for days at a time or sit in uncomfortable positions, and playing on his fears for himself and his family. Although excruciating for the victim, these tactics generally leave no permanent marks and do no lasting physical harm.[8]

The Geneva Convention, however, makes no distinctions of any kind between these tactics and the horrific possibilities I noted earlier. Torture is torture, it says in effect.

But is this not like saying a dead body is a dead body, as if we could not distinguish between accidental death, involuntary manslaughter, and outright murder? The interrogators Bowden interviewed weigh a situation in which the well-being of a captive sits on one side and "lives that might be saved by forcing him to talk" on the other.[9] To bring clarity to the situation, Bowden distinguishes between torture as the horrific practices about which no decent person has any doubts as to whether they constitute torture or not and, by contrast, forms of coercion that involve "moderate physical pressure" and that do no lasting physical damage.[10] It seems to be the case, as Bowden documents it, that techniques like solitary confinement and sensory deprivation often suffice to induce a prisoner to give up sensitive information about terrorist operations. The skilled interrogator often finds that the fear that something may happen is "more effective than any drug, tactic, or torture device.... The threat of coercion usually weakens or destroys resistance more effectively than coercion itself."[11] Forms of psychological pressure and the arts of deception and trickery—for example, telling a captive that others have capitulated so he might as well talk—are standard tools of the interrogator's trade, though some absolutists would forbid them, too. What interrogators learn quickly is that most people want to tell their stories. It is enough, then, to get them talking, for if you succeed, the prisoner keeps talking.

An Unhappy Subject Summed Up

Let's sum up this unhappy subject. Far greater moral guilt falls on a person in authority who permits the deaths of hundreds of innocents rather than choosing to "torture" one guilty or complicit person. One hopes and prays such occasions emerge only rarely. Were I the parent or grandparent of a child whose life might be spared, I confess, with regret, that I would want officials to rank their moral purity as far less important in the overall scheme of things than eliciting information that might spare my child or grandchild and all those other children and grandchildren. But I do not want a law to "cover" such cases, for, truly, hard cases do make bad laws. Instead, we work with a rough rule of thumb in circumstances in which we believe an informant might have information that would probably spare the lives of innocents. In a world of such probabilities, we should demur from Torture 1—the extreme forms of physical torment. But Torture 2, for which we surely need a different name, like coercive interrogation, may, with regret, be used. ("Torture lite," Bowden calls it.) This is a distinction with a difference.

One puts together in a single frame, then, normative condemnation of torture with appropriate consequentionalist considerations—What is to come? To condemn outright Torture 2, or coercive interrogation, is to lapse into a legalistic version of pietistic rigorism in which one's own moral purity is ranked above other goods. This is also a form of moral laziness. One repairs to a code rather than grappling with a terrible moral dilemma. The neighbor-regard in Christian moral thinking ranks concrete responsibility ahead of rigid rule-following. This neighbor-regard involves concern for forms of life and how best to make life at least slightly more just or, to cast it negatively, slightly less unjust. One is willing to pay a price and, if necessary, to incur moral guilt, when the lives of others are at stake.[12]

Notes

The title of this chapter reflects my indebtedness to Michael Walzer's classic essay "Political Action: The Problem of Dirty Hands," most of which is reprinted in chapter 3.

1. Clearly, I am simplifying each of these perspectives, especially utilitarianism, which comes in several varieties, e.g., rule utilitarianism, act utilitarianism, and so on. But this broad characterization of the direction these respective moral philosophies tend is correct.
2. The Protestant brief against casuistry was that it was "Jesuitical" and a way wily Jesuits used to wiggle out of various circumstances or to wheedle and maneuver people toward conclusions that were opposite what they began with. Casuistry took a major hit in the condemnations of Blaise Pascal and lost much credibility. Despite this, legal reasoning is primarily of a casuistical nature.
3. Walzer, "Political Action," p. 65 herein.
4. Ibid.
5. Kant's stringency infuriated the anti-Nazi theologian and martyr Dietrich Bonhoeffer, who declares that Kant carries the principle of not telling a lie to cruel absurdities. Bonhoeffer denounces the "fanatical devotee of truth" who "can make no allowance for human weakness" and who "betrays the community in which he lives." This version of 'truth' demands "its victims" even as the truth-teller remains "proud" and "pure." See Dietrich Bonhoeffer, *Ethics* (New York: Simon and Schuster, 1995), 361, 363.
6. Walzer, "Political Action," p. 68 herein.
7. Mark Bowden, "The Dark Art of Interrogation," *Atlantic Monthly*, October 2003, 51–76.
8. Ibid., 53.
9. Ibid., 54.
10. Ibid., 54.
11. Ibid., 60.
12. These concluding considerations emerged in correspondence with Randall Newman concerning Reinhold Niebuhr and the incompleteness of his spelling out of neighbor-love as a form of justice.

National Military Strategic Plan for the War on Terrorism

CHAIRMAN OF THE U.S. JOINT CHIEFS
OF STAFF

The U.S. Joint Chiefs of Staff are the leading officers in each of the country's armed services. It is their job to create a plan that puts into action the goals of the civilian leadership. On the face of it, the National Military Strategic Plan for the War on Terrorism is only a list of actions. Can you find in it examples of the "dirty hands" debate that Walzer and Elshtain represent? Does the National Military Strategic Plan list what military equipment is needed for success in the "War on Terror"? Why or why not?

Executive summary

The NMSP-WOT constitutes the comprehensive military plan to prosecute the Global War on Terrorism (GWOT) for the Armed Forces of the United States. This document reflects the lessons of the first four years of the Global War on Terrorism, including the findings and recommendations of the 9-11 Commission and a rigorous examination within the Department of Defense (DoD), personally led by the Secretary of Defense and the Chairman of the Joint Chiefs of Staff.

The NMSP-WOT outlines the Department's strategic planning and provides strategic guidance for military activities and operations in the GWOT. The document guides the planning and actions of the Combatant Commands, the Military Departments, Combat Support Agencies and Field Support Activities of the United States to protect and defend the homeland, attack terrorists and their capacity to operate effectively at home and abroad, and support mainstream efforts to reject violent extremism.

Strategic Environment

In the GWOT, violent extremism – in its various forms – is the primary threat to the United States, its allies, and interests. Groups and individuals who advocate extremist ideologies often see the United States and the West as obstacles to their ability to achieve their aims.

The terms "***extremist***" and "***moderate***" are used in this document as follows: *"Extremists"* are those who (1) oppose – in principle and practice – the right of people to choose how to live and how to organize their societies and (2) support the murder of ordinary people to advance extremist ideological purposes. *"Moderates"* or *"mainstream,"* refer to those individuals who do not support the extremists. The term *"moderate"* does not necessarily mean unobservant, secular or Westernizing. It applies to people who may differ from each other and from the average American in any number of ways except that they oppose the killing of ordinary people. The term "terrorist" refers to those who conduct terrorist acts.

National Military Strategic Plan for the War on Terrorism. 1 February 2006. Chairman of the Joint Chiefs of Staff. Washington, D.C. 20318.

Nature of the war

The United States is at war against extremists who advocate and use violence to gain control over others, and in doing so, threaten our way of life. The GWOT is a war to preserve ordinary peoples' ability to live as they choose, and to protect the tolerance and moderation of free and open societies. It is not a religious or cultural clash between Islam and the West, although our extremist enemies find it useful to characterize the war that way. These violent extremists see the U.S. and the West as primary obstacles to achieving their political ends. In fighting this global conflict, the United States must ally itself with partners around the world, especially those in the Muslim world who oppose domination by extremists.

The nature of free and open societies enables terrorist networks to take advantage of freedom of movement, communications, financial systems, and logistical support. Extremist networks are able to operate in and exploit seams between states, between military and police forces, and between international and local laws. Consequently, the United States and partner nations remain highly vulnerable to terrorist violence designed to undermine the international antiterrorist coalition and to cause some members to seek to "opt out" of the struggle.

The conditions that extremist networks exploit to operate and survive have developed over long periods. The effort to alter those conditions will require a long-term, sustained approach whose success is key to promoting an international environment inhospitable to terrorists and their supporters.

Nature of the enemy

The enemy is a transnational movement of extremist organizations, networks, and individuals – and their state and non-state supporters – which have in common that they exploit Islam and use terrorism for ideological ends. The Al Qa'ida Associated Movement (AQAM), comprised of al Qa'ida and affiliated extremists, is the most dangerous present manifestation of such extremism. Certain other violent extremist groups also pose a serious and continuing threat.

There is a direct relationship between the enemies' motivations and the willingness to use terror tactics. The enemies of the United States and its partners are motivated by extremist ideologies antagonistic to freedom, tolerance, and moderation. These ideologies have given rise to an enemy network of extremist organizations and their state sponsors and non-state supporters. Extremists use terrorism – the purposeful targeting of ordinary people – to produce fear to coerce or intimidate governments or societies in the pursuit of political, religious, or ideological goals. Extremists use terrorism to impede and undermine political progress, economic prosperity, the security and stability of the international state system, and the future of civil society.

All enemy networks rely on certain key *functions, processes,* and *resources* to be able to operate and survive. These three elements are an important basis for counter-network strategies and can be defined as follows:

- *Function* (Critical Capability): A specific occupation, role, or purpose.
- *Process:* A series of actions or operations (i.e., the interaction of *resources*) over time that bring about an end or results (i.e., a *function*).
- *Resource* (Critical Requirement): A person, organization, place, or thing (physical and non-physical) and its attributes. In network vernacular, a *resource* may also be referred to as a "node" and the interaction or relationship between nodes described as "linkage."

Specific functions, processes, and resources vary from group to group, network to network, and even from time to time. This demands an agile and adaptive approach to deny terrorists those critical elements that allow operation and survival of the network. A common lexicon and analytic framework is therefore essential to identify and describe these elements within the enemy's complex and ever-shifting network of networks. Such an approach facilitates ease, simplicity, and broad applicability at the strategic level within DoD and among the interagency and partner nations. As a strategic start-point, the terrorist network of networks is organized by NMSP-WOT into nine basic components for the further detailed study of its critical elements of operation and survival:

This categorization serves as a common lexicon for orienting and coordinating efforts against enemy networks.

National Strategy

Ends

The national strategic aims are to defeat violent extremism as a threat to our way of life as a free and open society; and create a global environment inhospitable to violent extremists and all who support them.

Ways

The U.S. Government strategy for GWOT is to continue to lead an international effort to deny violent extremist networks the components they need to operate and survive. Once we deny them what they need to survive, we will have won. In the mean time, we must deny them what they need to operate. This strategy has three elements and relies on three critical crosscutting enablers.

The key elements of the U.S. government GWOT strategy are: *protect and defend the homeland; attack terrorists and their capacity to operate effectively at home and abroad*; and *support mainstream Muslim efforts to reject violent extremism.* The three crosscutting enablers are: *expanding foreign partnerships and partnership capacity; strengthening capacity to prevent terrorist acquisition and use of WMD;* and *institutionalizing domestically and internationally the strategy against violent extremists.*

Means

Success in this war will rely heavily on the close cooperation among U.S. Government agencies and partner nations to integrate all instruments of U.S. and partner national power – diplomatic, information, military, economic, financial, intelligence, and law enforcement (DIMEFIL). The clandestine nature of terrorist organizations, their support by some populations and governments, and the trend toward decentralized control and integration into diverse communities worldwide complicate the employment of military power.

Mission for the Global War on Terrorism

The Department of Defense, as authorized under its chain of command and in coordination with other government agencies and coalition partners, will develop plans and, when directed:

Military Strategic Approach

The Armed Forces of the United States will support national and international activities to counter the enemy's ideology, support moderate alternatives, build capacities of partners, and attack the enemy to deny its key resources and functions. This strategy is expressed in terms of ends, ways, and means.

Ends

The Contingency Planning Guidance establishes four termination objectives as the military contribution to achieving these national strategic aims in the GWOT. These objectives and the mission expressed in this strategy account for the comprehensive military contribution to the GWOT. The CPG termination objectives can be found in the classified version of this document.

Ways

The U.S. government strategic elements and crosscutting enablers call for both direct and indirect military approaches. Direct approaches primarily focus on protecting our interests while attacking the enemy. Indirect approaches primarily focus on establishing conditions for others to achieve success.

The military contribution to this strategy focuses on the accomplishment of six strategic objectives:

Deny terrorists what they need to operate and survive

At the national military level, the armed forces focus efforts to deny the enemy the nine terrorist network components discussed earlier. This effort will identify global linkages among terrorist networks, and then arrange regional actions to achieve network-wide effects. The base plan proposes a five-step process to defeat violent extremism (comprised of mapping nodes and connections, identifying the **network**, developing an **action plan**, tying the plan to **metrics**, and **tracking** progress to determine effects). Doing this for all network components for all countries maps the network, identifies linkages, facilitates sharing "best practices," and informs capacity building efforts.

Enable partner nations to counter terrorism
While nations around the world must fight terrorist extremism within their own borders, many lack the capacity to do this. The armed forces will work with other agencies to enable our partners' success. This effort is key to creating a global environment inhospitable to terrorists.

Deny WMD/E proliferation, recover and eliminate uncontrolled materials, and increase capacity for consequence management
Military activities include efforts to: detect and monitor acquisition and development; conduct counterproliferation operations, security cooperation activities, WMD active and passive defense, and coordination of consequence management operations (logistics, health service support, and decontamination activities).

Defeat terrorists and their organizations
This military strategic objective directly addresses the enemy's ability to continue global terrorist operations. This requires continuous military operations to develop the situation and generate the intelligence that allows us to attack global terrorist organizations.

Counter state and non-state support for terrorism in coordination with other U.S. Government agencies and partner nations
The military contributes by setting conditions for the success of other U.S. Government agencies and coalition efforts.

Contribute to the establishment of conditions that counter ideological support for terrorism
Countering ideological Support for Terrorism attacks the enemy's strategic center of gravity – extremist ideology. To ensure unity of effort, the Department of Defense will coordinate closely with the Federal agencies assigned primary responsibility for this effort in the U.S. Government. The military's role in contributing to the establishment of conditions that counter enemy ideologies is critical. Among the ways that the military contributes are:

- **Security.** A secure environment allows moderates to express themselves without fear of intimidation.
- **Humanitarian Assistance.** These efforts are often key to demonstrating benevolence and goodwill abroad, reinforcing support for local governments and mitigating problems that extremists exploit to gain support for their cause.
- **Military-to-Military contacts.** The military's extensive footprint and access to foreign military leaders influence the way they think about the GWOT and the actions they take to counter violent extremists and promote moderates.
- **Conduct of Operations.** The way we conduct operations – choosing whether, when, where, and how – can affect ideological support for terrorism. Knowledge of indigenous population's cultural and religious sensitivities and understanding of how the enemy uses the U.S. military's actions against us, are considerations for military planning. The conduct of military operations should avoid undercutting the credibility and legitimacy of moderate authorities opposed to the extremists, while limiting the extremists ability to spread their ideology.
- **Military Information Operations (IO).** DoD has significant capabilities that can assist in amplifying the voices of moderates, while helping to counter extremists.

Means

The combination of the Combatant Commands, the Military Departments, the Combat Support Agencies, and the programs and resources of the Department of Defense constitute the military means for fighting the GWOT.

Conclusion

This National Military Strategic Plan is the result of close cooperation between the Office of the Secretary of Defense, the Joint Staff, and the Combatant Commands and Services. Building on the lessons learned over the past four years, it maps DoD's way ahead for the next few decades of this long struggle.

It is of supreme importance that the United States Military understand the nature of the threat and the nature of this war. This understanding is critical to the implementation of this strategy. Integral to the National Military Strategic Plan for the GWOT is the concept of "supporting mainstream efforts to reject violent extremism." All military members need an understanding of this critical element of the strategy. We must be aware of the culture, customs, language and philosophy of affected populations and the enemy, to more effectively counter extremism, and encourage democracy, freedom, and economic prosperity abroad.

It remains vital that the United States, our allies and partners face this enemy with a force of intelligent and culturally attuned professionals. Now is the time to invest in the human capital needed to combat this enemy for the coming decades.

From Global Village to Virtual Battlespace: The Colonizing of the Internet and the Extension of Realpolitik

MARY MCEVOY MANJIKIAN

For many of us, the Internet is simply a tool: we get the news; check up on the "status" of friends; or maybe download songs and movies, occasionally not quite legally. With the last activity we begin to enter the realm Professor Manjikian examines. The excerpt delves into the various ways in which government officials and scholars look at the possible military uses of cyberspace. Manjikian's description takes us back to IR theory perspectives that we studied in Part Two of this book. Which perspective fits how you perceive the Internet? What does Manjikian mean by the word "colonizing" in the title of this piece? Are there other areas of behavior that you believe have been invaded in this way?

From the earliest years of the Internet's creation, cyberspace has been distinguished from other types of political space because of three unique qualities: (i) its ability to mobilize users, particularly "outsiders" including those who have not been easily included in political systems using conventional means; (ii) its ability to quickly provide large quantities of information of uncertain

Manjikian, M. M. (2010), From Global Village to Virtual Battlespace: The Colonizing of the Internet and the Extension of Realpolitik. International Studies Quarterly, 54: 381–401.

or unregulated quality; and (iii) its ability to shrink distances between users, in some sense rendering conventional physical geography irrelevant. This paper presents three lenses for interpreting the significance of these developments: utopian, liberal, and realist. Evolving doctrines of cyberwarfare as put forth by China, Russia, and the United States in particular stress the ways in which cyberspace presents a unique security threat which may present greater advantages to nonstate actors engaged in unconventional warfare. Differing economic, political, and security policies derive from each lens.

> Governments of the Industrial World, you weary giants of flesh and steel, I come from Cyberspace, the new home of Mind. On behalf of the future, I ask you of the past to leave us alone. You are not welcome among us. You have no sovereignty where we gather.
>
> –Paul Barlow, a Declaration of the Independence of Cyberspace, 1996

> The Internet is the first thing that humanity has built that humanity doesn't understand, the largest experiment in anarchy that we have ever had.
>
> –Eric Schmidt[1]

> Anarchy is what states make of it.
>
> –Alexander Wendt

International Relations and the Internet: Reading Cyberpolitics

Few analysts would dispute the significance of the Internet in modern life. The Global Information Infrastructure provides a foundation for many features of the international economy, telecommunications, and transnational actions by individuals and groups of political actors. However, despite the Internet's undeniable presence in contemporary international society, international relations analysts have devoted remarkably little ink to pondering its evolution, its meaning, or its significance. We do not yet possess a coherent definition or theory of cyber power. We do not know how it relates to other aspects of power relations between states (such as economic capabilities, military capabilities or the capacity to mobilize a citizenry) in the international system. We lack a measure of cyber power and a ranking for which states are most "cyber powerful" or what makes them so. Is it, for example, a relative or an absolute capability, and is it merely the possession of this capability which matters, or is it a state's ability to deploy this capability on both an offensive and defensive level? Can cyber power be shared among states or must every state possess its own cyber power?

Two "Creation Stories"—Cyberliberalism vs. Cyberrealism

The thesis of this paper is that from the outset two different narratives have existed to describe cyberspace—its essence, its utility, and its relation to issues of state power. The stories differ in their basic assumptions, the terms they use, and their views of cyberspace's development. For the last 30 of so years, both stories have coexisted in a tense relationship with one story achieving prominence over the other at key junctures, usually as the result of historical events such as the 1991 Persian Gulf War or the terrorist attacks of September 11, 2001. The Internet's technical developers and their fellow academics tell a neoliberal story while the military and strategic studies community tells a neorealist story. Both stories acknowledge cyberspace as a new type of territory, with unique challenges as well as advantages for participants. However, the stories differ in three specific ways: in their understanding of the agent-structure debate as it applies to cyberspace; in their analysis of the likelihood of regulating actions within cyberspace; and in their understandings of whether cyberspace represents ungoverned or merely unclaimed territory. That is, both stories view cyberspace as anarchic while interpreting the significance and meaning of anarchy differently.

While both views have existed from the outset, over time both have become more fleshed out—providing specific (and varying) views on the subjects of territoriality, nationality, and the role of information within the rubric of cyber power. The realist view, in particular, has become more coherent as the result of developments tied to the first

Gulf War in 1991 and September 11. In addition, as cyberspace's economic functions have changed, notions of territoriality and citizenship have also been clarified.

The Liberal narrative: Cyberspace is a world apart

From the earliest days when the Internet existed in only its crudest form and was used only by a small subset of academics and computer professionals, liberal analysts have spoken about cyberspace's revolutionary potential. However, the liberal regime view is not a monolith. Since the beginning, the story has had two strands—a utopian strand and a more pragmatic one. Both are optimistic about cyberspace's democratizing and liberating potential and both view actor preferences as exogenous and evolving along with the system, which "learns" as it moves in a progressive, peaceful direction. However, utopians see cyberspace's development as an organic growth process, while regulators see the Internet evolving due to focused international cooperation. They emphasize that regulation is necessary in order to control antisocial practices and enable the technology to function.[2]

Utopians describe cyberspace as an organic entity, evolving largely by itself with little to no top-down regulation. They acknowledge no "blueprint" for what the Internet might finally look like—emphasizing instead its revolutionary potential to subvert existing power structures. In this view, the Internet is both a place and a "space"—where actors meet in a variety of structured and unstructured formats to exchange information. Cyberspace is a border-free civil society forming part of "the world in which we live."

The more pragmatic version of the liberal argument, however, describes cyberspace as an alternate universe created reflexively through human action where the physical world's old structure with its emphasis on power, identity, and wealth is less relevant. This relationship between developers and the system itself can best be described by referencing two phrases: "The code is the code" (Lips and Taylor 2008)—and "A map is a map" (Dodge and Kitchen 2003). The first phrase refers to Lessig's notion that the computer's code builder determines how data is treated within the Internet (whether it can be reproduced by outsiders and shared, whether the architect "owns" the code, and whether it can be altered by others). By making that coding decision, the builder determines which ethical and legal norms evolve regarding actions in cyberspace (Best and Wade 2007). Computer code thus constructs the legal code.

The second phrase—a map is a map—describes how the cartographers who began mapping the Internet's geography in 1995 engaged in both discovery and invention as they spontaneously found themselves making decisions about how that geography would ultimately look. That is, in deciding which categories to use for conceptualizing and visualizing pathways between data, the mapmakers ultimately ended up structuring the evolution of those pathways (Dodge and Kitchen 2003:73).

In addition, the two strands differ slightly regarding the overall goal of the system, with utopians emphasizing that the goal of the system is to provide information as a free good which is openly exchanged. Here, cyberspace is described as "apart" from traditional politics and operating by different rules and norms. It is as foreign as outer space.

The more pragmatic view, however, holds that information and information security is a collective good to be upheld by all players in the system through the development of Internet norms, the ability and will of Internet actors (including individuals, corporations, and states) to police themselves and their activities, and the development of regimes. As economic transactions began to occur over the Internet, actors worked together to establish trust, so that consumers could best be served within the institutions of the Internet (Pavlou, Anderson, Liang, and Xue 2007). The optimistic notion was that new entrants to the Internet system could be socialized into system values through the actions of other players, existing structures, and the philosophy of the cyberspace environment.

Here, cyberspace or "the global village" is regarded as extraterritorial and not belonging to any one actor or group of actors. It is unowned "commons" and should be the focus of international efforts to preserve it for all. It is, thus, less like outer space than like an ocean or the polar ice caps.

However, from the beginning, not all liberal social analysts were relentlessly optimistic about the opportunities afforded by the expansion of cyberspace. Indeed, the analyst Marshall McLuhan wrote about the "global village" yet noted presciently in 1974 that technology, including television, was capable of "ending the dichotomy between civilian and military" (McLuhan and Fiore 1974:134). He also noted that nearly every new technology introduced on earth has eventually been found to have a military component. In addition, the military analyst Chris Demchak (1999) sounds a note of caution in arguing that the interdependent nature of interactions between national actors in cyberspace actually renders them less, rather than more, secure—in effect increasing their vulnerability.

Detractors also cautioned throughout the 1990s against making the simplistic assumption that those who embraced technology and globalization were "internationalist," while those who did not were "nationalist." Rather, analysts pointed out that the Internet could serve as a door to the past as easily as it led to the future, allowing for the preservation of minority nationality languages and communities within the former Soviet Union (Gronskaya 2006) and even creating community for those suffering from Ost-algie or nostalgia for the former East Germany (Cooke 2002). Kaldor pointed to the role of technology and communication in rebuilding seemingly long-dormant nationalist feelings that ultimately led to the destruction of the former Yugoslavia (Kaldor 1999). In this scenario, the "new world" of the Internet could in effect be simply a reproduction of many of the social problems existing in the old world.

The Realist narrative: Cyberspace is business as usual

The realist narrative, in contrast, paints the increasing importance of communication technology (including satellite communication and later cyberspace communication) as a technological change in the existing international system—rather than a new creation. As early as the 1950s, according to Bruce Berkowitz, the US Department of Defense was aware of the ways in which information networks were forming along Cold War lines, allowing for the exchange of communications and intelligence between allies on both sides of the conflict (Berkowitz 2003:57). And in 1976, when the Internet was still in its infancy, the Boeing engineer Thomas Rona coined the phrase "information warfare," raising the possibility that US dependence upon information capabilities as a function of logistics could be a significant liability in warfare (Campen, Dearth, and Goodden 1996:1).

The realist view thus stresses that changes in information technology did not create a new entity. It merely caused the militaries of the United States, China, Russia, and Western Europe to adapt their existing strategies, goals, and methods of warfare. Technology's increasing role in the conduct of warfare was identified by Russian General Nikolai Ogarkov in the 1970s who (in line with a Marxist-Leninist worldview) described changes in the military-strategic environment as inevitable and unavoidable (Adelman 1985). The changed nature of warfare and an increasing emphasis on information warfare (IW) and electronic warfare (EW) was subsequently noted by the Chinese in the 1980s. And American military analysts integrated thinking about the changed nature of warfare into their analysis in the 1980s, using a variant of the Russians' terminology to identify a revolution in military affairs (RMA) (Mulvenon and Yang 1999; Siroli 2006). The "opening" of cyberspace was thus seen as an expansion of the existing domains of battle (air, land, sea, and space). Later evolutions in US military counterinsurgency policy and public affairs policy would come to reflect this stance.

From the 1980s onward, cyberspace was redefined as both an extension of the battlespace and an extension of the marketplace due to the development of e-commerce. And once issues of wealth and wealth-building began to require resolution within cyberspace, one might argue that these inequities made "war," including cyberwar, inevitable. Cyberspace was thus not a revolutionary space for the subversion of existing power structures within international relations, but instead a field for the overlay of traditional power structures onto this new surface. In addition, the development of e-commerce as well as the evolving notion that security within cyberspace could be provided privately (either by citizens or by hired moderators answerable to the specific private Internet environment) suggested that while cyberspace might be without a nationality or a gender, it was not without an economic ideology. Cyberspace was capitalist, not socialist, not based on barter or some other system—and by extension, it may be argued, cyberspace also was construed of as "western," perhaps even American.

Analysts noted that cyberspace had a temporal as well as a geographic dimension, as information technology helped to make intelligence and communication available more quickly (thus lifting Clausewitz's "fog of war"), as well as overcoming geographic distance between players in both conventional and unconventional warfare (Thomas 2002; Sullivan and Dubik 2003). As Major General Wang Pufeng, recognized as the founder of Chinese information warfare wrote, "Information warfare... constitutes a networkization of the battlefield, and a new model for the complete contest of time and space. At its center is the fight to control the information battlefield and thereby to influence or decide victory or defeat" (Yoshihara 2001: 328).

But the existence of this new domain did not in any way change the ways in which actors calculated the costs and benefits of action in the international sphere, nor did it change their aims. As General T. Michael Moseley, US Air Force Chief of Staff put it in 2007, the control of cyberspace (also known as information dominance or information superiority) was simply one facet of cross-domain dominance—which encompassed maneuvers on land, sea, air, space, and cyberspace (Moseley 2007:2). In the realist narrative, state and non-state actors bring their longstanding endogenous preferences—for relative power, defense against their neighbors and the expansion of territory and national interest—to the cyberspace game, essentially reproducing the security dilemma in the virtual world. Information warfare is a different kind of battle calling for different strategies and tactics, but its aims and goals are the same. Pre-existing conflicts, like the longstanding conflict between the People's Republic of China and Taiwan now also contain a cyberwarfare element (Yin and Taylor 2008:9–10). The existence of new technology and new terrain has simply added a new front to the battle. And a state like Japan, which has been constrained by the tenets of its constitution toward having only a Self-Defense Force, is now in the process of developing only defensive information technology (Yin and Taylor 2008:11).

In the realist view, cyberspace presents many unique advantages to the state actor—including the ability to act as a force multiplier by allowing a smaller opponent to defeat a larger opponent, sometimes by intimidation alone. That is, from the beginning, cyber power was seen as a useful deterrent, as well as an unconventional weapon (Strategic Deterrence Joint Operating Concept 2004:43–44). In evaluating cyber power as a deterrent, however, Chinese strategic analysts focused on the ways in which an adversary could be deterred from attacking if he viewed the costs of a responding Chinese "information strike" as so high as to render any attack unprofitable (Mulvenon and Yang 1999:199). American analysts, in contrast, focused on the ways in which cyberspace could be utilized as a WME or Weapon of Mass Effect, in effect altering the information available to enemy decision makers and changing their perceptions of the costs and benefits of an information strike (Strategic Deterrence Joint Operating Concept 2004:38–40).

Using cyberspace also meant planners could reduce force density through the shrinking of battlefield distances in both space and time, an advantage originally noted by China's military planners, but later cited as a unique advantage by many other nations, including Australia. Evans (2001:134) notes that Australian military strategists "bought into" the RMA beginning in 1994, as they felt it was ideally suited to Australia's low demography, advanced technology, and vast geography.

In addition, from the beginning, planners in the United States, China, UK and elsewhere were aware of the ways in which information warfare and the cyberspace environment could be used to disrupt the enemy's ability to carry out operations. This notion, that wars could be won not through the destruction of an opponent's military forces but rather through rendering them unable or unwilling to fight has been referred to as "control" by the Chinese who cite Sun Tzu as its originator, while

Western planners integrate this tactic more broadly into the field of effects-based operations or the quest for strategic paralysis (Fadok 1995; Batschelet 2002; Sawyer 2007:21).

Thus, as the realist narrative developed over time, many of cyberspace's unique features—including its amorphous, networked nature; the anonymity which it offers; and the speed and cheapness of transactions which can occur—were reconceptualized as dangerous. As Air Force Chief of Staff Michael Moseley noted in 2007, "perhaps for the first time in the history of warfare, the ability to inflict damage and cause strategic dislocation is no longer directly proportional to capital investment, superior motivation and training, or technological prowess" (Moseley 2007:5).

As a result of political developments since 9/11 (as well as legal and economic developments throughout the 1990s), the power narrative has focused on the establishment of Full Spectrum Information Dominance (Yurcik 1997:4), the launching of preemptive information strikes and a rhetoric stressing the Internet's unique open, anarchic system as a danger rather than an opportunity. Information is described as a device or a weapon rather than a collective good, while the Internet can be used as a force multiplier in achieving affects on target populations. Information dominance is preferred over regimes to protect one's interest in cyberspace. Cyberspace combatants now seek information dominance, the ability to access more information and more complete information more quickly than one's opponents in both the short and the long term.[3] Each incursion must be met with a like incursion and if possible, preemptive action must be taken to destroy the opponent's bandwidth

Table 1. Three Views of Cyberspace

	Utopian	*Regulatory*	*Realist*
Territory	Extraterritorial No neighborhoods Virtual world and real world are unrelated "Outer space"	International territory (like an ocean) No center Borders exist	Extraterritorial site of real world power Real estate, neighborhoods Sanctuaries, Dark Web Firewalls Centrally managed and allocated "spillover" from virtual world to real world
Power	Subvert existing power structures	Reproduce existing power structures	Strengthen existing power structures
Identity/ nationality	Disembodied, anonymous actors "Netizen" Internet renders nationality irrelevant	Digitized body possessing nationality Internet allows for nationality	Civilians to be defended by military Jihad represents "virtual imagined community" Internet is nation building
Credibility	Irrelevant	Principal-Agent Creation of trust	Zero-sum Good to be protected
Information	Infinite, shared	Free good Open Source Movement	Can be owned Weapon in fight for territory, credibility "preemptive" information strikes War of Ideas
Regulation	Communitarian Norms	Market-determined Self-policing	US as benevolent hegemon
Growth	Organic Autopoeisis	"Lex Informatica"—developer and social processes work to develop rules	Hybrid of centrally directed and evolving through code-writing

and increase one's own. What matters is to win strategic advantage, even adopting a "virtual scorched earth policy" if necessary (Shachtman 2007).

In the realist view, cyberspace (now known as "the virtual battlespace" rather than "the global village") is territory with borders, bad neighborhoods, and good neighborhoods, as well as dark places offering sanctuary to one's enemies. As simulations allow soldiers to meld their training in the real and virtual world, this has shaped how they understand, use, and formulate policy toward the Internet.

The following schematic illustrates major differences between the viewpoints. Here, there are three columns reflecting the schism between liberal views as well as the realist view (Table 1).

Information as Free Good vs. Information as Weapon

Utopian, liberal, and realist positions differ in their views of territory, citizenship, and strategic vulnerability. They also possess competing ideas about the meaning of information itself. Utopians see information as a free good which is preserved collectively while realists see information as a substance which could be owned, targeted, and weaponized.

The utopian framework—in which information is not subject to control—rests on two complementary notions: convergence and net neutrality. In Negroponte's scenario, media will eventually "converge" so that users own only one device which functions as telephone, cable television, and computer—and information will float between devices, infinite and incapable of being confined or directed.[4] Paul Barlow, the founder of the Electronic Frontier Foundation, a non-governmental organization dedicated to fighting for Internet "freedom" against what he saw as an increasing encroachment by government and private regulators—phrased it in his Declaration of the Independence of Cyberspace:

> Your increasingly obsolete information industries would perpetuate themselves by proposing laws, in America and elsewhere that claim to own speech itself throughout the world. These laws would declare ideas to be another industrial product, no nobler than pig iron. In our world, whatever the human mind can create can be reproduced and distributed infinitely at no cost. The global conveyance of thought no longer requires your factories to accomplish. (Barlow 1996)

Early Internet advocates also staunchly defended the principle of end-to-end use, or "net neutrality" which stated that all data on the Internet should be moved the same way, regardless of the content, destination, or source. This principle, also described as the "First Amendment of the Internet" means that all data should be equally available to anyone on the Internet, without any intervening principles of differential pricing, differential speeds for which information might be carried, or differential access which would make information available to some users but not others. Peer-to-peer file-sharing arrangements such as Napster meant that information was essentially free-flowing, unowned, and infinitely available.

In contrast, the regulatory view recognized the need for rules and norms on both the national and the international level regarding both the availability and the quality of information. Liberal strategies to regulate information have included the formation of professional organizations for those engaged in e-commerce and blogging, as noted above. Here, even academic citation indexes such as the IS Web of Science database—which ranks the relative influence of both academic journals and academic articles within those journals—can be read as regimes to regulate and control the quality of academic materials available on the Web[5] through the science of bibliometrics. Regulators also note that preexisting economic and political inequities mitigate against the ideal of free-flowing information, despite efforts to organize to make information more widely available. Despite initiatives like the One Laptop Per Child Program, a digital divide still exists, and as Leeder notes, even in countries like the US, more information is still consumed by those at the higher end of the socioeconomic spectrum (Leeder 2007:6).

Yet the liberal viewpoint (even the regulatory strand) is nonetheless optimistic about the ability of the Internet to provide timely, targeted political information—and as a result, to mobilize larger numbers of citizens to participate in and learn about the political process. The fact that 46% of Americans utilized at least one Internet source in gathering information about the 2008 presidential election is an indicator of the continuing power of the Internet to provide information, while the fact that 11% of users also posted an opinion or passed along information about the election through the Internet demonstrates its power to mobilize (Smith and Rainie 2008).

The realist, however, views these "information advantages" of cyberspace—including its ability to provide information to mobilize and empower the disenfranchised, as well as the ability of information itself to travel unimpeded in nonhierarchical ways—as strategic disadvantages and even vulnerabilities which threaten both cybersecurity and security in the conventional sense. Here, analysts stress three ideas—information warfare; networks of both ideas and humans, and the information arms race.

The realist position regarding strategic information vulnerability can be traced back to 1991. The 1991 Persian Gulf War has been described as the world's first high-tech war due to the overwhelming speed and effectiveness with which the US demolished the defenses put up by its Iraqi opponents, largely by sustaining large scale damage to their command and control structures. As encouraged as US military planners were by the win, they were also forced to acknowledge their nation's growing dependence on both EW and IW as strategic weapons, and the possibility that damage to these systems could render the US strategically vulnerable (Baker 1991; Maloney 1991).

In the years that followed, planners increasingly focused on overcoming strategic information vulnerability, with both US and Chinese analysts describing information operations as a center of gravity for determining military success (Thomas 2007:31). Hall describes the information center of gravity as "a confluence of streams of communication, automation, thinking, planning, and decision making. This confluence, whether it is found in physical or virtual space, is so important that its demise or manipulation can seriously jeopardize the success of a mission or task" (Hall 2003:28).

That is, gaining control of an adversary's information capabilities was crucial for gaining the initiative in battle, and Chinese doctrine first identified the possibility of making preemptive strikes on enemy centers of gravity (Thomas 2007:33). In this vein, two analysts, one a civilian from the Navy's Postgraduate School in Monterey, California, introduced the notion of cyberwar (or net war) in 1993, arguing that in future years, clashes might have a significant IW component (Arquilla and Ronfeldt 1993:81).

From the beginning, Western analysts were concerned with the fact that IW was a strategic advantage which did not depend on strength or organization, and thus it could be used (perhaps even more effectively) by smaller, irregular armies as well as by established powers like the United States. Thus, throughout the Balkan conflict in the late 1990s, analysts noted that irregular combatants were using information warfare, including the Internet and the sending of faxes, to carry their message directly to citizens and the media, as well as to distribute misinformation.

The realist thus regards information neither as free-flowing (as the utopians do) nor as capable of being regulated. As early as the 1980s, realists expressed the position that cyberspace represented not only a new arena for armed conflict—but also another arena for ideological conflict. According to this perspective, information has two qualities which make it a particularly effective weapon: First, it has an ideational quality (meaning that it can be deployed to carry ideas and change perceptions through psychological operations) and secondly, it has the ability to be targeted to a specific audience (or adversary) through the existence of multiple Internet "channels" for the purpose of informing and mobilizing citizens. The Air Force White Paper "Cornerstones of Information Warfare" in August 1995 described information itself as "a separate realm, potent weapon and lucrative target" (Rattray 2001:321).

The problem, however, with these advantages (ideation and targeting) is that they too are equally available to one's adversaries, and do not depend on any conventional military attributes, such as the size of one's force or even one's training or innate abilities in their deployment. In actuality, the existence of a large-scale conventional military force can actually be a *disadvantage* in deploying information weapons, as a system like the US military was a large, hierarchical bureaucracy in which getting the necessary clearance to issue a press release or set up a Web site in cyberspace might take hours or even days—while in contrast a nonstate actor like Al Qaeda which functioned in a network rather than a hierarchy could frequently post pictures of recent military victories within an hour of the incident, rather than hours or days later.

As cyberspace as a force multiplier was an advantage available to all combatants, all participants including the United States felt compelled to strive for "information dominance" in both offensive and defensive sectors. Arquilla, writing in 1999, quotes Harvard Professor Joseph Nye (who developed the notion of "soft power") on the importance of maintaining an "information edge."

Throughout the 1990s, analysts in Russia, China, and the United States formulated the concept of information dominance to describe the competitive relationship between actors who each strove to control information in cyberspace. Information dominance is a multifaceted or multidimensional objective with several key parts:

1. Each actor wants to be fastest in terms of gathering its own information and to stop his opponents from gathering the same information faster. This includes the objective of placing the adversary in a position of strategic paralysis where they are both unable to make a decision and unable to communicate the results of that decision further down the chain of command. Offensively, an actor can engage in attacks such as Denial of Service attacks which would swarm a system, causing it to shut down so that one's adversaries cannot access their data.
2. Each actor also wants to have the upper hand in terms of credibility, so that those available to be mobilized will be won to one side rather than the other. Each actor thus seeks to limit the other's access to those citizens available to be mobilized in whatever way possible—including the creation of decoy or doppelganger Web sites or "herding" citizens away from an adversary's Web site and toward yours (Moon 2007).

Information dominance (or information supremacy as it is described by the Chinese) is thus both a relative and an absolute capability—with speed seen as a relative capability and credibility seen as absolute.

Throughout the 1990s, actors including China and Russia carried out military exercises aimed at honing capabilities in both defensive and offensive information warfare strategies as well as providing training to nascent "information warriors." At this point, the competitive relationship between actors could be likened to a new arms race in which each side strove for information dominance. With the events of September 11, one could argue that the pace of this arms race merely escalated, with the notion of cyberterrorism providing a justification for applying the Bush Doctrine to cyberspace through the notion of preemptive information strikes.

Recently, US statements regarding offensive cyberwarfare have described attempts to preempt problems like Chinese attempts to hack into the Department of Defense communication network, as well as into British and German defense department computers. In addition, Lani Kass, who was appointed to head the Air Force Cyberspace Command in 2007, points to Iraqi attempts to jam US precision-location signals during the 2003 invasion, as well as attempts by outsiders to hack into military Web sites and even IED's in Iraq and Afghanistan (Convertino, DeMattei, and Knierim 2007).

It is perhaps in this third area—the question of information—where the utopian, liberal, and realist viewpoints diverge most sharply. Liberals regard information as a good to be preserved and regulated, whereas the realist viewpoint acknowledges the possibility that some types of information and the mechanisms used for transmitting this information should probably be destroyed. It is in this dichotomy that the optimism and pessimism of the two views are most sharply contrasted, and the openness and potentiality of one view shows up most starkly against the pessimism and fear of the other.

Conclusion

The aim of this paper was to ask how traditional international relations theories might be applied to make sense of what is fundamentally a novel situation, or one for which there is little, if any, historic precedent. What is particularly unusual about the cyberspace example, however, is the nature of the novel situation itself. In previous instances where analysts have debated the proper stance to take in a novel situation, novelty has generally been a result of a new type of foe—rather than a new type of terrain or international system. Indeed, in his *Social Theory of International Politics*, Alexander Wendt (1999) calls upon international relations theorists to exercise their imaginations in predicting how, for example, a nation like the US would react in encountering a new civilization (such as a race of aliens from outer space). He suggests that we might err on the side of caution, not wanting to anger a potential foe until we have a better sense of their strength and attitudes toward conflict.

However, thus far no one has explored the alternative scenario—in which the players are the same but the terrain or system is fundamentally different—nor has anyone begun to theorize about the ways in which players will adapt and change in response to this new terrain. The point of this paper has been less to theorize about the rightness or wrongness of any one approach to the conceptualization of the cyberspace system, than it has been to point out that this novel system can look completely different when viewed through a realist or a liberal lens. Cyberspace is either a space and place which offers potential for personal liberation, the creation of structures of international cooperation, and greater citizen mobilization and participation; or it is a dark, sinister extension of some of the most dangerous and ungoverned parts of our physical world, a new type of failed space with the potential to breed real threats which will quickly spill over into the real world. Different predictions about the likelihood of conflict in cyberspace and the potential for alliance building and cooperation follow logically from both viewpoints. It is likely that realist attempts to defend cyberspace, to form alliances for that defense, with initiatives to create new weapons in the defense of cyberspace, will continue alongside liberal efforts to regulate cyberspace and its intellectual and physical products, along with attempts to build greater international cooperation toward that end. An understanding of the various lenses used to visualize cyberspace will help to better predict and analyze initiatives undertaken by all players within the cyberspace system.

Notes

1. Quoted in Murray (2007:233).
2. I have borrowed these terms from Andrew Murray (2007).
3. Though I will not dwell in detail on these legal and economic developments, it is my contention that they have largely laid the groundwork for the neorealist understanding of the Internet, through establishing ideas of territoriality and borders. However it is doubtful that this understanding would have become as ensconced without the political developments spelled out here. For more on this point, see Goldsmith and Wu (2006).
4. In contrast, as described above, the military narrative also contains a convergence scenario—through in this scenario all of cyberspace eventually converges under the umbrella of electronic warfare.
5. For more on the influence of academic rating systems for data and information, see McLean, Blais, Garand, and Giles (2009).

References

Adelman, Jonathon. (1985) The Evolution of Soviet Military Doctrine, 1945-84. *Air University Review* 36 (3): 24–35. Available at http://www.airpower.maxwell.af.mil/airchronicles/airreview/1985/ mar-apr/adelman.html. (Accessed February 10, 2009.)

Anderson, W. (2008) Disrupting Threat Finances: Using Financial Information to Disrupt Terrorist Organizations. *Joint Special Operations University Report* 8 (3).

Arquilla, John, and David Ronfeldt. (1993) *Networks and Netwars: The Future of Terror, Crime and the Military.* Santa Monica, CA: Rand Corporation.

Arquilla, John, and David Ronfeldt. (1996) *The Advent of Netwar.* Santa Monica, CA: Rand Corporation.

Arquilla, John, and David Ronfeldt. (1999) *The Emergence of Noopolitik: Toward an American Information Strategy.* Santa Monica, CA: Rand Corporation.

Baker, Daniel. (1991) Deep Attack: Military Intelligence Task Force in Desert Storm. *Military Intelligence Professional Bulletin* 17 (40): 39–42.

Barlow, John Perry. (1996) *A Declaration of the Independence of Cyberspace.* Available at http://homes.eff.org/~barlow/Declaration-Final.html. (Accessed October 1, 2008.)

Batschelet, Allen W. (2002) *Effects-based Operations: A New Operational Model?* Carlisle Barracks, PA: US Army War College. Available at http://www.iwar.org.uk/military/resources/effect-based-ops/ebo.pdf. (Accessed August 14, 2008.)

Berkowitz, Bruce D. (2003) *The New Face of War: How War Will Be Fought in the 21st Century.* New York: Free Press.

Best, Michael L., and Keegan W. Wade. (2007) Democratic and Anti-democratic Regulators of the Internet: A Framework. *The Information Society* 23: 405–411.

Bosker, A. J. (2007) SECAF: Dominance in Cyberspace is Not Optional. Air Force Link, June 1. Available at http://www.af.mil/news/story.asp?id= 123055625. (Accessed March 12, 2009.)

Boyle, James. (2003) The Second Enclosure Movement and the Construction of the Public Domain. *Law and Contemporary Problems* 66 (33): 33–75.

Byerly, Carolyn. (2005) After September 11: The Formation of an Oppositional Discourse. *Feminist Media Studies* 5 (3): 281–294.

Campbell, David. (1998) *Writing Security: United States Foreign Policy and the Politics of Identity.* Minneapolis: University of Minnesota Press.

Campen, Alan, Douglas Dearth, and Thomas R. Goodden. (1996) *Cyber War: Security, Strategy, and Conflict in the Information Age.* Available at http://all.net/books/iw/iwarstuff/www.us.net/signal/ AIP/intro.html. (Accessed February 6, 2009.)

Cavelty, Myriam Dunn. (2008) *Power and Security in the Information Age: Investigating the Role of the State in Cyberspace.* London: Ashgate.

Convertino, Sebastian, Lou A. DeMattei, and Taimeri Knierim. (2007) *Flying and Fighting in Cyberspace.* Maxwell Air Force Base, AL: Air University Press.

Cooke, Paul. (2002) Surfing for Eastern Difference: Ost-algie, Identity and Cyberspace. *Canadian Journal of Germanic Studies* 40 (3): 202–221.

Demchak, Chris C. (1999) New Security in Cyberspace: Emerging Intersection between Military and Civilian Contingencies. *Journal of Contingencies and Crisis Management* 7 (4): 181–195.

Demchak, Chris. (2003) The Palestinian-Israeli Cyberwar. *Military Review* (March–April): 52–64.

Dodge, Martin, and Rob Kitchen. (2003) *Mapping Cyberspace.* New York: Routledge.

Doyle, John M. (2006) COIN of the Realm. *Aviation Week and Space Technology* 165 (16): 11–13.

Draft Russian Military Doctrine. (1999) Available at http://www.fas.org/nuke/guide/russia/doctrine/991009-draft-doctrine.htm. (Accessed February 5, 2009.)

Echevarria, Antulio. (2008) *Wars of Ideas and the War of Ideas.* Carlisle, PA: Strategic Studies Institute.

Evans, Michael. (2001) *Australia and the Revolution in Military Affairs.* Canberra, Australia: Land Warfare Studies Center.

Fadok, David S. (1995) *Airpower's Quest for Strategic Paralysis.* Maxwell Air Force Base, AL: Air University Press.

Feigenbaum, Evan. (2003) *China's Technowarriors: National Security and Strategic Competition from the Nuclear to the Information Age.* Stanford, CA: Stanford University Press.

Flichy, Patrice. (2007) *Internel Imaginaire.* Cambridge, MA: MIT Press.

Goldsmith, Jack L., and Tim Wu. (2006) *Who Controls the Internet? Illusions of a Borderless World.* New York: Oxford University Press.

Groc, Isabelle. (2008) *The Online Hunt for Terrorists.* PC Magazine, Available at http://www.eller.arizona.edu/docs/press/2008/02/PCMagazine_

The_Online_hunt_for_terrorists_Feb27_2008.pdf. (Accessed February 27, 2008.)

Gronskaya, Natalya. (2006) The Virtual Space of Language Policy: The Conflictual Nature of Linguistic Coexistence. *Russian Politics and Law* 44 (1): 42–54.

Hall, Wayne Michael. (2003) *Stray Voltage: War in the Information Age.* Annapolis, MD: Naval Institute Press.

Humphreys, Sal. (2008) Ruling the Virtual World: Governance in Massively Multiplayer Online Games. *European Journal of Cultural Studies* 11 (2): 149–171.

Kaldor, Mary. (1999) *New and Old Wars: Organized Violence in a Global Era.* Stanford, CA: Stanford University Press.

Kenny, Charles. (2006) *Overselling the Web? Development and the Internet.* Boulder: Lynne Riener.

Korteweg, Rem. (2008) Black Holes: On Terrorist Sanctuaries and Governmental Weakness. *Civil Wars* 10 (1): 60–71.

Krishna-Henzel, Sai Felicia. (2007) Cybersecurity: Perspectives on the Challenges of the Information Revolution. In *Power and Security in the Information Age: Investigating the Role of the State in Cyberspace*, edited by Myrian Dunn Cavelty, Victor Mauer, and Sai Felicia Krishna-Henzel. London: Ashgate.

Lachow, Irving, and Courtney Richardson. (2007) Terrorist Use of the Internet: The Real Story. *Joint Forces Quarterly* 45 (2): 11–16.

Leeder, Kim. (2007) Technology and Communication in the Environmental Movement. *Electronic Green Journal* 1 (25): 19–26.

Libicki, Martin. (2007) *Conquest in Cyberspace: National Security and Information Warfare.* Cambridge: Cambridge University Press.

Lips, Miriam, and Taylor J.A. (2008) The Citizen in the Information Polity: Exposing the Limits of the E-government Paradigm. *Information Polity* 13 (3–4): 139–152.

Maloney, Lawrence. (1991) What's Next for Smart War? *Design News* 47 (8): 1.

McLean, Iain, Andre Blais, James Garand, and Michael Giles. (2009) Comparative Journal Ratings: A Survey Report. *Political Studies Review* 7: 18–38.

McLuhan, Marshall, and Quentin Fiore. (1974) *War and Peace in the Global Village.* New York: Simon & Schuster, Inc.

Milone, Mark. (2003) National Infrastructure. *Knowledge, Technology & Policy* 16 (1): 75–103.

Moon, David B. (2007) Cyber-herding: Exploiting Islamic Extremists' Use of the Internet. Unpublished Thesis, Naval Postgraduate School. Available at http://stinet.dtic.mil/cgi-bin/ GetTRDoc?AD=ADA475919&location=U2&doc=GetTRDDoc.pdf. (Accessed August 11, 2008.)

Moseley, Michael. (2007) *The Nation's Guardians: America's 21st Century Air Force.* Available at http:// www.afa.org/CSAF_Whitepaper.pdf. (Accessed February 3, 2009.)

Mulvenon, James, and Richard Yang, Eds. (1999) *The People's Liberation Army in the Information Age.* Santa Monica, CA: Rand Corporation.

Murphy, Emma. (2006) Agency and Space: The Political Impact of Information Technologies in the Gulf Arab States. *Third World Quarterly* 27 (6): 1059–1083.

Murray, Andrew D. (2007) *The Regulation of Cyberspace: Control in the Online Environment.* New York: Routledge.

Nunes, Mark. (2005) Distributed Terror and the Ordering of Networked Social Space. *Media/Culture Journal* 7 (6): 1–3.

Olson, William J. (2007) Iraq and Global Insurgency: Dien Bien Phu or Khe Sanh. In *Warfare in the Age of Non-state Actors,* edited by Kendall Gott and Michael Brooks. Ft. Leavenworth, KS: Combat Studies Institute Press.

Pavlou, Paul, A. Anderson, Huigang Liang, and Yajiong Xue. (2007) Understanding and Mitigating Uncertainty in Online Exchange Relationships: A Principal-Agent Perspective. *MIS Quarterly* 31 (1): 105–137.

Pfister, Frederick W. (2007) Net Neutrality: An International Policy for the United States. *San Diego International Law Journal* 9: 173–185.

Posen, Barry. (2003) Command of the Commons: The Military Foundations of US Hegemony. *International Security* 28 (1): 5–46.

Rattray, Gregory. (2001) *Strategic Warfare in Cyberspace.* Cambridge, MA: MIT Press.

Sageman, Marc. (2008) The Next Generation of Terror. *Foreign Policy* (February 19): 36–42.

Sawyer, Ralph. (2007) *The Tao of Deception: Unorthodox Warfare in Historic and Modern China.* New York: Basic Books.

Scales, Robert H. (2007) The Army and the Future of Irregular Conflict. In *Warfare in the Age of Nonstate Actors,* edited by Kendall Gott and Michael Brooks. Ft. Leavenworth, KS: Combat Studies Institute Press.

Schonfeld, Erick. (2008) Six Months In and 600 Posts Later…The Worlds of Blogging and Journalism Collide. *Tech Crunch,* March 30. Available at http://www.techcrunch.com/2008/03/30/ six-months-in-and-six-hundred-posts-later-the-worlds-of-blogging-and-journalism-collide-in-my-brain. (Accessed February 5, 2009.)

Sewall, Sarah, John A. Nage, David H. Petraeus, and James Amos. (2007) *The US Army/Marine Corps Counterinsurgency Field Manual.* Chicago: University of Chicago Press.

Shachtman, Noah. (2007) Air Force Readying Cyber Strikes. Available at http://www.blog.wired.com/defense/2007/10/also-nsa-target.html. (Accessed October 13, 2008.)

Simonelis, Alex. (2005) A Concise Guide to the Major Internet Bodies. Available at http://www.acm.org/ubiquity/views/v6i5-simoneli.html. (Accessed September 1, 2009.)

Siroli, Gian Piero. (2006) Strategic Information Warfare: An Introduction. In *Cyberwar, Netwar and the Revolution in Military Affairs,* edited by Philippa Trevorrow, Steve Wright, David Webb, and Edward Halperin. New York: Palgrave Macmillan.

Smith, Aaron, and Lee Rainie. (2008) *The Internet and the 2008 Election.* Washington, DC: Pew Internet and American Life Project. Available at http://pewinternet.org. (Accessed February 12, 2009.)

Stein, Laura. (2008) Speech without Rights: The Status of Public Space on the Internet. *The Communication Review* 11: 1–23.

Sullivan, Gordon, and James Dubik. (2003) War in the Information Age. In *Envisioning Future Warfare,* edited by Gordon Sullivan and James Dubik. Ft. Leavenworth, KS: US Army Command and General Staff College Press.

Takehashi, Dean. (2008) Terrorists in Second Life. *Foreign Policy* (February 19): 93

Thomas, Timothy. (2002) Information Age De-Terror-Ence. *Military Review* (January–February): 31–37.

Thomas, Timothy. (2005) Chinese and American Network Warfare. *Joint Forces Quarterly* 38: 76–83.

Thomas, Timothy. (2007) *Decoding the Virtual Dragon.* Ft. Leavenworth, KS: Foreign Military Studies Office.

Weiss, Jeffrey. (2008) Exposing the Information Domain Myth: A New Concept for Air Force and Information Operations Doctrine. *Air and Space Power Journal* 23 (1): 49–63.

Wendt, Alexander. (1999) *Social Theory of International Politics.* Cambridge: Cambridge University Press.

Wynne, Michael. (2007) Flying and Fighting in Cyberspace. *Air Power Journal* 22 (1): 5–10.

Strategic Deterrence Joint Operating Concept. (2004) Washington, DC: Department of Defense. Available at http://www.dtic.mil/futurejointwarfare/concepts/sd_joc_v1.doc. (Accessed February 6, 2009.)

Yin, J., and Taylor P.M. (2008) Information Operations from an Asian Perspective: A Comparative Analysis. *Journal of Information Warfare* 7 (1): 1–23.

Yoshihara, Toshi. (2001) *Chinese Information Warfare: A Phantom Menace or Emerging Threat?* Carlisle, PA: Strategic Studies Institute.

Yurcik, William. (1997) Information Warfare: Legal & Ethical Challenges of the Next Global Battleground. Available at http://citeseerx.ist.psu.edu/viewdoc/downhload?=doi=10.1.1.15.2345&rep= rep1&type=pdf. (Accessed February 6, 2009.)

Zittrain, Jonathan. (2008) The Web's Dark Energy. *Technology Review* (July/August): 37.

Nuclear Weapons Reinforce Security and Stability in 21st-Century Asia

MUTHIAH ALAGAPPA

Professor Muthiah Alagappa offers a direct argument: Western security specialists have long asserted that nuclear weapons brought stability to US–USSR relations during the Cold War. Alagappa extends that argument to Asia. He does not claim that security should be based only on nuclear weapons; instead, Alagappa writes that because the weapons exist in Asia, policy planners should include the devices in their calculations. How does Alagappa structure his argument? In the mid-1990s Kenneth Waltz, in his exchange with Scott Sagan, made a similar argument about nuclear weapons in the developing world. How does Alagappa address Waltz's argument?

Continuing emphasis on non-proliferation and calls for elimination of nuclear weapons notwithstanding, it appears likely that nuclear weapons will persist and influence national security policies and strategies of major powers, as well as certain second-tier powers and isolated states in the foreseeable future. Initial anticipation in the West especially in the arms control and nonproliferation community of the decreasing security relevance of nuclear weapons was ill-founded. The effort in the last decade and a half to arrest and reverse the spread of nuclear weapons has not been any more successful than earlier ones. Leaders and governments in nuclear weapon states, their allies, and aspirants to the nuclear club believe that their nuclear forces or those of their allies can advance national security. Nuclear weapons, ballistic missiles, and strategic defense have entered or reentered the security thinking of the old, new, and prospective nuclear weapon states and their allies in a fundamentally different strategic environment and in a nuclear era that is substantially different from that of the Cold War. It is important to understand the security significance and roles of nuclear weapons in the new era, investigate national strategies for their employment, and explore their implications for international security, stability, and conflict resolution in the 21st century. This is particularly important in the broadly defined Asian security region which confronts serious security challenges and includes five of the seven declared nuclear weapon states (United States, Russia, China, India, Pakistan), one undeclared nuclear weapon state (Israel), two aspirant states (North Korea and Iran), and several states (Japan, South Korea, Taiwan and Australia) that rely on the American nuclear umbrella for their security.

Adapted from The Long Shadow: Nuclear Weapons and Security in 21st Century Asia. Edited by Muthiah Alagappa.

The grim scenarios associated with nuclear weapons in Asia frequently rely on worst-case political and military situations and draw upon a certain view of the role of nuclear weapons in Cold War Europe or on the claim that Europe's experience does not apply to Asia. Three contending views have been advanced on the consequence of nuclear weapons for peace and security in Europe during the Cold War. One view is that nuclear weapons contributed to the long peace and stability in Europe (Gaddis 1992; Jervis 1988; Waltz 2004). The second view does not contest the idea of a long peace but disputes that nuclear weapons contributed to it (Mueller 1988, 1998). The third view contests the claim that the Cold War was a period of stable peace. In this view, the nuclear standoff during the Cold War was highly dangerous and should be avoided. In terms of relevance for the contemporary era, some Western analysts (mostly non-proliferation scholars and advocates) argue that the contribution of nuclear weapons to the long peace in Europe would not apply to Asia. Asian countries are culturally different; their militaries view preventive war in a favorable light and are not interested in developing invulnerable strategic forces; and insecure command and control arrangements make them more prone to accidents and unauthorized use (Feaver 1992–93, 1993; Sagan 1994, 1995). Adherents of this perspective argue that the Indian, Pakistani, and most recently North Korean nuclear tests would set off a domino effect, with negative consequences for security and stability in Asia and the world. The view that nuclear weapons would contribute to insecurity and instability in Asia seems to have become dominant in the West. It resonates with and reinforces earlier views in Europe and the United States that Asia was ripe for rivalry and that its future would resemble the war-torn Europe of the nineteenth century (Buzan and Segal 1994; Friedberg 1993–94).

My Argument

The primary argument of this article is that although there could be destabilizing situations, on net, nuclear weapons have contributed to peace, security, and stability in Asia. This argument is supported on the following grounds. First, nuclear weapons have not fundamentally disrupted the regional distribution of power or intensified security dilemmas. In fact by assuaging the security concerns of weak and vulnerable states they promote stability in conflict prone dyads. Second, fear of the devastating consequences of a nuclear exchange prevents the outbreak and escalation of regional hostilities to full-scale war, strengthens the political and military status quo, and impels conflicting parties to freeze the conflict or explore a negotiated settlement. Third, the combination of minimum deterrence strategies and general deterrence postures enhances stability among major powers and avoids strategic arms races like that during the Cold War. Finally, nuclear weapons reinforce the trend in the region to circumscribe and transform the role of force in international politics.

The article further argues that the oftenposited destabilizing effects of nuclear weapons (dangers associated with new nuclear-weapon states, domino effect, preventive military action, and early use postures) have not materialized. There are indeed risks associated with nuclear weapons. However, they must be addressed on their own merits and not be advanced as a reason to deny the security relevance of nuclear weapons. The effort of the non-proliferation community to stop the spread of nuclear weapons on the basis of risks associated with nuclear weapons in the hands of "new" states generates an unproductive and futile debate. Arms are symptomatic of insecurity, not its cause. To be successful arms control policies must not only address the supply side but also deal with the demand side of the equation. The real cause of insecurity and armament lies in political disputes.

Two clarifications are in order. One, I am not arguing that security and stability in Asia rests only or even primarily on nuclear weapons. As I have argued elsewhere peace, stability, and prosperity in Asia since 1979 rests on several pillars (Alagappa 2003a). Nuclear weapons strengthen that peace and stability by reinforcing deterrence dominance and further circumscribing the offensive roles of force. Second, I am not making the case for unlimited proliferation on the ground that more may be better (Waltz 1995). My case is that that proliferation thus far has been gradual and has not undermined peace and stability as predicted. In fact gradual proliferation has reinforced peace and stability in Asia. Preventing proliferation should continue to be a key goal of the international community; proliferators must face serious cost and supply obstacles. In such context only countries that feel severely threatened will pursue the nuclear weapon route and the acquisition process will necessarily be prolonged. The international community will have opportunities and measures to stop specific acquisition(s) and/ or time to adjust to the changing nuclear situation. In addition to limiting and slowing proliferation, the nuclear order must be able to gradually accommodate new nuclear weapon states and promote deterrence and stability especially during potential moments of instability. Any attempt to freeze and rigidify the Cold War nuclear order will increase the gap between the formal regime and reality, weaken it, and possibly lead to its eventual collapse. I will deal with possible

No Fundamental Disruption in Power Distribution or Intensification of Security Dilemmas

Nuclear weapons have not disrupted or destabilized the overall distribution of power or fundamentally altered the patterns of amity and enmity in the Asian security region. The unipolar structure of the present system and the anticipated changes in the distribution of power in the Asian security region are consequences of change in the overall national power of states that has several dimensions. Military power is an important component of national power; and having nuclear weapons makes a significant difference in national military capability. However, military power by itself is not a sufficient basis for major power status. The enormous destructive power of nuclear weapons is also less fungible and less relevant to the pursuit of high priority non-traditional security goals. Nuclear weapons add to but are not a sufficient basis of national power.

The present dominance of the United States, the decline in the position of Russia, and the rise of China and India are not due to their nuclear weapon capabilities. U.S. dominance is grounded in its vast lead in several dimensions of power. Although Russia still has a formidable nuclear arsenal, it is not a superpower or even a top-tier regional power in Asia. China has long had nuclear weapons but only since the mid-1990s has it been recognized as a major power. The rapid and substantial increase in China's national power and the apprehension it creates are primarily due to its sustained high rate of economic growth, which in turn produces the resources for accumulating and exercising international power and influence. Likewise, the rise in the power and status of India is due in large measure to its economic growth, political stability, change in foreign policy, technological advancement, and human resource potential.

Although they do not affect the regional distribution of power, nuclear weapons strengthen weaker powers by canceling or mitigating the effects of imbalance in conventional and nuclear weapon capability and thereby reducing their strategic vulnerability. By threatening nuclear retaliation and catastrophic damage in the event of large-scale conventional or nuclear attack, and exploiting the risk of escalation to nuclear war, weaker powers with nuclear weapons constrain the military options of a stronger adversary. This is most evident in the cases of Pakistan, North Korea, and Israel. Pakistan is much weaker than India in several dimensions of national power. It suffered defeats in two of the three conventional wars it fought with India in the prenuclear era, with the 1971 war resulting in humiliating defeat and dismemberment. In the nuclear era, which dates from the late 1980s, Islamabad has been able to deter India from crossing into Pakistan proper and Pakistan-controlled Kashmir even in the context of Pakistani military infiltration into Indian-controlled Kashmir in 1999. India did not follow through with the limited-war option in 2001–02 because of the grave risk it entailed. India was also forced in part by the risk of nuclear war to engage in a comprehensive dialogue to explore settlement of disputes between the two countries, including the Kashmir conflict. Pakistan's nuclear arsenal has blunted the potency of India's large conventional military force. Although it has not canceled out all the consequences of the large power differential between the two countries, it has had significant constraining impact on India's military options and assuaged Pakistan's concern about the Indian threat.

The leveling and cautionary effects of nuclear weapons are also evident in the relationship of the weak and isolated North Korea with the vastly superior United States. Although North Korea does not have an operational nuclear arsenal and the United States can destroy that country many times over, the risk of quick and substantial damage to its forces and allies in the region induces caution and constrains U.S. military options. If in the future North Korea develops nuclear weapons and marries them to its missile capability, the risks associated with preventive military action against that country would multiply. Instead of simply suffering the will of the mighty United States, North Korea's nascent capability has provided it with security and bargaining leverage in its negotiations with major powers in the region (Park and Lee 2008). The security effect of an opaque nuclear force like that of Israel is more difficult to demonstrate, especially as that country also has superior conventional military capability. Nevertheless it is possible to argue that the Arab countries' tacit acceptance of Israel's nuclear deterrence posture has contributed to Israel's security and to regional stability by lowering the intensity of the Arab-Israeli conflict, and in some instances even contributed to peace settlements, like that between Israel and Egypt (Cohen 2008). Israel perceives nuclear weapons are the ultimate security guarantee. They enhance Israel's self-confidence and demonstrate its resolve to survive.

For non-nuclear weapon states like Japan and South Korea, the U.S. extended deterrence commitments have been a significant factor in assuaging their security vulnerabilities in the wake of the North Korean nuclear test. Both countries insisted on reaffirmation of the U.S. commitment, and Japan is exploring measures to increase the credibility of that commitment. In reassuring Japan, the U.S. commitment is a significant factor along with others in forestalling exploration of an independent nuclear option by that country. The U.S. commitment enables South Korea to maintain a nonnuclear posture, provides time to build a self-reliant defense capability, and is a fallback in dealing with a nuclear-armed North Korea.

As with structure, nuclear weapons have not fundamentally altered lines of amity and enmity in the Asian security region. The principal effect of nuclear weapons has been a function of strategies for their employment. Offensive strategies have intensified existing security dilemmas; but deterrence strategies have not. And deterrence has and continues to be the dominant role and strategy for the employment of nuclear weapons in Asia. Enmity in the India-Pakistan dyad, for example, dates to the partition of British India, their conflict over Kashmir, and Pakistan's quest for equality with India. Nuclear weapons have both ameliorated and intensified threat perceptions in this dyad. As noted earlier they have mitigated Pakistan's sense of insecurity by constraining India's military options. However, Pakistan's policy to exploit the risk of escalation to nuclear war to alter the political and territorial status quo in Kashmir, and India's coercive response to preserve or restore the status quo intensified both countries' vulnerabilities and threat perceptions, resulting in crisis situations early in the overt nuclear era. Since then, however, the situation has stabilized. A mixed strategic picture (conflict, dialogue, and negotiations between the two countries) along with other priorities and international pressure has helped to reduce the threat intensity between them. Recognition of the grave risks associated with offensive strategies under nuclear conditions is a factor as well. Although both countries continue to develop their nuclear and missile capabilities with reference to each other, the anxiety surrounding missile tests and military exercises has declined. Further, the crises precipitated by offensive strategies deepened the security interdependence between the two countries, providing a basis for limited confidence building and arms control measures to prevent unintended escalation of hostilities.

Likewise the enmity in U.S.-North Korea, North Korea-Japan, and North Korea-South Korea relations preceded the development of North Korean nuclear weapon capability. Although the North Korean nuclear test heightened the sense of insecurity in Japan and to a lesser degree in South Korea, it has not fundamentally altered the security situation in Northeast Asia. Should North Korea develop an operational arsenal and seek to use its nuclear weapons in an offensive manner that could intensify related security dilemmas. For reasons explained later, this is highly unlikely. Deterrence will be the primary role of North Korea's small nuclear weapon capability. Iran's nuclear quest may have the potential to alter the pattern of enmity and amity in the Middle East. A nuclear Iran is likely to intensify the Israel-Iran line of enmity and bring about change in Israel's nuclear posture, making nuclear weapons more prominent in Middle East security. The animosity between Iran and the Arab states may also intensify, while that between Israel and certain Arab states could become tempered.

Among the major powers, nuclear weapons have created apprehensions but not fundamentally altered the basis and nature of their security interaction, which is characterized by cooperation and conflict. The vastly superior American nuclear arsenal and especially Washington's emphasis on offensive and defensive strategies have raised concerns in Beijing and Moscow. Talk of U.S. nuclear primacy with a disarming capability created disquiet in these countries. The United States clarified that its offensive and defensive strategies are specifically directed at rogue states, and there is increasing doubt that the United States could develop effective strategic defense capabilities against China and Russia. Nevertheless, these countries can be expected to strengthen their strategic deterrent forces and increase their policy options in relation to the United States. At the same time, China has not abandoned its minimum deterrence strategy to engage in direct nuclear competition with the United States. The Chinese response has been deliberately indirect and muted. By retaining a posture of dynamic minimum deterrence and an NFU policy while continuing to modernize its nuclear force, China seeks to prevent deterioration of its security interaction with the United States. In the case of Russia, its strong opposition to the U.S. ballistic missile defense deployment in Eastern Europe and its suspension of the Conventional Forces in Europe Treaty further strained U.S.-Russia relations. However, Russia has not articulated a nuclear strategy to directly challenge or compete with the United States. The United States also does not appear to have altered its view of not treating Russia as an enemy state.

Nuclear weapons have not substantially altered Sino-Indian security interaction, which appears to be proceeding on dual tracks: engagement and cooperation along with mutual suspicion and quiet competition. Although China condemned the Indian nuclear tests, and India is concerned about the strategic imbalance, neither country has emphasized nuclear weapons in their relationship. India seeks to build a robust deterrent against China, but it has not pursued this goal with urgency. China too has deemphasized its nuclear force in relation to India. The low-key general deterrence postures of both countries reflect their common desire to improve bilateral relations.

Evidence from Asia supports the general proposition that arms per se including nuclear weapons are not the primary drivers of insecurity, but strategies for their employment may intensify or ameliorate insecurity. Except during 1999-2002 in India-Pakistan relations, deterrence has been the dominant role and strategy for employment of nuclear weapons in Asia.

Deterrence Dominance Promotes Stability

Only the United States is seeking to develop significant offensive and defensive nuclear weapon capabilities. Technological limitations, funding constraints, the relatively low cost of maintaining a strike force that can penetrate ballistic missile defense systems, the preference and capabilities (conventional and nuclear) of other states, and the generally stable strategic environment in the Asian security region are likely to limit the employment of nuclear weapons in these roles. The offensive and defensive roles of nuclear weapons are likely to remain marginal in utility and unlikely to surpass the deterrence role. Deterrence dominance advances stability by helping prevent the outbreak and escalation of regional hostilities, entrenching the political and military status quo by making the cost of violent change prohibitive, and impelling conflicting parties to explore peaceful settlement of disputes.

Help stabilize regional conflicts

Nuclear weapons contribute to regional stability by preventing the outbreak of major hostilities and their escalation to full-scale war in key regional conflicts across the Taiwan Strait, on the Korean peninsula, and over Kashmir. Nuclear weapons are relevant in the U.S.-PRC dimension of the Taiwan conflict. Beijing sees the implicit risk of escalation and the prospect of a nuclear retaliatory strike on the United States as inducing caution in Washington, deterring American military intervention, and compelling Washington to rein in independence oriented Taiwanese leaders. The American military objective is to deter Chinese military action against Taiwan and prevent unification by force. Although American deterrence is primarily conventional it inevitably includes a nuclear dimension. The 2002 NPR identifies Taiwan as a nuclear contingency. Although both the U.S. and China have not articulated a policy or strategy that will involve nuclear weapons, the risk of escalation is an ever-present possibility. That risk constrains the military options available to China and the United States and deters the outbreak of major hostilities making large-scale war unlikely. Similarly nuclear weapons help strengthen deterrence and stabilize the conflict on the Korean peninsula. North Korea feels more assured of its deterrence capability while South Korea is assured by the U.S. extended deterrence commitment. It is possible to argue that there has not been a deep crisis in the conflict across the Taiwan Strait to demonstrate the restraining and stabilizing effect of nuclear weapons and, further, that stability in the Taiwan and North Korea conflicts is due to a number of factors including conventional deterrence. It is difficult to refute these claims. The deterrence effect of nuclear weapons cannot be isolated and quantified in the absence of severe crisis. However, this does not imply irrelevance or that nuclear weapons do not contribute to stability.

The stabilizing effect of nuclear weapons may be better illustrated in India-Pakistan relations, as the crises between these two countries during the 1999–2002 period are often cited as demonstrating nuclear weapon-induced instability. Rather than simply attribute these crises to the possession of nuclear weapons, a more accurate and useful reading would ground them in Pakistan's deliberate policy to alter the status quo through military means on the premise that the risk of escalation to nuclear war would deter India from responding with full-scale conventional retaliation; and in India's response, employing compellence and coercive diplomacy strategies. In other words, particular goals and strategies rather than nuclear weapons per se precipitated the crises. Further, the outcomes of these two crises revealed the limited utility of nuclear weapons in bringing about even a minor change in the territorial status quo and highlighted the grave risks associated with offensive strategies. Recognition of these limits and the grave consequences in part contributed to the two countries' subsequent efforts to engage in a comprehensive dialogue to settle the many disputes between them. The crises also led to bilateral understandings and measures to avoid unintended hostilities.

Though it is too soon to take a long view, it is possible to argue that, like the Cuban missile crisis in 1962, the 1999 and 2001–02 crises between India and Pakistan mark a watershed in their strategic relations: the danger of nuclear war shifted their focus to avoiding a major war and to finding a negotiated settlement to bilateral problems. Large-scale military deployments along the common border, Pakistan-supported insurgent activities in India, and cross-border terrorism continue; and the two countries regularly conduct large-scale military exercises and test nuclear-capable missiles that have each other's entire territory within range. Despite these activities, the situation has become relatively less tense; stability with the ability to absorb shocks even like that created by the November 26terrorist attack in Mumbai has begun to characterize the bilateral relationship.

Assurance and stability in major power relations

Nuclear weapons feature primarily in deterrence and insurance roles in the interaction of major powers.

These roles are not threatening to other parties. The caution induced by nuclear weapons, their leveling effect, the strategic insurance they provide to cope with unanticipated contingencies, and general deterrence postures reduce anxieties and constrain the role of force in major power interaction. This enables major powers to take a long view and focus on other national priorities. In this context modernization of nuclear arsenals and the development of additional capabilities have proceeded at a moderate pace; they have produced responses but not intense strategic competition. The net effect has been stabilizing.

The stabilizing effect of nuclear weapons in the immediate security issue in Sino-American relations has been discussed earlier. Here I will discuss how deterrence dominance has enabled a measured Chinese response to the U.S. emphasis on offensive strategies and its development of strategic missile defense and helped avoid strategic competition. Perceiving the offensive strategies and BMD development as undermining the robustness of its strategic deterrent force, China seeks to strengthen the survivability of its retaliatory force and is attempting to develop capabilities that would threaten American space-based surveillance and communications facilities in the event of hostilities. However, these efforts are not presented as a direct challenge to or competition with the United States. Beijing has deliberately sought to downplay the modernization of its nuclear force. This is not simply deception, but a serious effort to develop a strong deterrent force without entering into a strategic competition with the United States, which it cannot win due to the huge imbalance in military capabilities and technological limitations. Strategic competition will also divert attention and resources away from the more urgent modernization goals. A strong Chinese strategic deterrent force blunts the military advantage of the United States, induces caution in that country, and constrains its military option in the event of hostilities.

India's strategic deterrence force does not compare with China's, but its nuclear, missile, and conventional military capability give New Delhi a relatively high degree of self-confidence in managing relations with Beijing. The insurance provided by its small nuclear force and strong conventional capability, combined with technological and resource limitations, and improving bilateral relations, explain India's gradual development of a nuclear deterrent capability against China. India's minimum deterrence nuclear posture and its gradual nuclear buildup also reassure China, which sees the United States as its principal security concern. In recent times, Japan has been more sensitive than India to China's nuclear force modernization and the development of North Korea's missile and nuclear capabilities. In part, this is due to the lack of its own nuclear weapon capability. However, Japan has not sought its own nuclear weapon capability to compete with China or North Korea, a move that could be unsettling. Instead it has sought reaffirmation of the U.S. extended deterrence commitment, denuclearization of the Korean peninsula, an increase in its own conventional military capability, and development of strategic defense, all of which can be stabilizing.

Reinforcing the Circumscription of Force

Finally nuclear weapons contribute to stability by circumscribing and transforming the role of force. In 2003, I argued that the offensive role of force in Asian international politics was declining and that assurance, deterrence, and defense were becoming the primary missions of Asian armed forces (Alagappa 2003b). I attributed the declining salience of the offensive role of force to several developments: the consolidation of Asian states and their willingness and ability to enter into international obligations; the general acceptance in Asia of the prevailing political and territorial status quo, which reduces the need for a forceful defense of a state's core interests and makes conquest and domination unacceptable; an increase in the political, diplomatic, and economic cost of using force in a situation of complex interdependence; and the impracticality of resolving conflicts through force. Over the past three decades, the use of force has been limited to border clashes, militant insurgencies, and occasional clashes at sea, where the danger of escalation is low. A major war could still occur, but the probability has declined dramatically since the early phase of the Cold War, when Asia was the site of several large-scale wars.

Nuclear weapons reinforce the declining salience of the offensive role of force in the Asian security region and increase the importance of deterrence, defense, and assurance. The logic of the enormous destructive power of nuclear weapons and the lack of defense against them also applies to Asia. None of the key regional conflicts can be resolved through the use of force, including conventional military force. The danger of escalation limits the offensive role of conventional military force among nuclear weapon states. The salience of deterrence and defense, already on the rise in the context of wide acceptance of the status quo, is now becoming entrenched. Nuclear weapons make nuclear deterrence and conventional defense the dominant strategies. Despite the U.S. effort to build a strategic defense system, deterrence dominance is likely to continue for the foreseeable future. Target nuclear weapon states can and will take measures to increase the robustness of their strategic deterrent forces. In situations of stark asymmetry, limited strategic defense may make a difference and make offensive use of force under nuclear conditions more attractive. However, it is unlikely to eliminate all uncertainty; continued caution is likely counsel against offensive military action.

References

Alagappa, Muthiah 2003a. "Introduction: Predictability and Stability Despite Challenges." In Asian Security Order: Instrumental and Normative Features, ed. Muthiah Alagappa, pp. 1–32. Stanford, Calif.: Stanford University Press.

——. 2003b. "Managing Asian Security: Competition. Cooperation and Evolutionary Change." In Asian Security Order: Instrumental and Normative Features, ed. Muthiah Alagappa, pp. 571–608. Stanford, Calif.: Stanford University Press.

Buzan, Barry, and Gerald Segal. 1994. "Rethinking East Asian Security." Survival 36 (2): 3–21.

Carter, Ashton B., and William J Perry. 2006. "If Necessary, Strike and Destroy: North Korea Cannot be Allowed to Test This Missile." Washington Post, June 22: A29.

Cohen, Avner. 2008. "Israel: A Sui Generis Proliferator." In *The Long Shadow: Nuclear Weapons and Security in 21st Century Asia.* Ed, Muthiah Alagappa. Stanford, CA: Stanford University Press.

Feaver, Peter. 1992–93. "Command and Control in Emerging Nuclear Nations." International Security 17 (3): 160–87.

——. 1993. "Proliferation Optimism and Theories of Nuclear Operations." Security Studies 2 (3/4): 159–91.

Friedberg, Aaron L. 1993–94. "Ripe for Rivalry: Prospects for Peace in a Multipolar Asia." International Security 18 (3): 5–33

Gaddis, John Lewis. 1992. The United States and the Cold War: Implications, Reconsiderations, Provocations. New York: Oxford University Press.

Hagerty, Devin T. 1998. The Consequences of Nuclear Proliferation Lessons from South Asia. Cambridge. Mass.: The MIT Press.

Jervis, Robert. 1988. The Political Effects of Nuclear Weapons." International Security, 13, Fall: 28–38.

——. 1989. The Meaning of the Nuclear Revolution: Statecraft and the Prospect of Armageddon Ithaca. N.Y.: Cornell University Press.

Kapur, S. Paul. 2006. Dangerous Deterrent Nuclear Weapons Proliferation and Conflict in South Asia. Stanford, Calif.: Stanford University Press.

Khan, Feroz Hassan, and Peter R. Lavoy 2008. "Pakistan: The Dilemma of Nuclear Deterrence." In *The Long Shadow: Nuclear Weapons and Security in 21st Century Asia.* Ed. Muthiah Alagappa. Stanford, CA: Stanford University Press.

Logan, Justin. 2006. The Bottom Line on Iran. The Costs and Benefits of Preventive War versus Deterrence. Washington, D.C., CATO Institute. Policy Analysis No. 583.

Lord. Winston 1993. "A New Pacific Community: Ten Goals of American Policy." Opening Statement of Confirmation Hearings: East Asian and Pacific Affairs. Washington, D.C. Subcommittee of the Senate Foreign Relations Committee Available at http://findarticles.com/p/articles/mi_m1584/is_n14_v4/ai_13784438/pg 8.

——. 1996. "U.S. Relations with Indonesia." Washington, D.C: Statement before the Subcommittee an East Asian and Pacific Affairs of the Senate Foreign Relations Committee, September 18. Available at http//dosfan.lin.uic.edu/ERC/ briefing/dispatch/ 1996/html/ Dispatchv7no38.html.

Morgan, Patrick M. 2003. Deterrence Now. Cambridge, UK: Cambridge University Press.

Mueller, John. 1988. "The Essential Irrelevance of Nuclear Weapons: Stability in the Postwar World." International Security, 13. Fall: 55–79.

——. 1998. "The Escalating Irrelevance of Nuclear Weapons." In *The Absolute Weapon Revisited: Nuclear Arms and the Emerging International Order*, eds. T. V. Paul, Richard J. Harknett, and James J. Wirtz Ann Arbor. The University of Michigan Press.

Park, John S., and Dang Sun Lee. 2008. "North Korea: Existential Deterrence and Diplomatic Leverage." In *The Long Shadow: Nuclear Weapons and Security in 21st Century Asia*. Ed. Muthiah Alagappa. Stanford. CA: Stanford University Press.

Perry, William 2006. "Proliferation on the Peninsula: Five North Korean Nuclear Crises." Annals of the American Academy of Political Science, 607. 1: 78–86.

Raas, Whitney, and Austin Long. 2007. "Osirak Redux? Assessing Israeli Capabilities to Destroy Iranian Nuclear Facilities." International Security 31 (4): 7–33.

Sugon, Scott D. 1994. "The Perils of Proliferation: Organization Theory. Deterrence Theory, and the Spread of Nuclear Weapons." International Security 18 (4): 66–107.

——. 1995. "More Will Be Worse." In *The Spread of Nuclear Weapons: A Debate*, ed. Scott D. Sagan and Kenneth Waltz, New York: W. W. Norton.

Sanger, David E., and William J. Broad. 2007. "U.S. Secretly Aids Pakistan in Guarding Nuclear Arms." New York Times. November 18. Available at http://www.nytimes.com/2007/11/18/washington/18nuke.html?8br=&pagewanted=all.

Waltz, Kenneth 1995. "More May Be Better." In The *Spread of Nuclear Weapons: A Debate*, ed. Scott D. Sagan and Kenneth Waltz. New York: W. W. Norton.

——. 2004. "Nuclear Myths and political Realities." In *The Use of Force: Military Power and International Politics*, ed. Robert J. Art and Kenneth N. Waltz. Boulder, Colo.: Rawman and Littlefield.

Darfur and the Failure of the Responsibility to Protect

ALEX DE WAAL

Responsibility to Protect (often stylishly shortened to R2P) was the name for one of the United Nations' post-Cold War peacekeeping initiatives. Many IR analysts and government officials thought the end of the Cold War would bring a renewed, more assertive role for United Nations peacekeeping operations. The conflict in the Darfur region of Sudan was a first major test of the R2P. De Waal examines this bloody multi-year war and offers explanations for its failure. Who is to blame for the war in Darfur? Does the conflict suggest limits to the Liberal Institutionalist model? Go back and look at the Waltz excerpt in Part Two. How would Waltz explain the violence in Sudan?

War in Darfur and International Responses

Darfur is a typical north-east African civil war,[1] consisting of multiple overlapping conflicts interspersed with large-scale offensives by the government army and its proxies and rebels. During 2001–2003, local disputes were exacerbated by the break-down of local governance and combined with the ambitions of a frustrated provincial elite to fuel an insurgency, which escalated more quickly and bloodily than either side anticipated. The government response was both ham-fisted and ruthless—characteristics of Khartoum's counter-insurgencies since the 1980s. The result was massacre, displacement and famine, an overall death toll probably exceeding 200,000, the deepening of distrust between Darfurians and the political leaders in Khartoum to the point of bitter hatred, and the fragmentation of Darfurian society into a state approaching anarchy, characterized by multiple local conflicts.

Darfur is a complex Sudanic society that straddles the desert and savanna.[2] An independent Muslim sultanate until 1916, Darfur became a neglected appendage to Sudan for a brief 40-year colonial interlude. The following 40 years of independent rule saw few developments in Darfurians' way of life, which remained desperately poor and underserviced. Worse, the civil war in neighbouring Chad spilled over into Darfur in the 1980s,[3] and the government in Khartoum turned a blind eye as militia drawn from Darfur's Arab tribes armed themselves with the support of their Chadian brethren and tried to seize land from their Fur and Masalit neighbours.[4] Throughout the 1990s, parts of Darfur intermittently erupted into conflict owing to a combination of the depredations of land-hungry Chadian Arab groups and Khartoum's penchant for addressing local conflicts by distributing arms to one side to suppress the other—a policy that almost always came down in favour of the Arabs.

DE WAAL, A. (2007), Darfur and the failure of the responsibility to protect. International Affairs, 83: 1039–1054.

While Darfur's conflicts smouldered, Sudan was engaged in a large and protracted civil war between the central government and the Sudan People's Liberation Army (SPLA). Commonly characterized as a war between north and south, this is better described as a connected set of wars between a dominant central elite claiming Islamic and Arab identity, and the peoples most marginalized by that elite, including southerners, the Nuba people of southern Kordofan, and a number of groups in eastern and south-eastern Sudan, all of them non-Arab, many of them non-Muslim. The basic pattern of grievances is shared by all the marginalized peoples: they were denied their share in political power and national wealth, and the government used divide-and-rule tactics to allow local militias to run amok and destroy their modest livelihoods.[5] In retrospect, the mystery is not why the war in Darfur broke out, but why it took so long to do so.

The Darfur rebels included the Sudan Liberation Movement/Army (SLM/SLA), with a broad base of support across Sudan's major ethnic groups (principally non-Arab but including some Arabs) and the Justice and Equality Movement (JEM), whose leaders have links with Sudan's Islamist movement. From the outset, the armed resistance was an amalgam of village defence groups and aspirant elites, divided on ethnic and political lines.[6] The main infrastructure for armed resistance was tribal, and the largest segments—Fur, Zaghawa and Masalit—rarely coordinated. Rivalry between the two SLA leaders, Abdel Wahid al Nur (Fur, with a following among diverse ethnic groups) and Minni Minawi (Zaghawa) became intense and bitter, and differences between these two and the leader of JEM, Khalil Ibrahim, were also significant. These divergences prevented the Darfur resistance from forming a united political front.

The main government proxies were the Janjaweed, from a segment of Darfur's camel-herding Arab tribes, and more recent Arab immigrants from Chad, who had their own territorial ambitious in Darfur. The Sudan government made a deal with these Arab groups whereby they were allowed to pursue their own agenda with impunity, in return for suppressing the rebellion. Other Darfurian Arabs initially remained outside the conflict, though some joined the counter-insurgency in 2003 and others were drawn in the following year as the rebels took the war to the east and south of Darfur.

Darfur's war gained international attention just as the negotiations to conclude the long-running hostilities between the central government and the SPLA were approaching conclusion in the Kenyan town of Naivasha. During the first half of 2004, the policy of the US-British-Norwegian troika that supported the Naivasha talks vacillated. One approach was to deal with Darfur as part of those negotiations, or at least stabilize Darfur before concluding the talks. The other approach, which won the day, was to proceed with completing the Comprehensive Peace Agreement while the Darfur problem remained unresolved. The decision in favour of the latter option was ultimately one of timing and feasibility. During 2004 attempts to obtain a robust ceasefire for Darfur, let alone a peace agreement, made little progress, in part because of the disorganization of the rebels. Neither the SPLA nor the international representatives wanted a north–south peace to be hostage to an unpredictable conflict in Darfur, so by default it was decided to address the two wars in sequence.

The Ndjamena Humanitarian Ceasefire Agreement, signed on 8 April 2004, was the basis for all subsequent diplomatic efforts on Darfur. It was a rushed agreement, which exists in two versions without an agreed text (the particular provision in dispute is the cantonment of the armed movements in assembly sites); although it allowed the African Union (AU) to dispatch ceasefire monitors, and subsequently a force to provide protection for those monitors and any civilians in the immediate vicinity of its operations, it contained no maps to enable the ceasefire monitors to do their job. On the basis of Ndjamena, the African Mission in Sudan (AMIS) had an impossible task. By improvising, and exceeding its mandated authority, AMIS achieved much in its first twelve months. However, any progress needed to be consolidated by a stronger mandate, a more realistic concept of operations, larger numbers and better logistics, and better finance. All these were promised by the AU and international donors, but not delivered.

The responses of the UN Security Council and the AU Peace and Security Council (PSC) consisted chiefly of ad hoe steps rather than a systematic or strategic approach to the crisis. The Ndjamena agreement became the foundation, not only for AMIS, but also for the UNSC's demands. While the Ndjamena text refers to the government's responsibility to 'neutralise armed militia', UNSC Resolution 1556 of 30 July 2004 went further and demanded the disarmament of the Janjaweed within 30 days, without defining either 'disarmament' or 'Janjaweed'. The UNSC then failed to monitor the implementation of its demand, let alone take action against Khartoum for failing to act. (In reality, the Sudan government was incapable of disarming the militia.) In August the UN demanded a series of steps to ensure security around displaced persons' camps but also failed to take any follow-up actions when Sudan government actions stalled. Later the UNSC adopted a resolution enabling it to identify individuals obstructing the peace process and sanction them, but it has used this instrument only slowly, sparingly and ineffectively.

Another piece of ad hoccery was the UNSC response to the US government decision that genocide had been committed in Darfur. In response to pressure from advocacy organizations and Congress, which believed that 'naming the situation in Darfur genocide would commit the US to action', specifically intervention,[7] in May 2004 the US State Department launched an investigation into whether the atrocities in Darfur qualified as genocide.[8] An investigative team sent to Chad concluded that the answer was yes. This was an important finding, not least because it broadens the usage of the term 'genocide' to include ethnically targeted killings, rapes and displacement perpetrated in the course of counter-insurgency, a significant expansion on the customary usage of the term to refer to attempts to eliminate entire populations. The State Department response to this finding, stated on 9 September 2004, was to affirm that genocide had been committed, but then to say that this would have no impact upon US policy. When the United States passed the issue to the UNSC a few days later the UNSC had no comparable luxury of continuing as before. Its initial response was to set up the International Commission of Inquiry into Darfur to examine the question. The ICID reported in February 2005 and the following month the UNSC referred the case to the International Criminal Court. There was no recent precedent for the UNSC deciding to pursue justice in advance of any workable peace process.[9]

Another significant international intervention on Darfur was the decision, adopted as a priority by the US government in the early summer of 2005, that AMIS should be handed over to a UN peacekeeping force. The stated rationale for this was that the UN would do a better job and that 'blue-hatting' of AU missions had worked in the past (e.g. in Burundi). It was certainly the case that the AU had never handled a peace support operation of the size and complexity required for Darfur, but at least the Constitutive Act of the AU provides for intervention in the case of gross violations of human rights or humanitarian crisis, a more liberal provision than anything in the UN Charter. Had the AU, UN and government of Sudan agreed promptly to this proposal, it could have been timely and effective. However, the secretariats and security council members of both AU and UN were reluctant, and Khartoum was opposed. Over the following two years, the greater part of US diplomatic energy and political capital was spent in the attempt to persuade the AU, UN and Sudan government to accept this policy. International forces in Darfur, rather than being a prop to a political policy, became the centrepiece of that policy. In the face of Khartoum's continuing opposition, on 31 August 2006 the UN Security Council adopted Resolution 1706, which invited Sudan's consent to a UN force—implying that if consent was not forthcoming, such a force might be dispatched without it.

The following week, President Omar al Bashir called the bluff of the US and UN Security Council by rejecting Resolution 1706. Bashir decided to draw a red line, and further tied down international political efforts on the details of the international force. A compromise proposal for a 'hybrid' AU–UN force was floated by the United States and China and adopted at a high-level meeting chaired by the UN Secretary General on 16 November. After another eight months of wrangling, the Security Council finally obtained Sudan's consent to the hybrid AU–UN force, the UN–African Union Mission in Darfur (UNAMID), which was duly mandated in Resolution 1769 of 31 July 2007, with its mandate, structure, size and talks determined with reference to a joint UN–AU assessment.[10] At the same time, AU and UN special envoys (Salim Ahmed Salim and Jan Eliasson respectively) began preparing for a new round of peace talks intended to bring all the rebel movements into a peace agreement, in the hope that there would be a peace to keep by the time UNAMID became operational in early 2008.

Over the period 2004–2007, the international community pursued a range of objectives for Darfur that included improving security and humanitarian access, supporting the CPA, obtaining justice at The Hague, seeking a negotiated peace, dispatching a UN force and punishing those standing in the way of these goals. The multiplicity of these goals impeded a clear and coherent strategy. Some actions demanded the impossible while others set unrealistic deadlines. Few were followed up. On the occasions that Khartoum met one demand, another was placed on the table.[11] With an internally dysfunctional regime facing a confused and inconsistent international community, it is unsurprising that little progress was made.

The Debate on Protection

It is exceptional for an international peacekeeping issue to seize and maintain the headlines in the way that UN troops did for Darfur. On 14 September 2006 the actor George Clooney addressed the UN Security Council and said that, should the Sudan government refuse to comply with Resolution 1706, 'You will simply need men with shovels and bleached white linen and headstones. In many ways, it's unfair, but it is, nevertheless, true that this genocide will be on your watch. How you deal with it will be your legacy, your Rwanda, your Cambodia, your Auschwitz.'[12] Two days later, tens of thousands of demonstrators donned blue hats to demand that Sudan allow in UN troops to stop genocide in Darfur. Many Darfurians, including those living in displaced persons' camps in the region and members of the diaspora, vested their hopes in the UN coming to 'save' them. An International Crisis Group report entitled *To save Darfur* was concerned overwhelmingly with UN troops.[13] Expectations of what UN troops would do were wildly inflated, including disarming the Janjaweed and physically protecting both displaced people and those returning home to their villages. Precisely this problem had been identified by the Brahimi Report some years earlier: 'Promising to extend such protection establishes a very high threshold of expectation. The potentially large mismatch between desired objective and resources available to meet it raises the prospect of continuing disappointment with United Nations follow-through in this area.'[14]

Throughout 2004–2006, the debate on the international military presence in Darfur focused on four major issues. The dominant question was whether the troops should be under AU or UN command. The labels used for the force identity obscured an agreement among all involved that a UN force would have a predominantly African character, and that a handover to the UN would involve the existing AMIS troops changing from green to blue helmets. If any troops from NATO countries were to be sent, they would be in small numbers only.

A second issue was the numbers of troops and their capabilities. It was generally agreed that the AMIS force was too small and poorly equipped. If AMIS or any UN successor organization was to take on the task of protecting displaced persons' camps and humanitarian supply routes, mounting monitoring patrols over large areas of Darfur, or even systematically supervising a ceasefire, it would have to be larger and be provided with more logistics and communications. If the force were to have the capability of deterring attack and, if necessary, calling upon reserves to fight its way out of a confrontation with a militia, then it would need additional armaments. More important than any of these issues, though rarely discussed, was the point that AMIS or its successor would also need larger numbers of civil and political affairs officers, to augment the modest contingent of two already stationed in Darfur.[15]

The third issue was the mandate. All agreed that the mandate of ceasefire monitoring arising from the Ndjamena agreement was insufficient, and that the additional mandate that enabled AMIS to protect civilians who were at risk when it encountered them during the course of its duties was also inadequate.[16] The principal question was whether the force should operate under Chapter VI or VII of the UN Charter.

A final issue was the financing of the force. The AU had no mechanism for obtaining sufficient financial contributions from its member states to support AMIS, because African countries did not have the ability to pay. Hence AMIS was funded by discretionary contributions from European and north American governments. A UN force authorized by the UNSC would be financed through mandatory assessed contributions by UN member states. Although more expensive than AMIS, this system was more reliable.

The question of the force's strategic purpose and concept of operations was not among the issues discussed, despite the efforts of professional staff within the UN Department of Peacekeeping Operations (DPKO). Many activists and some political leaders simply assumed that an international force could succeed in the Herculean task of providing physical protection to Darfurian civilians in the middle of continuing hostilities. The inflated expectations caused much dismay in the DPKO.

This public debate was matched by the internal debate in Addis Ababa, New York and Washington DC. The standard formula for describing AMIS was that it was overstretched, ill-equipped and undermandated. While these descriptions were accurate, they overlooked the question of what a larger and better-equipped force with a stronger mandate would actually be able to achieve.

In contrast to these intense debates, very little attention was paid to the concept of operations and strategic goal. This emphasis reflects the focus and content of the continuing debate on the responsibility to protect, which has concentrated on when and whether to intervene, not how to do so and with what aim in mind.[17] The International Crisis Group, one of the most vocal and influential participants in the debate on Darfur, simply assumed that the implementation of the responsibility to protect was achievable. For example, it criticized the provisions in the Darfur peace agreement providing for staged reciprocal disarmament by the parties under AMIS supervision, saying that the task of disarmament is 'usually left for peacekeepers', and that the lack of international security guarantees was the weakest element of the agreement.[18] In reality, disarmament is only very occasionally entrusted to a peace support operation (as in Sierra Leone) and is almost always voluntary. Coercive disarmament by UN forces is exceptional; and of the two notable instances when it has been attempted, by the UN operation in Somalia in 1993 and the United Nations Mission in the Democratic Republic of Congo (MONUC) French-led Operation Artemis in the DRC in 2005, the first was a complete failure and the second problematic.[19] The military capabilities of the Darfur militia are more comparable to those of the Somalia factions which humbled US special forces in Mogadishu than the eastern Congo rebels whom the UN partly disarmed.

Some military analysts have noted that only an invasion could fulfil the promise. For example, Jim Terrie writes that a 'robust peacekeeping force' 'will make some limited difference, but not enough of one, and will certainly fall well short of a "responsibility to protect"'.[20] Terrie argues for an intervention that 'removes Khartoum's influence in Darfur' and suggests that a force of 40,000–50,000 could accomplish this, without giving a basis for this calculation.

Erroneous and unrealistic expectations of what UN troops would do in Darfur, which were echoed and amplified by many Darfur activists in the United States and appeared to be endorsed by the extraordinarily high level of international diplomatic effort vested in bringing the UN to Darfur, fed inflated fears and hopes in Sudan.

The prospect of a UN force mandated under Chapter VII worried Khartoum. Those fears were aroused in part by the potential threat that a UN operation might pose, for example through being able to execute arrest warrants on behalf of the International Criminal Court, or by giving the UN Special Representative a military force with an open-ended mandate, and in part simply through suspicions of what the 'real' US agenda behind the plan might be—fears fuelled by US activities elsewhere in the Arab and Muslim world, and by the parallels made by some US politicians between 'saving' Kosovo and 'saving' Darfur.[21] It was not lost on Sudan's leaders that NATO's humanitarian intervention in Kosovo appears to be leading to the independence of the province. Meanwhile, the US government was also offering military training and assistance to the SPLA, many of whose members support the secession of southern Sudan in the referendum scheduled for 2011 in accordance with the Commonwealth Parliamentary Association (CPA). While the more moderate leaders in Khartoum, notably the vice-president Ali Osman Taha, argued that peace deals in the south and Darfur would lead to the United States normalizing relations and supporting the unity of Sudan, others, such as the security chief Nafie Ali Nafie, argued the contrary: that whatever concession was made, the United States would simply demand another one, until it achieved either regime change or the dismemberment of Sudan. Since 2005, Taha's influence has waned while Nafie's star has risen.

The promise of a UN force raised comparable expectations among the armed movements and their supporters. Abdel Wahid saw the possibility of an armed intervention comparable to those by NATO in Bosnia or Kosovo, and in the final negotiating session in Abuja made that demand of the Americans, considering any guarantee insufficient and refusing to sign the Darfur Peace Agreement (DPA).[22] Whether or not this was the critical factor in his refusal to sign, the prospect of being 'saved' by UN troops raised the hopes of Darfurians and made them consider any political compromises or offer of AMIS peacekeepers as an unacceptable second best.

In principle, the threat or promise of a robust coercive protection force can strengthen the hand of a mediator. In the case of the endgame of the Abuja negotiations, it had the reverse effect. The clamour for UN troops also had two other adverse impacts. First, it demoralized the AMIS troops stationed in Darfur. When the transition to the UN was first raised in the middle of 2005, AMIS troops were trying to do a difficult job under adverse circumstances, but in effect were told that they were the second-best option and would not be staying long, let alone reinforced and resupplied. Donor promises of funds were not fulfilled and at times the troops were not even paid. Any possibility of long-term planning in AMIS evaporated and morale began to decline.

Second and most important, it compromised the integrity of the peace process. In most circumstances, the political and diplomatic objective is to obtain a peace agreement, and a peacekeeping force is secondary to and supportive of that agreement. In Darfur, it was the other way round. The primary international objective was to dispatch a UN force, and the Abuja negotiations became a prop for achieving that. On 9 March 2006 Vice-President Taha indicated that, subsequent to signing a Darfur peace agreement, he would work to ensure that UN troops could be dispatched to Darfur. On the basis of this commitment (which Taha subsequently tried but failed to deliver), the deadline for the Abuja negotiations was decided and the negotiations were rushed to a conclusion. That rapid termination of talks meant that the text of the agreement was substantively deficient in important respects and, more significantly, that the process was too rushed to carry the armed movements along with it. Darfurians' central criticism of the Abuja process is that it was too hasty to retain their confidence.[23]

Operationalizing the R2P in Darfur

The success or failure of any peace support operation in Darfur will depend upon the long-term vision and strategy of the operation, and the intellectual leadership provided accordingly. It is only on the basis of such a concept of operations that the most fundamental question can be answered, namely: *What is the force there to do?* The mandate sets limits on what the force commander *may* do, especially in extremis, and the force numbers, logistics, armaments and political backing allow him to decide what he can attempt to do in specific instances up to the limits of the mandate. But only a concept of operations determines what counts as ultimate success, and hence the strategy he should adopt and tasks he will need to undertake. In turn, that concept of operations should be embedded not just in the mandate provided by his political masters (AU PSC or UNSC) but also in the security arrangements agreed by the warring parties in their ceasefire or peace agreement.

Darfur is the locus of several complex conflicts involving many different armed groups and, consequently, a range of different types and layers of conflict and threat. From the outset of the war, and especially once the shortcomings of the Ndjamena humanitarian ceasefire agreement had become clear, it was evident that a classic Chapter VI peacekeeping operation was insufficient. There were no sharp lines of territorial delineation between the parties, and there were numerous groups in possession of arms that were commanded neither by the Sudan armed forces nor by the rebel commanders represented at the peace talks. However, an outright invasion or air assault, as undertaken in Iraq, Afghanistan or Kosovo, was impracticable because of the unwillingness of NATO countries to commit the huge numbers of troops that would be required and to accept the casualties, cost and indefinite commitment required of a ground occupation. Something else was required. While armchair theorists in the United States and Brussels fantasized about sending special forces, cruise missiles or mercenaries, or dispatching the UN to confiscate the arms of the Janjaweed, and professional military officers attached to the UN DPKO or AMIS were tasked with an avalanche of practical and administrative details concerning maintaining the existing force or finding ways in which it could operate in tandem with the UN, the requirement of developing a concept of operations received very little attention.

At no point during the AMIS operation and the peace negotiations was an opportunity provided for systematically exploring a concept of operations for a Darfur peace support operation. The basis for such an exercise, namely field assessments in Darfur, an assessment of all armed groups on the ground (including militia and self-defence groups in addition to the armed forces of the government and the SLA and JEM) and a process of capacity-building and confidence-building among the commanders of the armed groups, was never established. This process was twice proposed by AU security advisers during 2005 and again in early 2006, but on each occasion it was dismissed as being an unnecessary luxury, requiring an estimated six to nine months, while a solution was required within six to eight weeks.

Nonetheless, during the Abuja negotiations and the subsequent months, some progress was made towards working out the central concepts under which a peace support mission could operate. Some of these discussions were conducted by the AU mediation's commission on security arrangements in Abuja and others by the joint UN DPKO–AU planning team for UNAMID. These exercises were unsatisfactory for a number of reasons. First, the Abuja security talks were focused on obtaining a text acceptable to the parties, without the benefit of an expert security assessment in the field. The parties were extremely reluctant to negotiate in any serious manner, and the mediators and international partners did not welcome any process that brought additional complexities to the mediation effort. The Sudan government repeatedly refused AU requests to attach additional military advisers to the mediation team, while the AU was reluctant to press the issue too hard because both the arguments with the government delegation and the advice of the experts would have slowed down a negotiation process that was already under extremely tight deadlines.[24] Of the security advisers present, several left in frustration while others felt their expertise was not adequately drawn upon. Second, many of Darfur's armed groups were not represented in the talks. The Arab militias were excluded on the assumption, increasingly tenuous, that they were represented by the government delegation. Important sections of the armed movements either were debarred from the talks altogether (e.g. the National Movement for Reform and Democracy) or were present but unable to participate in the talks (the 'Group of Nineteen' dissident SLA commanders). Third, technical advice was also ignored in the implementation phase. Neither the United States nor the AU fulfilled their commitments to take rapid practical steps to support key tasks such as verification of the positions of the forces or convene the working group on Janjaweed disarmament (in the latter case, because the AU Special Representative, in his own words, 'forgot'). However, the worst error, committed against the advice of the security commission, was to expel the non-signatory parties from the Ceasefire Commission. Finally, the immense logistical and administrative complexities of organizing an innovative hybrid UN–AU mission presented DPKO staff with an overwhelming burden of work, which left them too busy to develop strategic plans—an activity that was never demanded by their superiors!

Conclusion

The pursuit of the responsibility to protect in Darfur has not achieved its goal. Contrary to the position taken by the most ardent advocates of R2P, this article argues that this failure owes much to the inadequate conceptualization of the R2P, the inflated expectation that physical protection by international troops is indeed possible within the limits of the military strength envisaged, and the confused advocacy around the issue. It is possible that more concerted international pressure could have brought a bigger and better-equipped international force to Darfur earlier. That would, in itself, have been a positive development. But the expectation that such a force could 'save' Darfur is erroneous.

At the time of writing (September 2007), security for Darfurian civilians remains extremely poor. The main reason for this is multiple conflicts and lawlessness in Darfur, arising from the lack of an agreed and workable peace agreement, which in turn derives from the perfidy and ruthlessness of the Sudan government, and the incompetence and vanity of the leadership of the armed movements. Reviewing the failures to improve security in Darfur and especially the missed opportunity of the Abuja peace negotiations, it is clear that the fears expressed in the Brahimi Report over protection mandates are more prescient than the hope of a new era of international protection heralded by the International Commission on Intervention and State Sovereignty. In pursuit of an unachievable ideal, the international community has failed to achieve practical solutions that lay within its grasp.

Notes

1. Julie Flint and Alex de Waal, *Darfur: a short history of a long war* (London: Zed, 2005): Alex de Waal, ed., *War in Darfur and the search for peace* (Cambridge, MA: Harvard University Press. 2007).
2. R. S. O'Fahey, *State and society in Darfur* (London. Hurst. 1980), and *The Dar Fur sultanate* (London: Hurst. 2007).
3. Millard Burr and Robert O. Collins, *Darfur: the long road to disaster* (Princeton, NJ: Markus Wiener, 2006).
4. Ali Haggar, 'The origins and organization of the Janjaweed in Darfur', in de Waal, ed., *War in Darfur and the search for peace*, pp. 113–39.
5. Alex de Waal, 'Darfur's deadline: the final days of the Abuja peace process', in de Waal, ed., *War in Darfur and the search for peace*, pp. 267–83.
6. Julie Flint, 'Darfur's armed movements', in de Waal, ed., *War in Darfur and the search for peace*, pp. 140–72.
7. Rebecca Hamilton and Chad Hazlett, '"Not on our watch": the emergence of the American movement for Darfur'. in de Waal, ed., *War in Darfur and the search for peace*, pp. 337–66 at p. 342.
8. Samuel Totten and Eric Markusen, eds. *Genocide in Darfur: investigating the atrocities in the Sudan* (London: Routledge, 2006).
9. The case of violations committed during the war in the north of Uganda had already been referred to the ICC by the government of Uganda.
10. United Nations, 'Report of the Secretary General and the Chairperson of the African Union Commission on the hybrid operation in Darfur', letter dated 5 June 2007 from the Secretary General of the United Nations to the President of the Security Council, S/2007/307/Revi, 6 June 2007.
11. For example, on 16 April 2007 President Bashir agreed to the 'heavy support package' for AMIS,

one of the main US demands, and two days later President Bush announced that he would impose sanctions on Sudan after 30 days unless there was substantial progress on three issues, one of which was the deployment of the 'heavy support package'.

12. http://www.americanrhetoric.com/speeches/georgeelooneyumtednations.htm, accessed 14 Aug. 2007.
13. International Crisis Group, *To save Darfur*, report 105, 17 March 2006. The report devotes approximately seven times as much space to international forces than to the peace process. The ICG insists that it has treated peace and protection as equal priorities, but the balance of its reports and advocacy was skewed very heavily towards troops, especially when the peace process was in its critical stages.
14. UN General Assembly and Security Council, *Report of the Panel on United Nations Peace Operations* (the 'Brahimi Report'), A/55/305-S/2000/809, 2 Aug. 2000, para. 62.
15. The UN–AU assessment identified the need for both civil affairs officers and military liaison officers (UN, 'Report of the Secretary General and the Chairperson of the African Union Commission on the hybrid operation in Darfur', paras 66–8, 76).
16. AMIS's mandate was contained in the Addis Ababa Agreement on the Modalities for the Establishment of the Ceasefire Commission and the Deployment of Observers of 28 May 2004, and was expanded by the AU PSC to include a limited protection element in October 2004.
17. Victoria Holt and Tobias Berkman, *The impossible mandate? Military preparedness, the responsibility to protect and modern peace operations* (Washington DC: Henry L. Stimson Center, 2006).
18. International Crisis Group, 'Darfur's fragile peace agreement', policy briefing, 10 June 2006.
19. Holt and Berkman, *The impossible mandate?*, ch. 8.
20. Jim Terrie, 'Military options for Darfur', in David Mepham and Alexander Ramsbotham, eds. *Darfur: the responsibility to protect* (Pretoria and London: Institute of Social Studies/Institute for Public Policy Research. 2006), p. 36.
21. Anthony Lake, Susan Rice and Donald Payne, 'We saved Europeans. Why not Africans?', *Washington Post*, 2 Oct. 2006.
22. de Waal, 'Darfur's deadline', at p. 276.
23. Laurie Nathan, "The making and unmaking of the Darfur Peace Agreement', in de Waal, ed., *War in Darfur and the search for peace*, pp. 245–66.
24. Nathan, 'The making and unmaking of the Darfur Peace Agreement'.

Children in Global Politics

HELEN BROCKLEHURST

Twenty-first-century conflicts have been primarily at the intra-state level. Professor Helen Brocklehurst argues that these conflicts have increasingly relied on children as soldiers. This extract from her book *Who's Afraid of Children?* exposes the ways that states have long used children in their calculations of national security. As you read, please consider the following: What is a "child"? How have states manipulated that definition? Are male and female children treated differently? How do sub-state militias trap children in conflicts?

State-building and Family Planning

Harry Hendrick, in a history of child welfare in England, divides children into dualisms of bodies and minds. His study illustrates how the concept of the child changed as their physical and mental health was increasingly recognized as being of political significance.[1] Hendrick notes that changes in family structure, the welfare state, the Boer War, WWI and the British Empire played their part in changing perceptions of the child. The child's body rather than mind was of national interest to the British between 1870–1914, as the role of nutrition, welfare of the mother and medical care, were recognized as being of strategic importance in the propagation of much needed healthy soldiers. Society was informed by their government that 'an Empire such as ours requires a race vigorous and industrious and intrepid'.[2] As shown in Chapter 1, military requirements led to the demarcation of a period of childhood in medical science and practice. After the Boer war for example, the role of responsibility for child-care taking was stated in rather more direct terms. The British public were told that 'an unhealthy schoolchild is a danger to all society'.[3] In Canada, children were described as a national asset, a constituent part of the state's defenses, embodying the future of Canada. 'The Great War has impressed upon us as never before the grave necessity not only of conserving the children, but also of affording them every opportunity to develop normally. It has become a patriotic duty as well as a professional one'.[4] Pronatalist policies and attention to the relative birth rates of European states illustrate an increasing perception of children as future investments in terms of state manpower and security.[5]

Keep Britain Tidy

The corollary of generating and caring for larger numbers of younger people to shore up the future state was that their unhealthy counterparts necessarily drained resources which could further strengthen 'healthy' children. It was at this time that British nationals were needed to populate the Empire and these two factors alone prompted the British government's twin-track strategy of removing and exporting less desirable children from the British slums to the Dominions. Child emigration had already begun in the 1860s.[6] The forced or arranged mass migration of smaller bodies abroad dealt with unwanted children and acted as a safety valve on civil discontent, reducing numbers of the degenerate poor who posed dangers to respectable society. These children were seen as 'bricks with which the empire would be built – the young colonists of the future ... who would help to consolidate the Empire and form the living link between the Dominions and the mother country'.[7]

Children were thus a constituent part of nation-building, and the means employed to counter fear about declining birthrate. As Beveridge stated, reduced numbers of children could contribute to a decline of 'the security and influence of Great Britain'.[8] Opinion in the Dominions echoed this racial insecurity. In 1938 the Arehbishop of Perth had stated that 'if we do not supply from our own stock, we are leaving ourselves all the more exposed to the menace of the teeming millions of our neighboring Asian races'.[9] Many agencies in Britain, including Barnardo's, the Catholic Child Welfare Council, National Children's Homes and the Salvation Army, 'exported' children to Australia and New Zealand from 1850 until as recently as 1967. From the late 1860s, 10,000 children alone were sent to Canada.[10] In 1994 an article by Margaret Humphreys, entitled: 'Empty Cradles: one Woman's fight to Uncover Britain's Most Shameful secret', drove an ironically 'new found' moral panic over these grown up children, and through the media and churches, further publicity and compensation were sought.[11] Sherington notes how contrary to this drive, many of 'the lost children of empire' were not shamed but celebrated at the time by exporters and importers, the media and the family. A spectrum of complicity and victimhood is evident however. Children of Aboriginal and Torres Strait islander peoples were forcibly removed from their parents and fostered and assimilated into white society. This practice also remained legal until 1967.[12]

Such practices suggest that children were conceptualized as embodiments or potential vessels of national security or strength and also a conveniently mobile collective body that could be moved at will. A contemporary example might be shown in the mass baby-lift organized by the Americans when they left Vietnam in 1975. Vietnamese 'orphans' were taken from villages to prevent them from being further exposed to the Communist threat and given new adoptive parents in the United States.[13] In all these cases children's lesser size, strength and cognition may have allowed them to be subject to this attention and manipulated by the 'surrogate' state. Children may be particularly vulnerable to state manipulation if they are also homeless or without family. In practices not dissimilar to those outlined above, children in present day Central America are removed from the streets and killed. Their physical condition and presence can be regarded as sufficiently threatening to warrant their removal. Guatemalan street children, for example, have been targeted by government-sponsored hit squads in order to cleanse cities of sources of crime and evidence of poverty. The killing of small street children and child traders fulfils state requirements of public 'cleanliness'. In Colombia these children are described as *limpieza social*, or disposables. This 'social cleansing' – ridding the streets of vermin[14] – was first initiated in the 1950s by police squads to combat rising crime. There are up to 7.5 million children in Brazil's streets vulnerable to this practice which has attracted a great deal of attention in the West as a human rights abuse. Sixty-eight death squads are reportedly active in one neighborhood of Rio de Janeiro alone. The phenomenon has also been reported in India, Turkey, Bulgaria and Kenya,[15] and it is interesting that there is no such parallel practice in which homeless adults are targeted in the streets of their cities. In these examples children are physically moved and renationalized, or in the case of Latin America, 'taken out'.

Population wars

Children's presence may also be alluded to by states in the context of population policy and antinatalist and pronatalist practices. Children may feature prominently in discourses of population policy, though it is the mother, as container of the future child who is used and targeted in practice. In times of perceived national threat children may be essentialized as a number, reduced to a statistical concept. In Britain, children were invoked and motherhood deployed as a means of managing British identity, or of controlling what wasn't British identity:

> The concern for proper mothering was often couched in terms of national and imperial interests, and a concern for racial degeneration. Children were posited as 'citizens of tomorrow' and a 'national asset' upon which the future of the country and empire depended. Consequently, concern over the (white) British population's birthrate intensified. Fears over depopulation mushroomed and the focus turned to women and mothers as a site of the reproduction of the nation and the maintenance of racial health and purity. Women became 'mothers of the race'.[16]

French pronatalist policies during the Third Republic and Fascist Italy's 'battle for births', are evidence of the perception of children's increased numbers as an emblem and guarantor of state health. In 1919, the Italian government created 'Children's Colonies' – free summer holidays for thousands of children in order to preserve their health and Mussolini's closest advisors suggested annulling childless marriages and criminalizing celibacy.[17]

In war, however, the nationality as well as the number of children may become of paramount importance. Where territory is disputed and national identity under threat, pronatalist practices may be pursued with more urgency as an additional means of securing the political body. In Croatia for example, a legislative program to encourage the propagation of the Croatian family and the biological control of the nation was introduced.[18] Forced impregnation of women and the legal channeling of motherhood essentialised women's identity in relation to her capacity to bear children and childless women were specifically referred to as 'non-women'. Pronatalist practices may also serve as a dual strategy of violence and renationalization against the enemy, for example, in the mass rape of women. In the Serbian occupied territories of Bosnia Hercegovina and Croatia for example, Serbians have combined ethnic cleansing and population policy by committing mass rape and serial rape to populate and maintain the greater Serbian state. Women already pregnant prior to assaults had their fetuses removed[19] and women and girls interned in various types of Serbian concentration and rape/death camps were kept for at least 21 to 28 days to ensure pregnancy.

Evidence such as this is standard in accounts of the break-up of the former Yugoslavia. Though these children would be born of 'enemy' mothers they were forcibly conceived as part of the (re) nationalization of territory of which women's bodies formed a part. The rapists verbally emphasize that the women will give birth to their children.[20] The enemy was thus able to create a future national asset and a prize of war. Croatian and Bosnian men have also been attacked, specifically to make them sterile, to prevent them from fathering Croatian children. Survivor accounts detail systematic sterilization in various concentration camps by Serb forces using medical radiation, complete and partial castrations and beatings of the genitals.[21]

As has been shown, in times of state expansion and insecurity the propagation of more children may be high on the agenda. Conversely, in peace time the abundance of children may be rendered as a threat to the state, a souree of instability, rather than an example of 'national' health. Antinatalist practices may be enforced by states in order to slow down population growth. National policies and programs to influence population size and growth rates are particularly common in developing countries where a link has been established between population growth, economic security and the health of society. Egypt, India, the Philippines and Zambia each began population reform after the population size was shown to be hindering economic development. China has perhaps demonstrated the most aggressive and restricted population policy. Between 1977 and 1990 family planning was specifically linked to economic production[22] and from 1980 tight legislation forced families to have only one child per couple. As Yuval Davis points out however, it was concern for 'political security in the 3rd world which in turn would create security problems to the US' that in part provoked and funded these measures and invoked the necessary gendered and cultural frames of reference which helped to make it happen.[23] It is interesting to note that in the states which have implemented population reform and its associated antinatalist practices, surprisingly little 'political' debate has incurred.[24] From the 1990s the world's population has been deliberately and systematically imbalanced where there is pressure to reduce the number of children, though states may not even declare this gendered information in their census return.

This suggests that the sphere of the family and maternalism are not recognized as political by the majority of the polity, or that its political importance is deliberately played down. The latter is perhaps borne out by an example taken from Palestine where the sphere of child care is specifically identified as an 'antidote' to political participation. Palestinian women have noted that their family responsibilities and care of children are allowed to become extremely woman-oriented activities for the purpose of distracting, deterring and disassociating women from the sites of 'political' activities. Day-care centers, for example, are disallowed by the Israeli government and so children are seen and used as natural shackles on women in the community.[25] Children are encouraged to be 'seen to' by mothers, so that politics is not.

Workers, Laborers and Slaves

Children can play an active part in communities by securing themselves economically from an early age. Until the last decade, the children who sustained economies were barely even documented. Dominant paradigms of childhood illustrated earlier, have yielded little information on children as economic agents. Importantly this means that children's decisions or autonomy are ignored. Boyden and Levison have exposed the comprehensive nature of children's exclusion, the challenges for their appropriate inclusion and the numerous changes, recalculations and policy reforms necessitated through recognition of children as agents and participants in economic and social capital.[26] World wide, a majority of children's bodies – up to a billion, perhaps two billion – are contributing to the international economy. However in literature on the economy, children have been, and still are, subsumed within the category of adult workers or not documented at all if their labor is taking place informally, at home, within the family or unpaid. Disproportionately participating in labor, children are also, like women, disproportionately affected when structural reforms move them into the realm of goods and exchange. As suggested in the last section, children can perform roles, not by what they knowingly accomplish, but by their presence or constructed presence. A brief look at children in the global economy will first illustrate how children's bodies or presence can be commoditized, and then move on to illustrate some of the roles they perform and how they have been constructed.

Invisible girls

Natasha Nossent has shown that children, especially girl children are often missing from official statistics even as recently as a decade ago. The informal nature of their work and the gender of child laborers may have contributed to their invisibility and a downplaying of the scale of their presence and contribution. Girls in fact may be used as workers without acknowledgement of their labor by their families, employers or the state. She cites evidence of girls as young as three undertaking tasks in factories as servants and socialized into sewing forces from the age of four.[27] Nossent points out that reports such as those made by the ILO usually only refer to paid labor in a strictly defined 'formal' sector and as such many workers are not counted. 'Talk' of children working most often means boys. Given that 80 per cent of all child labor is estimated to be unpaid, many children are yet to be taken into account.

Most analysis of labor hides the vast numbers of children who work outside cities and in illegal occupations. Girls may not be considered to be 'workers' though they often work for longer hours than boys. Girls are also most often unpaid or paid less than boys for the same jobs. This gendered division of labor extends into other spheres of social life. According to Nossent: 'Girls spend their childhood close to the household domain while boys are encouraged to spend more time outside the home and thus participate in community affairs.'[28] Girls remain inside the community, doing the majority of the work. Boys, however, may have greater opportunities through their status as workers outside the home and also by their increased pay, enabling them to act within and represent the community. It could be argued, therefore, that the gendered division of labor within economies, allows boys to gain adult responsibilities and opportunities sooner than their female counterpart laborers.

Warfare

The earliest documented use of children being *active* in warfare begins with the mythologized Children's Crusade in 1212 where children set out to join the Christians fighting to capture the Holy Land, though most perished from exposure before reaching their battleground. Throughout history, children of soldiers have joined their parents and become involved in war as soon as they are physically capable. During the Napoleonic wars young boys joined the navy in such numbers that their ships were called 'nursery ships'. They could join up at the age of ten or eleven as officers' assistants suited to many small tasks. Frederick the Great of Prussia is recorded as allowing child soldiers to enlist from the age of eight. Armies raised through conscription however have since considerably reduced the need and opportunity for young boys to join the armed forces in many states.

The use of children in conflict has however increased as a consequence of the changing character of warfare, particularly in the late twentieth century. Total war and people's war, for example, have mobilized citizens outside the traditional boundaries of battlegrounds. During the final days of WWII, Hitler used thousands of children aged between eight and seventeen on the front line. Most died, perhaps in greater numbers because they had less experience than their adult counterparts.[29] New, lighter weaponry coupled with extreme poverty, Western training techniques and educational indoctrination have however considerably advanced the capacity of the child soldiers and young resistance fighters and with this also created new opportunities for children's abuse. Guerrilla war and very light weaponry alone make it possible for children to fight and kill from as young as six years. 'New rifles weigh less than 3 kilograms and fire 600 rounds a minute...making them genuine equalizers'.[30] African and Palestinian children have been at the forefront for change and participation in military activity. During the Palestinian *intifada* in the Israeli occupied territories, children and youths were the catalysts and initiators of violent strife against Israeli troops.[31] Stone throwing in Palestine has been elevated to a military art with specific roles assigned to children of all ages.[32]

Roles that children are given and/or take up war include:

- soldiers/combatants
- sex slaves and prostitutes
- human shields
- targets, killed or maimed or captured
- minesweepers
- 'consequences' of war rape
- stakeholders
- moral and political agents or agitators
- peacemakers.

The international age limit for soldiers' voluntary recruitment and use is currently set at sixteen and many are much younger than this. Over forty-five states now use approximately 300,000 child soldiers.[33] (Their lives are highly expendable and, as such, the total figure must run far higher.) It is estimated that the majority are active in government armed forces and the youngest are to be found in armed groups.[34] They may constitute 10 per cent of current combatants.[35] In addition girl soldiers are now occupying more silent, hidden or risky roles often forced to participate in sexual servicing of other eombatants as well as a range of roles upon which camps depend. The late recognition of girl soldiers and the consequent inadequacy of current disarmament, demobilisation and reintegration (DDR) attempts tells it own story.[36] Soldiering or armed combat roles do not assume that the child's status is shared or agreed by all parties concerned. These children may be solely in adult company, with other children, under the direction of adults, or even under the command of older children. They may be active agents with varying degrees of self-awareness. They may or may not be willing combatants. In today's conflicts the distinction between voluntary and enforced recruitment is often blurred, given the fact that militias may offer far more to children than just a life of combat. The more unstable a country is, the more the military may even resemble a safe harbor in some senses. Children may be motivated to enlist to ward off poverty and insecurity, attracted by the familial-style environment, food and clothing. Orphaned and traumatized children may 'simply' receive food or treats in return for using guns. Their role may primarily be a means of survival in the face of other threats: starvation, isolation, or abduction to name but a few. Children may therefore join to *live* – not to kill or be killed. Conversely, child soldiering may be experienced as a well-founded and complex site of development and apprenticeship, particularly in longstanding guerrilla campaigns. Groups such as the Tamil Tigers of Sri Lanka have been known to provide education integrated with military experience, tutoring boys from the age of nine in the importance of discipline, honesty and respect for the rights of ordinary citizens.[37] Here, child soldiers may be allowed to imitate adults in combat but only in specific positions that do not exceed their strengths or place them at risk of physical harm – 'apprentices' behind the frontline. They are also free to leave.

In the midst of a war, military obligations may come into force at an earlier age than is usual and child soldiers such as those in Africa may assume many of the responsibilities of an adult. Indeed conscription may be an initiation process into adulthood. Forced participation in war means that children now occupy a position in armies where they are capable of subjecting others and being subjected to the experiences of adults in war though, unlike some soldiers they may have no choice but to be soldiers.[38] Children's roles as soldiers may overlap with those of adults and some children may clearly relish taking control.

In Sierra Leone too, The Revolutionary United Front (RUF) deliberately broke down the social fabric of a community by letting children target adults.[39] Child soldiers may be specifically useful to armies by virtue of their childlike qualities, physically and mentally. Children, 'being small and inconspicuous' have been used as mini-messengers or spies.[40] Their ability to mingle and hide with crowds has meant that the Ugandan National Resistance Army has found an ideal use for them as hand-grenade throwers.

A significant change in child soldiering, thought to have been actually promoted by agencies from the West during the bitter proxy wars of the Cold War, is the deliberate use of children as combatants because of their perceived limitations or weaknesses. Children are increasingly used to play at 'dirty war' – doing the things that adults have thought of but do not want to do themselves or think that children can do better. A Renamo Party Delegate described his soldiers as working out 'quite nicely in the field. You know they always did what they were told to do, they were fiercely loyal and brave in battle.'[41] Children have also been encouraged to see war as a game, to not understand what they do so that they will have no inhibitions. In this way children have been manipulated differently compared to adults. They have been drugged into committing atrocities which adult soldiers refuse to do. The United Nations Operations Officer in Liberia commented that '[i]t's a children's war. Kids get promoted in rank for committing an atrocity. They can cut off someone's head without thinking'.[42] These children probably are thinking however. As a Save the Children field worker noted: '[c]hildren make awesome soldiers. Children are effective because they are easy to organize, and they don't ask questions. In wartime a commander wants total submission. You can get that only from a child.'[43] Again, it is unlikely that children do not have some 'questions' about what they are doing. It is also unlikely that they have the opportunity to ask them. Child soldiering is often cruelly dependent on naivety and vulnerability, qualities that cannot be lost at will (though it is arguable whether adults lose them in war either). Mimicking adults whilst high on drugs or 'playing the game' of war in Sierra Leone, such children are treated as neither child nor adult, victims nor aggressors but both.[44] Reports suggest that after political and military socialization some cannot distinguish their actions from fantasy. If these children survive they often attend rehabilitation centers to try and make sense of the atrocities that they were encouraged to participate in.[45] In Northern Uganda, the Lord's Resistance Army led by Joseph Kony has been abducting children since the 1990s. The army has now been cited by the UN as creating one of the most systematic and brutal humanitarian disasters in the world.

Young children are more vulnerable to harm than other soldiers by virtue of their susceptibility to terror and less developed faculties, though older children may be no less vulnerable than some adults and perhaps some are more resilient. The roles, circumstances and responses outlined above illustrate the ambiguities of children's status as combatants. The dominant representation of child soldiers however is unambiguously of persons who have attained premature adulthood though inhabiting a child's body. However as P.W. Singer notes, the prospect of ambush by such children is increasing, as evidenced in British Operation 'Barras', carried out by the Special Air Service (SAS) against the West Side Boys militia in Sierra Leone.[46]

The intergenerational status of children as embodiments of future internal stability is beginning to be recognized. Many studies of children in crisis situations have found that they respond differently to adults, and are in need of longer term care. Their mental and emotional experiences may lead to a different set of problems when they become adults. 'Approximately 50 per cent of children in Rwanda had seen other children killing, 66 per cent had witnessed massacres, and 56 per cent had seen their family killed.'[47] The cyclical impact of children's experience of war on their future has yet to be analyzed. It is possible, that the identification of the war child as weak being may be a short-sighted interpretation. Weakness and vulnerability are likely to manifest themselves in other ways when the child reaches adulthood, to the extent that the consequences may be quite profound. Weakness may be translated into agency later on, perhaps resilience or in defiance such as through future civil revenge killings. Though their situation is extraordinarily complex, Tutsi children who suffered in the Rwandan civil war of the 1970s have identified themselves as the aggressors of the recent Rwandan conflict.[48]

During the Iran-Iraq war, children's immaturity was deliberately employed to the Iranian army's advantage. Thousands of children were sent out into the battlefields as 'kamikaze' mine-sweepers.[49] The Minister of Education in Iran said that in 1987, 150,000 children (making up 60 per cent of its ranks) 'volunteered' to fight.[50] This was only possible because the children involved were first manipulated into believing that it was a worthwhile exercise. As a human rights lawyer has observed: '[t]hey received intense religious indoctrination, emphasizing the value of martyrdom to the Islamic faith. These children were sent into the minefields to clear mines for the advancing Iranian army, armed only with keys around their necks for opening the gates of heaven.'[51] When these atrocities came to light, Iran was widely criticized and the United Nations called for an end to this practice. The justification given by Iran reveals a different, if not gratuitous, assumption of the responsibilities of the child. An Iranian minister said: '[i]t was an honor for my country that those young people had become sufficiently mature to understand the seriousness of their country's situation. Their heroism and enthusiasm were based on the notion of martyrdom, which materialists are unable to understand'.[52] It is interesting that he did not call them 'children'. This example of martyrdom was made possible by political socialization and the manipulation of the belief system held by Iranian children. The following section will look at examples of how children's minds have been the object of a different form of political interest and appropriation.

Children's assimilation of military skills in their play and recreation may however be desired by states. The Soviet Ministry of Retail Trade declared in 1980 that:

> Military toys and war games are important from an educational point of view, as they arouse children's interest in, and knowledge of, military techniques, and war games also inspire patriotism.[53]

President Reagan, in an address to high school children in 1983 about 'Star Wars' styled video games, commented:

> Many young people have developed incredible hand-eye-brain coordination playing these games. The air force believes these kids will be outstanding pilots should they fly our jets. Watch a twelve-year-old take evasive action and score multiple hits while playing Space Invaders and you will appreciate the skills of tomorrow's pilots.[54]

Such superpower opinions clearly show that children in the Cold War were exposed to implicit training for war. Schooling may be used more explicitly to denigrate another state or ethnic group and to reproduce the values of the dominant groups within states.[55] Xenophobic teaching and curricula were employed in the former Yugoslavia in 1994 and in Serbian schools in Kosova. It may be an important factor in mobilizing xenophobic hostility.[56] Schools may use language as a means of cultural and social reproduction, and consequently schools and the curricula are one of the battlegrounds of a nation's secession, and one of the first areas to be reformed. The newly created Central Asian republic of Tajikistan reformed education by implementing the Tajik language and textbook reform within a flexible cultural curriculum to mirror ethnic diversity.[57] The Council of Europe has regularly initiated and assisted with cross-cultural history teaching programs in newly reformed states. For a recent report, Bush and Salterelli listed 'peace-destroying and conflict-maintaining' impacts of education that ageneies hope to counter:

- the uneven distribution of education as a means of creating or preserving positions of economic, social and political privilege
- education as a weapon in cultural repression
- denial of education as a weapon of war
- education as a means of manipulating history for political purposes
- education serving to diminish self-worth and encourage hate
- segregated education as a means of ensuring inequality, inferiority, and stereotypes
- the role of textbooks in impoverishing the imagination of children and thereby inhibiting them from dealing with conflict constructively.[58]

They note that 'restricted access to education should be viewed as an indicator of deteriorating relations between groups' and therefore 'a warning signal':[59]

> the systematic ethnic cleansing undertaken by the Serbian military forces in late 1999 was in no way a spontaneous event. The precursor to abuse on such a massive scale is the systematic dismantling of the social, political and economic institutions that provide order and stability for a community. This was certainly the case in Nazi Germany, and in Cambodia under Pol Pot.[60]

Children's comprehension about conflict and history may also be thought of as an important part of their identity and be managed by states through citizenship education and the formal transmission of inherited culture. Education and historiography, particularly history curricula and history teaching, remain the subject of contemporary debate in Great Britain.[61] The concept of *Education for Citizenship* was revived in 1990 to develop skills of 'tolerance and constructive questioning of the world around them', taught not as a substitute for but complementary to history.[62] An ethnically diverse British population also places a high degree of responsibility on the way British history is presented. Additionally international events illustrate lessons about human behavior which cannot be gleaned in any other subject. In a Working Committee Report on History in the National Curriculum,[63] Anthony Polonsky expressed the view that history was the intellectual discipline which appeared the most obvious means to transmit knowledge and understanding of the Holocaust. Despite its publicity, the Holocaust is still not a substantial element in WWII history teaching. Yet, the history of Nazi Germany is.

Notes

1. Harry Hendrick, *Child Welfare in England, 1872–1989* (London: Routledge, 1994).

2. Valeric Fildes, Lara Marks and Hilary Marland (eds), *Women and Children First: International and Infant Welfare 1870–1945* (London: Routledge, 1992), pp. 1 and 97.
3. Hendrick, *op. cit.*, p. 13.
4. In Cynthia R. Comaccio, 'The infant soldier: early child welfare efforts in Ontario', in Valerie Fildes, Lara Marks and Hilary Marland, (eds), *op. cit.*, p. 107.
5. Hendrick, *op. cit.*, p. 14.
6. *Ibid.*, p. 82.
7. *Ibid.*, p. 14.
8. *Ibid.*, p. 285.
9. Alexandra Frean, 'Empire's forgotten children strike back', *The Times*, 18 May 1998, p. 7.
10. Patriek, A. Dunae, 'Gender, generations and Social Class: the Fairbridge Society and British Child Migration to Canada, 1930–1960', in Jon Lawrence, Pat Starkey (eds), *Child Welfare and Social Action in the Nineteenth and Twentieth Centuries: International Perspectives* (Liverpool: Liverpool University Press, 2001), p. 82.
11. G. Sherington, 'Suffer Little Children': Between child migration as a study of journeyings between centre and periphery', *History of Education*, September 2003, vol. 32, no. 5, pp. 461–76.
12. See the 'Open letter from the International Supporters of Australian Native Title to H.M. Queen Elizabeth II', in *The Independent*, 19 June 1997.
13. Bridget Daly and Jenny Vaughan, *Children at War* (London: Macdonald, 1988), p. 25.
14. Susan Kobrin, 'Killed like cockroaches', *Amnesty*, January/February 1996, pp. 16–17.
15. Caroline Moorhead, 'All the world's children', in *Index on Censorship*, 2, 1997, p. 150.
16. Omnia Shakry, 'Schooled Mothers and Structured Play: Child Rearing in Turn-of-the Century Egypt', in Lila Abu-Lughod (ed.), *Remaking Women. Feminism and Modernity in the Middle East* (Princeton University Press, 1998), p. 133.
17. Maria Sophia Quine, *Population Politics in Twentieth Century Europe* (London: Routledge, 1996), p. 42.
18. Cynthia Enloe, *The Morning After: Sexual Politics at the End of the Cold War* (London: University of California Press, 1993), pp. 241–3.
19. Natalie Nenadic, 'Femicide: A framework for understanding Genocide', Diane Bell and Renate Kline, *Radically Speaking: Feminism Reclaimed* (London: Zed Books, 1996), pp. 458 and 459.
20. *Ibid.*, p. 460.
21. *Ibid.*, p. 459.
22. John W. Thomas and Merilee S. Grindle, 'Political Leadership and Policy Characteristics in Population Policy Reform', in Jason L. Finkle and C. Alison McIntosh (eds), *The New Politics of Population: Conflict and Consensus in Family Planning* (New York: Oxford University Press, 1994).
23. Nira Yuval Davis, *Gender and Nation* (Sage: London, 1997), p. 34.
24. *Ibid.*, p. 57.
25. Cynthia Enloe, *Bananas, Beaches and Bases: Making Feminist Sense of International Politics* (London: University of California Press, 1989), p. 58.
26. Jo Boyden and Deborah Levison, *Children as Economic and Social Actors in the Development Process*, Working Paper 1, Stockholm: Export Group on Development Issuses.
27. Nossent, *op. cit.*, p. 5.
28. Nossent, *op. cit.* p. 10
29. Jean Bethke Elshtain, 'Sovereignty, Identity, Sacrifice', in V. Spike Peterson (ed.), *Gendered States: Feminist (Re)Visions of International Relations Theory* (Boulder: Lynne Riener, 1992), p. 150.
30. Mark Frankel, *et al.*, 'Boy Soldiers: Special Report', *Newsweek*, 7 August 1995, p. 15.
31. Guy Goodwin-Gill and Ilene Cohn, *Child Soldiers* (Oxford: Clarendon, 1994), p. 22.
32. Ed Cairns, *Children and Political Violence* (London: Blackwell, 1996), pp. 112–13.
33. Alstri Halsan Høiskar, 'Under Age and Under Fire: An Enquiry into the Use of Child Soldiers 1994–8', *Childhood*, 8 (3), 2001 p. 342.
34. Rachel Harvey, *Children and Armed Conflict: A Guide to International and Humanitarian Human Rights Law* (Essex University and the International Bureau of Children's Rights: The Children and Armed Conflict Unit, 2003).
35. Peter W. Singer, 'Caution: Children at War', *Parameters*, Winter 2001–2002, pp. 40–56, at http://carlisle-www.army.mil/usawe/

Parameters/01winter/singer.htm accessed (20/10/04).

36. See works by Andy White, especially 'Children and Armed Conflict: Impact, Protection and Rehabilitation', Research Project. [Website] http://www.arts.ualberta.ca/childrenandwar/research_methodology.php.
37. Goodwin-Gill and Cohn, *op. cit.*, pp. 29, 97.
38. Bellamy, *op.cit.*, p. 17.
39. Jo Boyden (2003), *op. cit.*
40. Bellamy, *op. cit.*, p. 18.
41. Peter Nkhonjera, quoted in 'Children in Bondage', *World Press Review*, January 1996, Vol. 43, No. 1, p. 10.
42. Human Rights Watch, Africa, *Easy Prey: Child Soldiers in Liberia* (New York, 1995), p. 31.
43. Nkhonjera, *op. cit.*, p. 8.
44. Chris McGreal, 'Africa's child troops fuelled by drugs and revenge', *The Guardian*, 21 February 1995, p. 7.
45. *Ibid.*
46. Singer, P. W (2005), *Children at War* (Pantheon) and see also 'Western militaries confront child soldiers threat', *Jane's Intelligence Review*, January 2005.
47. See for example, Human Rights Watch, Africa, *Easy Prey: Child Soldiers in Liberia* (New York, Sept. 1995).
48. Anuradha Vittachi, *Stolen Childhood: In search of the rights of the child* (Cambridge: Polity Press), p. 46.
49. Bellamy, *op. cit.*, p. 18.
50. Kent, *op. cit.*, p. 85.
51. Carolyn Hamilton, *op. cit.*, p. 38.
52. *Ibid.*
53. *Ibid.*
54. Helen Caldicott, *Missile Envy: The Arms Race and Nuclear War* (New York: Bantam, 1984), p. 145.
55. David Coulby, 'European Curricula, Xenophobia and Warfare', *Comparative Education* Vol. 33, no. 1, p. 39.
56. *Ibid.*
57. See Nick Holdsworth, 'Tajiks opt for revival of the fittest', *Times Higher Education[al Supplement]*, 6 November 1998, p. 16.
58. Kenneth D. Bush, and Diana Salterelli (2000), *Two Faces of Education in Ethnic Conflict*, United Nations Children's Fund, Innocenti Research Centre, Italy, p. 34.
59. *Ibid.*, p. 9.
60. *Ibid.*, pp. 6–8.
61. Neil Burtonwood, 'Culture, Identity and the Curriculum,' *Education Review*, Vol. 48, no. 3, 1996, p. 227.
62. Blunkett David, 'The minister's view', *The Guardian Education Supplement*, 22 September 1998, p. 3.
63. John Plowright, 'Teaching the holocaust: A response to the report of a survey in the UK', *Teaching History*, No. 45, 1991, p. 28.

Trading Human Rights: How Preferential Trade Agreements Influence Government Repression

EMILIE M. HAFNER-BURTON

Quantitative methods often provide evidence contrary to expectations. Relying on extensive evidence, Hafner-Burton, of UC San Diego, demonstrates that the terms of preferential trade agreements can change the behaviors of governments that repress human rights. What pieces of data does Hafner-Burton select? How does Hafner-Burton account for long- and short-term changes in behaviors?

Human rights violations are pervasive.[1] As a substantial percentage of states repress their citizens, an increasingly dense set of formal treaties, conventions, and protocols have been designed to protect the inalienable rights of human beings—human rights agreements (HRAs). These agreements are different than other forms of international cooperation designed to overcome collective action problems and to internalize cross-border externalities. HRAs are designed to regulate sovereign governments' behaviors toward individuals, and a great many scholars of international law and politics believe they are a valuable source of domestic policy change, encouraging repressors to change their practices.[2] In the face of such optimism, however, many scholars are unconvinced. HRAs, scholars remind us, lack the engines of compliance that drive many other areas of international law; they supply no apparent material incentives to conform, and no superior power is authorized to compel observance of the law.[3] The debate is heated and unresolved.

Yet HRAs are no longer the only alternative for international regulation of domestic human rights policy. Few realize that the governance menu has recently expanded to include a growing number of formal institutions that embed human rights standards[4] into rules governing market access—preferential trade agreements (PTAs).[5] PTAs are a rapidly growing class of international institutions that govern market access between member states of an economic region.[6] Semi-autonomous from the global structure of the World Trade Organization (WTO),[7] PTAs frequently regulate spheres of social governance that increasingly include human rights standards. Some, such as the Euro-Mediterranean Association Agreements, supply "hard" standards that tie agreement benefits to member compliance with specific human rights principles. Others, such as the West African Economic and Monetary Union, supply "soft" standards that are only vaguely tied to market access and unconditional on member states' actions.[8]

My argument is a simple one about institutional design and influence. In the area of human rights, hard laws are essential: change in repressive behavior almost always requires legally binding obligations that are enforceable.[9] HRAs, on the whole, do not supply adequate enforcement, but there are strong reasons to expect that a growing number of PTAs with hard standards now govern state compliance with international human rights principles, with considerable potential to influence states' behaviors toward citizens. Indeed, these agreements may often be more effective than HRAs in changing the basic conduct of repressive governments toward greater protection for some fundamental rights. Certain PTAs enforce many principles of international law that most HRAs cannot. I offer three hypotheses.

First, most HRAs are not likely to effectively reduce violations most of the time. As I will elaborate in this article, HRAs are principally soft: they influence governments' human rights practices through persuasion rather than coercion, supplying weak obligations.[10] Persuading repressive actors to change their preferences for behavior requires a supply of convincing argumentation, a long-time horizon, simultaneous targeting of multiple actors, and access to the target abusers. HRAs, unfortunately, do not supply many of these conditions.

Second, PTAs are designed to enforce voluntary commitments to coordinate market policies at a transnational level. PTAs accordingly supply different mechanisms of influence, and they sometimes are designed to influence human rights. As I shall show, when PTAs supply soft human rights standards, they offer no capacity for coercive influence. Like HRAs, these agreements are at best designed to supply weak tools of persuasion and are unlikely to have any strong influence on government repression.

Third, when they implement hard standards, PTAs influence through coercion: they provide member governments with a mandate to protect certain human rights, while they supply the material benefits and institutional structures to reward and punish members' behavior. As I shall show, coercing repressive actors to change their behaviors requires a conditional supply of valuable goods wanted by target repressors. It does not require changing deeply held preferences for human rights and is likely to take place in a shorter time horizon. These agreements accordingly improve members' human rights by supplying the instruments and resources to change repressive actors' incentives to promote policy reforms that would not otherwise be implemented.

A Matter of Design: How HRAs and PTAs Change Governments' Behaviors

Although many scholars are optimistic that HRAs lacking hard standards are still capable of substantial influence on domestic policy, I argue the contrary: coercion is much more likely than persuasion (alone) to be effective. In the following section, I apply these claims to HRAs and PTAs, respectively, and develop three positive expectations about influencing human rights behaviors.

Human rights agreements

The international human rights regime is championed by a growing number of treaties and instruments designed to protect identifiable groups, such as women and children, as well as to protect all people against particular government behaviors, such as torture. At the heart of this regime are the UN Charter (Article 55) and seven international agreements that define a set of global regulations. Almost all states in the world have ratified one or more of these instruments.

This architecture of international law was principally constructed to influence through persuasion: to identify and classify which rights are globally legitimate, to provide a forum for the exchange of information regarding violations, and to sway governments and violators that laws protecting human rights are appropriate constraints on the nation-state that should be respected. Over the years, the regime has proven increasingly competent in supplying the instruments necessary to collect and exchange information on human rights violations, and to disseminate that information on a global scale.[11]

Despite this substantial capacity to classify and disseminate human rights norms and establish monitoring institutions, most agreements were not designed to influence through coercion, and those that were often fail to be effective: they remain quite soft.[12] Most HRAs supply no formal enforcement mechanisms[13] to provide or disrupt valuable exchange with a target state.[14] They offer no material rewards in exchange for better practices, and they cannot directly punish violators by with-holding valuable goods.[15] At their best, most HRAs influence by mobilizing human rights advocates and supplying repressors with information and legitimating motivations to internalize new norms of appropriate behavior.

There are therefore good reasons to be skeptical that most HRAs directly or frequently persuade repressive actors to change their human rights behaviors, especially among those who value repression highly. HRA's supply strong tools of moral suasion but offer few valuable incentives for repressors to change their beliefs about appropriate behaviors. They identify and lobby target individuals and groups, but they are often limited to accessing repressors that consent to be targeted to receive information. The exchange of information once it begins, usually takes place over many months, if not years, and repressive actors inside the targeted state may well have changed during this time. What is more, there is no single HRA effectively able to punish perpetrators of even the most egregious violations of human rights.[16]

The best case study evidence to date supports the argument. Risse and colleagues show that influence through persuasion depends crucially on the establishment of sustainable networks of advocates among domestic and transnational actors; that persuasion happens through several stages over time; and that the inculcation of new norms among the worst abusers often requires some coercive processes of instrumental bargaining, at least in the beginning.[17] Because repressors value the gains from repression highly, they often use repressive acts to effectively outlaw or restrict domestic human rights mobilization.

All told, HRAs rarely create the conditions necessary for state compliance with human rights because they are soft: persuasion, alone, is a weak mechanism of influence that does not supply strong enough incentives or commitment instruments to outweigh defection.

These agreements supply similar human rights influence properties as most HRAs: a set of principled ideas legitimating appropriate and accepted behavior among a community of states. Because the standards are soft—agreement benefits are unconditional on human rights behaviors—this class of institution supplies no coercive mechanisms of influence. If these organizations influence human rights at all, they influence through persuasion, and one should now expect that they are unlikely to change most repressors human rights beliefs or practices.

Other PTAs provide member governments with "harder" institutional channels to manage and enforce their policy commitments (that is, benefits that are in some way conditional on member states' actions). These PTAs do so by placing the language of human rights in an enforceable incentive structure designed to provide members with the economic and political benefits of various forms of market access. These benefits are supplied under conditions of compliance with the protection of human rights principles or laws identified in the agreement. Behavioral change is a side payment for market gains, enforced through threat (direct or tacit) to disrupt integration or exchange unless a trade partner complies with their human rights commitments specified in the contract. A list of PTAs offering standards, hard or soft, is available in the Appendix 1.

The Lomé and Cotonou Agreements are strong examples of these types of PTAs. Cotonou provides the new institutional structure for the European Community's (EC) largest financial and political framework for cooperation, offering nonreciprocal trade benefits for certain African, Caribbean, and Pacific (ACP) states, including nearly unlimited entry to the EC market for a wide range of goods. The agreement, which replaced successive Lomé Agreements, commits "Parties [to] undertake to promote and protect all fundamental freedoms and human rights, be they civil and political, or economic, social and cultural".[18] These principles are supported through a political dialogue designed to share information, to cultivate mutual understanding, and to facilitate the formation of shared priorities, including those concerning the respect for human rights (Article 8). Obligations are binding on recipients. They are supported by a review mechanism established in the consultation procedures of Article 96, which require habitual assessments of national developments concerning human rights.[19] Alongside the agreement are conditional financial protocols allocating resources available to eligible countries through the European Development Fund (EDF). When members are perceived to violate agreement terms, a variety of different actions can be taken to influence behavior. These include the threat or act of withdrawal of membership or financial protocols, as well as the enforcement of economic or political sanctions. Cotonou thus supplies strong elements of both coercion and persuasion.

This second category of agreement supplies coercion mechanisms of influence that most HRAs and all soft PTAs cannot supply. PTAs with hard standards can, under certain conditions, influence through coercion by changing repressive actors' costs and benefits of actualizing their preferences for repression. Consider again the abusive elite with strong preferences for repression. Where persuasion alone is likely to fail, hard standards can influence the problem of compliance without changing actors' preferences. They provide an economic motivation to promote human rights policy reforms that would not otherwise be implemented, and they do so in a relatively short time horizon. When institutionalized PTAs create new and valuable gains, hard agreements can also commit future elites with preferences for liberalization to human rights reforms they would not otherwise select. While influence through persuasion requires leveling a campaign to change a new leader's preferences for repression, influence through coercion requires only that the leader value the gains of integration more than the gains of repression. PTAs, moreover, may increase the costs of repression for any domestic actors that favor liberalization.

Hard PTAs are not a panacea for repression. They are likely to be much less effective in influencing armed opposition groups or governments under insurrection, where preferences for liberalization are low or absent among opponents. To be sure, not all leaders are likely to be influence by all agreements. Severely repressive elites that reap extensive benefits from repression that they value more than integration are apt to defect from agreements that offer only small gains or that require large-scale political upheaval. Moreover, target repressors that can secure an alternative supply of the goods achieved through cooperation without conditionality are likely to reject membership in PTAs that require human rights reforms.

Conclusion

When do states comply with international rules governing human rights? It has been often accepted that states regularly come to change their human rights behaviors when they are persuaded by international actors and institutions: international institutions can change states' preferences for behavior even when coercive instruments of enforcement are not available.[20] I do not contend in this article that institutions always fail to influence repression through persuasion, but I do argue that there are strong theoretical reasons to be skeptical that persuasion, alone, is likely to be effective much of the time. There is little evidence to show otherwise, and the failure of international human rights agreements to effectively bring about change in behaviors so much of the time should give us cause to rethink current optimism that HRAs can influence without coercion. Far from being counterproductive, some form of coercion may often be essential to bringing about better practices, although certainly not incompatible with most long-terms strategies of persuasion.[21] Moreover, PTAs may increasingly provide these instruments of coercion that the human rights regime so clearly lacks.

This argument has three core implications. First, human rights regimes alone rarely create the conditions necessary for state compliance with human rights because they are almost always soft, lacking the necessary mechanisms to supply strong incentives and commitment instruments to outweigh defection. Second, material and political rewards are often a more effective (and compatible) incentive structure to support the initial stages of compliance. Third, a growing number of PTAs have become part of a larger set of governing institutions enforcing better human rights practices. These agreements can supply limited human rights mandates and influence some governments to make marginal improvements in certain human rights behaviors; they can enforce the initial stages of compliance that most HRAs cannot.

It could easily be argued that PTAs are not ideal forums for human rights governance; that the WTO would be more effective in enforcing better practices; and that better designed HRAs would solve the problems of compliance. Nothing could be closer to the argument proposed here. International institutions have the greatest influence over state compliance with human rights principles when they offer substantial gains with some kind of coercive incentives, perhaps coupled with strategies of persuasion, to change the costs and benefits of repressive actors' behaviors. If the member states of the WTO could agree on a human rights clause linking the terms of trade to the protection of human rights, it could potentially begin to leverage some influence on world repression, and it could certainly empower human rights advocates fighting for reform.

The WTO today, however, provides no formal guidance with respect to member state compliance with international human rights laws or principles. Attempts to adopt even soft standards protecting workers rights have failed time and time again and they appear unlikely to succeed anytime in the near future.[22] Most human rights agreements are even further from any sort of institutional reform that could impose more enforceable rules of behavior.

PTAs, then, are certainly not ideal forms of human rights governance and they are not a replacement for human rights laws. They are among the only existing international institutions with some capacity to enforce compliance, and they may prove to be one of the more effective available means of implementing very basic human rights values into practice, although partial and imperfect.

Notes

1. Last year, Amnesty International documented human rights abuses in 151 countries and territories. Amnesty International Report 2003.
2. See Rosati 2001; Lutz and Sikkink 2000; Risse, Ropp, and Sikkink 1999; Koh 1998; and Franck 1988. Hathaway 2002 argues that leading perspectives on international law assume that states intend to comply with their internal legal commitments. This assumption, commonly applied to HRAs, has been widespread among international lawyers and scholars but seldom tested.
3. See Hafner-Burton and Tsutsui 2005; Hathaway 2002; and Donnelly 1986.
4. A standard is an acknowledged behavioral criterion established by authority, custom, or general consent as a model or example. See Merriam-Webster Unabridged online Dictionary, available at <http:// www.m-w.com/cgr-bin/dictionary> accessed 6 May 2005.
5. I define PTAs in the broadest sense possible to include preferential trade instruments of many kinds, including unilateral preferential schemes, bilateral and regional agreements, and reciprocal and nonreciprocal agreements.
6. See De Melo and Panagariya 1993; Mansfield 1998; Mattli 1999; and McCall Smith 2000.
7. WTO members participating in PTAs are required to meet a set of preferential trading conditions defined in the text of GATT Article XXIV, Ad Article XXIV, and its updates, which include the 1994 Understanding on the Interpretation of Article XXIV of the General Agreement on Tariffs and Trade, as well as the text of GATS Article V. Note that many PTAs are not notified to the WTO.
8. Abbott and Snidal 2000 identify variation in international legalization: hard laws are legally binding obligations that are precise and that delegate authority for interpreting and implementing the law; while soft laws are those that deviate from hard along several dimensions. The use of hard and soft law through the remainder of this article invokes Abbott and Snidal's attention to variation but simplifies by identifying one primary distinguishing characteristic: conditionality. Hard PTA standards establish enforceable conditions for integration, while soft standards

appeal to voluntary principles of cooperation that do not require behavioral change to receive market access benefits. Abbott and Snidal 2000, 421.

9. This view stands in sharp contrast to the belief that coercion is unnecessary or counterproductive: that governments often conform to global human rights laws out of concern for legitimacy, even when laws are powerless to enforce compliance; and that coercion necessarily produces adverse consequences on the enjoyment of human rights. See Goodman and Jinks 2004; Johnston 2001; Payne 2001; Price 1998; Helfer and Slaughter 1997; Finnemore 1996; Koh 1996–97; Franck 1990; Henkin 1979; as well as Bossuyt 2000. For an exception, see Martin and Sikkink 1993.
10. HRAs, as with PTAs, vary in their degree of institutionalization, and exceptions to this claim are discussed in later sections of the article.
11. The major treaties furnish UN committees that formally provide a reporting and oversight function.
12. There is today only one major exception to this claim: the European human rights system supplies a unique set of instruments to enforce the Council of Europe's commitment to uphold HRAs. Almost all members have adopted the Convention for the Protection of Human Rights and Fundamental Freedoms into national law, obligating national courts to enforce the agreement's provisions. The European Court of Human Rights is the superior arbitrator of disputes concerning noncompliance with human rights standards under the Convention, acting as a subsidiary to national enforcement in cases of failure. Europe, however, is exceptional. The vast majority of HRAs provide softer standards that are voluntary and weakly enforceable at best. See Cleveland 2001b. The Organization of American States (OAS) offers the closest comparison. The Commission monitors observance of treaty obligations for all states committed to the American Convention on Human Rights, while the Court monitors compliance under the Convention for states that have also recognized the compulsory jurisdiction of the Court. Yet OAS political bodies routinely fail to support or enforce the recommendations of the Commission or the judgments of the Court, and human rights standards remain effectively soft. See Dulitzky 1999; and Davidson 1997.
13. Small steps toward legal enforcement have only recently begun at the global level through the formation of the International Criminal Court (ICC), as well as at the regional level through courts such as the European and Inter-American Courts of Human Rights, and the state level through the two International Criminal Tribunals in the Former Yugoslavia and Rwanda. These institutions signal an important step toward management of human rights, but they nevertheless remain extremely limited in their jurisdiction and in their effectiveness to provide repressive states with the incentives to protect human rights.
14. See Cottier 2002; and Goodman and Jinks 2004.
15. Donnelly 1986.
16. See Cleveland 2001a and 2001b.
17. Risse, Ropp, and Sikkink 1999.
18. Articles 9, 13, and 26.
19. Lomé IV provided a similar hard standard in Article 366a.
20. Although influence through coercion is almost always beyond the scope of HRAs, many scholars that remain convinced of HRA influence without hard standards also recognize that coercive instruments can be important tools to enforce better practices, and that human rights advocates frequently employ material incentives to proffer norms of better behavior. See, for example, Keck and Sikkink 1998; and Risse, Ropp, and Sikkink 1999. Others support the general views of Chayes and Chayes 1998 by arguing that coercive enforcement is likely to be unproductive, imposing high costs with little behavioral gain. See note 22.
21. Strategies of economic coercion can also have persuasive effects overtime, as repeated punitive interactions may contribute to the recognition and domestic internalization of the disputed norm. For a similar argument with respect to unilateral economic sanctions, see Cleveland 2001b.
22. The adoption of rules designed to protect citizens' rights into trade agreements had limited precedent in the pre-GATT era, although the issue of human rights emerged most forcefully during

the Uruguay Round. See Francioni 2001. Several countries sought to reintroduce a narrow set of labor rights into the legal architecture of the organization. Perceiving this initiative as protectionist and imperialist, many countries of the developing world launched a campaign to prevent the incorporation of core labor standards into global trade doctrine. See McCrudden and Davies 2000. These disputes eventually led to the 1996 Singapore compromise declaring that the WTO is not the competent body to redress concerns for members' compliance with international labor laws. The compromise was upheld in Seattle (1999), Doha (2001), and Cancun (2003).

References

Abbott, Kenneth W, and Duncan Snidal. 2000. Hard and Soft Law in International Governance, *International Organization* 54 (3):421–56.

——. 2001. International 'Standards' and International Governance. *Journal of European Public Policy* 8 (3):345–70.

Amnesty International. 2003. Annual Report. Available at <http://web.amnesty.org/report2003/index-eng>. Accessed 28 March 2005.

Anderson, Craig A. 1989. Causal Reasoning and Belief Perseverance. In *Proceedings of the Society for Consumer Psychology*, edited by D. W. Schumann, 115–20. Knoxville: University of Tennessee Press.

Austin, John, and Sarah Austin. 1861. *The Province of Jurisprudence Determined.* 2d ed. London: J. Murray.

Axelrod, Robert M. 1984. *The Evolution of Cooperation.* New York: Basic Books.

Bossuyt, Marc. 2000. The Bossuyt Report: The Adverse Consequences of Economic Sanctions on the Enjoyment of Human Rights. Working Paper E/CN.4/Sub.2/2000/33. Prepared for submission to the UN Commission on Human Rights, Subcommission on the Promotion and Protection of Human Rights.

Brandtner, Barbara, and Allan Rosas. 1999. Trade Preferences and Human Rights. In *The EU and Human Rights*, edited by Philip Alston, Mara Bustelo and James Heenan, 699–722. New York: Oxford University Press.

Bulterman, Mielle. 1999. Human Rights Dimensions of the Lomé Convention. *Netherlands Quarterly of Human Rights* 1:83.

Bulterman, Mielle, Aart Hendriks, and Jacqueline Smith, eds. 1998. *To Baehr in Our Minds: Essays on Human Rights From the Heart of the Netherlands.* Utrecht: SIM, Netherlands Institute of Human Rights.

Bulterman, Mielle, and Martin Kuijer. 1996. *Compliance with Judgments of International Courts.* Boston: Martinus Nijhoff.

Chayes, Abram, and Antonia Handler Chayes. 1990. From Law Enforcement to Dispute Settlement: A New Approach to Arms Control Verification and Compliance. *International Security* 14 (4):147–64.

——. 1993. On Compliance. International Organization 47 (2):175–205.

——. 1998. *The New Sovereignty: Compliance with International Regulatory Agreements.* Cambridge, Mass.: Harvard University Press.

Cingranelli, David L., and David L. Richards. 1999. Respect for Human Rights After the End of the Cold War. *Journal of Peace Research* 36 (5):511–34.

Cleveland, Sarah H. 2001a. Human Rights Sanctions and the World Trade Organization. In *Environment, Human Rights & International Trade*, edited by Francesco Francioni, 199–261. Portland, Ore: Hart.

——. 2001b. Norm Internalization and U.S. Economic Sanctions. *Yale Journal of International Law* 1:1–102.

Cottier, Thomas. 2002. Trade and Human Rights: A Relationship to Discover. *Journal of International Economic Law* 5 (1):111–32.

Crawford, Gordon. 1998. Human Rights and Democracy in EU Development Co-operation: Towards Fair and Equal Treatment. In *European Union Development Policy*, edited by Marjorie Lister, 131–78. London: Macmillan.

Davidson, Scott. 1997. *The Inter-American Human Rights System.* Brookfield, Vt.: Ashgate Publishing.

De Melo, Jaime, and Arvind Panagariya. 1993, *New Dimensions in Regional Integration.* New York: Cambridge University Press.

Donnelly, Jack. 1986. International Human Rights: A Regime Analysis. *International Organization* 40 (3):599–642.

Downs, George W., David M. Rocke, and Peter N. Barsoom. 1996. Is the Good News About Compliance Good News about Cooperation? *International Organization* 50 (3):379–406.

Drezner, Daniel W. 2003. The Hidden Hand of Economic Coercion. *International Organization* 57 (3):643–59.

Dulitzky, Ariel E. 1999. Book Review: The Inter-American Human Rights System by Scott Davidson. *European Journal of International Law* 10 (2):475–77.

Eaton, Jonathan, and Maxim Engers. 1999. Sanctions: Some Simply Analytics. *American Economic Review* 89 (2):409–14.

European Commission. 1997. Agenda 2000—Commission Opinion on Slovakia's Application for Membership in the European Union (Doc/97/20). Brussels: European Commission. Available at <http:// www.europa.eu.int/comm/enlargement/dwn/opinions/slovakia/sk-op-en.pdf>. Accessed 28 March 2005.

——. 1998a. Communication from the Commission to the Council "Regarding the Conclusion of Consultations with Togo under Article 366a of the Lomé Convention" (SEC 1956 Final, 25 November, 2). Brussels: European Commission.

——. 1998b. Evaluation du Programme d'Action Immédiate de Réhabilitation (November 1998—Ref. 951452). Brussels: European Commission.

——. 1999a. Commission Proposal for a Council Decision "Concluding Consultations with the Comoros under Article 366 of the Lomé Convention and Taking Appropriate Measures" (COM 695 Final, 16 December). Brussels: European Commission.

——. 1999b. Communication from the to the Council "On Conclusion of Consultations with Niger Pursuant to Article 366 of the Lomé Convention and Taking Appropriate Measures" (COM 350 Final, 8 July). Brussels: European Commission.

——. 1999e. *Regular Report from the Commission on Slovakia's Progress Towards Accession.* Brussels: European Commission. Available at (http:// www.europa.eu.int/comm/enlargement/report_10_99/pdf/en/slovakia_en.pdf). Accessed 28 March 2005.

——. 2000a. Communication from the Commission to the Council "On the Opening of Consultations with the Republic of Fiji Islands under Article 366 of the Lomé Conventions" (COM 460 Final, 24 July, 2). Brussels: European Commission.

——. 2000b. External Evaluation of Community Aid Concerning Positive Actions in the Field of Human Rights and Democracy in the ACP Countries. Vol. 28, August (SCR F5). Brussels: European Commission.

——. 2000c. Follow-Up to the First Summit between Latin America, Caribbean and the European Union (COM 670 Final, 31 October). Brussels: European Commission.

——. 2000d. To Prepare the Fourth Meeting of Euro-Mediterranean Foreign Ministers, "Reinvigorating the Barcelona Process" (COM 497 Final, 6 September). Brussels: European Commission.

——. 2001a. Proposal for a Council Decision "Concluding Consultations with Cote D'Ivoire under Artiele 96 of the Cotonou Agreement" (COM 290 Final, 28 May). Brussels: European Commission.

——. 2001b. The European Union's Role in Promoting Human Rights and Democratisation in Third Countries (COM 252 Final). Brussels: European Commission.

——. 2003. Comprehensive Monitoring Report on Slovakia's Preparations for Membership. Brussels: European Commission.

European Council. 2003. *EU Annual Report on Human Rights* (13449/03 COHOM 29). Brussels: European Council.

Fierro, Elena. 2003. *The EU's Approach to Human Rights Conditionality in Practice.* The Hague, Netherlands: Martinus Nijhoff.

Finnemore, Martha. 1996. *National Interests in International Society, Cornell Studies in Political Economy.* Ithaca, N.Y.: Cornell University Press.

Finnemore, Martha, and Kathryn Sikkink. 1998. International Norm Dynamics and Political Change. *International Organization* 52 (4):887–917.

Francioni, Francesco. 2001. Environment, Human Rights and the Limits of Free Trade. In *Environment, Human Rights & International Trade*, edited by F. Franeioni, 1–26. Portland, Ore.: Hart.

Franck, Thomas M. 1988. Legitimacy in the International System. *American Journal of International Law* 82 (4):705–58.

——. 1990. *The Power of Legitimacy Among Nations.* Oxford: Oxford University Press.

——. 1995. *Fairness in International Law and Institutions.* New York: Clarendon Press.

Frankel, Jeffrey A., Ernesto Stein, and Shang-Jin Wei. 1996. Regional Trading Arrangements: Natural or Supernatural? *American Economic Review* 86 (2):52–56.

Goodman, Ryan, and Derek Jinks. 2004. How to Influence States: Socialization and International Human Rights Law. *Duke Law Journal* 54 (3), 2004.

Grether, Jean-Marie, and Marcelo Olarreaga. 1998. Preferential and Non-Preferential Trade Flows in World Trade. Staff Working Paper ERAD-98-10. Washington, D.C: World Trade Organization.

Hafner-Burton, Emilie M. 2004. Forum Shopping for Human Rights: Who Chooses Preferential Trade? Paper presented at the workshop on Forum Shopping and Global Governance at the European University Institute, Florence, Italy, 23–24 April. Available at <http://www.stanford.edu/~emiliehb>. Accessed 28 March 2005.

——. 2005. Right or Robust? The Sensitive Nature of Political Repression in an Era of Globalization. Journal of Peace Research. Available at <http://www.stanford.edu/~emiliehb>. Accessed 28 March 2005.

Hafner-Burton, Emilie M., and Kiyoteru Tsutsui. 2005. Human Rights in a Globalizing World: The Paradox of Empty Promises. American Journal of Sociology 110 (5):1373–1411. Available at <http://www.stanford.edu/~emiliehb>. Accessed 28 March 2005.

Hathaway, Oona A. 2002. Do Human Rights Treaties Make a Difference? Yale Law Journal III (8):1935–2042.

Hazelzet, Hadewych A. 2001. Carrots or Sticks? EU and US Reactions to Human Rights Violations (1989–2000). Ph.D. diss., European University Institute, Florence, Italy.

——. 2004. Suspension of Development Co-Operation: An Instrument to Promote Human Rights and Democracy? Centre Européen de Gestion des Politiques de Développement (ECPDM) Discussion Paper. Maastricht, Netherlands: ECPDM.

Helfer, Laurence R., and Anne-Marie Slaughter. 1997. Toward a Theory of Effective Supranational Adjudication. Yale Law Journal 107 (2):273–391.

Helson, Arthur C., and Robert P. DeVecchi. 2000. Human Rights, Humanitarian Intervention & Sanctions. Council on Foreign Relations Issue Brief. Washington, D.C: Council on Foreign Relations.

Henderson, Conway W. 1991. Conditions Affecting the Use of Political Repression. Journal of Conflict Resolution 35 (1):120–42.

——. 1993. Population Pressures and Political Repression. Social Science Quarterly 74 (2):323–33.

Henkin, Louis. 1979. How Nations Behave: Law and Foreign Policy. 2d ed. New York: Council on Foreign Relations/Columbia University Press.

Howard, Rhoda, and Jack Donnelly. 1986. Human Dignity, Human Rights, and Political Regimes. American Political Science Review 80 (3):801–18.

Johnston, Alastair Iain. 2001. Treating International Institutions as Social Environments. International Studies Quarterly 45 (4):489–90.

Kahler, Miles, and David A. Lake. 2003. Governance in a Global Economy: Political Authority in Transition. Princeton, N.J.: Princeton University Press.

Keck, Margaret E., and Kathryn Sikkink. 1998. Activists Beyond Borders: Advocacy Networks in International Politics. Ithaca, N.Y.: Cornell University Press.

Keohane, Robert O. 1984. After Hegemony: Cooperation and Discord in the World Political Economy. Princeton, N.J.: Princeton University Press.

King, Toby. 1999. Human Rights in European Foreign Policy: Success or Failure for Post-Modern Diplomacy? European Journal of International Relations 10 (2):313–37.

Kirkpatrick, Jeane. 1979. Dictatorships and Double Standards. Commentary 68 (5):34–45.

Koh, Harold Hongju. 1996–97. Why Do Nations Obey International Law? Yale Law Journal 106 (8):2599–659.

——. 1998. How Is International Human Rights Law Enforced? Indiana Law Journal 74 (4):1397–417.

Kratochwil, Friedrich V. 1989. Rules, Norms, and Decisions: On the Conditions of Practical and Legal Reasoning in International Relations and Domestic Affairs. Cambridge: Cambridge University Press.

Krauthammer, Charles. 1989. The Curse of Legalism: International Law? It's Purely Advisory. New Republic 201 (19):44–47.

Lutz, Ellen L., and Kathryn Sikkink. 2000. International Human Rights Law and Practice in Latin America. International Organization 54 (3):633–59.

Mansfield, Edward D. 1998. The Proliferation of Preferential Trading Agreements. Journal of Conflict Resolution 42 (5):523–43.

Martin, Lisa L. 1992. Coercive Cooperation: Explaining Multilateral Economic Sanctions. Princeton, N.J.: Princeton University Press.

——. 1993. The Rational State Choice of Multilateralism. In Multilateralism Matters: The Theory and Praxis of an Institutional Form, edited by John G. Ruggie, 91–122. New York: Columbia University Press.

——. 1998. Evasive Maneuvers? Reconsidering Presidential Use of Executive Agreements. In Strategic Politicians, Institutions, and Foreign Policy, edited by Randolph M. Siverson, 51–77. Ann Arbor: University of Michigan Press.

——. 2000. Democratic Commitments: Legislatures and International Cooperation. Princeton, N.J.: Princeton University Press.

Martin, Lisa L., and Kathryn Sikkink. 1993. U.S. Policy and Human Rights in Argentina and Guatemala, 1973–1980. In Double-Edged Diplomacy: International Bargaining and Domestic Politics, edited by Peter Evans, Harold Jacobson, and Robert Putnam, 330–62. Berkeley: University of California Press.

Mattli, Walter. 1999. The Logic of Regional Integration: Europe and Beyond. Cambridge: Cambridge University Press.

McCall Smith, James. 2000. The Politics of Dispute Settlement Design: Explaining Legalism in Regional Trade Pacts. International Organization 54 (1):137–80.

McCrudden, Christopher, and Anne Davies. 2000. A Perspective on Trade and Labour Rights. Journal of International Economic Law 3 (1):43–62.

Mearsheimer, John J. 1994/1995. The False Promise of International Institutions. International Security 19 (3):5–49.

Meyer, John W., John Boli, George M. Thomas, and Francisco O. Ramirez. 1997. World Society and the Nation-State. American Journal of Sociology 103 (1):144–81.

Miller, Vaughne, 2004. The Human Rights Clause in the EU's External Agreements. International Affairs and Defence, House of Commons Library Research Paper 04/33. London: House of Commons. Available at <http://66.102.9.104/search?q=cache:BDfad6HTPmkJ:www.parliament.uk/commons/lib/research/rp2004/rp04-033.pdf+The+Human+Rights+Clause+in+the+EU%27s+External+Agreements&hl=en>. Accessed 28 March 2005.

Mitchell, Neil, and James McCormick. 1988. Economic and Political Explanations of Human Rights Violations. World Politics 40 (4):476–98.

Mitchell, Ronald B. 1993. Compliance Theory: A Synthesis. Review of European Community and International Environmental Law 2 (4):327–34.

Moravcsik, Andrew. 1995. Explaining International Human Rights Regimes: Liberal Theory and Western Europe. European Journal of International Relations 1 (2):157–89.

——. 2000. The Origins of Human Rights Regimes: Democratic Delegation in Postwar Europe. International Organization 54 (2):217–52.

Nowak, Manfred. 1999. Human Rights "Conditionality" in Relation to Entry to, and Full Participation in, the EU. In The EU and Human Rights, edited by Philip Alston, Mara Bustelo, and James Heenan, 687–98. New York: Oxford University Press.

Office of the United States Trade Representative. 2001. Comprehensive Report of the President of the United States, U.S. Trade and Investment Policy Toward Sub-Saharan Africa and Implementation of the African Growth and Opportunity Act. The First of Eight Annual Reports. Washington, D.C.: Government Printing Office.

——. 2002. Comprehensive Report of the President of the United States, U.S. Trade and Investment Policy Toward Sub-Saharan Africa and Implementation of the African Growth and Opportunity Act. The

Second of Eight Annual Reports. Washington, D.C.: Government Printing Office.

——. 2003. Comprehensive Report of the President of the United States, U.S. Trade and Investment Policy Toward Sub-Saharan Africa and Implementation of the African Growth and Opportunity Act. The Third of Eight Annual Reports. Washington, D.C.: Government Printing Office.

Organization for Economic Co-operation and Development (OECD). 1996. Trade, Employment and Labour Standards: A Study of Core Worker's Rights and International Trade (11–12). Paris: OECD.

Oneal, John R., and Bruce M. Russett. 1999. The Kantian Peace—The Pacific Benefits of Democracy, Interdependence, and International Organizations, 1885–1992. World Politics 52 (1):1–37.

Payne, Rodger A. 2001. Persuasion, Frames, and Norm Construction. European Journal of International Relations 7 (1):37–61.

Petersmann, Ernst-Ulrich. 1997. International Trade Law and the GATT/WTO Dispute Settlement System. Boston: Kluwer Law International.

Poe, Steven C., and C. Neal Tate. 1994. Repression of Human Rights to Personal Integrity in the 1980s: A Global Analysis. American Political Science Review 88 (4):853–72.

Poe, Steven, C. Neal Tate, and Linda Camp Keith. 1999. Repression of the Human Right to Personal Integrity Revisited: A Global Cross-National Study Covering the Years 1976–1993. International Studies Quarterly 43 (2):291–313.

Price, Richard. 1998. Reversing the Gun Sights: Transnational Civil Society Targets Land Mines. International Organization 52 (3):613–44.

Pritchard, Kathleen. 1989. Human Rights and Development: Theory and Data. In Human Rights and Development: International Views, edited by D. P. Forsythe, 329–47. London: Macmillan.

Rai, Milan, and Eden, Douglas. 2001. Can We Ever Justify Economic Sanctions? Ecologist (4):24–27.

Richards, David L., Ronald D. Gelleny, and David H. Sacko. 2001. Money with a Mean Streak? Foreign Economic Penetration and Government Respect for Human Rights in Developing Countries. International Studies Quarterly 45 (2):219–39.

Riedel, Eibe, and Martin Will. 1999. Human Rights Clauses in External Agreements of the EC. In The EU and Human Rights, edited by Philip Alston, Mara Bustelo, and James Heenan, 723–54. New York: Oxford University Press.

Risse, Thomas, Stephen C. Ropp, and Kathryn Sikkink, eds. 1999. The Power of Human Rights: International Norms and Domestic Change. Cambridge: Cambridge University Press.

Rosati, Kristen B. 2001. International Human Rights Treaties Can Make a Difference. U.S. Implementation of Article 3 of the United Nations Convention Against Torture. Human Rights 28 (1):14–16.

Ruggie, John Gerard. 1998. Constructing the World Polity: Essays on International Institutionalization. New York: Routledge.

Schwitzgebel, Eric. 1999. Gradual Belief Change in Children. Human Development 42 (1):283–96.

Singer J. David, and Melvin Small. 1994. Correlates of War Project: International and Civil War Data, 1816–1992 (ICPR 9905). Ann Arbor, MI: Inter-University Consortium for Political and Social Research.

Slusher, Morgan, and Craig A. Anderson. 1996. Using Causal Persuasive Arguments to Change Beliefs and Teach New Information: The Mediating Role of Explanation Availability and Evaluation Bias in the Acceptance of Knowledge. Journal of Educational Psychology 88 (1):t10–22.

Steiner, Henry J., and Philip Alston. 1996. International Human Rights in Context: Law, Politics, Morals: Text and Materials. Oxford: Clarendon Press.

Winters, L. Alan. 1996. Regionalism Versus Multilateralism. Policy Research Working Paper 1687. Washington, D.C.: World Bank.

Yarbrough, Beth V., and Robert M. Yarbrough. 1997. Dispute Settlement in International Trade: Regionalism and Procedural Coordination. In The Political Economy of Regionalism, New Directions in World Politics, edited by Edward Mansfield and Helen V. Milner, 134–63. New York: Columbia University Press.

Young, Oran R. 1994. International Governance: Protecting the Environment in a Stateless Society. Ithaca, N.Y.: Cornell University Press.

Preventing and Transforming Conflict Nonviolently

SANAM NARAGHI ANDERLINI

Sanam Naraghi Anderlini has advised UN agencies, the UK government, and NGOs on steps for peace promotion. This extract presents an example of the ways in which conflict resolution can happen without a military solution. Anderlini contends that there are specific early warning signs that a violent conflict is developing. What are those signs? What methods can non-state actors use to prevent a conflict from escalating? Do you find Anderlini's proposals convincing? Why or why not? On what IR theory perspective do you base your opinion?

> Could we have managed [the threat of Saddam Hussein] by means other than a direct military intervention? Well, maybe we could have.
>
> —Richard Perle, former chair of the Pentagon's Defense Policy Board, November 2006[1]

> Just people cannot follow unjust laws....We seem to be the only people bravely standing in the street, owning the street, commanding it....And so they [the police] felt they had to trample upon as much harder....But we have a slogan: "Strike a woman and you strike a rock." We are not going to be deterred.
>
> —Jenni Williams, founder, WOZA. 2005[2]

In 2002, a US-led war against Saddam Hussein's regime in Iraq was inevitable in the minds of most people. In Washington and London, discussions among policy pundits and analysts had moved beyond the prevention of war into the realm of possible scenarios in the aftermath and detailed plans and recommendations for "winning the peace."[3] In the midst of this, a group of women in shades of pink took a different stand. Calling themselves "Code Pink" in response to the Bush administration's color-coded warnings against the threat of terror, the US-based group defined itself as "a women-led and women-initiated grassroots peace and social justice movement dedicated to stopping the war in Iraq, preventing future wars and redirecting our country's resources into life-affirming activities: education, health care, veteran's benefits and social services."[4]

Code Pink led protests, mobilized women and men, opened chapters across the United States and internationally, and became an organized movement. In the same year, in Zimbabwe, the government-induced economic crisis and descent into mass poverty were accelerating. In response, Women of Zimbabwe Arise (WOZA), officially formed in 2003, also started peaceful but noisy public protests against the government. In its first demonstration. WOZA took to pot banging on the streets of Harare, protesting violence against women. At its second gathering, the women, representing a cross section of Zimbabwean society, protested the increasingly harsh government policies by handing out roses to symbolize love. "We challenge the love of power, with the power of love." says WOZA founder Jenni Williams, veteran of twenty-five arrests.[5]

Across the world in Venezuela, the pot-banging tactic has also been at work. Protesting President Hugo Chavez's encroachment on democratic freedoms from 2000 to 2005, women in Venezuela adopted nonviolent strategies to protest his actions. Firmly identifying themselves as women, mothers, sisters, daughters, and grandmothers, they joined the broader resistance movement and adopted three strategies: protest and persuasion, noncooperation, and intervention.[6] They initiated community meetings to discuss nonviolent strategies for protest and mobilized to collect signatures for a referendum in 2004. Waving flags and blowing whistles, banging pots and shouting slogans, they often accounted for over 50 percent of the protesters.

Code Pink did not succeed in preventing the onset of the Iraq War. Will WOZA or the women of Venezuela succeed in bringing about change nonviolently? Difficult to predict; for every attempt at a Czech-like Velvet Revolution, there are countless other instances where nonviolent demands for change have ended with state-sponsored and even communal violence. That is ironic. The need to prevent violent expression of conflict is an easy concept to grasp. Yet avoiding overt violent conflict remains a critical challenge for most societies struggling for peaceful transition from oppression to coexistence and democracy.

No society wants violence, so much so that the tolerance threshold for oppression, poverty, fear, and abuse is extremely high in most instances. The horrors and unpredictability of war are too well-known, and violence is not the route that most people wish to follow. Yet preventing violent conflict and civil wars is proving to be an elusive challenge.[7]

Even in the case of the US war on Iraq, those opposing the war could offer no viable alternative way of dealing with Saddam Hussein. Some argued for the maintenance of international sanctions and isolation, which had hardened the regime's grip on the country. But in taking that stance they were implicitly willing to leave the Iraqi people at the mercy of the Hussein regime for a further indeterminate period. Talk of lifting the sanctions or exploring alternative long-term solutions was either limited or never fully aired. The space for deliberations was heavily circumscribed by the political class and the media. The mass public demonstrations had no effect. By the time the Iraq invasion began in March 2003, the trajectory of violence was not a surprise. Like the wars in Kosovo and the Democratic Republic of Congo in 1998, we watched as the inevitable became reality.

Throughout the late 1990s, the idea of conflict prevention—particularly in the context of intrastate conflicts—captured the imagination and pockets of many European nations and through them the European Commission. The term conflict prevention became internationally accepted shorthand for describing the prevention of the outbreak, escalation, or resurgence of armed conflict.[8] In the United States, the Carnegie Commission on Preventing Deadly Conflict (1994–1999) made distinctions between direct (short-term) conflict prevention that aims to halt the rise of violence and structural (long-term) prevention that seeks to address the root political, social, and economic causes of conflict so that it can be resolved and transformed nonviolently.[9] In practice, however, much of the developments in the field of conflict prevention have focused on the direct/short-term approach in situations of state fragility or collapse, with a primary focus on the actions of international agencies or actors rather than the capacities and potential of national actors or civil society.

The international nongovernmental community also continued its efforts and activism. The establishment of the International Criminal Court (ICC) as a means of prosecuting and preventing war crimes and crimes against humanity was a key mechanism of the broader discourse of conflict prevention. The September 11, 2001, attacks in the United States shocked the Western world into registering the threat posed by nonstate actors, within and across national borders. The knee-jerk reaction in the United States was to beef up military responses and define virtually all nonstate armed groups as "terrorists." But the 9/11 attacks also provoked a significant shift in thinking about "nontraditional" security threats, the nature of violent conflicts, and the range of actors involved.[10]

The concept of conflict prevention, which in the mid-1990s was absent from the lexicon of international policymakers, is not only widely used but has spawned an ever-evolving field of study, policy, and practice. In the process it has become increasingly nebulous and all-encompassing. As a concept, it is everything to everybody: violence prevention, prevention of escalation, prevention of resurgence that merges with postconflict reconstruction and even nation building. All for good reason: successful peacebuilding is effective conflict prevention. Increased attention to "fragile states" is also an important development, but the dilemma remains of addressing seemingly strong states, where governments not only have a monopoly over the use of violence but also are not shy about using oppressive measures to quell dissent. Political sensitivity, together with a conflation of terms, has led to oversight of cases where the state is strong but conflict with society is rife, where violence has not erupted but a sociopolitical pressure cooker is evident, and where state-sponsored aggression is rampant. Iraq a decade ago. Zimbabwe today, perhaps Iran tomorrow: the outstanding challenge is how to resolve the conflict that exists, without violence and without suppressing the legitimate grievances of all parties. Who should and could be involved?

The International Context: Developments in Conflict Prevention

The end of the Cold War and the demise of the Soviet Union as a superpower led in part to the onslaught of violent conflict within states and across state boundaries, often perceived to be artificially drawn by former colonial rulers. Existing global institutions, driven by member states guarding their sovereignty and sensitive to external intervention, have struggled to prevent, avert, and respond to such conflicts effectively. Nonetheless, the 2005 Human Security Report indicates that from 1991 to 2004, despite conventional wisdom, 28 armed struggles for self-determination started or restarted, while 43 were contained or ended. There has been a decline not only in international but also internal conflicts.[11] The end of colonialism, a decline in proxy wars, growing economic interdependence and democratization, and a growing aversion to war are contributing factors, but the UN is also credited. There has been "a dramatic increase in preventive diplomacy and peacemaking,"[12] the report says. Statistics tell the story more clearly. From the late 1980s to the early 2000s, the UN became more involved in peacemaking (stopping ongoing wars), increasing the number of its interventions from four to fifteen; its postconflict peace operations rose from seven to sixteen.[13]

It is the number of preventive missions (prior to the outbreak of conflict) that indicate the difficulty that still exists. From 1990 to 2002, UN-led preventive missions increased from one to six.[14] The UN Preventive Deployment Mission to Macedonia (UNPREDEP), established in 1995, is among the six. But information about discreet UN diplomatic and political initiatives that prevented potential conflicts elsewhere, between states or within states, is not readily available.

The Limits of the UN

Particularly in matters of peace and security, the UN, as an organization of member states, has no independent decisionmaking authority outside its membership. Despite the changing nature of warfare, the institution remains severely restricted in its ability to intervene in the internal affairs of a sovereign state. In 1992, then UN Secretary-General Boutros Boutros-Ghali published the groundbreaking *Agenda for Peace,* challenging the international community to address the phenomenon of internal conflict through the application of conflict prevention policies to prevent the outbreak and emergence of violence, stop the spread of violence, and deter the resurgence/reemergence of violence in situations where cease-fires or peace had been reached.[15]

The idea was seductive, the practice ineffectual. Two years later, as Yugoslavia splintered, bled, and burned and Rwanda exploded, the world watched and the Security Council debated the applicability of the term genocide to the ongoing slaughter of some 800,000 people in the tiny African country. The decision to avoid the use of the term genocide freed the international community of its obligation to intervene.

In this vacuum of silence, civil society organizations, ranging from traditional human rights groups to newly minted conflict resolution entities, found a space and a common voice. They drew attention to the changed nature of warfare and an end to the familiar boundaries of battleground versus civilian community. Civil wars, they said, are fought in homes and villages. Civilians make up 90 percent of the dead and injured. Trust and security are ripped aside in civil war, and peace cannot be made solely by military and political leaders. They advocated for a broader inclusion of civil society in the prevention and resolution of intrastate violent conflicts. They also called for increased and earlier intervention on the part of the international community. Others, notably Francis Deng, the former UN special representative for internally displaced persons (IDPs), tackled the question of state sovereignty from a different angle, suggesting that sovereignty came with the responsibility to protect citizens, not the right to oppress them.[16]

Gendered Indicators and Early Warning

From an analytical standpoint, the evolution and use of conflict early warning indicators is among the more developed aspects of the field. Such indicators cover a range of security, political, economic, and sociocultural issues. They can be divided into three categories. First, structural indicators provide an assessment of the baseline state of a country, ranging from its political nature to economic conditions, the historic role of the military, and sociocultural traditions. Second, proximate indicators relate to noticeable trends or changes that emerge. For example, if military spending has been stagnant for an extended period of time but begins to increase in a recognizable trend, it can be viewed as a proximate indicator. Similarly, changes in the status or treatment of minority groups or sectors of society are proximate indicators. Finally, there are triggers or indicators that, when viewed in the wider context of the structural and proximate developments, can be identified as catalysts for violence. For example, a state of perpetual bad governance, overlaid with a political crisis and accusations of electoral fraud, can erupt into public violence as it did in the Solomon Islands in 2006. Ideally, of course, those monitoring and analyzing the situation should be able to predict the escalation and put in place mechanisms to avert the violence. In practice, more often than not, the international community is still reacting. Sometimes it is caught off guard, as in the case of Timor Leste, where violence erupted in the spring of 2006, only a year after the UN's peacekeeping mission ended and was replaced by a small political office. Other times, the UN is unable to take early enough action because the sovereign state is unwilling to concede that there is trouble brewing.

The field of conflict early warning, like other aspects of peace and security work, has largely neglected consideration of what happens to women and the integration of women's experiences as indicators and potential warning signs in the monitoring and analysis of conflict. To be fair, much of the early work done on conflict indicators and analysis is indifferent to the direct experiences of women *and* men.[17] In effect, issues relating to gender dynamics, either as variables of analysis or as the basis for early warning indicators, are poorly considered. To a large extent gender relations should be considered in sociocultural analysis. But there is a gap. Such analyses overlook the role of men and women within a society, their access to and control of power and resources, forms of discrimination, the opportunities available to them and the constraints on them, and socially sanctioned notions of masculinity and femininity that often play into conflict. The indicators that do appear relate to broader developmental issues—literacy, maternal mortality, employment—rather than in relation to conflict dynamics, as part of the trends or triggers of conflict.

Canaries in the coal mine

Their first argument is analogous to the canary in the coal mine metaphor.[18] Deterioration or changes in the status of men or women can be the earliest signs of conflict trends that might lead to violence. For example, one of the earliest signs of the spread of less tolerant forms of Islam is the noticeable increase in Muslim women wearing head scarves in public and the decrease in their participation in public affairs. In France, the spread of extremist Islamism and the crisis brewing in the Parisian suburbs that ignited in riots in 2006 were preceded by an increase in "honor killings" and violence against women in immigrant North African communities.[19] In Iraq, the US invasion helped unleash religious fervor and crime, and among the first casualties was the status of women. Women's increased use of the hijab (Islamic covering) and the absence of girls and young women from schools indicated growing insecurity and intolerance.

The targeting of women is not limited to any one country. Too often women's roles and position in society are among the first to be circumscribed. Their employment, their freedom of movement, their dress, and legislation governing their citizenship, as well as a rise in sexual violence and parallel decline in prosecution of such crimes, are among the earliest indicators of increased social and political intolerance. That was the case among Serbian women, says Sarah Maguire, human rights lawyer and adviser to the UK's Department for International Development (DFID). "Domestic violence spiked as the Balkans conflict escalated in the 1990s, yet the authorities did not heed the calls coming into domestic violence hotlines."[20]

On the same basis, what women know is also important. In Sierra Leone in the late 1990s, women watched as arms were shipped in overnight along the river. Interviewed in 2001 for a UN study, one spoke of wanting to alert the international peacekeeping forces of the buildup to another attack, but she had no means of gaining access to the relevant officials.[21] In 2006, in the Solomon Islands, women's groups predicted an outbreak of violence based on corruption in the run-up to the parliamentary elections. Again, they had no access or direct mechanism to communicate with the regional peacekeeping authorities.[22]

Ignorance of gender dynamics can also lead to oversight of fundamental causes of conflict. For example, the promotion of hypermasculinity or perceptions of manhood as being intrinsically related to violence can be indicative of social forces influencing men. Prior to the outbreak of war in the Balkans, the situation and activities of young men should have been a warning of the emerging threat and nature of violence that ensued. Many unemployed and disenfranchised were readily recruited by hypernationalists into "soccer teams" and indoctrinated with ethnic hatred. According to some experts, many of the teams fed into the militias and armed gangs that terrorized the region as the war spread.[23]

Such oversight can also result in a lack of understanding of the gendered impact of conflict. An increase in violence against women, for example, impedes their ability to engage in development-related activities, reduces productivity, and affects their levels of employment. Restrictions on movement and random arrests of men have direct and indirect consequences for men and women. The situation in Palestine following the collapse of the Oslo process in 2000 illustrates this point. In 2004 over 50 percent of Palestinian men were unemployed.[24] The implications for the men—ranging from depression to increased inclination or propensity to engage in violence against Israel—are significant. Coupled with the direct and indirect impact on women—increased economic burden, greater risk of domestic violence due to the frustration, humiliation, and presence of men in closed spaces—this situation creates new and complex social dynamics that need to be addressed if the goal is to prevent the escalation of violent conflict.

The argument can be extended further: being mindful of the changing circumstances or portrayal of men and women can be indicative of the type of violence that might arise. Where there is a marked increase in sexual violence against women, it is likely that such violence will characterize any emerging conflict. Yet internationally, the use of indicators relating to the changed status of men and women is limited and ad hoc. Within the UN system, for example, an increase in sexual violence is among the signs monitored in the context of genocide prevention, but it does not feature particularly in other areas of analysis.

Knowledge of the relationship between genocide and sexual violence has much to do with the history of Rwanda's descent into genocide. Reflecting on the buildup to the 1994 genocide, Elizabeth Powley notes the deliberate attack on women by extremist Hutu propaganda.[25] "One popular tract, the 'Hutu Ten Commandments,' was circulated widely and read aloud at public meetings," she writes.

> It portrayed Tutsi women as deceitful "temptresses" and urged Hutu women to protect Hutu men from treacherous influences. Three of the commandments addressed gender relations:
>
> 1. Each Hutu man must know that the Tutsi woman, no matter whom, works in solidarity with her Tutsi ethnicity. In consequence, every Hutu man is a traitor: who marries a Tutsi woman; who makes a Tutsi woman his concubine: who makes a Tutsi woman his secretary or protégé.
> 2. Every Hutu man must know that our Hutu girls are more dignified and more conscientious in their roles as woman, wife, and mother. Aren't they pretty, good secretaries and more honest!
> 3. Hutu women, be vigilant; bring your husbands, brothers, and sons to reason![26]

These indicators were particularly blatant, and in retrospect, it is clear that the propaganda would very likely lead to sexual violence against women. As the genocide unfolded in April 1994, Tutsi women, particularly the educated and the young, were among the key victims. The violence they endured was deliberately sexual, including rape and torture, breast oblations, and forced incest and pregnancy. As in Bosnia, Darfur, and elsewhere, the sexual nature of the attacks is a particularly cruel means of attempting to destroy family ties and the very notion of ethnicity through forced pregnancies. In societies where men's honor is bound by their ability to protect their family, sexual attacks on women are also a means of bringing shame and dishonor to men. In effect, men communicate with each other through attacks on women: thus women's bodies are literally the front lines and battlefields of many contemporary wars.

Indicators relating to women can also be used to monitor potentially positive trends. In Iran, since the 1979 revolution that brought the Islamic government to power, women have been the barometers of society, as the regime systematically sought to curtail their rights. Their presence and activities in the public sphere, education, and political participation have signaled the extent to which the government is adhering to its extremist ideology. In turn women have used their physical appearance, including the Islamic dress codified by law, to resist the state's control. The long, dark-colored overcoats (manteaux) of the early 1980s have long been relinquished in favor of shorter, tighter, lighter, more colorful fabrics. Head scarves are worn with flourish. Makeup, once severely restricted and monitored by black-hooded women patrolling the streets, is evident throughout the cities. Women have also fought against legislative restrictions. Educational courses in the scientific fields closed to them in the 1980s have, through intense pressure, been opened. By 2004, women—who had once been threatened with exclusion from the university—represented over 60 percent of the undergraduate population. Even birthrates have dropped from an average high of 8.1 children to below 2 births per woman in 2005.[27]

Finally, understanding the gendered implications of a situation should in theory lead to political and humanitarian interventions that address the vulnerabilities specific to women and men. In Darfur's camps, displaced women are at daily risk of sexual assault and rape, particularly when they leave designated camp areas to search for firewood. This is not a new phenomenon; it is reality in many situations where women are forced into displacement. In practice, however, interventions to help prevent the extent of rape (either through the provision of alternative forms of cooking and heating material, better security, or otherwise) have been delayed and limited. Rape prevention should be a priority for all international actors. But it isn't. Rather, within the international community, there remains a culture of reaction and seeming acceptance of the inevitability of such attacks, characterized by the scramble to provide emergency kits (for the care of rape victims).[28] There is rarely consultation with women themselves to garner their views and opinions about the threats they face and possible solutions. Instead, as in the case of Darfur, the men or tribal leaders (often self-nominated) are consulted.[29]

In sum, indicators that highlight men's and women's experiences can enhance international efforts to prevent violence and ensure more effective and better-timed responses in political, humanitarian, and developmental terms. Consultations with men and women themselves are critical. First, they can show aid agencies which actions are acceptable. Second, those consulted may have alternative strategies and capacities that could be drawn upon and strengthened.

Conclusion

Are women relevant to conflict prevention? Clearly they are. Information from and about them provides insight into a society. They are also important change agents. Women's actions to prevent the rise of violence and promote change through nonviolent means are important to recognize and support. But alone they cannot prevent the next violent conflict—prompted by the United States or resulting from state-induced oppression in the Middle East. Africa, or Latin America. If the timing is right, women can mobilize effectively. Supported by other sectors in their own society, they can tip the balance away from violence. But like others, particularly in the initial stages, they can be swayed by manipulation of identity politics and paralyzed with fear. The result is, too often, when they do enter the fray, the fighters are already recruited and the arms distributed. Their warnings against political manipulation, holding back their sons and daughters, street protests—silent or noisy—even coming together across the lines of conflict, are not enough to stop the tidal wave of war.

Notes

1. David Rose. "Neo Culpa," *Vanity Fair*, November 2006, available at http://www.vanityfair.com/politics/features/2006/12/neocons200612.
2. "Zimbabwean Activist Vows to Fight On." Amnesty International, May 2005. available at http://web.amnesty.org/wire/May2005/WOZA.
3. Think tanks such as the US Institute of Peace, the Council on Foreign Relations, the Center for Strategic and International Studies, and others ran seminars and roundtable discussions and issued reports with recommendations on effective post-conflict operations and "winning the peace."
4. Information available at http://www.codepink4peace.org/article.php?id=347, retrieved December 16, 2005.
5. Jenni Williams, presentation at the Woodrow Wilson Center for International Scholars and in discussion with the author, Washington, DC, September 2005.
6. Alexandra Balandia Ruizpineda. "Women in the Nonviolent Resistance Movement in Venezuela," in *Conflict Prevention and Transformation: Women's Vital Contributions* (Washington, DC: Hunt Alternatives Fund. 2005).
7. The Iraq War proves that even interstate wars are difficult to prevent.
8. Reports of the Carnegie Commission on Preventing Deadly Conflict are available at http://www.carnegie.org/sub/research.
9. Carnegie Commission on Deadly Conflict, *Preventing Deadly Conflict, Final Report*. Carnegie Commission of New York. 1999, available at http:// wwics.si.edu/subsites/cepde/pubs/rept97/finfr.htm.
10. Examples of this debate include Carlu Koppell and Anita Sharma. *Preventing the Next Wave of Conflict: Understanding Non-traditional Threats to Global Security* (Washington, DC: Woodrow Wilson Center for International Scholars. 2003).
11. The Human Security Center at the University of British Columbia, *Human Security Report 2005: War and Peace in the Twenty-First Century* (Oxford. UK: Oxford University Press, 2005), pp. 147–155.
12. Ibid.
13. Ibid.
14. The Human Security Center at the University of British Columbia, *Human Security Report 2005*, pp. 147–155, available at http://www.humansecurityreport.info, retrieved July 18. 2006.

15. *An Agenda for Peace: Preventive Diplomacy, Peacemaking, and Peace-keeping* (New York: UN. 1992), available at http://www.un.org/docs/SG/agpeace.html.
16. For more on this discussion, see Francis Deng and Roberta Cohen, *Masses in Flight: The Global Crisis of Internal Displacement* (Washington, DC: Brookings Institution, 1998).
17. For a selection of early conflict indicators developed by a cross section of research institutions, see *Conflict and Peace Analysis and Response Manual*, 2nd edition (London: FEWER, 1999), Annex 1, available at http://www .reliefweb.int/library/documents/studman2.pdf.
18. In the nineteenth century, coal miners took a canary with them into the mine as an early warning sign of toxic fumes. Canaries are particularly sensitive to colorless, odorless futnes. If the canary showed signs of distress, it indicated that the air was not safe.
19. Jan Goodwin, "International Report," *Marie Claire*, November 1, 2005, available at http://www.accessmylibrary.com.
20. Discussions with the author. London, July 2006.
21. Ellen Johnson-Sirleaf and Elizabeth Rehn, *Women, War, and Peace* (New York: UNIFEM. 2002).
22. Women activists discussed their situation with the author. Fiji, June 2006.
23. These views were shared with the author by a former senior diplomat from the region. New York, January 2005.
24. International Labour Organization. *Situation of Workers in Occupied Arab Territories Continues to Deteriorate.* press release (Geneva: ILO. May 27, 2005), available at http://www.ilo.org, retrieved July 26, 2006.
25. Elizabeth Powley, *Strengthening Governance: The Role of Women in Rwanda's Transition* (Washington, DC: Hunt Alternatives Fund, 2004).
26. Elizabeth Powley, quoting Heather B. Hamilton. "Rwanda's Women: The Key to Reconstruction," in "The Future of the African Great Lakes Region," *Journal of Humanitarian Assistance* 3, May 19, 2002, available at http://www.jha.ae/greatlakes/b001.htm.
27. Index Mundi, *Iran Total Fertility Rate*, 2006, available at http://www.indexmundi.com/iran/total_fertility_rate.html.
28. For more information, see Bernard Broughton and Sarah Maguire, *The Interagency Real-Time Evaluation of the Humanitarian Response to the Darfur Crisis* (New York: United Nations, January 2006), p. 33. available at documents.wfp.org/stellent/groups/public/documents/reports/wfp092382.pdf.
29. Ibid.

Useful Internet Resources

Amnesty International, www.amnesty.org

European Human Rights Centre, http://www.ehrcweb.org/

First World War.com/Vintage Photographs/Home Front: http://www.firstworldwar.com/photos/homefront.htm

Global Security: Reliable Security Information: http://www.globalsecurity.org/: This website has an extensive section of information about the armed forces of most countries. It also has current news from the world of international security.

Human Rights Watch, www.hrw.org

Imperial War Museum: http://www.iwm.org.uk/: The definitive war museum has a large and growing online collection.

International Atomic Energy Agency: www.iaea.org: The international organization created to control the dissemination of nuclear technology. More recently at the center of debate regarding Iran's nuclear program.

International Institute for Strategie Studies/International Institute for Strategie Studies: http://www.iiss.org/: An academic source for information about international policy

International Physicians for the Prevention of Nuclear War: http://www.ippnw.org/NukeEPWsFull.html: A leading NGO committed, as its name suggests, to ending the threat of nuclear war

Terrorism Files: www.terrorismfiles.org: A useful collection of news items, terrorist group overviews, individuals, and incidents

Terrorism Research Center: www.Terrorism.com: This useful site has an excellent links section, including links to relevant reports and terrorism news.

This is Baader-Meinhof: www.baader-meinhof.com: This site contains information related to transnational terrorism and in particular the German Baader-Meinhof group.

United Nations Development Program, www.undp.org

Center for World Indigenous Rights, http://cwis.org/

Discussion Questions and Activities

1. Discuss the concept of revolution in military affairs by comparing and contrasting the strategie bombing campaigns against Germany and Japan during the Second World War with the 1991 campaign against Iraq.
2. Discuss nuclear proliferation from the perspective of countries in the developing world.
3. Compare and contrast "guerrillas as freedom fighters" versus. "guerrillas as terrorists." Cases to explore: Molly Malones, IRA, Stern Gang, Viet Cong, PLO, Sendero Luminoso, Al-Qaeda.
4. Research a political or religious group that has used terrorist methods. Present your findings in class.
5. Discuss the methods states employ to combat terror. Include the moral and ethical aspects, comparing these with practical and political aspects.
6. Research the human rights records of several countries from each of these regions: Africa, Asia, Europe, Oceania, and North and South America. Correlate your findings with economic statistics found at http://www.imf.org. Do any patterns emerge?

GLOBAL ECONOMY AND TRADE: READING SELECTIONS

Fiscal Policy and Structural Fiscal Challenges

JOHN LIPSKY

John Lipsky, First Deputy Managing Director of the International Monetary Fund, gave this speech at the 2011 China Development Forum. Because of his position within one of the central institutions of globalization, Lipsky's remarks might provide us with the IMF's analysis of the ongoing global economic recession in addition to hints about what the organization planned to do in the future. Were you surprised by anything in Lipsky's speech? How might a person writing from the Marxist, Constructivist, or Feminist perspective respond to this speech?

It's a great pleasure and honor to be invited to address this year's Development Forum. Many notable changes have occurred since I participated in last year's Forum, and I am grateful for the opportunity to discuss them with you today.

Although the world's attention has been focused during the past week on the impact of the tragic Japanese earthquake – and on the terrible suffering that it has caused – on balance, the economic and financial news of the past year has been positive. Most important, global economic growth has been advancing at a much faster pace than the average annual expansion of the past 20 years. Our *World Economic Outlook* forecast anticipates global growth this year of almost 4½ percent, following the 5 percent gain registered last year.

The current solid global growth rate obscures some more difficult details, however. As anticipated – and as has been the case for many years – emerging economies are growing much more rapidly than advanced economies. While this is neither new nor surprising, the current growth rates nonetheless imply challenges for both groups of economies. With the advanced economies expanding at an annual average rate of about 2½ percent, growth simply is not strong enough to reduce quickly the substantial margins of unused capacity that resulted from the Great Recession of 2008/2009. In particular, job growth remains sluggish in most advanced economies, and as a result, unemployment rates remain high and consumption gains remain no better than moderate.

In contrast, the emerging economies are growing at a 6½ percent annual rate. Of course, these economies in general escaped the Great Recession without the damaged financial systems, depleted household balance sheets and high public debt that have hampered recoveries in the advanced economies. As a result, their post-recession expansion is being driven by domestic demand as well as by the rebound in global trade.

Despite the contrast in growth rates, both sets of economies face near-term and longer-term challenges. In advanced economies, reducing unemployment is a priority. At the same time, however, public debt is piling up to unprecedented

John Lipsky, Fiscal Policy and Structural Fiscal Challenges, International Monetary Fund, March 20, 2011.

heights, creating worries in many advanced countries about fiscal sustainability. In fact, IMF analysis indicates that advanced economy fiscal deficits will average about 7 percent of GDP in 2011, and the average public debt ratio will exceed 100 percent of GDP for the first time since the end of World War II.

As is increasingly obvious, such a fiscal trend simply is not sustainable. While expansionary fiscal policy actions helped to save the global economy from a far deeper downturn, the fiscal fallout of the crisis must be addressed before it begins to impede the recovery, and to create new risks. The central challenge is to avert a potential future fiscal crisis, while at the same time create jobs and support social cohesion.

The situation is quite different in many key emerging economies. Although fiscal sustainability is not a major near-term concern, in general both monetary and budget policies in these economies are still expansionary – reflecting earlier anti-crisis measures – despite evaporating margins of excess capacity and accelerating inflation. With early signs of overheating becoming visible, the need is clear for near-term fiscal and monetary policy adjustment.

I will focus the balance of my remarks today on fiscal policy and structural fiscal challenges, particularly in the advanced economies, but also in many emerging economies. I also will discuss the role of fiscal policy in the global rebalancing process.

Advanced Economy Challenges

The immediate fiscal task among the advanced countries is to credibly reduce deficits and debts to sustainable levels, while remaining consistent with achieving the economy's long-term growth potential and reducing unemployment. Achieving the fiscal adjustment alone is no small task: The reduction in advanced economies' cyclically adjusted primary budget balance that will be needed to bring debt ratios back to their pre-crisis levels within the next two decades is very large—averaging around 8 percent of GDP – although there is considerable variation across countries. Large gross financing requirements—averaging over 25 percent of GDP both this year and next—only add to the urgency of creating credible medium-term fiscal adjustment plans.

Up to now, the advanced economies have been fortunate in one important way: Low interest rates have kept debt service burdens manageable, despite the recent large increases in public debt outstanding. In particular, the G7 countries' interest payments on government debt outstanding have remained broadly stable at 2¾ percent of GDP over the last three years, even as debt to GDP ratios increased by over 25 percentage points.

This combination of rising debt but stable debt service payments is not likely to continue for long, however. Higher deficits and debts – together with normalizing economic growth – sooner or later will lead to higher interest rates. Evidence suggests that an increase in the debt to GDP ratio of 10 percentage points is associated with a rise in long-term interest rates of 30 to 50 basis points.

Given the post-crisis rise in debt ratios – and the projected medium-term increase in public debt – long-term bond yields could rise by 100 to 150 basis points for this cause alone. Were rates to rise even by the lower end of this estimated range, debt servicing costs for the G7 economies could increase by around 1½ percentage points of GDP by 2014 – to a total of around 4¼ percent of GDP. Moreover, our estimates suggest that maintaining public debt at its post-crisis ratio to GDP over the medium term could reduce potential growth in advanced economies by as much as ½ percentage point of GDP annually. Econometric analysis indicates that, on average, each 10 percentage point increase in the debt ratio leads to a slowdown in real GDP growth of around 0.15 percentage points per year, mostly through an adverse effect on investment, but also through lower productivity growth.

Clearly, it will take quite some time for the advanced countries to restore their debt ratios to prudent levels. While this has been widely recognized already, the crisis-related sharp rise in debt outstanding has heightened the public's awareness that it is no longer sufficient to discuss prospects for fiscal consolidation. Rather, the time has arrived for generating concrete action plans, and in many cases it is time to begin implementing such plans. The cost of excessive delay could be very high: Recent experience demonstrates that financial markets can be slow to react to policy slippages, but they can react decisively—even excessively—once they do.

Many advanced economies, particularly in Europe, are acting this year to reduce fiscal deficits. A key fiscal policy task in the euro area will be to implement already-promulgated consolidation plans, that in some cases are exceptionally ambitious. Of course, these plans are being complimented by the development of a comprehensive pan-European approach for supporting member countries that are under market pressure because of excessive debt and deficits. In these cases, fiscal adjustment is one part of the solution.

At their recent EU Council meeting, European leaders agreed to raise the effective lending capacity of the newly-formed European Financial Stability Facility (EFSF) to E440 billion, and agreed on the key parameters of the future European Stability Mechanism (ESM). However, there are many details yet to be worked out and implemented before these new initiatives will be fully operational. Nonetheless, these initiatives, among other things, are intended to make more credible the process of medium-term fiscal consolidation and long-term budget control.

Of course, the two largest advanced economies—the United States and Japan—have deferred consolidation. The US authorities previously had announced plans to reduce the federal deficit by about 2 percent of GDP in the current fiscal year. In response to weaker than expected economic data – including disappointing employment growth – they announced a new package of stimulus measures consisting of tax cuts and new spending – that will increase the deficit by about ¼ percent of GDP.

Looking forward, a credible US fiscal consolidation program will likely have to encompass three elements: First, a set of near-term actions that will help to convince financial market participants and others of the United States authorities' serious intent. Second, some sort of policy anchor – perhaps a medium-term target for the debt/GDP ratio – that will serve as a guide to the intended trajectory for future fiscal consolidation; and third, a credible medium-term approach to revenue and spending plans that will lead plausibly to the intended medium-term target. President Obama's Fiscal Commission has done a good job in identifying several measures both on the revenue and expenditure side for medium-term fiscal consolidation. In particular its proposals for tax reform and steps to reduce long-term entitlement pressures are very useful.

In the case of Japan, the tragic recent events inevitably create the need for a supplementary budget – most likely including short-term increases in public expenditures in order to provide disaster relief, as well as to help finance reconstruction spending. Nonetheless, Japanese authorities will be expected eventually to stabilize market expectations by providing guidance regarding a credible medium-term adjustment plan that will encompass both revenue and expenditure reforms.

It seems very likely that advanced economies' fiscal adjustment will include measures to reduce primary spending, as spending ratios already are relatively high in most of these countries. Given the size of the required fiscal adjustment in many countries, revenue measures also are likely to form part of the solution, especially in countries with large adjustment needs.

Without a doubt, innovative thinking is in order regarding possible future revenue measures. Of the 8 percent of GDP average primary balance adjustment referred to earlier, as much as one-third may have to come from additional revenues, although there will be significant variations across countries. Analysis carried out by the IMF's Fiscal Affairs Department – and summarized in the IMF's new semi-annual *Fiscal Monitor* publication – highlights that consumption taxes may prove to be an important source of potential revenues.

In particular, the IMF has endorsed earlier plans by the Japanese authorities to reduce the budgetary shortfall in part by increasing the rate on Japan's Value-Added Tax (VAT). Like many fiscal policy experts, Fund staff also have suggested that a VAT should be considered as a potential innovation for US deficit-reduction efforts, along with targeted income-based safeguard measures to protect low-income groups.

More generally, classic tax reforms – encompassing broadening tax bases while simplifying rules and rates – would be appropriate in most advanced economies. At the same time, it would be important to review the increasingly significant role of tax expenditures. Tax expenditures are special provisions providing tax reductions for specified activities, equivalent in economic effect with regard to the deficit as direct government spending. Rolling back tax expenditures would bring in substantial revenue—they amount to as much as 5 percent of GDP in several of the largest economies—while also improving both the efficiency and fairness of tax systems. One of the key areas where action could be taken includes mortgage deductions. The United Kingdom's recent experience has demonstrated that this can be done without major dislocations if phased in over time.

Action could also be useful to rein in special incentives in the corporate sector related to depreciation and other credits. These are win-win reforms, in that they could help to reduce deficits while reducing distorting incentives that work via the tax system. At the same time, the broad area of environmental concerns will encourage the opposite, namely the introduction of measures that produce desirable distortions intended to correct specific market imperfections.

To be credible, any advanced economy fiscal consolidation strategy must deal with the cost of entitlements that are a – if not **the** – key driver of long-term spending pressures. Of course, health care-related spending reforms will have to form a central part of any budget strategy. New projections by IMF staff show that for advanced economies, public spending on health care alone is expected to rise on average by 3 percent of GDP over the next two decades. Thus, for any budget consolidation plan to be credible, it must deal with the reality of rising health care costs. Inevitably, successful reforms in this area will include effective spending controls, but also bottom-up reforms that will improve the efficiency of health care provision.

While old-age pension spending is in somewhat better shape in some countries, others countries still face long-term solvency challenges. After all, public pension spending in advanced economies is projected to increase on average by over 1 percent of GDP by 2030 with the increase exceeding 2 percent in a quarter of the economies. In some instances, however, forecasts may be based on optimistic assumption, including regarding productivity growth.

Another key point: good institutions are needed to underpin good policy. In the fiscal area, institutions such as independent fiscal agencies, using fiscal rules, strong medium-term fiscal frameworks, close monitoring of out-turns, and coordination across levels of government are keys to success. Fiscal transparency should remain a principal policy goal. Unfortunately, this already has been a victim of the crisis as some countries resort to accounting tricks to artificially boost reported revenues or lower to spending.

These include using pension contributions to provide an immediate boost to revenues while the associated pension liability will translate into spending only in the future; or increasing expenditures but keeping the headline deficit in check by guaranteeing loans and running up other contingent liabilities. Such accounting strategies paint a false picture and should be avoided. In this respect, a key role can be played by independent surveillance by international financial institutions, for example with reports on compliance with fiscal standards, such as the IMF's code of fiscal transparency.

Fiscal adjustment will not be painless, especially on the scale that will be required. With unemployment so high for so long, targeted measures geared towards job creation and alleviating the costs of joblessness make sense in some countries—within the context of an overall adjustment strategy. Such measures could include extensions of unemployment benefits, short-term work schemes, job subsidies targeted at vulnerable groups, or active labor market policies that focus on training and education. Fiscal adjustment can be fair, and it can be done in a way to protect the most vulnerable. Indeed, adjustment will be sustainable only if it is achieved in a way that ensures that costs of adjustment—and the benefits of recovery—are distributed equitably across society.

Emerging Market Challenges

I will now turn to the emerging economies, where the fiscal situation may appear less worrying. Fiscal deficits in these economies fell last year – to average 3 percent of GDP – and they will decline again this year. Debt ratios are also much lower than in the advanced economies, around 37 percent of GDP.

But the fiscal house might not be as sturdy as it first appears. In some instances, the favorable picture reflects strong capital inflows, low interest rates, buoyant asset prices, and currently high commodity prices. At the same time, inflationary pressures are broadening beyond food and energy prices, especially in Asia. And fiscal buffers need to be rebuilt to protect against sudden reversals in capital flows.

For all these reasons, a tighter fiscal stance than currently envisaged will be needed in the *near term* in many emerging economies. Underlying fiscal balances should be improving much faster than they in fact are. At a minimum, spending pressures should be resisted and revenue over-performance saved in full. But once again, the poor must be protected—targeted measures to protect the most vulnerable in the face of rising commodity prices are a key element of social solidarity.

Shifting to the *medium term*, while fiscal challenges vary, increases in government spending are likely. Some countries will need reforms in order to help boost consumption; others need greater investment in infrastructure. Especially in Asia, many countries plan to increase health care spending with the goal of raising access and coverage. Many emerging economies also intend to improve social safety nets in order to support the vulnerable, to increase consumption by reducing precautionary savings, and reduce to reduce inequality.

The main challenge is to improve these safety nets while preserving long-term fiscal sustainability. Many emerging market countries need to manage the required increase in the size of government without adding to risks of overheating in the near term. This will require a skillful combination of both expenditure and tax reforms.

Global Rebalancing

Many of the measures I have been discussing—by both advanced and emerging economies— also would help reduce global imbalances, which are on the rise again, and are expected to continue rising over the medium term. Growth in economies with large external deficits, like the United States, is still being driven by domestic demand. And growth in economies with large external surpluses is still too reliant on exports. For example, we expect China's current account balance to increase again over the coming years, after bottoming out in 2010. Current account surpluses are expected to decrease only marginally in many other Asian economies. And with the US current account deficit not expected to fall further over the next few years, global imbalances could widen again, putting the sustainability of the recovery at risk.

In the short run, the fiscal adjustment being undertaken or planned in some deficit countries will help to moderate imbalances, although the impact will be somewhat offset by the need to rebuild fiscal buffers in surplus emerging economies. In the medium to long run, however, many of the measures I have outlined would help tackle the distortions at the root of persistent imbalances.

For instance, increasing consumption taxation and eliminating tax exemptions that effectively subsidize debt would help raise national savings and reduce the external deficits. In emerging market economies, the development of social safety nets—particularly pensions and broader healthcare provisions—would weaken incentives for excessive precautionary savings. In addition, eliminating policies that distort exchange rates markets would contribute to an internal rebalancing of the sources of growth, as the wealth and income effects of an appreciating currency boost domestic consumption in surplus countries. This is well known, and widely accepted.

Conclusion

In sum, there is no doubt that given the evolution of the recovery, countries are grappling with increasingly-complex and increasingly-diverse challenges. This is certainly true of fiscal policy. But to move toward a future of strong, sustainable, and balanced growth, these fiscal challenges need to be addressed urgently. The time for action is now.

Thank you for your attention.

Making Globalization Work

JOSEPH E. STIGLITZ

The title of this extract gives away Stiglitz's position on economic globalization: it is not working, at least for the benefit of most people. Therefore, as we read this piece from the Nobel Prize-winning economist, we should look for the proof Stiglitz offers to support his claim. Which institutions are working? Which are not? Who benefits from economic globalization as it operates now? Does Stiglitz genuinely expect reforms to occur?

In a vast field on the outskirts of Mumbai, activists from around the world gathered for the World Social Forum in January 2004. The first Forum to be held in Asia, this meeting had a very different feel from chose held in Porto Alegre, Brazil, in the four previous years. Over 100,000 people attended the week-long event, and the scene was, like India itself, a colorful crush of humanity. Fair trade organizations staffed rows of stalls selling handmade jewelry, colorful textiles, and housewares. Banners strung along the streets proclaimed, "HANDLOOM IS A BIGGEST EMPLOYMENT SOURCE IN INDIA." Columns of demonstrators banged drums and chanted slogans as they wended their way through the crowds. Loincloth-clad groups of *dalit* activists (members of the castes that used to be known as untouchables), representatives of workers' rights organizations and women's groups, the UN and non-governmental organizations (NGOs) all rubbed shoulders. Thousands gathered in temporary meeting halls the size of aircraft hangars to hear a program of speakers that included former Irish president Mary Robinson (former UN High Commissioner for Human Rights, 1997–2002) and Nobel Peace Prize winner Shirin Ebadi. It was hot and humid and there were crowds everywhere.

Many conversations took place at the World Social Forum. There was debate about how to restructure the institutions that run the world and how to rein in the power of the United States. But there was one overriding concern: globalization. There was a consensus that change is necessary, summed up in the motto of the conference: "Another world is possible." The activists at the meeting had heard the promises of globalization—that it would make everyone better off; but they had seen the reality: while some were in fact doing very well, others were worse off. In their eyes, globalization was a big part of the problem.

Globalization encompasses many things: the international flow of ideas and knowledge, the sharing of cultures, global civil society, and the global environmental movement. This book, however, is mostly about economic globalization, which entails the closer economic integration of the countries of the world through the increased flow of goods and services, capital, and even labor. The great hope of globalization is that it will raise living standards throughout the world: give poor countries access to overseas markers so that they can sell their goods, allow in foreign investment that will make new products at cheaper prices, and open borders so that people can travel abroad to be educated, work, and send home earnings to help their families and fund new businesses.

I believe that globalization has the potential to bring enormous benefits to those in both the developing and the developed world. But the evidence is overwhelming that it has failed to live up to this potential. Economics has been driving globalization, especially through the lowering of communication and transportation costs. But politics has shaped it. The rules of the game have been largely set by the advanced industrial countries—and particularly by special interests within those countries—and, not surprisingly, they have shaped globalization to further their own interests. They have not sought to create a fair set of rules, let alone a set of rules that would promote the well-being of those in the poorest countries of the world.

After speaking at the World Social Forum, Mary Robinson, Delhi University chancellor Deepak Nayaar, International Labout Organization president Juan Somavia, and I were among the few who went on to the World Economic Forum in Davos, the Swiss ski resort where the global elite gather to mull over the state of the world. Here, in this snowy mountain town, the world's captains of industry and finance had very different views about globalization from those we heard in Mumbai.

The World Social Forum had been an open meeting, bringing together vast numbers from all over the world who wanted to discuss social change and how to make their slogan, "Another world is possible," a reality. It was chaotic, unfocused, and wonderfully lively—a chance for people to see each other, make their voices heard, and to network with their fellow activists. Networking is also one of the main reasons that the movers and shakers of the world attend the invitation-only event at Davos. The Davos meetings have always been a good place to take the pulse of the world's economic leaders. Though largely a gathering of white businessmen, supplemented by a roster of government officials and senior journalists, in recent years the invitation list has been expanded to include a number of artists, intellectuals, and NGO representatives.

In Davos there was relief, and a bit of complacency. The global economy, which had been weak since the bursting of the dot-com bubble in America, was finally recovering, and the "war on terror" seemed to be under control. The 2003 gathering had been marked by enormous tension between the United States and the rest of the world over the war in Iraq, and still earlier meetings had seen disagreement over the direction which globalization was taking. The 2004 meeting was marked with relief that these tensions had at least been modulated. Still there was worry about American unilateralism, about the world's most powerful country imposing its will on others while preaching democracy, self-determination, and human rights. People in the developing world had long been worried about how global decisions—decisions about economics and politics that affected their lives—were made. Now, it seemed, the rest of the world was worried also.

I have been going to the annual meetings at Davos for many years and had always heard globalization spoken of with great enthusiasm. What was fascinating about the 2004 meeting was the speed with which views had shifted. More of the participants were questioning whether globalization really was bringing the promised benefits—at least to many in the poorer countries. They had been chastened by the economic instability that marked the end of the twentieth century, and they worried about whether developing countries could cope with the consequences. This change is emblematic of the massive change in thinking about globalization that has taken place in the last five years all around the world. In the 1990s, the discussion at Davos had been about the virtues of opening international markets. By the early years of the millennium, it centered on poverty reduction, human rights, and the need for fairer trade arrangements.

At a Davos panel on trade, the contrast in views between the developed and developing countries was especially marked. A former World Trade Organization official said that if trade liberalization—the lowering of tariffs and other trade barriers—had not fully delivered on its promise of enhanced growth and reduced poverty, it was the fault of the developing countries, which needed to open their markets more to free trade and globalize faster. But an Indian running a micro-credit bank stressed the downside of free trade for India. He spoke of peanut farmers who could not compete with imports of Malaysian palm oil. He said it was increasingly difficult for small and medium-sized businesses to get loans from banks. This was not surprising. Around the world, countries that have opened up their banking sectors to large international banks have found that those banks prefer to deal with other multinationals like Coca-Cola, IBM, and Microsoft. While in the competition between large international banks and local banks the local banks often appeared to be the losers, the teal losers were the local small businesses that depended on them. The puzzlement of some listeners, convinced that the presence of international banks would unambiguously be better for everyone, showed that these businessmen had paid little attention to similar complaints from Argentina and Mexico, which saw lending to local companies dry up after many of their banks were taken over by foreign banks in the 1990s.

At both Mumbai and Davos, there was discussion of reform. At Mumbai, the international community was asked to create a fairer form of globalization. At Davos, the developing countries were enjoined to rid themselves of their corruption, to liberalize their markets, and to open up to the multinational businesses so well represented at the meeting. But at both events there was an understanding that something had to be done. At Davos the responsibility was placed squarely on the developing countries; at Mumbai, it was on the entire international community.

The Two Faces of Globalization

In the early 1990s, globalization was greeted with euphoria. Capital flows to developing countries had increased sixfold in six years, from 1990 to 1996. The establishment of the World Trade Organization in 1995—a goal that had been sought for half a century—was to bring the semblance of a rule of law to international commerce. Everyone was supposed to be a winner—those in both the developed and the developing world. Globalization was to bring unprecedented prosperity *to all.*

No wonder then that the first major modern protest against globalization—which took place in Seattle in December 1999, at what was supposed to be the start of a new round of trade negotiations, leading to further liberalization—came as a surprise to the advocates of open markets. Globalization had succeeded in unifying people from around the world—against globalization. Factory workers in the United States saw their jobs being threatened by competition from China. Farmers in developing countries saw their jobs being threatened by the highly subsidized corn and other crops from the United States. Workers in Europe saw hard-fought-for job protections being assailed in the name of globalization. AIDS activists saw new trade agreements raising the prices of drugs to levels that were unaffordable in much of the world. Environmentalists felt that globalization undermined their decades-long struggle to establish regulations to preserve our natural heritage. Those who wanted to protect and develop their own cultural heritage saw too the intrusions of globalization. These protestors did not accept the argument that, economically at least, globalization would ultimately make everybody better off.

Globalization may have helped some countries—their GDP, the sum total of the goods and services produced, may have increased—but it had not helped most of the people even in these countries. The worry was that globalization might be creating rich countries with poor people.

Of course, those who are discontented with economic globalization generally do not object to the greater access to global markets or to the spread of global knowledge, which allows the developing world to take advantage of the discoveries and innovations made in developed countries. Rather, they raise five concerns:

- The rules of the game that govern globalization are unfair, specifically designed to benefit the advanced industrial countries. In fact, some recent changes are so unfair that they have made some of the poorest countries actually worse off.

- Globalization advances material values over other values, such as a concern for the environment or for life itself.
- The way globalization has been managed has taken away much of the developing countries sovereignty, and their ability to make decisions themselves in key areas that affect their citizens' well-being. In this sense, it has undermined democracy.
- While the advocates of globalization have claimed that everyone will benefit economically, there is plenty of evidence from both developing and developed countries that there are many losers in both.
- Perhaps most important, the economic system that has been pressed upon the developing countries—in some cases essentially forced upon them—is inappropriate and often grossly damaging. Globalization should not mean the Americanization of either economic policy or culture, but often it does—and that has caused resentment.

The last is a topic that touches both those in developed and developing countries. There are many forms of a market economy—the American model differs from that of the Nordic countries, from the Japanese model, and from the European social model. Even those in developed countries worry that globalization has been used to advance the "Anglo-American liberal model" over these alternatives—and even if the American model has done well as measured by GDP, it has not done well in many other dimensions, such as the length (and, some would argue, the quality) of life, the eradication of poverty, or even the maintenance of the well-being of those in the middle. Real wages in the United States, especially of those at the bottom, have stagnated for more than a quarter century, and incomes are as high as they are partly because Americans work far longer hours than their European counterparts. If globalization is being used to advance the American model of a market economy, many elsewhere are not sure they want it. Those in the developing world have an even stronger complaint—that globalization has been used to advance a version of market economics that is more extreme, and more reflective of corporate interests, than can be found even in the United States.

Globalization and poverty

Critics of globalization point to the growing numbers of people living in poverty. The world is in a race between economic growth and population growth, and so far population growth is winning. Even as the percentages of people living in poverty are falling, the absolute number is rising. The World Bank defines poverty as living on less than $2 a day, absolute or extreme poverty as living on less than $1 a day.

Think for a minute what it means to live on one or two dollars a day. Life for people this poor is brutal. Childhood malnutrition is endemic, life expectancy is often below fifty years, and medical care is scarce. Hours are spent each day searching for fuel and drinkable water and eking out a miserable livelihood, planting cotton on a semi-arid plot of land and hoping that this year the rains will not fail, or in the backbreaking toil of growing rice in a meager half acre, knowing that no matter how hard one works there will be barely enough to feed one's family.

The sad truth, however, is that outside of China, poverty in the developing world has increased over the past two decades. Some 40 percent of the world's 6.5 billion people live in poverty (a number that is up 36 percent from 1981), a sixth—877 million—live in extreme poverty (3 percent more than in 1981). The worst failure is Africa, where the percentage of the population living in extreme poverty has increased from 41.6 percent in 1981 to 46.9 percent in 2001. Given its increasing population, this means that the number of people living in extreme poverty has almost doubled, from 164 million to 316 million.

Historically, Africa is the region most exploited by globalization: during the years of colonialism the world took its resources but gave back little in return. In recent years, Latin America and Russia have also been disappointed by globalization. They opened up their markets, but globalization did not deliver on its promises, especially to the poor.

Insecurity was one of the major concerns of the poor; a sense of powerlessness was another. The poor have few opportunities to speak out. When they speak, no one listens; when someone does listen, the reply is that nothing can be done; when they are told something can be done, nothing is ever done. A remark in the World Bank report, from a young woman in Jamaica, captures this sense of powerlessness: "Poverty is like living in jail, living under bondage, waiting to be free."

What is true for poor people is too often true for poor countries. While the idea of democracy has spread and more countries have free elections than, say, thirty years ago, developing countries find their ability to act eroded both by new constraints imposed from outside and by the weakening of their existing institutions and arrangements to which globalization has contributed. Consider, for instance, the demands imposed on developing countries as a condition for aid. Some might make sense (though not all, as we will see in chapter 2). But that is not the point. Conditionality undermines domestic political institutions. The electorate sees its government bending before foreigners or giving into international institutions that it believes to be run by the United States. Democracy is undermined; the electorate feels betrayed. Thus, although globalization has helped spread the idea of democracy, it has, paradoxically, been managed in a way that undermines democratic processes within countries.

Moreover, it is perceived—quite rightly, I think—that the way globalization is currently managed is not consistent with democratic principles. Little weight is given, for instance, to the voices and concerns of the developing countries. At the International Monetary Fund, the international institution charged with oversight of the global financial system, a single country—the United States—has effective vero. It is not a question of one man one vote, or one country one vote: dollars vote. The countries with the largest economies have the most votes—and it is not even today's dollars that count. Votes are determined largely on the basis of economic power at the time the IMF was established sixty years ago (with some adjustments since). China, with its burgeoning economy, is underrepresented. As another example, the head of the World Bank, the international organization charged with promoting development, has always been appointed by the president of the United Stares (without even having to consult his own Congress). American politics, not qualifications, are what matters: experience in development, or even experience in banking, is not requited. In two instances—the appointments of Paul Wolfowitz and Robert MacNamara—the background was defense, and both these former secretaries of defense were associated with discredited wars (Iraq and Vietnam).

Reforming Globalization

The globalization debate has gone from a general recognition that all was not well with globalization and that there was a real basis for at least some of the discontent to a deeper analysis that links specific policies with specific failures. Experts and policymakers now agree on the areas where change has to take place.

There are many things that must be done. Six areas where the international community has recognized that all is not well illustrate both the progress that has been made and the distance yet to go.

The pervasiveness of poverty

Poverty has, at last, become a global concern. The United Nations and multinational institutions such as the World Bank have all begun focusing more on poverty reduction. In September 2000, some 150 heads of state or government attended the Millennium Summit at the United Nations in New York and signed the Millennium Development Goals, pledging to cut poverty in half by 2015. They recognized the many dimensions to poverty—not just inadequate income, but also, for instance, inadequate health care and access to water.

Until recently, IMF perspectives have been paramount in economic policy discussions, and the IMF traditionally focused on inflation rather than on wages, unemployment, or poverty. Its view was that poverty reduction was the mandate of the World Bank, while its own mandate was global economic stability. But focusing on inflation and ignoring employment led to the obvious result: higher unemployment and more poverty. The good news is that, at least officially, the IMF has now made poverty reduction a priority.

By now it has become clear that opening up markets (taking down trade barriers, opening up to capital flows) *by itself* will not "solve" the problem of poverty; it may even make it worse. What is needed is both more assistance and a fairer trade regime.

The need for foreign assistance and debt relief

At Monterrey, Mexico, in March 2002 at the International Conference on Financing for Development, which was attended by 50 heads of state or government and 200 government ministers, among others, the advanced industrial countries committed themselves to substantial increases in assistance—to 0.7 percent of their GDP (though so far few countries have lived up to those commitments, and some—especially the United States—are a far way off). In tandem with the recognition that aid should be increased has come a broad agreement that more assistance should be given in the form of grants and less in loans—not surprising given the constant problems in repaying the loans.

Most telling of all, however, is the altered approach to conditionality. Countries seeking foreign aid are typically asked to meet a large number of conditions; for instance, a country may be told that it must quickly pass a piece of legislation or reform social security, bankruptcy, or other financial systems if it is to receive aid. The enormous number of conditions often distracted governments from more vital tasks. Excessive conditionality was one of the major complaints against the IMF and the World Bank. Both institutions now admit that they went overboard, and in the last five years they have actually greatly reduced conditionality.

The aspiration to make trade fair

Trade liberalization—opening up markets to the free flow of goods and services—was supposed to lead to growth. The evidence is at best mixed. Part of the reason that international trade agreements have been so unsuccessful in promoting growth in poor countries is that they were often unbalanced: the advanced industrial countries were allowed to levy tariffs on goods produced by developing countries that were, on average, four times higher than those on goods produced by other advanced industrial countries. While developing countries were forced to abandon subsidies designed to help their nascent industries, advanced industrial countries were allowed to continue their own enormous agricultural subsidies, forcing down agricultural prices and undermining living standards in developing countries.

The limitations of liberalization

In the 1990s, when the policies of liberalization failed to produce the promised results, the focus was on what the developing countries had failed to do. If trade liberalization did not produce growth, it was because the countries had not liberalized enough, or because corruption created an unfavorable climate for business. Today, even among many of the advocates of globalization, there is more awareness of shared blame.

The most hotly contested policy issue of the 1990s was capital market liberalization, opening up markets to the free flow of short-term, hot, speculative money. The IMF even tried to change its charter at its annual meeting in 1997, held in Hong Kong, to enable it to push countries to liberalize. By 2003, even the IMF had conceded that, at least for many developing countries, capital market liberalization had led not to more growth, just to mote instability.

Trade and capital market liberalization were two key components of a broader policy framework, known as the Washington Consensus—a consensus forged between the IMF (located on 19th Street), the World Bank (on 18th Street), and the U.S. Treasury (on 15th Street)—on what constituted the set of policies that would best promote development. It emphasized downscaling of government, deregulation, and rapid liberalization and privatization. By the early years of the millennium, confidence in the Washington Consensus was fraying, and a post-Washington Consensus consensus was emerging.

Protecting the environment

A failure of environmental stability poses an even greater danger for the world in the long run. A decade ago, concern about the environment and globalization was limited mostly to environmental advocacy groups and experts. Today, it is almost universal. Unless we lessen environmental damage, conserve on our use of energy and other natural resources, and attempt to slow global warming, disaster lies ahead. Global warming has become a true challenge of globalization. The successes of development, especially in India and China, have provided those countries the economic wherewithal to increase energy usage, but the world's environment simply cannot sustain such an onslaught. There will be grave problems ahead if everybody emits greenhouse gases at the rate at which Americans have been doing so. The good news is that this is, by now, almost universally recognized, except in some quarters in Washington; but the adjustments in lifestyles will not be easy.

A flawed system of global governance

There is now also a consensus, at least outside the United States, that something is wrong with the way decisions are made at the global level; there is a consensus, in particular, on the dangers of unilateralism and on the "democratic deficit" in the international economic institutions. Both by structure and process, voices that ought to be heard are not. Colonialism is dead, yet the developing countries do not have the representation that they should.

There is a growing consensus both that there is a problem of governance in the international public institutions like the IMF that shape globalization and that these problems contribute to their failures. At the very least, the democratic deficit in their governance has contributed to their lack of legitimacy, which has undermined their efficacy—especially when they speak on issues of democratic governance.

The Nation-State and Globalization

Some 150 years ago, the lowering of communication and transportation costs gave rise to what may be viewed as the earlier precursor of globalization. Until then, most trade had been local; it was the changes of the nineteenth century that led to the formation of national economies and helped to strengthen the nation-state. New demands were put on government: markets might be producing growth, but they were accompanied by new social, and in some cases even economic, problems. Governments took on new roles in preventing monopolies, in laying the foundations of modern social security systems, in regulating banks and other financial institutions. There was mutual reinforcement: success in these endeavours helped shape and strengthen the process of nation building, and the increased capabilities of the nation-state led to greater success in strengthening the economy and enhancing individual well-being.

The conventional wisdom that the United States' development was the result of unfettered capitalism is wrong. Even today, the U.S. government, for instance, plays a central role in finance. It provides, or provides guarantees for, a significant fraction of all credit, with programs for mortgages, student loans, exports and imports, cooperatives, and small businesses. Government not only regulates banking and insures depositors but also tries to ensure that credit flows to underserved groups and, at least until recently, to all regions in the country—not just the big money centers.

Increasingly, a government's inability to control the actions of individuals or companies is also limited by international agreements that impinge on the right of sovereign states to make decisions. A government that wants to ensure that banks lend a certain fraction of their portfolio to underserved areas, or to ensure that accounting frameworks accurately reflect a company's true status, may find it is unable to pass the appropriate laws. Signing on to international trade agreements can prevent governments from regulating the influx and outflow of hot, speculative money, even though capital market liberalization can lead to economic crises.

The nation-state, which has been the center of political and (to a large extent) economic power for the past century and a half is being squeezed today—on one side, by the forces of global economics, and on the other side, by political demands for devolution of power. Globalization—the closer integration of the countries of the world—has resulted in the need for more collective action, for people and countries to act together to solve their common problems. There are too many problems—trade, capital, the environment—that can be dealt with only at the global level. But while the nation-state has been weakened, there has yet to be created at the international level the kinds of democratic global institutions that can deal effectively with the problems globalization has created.

In effect, economic globalization has outpaced political globalization. We have a chaotic, uncoordinated system of global governance without global government, an array of institutions and agreements dealing with a series of problems, from global warming to international trade and capital flows. Finance ministers discuss global finance matters at the IMF, paying little heed to how their decisions affect the environment or global health. Environment ministers may call for something to be done about global warming, but they lack the resources to back up those calls.

As the nation-state developed, individuals felt connected to others within the nation—not as closely as to those in their own local community, but far more closely than to those outside the nation-state. The problem is that, as globalization has proceeded, loyalties have changed little. War shows these differences in attitude most dramatically: Americans keep accurate count of the number of U.S. soldiers lost, but when estimates of Iraqi deaths, up to fifty times as high, were released, it hardly caused a stir. Totture of Americans would have generated outrage; torture by Americans seemed mainly to concern those in the antiwar movement; it was even defended by many as necessary to protect the United States. These asymmetries have their parallel in the economic sphere. Americans bemoan the loss of jobs at home, and do not celebrate a larger gain in jobs by those who are far poorer abroad.

Today, there is an understanding that many of the problems with globalization are of our own making—are a result of the way globalization has been managed. I am heartened as I see mass movements, especially in Europe, calling for debt relief, and as I see the leaders of most of the advanced industrial countries calling for a fairer trade regime, doing something about global warming, and committing themselves to cutting poverty in half by 2015. But there is a gap between the rhetoric and the reality—and many of these leaders are ahead of the people in their democracies, who may be fully committed to these lofty goals, but only so long as it does not cost them anything.

Demise of the Anglo-American Model of Capitalism

WONHYUK LIM

Wonhyuk Lim, a Korean economist, writes that the global financial collapse that began in 2008 killed the model of neo-liberal capitalism. What, according to Lim, were the features of this economic model? Which politicians and academics advocated neo-liberalism? Why? What does Lim say will replace neo-liberalism?

Though couched in geographical terms, "the Anglo-American model of capitalism" does not represent some permanent model of capitalism prevailing in Britain and America. Rather, it refers to the brand of capitalism that has essentially sought to dismantle the postwar welfare state through privatization, deregulation, and regressive tax and social policies in the name of promoting economic efficiency. Its neo-liberal philosophy is characterized by a strong distrust of the government and an equally strong faith in the market, and its ambitious liberalization program extends beyond real markets to financial markets, where herd behavior and systemic risks pose significant challenges. This brand of capitalism takes an aggressively hostile approach toward labor unions and subscribes to "supply-side economics," or the "trickle-down" theory of income generation and distribution.

Initially popularized by Margaret Thatcher and Ronald Reagan, the Anglo-American model of capitalism enjoyed its heyday right after the collapse of the Soviet Bloc in the early 1990s, but widening income disparities and repeated economic crises over the past decade have reduced its appeal around the world. Although it successfully eliminated the excesses of the postwar welfare state, its attack on the government and worship of the market failed to deliver broad-based, sustained growth. The current global financial crisis, combined with the resurgence of progressive politics, is likely to hasten its demise and usher in a new era of expanded role for the government and strengthened financial supervision on a global scale. Although the advocates of the Anglo-American model of capitalism have tended to present it as an embodiment of irrefutable economic principles, it was actually a product of political and commercial calculations. Understanding its rise and fall would shed light on the new balance that is likely to be reached between the government and the market in the wake of the current crisis.

The intellectual underpinning of the Anglo-American model of capitalism initially began as a critique of totalitarianism but soon evolved into a revolt against state intervention in general. Criticizing John Maynard Keynes as well as Karl Marx in the 1930s and 1940s, Friedrich von Hayek asserted that state intervention would threaten human liberty and place society on the "Road to Serfdom"—even if this state intervention was

Wonhyuk Lim's "Demise of the Anglo-American Model of Capitalism," *Global Asia*, Vol. 3, No. 4, pages 58–60.

supported and demanded by a free democratic political process. Hayek also argued that due to information and incentive problems, planning would prove inferior to market mechanisms in co-ordinating economic production. His claim stood in contrast to the theory of the firm advanced by Ronald Coase, who took a much more balanced view on the merits and demerits of markets versus hierarchies based on the concept of transaction costs. The implicit anti-democratic bias and intellectual extremism inherent in Hayek's writings prevented him from gaining a great deal of popularity for a long time.

In fact, the guiding economic principle for western nations after the Great Depression and World War II was, in many ways, the opposite of what Hayek prescribed. It was probably a surprise to Hayek that the welfare state model based on social democracy ushered in a remarkable period of broad-based growth. In the United States, for instance, annual productivity growth averaged 2.8 percent from 1948 to 1973, and progressive taxation and pro-labor policy significantly reduced income disparities and created a robust middle class in what is commonly called "the Great Compression."

However, the very success of the postwar welfare state sowed its own demise. As Michael Kalecki foresaw, full employment greatly strengthened labor unions' hands and led to excessive welfare demands and practices that alienated not only the rich but eventually the middle class as well. The stagflation of the 1970s amplified the public's disenchantment with these excesses, even though they continued to value the social safety net provided by the state. Conservative politicians such as Thatcher and Reagan saw an opportunity to dismantle the welfare state, and adroitly combined the rhetoric of individual liberty and free enterprise with thinly veiled appeals to not-so-lofty instincts of the electorate such as racism. It is in this context that the Anglo-American model of capitalism was born and Hayek's theory gained popularity.

Although the actual economic records of Thatcher and Reagan left much to be desired, the collapse of the Soviet Bloc ushered in a triumphant era for the Anglo-American model of capitalism. To a critical observer, it was "[a]n era of unbridled deregulation, wealth-enhancing perks for the already well-off, and miserly indifference to the poor and middle class; of the recasting of greed as goodness, the equation of bellicose provincialism with patriotism, the reframing of bigotry as small-town decency." (Judith Warner blog, Nov. 6, 2008, *New York Times*) In development economics, this brand of capitalism found its expression in the Washington Consensus, which preached privatization, market liberalization, and macroeconomic stabilization. Its advocates typically missed the irony of huge macroeconomic imbalances in the United States and aggressively pushed for financial globalization, whether emerging markets—and for that matter, advanced industrial nations—were prepared for it or not.

Had the Anglo-American model of capitalism produced broad-based, sustained growth, its appeal might have lasted. Unfortunately, it could not. In the developing world, the Washington Consensus failed to deliver tangible benefits. By comparison, East Asian countries that judiciously combined market mechanisms with selective state intervention generated "rapid, shared growth." In advanced industrial nations, the Anglo-American model of capitalism increasingly produced social disparities and economic insecurity, even as it yielded solid productivity gains. In the United States, for instance, annual productivity growth averaged 2.5 percent between 2000 and 2007, but the median income declined by $2,010 in the same period. The portrayal of the government as an embodiment of corruption and incompetence became a self-fulfilling prophecy as key posts were filled with corrupt and incompetent people and essential services were privatized with little oversight. The faith in the self-regulating capability of the market suffered a heavy blow as the current global financial crisis revealed the corruption and incompetence of those who were entrusted with other people's money. In addition, the swift propagation of shocks and rapid rise in systemic risks confirmed that financial markets are different from real markets and demonstrated the need to establish a global financial supervision framework commensurate with the global reach of financial institutions. The intellectual and philosophical premises of the Anglo-American model of capitalism were never as solid as its advocates claimed, and after a generation of political dominance, reality finally caught up with it.

Does Globalization Spell the End of Nation-State?

KAVALJIT SINGH

Many analysts of globalization contend that the phenomenon has transformed nearly every aspect of states' economic and political lives, domestically and internationally. Kavaljit Singh, an economist based in India, strongly disagrees with this assertion. How does Singh structure his argument? What does Singh assert globalization is doing to state sovereignty? What kinds of proof does he offer? Does he agree or disagree with Stiglitz and Lim?

> The nation state has rapidly become an unnatural, even dysfunctional, unit in terms of which to think about or organize economic activity... Nation states are dinosaurs waiting to die.
>
> *Kenichi Ohmae*

Many commentators are of the viewpoint that the ascendancy of globalization leads to the demise of nation-state.[1] It is claimed that globalization processes are creating a truly 'global' economy dominated by transnational corporations and financial markets in which political boundaries are no longer relevant. Further, it is asserted that economics have been integrated in global economy in such a manner that national level policy solutions have become obsolete. Not only hyper-globalists, even some well meaning anti-globalists also share similar false notions. Such a superficial understanding fails to capture the essence of the complex relationship between globalization and nation-state. There is no denying that the growing domination of transnational capital in various forms poses new challenges to pursue independent economic policy making and promote redistributive policies but it would be off the mark to conclude that the nation-state would wither away or become irrelevant.

If globalization was perceived to destroy nation-states, then it has completely failed to do so. Far from vanishing, several new states have been formed in the past two decades and many more could be expected in the times to come. At present, there are 192 independent nation-states, compared to just 70 in 1946.

In contrast to the claims made by the hyper-globalists, borders still matter. There are very few regions in the world where border disputes have altogether disappeared. Regardless of its geographical location, private capital (domestic or transnational) operates within a particular national jurisdiction.

Those who augur the demise of the nation-state under the impact of globalization simply ignore the fact that political power still resides in the arena of nation-state and pressures generated by national social and political institutions and interest groups shape the final policy outcomes. Unlike states, transnational capital lacks sovereign power to enforce its agenda.

Kavaljit Singh, *Questioning Globalization*. Zed Books, 2005.

How Global Is Globalization?

Contrary to neoliberal presumptions, the contemporary world economy is far from being truly 'global.' Bulk of trade, production and financial flows are still concentrated in a handful of developed countries. The following facts corroborate the viewpoint that globalization is by no means a truly 'global' and even process:

- FDI flows are highly concentrated and unevenly distributed around the world. Although FDI flows have increased in developing countries, over two-thirds of flows are concentrated among the members of the Triad—the US, EU and Japan.
- Around 90 per cent of the world's top 100 non-financial TNCs are headquartered in the Triad.
- There are very few truly stateless 'global' TNCs. There is no denying that in an era of declining constraints on capital mobility and the attraction of low wages in the developing countries, TNCs are shifting production abroad. But only low value, labor-intensive activities are being shifted to the developing countries while strategic operations such as research and development (R&D), headquarters and financial management continue to be located in the home country. Besides, the board of directors and senior management personnel predominantly belong to the home country. A large majority of shareholders also belong to the home country. Even in instances where globalization of strategic operations such as R&D has taken place, it has remained a regional phenomenon.
- Over 85 per cent of production in the developed countries is for the domestic market.
- With few exceptions, transnational corporations are still dependent on home markets. Take the case of international banks. Despite considerable acquisition of assets abroad, most international banks' assets still remain in their domestic markets. To illustrate, Citigroup with operations in more than 100 countries cannot be portrayed as a truly 'global' bank because the bulk of its assets are in the US. With only 34 per cent of assets held outside the US, Citigroup is essentially a domestic US bank. Just 30 banks worldwide have more than one-third of their total assets outside their domestic markets.
- Instead of becoming stateless 'global' enterprises, most TNCs are deeply rooted in their national societies and maintain their distinct social, economic, and political value systems. Paul Doremus and his colleagues in their book, *The Myth of the Global Corporation*, have unveiled how American, German and Japanese transnational corporations are embedded in the history, culture, and economic systems of their respective home societies.[2]
- Most TNCs maintain close ties with their home country governments.

Unlike the present phase of globalization, international labor migration was mammoth during that period, as there was no restrictions on the movement of people across borders. Nowadays immigration controls are much tighter than ever.

Have States Become Powerless and Obsolete?

First, not all states have become powerless under the influence of transnational capital as there are significant variations across countries. As noted by Ha-Joon Chang, the influence of transnational capital on individual states is highly uneven and varies from issue to issue.[3] The degree of influence is largely dependent on the size, military strength and power of states. Admittedly, the globalization processes may have weakened the bargaining powers of smaller and weaker states but there are hardly any examples where the entire state structures have collapsed for prolonged period. Even in certain African countries where the collapse of state structures is somewhat evident, the collapse had more to do with the domestic social and political reasons. On the other hand, powerful states (for instance, US) still retain considerable clout to pursue domestic and international policies suiting their national interests.

The national policy response to globalization processes also varies across countries. For instance, some governments have allowed complete takeover of domestic assets by transnational capital while other governments have forced mergers and acquisitions among domestic entities to ensure that they can effectively compete with transnational capital. Besides, there are several instances where governments, particularly those belonging to the developed world, have resorted to protectionist measures to safeguard domestic economic sectors.

Second, the budgets of governments have not diminished with the adoption of open economy. In most highly integrated countries, government spending is increasing, rather than declining. Government spending accounts as much as half of their national income in many developed countries.

Third, privatization of public sector enterprises does not necessarily mean overall decline in state intervention in the economy. Privatization may lead to a decline in the public ownership but there might be an increase in the state regulation through the establishment of regulatory authority, competition policy, disclosure norms and other new policy measures.

Fourth, it is likely that the role of the state may reduce in certain sectors of economy but it may expand significantly elsewhere. Similarly, the repressive powers of the governments may also expand. In the wake of globalization, the repressive powers of many states have expanded rather than shrinking. Increasingly, states are taking recourse to anti-democratic methods to suppress social and political movements seeking genuine democratization. There have been several instances (e.g., Shell in Nigeria and mass protests against adjustment programs in Mexico, Argentina, Venezuela and Indonesia) where the governments took to repressive measures against their own people in order to protect the interests of transnational capital. The rise in repressive measures in the name of preserving 'law and order' and maintaining a favorable investment climate has grave implications for the human rights (particularly economic and social rights) of vast majority of people. In the developed world too, repressive powers are increasing. In the aftermath of September 11, 2001 attacks, the Bush administration enacted several draconian laws to curb democratic freedom and rights. Many other countries have imposed similar repressive measures too.

Lastly, the term deregulation could be misleading as semantically it means re-regulation. For instance, the captains of global capital demand strong regulation of trade union activity while insisting on complete deregulation of wages and labor markets.

Can Globalization Survive without Nation-States?

As propagated, globalization is neither a natural nor an autonomous phenomenon. Rather it has been shaped by the complex and dynamic set of interactions between transnational capital and nation-states. The present phase of globalization could not have proceeded without the active participation of states through liberalization of trade, foreign investment and industrial policies. A favorable international political environment created and sustained by certain powerful states, particularly the US, played a crucial role in the aggrandizement of transnational capital in the post-World War II era.

In contrast to the popular perception, states play an indispensable role in the advancement and sustenance of contemporary globalization. The world economy is still governed by nation-states, along with several inter-state institutional arrangements created and sustained by them. Undoubtedly the character of the state has changed profoundly over the years but the state and inter-state institutional arrangements manage and steer contemporary world economy. The role of certain powerful states in shaping the contours of contemporary world economy is well recognized.

On its own, transnational capital lacks the necessary power and ability to mould the world economy in its favor. Rather, it strives for the support of nation-states and inter-state institutions to shape the contemporary world economy.[4] Undeniably, financial markets have become powerful with trillions of dollars moving across the borders daily but cross-border movement of funds was primarily made possible by the removal of capital controls by governments (willingly or unwillingly) since the mid-1970s.

In the global capitalism context, nation-states provide the framework within which all markets operate. The notion of 'free market' is a myth as all markets are governed by regulations. Though the nature and degree of regulation may vary from market to market. Even the much-claimed self-regulation model would be illegitimate if it is not backed by the government decree. In fact, it is impossible to conceive contemporary globalization without laws, and laws do not exist outside the realm of nation-states. Even the global rules on trade and investment enforced by international institutions (for instance, WTO) are not independent of nation-states.

In addition, state intervention is also necessary to prevent and correct market failures. There are innumerable instances of market failures with huge social costs throughout the world. Although all markets are imperfect and liable to fail, financial markets are more prone to failure because of asymmetric information, herd behavior and self-fulfilling panics.[5] These factors make financial markets more inefficient and volatile. Due to its speculative behavior, finance capital would collapse on its own in the absence of state regulations.

Corporate world relies on state apparatus for providing financial stability. Majority of TNCs will suffer losses if the volatility in exchange rates is not tamed by international policy coordination. On numerous occasions, powerful states have coordinated their policies and deliberately intervened in the foreign exchange markets to bring financial stability. For instance, the Plaza and Louvre Accords among the G-7 countries in the 1980s were attempts to establish greater international currency stability. In the aftermath of Southeast Asian financial crisis, countries from the region have coordinated their policies and launched regional arrangements such as Asian Bond Fund and currency swap agreements to protect their economics from volatile capital flows. In 1997, Japan also proposed the establishment of an Asian Monetary Fund to address regional monetary issues.

Private capital (domestic or transnational) still relies on state resources in several areas, particularly physical infrastructure such as roads, railways, airports, seaports and telecommunications. In addition, it also relies on state resources for providing human infrastructure (educated workforce), research and development, tax concessions as well as direct financial support. The tax concessions and huge subsidies to Boeing Corporation and Airbus Industries are shining examples of financial support to big corporations. In the aftermath of the attacks on the World Trade Center and Pentagon on September 11, 2001, the US administration approved $15 billion bailout package for the airline industry. While over 500000 employees who lost their jobs in the wake of attacks on the World Trade Center did not receive any financial support.

While arguing that the globalization processes are deeply embedded with the state, one is not negating the existence of conflicts between transnational capital and states. Since the *raison d'être* of these two entities are different, conflicts are unlikely to disappear. As opposed to transnational capital with its single-minded pursuit of profit maximization, national governments have to carry out diverse economic, social and political tasks to meet the needs of their citizens. These conflicts would persist as victims of globalization look upon the state institutions to provide them economic and social security.

International Institutional Arrangements and Globalization

Since 1945, the world has witnessed a plethora of international institutional arrangements. In addition, a large number of declarations, conventions and treaties in economic and political affairs have been signed by nation-states.

International institutional arrangements including the EU, UN, NATO, IMF, World Bank, WTO, OECD and Bank for International Settlement are not independent entities but have been created and nurtured by nation-states. The World Bank and the IMF, for instance, are not controlled by private financiers and large transnational banks but by a handful of creditor states.

Inter-state institutional arrangements are essentially governed by the balance of power among member-countries. Due to unequal power relations, certain powerful states exert considerable influence in deciding the policy framework of these institutions. The US, in particular, has had a decisive say in determining the policy agenda of many institutional arrangements. The US domination of multilateral financial institutions such as the World Bank and the IMF is well known. It is also a well-established fact that the EU and US enjoy a disproportionate influence on the agenda of global trade regime enforced by the WTO. Within the highly integrated EU, the influence of certain powerful states such as Germany, UK and France has not diminished despite 10 new countries joined it in 2004.

Nevertheless, it needs to be underscored that the growing influence of inter-state institutions such as IMF, World Bank and WTO has not completely put an end to domestic economic policy making by the national governments. Irrespective of the degree of globalization, the role of nation-state would remain paramount in performing several functions including regulation and supervision of markets; social cohesion and political stability; and guarantor of the rule of the law.

Is Globalization Irreversible?

The oft-repeated assertion that political processes cannot reverse the march towards economic globalization is more a myth than reality. Economic globalization has been reversed by domestic political processes in the past and therefore could be reversed in the future. All public policies are the products of pressures generated by social and political institutions in a given society and are liable to change. If labor-friendly policies could be reversed to serve the interests of private capital, investor-friendly policies could also face the same fate.

There is nothing sacrosanct about the economic globalization processes. History is replete with instances where the pendulum had swung in the opposite direction due to unanticipated events. The advancement of earlier phase of globalization was scuttled by a series of events including World War I, the Great Depression and World War II. Whether the contemporary phase of globalization would face the same fate by such unforeseen events remains open to question.

In contrast to popular presumptions, there are alternatives. Nevertheless, it is the wider national and international context that determines the choice of particular policy alternatives. Within the present global capitalism context, a strategy calling for complete delinking of domestic economy from world economy or autarky may not succeed. While a strategy based on curbing unbridled financial liberalization and selective delinking from speculative funds is likely to succeed. There have been several attempts by countries to resist short-term, speculative financial flows in the late 1990s. The experiences of countries such as Malaysia, Chile and China show that selective delinking is not only desirable but also feasible. The terms and conditions of linkages with global financial flows should be decided democratically by people rather than by international financial institutions and private investors. If peoples' movements are strong, alert and influential, there is every possibility of devising an investment strategy which allows only such financial flows that are beneficial to the domestic economy. This does not mean that countries should blindly attract long-term FDI and other types of financial flows. As discussed in Chapter 2, the cost of FDI flows can be debilitating as capital can move out through royalty payments, dividends, imports as well as other legal and illegal means.

Delinking from speculative financial flows could be followed by alterating trade and investment agreements which disproportionately benefit transnational capital. The alternative development strategy should include enlarging the rights of governments over transnational capital through policy measures such as tough competitive laws, increased corporate taxes, capital controls, taxes on speculative investments, and stricter labor and environmental regulations.

However, fundamental reorientation of domestic economy is not viable without democratization of state and domestic arrangements of political power. In other words, a democratic and accountable state can act as a bulwark against the present trajectory of globalization besides broadening the space for alternative developmental strategy.

Globalization, Ethnicity and Nation-State

Over the years, nation-states have increasingly come under attack from ethnic nationalism. There is *per se* nothing wrong with the assertion of ethnic identity but it becomes a serious problem when ethnicity based on chauvinistic agenda is politicized to capture power and unleash a reign of terror against other ethnic groups. In many parts of the world, fundamentalist movements based on ethnic, religious or linguistic identities are challenging the integrity of existing states in several ways. Some ethnic movements are demanding greater autonomy while others are seeking complete independence. Diverse forms of fundamentalist movements and ethnic conflicts have mushroomed in Europe, Latin America, Africa and Asia. Though majority of ethnic conflicts and civil wars are located in the poorest regions of the world. Ethnic conflicts in Indonesia, Rwanda, Somalia and Sudan are examples of this phenomenon.

Escalation in the frequency of ethnic conflicts could be gauged from the alarming rise in the scale of civil wars in the 1990s. In this decade, most wars were fought on ethnic rather than on ideological grounds. In the late 1980s and early 1990s, formation of new states based on ethnicity witnessed a sharp rise and over 20 new states were formed after the collapse of USSR and Yugoslavia. Since then several new states have been formed and many more are expected in the future.

The detailed analysis of causes behind the rise of ethnic nationalism is beyond the scope of this book. The linkages between globalization processes and the rise of ethnic nationalism are noticeable. But it would be an exaggeration to attribute the rise of ethnicity entirely to economic globalization processes since many fundamentalist movements existed even before the onset of present phase of globalization.

A closer examination of several ethnic conflicts reveals that these often originate due to unequal distribution of wealth and power. Massive job losses and unemployment due to global economic restructuring has exacerbated economic inequalities and social unrest. These conditions, in turn, create an atmosphere in which security and identities are perceived to be under threat. With the decline of class-based politics, fundamentalist movements have been successful in mobilizing the losers from globalization processes on the basis of ethnic, religious or national identity. It comes as no surprise that the social base of fundamentalist movements largely consists of the poor and disadvantaged groups who join these movements to regain their lost identity and economic stability through the capture of state power. Yet it needs to be noted that ethnic movements are not seeking complete collapse of nation-states rather they wish to create new nation-states based on their own ethnic identities.

Concluding Remarks

The world economy is still governed by nation-states, along with several inter-state institutional arrangements created and sustained by them. States have played an indispensable role in the advancement and sustenance of contemporary globalization. On its own, transnational capital cannot mould the world economy in its favor. Rather, it strives for the support of nation-states and inter-state institutions to shape the contemporary world economy.

No denying that contemporary economic globalization poses new challenges to national authorities but it would be erroneous to conclude that the nation-states would cease to exist. Despite global integration coupled with multilayered apparatus of governance, the state will remain a key player in both domestic and international economic affairs.

Notes and References

1. Kenichi Ohmae is an ardent supporter of this thesis. For detailed account of his arguments, see Kenichi Ohmae, *The Borderless World*, Collins, London, 1990; and Kenichi Ohmae, *The End of the Nation State*, Free Press, New York, 1995.
2. For details, see Paul N. Doremus, William W. Keller, Louis W. Pauly and Simon Reich, *The Myth of the Global Corporation*, Princeton University Press, Princeton, 1998.
3. For details, see Ha-Joon Chang, *Globalisation, Economic Development and the Role of the State*, Zed Books, London and New York, 2003.
4. The role of nation-state in shaping and nurturing contemporary phase of globalization has been well-documented by several analysts. In particular see, Eric Helleiner, *States and the Re-emergence of Global Finance*, Cornell University Press, Ithaca, 1994; Saskia Sassen, *Losing Control? Sovereignty in an Age of Globalization*, Columbia University Press, New York, 1996; Samir Amin, *Capitalism in the Age of Globalization*, Madhyam Books, Delhi, 1997; Peter Dicken, *Global Shift*, Chapman, London, 1998; Linda Weiss, *The Myth of the Powerless State: Governing the Economy in a Global Era*, Polity Press, Cambridge, 1998; John Gray, *False Dawn*, Granta, London, 1998; Boris Kagarlitsky, *The Twilight of Globalization: Property, State and Capitalism*, Pluto Press, London, 2000; Noam Chomsky, *Profit Over People: Neoliberalism and Global Order*, Madhyam Books, Delhi, 1999; and James Petras and Henry Veltmeyer, *Globalization Unmasked: Imperialism in the 21st Century*, Madhyam Books, Delhi, 2001.
5. For detailed information on the failures of financial markets and financial crises, see Kavaljit Singh, *Taming Global Financial Flows: Challenges and Alternatives in the Era of Financial Globalization*, Zed Books, London, 2000.

What Do Undergrads Need to Know about Trade?

PAUL KRUGMAN

A winner of the Nobel Prize for Economics and a professor of the discipline, Paul Krugman is noted for his ability to explain complex ideas in a manner that non-specialists can understand. In this chapter from a collection of essays compiled in 1996, Krugman sets out to explain trade policy. What is his central argument? How does he structure the presentation? Why does he call "nonsense" many of the ideas that students learn in intro survey courses?

Few of the undergraduates who take an introductory course in economics will go on to graduate study in the field, and indeed most will not even take any higher-level economics courses. So what they learn about economics will be what they get in that first course. It is now more important than ever before that their basic training include a solid grounding in the principles of international trade.

I could justify this assertion by pointing out that international trade is now more important to the U.S. economy than it used to be. But there is another reason, which I think is even more important: the increased *perception* among the general public that international trade is a vital subject. We live in a time in which Americans are obsessed with international competition, in which Lester Thurow's *Head to Head* is the nonfiction best-seller, and Michael Crichton's *Rising Sun* tops the fiction list. The news media and the business literature are saturated with discussions of America's role in the world economy.

The problem is that most of what a student is likely to read or hear about international economics is nonsense. What I want to argue in this paper is that the most important thing to teach our undergrads about trade is how to detect that nonsense. That is, our primary mission should be to vaccinate the minds of our undergraduates against the misconceptions that are so predominant in what passes for educated discussion about international trade.

I. The Rhetoric of Pop Internationalism

As a starting point, I would like to quote a typical statement about international economics. (Please ignore the numbers for a moment.) Here it is: "We need a new economic paradigm, because today America is part of a truly global economy.[1] To maintain its standard of living, America now has to learn to compete in an ever tougher world marketplace.[2] That's why high productivity and product quality have become essential.[3] We need to move the American economy into the high-value sectors[4] that will generate jobs[5] for the future. And the only way we can be competitive in the new global economy is if we forge a new partnership between government and business."[6]

OK, I confess: it's not a real quotation. I made it up as a sort of compendium of popular misconceptions about international trade. But it certainly sounds like the sort of thing one reads or hears all the time—it is very close in content and style to the still-influential manifesto by Ira Magaziner and Robert Reich (1982), or for that matter to the presentation made by Apple Computer's John Sculley at President-elect Clinton's Economic Conference last December. People who say things like this believe themselves to be smart, sophisticated, and forward-looking. They do not know that they are repeating a set of misleading clichés that I will dub "pop internationalism."

It is fairly easy to understand why pop internationalism has so much popular appeal. In effect, it portrays America as being like a corporation that used to have a lot of monopoly power, and could therefore earn comfortable profits in spite of sloppy business practices, but is now facing an onslaught from new competitors. A lot of companies are in that position these days (though the new competitors are not necessarily foreign), and so the image rings true.

Unfortunately, it's a grossly misleading image, because a national economy bears very little resemblance to a corporation. And the ground-level view of businessmen is deeply uninformative about the inherently general-equilibrium issues of international economics.

So what do undergrads need to know about trade? They need to know that pop internationalism is nonsense—and they need to know *why* it is nonsense.

II. Common Misconceptions

I inserted numbers into my imaginary quotation to mark six currently popular misconceptions that can and should be dispelled in an introductory economics course.

1. "We need a new paradigm...." Pop internationalism proclaims that everything is different now that the United States is an open economy. Probably the most important single insight that an introductory course can convey about international economics is that it does *not* change the basics: trade is just another economic activity, subject to the same principles as anything else.

James Ingram's (1983) textbook on international trade contains a lovely parable. He imagines that an entrepreneur starts a new business that uses a secret technology to convert U.S. wheat, lumber, and so on into cheap high-quality consumer goods. The entrepreneur is hailed as an industrial hero; although some of his domestic competitors are hurt, everyone accepts that occasional dislocations are the price of a free-market economy. But then an investigative reporter discovers that what he is really doing is shipping the wheat and lumber to Asia and using the proceeds to buy manufactured goods—whereupon he is denounced as a fraud who is destroying American jobs. The point, of course, is that international trade is an economic activity like any other and can indeed usefully be thought of as a kind of production process that transforms exports into imports.

It might, incidentally, also be a good thing if undergrads got a more realistic quantitative sense than the pop internationalists seem to have of the limited extent to which the United States actually has become a part of a global economy. The fact is that imports and exports are still only about one-eighth of output, and at least two-thirds of our value-added consists of nontradable goods and services. Moreover, one should have some historical perspective with which to counter the silly claims that our current situation is completely unprecedented: the United States is not now and may never be as open to trade as the United Kingdom has been since the reign of Queen Victoria.

2. "Competing in the world marketplace:" One of the most popular, enduring misconceptions of practical men is that countries are in competition with each other in the same way that companies in the same business are in competition. Ricardo already knew better in 1817. An introductory economics course should drive home to students the point that international trade is not about competition, it is about mutually beneficial exchange. Even more fundamentally, we should be able to teach students that imports, not exports, are the purpose of trade. That is, what a country gains from trade is the ability to import things it wants. Exports are not an objective in and of themselves: the need to export is a burden that a country must bear because its import suppliers are crass enough to demand payment.

One of the distressing things about the tyranny of pop internationalism is that there has been a kind of Gresham's Law in which bad concepts drive out good. Lester Thurow is a trained economist, who understands comparative advantage. Yet his recent book has been a best-seller largely because it vigorously propounds concepts that unintentionally (one hopes) pander to the clichés of pop internationalism: "Niche competition is win–win. Everyone has a place where he or she can excel; no one is going to be driven out of business. Head-to-head competition is win–lose." (Thurow, 1992 p. 30). We should try to instill in undergrads a visceral negative reaction to statements like this.

3. "Productivity:" Students should learn that high productivity is beneficial, not because it helps a country to compete with other countries, but because it lets a country produce and therefore consume more. This would be true in a closed economy; it is no more and no less true in an open economy: but that is not what pop internationalists believe.

I have found it useful to offer students the following thought experiment. First, imagine a world in which productivity rises by 1 percent annually in all countries. What will be the trend in the U.S. standard of living? Students have no trouble agreeing that it will rise by 1 percent per year. Now, however, suppose that while the United States continues to raise its productivity by only 1 percent per year, the rest of the world manages to achieve 3-percent productivity growth. What is the trend in our living standard?

The correct answer is that the trend is still 1 percent, except possibly for some subtle effects via our terms of trade; and as an empirical matter changes in the U.S. terms of trade have had virtually no impact on the trend in our living standards over the past few decades. But very few students reach that conclusion—which is not surprising, since virtually everything they read or hear outside of class conveys the image of international trade as a competitive sport.

An anecdote: when I published an op-ed piece in the *New York Times* last year, I emphasized the importance of rising productivity. The editorial assistant I dealt with insisted that I should "explain" that we need to be productive "to compete in the global economy." He was reluctant to publish the piece unless I added the phrase—he said it was necessary so that readers could understand why productivity is important. We need to try to turn out a generation of students who not only don't need that kind of explanation, but understand why it's wrong.

4. "High-value sectors:" Pop internationalists believe that International competition is a struggle over who gets the "high-value" sectors. "Our country's real income can rise only if (1) its labor and capital increasingly flow toward businesses that add greater value per employee and (2) we maintain a position in these businesses that is superior to that of our international competitors" (Magaziner and Reich. 1982 p. 4).

I think it should be possible to teach students why this is a silly concept. Take, for example, a simple two-good Ricardian model in which one country is more productive in both industries than the other. (I have in mind the one used in Krugman and Maurice Obstfeld [1991 pp. 20–1]. The more productive country will, of course, have a higher wage rate, and therefore whatever sector that country specializes in will be "high value," that is, will have higher value-added per worker. Does this mean that the country's high living standard is the result of being in the right sector, or that the poorer country would be richer if it tried to emulate the other's pattern of specialization? Of course not.

5. "Jobs:" One thing that both friends and foes of free trade seem to agree on is that the central issue is employment. George Bush declared the objective of his ill-starred trip to Japan to be "jobs, jobs, jobs;" both sides in the debate over the North American Free Trade Agreement try to make their case in terms of job creation. And an astonishing number of free-traders think that the reason protectionism is bad is that it causes depressions.

It should be possible to emphasize to students that the level of employment is a macroeconomic issue, depending in the short run on aggregate demand and depending in the long run on the natural rate of unemployment, with microeconomic policies like tariffs having little net effect. Trade policy should be debated in terms of its impact on efficiency, not in terms of phony numbers about jobs created or lost.

6. "A new partnership:" The bottom line for many pop internationalists is that since U.S. firms are competing with foreigners instead of each other, the U.S. government should turn from its alleged adversarial position to one of supporting our firms against their foreign rivals. A more sophisticated pop internationalist like Robert Reich (1991) realizes that the interests of U.S. *firms* are not the same as those of U.S. *workers* (you may find it hard to believe that anyone needed to point this out, but among pop internationalists this was viewed as a deep and controversial insight), but still accepts the basic premise that the U.S. government should help our industries compete.

What we should be able to teach our students is that the main competition going on is one of U.S. industries against *each other*, over which sector is going to get the scarce resources of capital, skill, and, yes, labor. Government support of an industry may help that industry compete against foreigners, but it also draws resources away from other domestic industries. That is, the increased importance of international trade does not change the fact the government cannot favor one domestic industry except at the expense of others.

Now there are reasons, such as external economies, why a preference for some industries over others may be justified. But this would be true in a closed economy, too. Students need to understand that the growth of world trade provides no additional support for the proposition that our government should become an active friend to domestic industry.

III. What We Should Teach

By now the thrust of my discussion should be clear. For the bulk of our economics students, our objective should be to equip them to respond intelligently to popular discussion of economic issues. A lot of that discussion will be about international trade, so international trade should be an important part of the curriculum.

What is crucial, however, is to understand that the level of public discussion is extremely primitive. Indeed, it has sunk so low that people who repeat silly clichés often imagine themselves to be sophisticated. That means that our courses need to drive home as clearly as possible the basics. Offer curves and Rybczinski effects are lovely things. What most students need to be prepared for, however, is a world in which TV "experts," best-selling authors, and $30,000-a-day consultants do not understand budget constraints, let alone comparative advantage.

The last 15 years have been a golden age of innovation in international economics. I must somewhat depressingly conclude, however, that this innovative stuff is not a priority for today's undergraduates. In the last decade of the 20th century, the essential things to teach students are still the insights of Hume and Ricardo. That is, we need to teach them that trade deficits are self-correcting and that the benefits of trade do not depend on a country having an absolute advantage over its rivals. If we can teach undergrads to wince when they hear someone talk about "competitiveness," we will have done our nation a great service.

References

Crichton, Michael *Rising Sun*, New York: Knopf, 1992.

Ingram, James, *International Economics*, New York: Wiley, 1983.

Krugman, Paul and Obstfeld Maurice, *International Economics: Theory and Policy*. New York: Harper Collins. 1991.

Magaziner, Ira and Reich, Robert, *Minding America's Business*, New York: Random House, 1982.

Reich, Robert, *The Work of Nations*, New York: Knopf, 1991.

Thurow, Lester, *Head to Head*, New York: William Morrow, 1992.

Weathering the Storm: The Impact of the Global Financial Crisis on Asia

CHOONG YONG AHN

Choong Yong Ahn, a South Korean economist who has worked in government and academic positions, makes the case that because of the East Asia's experience with previous economic hard times in 1997, the region is better prepared to cope with the global recession that began in 2008. What methods did the states of the region employ? Would these measures succeed in other regions, or is there a distinctive "Asian" culture? What evidence does Ahn present?

The financial crisis that struck Asia in 1997-98 left a path of destruction that had a profound impact on the region. Measures taken since then to strengthen the financial system and reshape economic policies helped Asia withstand the latest global crisis much better than the US or Europe, writes South Korean economist Choong Yong Ahn. But more needs to be done, he argues.

The financial crisis that started in the US in 2007 and then spread to the rest of the world has been notable for its depth and severity and the degree to which it threatened the stability and even the existence of the global financial system. But what was equally notable from an Asian perspective was how countries in this region, especially the emerging economies, weathered the storm relatively well compared to the US and Europe. This is especially pertinent given that the last major financial crisis, in 1997-98, started in Asia and prompted critics to say the region's financial policies and practices exposed it to great peril.

During that crisis, the backward and shallow financial systems embedded in East Asia's high-growth regimes caused systemic risks despite the "miracle" economic performance of the region in preceding decades. This time around, Asian economies, especially the export-oriented ones, have been seriously affected not by internal financial problems but by the external financial shocks from advanced economies. Thanks to some commendable financial and corporate-sector reforms adopted since the earlier crisis, many Asian economies this time are experiencing a V-shaped recovery in which they bounce back earlier than expected from the worst global downturn since the Great Depression in the 1930s.

The present crisis spread to Asia through the collapse of external demand for Asian exports. To a lesser extent, reduced demand for Asian services in the form of fewer tourists and slower demand for immigrant labor also contributed to the region's economic downturn. However, the negative impact of the crisis on Asian economies has been less serious than a decade ago. China and India, although temporarily and seriously affected, quickly regained their high-growth path followed by many of their neighbors, putting the region on a solid recovery track.

Choong Yong Ahn's "Weathering the Strom: The Impact of the Global Financial Crisis on Asia," *Global Asia*, Vol. 5, No. 1, Spring 2010, pp 58–68. Reproduced with the permission of *Global Asia*.

Contagion Channels and the Impact of the Crisis on Asia

There are two major ways that the current crisis is transmitted to Asia. The first is trade linkage between Western economies and emerging Asia. The second is a "sudden stop" in net private-capital inflows. Despite the beating the region took during the Asian financial crisis, the circumstances were quite different this time. First, the crisis originated in the West and spread to Asia largely through a collapse in world trade. Second, the collapse in external demand hit the region hard as industrial production contracted sharply with the fall in exports. Finally, extreme volatility in global commodity markets created additional uncertainty.

Fortunately, Asian economies had limited direct exposure to the toxic assets that originated in US banks, mortgage lenders, hedge funds and other financial companies. Various financial indicators and banking sector data suggest that Asia's financial systems were rather well prepared for this crisis (see Table 1). Risk-weighted capital-adequacy ratios in the region's banks – at above 10 percent – have provided a strong capital cushion in the face of the severe downturn in the real economy and a substantial pull-out of Western portfolio investment from Asia. Since the financial crisis of 1997–98, most of the crisis-hit Asian economies have adopted the Bank for International Settlement's (BIS) capital adequacy rules – which are the global benchmark for sound banking – as the most important criteria for maintaining a robust banking system.

Overall, non-performing loans were also quite low as a share of total loans, banks were well capitalized and reliance on credit lines from Western banks was minimal. Table 2 shows that the ratios of non-performing loans as a percentage of commercial bank loans are down substantially from the high average ratios observed during 2000-2004. China, Indonesia, Malaysia, the Philippines and Thailand improved a great deal. However, stock prices in Asia were closely linked to global markets and suffered badly in 2008 and until at least the third quarter of 2009.

Despite the relative robustness of the banking system in Asia, the synchronized recession in advanced economies led to a collapse in external demand across the region and severely hurt growth in export-oriented Asian economies. Table 3 shows that most Asian economies experienced a severe contraction of exports, especially if one looks at the quarterly rate of increase of exports between the first quarter of 2007 and the second quarter of 2009. Beginning in the fourth quarter of 2008, most Asian economies experienced a dramatic drop in year-on-year quarterly exports. The contraction accelerated into 2009, with declines in exports reaching more than 30 percent for a number of countries.

The three largest economics in Northeast Asia – China, Japan and South Korea – have responded differently in terms of export performance. Japan appears to have suffered the greatest reduction in exports, with year-on-year exports falling by 40.3 percent and 34 percent in the first quarter and second quarter of 2009, respectively. Additionally, as late in the crisis as the fourth quarter of 2008, China was still seeing export growth of 4.3 percent, while Japan and South Korea saw their exports contract by 9.4 percent and 9.9 percent, respectively (see Table 4).

Unfortunately, the newly industrialized and export-dependent economies suffered most from the collapse of international trade and had the most severe contractions in industrial production as firms drew down inventories and suspended production. As supply chains reacted to the reduction of demand, the rate of decline in imports quickly matched that of exports. In addition, the reduced demand for Asian services such as tourism and slower demand for immigrant labor from Asia also slowed growth. Table 5 shows that the greater the share of exports in gross domestic product (GDP), the lower the growth rate. Singapore, Hong Kong, China, Malaysia and Taiwan were all cases in point.

In terms of percentage change in GDP growth, Goldstein and Xie (2009) further show that Singapore, Hong Kong, Malaysia and South Korea experienced the largest drops (more than nine percentage points) between 2007 and 2009, while the rest of Asia's emerging economies contracted in the range of minus 3.8 to minus 7.9 percentage points (Table 6).

In the wake of the present global downturn, both China and India have managed respectable positive growth rates, while the rest of Asia's major economies are forecast to register negative or near zero growth. Both China and India's growth has provided emerging

Table 1. Risk-Weighted Capital Adequacy Ratos as Percentage of Risk-Weighted Assets

	2000-04 ave. (%)	2008 (%)	2009 (%)
China	−2.3	8.2	n/a
Hong Kong	16.1	14.7	15.6
Indonesia	18.7	16.8	17.8
South Korea	10.7	12.7	13.4
Malaysia	13.4	12.2	13.7
Philippines	17.0	15.7	n/a
Singapore	17.7	14.3	n/a
Taiwan	10.5	10.8	n/a
Thailand	13.2	14.1	15.2

Source: Asian Development Bank, Asia Economic Monitor. July 2009. p. 22.

Table 2. Non-Performing Loans as a Percentage of Commercial Bank Loans

	2000-04 ave. (%)	2008 (%)	2009(%)
China	21.0	2.5	2.0
Hong Kong	4.0	1.2	1.5
Indonesia	10.2	3.2	3.6
South Korea	3.1	1.2	1.5
Malaysia	8.9	2.2	2.2
Philippines	14.8	3.5	3.7
Singapore	5.3	1.4	n/a
Taiwan	5.2	1.5	n/a
Thailand	13.5	5.3	5.5

Source: Asian Development Bank, Asia Economic Monitor, July 2009. p. 24

Table 3. Year-on-Year Quarterly Export Growth Rates of Major East Asian Economies (%)

	2007				2008				2009	
	QI	Q2	Q3	Q4	QI	Q2	Q3	Q4	QI	Q2
South Korea	16.0	13.5	8.3	19.0	18.5	22.7	26.1	−9.5	−24.8	−20.7
China	27.9	27.4	26.2	22.2	21.3	22.3	23.0	4.3	−19.8	−23.4
Japan	11.9	7.5	7.8	14.3	23.1	17.7	9.4	−10.5	−37.8	−34.3
Indonesia	13.9	15.6	9.4	14.1	31.9	29.6	27.9	−5.6	−31.8	−26.2
Malaysia	7.6	7.8	6.9	16.1	19.2	28.9	21.4	−12.9	−28.9	−33.3
Philippines	9.4	4.6	2.3	9.9	2.8	5.5	4.1	−22.3	−36.8	−28.9
Singapore	9.8	7.2	8.5	14.8	21.2	26.4	21.0	−13.9	−32.7	−30.7
Thai land	20.7	17.4	13.7	25.1	19.1	28.6	26.0	−10.4	−19.9	−26.1
Vietnam	18.6	19.9	15.8	33.5	26.9	32.3	44.8	4.7	4.8	−14.7
Cambodia	14.8	17.1	7.7	20.4	8.3	12.5	4.6	−6.3	−0.6	−6.9
Laos	6.4	−3.5	22.1	25.5	39.4	17.8	39.2	−6.5	1.2	−6.7

Source: CEIC [online]: Global Insight [online].

Table 4. China, Japan and South Korea Quarterly Export Growth Rates (%)

	China		Japan		South Korea	
	Q on Q	Y on Y	Q on Q	Y on Y	Q on Q	Y on Y
2008 Q1	−9.9	21.3	2.0	20.3	−3.7	17.4
2008 Q2	17.8	22.3	−0.5	17.5	15.1	23.1
2008 Q3	13.2	23.1	2.8	13.0	0.4	27.0
2008 Q4	−13.1	4.3	−13.2	−9.4	−19.1	−9.9
2009 Q1	−30.8	−19.8	−32.8	−40.3	−19.9	−25.0
2009 Q2	12.4	−23.5	10.1	−34.0	22.2	−20.4

Source: Korea Trade Association (online)

Table 5. Exports Share and GDP Growth of Selected Emerging East Asia (%)

	GDP growth (Q1 2009)
Singapore	−9.6
Hong Kong	−7.8
Malaysia	−6.2
Vietnam	3.1
Taiwan	−10.2
Thailand	−7.1
South Korea	−4.2
China	6.1
Philippines	0.4
Indonesia	4.4

Share of Exports to GDP (2008)

0 50 100 150 200

Source: Asian Development Bank. Asia Economic Monitor, July 2009. p. 5.

Table 6. Slowdown in Economic Growth in 2007-09 by Individual Asian Economies (%)

	2007	2008	2009	2009-07
Singapore	7.8	1.1	−10	−17.8
Hong Kong	6.4	2.5	−4.5	−10.8
Malaysia	6.3	4.6	−3.5	−9.8
South Korea	5.1	2.2	−4	−9.1
Thailand	4.9	2.6	−3	−7.9
Philippines	7.2	4.6	0	−7.2
China	13	9	6.5	−6.5
India	9.3	7.3	4.5	−4.8
Indonesia	6.3	6.1	2.5	−3.8

Source: Goldstein, Morris and Xie (2009)

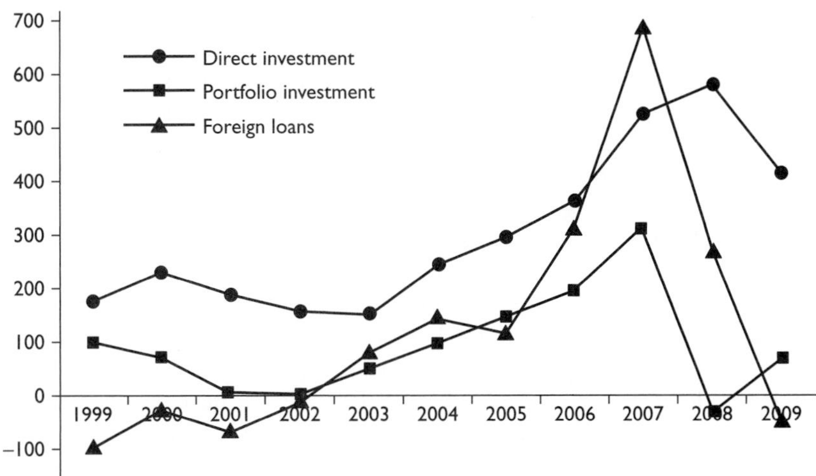

Figure 1. Capital Flow to Emerging Economies, 1999-2009 (US$ Billion)
Tong and Wei (2009): IMF's World Economic Outlook database. The sample includes 24 emerging economies.

Asian economies with a substantial cushion to mitigate the negative global impacts.

As shocks from the financial contagion strongly reverberated around the world in late 2008, Asian equity and bond markets could not escape the asset-price implosion and contraction in trade credit. Following the failure of Lehman Brothers in September 2008, frightened depositors were even tempted to withdraw funds on any rumor that a particular bank was exposed to losses.

In addition to the downfall in export demand, both portfolio investment and foreign loans into 24 emerging Asian economies have continued to drop sharply since the present crisis started to show its early symptoms in mid-2007, as shown in Figure 1. One year later, foreign direct investment inflows from the major industrial economies tumbled in the midst of the global financial panic after September-October 2008. Some have described this phenomenon as "financial protectionism." However, the sudden stop of net capital inflow to emerging Asia amounting to 2 percent of GDP was considerably smaller than what occurred during the Asian financial crisis and was also far smaller than Europe's 11 percent of GDP.

Table 7 indicates that global foreign direct investment (FDI) inflows and outflows fell by more than 10 percent in 2008. As a result, the global FDI inward stock reduced by 4.8 percent in the same year. The credit de-leverage was also reflected in elevated spreads of Asian bonds. Together, the impact on investment became severe. As exports fell in most Asian economies, unemployment in much of the region also rose by 0.5 to 2.5 percentage points, notably in Hong Kong, Singapore and Taiwan from Q3 of 2008 to Q1 of 2009 (ADB 2009b).

An interesting difference between the current crisis and the Asian financial crisis is that those Asian economies that were hit hardest during the previous crisis fared much better this time around than those that had an easier time in 1997-1998 (see Table 8). Indonesia and Taiwan, for example, exhibited almost mirror-image performance during these two crisis periods. Indonesia was the most severely hit economy a decade ago, but emerged with the second-highest growth this time around.

Which industries in Asia had the worst time of it during this crisis, especially in export-dependent economies? It is well known that manufactured exports have much higher income elasticity than primary commodities, and hence the demand for the former can fall very sharply during recessions in major export markets, especially the US market due to its cyclical sensitivity.

The Asian Development Bank (2009) reports that the electronics industry is more dependent on the so-called Group of Three (G-3) markets – the US, Eurozone and Japan – than other industries, that intra-Asian trade in electronics parts and components is larger than any other industry because of the dense supply chain networks in the region, and that electronics products display a high income elasticity. Furthermore, the medium- and high-tech products produced by Asia's manufacturing exporters – especially electronics, motor vehicles, and capital goods – are highly sensitive to the very uncertainties and disruptions that occurred during this crisis.

A Quicker Rebound than Expected

Despite the relatively heavy dependence on exports and investment in the region, by the second quarter of 2009 most Asian developing economies were escaping from the slump, driven by a recovery in industrial production and rallies in equities and other assets. In the wake of the Asian economic crisis, economies here emerged rapidly as a result of favorable external economic conditions. By what means will developing Asia be able to put its economy back on track this time, given the continued weak demand in major export markets such as the US and Europe? Clearly, it will have to generate new demand through sources other than exports, given the likelihood of a prolonged recession in advanced Western economies and global trade imbalances.

Table 7. Selected Indicators of Foreign Direct Investment

	Value at Current Prices (US$b)				Average Annual Growth Rate (%)				
	1982	1990	2007	2008	1996-2000	2005	2006	2007	2008
FDI Inflow	58	207	1,979	1,697	39.4	32.4	50.1	35.4	−14.2
FDI Outflow	27	239	2,147	1.858	35.6	-5.4	58.9	53.7	−13.5
FDI inward stock	790	1942	15,660	14,909	16.0	4.6	23.4	26.2	−4.8
FDI outward stock	579	1786	16,227	16,206	16.9	5.1	22.2	25.3	−0.1
Income on inward FDI	44	74	1,182	1,171	13.3	32.8	23.3	21.9	−0.9
Income on outward FDI	46	120	1,252	1,273	10.3	28.4	18.4	18.5	1.7
Cross-border M&A	n/a	112	1,031	673	62.9	91.1	38.1	62.1	−34.7
Sales of foreign affiliates	2,530	6,026	31,764	30,311	8.1	5.4	18.9	23.6	−4.6

Source: UNCTAD, World Investment Report 2009-Transnational Corporations, Agricultural Production and Development, Table 1.6

Table 8. Quarterly GDP Growth Rate of Selected Asian Economies (%)

	Q1 1997 to Q4 1998 Lowest	Q1 2009 Latest
China	7.20	6.10
Hong Kong	−8.06	−7.79
Indonesia	−18.26	4.37
South Korea	−8.12	−4.25
Malaysia	−11.18	−6.17
Philippines	−2.42	0.45
Singapore	−4.20	−9.6
Taiwan	3.31	−10.24
Thailand	−13.92	−7.11

Source: Asian Development Bank, Asia Economic Monitor, July 2009, p. 4

In line with the global policy guidelines suggested by recent meetings of the Group of 20 (G-20) nations, almost every large economy in developing Asia has implemented various measures to stimulate aggregate demand through fiscal and monetary expansion. In turn, households were relatively quick to spend fiscal windfalls that came in the form of tax cuts and income support, giving a fillip to consumption that began to boost GDP by the second quarter of 2009.

The Asian Development Bank (2009b) reports that fiscal stimuli in Asian developing economies averaged 7.1 percent of nominal 2008 GDP. The emphasis placed by governments to boost demand through discretionary fiscal measures differed, but the boost from the stimulus was strong enough to arrest the decline in GDP growth, even though automatic stabilizers are fairly weak across most countries in the region. For example, almost all of China's 4 trillion yuan stimulus package went to infrastructure projects or other types of construction activity. In contrast, Hong Kong emphasized tax cuts, public housing rent reductions and other forms of household income support. South Korea opted for a mix of tax cuts and expenditure measures.

On the monetary side, most Asian economies have reduced interest rates to provide liquidity to boost investment and expenditure on durable goods. For example, the Bank of Korea reduced its policy rate by 325 basis points from October 2008 to February 2009, and kept the rate at 2 percent through August. Bank Indonesia brought down its policy rate by 300 basis points from December 2008 to August 2009 to a record low of 6.5 percent. Likewise, the Reserve Bank of India cut its policyrate substantially (by 425 basis points) and injectedliquidity into banks. It also raised deposit rates available tonon-resident Indian savers. A general softening ofinflationary pressures and lower prices for commoditiesand energy helped Asian monetary authorities easemonetary policy.

Developing Asia's Economic Prospects

Developing Asia is leading the global economic recovery with a strong rebound in GDP growth that began in the second quarter of 2009. The fiscal and monetary actions taken by governments throughout the region — especially China, South Korea, India, Indonesia and Vietnam — spurred the resurgence.

Recently, the ADB raised its forecasts for GDP growth for developing Asia as a whole from those given in early 2009. The region is now projected to grow by 3.9 percent in 2009 and 6.4 percent in 2010, up from earlier forecasts of 3.4 percent and 6.0 percent, respectively.

One reason that developing Asia has recovered faster than the rest of the world is the relative robustness of its financial sector, which provided a buffer against the global financial turmoil. The strong fiscal position of most large economies in developing Asia also enabled them to pursue expansionary fiscal policies. Existing high savings rates and low levels of house hold debt made consumers more amenable to spending the additional income from the fiscal stimulus measures (ADB 2009b).

With external demand from the main industrial countries still relatively weak, however, it will be difficult for developing Asia to return to the high growth rates achieved in 2006–2007. Growth in 2010 will only return to about 6 percent to 7 percent compared to growth of 9 percent to 10 percent prior the crisis.

Fortunately, the resumption of growth has taken place against a backdrop of low inflation or even mild deflation. The region as a whole has benefited from the steep slide in oil prices and from the improved supply of food and raw materials. Despite the sharp fall in short-term interest rates engineered by central banks and the pumping of liquidity into financial markets, the threat of inflation remains muted.

More recently, there has been an apparent recovery of portfolio capital flowing into the region as equities markets have rallied. Less foreign direct investment (FDI) is coming into the region but there are early signs that multinational enterprises, having sharply reduced unwanted inventories, are now in a position to increase production. In addition, industrial output is on the rise in China, South Korea and Singapore after the deep plunges in the fourth quarter of 2008 and the first quarter of 2009. There are also signs that lending by the banking system is reviving. Much of this is going into domestic demand-driven sectors such as consumer credit for purchases of durable goods, but much of it may also be going into stock and real estate markets.

Once the effects from fiscal stimulus packages wear off, it will be essential that domestic consumption and private investment take over as the drivers of growth. Rebalancing Asian growth through increasing domestic investment and consumption relative to income will help keep momentum behind the global recovery. In some instances, structural reforms in the corporate and banking sectors — as well as industrial restructuring towards more labor-intensive service sectors — need to be stepped up to rekindle growth. Fortunately though, most developing Asian economies have relatively low debt-to-GDP ratios and are on a sound fiscal footing.

Issues and Challenges

There are at least two key points that emerge from my analysis so far. The first is that emerging Asia was not able to "decouple" from the crisis in the advanced economies. The second is that Asia's improved fundamentals resulted in a quicker than expected recovery relative to the rest of the world. Given the financial contagion and the on-going process of globalization, several issues and challenges present themselves.

I. Coordination of an exit strategy

Recovery is under way, so when is it appropriate to exit from expansionary fiscal and monetary policies? As long as the recovery remains fragile and subject to serious downside risks, the implementation of an exit strategy by Asian economies should be very cautious and must be coordinated with the world's other major economies. Global trade prospects should be carefully assessed, even though the low point in world trade volume may have been reached in the first quarter of 2009. Both imports and exports are still well below levels attained a year earlier. Hence, continuing the expansionary stance is warranted until global markets and demand are on a firm recovery path.

One consequence of expansionary monetary policies is that they may create asset bubbles if their duration and strength exceed desired levels. Asian equity markets, along with those around the world, have rallied in hopeful anticipation of global economic recovery and regional recovery faster than other parts of the world.

However, the region's asset price rally is also being fueled by excess liquidity from expansionary monetary policies.This overhang is finding its way into equity and property markets to cause asset-price inflation that may pose a threat to the soundness of the region's financial systems. Under these circumstances, a failure to tighten monetary policy atsome point will create conditions that are conducive to the formation of bubbles. A downward correction in assetprices is warranted, despite some painful consequences for the financial system and the economy, as best illustrated by the bursting of East Asia's asset bubbles in 1997-98 and the recent US housing bubble.

II. Rebalancing extra-regional exports and intra-regional domestic demand

The economic prospects for developing Asia this year are promising, but it is likely that growth will remain well below the average performance of pre-crisis years. The region will only be able to achieve a fully-fledged high-growth path if the global economy succeeds in growing closer to its potential. A major challenge in this context is whether Asia can adjust to long-standing global trade imbalances by striking an optimal balance between export orientation and increased reliance on domestic demand-driven growth. Looking ahead to the next decade, it is likely that demand from advanced economies is not going to be as robust as it used to be. This implies that Asia needs to shift from a growth model that relies excessively on exports (especially to markets outside the region) to one that relies more on domestic demand within Asia.

Emerging Asia's rising prosperity in the past two decades or so has been closely associated with its outward orientation to foreign trade. Indeed, many other developing countries have attempted to emulate the success stories of East Asian tiger economies. Although trade orientation became the symbol of the Asian model, liberalization and openness to cross-border flows of capital and labor also played an important role in the region's success.

Yet excessive openness is not without risks, as witnessed by the two major crises in a decade. The 1997-98 Asian financial crisis had its roots in the sudden reversal of capital inflows into the region's financial institutions, which were overexposed to foreign borrowings, and this made it impossible to maintain exchange-rate pegs to the dollar. This time, a sudden stop in private capital inflows into emerging Asian markets, coupled with capital withdrawals, caused extreme exchange-rate volatility, as was seen especially in the case of the South Korean won in late 2008 and early 2009.

III. Expansion of intra-regional trade

More specifically, the region's heightened reliance on external demand for growth hindered consumption and catalyzed an accumulation of foreign reserves, which was widely seen as insurance against a repeat of the 1997-98 crisis. This reliance left the region vulnerable to the synchronized collapse of the major industrial economies. To counter this, trade within Asia should be pursued by encouraging cross-border production networks and consuming final goods inside Asia.

One way of effectively creating significant intra-regional demand in East Asia is to forge an East Asian free trade agreement (FTA) benchmarked against the integration process of the European Union. There are some signs that the atmosphere for such an endeavor is becoming more favorable. The Asian financial crisis triggered a rising sense of East Asian identity and, as a result, in November 1999, the ASEAN + 3 (China, Japan and South Korea) Summit released a joint statement on East Asian cooperation. Among the notable developments that have occurred include the so-called Chiang Mai Initiative (CMI), which involves a regional currency swap to provide financial help and support mechanisms in the event of another currency crisis, and trade integration efforts through intra-regional FTAs. ASEAN has concluded bilateral FTAs with China, Japan and South Korea, and ASEAN + 3 should seriously consider a regionwide FTA that would help realize potential benefits from geographical proximity, complementary endowments of production factors and growing economic ties.

For merchandise trade, a broader customer base for final goods is needed. Strengthening intra-regional trade can help reduce developing Asia's overdependence on the major industrial economies and remedy unsustainable current account imbalances. For policy-makers in Asia, the decision to accelerate economic growth and job creation through cross-border movements of goods and services, capital and labor must be made within Asia.

IV. Halting protectionist measures

While the world's major economies employ economic stimulus packages to ensure a recovery from the current economic slump, trade officials and export-dependent economies are worried about creeping protectionism in the EU, the US, China, Russia and other countries. Given rising unemployment and tremendous uncertainties in the financial markets, many economic recovery measures adopted by major economies come with a high risk of protectionism.

Unlike traditional forms of protectionism such as higher tariffs, new forms of protectionism are more subtle and indirect, such as subsides tied to "buy local" programs that favor domestic industries at the expense of international competitors. Such actions could well do more harm than good by choking off trade and provoking a downward spiral of tit-for-tat actions worldwide. If this happens, negotiated tariff reductions would be meaningless if countries could simply use taxes or subsidies to discriminate in favor of local products. The prospect of such policies underpins the rising concerns about protectionism and economic nationalism in economic recovery efforts.

Given these protectionist symptoms, the G-20 leaders, however, agreed to freeze trade protectionist measures and declared the critical importance of rejecting protectionism and refraining from raising new barriers to investment ortrade in goods and services. They also called on leaders to reinvigorate efforts to get the World Trade Organization's Doha Round back on track. Protectionism at this critical point in the global economic downturn would harm the spirit of cooperation that is needed for global economic recovery. The G-20 should go further, in my view, and take specific actions to liberalize trade.

To ensure a robust revival of world trade in coming years, large Asian economies could take up the mantle of the Doha Round. An example is India's hosting of the meeting of trade ministers in New Delhi in September 2009, aiding the G-20's goal of reaching agreement on the Doha Round by the end of 2010. Efforts to head off protectionist tendencies are still important as governments continue to implement stimulus packages that involve procurement of tradable goods and services. The G-20 consultations provide an excellent opportunity for developing Asia to push the trade talks forward. There are also opportunities for successful agricultural negotiations as the G-3 economies have proposed to step up assistance for agricultural development.

V. In search of sustainable growth models

As world leaders turn greater attention to combating climate change, it is critical that those efforts do not undermine half a century of world trade opening. The US passed a climate bill that would impose trade penalties on countries that do not accept limits on carbon emissions. The EU has already approved the idea of an "equalization" levy on imports from countries that have not agreed to cut emissions. Such unilateral sanctions are unlikely to work and are more likely to provoke a dangerous protectionist trade war. The main reason trade and climate change are linked is that the damage inflicted by greenhouse gases is not mainly local and regional. If big emitters do not cut back, atmospheric concentrations of greenhouse gases will continue to rise dangerously, no matter what the rest of the world does. There are precedents for using trade measures for environmental goals. The WTO has suggested that levying taxes at the border on the carbon contents of imports would be acceptable if they are devised properly. Such tariffs, though, must be part of an international agreement on climate change.

An international accord that includes trade-related enforcement must also include commitments on emission reductions all around, as well as financial aid for poor countries to meet the caps without sacrificing economic growth. How can we set up clear guidelines to identify and quantify transgressions and establish appropriate countermeasures? It must not open a back door for protectionism.

Summary and Policy Implications

I have examined how the worst global economic downturn since the Great Depression has affected Asia. After a painful restructuring of its economic system following the 1997-98 financial crisis, Asian economies this time appear to be successfully weathering the global downturn. Financial globalization needs to be effectively managed so that capital flows do not become a source of instability. This requires policy changes and domestic financial market development to create an environment that both fosters Asian intermediation for its huge savings and foreign exchange reserves and that attracts long-term foreign investment.

An excessive opening of domestic capital markets without clear monitoring on hedge fund flows and appropriate corrective mechanisms, exacerbated the current crisis in Asia. Under the G-20 process, Asian G-20 members Japan, China, India, Indonesia and South Korea should play an important role in designing a new global financial architecture. Emerging Asian economies still harbor weaknesses in their financial systems, especially in risk management. As we learned during the Asian financial crisis and the current crisis, emerging Asia should continue to improve its financial system by adopting the most advanced best practices.

Excessive exchange-rate volatility also needs to be avoided while global trade imbalances are addressed by expanding intra-regional demand for finished as well as intermediate goods. Labor mobility has provided foreign exchange flows that have proven to be reliable even in times of crisis. Policies and institutional changes to ease the transfer of remittances can enhance the benefits of tapping into the international labor market.

Also, Asia's economies should promote efficiency in the functioning of their financial systems along with manufacturing efficiency.

Finally, emerging Asia should continue to accelerate the ongoing process of regional integration in the form of an ASEAN +3 FTA and gradual moves toward creating an East Asian Community.

References

Ahn, Choong Yong (2001), "Financial and Corporate Sector Restructuring in South Korea: Accomplishments and Unfinished Agenda," The Japanese Economic Review, Vol. 52, No. 4.

Ahn, Choong Yong (2008), "South Korea: Wary of Another Financial Crisis," Global Asia, Vol. 3, No. 4.

Ahn, Choong Yong and Inkyo Cheong (2007), "A Search for Closer Economic Relations in East Asia," The Japanese Economic Review, Vol. 58, No. 2.

Asian Development Bank (2009a), Asian Development Outlook 2009: Rebalancing Asia's Growth. pp. 51-124.

Asian Development Bank (2009b), Asian Development Outlook 2009 Update: "Developing Asia's response to the turmoil," pp. 26-32.

Asian Development Bank (2009c), Asia Economic Monitor, July.

Baily, Martin Neil, Robert E. Litan, and Matthew S. Johnson (2008), "The Origins of the Financial Crisis," Initiative on Business and Public Policy.

Goldstein, Morris and Daniel Xie (2009), "Impact of Financial Crisis on Emerging Asia," Peterson Institute for International Economics, Working Paper, 09-11.

Gregor Eder, Michaela Grimm (2009), "Asia and the Global Economic Crisis: Challenges and Opportunities," Allianz, June 3, 2009.

World Bank (2009)."Prospects for the Global Economy," June.

World Trade Organization (2009)."Global Crisis Requires Global Solutions," 2009 News Report on Recent Developments. 13 July.

Women and Globalization: A Study of 180 Countries, 1975–2000

MARK M. GRAY, MIKI CAUL KITTILSON, AND WAYNE SANDHOLTZ

The authors of this piece seek to apply complex quantitative methods to answer a simple question: Has globalization improved life for women around the world? Gray, Kittilson, and Sandholtz examine both material and ideational factors in their analysis. This begs the question: If a person has a better standard of living, does it matter if the society does not grant legal or emotional equality? How does this study address this question? Do you think it is more important to have possessions or equal legal status?

How do rising levels of international interconnectedness affect the social, economic, and political conditions for women? Competing hypotheses are easy to identify. Indeed, research on gender and international relations sometimes offers clear propositions but seldom submits them to broad, quantitative testing. This article begins to fill that gap. We expect to find a considerably mixed picture: some women will benefit from globalization and some will be hurt; the status of women will improve in some respects but not others. Nevertheless, we advance the hypothesis that, on balance and over time, increasing cross-national exchange and communication lead to improvements in women's status and equality.[1] We argue that both economic factors and ideational or normative effects support that proposition. Economic aspects of globalization bring new opportunities and resources to women. But equally important, globalization promotes the diffusion of ideas and norms of equality for women; although some societies resist such notions, others gradually abandon rules and practices that have functioned to subordinate and constrain women.

Why should a study focus on the effects of globalization for women and not for other groups of people? First, in assessing the condition of women, we take seriously the basic insight of feminist and gender analysis approaches that the absence of gender in theoretical and empirical research leads to distortion, or even blindness, with respect to ubiquitous social and political phenomena. Second, we note that gender is one of the few modes of differentiation that has social, cultural, political, and economic implications everywhere in the world. As Youngs puts it, all institutions involve the "exercise of power to the advantage of some and the disadvantage of others," and "gender is a pervasive basis for such differentiations."[2] The 1995 *Human Development Report* declares, on the basis of numerous indicators, "in no society today do women enjoy the same opportunities as men."[3] In the 1999 *Human Development Report*, both of the composite measures, the "gender empowerment measure" and the "gender development index," "show disparities in every country."[4] In other words, focusing on women allows us to investigate the effects of internationalization on a group that is disadvantaged, to a greater or lesser extent, in every country in the world.

Finally, although numerous social scientists have offered arguments as to the consequences of globalization for women, these propositions have generally been cast at a relatively high level of theoretical abstraction. Some studies include an empirical dimension, usually in the form of ethnographic or case study material. We hope to contribute to these conversations by analyzing quantitative data from about 180 countries. It is not our contention that only statistical methods can answer all the questions—far from it. But quantitative analysis can provide powerful evidence for or against some key propositions.

Theories and Hypotheses

In most political science research on globalization and internationalization,[5] the focus has been, implicitly or explicitly, on economic transactions across national frontiers.[6] But transnational economic ties via trade, investment, and corporate alliances and production networks constitute only one dimension of globalization. International communications are as important as economic exchange. Transborder interchange can involve people, ideas, information, fashions, and tastes. Cross-national communication occurs through travel and tourism, telecommunications, and the Internet. Many forms of transnational interchange include both economic and sociocultural dimensions. For instance, migration has powerful economic causes and effects, as well as cultural repercussions in both sending and receiving countries. Transnational media and entertainment activities (movies, television, music, news, and information) are simultaneously business and cultural phenomena.

Our analysis of the gendered effects of globalization includes two principal dimensions. The first has to do with economic resources and opportunities. The second concerns the spread of norms and ideas regarding the place of women in social, political, and economic life.

Economic arguments

Economic arguments on the effects of globalization on women fall into two broad groups, one intensely critical and the other basically optimistic, but with reservations and qualifications. From the critical point of view, economic globalization has largely negative consequences for women. Globalization confines women to low-pay, low-status, often part-time jobs that reinforce their subordination and perpetuate the devalorization of women's work in most societies.[7] Demand among multinational firms for cheap, flexible labor has encouraged offshore production using low-paid women. Women, however, remain excluded from the more stable and higher-paying jobs in heavy industry.[8] In Pettman's account, globalization (defined as increasing capital mobility, trade, and offshore manufacturing) leads to an "increasing feminization of labor," because women continue to be "constructed as dependents" and thus confined to the worst-paying jobs.[9] The removal of barriers to transnational investment, far from empowering women, has brought them dismal jobs in offshore production sites where women are subject to sexual discrimination and harassment. Furthermore, competition from foreign firms undercuts efforts to help women launch local "microenterprises."[10] Some within the critical camp acknowledge that the picture for women as workers in an era of mobile capital is somewhat mixed but see it as largely discouraging. Some women may benefit from new jobs, but their "work is highly exploitative and features low wages, poor working conditions, suppression of trade unions, and little opportunity for security or advancement."[11]

In addition, the structural adjustment and market liberalization policies that have accompanied globalization are particularly damaging to women. These policies lead to cuts in public-sector jobs that are often disproportionately held by women, undercut social programs that benefit women, and inhibit labor organization by women.[12] Further, in an increasingly volatile economic context, women are often the first to suffer in times of financial crisis. Evidence from the Asian financial crisis shows that women were more likely than men to lose their jobs.[13] Another argument is that industrial development causes environmental damage that disproportionately degrades life for women in developing countries. Women suffer the most from ecological problems because they are responsible for most family sustenance; finding food and fuel becomes harder, and diets suffer.[14]

No scholarship on globalization and women takes an unabashedly positive view. The alternative to the critical position is a qualified one that posits, on balance, economic advantages in the form of greater agency for women in an era of globalization. The primary advantage centers on enhanced prospects for nonhousehold employment. Indeed, globalization, including greater openness to foreign direct investment (FDI), has led to a massive infusion of women into job markets.[15] Especially in the lower-income countries, foreign multinationals often make better-paying jobs available to women. Sassen, cited earlier on the negative implications of globalized production, in fact recognizes the mixed impact of globalization for women's jobs: "On the one hand, they [women] are constituted as an invisible and disempowered class of workers....On the other hand, the access to wages and salaries (even if low), the growing feminization of the job supply, and the growing feminization of business opportunities...alter the gender hierarchies in which they [women] find themselves."[16]

Many analysts note that improved employment possibilities for women are not an unalloyed good. For instance, Levidow argues that though such offshore production brings women economic benefits, working for foreign manufacturers (in this case in the semiconductor industry) can be alienating and unhealthful and not necessarily terribly empowering.[17] In a superb ethnographic study of Thai women who migrated to Bangkok to work, Mills captures that sense of ambivalence. She writes that she expected to encounter much more disenchantment and unhappiness than she found, and that the women felt a real "strength of purpose and sense of personal agency." Her study balances the difficulties and alienation of factory work against the women's perceptions of empowerment from earning money and living on their own in the city: "They are neither victims pure and simple nor free and unfettered actors."[18]

Thus, at a minimum, with globalization, more women have more options for income-producing employment. More numerous job opportunities mean more ways to get out of unequal relations; these options give women more chances to take their labor and skills elsewhere.[19] One of the first places where women benefit from enhanced employment opportunities is the household. Sassen cites extensive research showing that with regular wage work, "women gain greater personal autonomy and independence....[They] gain more control over budgeting and other domestic decisions and greater leverage in requesting help from men in domestic chores."[20] As households become more dependent on female incomes, the status and relative power of women improve.[21]

Diffusion of norms and ideas

International interactions, in addition to whatever economic or material purpose they have, inevitably depend on, and work to diffuse, norms and ideas. Cross-border interactions always rely on a basis of shared norms. The more transnational activity people engage in, the more they absorb ideas and norms prevailing in international society. In other words, we posit a socialization effect. Socialization is a process through which actors learn the ideas, values, and norms of the social contexts in which they interact.[22] International organizations are, among other things, forums for socialization and learning. At times they are also purposeful "teachers of norms."[23] The more a country's citizens and organizations participate in, and value, these transnational networks of exchange, communication, and organization, the more likely they are to absorb international ideas and norms.[24]

To the extent that a country internalizes norms and ideas diffused through cross-national interactions, it incorporates those norms and ideas into its domestic policies, laws, and institutions.[25] It is the relationship among international interactions, socialization, and internalization that leads us to hypothesize a link between a country's level of integration in international society and the political, economic, and social condition of its women.

The key question then becomes, which norms and ideas in international society have a bearing on the status of women? In recent decades, a number of international conferences, conventions, and declarations have promoted a variety of norms and ideas designed to improve the lot of women. They address health, nutrition, and physical quality of life; personal security; employment and income; participation in politics and government; and social status. Of course, increased attention to women's rights (as much of the discourse has been framed) in international forums did not simply emerge on its own. It has been the product of "a form of feminism with an internationalist orientation."[26] Internationalist feminism has been the work of a broad range of women's activist and advocacy groups that have pressured both national governments and international organizations.[27] Links among local, national, and international women's groups have created "transnational issue networks...that can exchange information, ideas, and political support."[28] In this section, we summarize the interactions among two major international governmental organizations, the United Nations (UN) and Word Bank, and transnational issue networks that have promoted the diffusion of ideas and norms supporting improvements in the status of women.

From its inception, the UN has addressed issues concerning women. In the late 1940s and 1950s, the UN established a Commission on the Status of Women,[29] and sponsored a Convention on the Political Rights of Women. After a long lapse, the UN declared a "Decade for Women" (1976 to 1985) and held a series of international conferences on women: in 1980 (Copenhagen), 1985 (Nairobi), and 1995 (Beijing). The conferences established a Bill of Female Rights; addressed violence against women and women's health, employment, education, and poverty; and culminated in 1995 with the *Platform for Action*. UN conferences on women have served as "lightning rods that have helped to channel the collective buzz of ideas and energy emanating from the global women's movement into prescriptions for and commitments to policy action at the level of nation-states."[30] The Beijing conference, and later the UN General Assembly, endorsed an innovative approach to addressing women's inequality called "gender mainstreaming," which calls for governments to make gender equality an explicit and central part of all policy and planning.

The UN conferences also fostered the growth of a transnational feminist movement.[31] Nongovernmental organizations (NGOs) held meetings parallel to the UN conferences. Attendance at the NGO forums grew considerably over time—from 1,000 in 1975 to 30,000 in 1995.[32] These grassroots connections complement and support the connections made among official governmental delegates.

The increasing number and activism of women's NGOs ensured that other UN conferences and specialized agencies would also address the gender dimension.[33] For example, since the early 1980s, under the rubric of Women in Development, the UN Development Program has considered the impact of its programs and policies on women.[34] Women's concerns have figured prominently in a variety of UN conferences, especially in the 1990s, including the 1994 Earth Summit in Rio de Janeiro, the 1995 International Conference on Population and Development, the 1993 World Conference on Human Rights, and the 1995 World Summit for Social Development.[35]

Finally, the UN's heightened awareness of gender inequality spurred its General Assembly to adopt the Convention on the Elimination of All Forms of Discrimination Against Women (CEDAW) in 1979, calling for government action on several policies designed to support women, such as maternity leave and access to childcare.[36] Although many nations did not ratify it, including the United States, CEDAW became the main international legal document on women's rights.[37] Its existence created a source of legitimacy with which women could justify their claims to their national governments.[38]

Conclusion

The evidence presented in our analysis shows that global norms and institutions make a difference for the quality of life and status of women. We have found that more often than not, when domestic cultures are more open to international influences, outcomes for women improve, as measured by health, literacy, and participation in the economy and government. Membership in the UN and World Bank, along with international trade and investment activity, are frequently associated with improved outcomes for women. But the most consistently important factor across models is ratification of CEDAW. Participation in this agreement has played a role in increasing female levels of literacy, participation in the economy, and representation in parliament. Further, our analysis confirms that the effects of CEDAW are independent; ratification of CEDAW and positive changes for women on the dependent variables cannot be attributed to underlying domestic factors. Finally, with respect to life expectancy and illiteracy, our models show that at least some forms of international integration not only produce absolute gains for women but also contribute to greater equality vis-à-vis men.

In examining the "rising tide" of changes in women's roles around the world, Inglehart and Norris argue that cultural change is necessary for institutional change, which ultimately brings improvements in women's lives.[39] We concur: changes in attitudes and values are key to women achieving greater equality. Yet our analysis suggests that this process is not unidirectional. In a mutually reinforcing manner, changes in institutions can alter culture. Participation in international organizations and treaties designed to promote women's equality can shape national attitudes. In this way, institutions such as CEDAW may act as mechanisms for change.

Finally, though our findings do support the conclusion that, on balance, expanding international ties open the way to improvements in the quality of life and status of women, they in no way imply that globalization is good for all women everywhere. Where international trade and investment erode traditional local economies or degrade the environment, women as well as men suffer. When transnational enterprises create new jobs in one country, they may well eliminate them in another, diminishing economic opportunity and standards of living. But our initial proposition seems to hold up: increasing international exchange and communication create new opportunities for income-generating work and expose countries to norms that, in recent decades, have promoted equality for women. International norms and institutions can, at a minimum, give women one more source of leverage in pressing for domestic reforms. Advocates of equality for women at the national level can insist that their governments measure up to international standards and commitments. Because our findings have these practical implications for political bargaining over women's issues, future research may shed light on the national processes behind these large-scale shifts. By moving between the aggregate level and in-depth studies of particular cases, it may be possible to more fully draw out some of the mechanisms behind these relationships, including the role of women's groups in leveraging policy changes from international agreements such as CEDAW.

Notes

1. We give careful consideration to our choice of terms "status" and "conditions for women" here. Although these terms may connote a passive role for women, we recognize that women actively shape their environments. We argue that favorable conditions in women's lives provide greater opportunity for empowerment. We avoid the terms "equality" and "empowerment" in instances where we can only measure changes for women in absolute terms (not relative to men).

2. Youngs 2000, 12-13.
3. United Nations Development Programme 1995, 29.
4. United Nations Development Programme 1999.
5. We use the terms "globalization" and "internationalization" interchangeably. Both refer to transborder movements of goods, services, capital, people, ideas, information, and symbols. The terms imply that countries are becoming increasingly interconnected through rising levels of cross-border interactions.
6. See Milner and Keohane 1996, 4; Wade 1996; Greider 1997; Rodrik 1997; Prakash and Hart 1999, 3; and Smith, Solinger, and Topik 1999, 3-9.
7. See Enloe 1990, chap. 7; Moghadam 1999; and Mason 1986.
8. Sassen 1998, chap. 6.
9. Pettman 1996, 163-67.
10. Sforza 1999.
11. Wright 1995, 864.
12. See Ward 1990; Afshar and Dennis 1992; Benerfa and Feldman 1992; Elson 1995; and Lorentzen and Turpin 1996, 3-4; and Pettman 1996, 168.
13. Singh and Zammit 2000.
14. See Lorentzen and Turpin 1996, 5; and Mies 1996, 13.
15. Standing 1989.
16. Sassen 1996, 26.
17. Levidow 1996.
18. Mills 1999, 11.
19. Dau-Schmidt 1996.
20. Sassen 1996, 27.
21. See Gladden 1993; Afshar 1998; and Afshar and Barrientos 1999.
22. Eckstein 1988, 791.
23. Finnemore 1993.
24. Sandholtz and Gray 2003.
25. See Cortell and Davis 1996; Koh 1998; Wendt 1999; and Cortell and Davis 2000.
26. Prügl and Meyer 1999, 3.
27. See Keck and Sikkink 1998; Naples and Desai 2002.
28. Prügl and Meyer 1999, 9.
29. United Nations 1988.
30. True and Mintrom 2001, 48-49.
31. See Nelson and Chowdhury 1994; Keck and Sikkink 1998; and Stienstra 2000.
32. True and Mintrom 2001.
33. Joachim 2003.
34. See Kardam 1991; and Goetz 1997.
35. See Tinker 1999, 99; Higer 1999; and Miller 1999.
36. United Nations 1988.
37. Keck and Sikkink 1998.
38. Bernard 1987.
39. Inglehart and Norris 2003.

References

Afshar, Haleh, ed. 1998. *Women and Empowerment: The Politics of Development*. Basingstoke, England: Macmillan.

Afshar, Haleh, and Stephanie Barrientos. 1999. Introduction: Women, Globalization, and Fragmentation. In *Women, Globalization, and Fragmentation in the Developing World*, edited by Haleh Afshar and Stephanie Barrientos, 1–17. New York: St. Martin's.

Afshar, Haleh, and Carolyne Dennis, eds. 1992. *Women and Adjustment Policies in the Third World*. Basingstoke, England: Macmillan.

Ahmed, Manzoor. 1992. Literacy in a Larger Context. *Annals of the American Academy of Political and Social Science* 520 (March):32–35.

Apodaca, Clair. 1998. Measuring Women's Economic and Social Rights Achievement. *Human Rights Quarterly* 20 (1):139–72.

Atkeson, Lonna Rae. 2003. Not All Cues Are Created Equal: The Conditional Impact of Female Candidates on Political Engagement. *Journal of Politics* 65 (4):1040–61.

Baltagi, Badi, and Qi Li. 1990. A Lagrange Multiplier Test for Error Components Model with Incomplete Panels. *Econometric Reviews* 9 (1):103–107.

Banks, Arthur S. 2000. Cross-National Time-Series Data Archive. Binghamton, N.Y.: Databanks International.

Barrett, David, George Kurian, and Todd Johnson. 2001. *World Christian Encyclopedia: A Comparative Study of Churches and Religions in the Modern World*. Oxford: Oxford University Press.

Beck, Nathaniel, and Jonathan Katz. 1995. What to Do (and Not to Do) with Time-Series Cross-Section

Data. *American Political Science Review* 89 (3):634–47.

Beckwith, Karen. 1992. Comparative Research and Electoral Systems: Lessons from France and Italy. *Women & Politics* 12 (4):1–33.

Belloc, Nedra Bartlett. 1950. Labor-Force Participation and Employment Opportunities for Women. *Journal of the American Statistical Association* 45 (251):400–10.

Beneria, Lourdes, and Shelley Feldman, eds. 1992. *Unequal Burden: Economic Crises, Persistent Poverty, and Women's Work*. Manchester, England: Manchester University Press.

Bernard, Jesse. 1987. *The Female World from a Global Perspective*. Bloomington: Indiana University Press.

Bongaarts, John, and Griffith Feeney. 2002. How Long Do We Live? *Population and Development Review* 28 (1):13–29.

Breusch, Trevor, and Adrian Pagan. 1980. The Lagrange Multiplier Test and Its Applications to Model Specification in Econometrics. *Review of Economic Studies* 47 (1):239–53.

Brysk, Alison. 2005. Global Good Samaritans? Human Rights Policy in Costa Rica. *Global Governance* 11 (4):445–66.

Carceles, Gabriel. 1990. World Literacy Prospects at the Turn of the Century: Is the Objective of Literacy for All by the Year 2000 Statistically Plausible? *Comparative Education Review* 34 (1): 4–20.

Celik, Yasemin. 2004. The Effect of the CEDAW on Women's Rights in Turkey. Paper presented at the 100th Annual Meeting of the American Political Science Association, Chicago, September.

Cichowski, Rachel. 2001. Judicial Rulemaking and the Institutionalization of EU Sex Equality Policy. In *The Institutionalization of Europe*, edited by Alec Stone Sweet, Wayne Sandholtz, and Neil Fligstein, 113–36. Oxford: Oxford University Press.

——. 2002. Women's Transnational Activism and the Evolution of European Sex Equality Policy. In *Women's Activism and Globalization*, edited by Nancy Naples and Manisha Desai, 220–38. New York: Routledge.

Clark, Robert, and Richard Anker. 1993. Cross-National Analysis of Labor Force Participation of Older Men and Women. *Economic Development and Cultural Change* 41 (3):489–512.

Clark, Roger, Thomas W. Ramsbey, and Emily Stier Adler. 1991. Culture, Gender, and Labor Force Participation: A Cross-National Study. *Gender and Society* 5 (1):47–66.

Collver, Andrew, and Eleanor Langlois. 1962. The Female Labor Force in Metropolitan Areas: An International Comparison. *Economic Development and Cultural Change* 10 (4):367–85.

Cook, Chris, and Whitney Walker. 2001. *The Facts on File World Political Almanac: From 1945 to the Present*. New York: Checkmark Books/Facts on File.

Cooney, Rosemary Santana. 1975. Female Professional Work Opportunities: A Cross-National Study. *Demography* 12 (1):107–20.

Coriden, James A., Thomas J. Green, and Donald E. Heintschel, eds. 1985. *The Code of Canon Law: A Text and Commentary*. New York: Paulist Press/Canon Law Society of America.

Cortell, Andrew P., and James W. Davis Jr. 1996. How Do International Institutions Matter? The Domestic Impact of International Rules and Norms. *International Studies Quarterly* 40 (4):451–78.

——. 2000. Understanding the Domestic Impact of International Norms: A Research Agenda. *International Studies Review* 2 (1):65–87.

Cotter, David A., Joan M. Hermsen, and Reeve Vanneman. 2001. Women's Work and Working Women: The Demand for Female Labor. *Gender and Society* 15 (3):429–52.

Darcy, R., Susan Welch, and Janet Clark. 1994. *Women, Elections, and Representation*. Lincoln: University of Nebraska Press.

Dau-Schmidt, Kenneth G. 1996. Dividing the Surplus: Will Globalization Give Women a Larger or Smaller Share of the Benefits of Cooperative Production? *Indiana Journal of Global Legal Studies* 4 (1):51–58.

Duverger, Maurice. 1955. *The Political Role of Women*. Paris: UN Economic and Social Council.

Eckstein, Harry. 1988. A Culturalist Theory of Political Change. *American Political Science Review* 82 (3):789–804.

Elgstrom, Ole. 2000. Norm Negotiations: The Construction of New Norms Regarding Gender and Development in EU Foreign Aid Policy. *Journal of European Public Policy* 7 (3):457–76.

Ellis, Evelyn. 1998. *European Community Sex Equality Law*. Oxford: Oxford University Press.

Elson, Diane, ed. 1995. *Male Bias in the Development Process*. Manchester, England: Manchester University Press.

Engels, Friedrich. [1884] 1942. *The Origin of the Family, Private Property and the State*. Reprint, New York: International Publishers.

Enloe, Cynthia. 1990. *Bananas, Beaches & Bases: Making Feminist Sense of International Politics*. Berkeley: University of California Press.

Finnemore, Martha. 1993. International Organizations as Teachers of Norms: The United Nations Educational, Scientific, and Cultural Organization and Science Policy. *International Organization* 47 (4):565–97.

Freedom House. 2003. *Annual Survey of Freedom Country Scores 1972–73 to 1999–00*. Available at (http://www.freedomhouse.org/ratings/index.htm). Accessed 23 January 2006.

Gladden, Kathleen. 1993. Women in the Global Economy: A Case Study of Garment Workers in Colombia. Michigan State University, Women and International Development Program Working Paper 236.

Goetz, Anne Marie, ed. 1997. *Getting Institutions Right for Women in Development*. New York: St. Martin's Press.

Gould, William. 2001. *Interpreting the Intercept in the Fixed-Effects Model*. StataCorp. Available at (http://www.stata.com/support/faqs/stat/xtreg2.html);. Accessed 23 January 2006.

Greider, William. 1997. *One World, Ready or Not: The Manic Logic of Global Capitalism*. New York: Simon & Schuster.

Hafner-Burton, Emilie, and Mark A. Pollack. 2002. Mainstreaming Gender in Global Governance. *European Journal of International Relations* 8 (3):339–73.

Hausman, Jerry. 1978. Specification Tests in Econometrics. *Econometrica* 46 (6):1251–71.

Heston, Alan, Robert Summers, and Bettina Aten. 2002. *Penn World Table Version 6.1*. Philadelphia: Center for International Comparisons at the University of Pennsylvania.

Higer, Amy J. 1999. International Women's Activism and the 1994 Cairo Population Conference. In *Gender Politics in Global Governance*, edited by Mary K. Meyer and Elisabeth Prügl, 122–41. Lanham, Md.: Rowman & Littlefield.

High-Pippert, Angela, and John Comer. 1998. Female Empowerment: The Influence of Women Representing Women. *Women & Politics* 19 (4):51–66.

Hoskyns, Catherine. 1996. *Integrating Gender*. London: Verso.

Inglehart, Ronald. 1990. *Culture Shift in Advanced Industrial Society*. Princeton, N.J.: Princeton University Press.

——. 1997. *Modernization and Postmodernization: Cultural, Economic, and Political Change in 43 Societies*. Princeton, N.J.: Princeton University Press.

Inglehart, Ronald, and Pippa Norris. 2003. *Rising Tide: Gender Equality and Cultural Change Around the World*. Cambridge: Cambridge University Press.

International-Parliamentary Union. 1995. *Women in Parliaments 1945–1995: A World Statistical Survey*. Geneva: International-Parliamentary Union.

——. 2003. *Women in National Parliaments*. Available at (http://www.ipu.org/wmn-e/world.htm). Accessed 23 January 2006.

Joachim, Jutta. 2003. Framing Issues and Seizing Opportunities: The UN, NGOs, and Women's Rights. *International Studies Quarterly* 47 (2):247–74.

Johnston, Jack, and John DiNardo. 1997. *Econometric Methods*. New York: McGraw Hill.

Jupille, Joseph, and James Caporaso. 2001. The Europeanization of Gender Equality Policy and Domestic Structural Change. In *Transforming Europe: Europeanization and Domestic Change*, edited by Maria Green Cowles, James Caporaso, and Thomas Risse, 21–43. Ithaca, N.Y.: Cornell University Press.

Kardam, Nuket. 1991. *Bringing Women In: Women's Issues in International Development*. Boulder, Colo.: Lynne Rienner.

Keck, Margaret E., and Kathryn Sikkink. 1998. *Activists Beyond Borders: Advocacy Networks in International Politics*. Ithaca, N.Y.: Cornell University Press.

Koh, Harold Hongju. 1998. The 1998 Frankel Lecture: Bringing International Law Home. *Houston Law Review* 35 (3):623–81.

Lakeman, Enid. 1994. Comparing Political Opportunities in Great Britain and Ireland. In *Electoral Systems in Comparative Perspective*, edited by Wilma Rule and Joseph Zimmerman, 45–53. Westport, Conn.: Greenwood Press.

Levidow, Les. 1996. Women Who Make the Chips. In *Women, Work, and Gender Relations in Developing Countries: A Global Perspective*, edited by Parvin Ghorayshi and Claire Belanger, 43–56. Westport, Conn.: Greenwood.

Lorentzen, Lois Ann, and Jennifer Turpin. 1996. Introduction: The Gendered New World Order. *In The Gendered New World Order: Militarism, Development, and the Environment*, edited by Lois Ann Lorentzen and Jennifer Turpin, 1–12. New York: Routledge.

Mason, Karen Oppenheim. 1986. The Status of Women: Conceptual and Methodological Issues in Demographic Studies. *Sociological Forum* 1 (2):284–300.

Matland, Richard E. 1993. Institutional Variables Affecting Female Representation in National Legislatures: The Case of Norway. *Journal of Politics* 55 (3):737–755.

Matland, Richard E., and Donley T. Studlar. 1996. The Contagion of Women Candidates in Single-Member District and Proportional Representation Systems: Canada and Norway. *Journal of Politics* 58 (3):707–33.

Meier, Kenneth J., Warren S. Eller, Robert D. Wrinkle, and J. L. Polinard. 2001. Zen and the Art of Policy Analysis: A Response to Nielsen and Wolf. *Journal of Politics* 63 (2):616–29.

Meyer, Mary K. 1999. Negotiating International Norms: The Inter-American Commission of Women and the Convention on Violence Against Women. In *Gender Politics in Global Governance*, edited by Mary K. Meyer and Elisabeth Prügl, 58-71. Lanham, Md.: Rowman & Littlefield.

Mies, Maria. 1996. *Women, Food, and Global Trade*. Bielefeld, Germany: Institut für Theorie and Praxis der Subsistenz.

Miller, Alice M. 1999. Realizing Women's Human Rights: Nongovernmental Organizations and the United Nations Treaty Bodies. In *Gender Politics in Global Governance*, edited by Mary K. Meyer and Elisabeth Prügl, 161–76. Lanham, Md.: Rowman & Littlefield.

Mills, Mary Beth. 1999. *Thai Women in the Global Labor Force*. New Brunswick, N.J.: Rutgers University Press.

Milner, Helen V., and Robert O. Keohane. 1996. Internationalization and Domestic Politics: An Introduction. In *Internationalization and Domestic Politics*, edited by Robert O. Keohane and Helen V. Milner, 3–24. Cambridge: Cambridge University Press.

Moghadam, Valentine. 1999. Gender and Globalization: Female Labor and Women's Mobilization. *Journal of World Systems Research* 5 (2):367–88.

Murphy, Josette. 1997. *Mainstreaming Gender in World Bank Lending*. Washington, D.C.: World Bank.

Naples, Nancy, and Manisha Desai, eds. 2002. *Women's Activism and Globalization*. New York: Routledge.

Nelson, Barbara, and Najma Chowdhury. 1994. *Women and Politics Worldwide*. New Haven: Yale University Press.

Norris, Pippa. 1993. Conclusions. In *Gender and Party Politics*, edited by Joni Lovenduski and Pippa Norris, 309–30. London: Sage Publications.

——. 1996. Legislative Recruitment. In *Comparing Democracies: Elections and Voting in Global Perspectives*, edited by Lawrence LeDuc, Richard Niemi, and Pippa Norris, 184-216. London: Sage Publications.

Oakes, A., and Elizabeth Almquist. 1993. Women in National Legislatures: A Cross-National Test of Macrostructural Gender Theories. *Population Research and Policy Review* 12 (1):71–81.

O'Brien, Joanne, and Martin Palmer. 1993. *The State of Religion Atlas*. New York: Touchstone.

O'Regan, Valerie. 2000. *Gender Matters: Female Policymakers' Influence in Industrialized Nations*. Westport, Conn.: Praeger.

Paxton, Pamela. 1997. Women in National Legislatures: A Cross-National Analysis. *Social Science Research* 26 (4):442–64.

Perl, Paul. 2006. Are Former Catholic Women Over-Represented Among Protestant Clergy? *Sociology of Religion* 66 (4):359–80.

Pettman, Jan Jindy. 1996. *Worlding Women: A Feminist International Politics*. New York: Routledge.

Pollack, Mark A., and Emilie Hafner-Burton. 2000. Mainstreaming Gender in the European Union. *Journal of European Public Policy* 7 (3):432–56.

Prakash, Aseem, and Jeffrey A. Hart. 1999. Globalization and Governance: An Introduction. In *Globalization and Governance*, edited by Aseem Prakash and Jeffrey A. Hart, 1–24. London: Routledge.

Prügl, Elisabeth, and Mary K. Meyer. 1999. Gender Politics in Global Governance. In *Gender Politics in Global Governance*, edited by Mary K. Meyer and Elisabeth Prügl, 3–16. Lanham, Md.: Rowman & Littlefield.

Ram, Rati. 1998. Forty Years of the Life Span Revolution: An Exploration of the Roles of "Convergence," Income and Policy. *Economic Development and Cultural Change* 46 (4):849–57.

Reynolds, Andrew. 1999. Women in the Legislatures and Executives of the World: Knocking at the Highest Glass Ceiling. *World Politics* 51 (4):547–72.

Rodgers, G. B. 1979. Income and Inequality as Determinants of Mortality: An International Cross-Section Analysis. *Population Studies* 33 (2):343–51.

Rodrik, Dani. 1997. *Has Globalization Gone Too Far?* Washington, D.C.: Institute for International Economics.

Rojas, Roberto. 2001. Los Derechos Humanos en la Politica Exterior Costarricense. *Revista Costarricense de Politica Exterior* 1 (1):5–14.

Rule, Wilma. 1987. Electoral Systems, Contextual Factors, and Women's Opportunity for Election to Parliament in Twenty-Three Democracies. *Western Political Quarterly* 40 (3):477–98.

Rule, Wilma, and Joseph Zimmerman. 1994. *Electoral Systems in Comparative Perspective: Their Impact on Women and Minorities*. Westport, Conn.: Greenwood Press.

Sandholtz, Wayne, and Mark M. Gray. 2003. International Integration and National Corruption. *International Organization* 57 (4):761–800.

Sassen, Saskia. 1996. Toward a Feminist Analytics of the Global Economy. *Indiana Journal of Global Legal Studies* 4 (1):7–42.

——. 1998. *Globalization and Its Discontents*. New York: New Press.

Schwartz, Nancy L. 1988. *The Blue Guitar: Political Representation and Community*. Chicago: University of Chicago Press.

Semyonov, Moshe. 1980. The Social Context of Women's Labor Force Participation: A Comparative Analysis. *American Journal of Sociology* 86 (3):534–50.

Sforza, Michele. 1999. *Globalization, the Multilateral Agreement on Investment, and the Increasing Economic Marginalization of Women*. Washington, D.C.: Preamble Center.

Simmons, Beth. 2004. International Law Compliance and Human Rights. Paper presented at the 45th Annual Meeting of the International Studies Association, Montreal, Canada, March.

Singh, Ajit, and Ann Zammit. 2000. International Capital Flows: Identifying the Gender Dimension. *World Development* 28 (7):1249–68.

Smith, David A., Dorothy J. Solinger, and Steven C. Topik. 1999. Introduction. In *States and Sovereignty in the Global Economy*, edited by David A. Smith, Dorothy J. Solinger, and Steven C. Topik, 1–19. London: Routledge.

Standing, Guy. 1989. Global Feminization Through Flexible Labor. *World Development* 17 (7): 1077–95.

Stienstra, Deborah. 2000. Dancing Resistance from Rio to Beijing: Transnational Women's Organizing and UN Conferences 1992–6. In *Gender and Global Restructuring*, edited by Marianne Marchand and Anne Sisson Runyan, 209–24. London: Routledge.

Stimson, James. 1985. Regression in Space and Time: A Statistical Essay. *American Journal of Political Science* 29 (4):914–947.

Stromquist, Nelly P. 1990. Women and Illiteracy: The Interplay of Gender Subordination and Poverty. *Comparative Education Review* 34 (1):95–111.

Sweeney, Shawna E. 2004. Global Transformations, National Institutions, and Women's Rights: A Cross-National Comparative Analysis. Paper presented at the 100th Annual Meeting of the

American Political Science Association, Chicago, September.

Tinker, Irene. 1999. Nongovernmental Organizations: An Alternative Power Base for Women? In *Gender Politics in Global Governance*, edited by Mary K. Meyer and Elisabeth Prügl, 88–104. Lanham, Md.: Rowman & Littlefield.

True, Jacqui, and Michael Mintrom. 2001. Transnational Networks and Policy Diffusion: The Case of Gender Mainstreaming. *International Studies Quarterly* 45 (1):27–57.

UNAIDS: Joint United Nations Programme on HIV/AIDS. 2003. UNAIDS. Available at <http:// www.unaids.org>. Accessed 23 January 2006.

United Nations. 1988. *Compendium of International Conventions Concerning the Status of Women*. Doc. No. ST/CSDHA/3. New York: United Nations.

United Nations. 1999. *United Nations Women's Indicators and Statistics Database*. Wistat Version-4, CD-ROM. New York: UN.

——. 2003. *Convention on the Elimination of All Forms of Discrimination against Women: States Parties*. Available at <http://www.un.org/womenwatch/daw/cedaw/states.htm>. Accessed 23 January 2006.

——. 2005. *Growth in United Nations Membership, 1945–2005*. Available at <http://www.un.org/overview/growth.htm>. Accessed 23 January 2006.

United Nations Conference on Trade and Development. 2005. Foreign Direct Investment Database. Available at (http://www.unctad.org). Accessed 23 January 2006.

United Nations Development Programme. 1995. *Human Development Report 1995*. New York: Oxford University Press.

——. 1999. *Human Development Report 1999*. New York: Oxford University Press.

United Nations Division for the Advancement of Women. 2005. Convention on the Elimination of All Forms of Discrimination against Women. Available at (http://www.un.org/womenwatch/daw/ccdaw/). Accessed 23 January 2006.

United Nations Programme on HIV/AIDS. 1998. The United Nations on the Impact of HAIV/AIDS on Adult Mortality in Sub-Saharan Africa. *Population and Development Review* 24 (3):655–58.

Wade, Robert. 1996. Globalization and Its Limits: Reports of the Death of the National Economy are Greatly Exaggerated. In *National Diversity and Global Capitalism*, edited by Suzanne Berger and Ronald Dore, 60–88. Ithaca, N.Y.: Cornell University Press.

Ward, Kathryn, ed. 1990. *Women Workers and Global Restructuring*. Ithaca, N.Y.: ILR Press.

Waylen, Georgina. 1996. *Gender in Third World Politics*. Boulder, Colo.: Lynne Rienner.

Weiss, Anita. 2003. Interpreting Islam and Women's Rights. *International Sociology* 18 (3):581–600.

Weldon, S. Laurel. 2002. *Protest, Policy, and the Problem of Violence Against Women: A Cross National Comparison*. Pittsburgh: University of Pittsburgh Press.

Wendt, Alexander. 1999. *Social Theory of International Politics*. Cambridge: Cambridge University Press.

West, Lois A. 1999. The United Nations Women's Conferences and Feminist Politics. In *Gender Politics in Global Governance*, edited by Mary K. Meyer and Elisabeth Prügl, 177–93. Lanham, Md.: Rowman & Littlefield.

Wilensky, Harold. 1968. Women's Work: Economic Growth, Ideology and Social Structure. *Industrial Relations* 7:235–52.

Wilson, Chris. 2001. On the Scale of Global DemographicConvergence1950-2000.*Population and Development Review* 27 (1):155–71.

World Bank. 2000. *The World Development Indicators 2000*. Washington, D.C.: World Bank.

——. 2006. *Member Countries*. Available at <http://web.worldbank.org/WBSITE/EXTERNAL/ EXTABOUTUS/0,,contentMDK:50004946~menuPK:271153~pagePK:34542~piPK:36600~theSitePK:29708,00.html). Accessed 23 January 2006.

Wright, Shelley. 1995. Women and the Global Economic Order: A Feminist Perspective. *American University Journal of International Law and Policy* 10 (2):861–87.

Youngs, Gillian. 2000. Embodied Political Economy or and Escape from Disembodied Knowledge. In *Political Economy, Power and the Body: Global Perspectives*, edited by Gillian Youngs, 11–30. Houndmills, England: Macmillan Press.

Need versus Greed

JEFFREY D. SACHS

Professor Sachs is a world-renowned advisor on sustainable development to governments around the world. From 2002 to 2006 he was Director of the United Nations Millennium Project. His extensive written work freely crosses the line between the academic and policy-making realms. According to Sachs, how has economic growth in developing countries been a mixed blessing? Without what Sachs calls "greed," how can we meet the "need" of people around the world? Can you identify a specific theoretical perspective in Sachs' essay? What evidence supports your view?

India's great moral leader Mohandas Gandhi famously said that there is enough on Earth for everybody's need, but not enough for everybody's greed. Today, Gandhi's insight is being put to the test as never before.

The world is hitting global limits in its use of resources. We are feeling the shocks each day in catastrophic floods, droughts, and storms – and in the resulting surge in prices in the marketplace. Our fate now depends on whether we cooperate or fall victim to self-defeating greed.

The limits to the global economy are new, resulting from the unprecedented size of the world's population and the unprecedented spread of economic growth to nearly the entire world. There are now seven billion people on the planet, compared to just three billion a half-century ago. Today, average per capita income is $10,000, with the rich world averaging around $40,000 and the developing world around $4,000. That means that the world economy is now producing around $70 trillion in total annual output, compared to around $10 trillion in 1960.

China's economy is growing at around 10 per cent annually. India's is growing at nearly the same rate. Africa, long the world's slowest-growing region, is now averaging roughly 5 per cent annual GDP growth. Overall, the developing countries are growing at around seven per cent per year, and the developed economies at around 2 per cent, yielding a global average of around 4.5 per cent.

Greed for Growth

This is very good news in many ways. Rapid economic growth in developing countries is helping to alleviate poverty. In China, for example, extreme poverty has been cut from well over half of the population 30 years ago to around 10 per cent or less today.

Yet there is another side to the global growth story that we must understand clearly. With the world economy growing at 4-5 per cent per year, it will be on a path to double in size in less than 20 years. Today's $70 trillion world economy will be at $140 trillion before 2030, and $280 trillion before 2050 if we extrapolate from today's growth rate.

Jeffrey D. Sachs, "Need versus Greed" March 4, 2011. Al Jazeera English. http://english.aljazeera.net/indepth/opinion/2011/03/20113313330192433.html.

Our planet will not physically support this exponential economic growth if we let greed take the upper hand. Even today, the weight of the world economy is already crushing nature, rapidly depleting the supplies of fossil-fuel energy resources that nature created over millions of years, while the resulting climate change has led to massive instabilities in terms of rainfall, temperature, and extreme storms.

We see these pressures every day in the marketplace. Oil prices have surged to more than $100 per barrel, as China, India, and other oil-importing countries join the United States in a massive scramble to buy up supplies, especially from the Middle East. Food prices, too, are at historical highs, contributing to poverty and political unrest.

Environmental Stress

On the one hand, there are more mouths to feed, and with greater purchasing power on average. On the other hand, heat waves, droughts, floods, and other disasters induced by climate change are destroying crops and reducing the supplies of grains on world markets. In recent months, massive droughts have struck the grain-producing regions of Russia and Ukraine, and enormous floods have hit Brazil and Australia; now, another drought is menacing northern China's grain belt.

There is something else hidden from view that is very dangerous. In many populous parts of the world, including the grain-growing regions of northern India, northern China, and the American Midwest, farmers are tapping into groundwater to irrigate their crops.

The great aquifers that supply water for irrigation are being depleted. In some places in India, the water table has been falling by several meters annually in recent years. Some deep wells are approaching the point of exhaustion, with salinity set to rise as ocean water infiltrates the aquifer.

A calamity is inevitable unless we change. And here is where Gandhi comes in. If our societies are run according to the greed principle, with the rich doing everything to get richer, the growing resource crisis will lead to a widening divide between the rich and the poor – and quite possibly to an increasingly violent struggle for survival.

Class Conflict

The rich will try to use their power to commandeer more land, more water, and more energy for themselves, and many will support violent means to do so, if necessary. The US has already followed a strategy of militarisation in the Middle East in the naïve hope that such an approach can ensure secure energy supplies. Now competition for those supplies is intensifying, as China, India, and others bid for the same (depleting) resources.

An analogous power grab is being attempted in Africa. The rise in food prices is leading to a land grab, as powerful politicians sell foreign investors massive tracts of farmland, brushing aside the traditional land rights of poor smallholders. Foreign investors hope to use large mechanised farms to produce output for export, leaving little or nothing for the local populations.

Everywhere in the leading countries – the US, the United Kingdom, China, India, and elsewhere – the rich have enjoyed soaring incomes and growing political power. The US economy has been taken over by billionaires, the oil industry, and other key sectors. The same trends threaten the emerging economies, where wealth and corruption are on the rise.

If greed dominates, the engine of economic growth will deplete our resources, push the poor aside, and drive us into a deep social, political, and economic crisis. The alternative is a path of political and social cooperation, both within countries and internationally. There will be enough resources and prosperity to go around if we convert our economies to renewable energy sources, sustainable agricultural practices, and reasonable taxation of the rich. This is the path to shared prosperity through improved technologies, political fairness, and ethical awareness.

Useful Internet Resources

Foundation for Sustainable Development, www.fsdinternational.org: an NGO that promotes community development projects
Gapminder, www.gapminder.org
International Monetary Fund, www.imf.org
Oxfam International, www.oxfam.org: perhaps the most famous antipoverty NGO, with projects and programs globally
Public Citizen NAFTA page, http : //www, citizen, org/trade/nafta/
Organization for Economic Cooperation and Development, http://www.oecd.org
The Group of Twenty, http://www.g20.org/
United Nations Conference on Trade and Development, www.unctad.org
World Bank, www.worldbank.org
World Food Program, www.wfp.org: a UN agency
World Trade Organization, www.wto.org

Discussion Questions and Activities

1 Analyze the ways in which development affects global civil society.
2. Research the style of European colonial rule for states in the developing world. To what extent does the current level of economie development, poverty, and hunger correlate with style of colonial rule? Are some developing states better off than others?
3. What are the pros and cons of the global food regime established since the Second World War?
4. Account for the increasing gap between rich and poor states and people after 50 years of official development policies.
5. Use a gendered lens to explore the nature of global poverty.
6. Is the recent World Bank focus on poverty reduction evidence of a change of direction by the Bank?

GLOBAL ENVIRONMENT: READING SELECTIONS

The Tragedy of the Commons

GARRETT HARDIN

This extract from Garrett Hardin's essay offers the reader a stark question: what will policy-makers do to address the apparent inability to provide enough food for the world's increasing population? Although it originally appeared in the journal *Science,* in many ways it is a work of historical interpretation and political science. Into which of the theory perspectives would you locate Hardin's essay? Why? Have advances in agronomy and other sciences reduced the threat of global starvation since 1968, when Hardin wrote this essay? If, as a Constructivist might suggest, instead of "tragedy" Hardin had used "dilemma," would the policy options seem less bleak?

We can make little progress in working toward optimum population size until we explicitly exorcize the spirit of Adam Smith in the field of practical demography. In economic affairs, *The Wealth of Nations* (1776) popularized the "invisible hand," the idea that an individual who "intends only his own gain," is, as it were, "led by an invisible hand to promote…the public interest" (*1*). Adam Smith did not assert that this was invariably true, and perhaps neither did any of his followers. But he contributed to a dominant tendency of thought that has ever since interfered with positive action based on rational analysis, namely, the tendency to assume that decisions reached individually will, in fact, be the best decisions for an entire society. If this assumption is correct it justifies the continuance of our present policy of laissez-faire in reproduction. If it is correct we can assume that men will control their individual fecundity so as to produce the optimum population. If the assumption is not correct, we need to reexamine our individual freedoms to see which ones are defensible.

Tragedy of Freedom in a Commons

The rebuttal to the invisible hand in population control is to be found in a scenario first sketched in a little-known pamphlet (*2*) in 1833 by a mathematical amateur named William Forster Lloyd (1794–1852). We may well call it "the tragedy of the commons," using the word "tragedy" as the philosopher Whitehead used it (*3*): "The essence of dramatic tragedy is not unhappiness. It resides in the solemnity of the remorseless working of things." He then goes on to say, "This inevitableness of destiny can only be illustrated in terms of human life by incidents which in fact involve unhappiness. For it is only by them that the futility of escape can be made evident in the drama."

The tragedy of the commons develops in this way. Picture a pasture open to all. It is to be expected that each herdsman will try to keep as many cattle as possible on the commons. Such an arrangement may work reasonably satisfactorily for centuries because tribal wars, poaching, and disease keep the

Excerpted from Garrett Hardin's, "The Tragedy of the Commons," *Science*, Vol. 162, No. 3859 (13 Dec. 1968); pages 1244–1248. Reproduced with permission.

numbers of both man and beast well below the carrying capacity of the land. Finally, however, comes the day of reckoning, that is, the day when the long-desired goal of social stability becomes a reality. At this point, the inherent logic of the commons remorselessly generates tragedy.

As a rational being, each herdsman seeks to maximize his gain. Explicitly or implicitly, more or less consciously, he asks, "What is the utility *to me* of adding one more animal to my herd?" This utility has one negative and one positive component.

1) The positive component is a function of the increment of one animal. Since the herdsman receives all the proceeds from the sale of the additional animal, the positive utility is nearly +1.

2) The negative component is a function of the additional overgrazing created by one more animal. Since, however, the effects of overgrazing are shared by all the herdsmen, the negative utility for any particular decision-making herdsman is only a fraction of −1.

Adding together the component partial utilities, the rational herdsman concludes that the only sensible course for him to pursue is to add another animal to his herd. And another; and another.... But this is the conclusion reached by each and every rational herdsman sharing a commons. Therein is the tragedy. Each man is locked into a system that compels him to increase his herd without limit—in a world that is limited. Ruin is the destination toward which all men rush, each pursuing his own best interest in a society that believes in the freedom of the commons. Freedom in a commons brings ruin to all.

Some would say that this is a platitude. Would that it were! In a sense, it was learned thousands of years ago, but natural selection favors the forces of psychological denial (*4*). The individual benefits as an individual from his ability to deny the truth even though society as a whole, of which he is a part, suffers. Education can counteract the natural tendency to do the wrong thing, but the inexorable succession of generations requires that the basis for this knowledge be constantly refreshed.

Pollution

In a reverse way, the tragedy of the commons reappears in problems of pollution. Here it is not a question of taking something out of the commons, but of putting something in—sewage, or chemical, radioactive, and heat wastes into water; noxious and dangerous fumes into the air; and distracting and unpleasant advertising signs into the line of sight. The calculations of utility are much the same as before. The rational man finds that his share of the cost of the wastes he discharges into the commons is less than the cost of purifying his wastes before releasing them. Since this is true for everyone, we are locked into a system of "fouling our own nest," so long as we behave only as independent, rational, free-enterprisers.

The tragedy of the commons as a food basket is averted by private property, or something formally like it. But the air and waters surrounding us cannot readily be fenced, and so the tragedy of the commons as a cesspool must be prevented by different means, by coercive laws or taxing devices that make it cheaper for the polluter to treat his pollutants than to discharge them untreated. We have not progressed as far with the solution of this problem as we have with the first. Indeed, our particular concept of private property, which deters us from exhausting the positive resources of the earth, favors pollution. The owner of a factory on the bank of a stream—whose property extends to the middle of the stream—often has difficulty seeing why it is not his natural right to muddy the waters flowing past his door. The law, always behind the times, requires elaborate stitching and fitting to adapt it to this newly perceived aspect of the commons.

The pollution problem is a consequence of population. It did not much matter how a lonely American frontiersman disposed of his waste. "Flowing water purifies itself every 10 miles," my grandfather used to say, and the myth was near enough to the truth when he was a boy, for there were not too many people. But as population became denser, the natural chemical and biological recycling processes became overloaded, calling for a redefinition of property rights.

How To Legislate Temperance?

Analysis of the pollution problem as a function of population density uncovers a not generally recognized principle of morality, namely: *the morality of an act is a function of the state of the system at the time it is performed* (5). Using the commons as a cesspool does not harm the general public under frontier conditions, because there is no public; the same behavior in a metropolis is unbearable. A hundred and fifty years ago a plainsman could kill an American bison, cut out only the tongue for his dinner, and discard the rest of the animal. He was not in any important sense being wasteful. Today, with only a few thousand bison left, we would be appalled at such behavior.

In passing, it is worth noting that the morality of an act cannot be determined from a photograph. One does not know whether a man killing an elephant or setting fire to the grassland is harming others until one knows the total system in which his act appears. "One picture is worth a thousand words," said an ancient Chinese; but it may take 10,000 words to validate it. It is as tempting to ecologists as it is to reformers in general to try to persuade others by way of the photographic shortcut. But the essense of an argument cannot be photographed: it must be presented rationally—in words.

That morality is system-sensitive escaped the attention of most codifiers of ethics in the past. "Thou shalt not..." is the form of traditional ethical directives which make no allowance for particular circumstances. The laws of our society follow the pattern of ancient ethics, and therefore are poorly suited to governing a complex, crowded, changeable world. Our epicyclic solution is to augment statutory law with administrative law. Since it is practically impossible to spell out all the conditions under which it is safe to burn trash in the back yard or to run an automobile without smog-control, by law we delegate the details to bureaus. The result is administrative law, which is rightly feared for an ancient reason—*Quis custodiet ipsos custodes?*—"Who shall watch the watchers themselves?" John Adams said that we must have "a government of laws and not men." Bureau administrators, trying to evaluate the morality of acts in the total system, are singularly liable to corruption, producing a government by men, not laws.

Prohibition is easy to legislate (though not necessarily to enforce); but how do we legislate temperance? Experience indicates that it can be accomplished best through the mediation of administrative law. We limit possibilities unnecessarily if we suppose that the sentiment of *Quis custodiet* denies us the use of administrative law. We should rather retain the phrase as a perpetual reminder of fearful dangers we cannot avoid. The great challenge facing us now is to invent the corrective feedbacks that are needed to keep custodians honest. We must find ways to legitimate the needed authority of both the custodians and the corrective feedbacks.

Freedom To Breed Is Intolerable

The tragedy of the commons is involved in population problems in another way. In a world governed solely by the principle of "dog eat dog"—if indeed there ever was such a world—how many children a family had would not be a matter of public concern. Parents who bred too exuberantly would leave fewer descendants, not more, because they would be unable to care adequately for their children. David Lack and others have found that such a negative feedback demonstrably controls the fecundity of birds (6). But men are not birds, and have not acted like them for millenniums, at least.

If each human family were dependent only on its own resources; *if* the children of improvident parents starved to death; *if*, thus, overbreeding brought its own "punishment" to the germ line—*then* there would be no public interest in controlling the breeding of families. But our society is deeply committed to the welfare state (7), and hence is confronted with another aspect of the tragedy of the commons.

In a welfare state, how shall we deal with the family, the religion, the race, or the class (or indeed any distinguishable and cohesive group) that adopts overbreeding as a policy to secure its own aggrandizement (8)? To couple the concept of freedom to breed with the belief that everyone born has an equal right to the commons is to lock the world into a tragic course of action.

Conscience Is Self-Eliminating

It is a mistake to think that we can control the breeding of mankind in the long run by an appeal to conscience. Charles Galton Darwin made this point when he spoke on the centennial of the publication of his grandfather's great book. The argument is straightforward and Darwinian.

People vary. Confronted with appeals to limit breeding, some people will undoubtedly respond to the plea more than others. Those who have more children will produce a larger fraction of the next generation than those with more susceptible consciences. The difference will be accentuated, generation by generation.

In C. G. Darwin's words: "It may well be that it would take hundreds of generations for the progenitive instinct to develop in this way, but if it should do so, nature would have taken her revenge, and the variety *Homo contracipiens* would become extinct and would be replaced by the variety *Homo progenitivus*" (9).

The argument assumes that conscience or the desire for children (no matter which) is hereditary—but hereditary only in the most general formal sense. The result will be the same whether the attitude is transmitted through germ cells, or exosomatically, to use A. J. Lotka's term. (If one denies the latter possibility as well as the former, then what's the point of education?) The argument has here been stated in the context of the population problem, but it applies equally well to any instance in which society appeals to an individual exploiting a commons to restrain himself for the general good—by means of his conscience. To make such an appeal is to set up a selective system that works toward the elimination of conscience from the race.

Pathogenic Effects of Conscience

The long-term disadvantage of an appeal to conscience should be enough to condemn it; but has serious short-term disadvantages as well. If we ask a man who is exploiting a commons to desist "in the name of conscience," what are we saying to him? What does he hear?—not only at the moment but also in the wee small hours of the night when, half asleep, he remembers not merely the words we used but also the nonverbal communication cues we gave him unawares? Sooner or later, consciously or subconsciously, he senses that he has received two communications, and that they are contradictory: (i) (intended communication) "If you don't do as we ask, we will openly condemn you for not acting like a responsible citizen"; (ii) (the unintended communication) "If you *do* behave as we ask, we will secretly condemn you for a simpleton who can be shamed into standing aside while the rest of us exploit the commons."

Mutual Coercion Mutually Agreed upon

The social arrangements that produce responsibility are arrangements that create coercion, of some sort. Consider bank-robbing. The man who takes money from a bank acts as if the bank were a commons. How do we prevent such action? Certainly not by trying to control his behavior solely by a verbal appeal to his sense of responsibility. Rather than rely on propaganda we follow Frankel's lead and insist that a bank is not a commons; we seek the definite social arrangements that will keep it from becoming a commons. That we thereby infringe on the freedom of would-be robbers we neither deny nor regret.

The morality of bank-robbing is particularly easy to understand because we accept complete prohibition of this activity. We are willing to say "Thou shalt not rob banks," without providing for exceptions. But temperance also can be created by coercion. Taxing is a good coercive device. To keep downtown shoppers temperate in their use of parking space we introduce parking meters for short periods, and traffic fines for longer ones. We need not actually forbid a citizen to park as long as he wants to; we need merely make it increasingly expensive for him to do so. Not prohibition, but carefully biased options are what we offer him. A Madison Avenue man might call this persuasion; I prefer the greater candor of the word coercion.

To many, the word coercion implies arbitrary decisions of distant and irresponsible bureaucrats; but this is not a necessary part of its meaning. The only kind of coercion I recommend is mutual coercion, mutually agreed upon by the majority of the people affected.

To say that we mutually agree to coercion is not to say that we are required to enjoy it, or even to pretend we enjoy it. Who enjoys taxes? We all grumble about them. But we accept compulsory taxes because we recognize that voluntary taxes would favor the conscienceless. We institute and (grumblingly) support taxes and other coercive devices to escape the horror of the commons.

An alternative to the commons need not be perfectly just to be preferable. With real estate and other material goods, the alternative we have chosen is the institution of private property coupled with legal inheritance. Is this system perfectly just? As a genetically trained biologist I deny that it is. It seems to me that, if there are to be differences in individual inheritance, legal possession should be perfectly correlated with biological inheritance—that those who are biologically more fit to be the custodians of property and power should legally inherit more. But genetic recombination continually makes a mockery of the doctrine of "like father, like son" implicit in our laws of legal inheritance. An idiot can inherit millions, and a trust fund can keep his estate intact. We must admit that our legal system of private property plus inheritance is unjust—but we put up with it because we are not convinced, at the moment, that anyone has invented a better system. The alternative of the commons is too horrifying to contemplate. Injustice is preferable to total ruin.

Recognition of Necessity

Perhaps the simplest summary of this analysis of man's population problems is this: the commons, if justifiable at all, is justifiable only under conditions of low-population density. As the human population has increased, the commons has had to be abandoned in one aspect after another.

First we abandoned the commons in food gathering, enclosing farm land and restricting pastures and hunting and fishing areas. These restrictions are still not complete throughout the world.

Somewhat later we saw that the commons as a place for waste disposal would also have to be abandoned. Restrictions on the disposal of domestic sewage are widely accepted in the Western world; we are still struggling to close the commons to pollution by automobiles, factories, insecticide sprayers, fertilizing operations, and atomic energy installations.

Every new enclosure of the commons involves the infringement of somebody's personal liberty. Infringements made in the distant past are accepted because no contemporary complains of a loss. It is the newly proposed infringements that we vigorously oppose; cries of "rights" and "freedom" fill the air. But what does "freedom" mean? When men mutually agreed to pass laws against robbing, mankind became more free, not less so. Individuals locked into the logic of the commons are free only to bring on universal ruin once they see the necessity of mutual coercion, they become free to pursue other goals. I believe it was Hegel who said, "Freedom is the recognition of necessity."

The most important aspect of necessity that we must now recognize, is the necessity of abandoning the commons in breeding. No technical solution can rescue us from the misery of overpopulation. Freedom to breed will bring ruin to all. At the moment, to avoid hard decisions many of us are tempted to propagandize for conscience and responsible parenthood. The temptation must be resisted, because an appeal to independently acting consciences selects for the disappearance of all conscience in the long run, and an increase in anxiety in the short.

The only way we can preserve and nurture other and more precious freedoms is by relinquishing the freedom to breed, and that very soon. "Freedom is the recognition of necessity"—and it is the role of education to reveal to all the necessity of abandoning the freedom to breed. Only so, can we put an end to this aspect of the tragedy of the commons.

References

1. A. Smith, *The Wealth of Nations* (Modern Library, New York, 1937), p. 423.
2. W. F. Lloyd, *Two Lectures on the Checks to Population* (Oxford Univ. Press, Oxford, England, 1833), reprinted (in part) in Population, Evolution, and Birth Control, G. Hardin, Ed. (Freeman, San Francisco, 1964), p. 37.
3. A. N. Whitehead, *Science and the Modern World* (Mentor, New York, 1948), p. 17.
4. G. Hardin, Ed. *Population, Evolution, and Birth Control* (Freeman, San Francisco, 1964), p. 56.
5. J. Fletcher, *Situation Ethics* (Westminster, Philadelphia, 1966).
6. D. Lack, *The Natural Regulation of Animal Numbers* (Clarendon Press, Oxford, 1954).
7. H. Girvetz, *From Wealth to Welfare* (Stanford Univ. Press, Stanford, Calif., 1950).
8. G. Hardin, *Perspec. Biol. Med.* **6**, 366 (1963).
9. S. Tax, Ed., *Evolution after Darwin* (Univ. of Chicago Press, Chicago, 1960), vol. 2, p. 469.

Preparing for an Uncertain Global Food Supply: A New Food Assistance Convention

C. STUART CLARK

Twin pressures—global population growth and the effects of climate change—present immediate challenges to the world's food supply. The current global food regime that Clark describes is state-centric and depends upon food-surplus states sharing their blessings with food-deficit states. How might a Realist, Liberal, or Marxist scholar explain the shortcomings of the Food Aid Convention? What are the ways in which ecological factors, market forces, and state sovereignty help to explain the rules of the Food Aid Convention?

Over the past decade, a growing consensus has emerged that the global human food supply is becoming increasingly vulnerable to serious disruptions. These disruptions are likely to be regional in nature but may also have global implications, as they did in the early months of 2008. Food system disruptions can have profoundly destabilizing effects on the affected countries and beyond. There is therefore a strong rationale for designing a global food "safety net" that can bridge the disruption of these food supplies.

The Food Aid Convention (FAC) is the only treaty that provides a predictable multilateral mechanism for making food transfers available in response to structural food deficits and food crises. The current version of the treaty was renegotiated almost a decade ago and in many key aspects has been rendered less and less suited to contemporary

C. Stuart Clark, Preparing for an Uncertain Global Food Supply, in *The Global Food Crisis: Governance Challenges and Opportunities*, by Jennifer Clapp and Marc J. Cohen. Wilfrid Laurier University Press, 2009. Pp 95–101.

realities. Although its reform has been stalled by agricultural trade negotiations at the World Trade Organization (WTO), there is a growing consensus among the current member states that now is the time to seek significant changes, through reform of the Rules of Procedure and/or renegotiation of the convention itself. Either option has the potential to provide a global food safety net.

Discussions have already begun about the nature of any new or reformed convention, examining ideas such as:

- modifying the commitment structure to permit greater flexibility in the nature of countable contributions (e.g., non-food transfers such as vouchers and cash transfers, micronutrient supplements, cash contributions toward the costs associated with another members' commodity contributions):
- improving the effectiveness of food assistance activities by implementing a system of periodic reviews of selected interventions;
- broadening participation in the convention to include recipient countries who undertake to adhere to a code of conduct for food assistance effectiveness; and
- implementing a rights-based approach by linking the overall commitment level to a reliable measure of need and using a prorated formula for member contributions.

The broadening of the application of the FAC has led many proponents to promote the changing of the title to "Food Assistance Convention," underscoring the use of tools beyond food aid to increase food consumption among food-insecure people. The outcome of these negotiations could significantly improve the governance of international food security by ensuring a just allocation of food supplies for future major food crises.

Background to the Food Aid Convention

The FAC was established in 1967 in conjunction with the Kennedy Round negotiations of the General Agreement on Tariffs and Trade. Its original purpose was to provide an agreed-upon framework to regulate the use of food aid as a mechanism to utilize surplus food stock, in particular to minimize the disruption of the international trade in cereals and to provide a reliable minimum quantity of food aid. The initial membership included all the major wheat-exporting countries and some of the major cereals-importing countries. The FAC has been renegotiated five times, resulting in changes in the overall quantities of food aid, the range of "countable" commodities, and the agreed-upon purpose and qualifications for food aid transactions.

Within certain convention periods there were adjustments in commitment levels, usually based on unilateral notifications by donors. Other changes during the past twenty-five years have included local purchase flexibility (FAC 1986) and an increase in the number of countries on the eligible recipients list, most notably the addition of the emerging economies of the former Soviet Union in the 1995 convention. The range of eligible food commodities was increased, extending beyond cereals to include limited amounts of pulses, edible oil, root crops, skim milk powder, sugar, seeds, and micronutrient fortification/supplementation (FAC 1995; FAC 1999). Eligible costs were adjusted to include those associated with transport in the case of internationally recognized emergency situations (FAC 1999).

The most recent FAC was due for renegotiation in 2002 but has been extended several times pending the conclusion of Doha Round WTO negotiations on trade disciplines for food aid. Although these negotiations are not yet complete, there is sufficient closure on the food aid discussions for member states to begin discussion on FAC reform.

This renegotiation comes at a particularly important moment. Food aid needs have risen steadily over recent years, reflecting continuing low investment in agriculture and rural development, unfair agricultural trade relationships and the growing impact of climate change, which is expected to steadily reduce food production in equatorial countries. At the same time, total food aid availability has declined, with rising prices decreasing budgetary allocations for food aid. Because food is such a basic necessity, acute food shortages can quickly lead to serious political instability, particularly in urban areas. If such instability arose in several countries at the same time, the threat to the international economic and political systems would be severe. In this context, the existence of an adequate global food aid safety net may be a key element in ensuring global economic and political stability.

The Value of the Food Aid Convention

There has been considerable debate about the value of the FAC, most notably by Charlotte Benson (2000) and, more recently, by Hoddinott, Cohen, and Barrett. (2008). On the positive side it has been noted that the Food Aid Convention is the sole international treaty that guarantees a minimum transfer of resources between (mostly) Organization for Economic Co-operation and Development (OECD) countries and developing countries. By specifying a minimum quantity of food, it provides some protection from reductions in food aid availability when the food prices rise suddenly as they did in early 2008. In principle it is therefore a legal instrument for providing an international food safety net, a fact that could be of great importance in the volatile years ahead.

In practice, the FAC has fallen short of its potential. Benson points out that the total commitment level of the FAC has generally been well below the actual food aid levels, suggesting that at least some convention members set their commitment levels so low that they are unlikely to fall below them. Despite this, meeting the convention commitments has been a significant factor in some member states' allocation of resources, even though at times they threatened to weaken their commitments. The strong domestic political profile of food aid in some member states may also support the claim that these resources have been at least partially additional to other aid flows.

There are several other criticisms of the current convention. Some critiques focus on the complexities of the rules and procedures. In particular, it has a very complex and non-transparent method for rendering the quantities of a wide range of permissible commodities, delivered through several different modalities, into a single unit of food aid, the "wheat-equivalent tonne."[1] It also has complex and sometimes perverse rules regarding the accounting of transportation costs—most recently the inability to count transportation costs paid for the transport of non-member food aid shipments (e.g., Indian wheat provided for food emergencies in neighbouring countries).

Further critiques focus on what the convention fails to do. For example, it fails to fully recognize the importance of the nutritional adequacy of food aid, particularly the important role of micronutrient supplementation. There has also been a failure to implement the convention provisions that focus on ensuring the effectiveness of food aid. Although these are aspirational in nature, there is much that could be done to give them substance. The convention also fails to provide adequate representation to recipients because it limits its membership to donors only. This is a direct challenge to the emerging aid consensus represented by the Paris Declaration on Aid Effectiveness that recipients must also be represented. Finally, it lacks transparency in that reports of member compliance with their commitments are not publicly released and have been difficult or impossible to obtain.

Despite these weaknesses, most member states think that scrapping the convention would carry an unacceptably high political price—particularly in the context of an increasing need for food-related transfers due to climate change-related emergencies and instability, and volatility on world food markets. The principal debate now centres on how much to change the convention and in what direction.

Conversion to a Food Assistance Convention

Observers of the FAC have been looking for ways to "retool" the convention to better suit current best practices. The inclusion of vouchers and cash transfers to the traditional food transfer has given rise to the call for a Food Assistance Convention. The Trans-Atlantic Food Assistance Dialogue

(TAFAD), an NGO coalition, has been one of the most active voices in this debate to date. TAFAD is made up of most of the major North American and European food aid programming NGOs and issued its first proposals for a new Food Aid Convention in August 2006. TAFAD called for several major changes to the convention in the context of meeting the first Millennium Development Goal—to halve, between 1990 and 2015, the proportion of people who suffer from hunger and the proportion of people whose income is less than US$1 per day.

In May 2007, the German Government convened an international conference, "Food Aid—Exploring the Challenges." which focused its attention on the future of the convention. The conference was attended by representatives of all but one of the FAC member states, ten recipient countries, and many NGOs and research organizations. The result of the conference, dubbed the "Berlin Consensus" (Cohen and Weingärten 2007), called for the following reforms to the convention:

1. Broaden the convention to include all food assistance tools—food transfers, vouchers, and cash transfers.
2. Make the overall commitment level meaningful (related to some measure of need for food aid).
3. Provide greater transparency in commitment performance and ensure the evaluation of the quality of food aid activities.
4. Increase participation of other stakeholders, especially recipient governments.
5. More closely integrate the convention with other international food security arrangements (e.g., reform of the FAO Committee on Food Security).

Since the Berlin Conference, discussion has continued on the possibility of an International Food Assistance Convention, particularly supported by the European Union, with interest shown by Canada. Particular challenges relate to the quantification of commitments when applied to food, vouchers, and cash, particularly if the convention is to retain its commitment to a quantity of food rather than a quantity of money.

A Further Development?—The Integration of a Human Rights Approach

Some of the member states and the TAFAD group have shown their support for a stronger human rights orientation for a new convention. The Human Right to Adequate Food, already recognized in the United Nations International Covenant on Economic, Social, and Cultural Rights, has received increasing attention in recent years. This Right to Food orientation would apply at two levels—ensuring that food aid activities do not interfere with the right to food of either the recipients or adjacent populations, and ensuring that the overall commitment is sufficient to support meeting the need for food aid.

Conclusion

The renegotiation of the Food Aid Convention will provide an important opportunity to strengthen the global food security architecture as we enter an era of increasing instability in the world's food systems. It provides a tangible means of contributing to such internationally recognized goals as the first Millennium Development Goal. But the Food Aid Convention is currently like a T-shirt in a blizzard—better than nothing but certainly not up to the task. Nevertheless, the basic structure of the convention is sound, and, with appropriate and modest changes, it could become an important symbol of the international community's ability to work together to address common hunger challenges. Whether or not its members rise to this challenge will depend very much on whether political support can be successfully generated, especially in difficult economic times.

Note

1. Beyond the semantic objection of referring to all food aid as wheat, the real of finding a system to add up so many "apples and oranges" is not insignificant.

Works Cited

Benson, Charlotte (2000). "The Food Aid Convention: An Effective Safety Net." *In Food Aid and Human Security*, ed. E. J. Clay and O. Stokke. London: Frank Cass.

Cohen, Marc J., and L. Weingärten (2007). "Food Aid: Exploring the Challenges." Conference report from Food Aid: Exploring the Challenges. Berlin: Federal Ministry for Economic Cooperation and Development. 2–4 May.

Food and Agriculture Organization of the United Nations (2005). "Voluntary Guidelines to Support the Progressive Realization of the Right to Adequate Food in the Context of National Food Security." Rome.

Hoddinott, John. Marc Cohen, and Christopher Barrett (2008). "Renegotiating the Food Aid Convention: Background, Context and Issues." *Global Governance* 14, no. 3: 283–304.

Sphere Project (2004). "Humanitarian Charter and Minimum Standards in Disaster Response." Oxford: Oxfant Publishing.

United Nations (1986). "Food Aid Convention, 1986." London. 13 March.

—— (1995). "Food Aid Convention, 1995." Geneva. 1 April.

—— (1999). "Food Aid Convention, 1999." London. 13 April.

Out of Chaos, a Shining Star? Toward a Typology of Green States

PETER CHRISTOFF

In many ways Christoff's essay is a very good way to end a book about the past, present, and future of global politics. What is a "green state'? What are the characteristics of a green state? What must a state do to make the transition to the status of green state? Does Christoff's essay refute Hardin's findings on the tragedy of the commons? What evidence does Christoff present?

Over the past thirty years both industrialized and industrializing states have shown an astonishingly uniform shift in their intentions, if not capacities, to deal with environmental problems. Indeed, few countries are now without an environmental ministry, or waste management and pollution abatement programs, or laws establishing nature reserves and protecting native flora and fauna. Most states have sought to give direction and impetus to ecological modernization through national green plans of varying levels of sophistication and implementation. Together, these changes have been articulated through the evolving international discourse of sustainable development, overwritten by the demands of international environmental regimes, and responsive to the new wave of global environmental issues. Are we seeing here the birth of the green state,[1] emerging—as Nietzsche might have put it—"out of chaos, a shining star"?

On the other hand, over roughly the same period, the institutional burdens and fiscal demands on the welfare state have grown, despite attempts at welfare capping by social democrats and welfare retrenchment by neoliberals. Given demographic projections and associated pressure for aged care and health services, these burdens are likely to continue to grow.[2] Environmental problems will add to them. So, what then might this green state or ecostate, look like in future, and what relationship does it have to the (social) welfare state?

Indeed, how useful is it to talk of the ecostate as such? Huber and Stephens have observed that since publication of Esping-Andersen's *The Three Worlds of Welfare Capitalism*[3] in 1990, "the dominant approach to the study of welfare states in advanced capitalist democracies has been to study variations in welfare state provisions through the typology of three or four types of 'welfare state regimes.' "[4]

Saving Paradise

Just three months after the arrival of the First Fleet and the start of European colonization of Australia early in 1788, Philip Gidley King, Governor of the penal colony of Norfolk Island, issued Australia's first environmental regulation when he ordered his subjects "not to cut down or destroy" the island's plantain trees. This first attempt at resource conservation preceded growing awareness of the environmental limitations of the fledgling Antipodean colonies. Soil erosion and salinity were observed as early as the 1830s.[5] By the mid-1850s certain tree species had been entirely logged out, and the need for both forest and water conservation were frequently debated in Victoria and South Australia by the 1860s.[6]

As a result, during the latter part of the nineteenth century, Royal Commissions inquired into the impacts of land clearing for agriculture and of gold mining on colonial timber and water supplies. These inquiries led to the establishment of public bodies such as Water Boards, Forest Commissions, and Departments of Agriculture and Lands, and the proclamation of laws (or attempts at legislation)[7] to regulate logging, land clearing, and water use—activities central to Australia's burgeoning rural economy—in most Australian States by the start of the twentieth century. Richard Grove observes that similar resource conservation regimes were common among French and British colonies in the ninetienth century.[8]

The dissemination of new frontier-breaking techniques and inventions—new types of plough and, later, tractors, bulldozers, and chainsaws—resulted in settler societies' often experiencing similar environmental problems in tandem, as occurred with the Dust Bowl erosion crises that affected both the U.S. Midwest and semiarid Australia during the 1930s and 1940s. Unsurprisingly, from the 1860s onward, these common experiences and crises encouraged the rapid transnational transmission of ideas about resource conservation and regulation between scientists and administrators across the oceans. Indeed, some Australian laws were regarded as mere "crude copies" of contemporary U.S. legislation,[9] following a practice that continued well into the twentieth century. In all, the resulting transfers of species, technologies, techniques, and laws encouraged what might be called a common environmental sensibility and similar institutional frameworks.[10]

Separately, during the late nineteenth and early twentieth centuries, Australia's colonies and then States looked mainly to British regulatory innovations to ameliorate the effects of industrialization and urbanization on human health and welfare, and to counter local public concerns about sanitation and disease. During the mid- to late nineteenth century, Sydney and especially Melbourne experienced intense industrialization and rapid urbanization that in turn led to water shortages, dramatic failures in water and air quality, and the cholera and typhoid plagues that periodically threatened both settlements. Melbourne in the late nineteenth century was often described as standing "ankle deep in its own wastes."[11] The citizens of Sydney complained about the impact of raw sewage as it accumulated in the harbor, "rendering all business occupations upon its shores disgustingly offensive."[12]

As a result, late in the nineteenth century, public bodies based on British models were established in most Australian capital cities to limit pollution, regulate industry, manage urban open space, parks, and gardens, and provide or supervise the development of infrastructure for clean water, sewerage, and the disposal of domestic and industrial waste. Regulations governing industrial pollution of air and water were also devised at this time under various new health laws, then revised during the 1950s, and further refined and consolidated when environmental protection agencies—modeled on the 1969 U.S. EPA legislation and agency—were established in New South Wales, Victoria, and Western Australia in the early 1970s and the remaining States during the early 1990s.[13] Together, these developments overwhelmingly reflected anthropocentric concern over the effects of environmental degradation on human well-being, or what Robyn Eckersley has called human welfare ecology.[14]

In addition, one can discover in Australia a third, parallel albeit subordinate, narrative of environmental history—this one relating to an aesthetic and moral concern for nature. This too is reflected in aspects of early state development and behavior. In *The Colonial Earth*, Bonyhady emphasizes that the regulatory prohibition of 1790, intended to protect the petrels of Norfolk Island, was inspired by something more than a merely utilitarian calculus. The birds were being slaughtered for their flesh and also taken for their eggs. Since, initially, "the birds were superabundant, there was no market for them, but there was a limited market for their eggs," birds found without eggs were sometimes released whereas those carrying eggs sometimes had their eggs cut out, leaving the still-live petrels "to become a nuisance round the hills."[15] Lieutenant Ralph Clark regarded this as "one of the Crueles[t] things which I think I Ever herd" and hoped "Some of them will be caught at this Cruel work for the Sake of making an example of them."[16] Laws soon enacted to stop such cruelty broadly reflected the new sentiments toward nature emergent in Europe during the period from 1500 to 1800 and then rising to the fore.[17]

And then there was the influence of widespread fascination with the natural wonders of the Antipodes. From the first moments of European discovery, artists painted, and visitors and settlers wrote about, its strange birds, fish, plants, natives, and landscapes. Bonyhady comments that "the invaders loved birds. Their letters, despatches and books attest to their delight in the 'astonishing variety' and 'uncommonly beautiful plumage' of Australia's novel species."[18] Between the late eighteenth and the early twentieth centuries, scientists and artists established and educated colonial and international interest in Australian species. In doing so, they created the cultural foundations for domestic political and legal action for the preservation of nature.[19] Fascination with this new but threatened realm spurred enactment of wildlife protection laws, which emerged in several phases. Before 1900 they concentrated on providing sporadic and ineffectual protection for hunted emblematic species.[20] From about 1900 to 1920, reflecting greater public concern, statutes offered continuous but still ineffectual protection in limited areas. After the 1920s more comprehensive legislation was articulated, first at State level[21] and then, from 1972 onward, nationally, in response to environmentalist pressure.

Preservationist concerns also combined with and later overwhelmed the early push for the conservation of scenic sites and recreational areas. The National Park (later, Royal National Park) on the coast just south of Sydney was Australia's and the world's first officially designated national park. Proclaimed in 1879, fifteen years after the reservation of Yosemire in the United States, it was intended to provide "a national domain for rest and recreation...for the use of the public forever" and became, as Anderson puts it, "a sanctuary for the pale-faced Sydneyites fleeing the pollution—physical, mental, and social—of that densely packed city" rather than a sanctuary for natural flora and fauna.[22] By contrast, Victoria's Fern Tree Gully, a "much loved destination for excursionists since the 1860s"[23] was set aside in 1887 both as a recreational reserve and as a public park to protect its exotic vegetation, and Wilson's Promontory, also in Victoria, was (temporarily) reserved in 1898 under the Lands Act for a national park for public recreation and to preserve flora and fauna. This trend toward setting aside parks for both human welfare and nature conservation was also common in other States. From the 1930s on, the various bushwalking, wild life preservation, and forest conservation clubs began to display the features of a social movement (shared networks, unifying discursive framework, collective and sometimes coordinated approach to political action). By the 1970s their leading arguments for reservation were predominantly preservationist in intent, and by the 1990s Australia's national parks were being regarded, by environmentalists and governments alike, as a core component of a larger strategy for the protection of national biodiversity.

In all, the foundations of the environmental aspects of the Australian state—its European-style environmental institutions and agencies, established to conserve natural resources, limit pollution and disease, and preserve nature, and associated actions and expenditures—date almost from the moment of white settlement over two hundred years ago. It is this long history, substantially influenced by three or four waves of global environmental concern,[24] which underlies the rapid growth of additional environmental institutions in Australia during the last part of the twentieth century.

Crisis and Reform

The last two decades have seen a period of exceptional innovation for Australia's environmental institutions. In 1983 the newly elected Hawke Labor government confronted both political and economic crises in Australia. It inherited a deteriorating balance of payments, an elevated budget deficit, and unprecedented levels of unemployment—problems common to a number of other welfare states at this time. Faced with an immediate flight of capital, Prime Minister Bob Hawke and his Treasurer and successor Paul Keating floated the exchange rate, deregulated the finance sector, and relaxed regulatory controls over transboundary capital movements (especially overseas borrowing). Throughout the remainder of the 1980s, Labor sought to enhance economic competitiveness and hasten the integration of the national economy into international markets. It reduced tariff barriers by increasing the manufacturing sector's exposure to import competition and selectively targeted manufacturing industry sectors with incentives intended to promote export enhancement.[25] In retrospect, many of these steps merely weakened the Australian state's capacity to direct and implement fiscal and industry policies.

The new Labot government also swiftly rewarded the environmental movement. In the run-up to the 1983 election, the national Fraser coalirion government had refused to protect the iconic, untamed, and World Heritage–listed Franklin River from damming by Tasmania's State government. It regarded this issue as a State matter under Australia's Constitution. Labor, in opposition, vowed if elected to save the river. It would empower itself to trump the Tasmanian government by enacting Commonwealth legislation that reflected the requirements of the World Heritage Convention. The environmental movement mounted an unprecedented national electoral campaign that delivered a crucial proportion of the vote and power to Labor. The Hawke government's first law delivered on Labor's promise, and the Franklin was saved.

Each of these domestic developments—economic and environmental—defined the national settings for green politics and policy during the latter part of the decade. The international context for domestic environmental politics also changed profoundly through the 1980s. The symbolic, political, and economic dimensions of conflicts between environmental preservation and economic development intensified, and by the close of the 1980s the environment had risen high on the Australian political agenda. Environmental conflict had generated legitimation crises for both State and national governments in relation to their facilitation of resource development and appeared to challenge their capacity for economic management by forcing "policy on the run." By 1990 a political conjuncture unique in Australian history offered opportunities for environmental institutional development.

Paradise Deferred

The alignment of factors that had enabled environmental issues and institutional reform to rise on the political agenda between 1989 and late 1991 collapsed soon afterwards. A new recession pushed formal unemployment in Australia to an all-time peak of over 12 percent. The discourse of economic crisis again dominated the media and political and policy debates, and media fatigue with the environment reduced the profile of green issues. Newly articulated political responses to critical global concerns such as climate change and ozone depletion convinced the general public that these were now being addressed effectively, and popular concern about the environment declined in relation to other issues. The conjunctural opportunity for significant environmental institutional transformation had been largely squandered. As environmental politics became increasingly marginalized, key national green policy experiments from the earlier period, including the ESD strategy, were wound down, the Resource Assessment Commission was closed, and the Commonwealth EPA reduced in size and then dismantled.

Meanwhile, other initiatives, such as an Inter-Governmental Agreement on the Environment (IGAE)[26] and the National Forests Policy Agreement (NFPA), were deliberately pursued because of their capacity to systematize and normalize environmental policy relations with the States. The IGAE defined a federal process for creating national environment protection measures and minimum, nationally uniform standards for air and water quality, toxic waste management, and so on, through mirror legislation enacted by all States, Territories, and the Commonwealth. The NFPA proposed the establishment of regional forest agreements based on accredited State assessment processes. These regional agreements were intended to finally resolve conflict over harvesting in native forests by reserving 15 percent of remaining forest ecosystems and releasing the remainder for logging—in effect providing those resource security arrangements the environmental movement had successfully rejected in the early 1990s. In other words, while on the one hand the integrative, *centralizing* green state-building initiatives of the ESD strategy were ignored, *federalist* processes were extended to rationalize, systematize and standardize environmental policy-making, resource management, and environmental conditions nationally *without* effecting a transfer of powers to central government.

As the 1990s progressed, the other major national strategic initiative of the earlier period—the National Greenhouse Response Strategy—was constrained and weakened by the counteraction of the fossil fuel industries and their champions within the national economic ministries and inside Cabinet. Arguments about the importance of fossil fuel exports for the national economy and of low fossil fuel-based energy costs to Australia's international competitive advantage dominated debate over a national carbon tax in 1994 and later underpinned the Australian government's stance seeking and winning additional CO_2 emissions capacity during the Kyoto Climate Change Protocol negotiations in 1997 while blocking endorsement of the Protocol itself.

Green State, Ecostate, or Environmental State?

I want now to set this specific environmental political history in a broader theoretical context. In the well-established debate over the nature and origins of the social welfare state, arguments have revolved around when individual welfare states came into being, what were the major factors behind their emergence, and whether any patterns are common across national examples. Similar questions may be asked about the sources, characteristics, trajectory, and likely success of the state's environmental provisions.

Marxists, neo-Marxists, and others have argued that the welfare state arose as a functional response to the logic and structural needs of capitalism. For instance, in emphasizing the welfare state's role in securing and fostering capital accumulation, Claus Offe has argued in this regard that two modes of state intervention—allocative and productive—may be identified. The allocative mode refers to the state's regulatory (and strategic) capacity, which "creates and maintains the conditions of accumulation in a purely authoritative way" in both private and public sectors. By contrast, the productive mode describes state intervention in those areas of economic activity where the market has failed to provide the material conditions necessary for capital accumulation, because of the initial cost, risk, or low returns associated with investment. In Australia during much of the twentieth century, for instance, the state was heavily committed to the provision of health and education and also to "socialized production" through the direct provision of air, sea, and rail transport, dams, banking, and telecommunications services, in a large country with a low population.

Others, arguing that the welfare state was fashioned by and represents a victorious embodiment of the struggles of an emergent organized working class, and the rise of social citizenship and social democracy, place greater emphasis on forces in civil society. Despite historical differences between individual states, broadly speaking, the welfare state, through its provision of social pensions and public health, education, housing, and transport, has ameliorated the worst impacts of capitalism and improved the lot of those it assists as a result of these victories. (By contrast, neo-Marxists such as Offe and Habermas consider the welfare state to be an institutionalized response to the threats posed by social movements to capitalism, and therefore in significant part fashioned around and engaged in the legitimation of capital accumulation and in the pacification of dissent). However, whether the emphasis is on struggle or resistance, there is agreement that differences in patterns of welfare provision exist and that these reflect the specific political and institutional histories of individual states. These may nevertheless be typified or classified in various ways, for instance, as by Esping-Andersen, who classified welfare regimes as market-supporting or market-usurping and welfare states as liberal, conservative, or social democratic.

It is essential to read the environment into these debates. For example, aspects of state environmental activity are clearly market-supporting and intended to assist capital reproduction. They may be considered, in Offe's sense, productive (providing funding or infrastructure like dams or logging roads, and state-funded research to boost primary production and expenditure on environmental amelioration in order to sustain the quality of natural resources as a factor of production) or allocative (regulating uniform access to, and stable conditions and quality of, natural resources). While facilitating economic growth and capital accumulation overall, the state's environmental interventions can be considered to be defensive and remedial (for instance, repairing land degradation that may threaten future farm productivity) or proactive (legislating or establishing reserves to conserve natural resources for the future, or implementing regularions that will limit future costs associated with environmental damage).

Clearly, what has been left out of the frame to this point is the state's ambivalent normative stance over the uses of nature. Increasingly the state is morally and materially divided against itself along a green fracture line, one evidenced in the combative stance taken by state environmental agencies versus their resource-exploiting counterparts in agriculture, mining, or energy. Institutionally, most advanced industrial states embody a series of historical compromises over conflicting demands in this realm. Indeed, departments of environment and environmental laws are in significant part the outcomes of contested interventions by green groups and ecological citizens. Certain of these responses operate *despite* and *against* the imperative to capital accumulation by decommodifying nature, for instance, by "locking up valuable resources" as the timber and mining industries in Australia are so fond of saying, for the benefits of nonmaterial human needs and for nature.

Differing emphases on state functions and imperatives have also shaped narratives about the origins of specific welfare states. The establishment of a national social security scheme or of state-funded health and education; enactment of the first comprehensive national laws to regulate salaries, limit working hours, and improve conditions for labor; the first clear signs of an emergent policy debate about founding the national welfare state; or when a certain significant percentage of the national budget or of national GDP is devoted to social welfare expenditure may be taken as initiating or defining features of the welfare state.

Foregrounding crucial legislative innovation, or the creation of foundational state agencies, or the establishment of critical funding arrangements, or the rise of specific discourses and their political champions, as signposts marking the start of the social or environmental characteristics of the welfare state will therefore define a different chronology and canvas for the historical trajectory and cultural and legal foundations of the environmental or green state. In what follows, I consider a range of these factors and use a broader rather than narrower template of functions to frame the historical canvas of the (social and environmental) welfare state.

Green states, were they to exist, would be characterized by the predominance of types of state activity aimed at strong ecological modernization. Here state activity would have, centrally, a driving and predominant moral purpose in directing social and economic activity toward ecologically sustainable (and socially just) outcomes. It would incorporate at its heart recognition of environmental constraints on material activity, and this would be reflected in institutional developments that substantially benefit nature in addition to or apart from human welfare. Significant state capacity for ecologically sustainable development would be evident in the following areas:

- *Consensus formation*. The state, in its activities, would be highly inclusive of civil society in institutions and processes for the deliberative consideration of programs for substantial ecologically bounded economic and social change.
- *Strategic planning*. The state would provide the capacity for (or facilitate) long-term integrative social and economic planning aimed at ecological sustainability with horizons beyond those available or meaningful to actors in specific industry or social sectors.
- *Policy coordination and integration*. This would occur both within the state and across sectors of economic activity and civil society in ways that enabled and guaranteed effective ecological governance by ensuring that ecological concerns were effectively incorporated into all decision making.
- *Implementation*. The state would also ensure that resources were available for appropriate regulatory, monitoring, allocative, and productive tasks.

These capacities would also necessarily be such as to enable the green state to participate effectively in various forms of international environmental governance.

By contrast, one may now talk of two types of welfare state. *Social welfare states* may be characterized by the predominance of well-developed state social welfare capacities and functions that ensure the reproduction and legitimization of capital accumulation, with major environmental problems or issues often barely recognized or disregarded as externalities. (Many socialist states fitted into this mold.) By contrast, *environmental welfare states* are distinguished by their developed capacity to engage in weak ecological modernization. These states predominantly engage in environmental activity that ensures the reproduction and legitimization of a "nature-blind" form of capital accumulation or which meets short-term human welfare requirements. However nonmaterial ecological considerations and longer-term environment-related human welfare requirements remain incidental to or subordinated to these functions.

These types of state may in turn be set apart from two types of neoliberal states: *"Classical" neoliberal states*, which manifest weak state social and environmental welfare capacity and a strong bias toward market-oriented solutions in these and other policy domains, may be distinguished from *environmental neoliberal states*, which manifest weak state social welfare capacity and a strong bias toward market-oriented solutions to social welfare problems but have developed, in parallel, a moderate to strong environmental welfare capacity.

Last, for the sake of analytical completeness, it is possible to conceive of an *ecofascist state*, which places priority on ecological values at the expense of social welfare and human rights—one akin to those authoritarian states proposed by neo-Malthusians and ecosurvivalists in the early 1970s.

First, when can we say that we *have* an environmental welfare state, or environmental neoliberal state, or a green state? Pierson uses three criteria to mark the establishment of a social welfare state. These are the dates of introduction of social insurance and of the extension of social citizenship, and the growth of public expenditure on social welfare to over 3 percent of GNP. Additional criteria, similar to those mentioned earlier and in table 2.2, could be employed to mark the existence of, for instance, an environmental welfare state, including the date significant public institutions and laws relating to pollution and the protection of nature were founded or enacted, and the growth of a significant public environmental budget (although it is clear that the level of public budget committed to the environment would have to be commensurate with national need rather than simply based on some simple hurdle requirement).

Using Pierson's criteria and other distinctions described earlier, Australia, it could be argued, now has autonomous and significant national and subnational environmental institutions and laws and a major national environmental remediation program (the Natural Heritage Trust). But its citizens, while now able to vote for a green party with a clearly defined ecological program, still do not have real legal standing on environmental matters, and so the criterion of full environmental (let alone ecological) citizenship is not met. Meanwhile, even if one considered total national expenditure (not just Commonwealth but also State and local government outlays) to include some very marginally environmental activities like waste disposal to total some $A 5 billion, this amount not only is less than 3 percent of Australian GNP but, more important, is well below the sum *needed* for environmental remediation and environmental infrastructural transformation, and less than that currently afforded in hidden subsidies to environmentally destructive activities such as fossil fuel exploitation and land clearing. In all, while Australia during the early 1990s began developing features of a weak environmental welfare state, in the early 2000s it is probably more accurately classified an environmental neoliberal state, according to the typology offered in table 2.1.

Second, to what extent is the history of the emergence of the environmental welfare or green state *synchronous* with, or *dependent* and *founded* on, the development of the social welfare state—and if not, why not? In the Australian case, the historical relationship is clearly not straightforward. One can conclude that a significant and persistent disjuncture exists between developments in different parts of the Australian (welfare) state and also that it is impossible to argue that the Australian environmental state simply evolved out of the social welfare state. Nor can claims for simple historical succession—the evolution of a social welfare state into an environmental welfare state and then, possibly, a green state—be sustained. The argument for parallels in development between, first, one welfare state form (the social welfare state) and then the next (the ecostate), as suggested by Meadowcroft, may not hold up to close scrutiny.

Third, what forces drive the environmental welfare state's development, and how do these relate to the sources of the social welfare state? To what extent is the fate or *trajectory* of the various environmental or green states linked to or autonomous of that of the social welfare state? The Australian instance suggests that these links are indirect, complex, and politically charged and include the long institutional history of a state as much as its immediate circumstances. It is also clear that ecological crisis—about global issues such as climate change or domestic issues such as the fate of threatened forests or species—can influence political mobilization and action in ways that are not dependent on, that take the heat out of, that even draw attention away from, other (social or economic) policy issues.

Even if the state were capable of retreating from or even shedding its historically accrued responsibilities for certain allocative and productive functions—those relating to social reproduction—the intensification of (global) environmental crisis means the state is increasingly being pressed to perform a green welfare function by organizing and funding remediation, infrastructure provision, research and implementation, and regulating environmental degradation in the environmental domain. As the Australian example suggests, these costs, while still marginal now, are likely to become a profound political and economic burden in the future (given climate change). Although industrialized states have moved to deal with these demands in ways that are culturally and situation specific,

Table 2.1. Toward a Typology of Environmental States

Type of State	Characteristics	Examples
Green state	Strong ecomodernization through • High levels of state environmental capacity and intervention, and of integration of economic, social welfare, and environmental welfare policies • Strong cultural and political institutionalization of ecological values • High levels of ecocitizenship—state highly inclusive • High commitment to biocentric values • High commitment to human welfare environmentalism • Strong budgetary commitment to both human welfare environmental and ecocentric issues	
Environmental welfare state	Weak ecomodernization through • Moderate state environmental capacity and intervention • Weak institutionalization of ecological values, with human-oriented (social and environment) welfare, including resource conservation, predominant • Moderate levels of ecocitizenship—state moderately inclusive • Low commitment to biocentric values • High commitment to human welfare environmentalism • Moderate budgetary commitment to ecological issues	Sweden, Netherlands
Social welfare state		Socialist Hungary
Neoliberal state		
Environmental neoliberal state	Very weak ecomodernization through • Weak state environmental capacity and intervention—strongly market-oriented • Weak institutionalization of environmental values • State concentration on resource conservation and environmental remediation • Low levels of ecocitizenship—exclusionary state • Low commitment to biocentric values • Moderate to high commitment to human welfare environmentalism • Weak to moderate budgetary commitment to social and environment welfare	Australia, United States
Ecofascist state	Strong ecomodernization through • Strong institutionalization of ecological values built around a neo-Malthusian outlook • High levels of state environmental capacity and actual intervention • Authoritarian political characteristics • Very low levels of ecocitizenship and democracy—state profoundly exclusionary • High commitment to biocentric values • Low commitment to human welfare environmentalism • (Possibly) strong budgetary commitment, especially to ecocentric issues/values	

and sometimes seemingly contradictory across states, there is also a divergence of environmental policy responses and institutional tendencies in this domain across the OECD.

In conclusion, I would suggest that claims for a teleological development from social welfare state to green state do not hold. Historically, some environmental characteristics of the state precede its social welfare aspects (at least in Australia), and there are also clear instances of states' being wound back from stronger to weaker positions on matters of ecological sustainability in recent political times. Yet even if the collective trajectory of states appeared to be toward strengthening national environmental capacity in response to intensifying environmental pressures—the argument underlying Meadowcroft's notion of the emerging ecostate—this development would require more nuanced description of the potentially very different types of environmental welfare state that might be emerging. For that reason, this chapter has sought to provide a better means to describe individual states and their environmental capacities, and to assess their future development not merely against institutional precedents but against present and future ecological trends and needs.

Notes

1. Throughout this chapter, I use *state* to refer to the concept in general and *State* to refer to Australia's subnational unit of government.
2. On whether this may constitute a serious crisis, see Kaufmann (2001).
3. Esping-Andersen (1990).
4. Huber and Stephens (2001, 107).
5. Robertson (1898).
6. Powell (1976, 60).
7. For instance, in *Environmental Management in Australia* (1976), Powell comments that "Forest Bills were introduced into the Victorian Parliament in 1879, 1881, 1887 and 1892 but none became law" (124). The first Victorian Forests Act was passed in 1907.
8. Richard Grove (1995).
9. Powell (1976, 130).
10. See also Grove (1995); Grove (1997); and Tyrell (1999).
11. See Dunstan (1984); Dunstan (1985).
12. Coward (1976, 9).
13. See Christoff (1999).
14. Eckersley (1992).
15. Bonyhady (2000, 30–31).
16. Cited in Bonyhady (2000, 31).
17. See Thomas (1983).
18. Bonyhady (2000, 14).
19. Moyal (1986); Finney (1993).
20. In 1861, Tasmania enacted a law preventing the taking of the black swan, the first statute to provide limited protection for a native species.
21. See Walker (1991); Harris (1956, ch. 1).
22. Esther Anderson (2000, 4).
23. Esther Anderson (2000, 52).
24. These waves occurred during the mid-nineteenth century (the rise of the resource conservation movement), the end of the nineteenth century (the movement for urban planning and sanitation, and the rise of species preservation), during the 1970s (antipollution and nature conservation movements, leading to departments of conservation, U.S. style environmental protection agencies and national parks authorities, and a new emphasis on ecological preservation), and during the 1980s and early 1990s (in response to global threats—particularly climate change and ozone depletion—and leading to sustainability planning).
25. The effort was largely unsuccessful, resulting instead in a significant loss of employment in the textile, clothing, and footwear industries, where tariff reductions permitted competition with cheaper overseas goods and hastened transfer of manufacturing to offshore havens of low-cost labor.
26. The Inter-Governmental Agreement on the Environment (IGAE) codified environmental powers between Commonwealth, State, and local government spheres and reinforced the States' power as environmental managers after almost

References

Anderson, Esther. 2000. *Victoria's National Parks, a Centenary History*, Melbourne: Parks Victoria/ State Library of Victoria.

Bonyhady, Tim. 2000. *The Colonial Earth*. Melbourne: Miegunyah Press

Christoff, Peter. 2000. Environmental Citizenship. In *Rethinking Australian Citizenship*, ed. Wayne Hudson and John Kane, 200–214. Cambridge: Cambridge University Press.

Christoff, Peter. *1996 In Reverse: Australia's Environmental Performance 1992–2002*. Melbourne: ACF/ ACFOAI Greenpeace Australia-Pacific.

Christoff, Peter. 1996. Ecological Modernisation, Ecological Modernities. *Environmental Politics* 5 (4): 476–500.

Christoff, Peter. 1998a. From Global Citizen to Renegade State: Australia at Kyoto. *Arena Journal* 10: 113–128.

Christoff, Peter. 1998b. Degreening Government in the Garden State: Environment Policy under the Kennett Government. *Environmental and Planning Law Journal* 15 (I): 10–32.

Christoff, Peter. 1999. Regulating the Urban Environment. In *Serving the City: the Crisis in Australia's Urban Services*, ed. Patrick Troy, 34–59. Sydney: Pluto Press.

Coward, D. 1976. From Public Health to Environmental Amenity. In *Sydney's Environmental Amenity, 1970–1975: A Study of the System of Waste Management and Pollution Control*, ed. Noel Butlin, 4–26. Canberra: Australian National University.

Dunstan, David. 1985. Dirt and Disease. In *The Outcasts of Melbourne*, ed. G. Davidson, D. Dunstan, and C. McConville, 140–171. Sydney: Allen and Unwin

Dunstan, David. 1984. *Governing the Metropolis: Politics, Technology and Social Change in a Victorian City: Melbourne 1850–1891*. Melbourne: Melbourne University Press.

Eckersley, Robyn. 1992. *Environmentalism and Political Theory Albany:* State University of New York Press

Esping-Andersen, Gosta. 1990. *The Three Worlds of Welfare Capitalism*. Cambridge: Polity.

Finney, Colin. 1993. *Paradise Revealed: Natural History in Nineteenth-Century Australia*. Melbourne: Museum of Victoria.

Grove, Richard. 1997. *Ecology, Climate and Empire: Colonialism and Global Environmental History 1400–1940*. Cambridge: Whitehorse Press.

Grove, Richard. 1995. *Green Imperialism: Colonial Expansion, Tropical Island Edens and the Origins of Environmentalism*. New York: Cambridge University Press.

Harris, Thistle Y. 1956. *Naturecraft in Australia*. London: Angus and Robertson

Huber, Evelyne, and John D. Stephens. 2001. Welfare State and Production Regimes in the Era of Retrenchment. *In The New Politics of the Welfare State*, ed. Paul Pierson, 107–145. Oxford: Oxford University Press.

Moyal, Ann. 1986. A *Bright and Savage Land: Scientists in Colonial Australia*. Sydney: Collins.

Powell, Joe M. 1976. *Environmental Management in Australia 1788–1914*. Melbourne: Oxford University Press.

Productivity Commission. 1999, *Implementation of Ecologically Sustainable Development by Commonwealth Departments and Agencies: Inquiry Report. Report No.* 5. Canberra: Productivity Commission.

Robertson, John. 1898. Letter to Governor LaTrobe. September 20 1853. In *Letters from Victorian Pioneers*, ed. T. H. Bride, 3 4 3 5. Melbourne: Brain, Govt. Printer.

Thomas, Keith. 1983. *Man and the Natural World: Changing Attitudes in England 1500–1800*. London: Allen Lane/Penguin Books.

Tyrell, Ian. 1999. *True Gardens of the Gods: Californian-Australian Environmental Reform, 1860–1930*. Berkeley: University of California Press.

Walker R. B. 1991. Fauna and Flora Protection in New South Wales 1866–1948. *Journal of Australian Studies* 28 (March): 17–28.

The Rise of Complex Terrorism

THOMAS HOMER-DIXON

Professor Homer-Dixon was one of the first IR specialists who wrote about the connections between environmental scarcity and national security. As a result, this excerpt is interesting on at least two levels. First, Homer-Dixon warns us about the potential effects of our increasingly technology-dependent society. Second, *Foreign Policy*, the journal in which this article appeared, is a publication that can influence policy-makers within governments. Did Homer-Dixon's argument convince you? Why, or why not? If you were a government official, what specific policy changes would you make?

Modern societies face a cruel paradox: Fast-paced technological and economic innovations may deliver unrivalled prosperity, but they also render rich nations vulnerable to crippling, unanticipated attacks. By relying on intricate networks and concentrating vital assets in small geographic clusters, advanced Western nations only amplify the destructive power of terrorists—and the psychological and financial damage they can inflict.

It's 4 a.m. on a sweltering summer night in July 2003. Across much of the United States, power plants are working full tilt to generate electricity for millions of air conditioners that are keeping a ferocious heat wave at bay. The electricity grid in California has repeatedly buckled under the strain, with rotating blackouts from San Diego to Santa Rosa.

In different parts of the state, half a dozen small groups of men and women gather. Each travels in a rented minivan to its prearranged destination—for some, a location outside one of the hundreds of electrical substations dotting the state; for others, a spot upwind from key, high-voltage transmission lines. The groups unload their equipment from the vans. Those outside the substations put together simple mortars made from materials bought at local hardware stores, while those near the transmission lines use helium to inflate weather balloons with long silvery rails. At a precisely coordinated moment, the homemade mortars are fired, sending showers of aluminum chaff over the substations. The balloons are released and drift into the transmission lines.

Simultaneously, other groups are doing the same thing along the Eastern Seaboard and in the South and Southwest. A national electrical system already under immense strain is massively short-circuited, causing a cascade of power failures across the country. Traffic lights shut off. Water and sewage systems are disabled. Communications systems break down. The financial system and national economy come screeching to a halt.

Sound far-fetched? Perhaps it would have before September 11, 2001, but certainly not now. We've realized, belatedly, that our societies are wide-open targets for terrorists. We're easy prey because of two key trends: First, the growing technological capacity of small groups and individuals to destroy things and people; and, second, the increasing vulnerability of our economic and technological systems to carefully aimed attacks. While commentators have devoted considerable ink and airtime to the first of these trends, they've paid far less attention to the second, and they've virtually ignored their combined effect. Together, these two trends facilitate a new and sinister kind of mass violence—a "complex terrorism" that threatens modern, high-tech societies in the world's most developed nations.

Our fevered, Hollywood-conditioned imaginations encourage us to focus on the sensational possibility of nuclear or biological attacks—attacks that might kill tens of thousands of people in a single strike. These threats certainly deserve attention, but not to the neglect of the likelier and ultimately deadlier disruptions that could result from the clever exploitation by terrorists of our societies' new and growing complexities.

Weapons of Mass Disruption

The steady increase in the destructive capacity of small groups and individuals is driven largely by three technological advances: more powerful weapons, the dramatic progress in communications and information processing, and more abundant opportunities to divert nonweapon technologies to destructive ends.

Consider first the advances in weapons technology. Over the last century, progress in materials engineering, the chemistry of explosives, and miniaturization of electronics has brought steady improvement in all key weapons characteristics, including accuracy, destructive power, range, portability, ruggedness, ease-of-use, and affordability. Improvements in light weapons are particularly relevant to trends in terrorism and violence by small groups, where the devices of choice include rocket-propelled grenade launchers, machine guns, light mortars, land mines, and cheap assault rifles such as the famed AK-47. The effects of improvements in these weapons are particularly noticeable in developing countries. A few decades ago, a small band of terrorists or insurgents attacking a rural village might have used bolt-action rifles, which take precious time to reload. Today, cheap assault rifles multiply the possible casualties resulting from such an attack. As technological change makes it easier to kill, societies are more likely to become locked into perpetual cycles of attack and counterattack that render any normal trajectory of political and economic development impossible.

Meanwhile, new communications technologies—from satellite phones to the Internet—allow violent groups to marshal resources and coordinate activities around the planet. Transnational terrorist organizations can use the Internet to share information on weapons and recruiting tactics, arrange surreptitious fund transfers across borders, and plan attacks. These new technologies can also dramatically enhance the reach and power of age-old procedures. Take the ancient *hawala* system of moving money between countries, widely used in Middle Eastern and Asian societies. The system, which relies on brokers linked together by clan-based networks of trust, has become faster and more effective through the use of the Internet.

Information-processing technologies have also boosted the power of terrorists by allowing them to hide or encrypt their messages. The power of a modern laptop computer today is comparable to the computational power available in the entire U.S. Defense Department in the mid-1960s. Terrorists can use this power to run widely available state-of-the-art encryption software. Sometimes less advanced computer technologies are just as effective. For instance, individuals can use a method called steganography ("hidden writing") to embed messages into digital photographs or music clips. Posted on publicly available Web sites, the photos or clips are downloaded by collaborators as necessary. (This technique was reportedly used by recently arrested terrorists when they planned to blow up the U.S. Embassy in Paris.) At latest count, 140 easy-to-use steganography tools were available on the Internet. Many other off-the-shelf technologies—such as "spread-spectrum" radios that randomly switch their broadcasting and receiving signals—allow terrorists to obscure their messages and make themselves invisible.

The Web also provides access to critical information. The September 11 terrorists could have found there all the details they needed about the floor plans and design characteristics of the World Trade Center and about how demolition experts use progressive collapse to destroy large buildings. The Web also makes available sets of instructions—or "technical ingenuity"—needed to combine readily available materials in destructive ways. Practically anything an extremist wants to know about kidnapping, bomb making, and assassination is now available online. One somewhat facetious example: It's possible to convert everyday materials into potentially destructive devices like the "potato cannon." With a barrel and combustion chamber fashioned from common plastic pipe, and with propane as an explosive propellant, a well-made cannon can hurl a homely spud hundreds of meters—or throw chaff onto electrical substations. A quick search of the Web reveals dozens of sites giving instructions on how to make one.

Finally, modern, high-tech societies are filled with supercharged devices packed with energy, combustibles, and poisons, giving terrorists ample opportunities to divert such nonweapon technologies to destructive ends. To cause horrendous damage, all terrorists must do is figure out how to release this power and let it run wild or, as they did on September 11, take control of this power and retarget it. Indeed, the assaults on New York City and the Pentagon were not low-tech affairs, as is often argued. True, the terrorists used simple box cutters to hijack the planes, but the box cutters were no more than the "keys" that allowed the terrorists to convert a hightech means of transport into a high-tech weapon of mass destruction. Once the hijackers had used these keys to access and turn on their weapon, they were able to deliver a kiloton of explosive power into the World Trade Center with deadly accuracy.

High-tech Hubris

The vulnerability of advanced nations stems not only from the greater destructive capacities of terrorists, but also from the increased vulnerability of the West's economic and technological systems. This additional vulnerability is the product of two key social and technological developments: first, the growing complexity and interconnectedness of our modern societies; and second, the increasing geographic concentration of wealth, human capital, knowledge, and communication links.

Consider the first of these developments. All human societies encompass a multitude of economic and technological systems. We can think of these systems as networks—that is, as sets of nodes and links among those nodes. The U.S. economy consists of numerous nodes, including corporations, factories, and urban centers; it also consists of links among these nodes, such as highways, rail lines, electrical grids, and fiber-optic cables. As societies modernize and become richer, their networks become more complex and interconnected. The number of nodes increases, as does the density of links among the nodes and the speed at which materials, energy, and information are pushed along these links. Moreover, the nodes themselves become more complex as the people who create, operate, and manage them strive for better performance. (For instance, a manufacturing company might improve efficiency by adopting more intricate inventory-control methods.)

Complex and interconnected networks sometimes have features that make their behavior unstable and unpredictable. In particular, they can have feedback loops that produce vicious cycles. A good example is a stock market crash, in which selling drives down prices, which begets more selling. Networks can also be tightly coupled, which means that links among the nodes are short, therefore making it more likely that problems with one node will spread to others. When drivers tailgate at high speeds on freeways, they create a tightly coupled system: A mistake by one driver, or a sudden shock coming from outside the system, such as a deer running across the road, can cause a chain reaction of cars piling onto each other. We've seen such knock-on effects in the U.S. electrical, telephone, and air traffic systems, when a failure in one part of the network has sometimes produced a cascade of failures across the country. Finally, in part because of feedbacks and tight coupling, networks often exhibit nonlinear behavior, meaning that a small shock or perturbation to the network produces a disproportionately large disruption.

Terrorists and other malicious individuals can magnify their own disruptive power by exploiting these features of complex and interconnected networks. Consider the archetypal lone, nerdy high-school kid hacking away at his computer in his parents' basement who can create a computer virus that produces chaos in global communications and data systems. But there's much more to worry about than just the proliferation of computer viruses. A special investigative commission set up in 1997 by then U.S. President Bill Clinton reported that "growing complexity and interdependence, especially in the energy and communications infrastructures, create an increased possibility that a rather minor and routine disturbance can cascade into a regional outage." The commission continued: "We are convinced that our vulnerabilities are increasing steadily, that the means to exploit those weaknesses are readily available and that the costs [of launching an attack] continue to drop."

Terrorists must be clever to exploit these weaknesses. They must attack the right nodes in the right networks. If they don't, the damage will remain isolated and the overall network will be resilient. Much depends upon the network's level of redundancy—that is, on the degree to which the damaged node's functions can be offloaded to undamaged nodes. As terrorists come to recognize the importance of redundancy, their ability to disable complex networks will improve. Langdon Winner, a theorist of politics and technology, provides the first rule of modern terrorism: "Find the critical but nonredundant parts of the system and sabotage...them according to your purposes." Winner concludes that "the science of complexity awaits a Machiavelli or Clausewitz to make the full range of possibilities clear."

The range of possible terrorist attacks has expanded due to a second source of organizational vulnerability in modern economies—the rising concentration of high-value assets in geographically small locations. Advanced societies concentrate valuable things and people in order to achieve economies of scale. Companies in capital-intensive industries can usually reduce the per-unit cost of their goods by building larger production facilities. Moreover, placing expensive equipment and highly skilled people in a single location provides easier access, more efficiencies, and synergies that constitute an important source of wealth. That is why we build places like the World Trade Center.

In so doing, however, we also create extraordinarily attractive targets for terrorists, who realize they can cause a huge amount of damage in a single strike. On September 11, a building complex that took seven years to construct collapsed in 90 minutes, obliterating 10 million square feet of office space and exacting at least $30 billion in direct costs. A major telephone switching office was destroyed, another heavily damaged, and important cellular antennas on top of the towers were lost. Key transit lines through southern Manhattan were buried under rubble. Ironically, even a secret office of the U.S. Central Intelligence Agency was destroyed in the attack, temporarily disrupting normal intelligence operations.

Yet despite the horrific damage to the area's infrastructure and New York City's economy, the attack did not cause catastrophic failures in U.S. financial, economic, or communications networks. As it turned out, the World Trade Center was not a critical, nonredundant node. At least it wasn't critical in the way most people (including, probably, the terrorists) would have thought. Many of the financial firms in the destroyed buildings had made contingency plans for disaster by setting up alternate facilities for data, information, and computer equipment in remote locations. Though the NASDAQ headquarters was demolished, for instance, the exchange's data centers in Connecticut and Maryland remained linked to trading companies through two separate connections that passed through 20 switching centers. NASDAQ officials later claimed that their system was so robust that they could have restarted trading only a few hours after the attack. Some World Trade Center firms had made advanced arrangements with companies specializing in providing emergency relocation facilities in New

Jersey and elsewhere. Because of all this proactive planning—and the network redundancy it produced—the September 11 attacks caused remarkably little direct disruption to the U.S. financial system (despite the unprecedented closure of the stock market for several days).

But when we look back years from now, we may recognize that the attacks had a critical effect on another kind of network that we've created among ourselves: a tightly coupled, very unstable, and highly nonlinear psychological network. We're all nodes in this particular network, and the links among us consist of Internet connections, satellite signals, fiber-optic cables, talk radio, and 24-hour television news. In the minutes following the attack, coverage of the story flashed across this network. People then stayed in front of their televisions for hours on end; they viewed and reviewed the awful video clips on the CNN Web site; they plugged phone lines checking on friends and relatives; and they sent each other millions upon millions of e-mail messages—so many, in fact, that the Internet was noticeably slower for days afterwards.

Along these links, from TV and radio stations to their audiences, and especially from person to person through the Internet, flowed raw emotion: grief, anger, horror, disbelief, fear, and hatred. It was as if we'd all been wired into one immense, convulsing, and reverberating neural network. Indeed, the biggest impact of the September 11 attacks wasn't the direct disruption of financial, economic, communications, or transportation networks—physical stuff, all. Rather, by working through the network we've created within and among our heads, the attacks had their biggest impact on our collective psychology and our subjective feelings of security and safety. This network acts like a huge megaphone, vastly amplifying the emotional impact of terrorism.

To maximize this impact, the perpetrators of complex terrorism will carry out their attacks in audacious, unexpected, and even bizarre manners—using methods that are, ideally, unimaginably cruel. By so doing, they will create the impression that anything is possible, which further magnifies fear. From this perspective, the World Trade Center represented an ideal target, because the Twin Towers were an icon of the magnificence and boldness of American capitalism. When they collapsed like a house of cards, in about 15 seconds each, it suggested that American capitalism was a house of cards, too. How could anything so solid and powerful and so much a part of American identity vanish so quickly? And the use of passenger airplanes made matters worse by exploiting our worst fears of flying.

Unfortunately, this emotional response has had huge, real-world consequences. Scared, insecure, grief-stricken people aren't ebullient consumers. They behave cautiously and save more. Consumer demand drops, corporate investment falls, and economic growth slows. In the end, via the multiplier effect of our technology-amplified emotional response, the September 11 terrorists may have achieved an economic impact far greater than they ever dreamed possible. The total cost of lost economic growth and decreased equity value around the world could exceed a trillion dollars. Since the cost of carrying out the attack itself was probably only a few hundred thousand dollars, we're looking at an economic multiplier of over a millionfold.

The Weakest Links

Complex terrorism operates like jujitsu—it redirects the energies of our intricate societies against us. Once the basic logic of complex terrorism is understood (and the events of September 11 prove that terrorists are beginning to understand it), we can quickly identify dozens of relatively simple ways to bring modern, high-tech societies to their knees.

How would a Clausewitz of terrorism proceed? He would pinpoint the critical complex networks upon which modern societies depend. They include networks for producing and distributing energy, information, water, and food; the highways, railways, and airports that make up our transportation grid; and our healthcare system. Of these, the vulnerability of the food system is particularly alarming [see sidebar on opposite page]. However, terrorism experts have paid the most attention to the energy and information networks, mainly because they so clearly underpin the vitality of modern economies.

The energy system—which comprises everything from the national network of gas pipelines to the electricity grid—is replete with high-value nodes like oil refineries, tank farms, and electrical substations. At times of peak energy demand, this network (and in particular, the electricity grid) is very tightly coupled. The loss of one link in the grid means that the electricity it carries must be offloaded to other links. If other links are already operating near capacity, the additional load can cause them to fail, too, thus displacing their energy to yet other links. We saw this kind of breakdown in August 1996, when the failure of the Big Eddy transmission line in northern Oregon caused overloading on a string of transmission lines down the West Coast of the United States, triggering blackouts that affected 4 million people in nine states.

Substations are clear targets because they represent key nodes linked to many other parts of the electrical network. Substations and high-voltage transmission lines are also "soft" targets, since they can be fairly easily disabled or destroyed. Tens of thousands of miles of transmission lines are strung across North America, often in locations so remote that the lines are almost impossible to protect, but they are nonetheless accessible by four-wheel drive. Transmission towers can be brought down with well-placed explosive charges. Imagine a carefully planned sequence of attacks on these lines, with emergency crews and investigators dashing from one remote attack site to another, constantly off-balance and unable to regain control. Detailed maps of locations of substations and transmission lines for much of North America are easily available on the Web. Not even all the police and military personnel in the United States would suffice to provide even rudimentary protection to this immense network.

The energy system also provides countless opportunities for turning supposedly benign technology to destructive ends. For instance, large gas pipelines, many of which run near or even through urban areas, have huge explosive potential; attacks on them could have the twin effect of producing great local damage and wider disruptions in energy supply. And the radioactive waste pools associated with most nuclear reactors are perhaps the most lethal targets in the national energy-supply system. If the waste in these facilities were dispersed into the environment, the results could be catastrophic. Fortunately, such attacks would be technically difficult.

Even beyond energy networks, opportunities to release the destructive power of benign technologies abound. Chemical plants are especially tempting targets, because they are packed with toxins and flammable, even explosive, materials. Security at such facilities is often lax: An April 1999 study of chemical plants in Nevada and West Virginia by the U.S. Agency for Toxic Substances and Disease Registry concluded that security ranged from "fair to very poor" and that oversights were linked to "complacency and lack of awareness of the threat." And every day, trains carrying tens of thousands of tons of toxic material course along transport corridors throughout the United States. All a terrorist needs is inside knowledge that a chemical-laden train is traveling through an urban area at a specific time, and a well-placed object (like a piece of rail) on the track could cause a wreck, a chemical release, and a mass evacuation. A derailment of such a train at a nonredundant link in the transport system—such as an important tunnel or bridge—could be particularly potent. (In fact, when the U.S. bombing campaign in Afghanistan began on October 7, 2001, the U.S. railroad industry declared a three-day moratorium on transporting dangerous chemicals.) Recent accidents in Switzerland and Baltimore, Maryland, make clear that rail and highway tunnels are vulnerable because they are choke points for transportation networks and because it's extraordinarily hard to extinguish explosions and fires inside them.

Modern communications networks also are susceptible to terrorist attacks. Although the Internet was originally designed to keep working even if large chunks of the network were lost (as might happen in a nuclear war, for instance), today's Internet displays some striking vulnerabilities. One of the most significant is the system of computers—called "routers" and "root servers"—that directs traffic around the Net. Routers represent critical nodes in the network and depend on each other for details on where to send packets of information. A software error in one router, or its malicious reprogramming by a hacker, can lead to errors throughout the Internet. Hackers could also exploit new peer-to-peer software (such as the information-transfer tool Gnutella) to distribute throughout the Internet millions of "sleeper" viruses programmed to attack specific machines or the network itself at a predetermined date.

The U.S. government is aware of many of these threats and of the specific vulnerability of complex networks, especially information networks. President George W. Bush has appointed Richard Clarke, a career civil servant and senior advisor to the National Security Council on counterterrorism, as his cyberspace security czar, reporting both to Director of Homeland Security Tom Ridge and National Security Advisor Condoleezza Rice. In addition, the U.S. Senate recently considered new legislation (the Critical Infrastructure Information Security Act) addressing a major obstacle to improved security of critical networks: the understandable reluctance of firms to share proprietary information about networks they have built or manage. The act would enable the sharing of sensitive infrastructure information between the federal government and private sector and within the private sector itself. In his opening remarks to introduce the act on September 25, 2001, Republican Sen. Bob Bennett of Utah clearly recognized that we face a new kind of threat. "The American economy is a highly interdependent system of systems, with physical and cyber components," he declared. "Security in a networked world must be a shared responsibility."

Preparing for the Unknown

Shortly following the September 11 attacks, the U.S. Army enlisted the help of some of Hollywood's top action screenwriters and directors—including the writers of *Die Hard* and *McGyver*—to conjure up possible scenarios for future terrorist attacks. Yet no one can possibly imagine in advance all the novel opportunities for terrorism provided by our technological and economic systems. We've made these critical systems so complex that they are replete with vulnerabilities that are very hard to anticipate, because we don't even know how to ask the right questions. We can think of these possibilities as "exploitable unknown unknowns." Terrorists can make connections between components of complex systems—such as between passenger airliners and skyscrapers—that few, if any, people have anticipated. Complex terrorism is particularly effective if its goal is not a specific strategic or political end, but simply the creation of widespread fear, panic, and economic disruption. This more general objective grants terrorists much more latitude in their choice of targets. More likely than not, the next major attack will come in a form as unexpected as we witnessed on September 11.

What should we do to lessen the risk of complex terrorism, beyond the conventional counterterrorism strategies already being implemented by the United States and other nations? First, we must acknowledge our own limitations. Little can be done, for instance, about terrorists' inexorably rising capacity for violence. This trend results from deep technological forces that can't be stopped without producing major disruptions elsewhere in our economies and societies. However, we can take steps to reduce the vulnerabilities related to our complex economies and technologies. We can do so by loosening the couplings in our economic and technological networks, building into these networks various buffering capacities, introducing "circuit breakers" that interrupt dangerous feedbacks, and dispersing high-value assets so that they are less concentrated and thus less inviting targets.

These prescriptions will mean different things for different networks. In the energy sector, loosening coupling might mean greater use of decentralized, local energy production and alternative energy sources (like small-scale solar power) that make individual users more independent of the electricity grid. Similarly, in food production, loosening coupling could entail increased autonomy of local and regional food-production networks so that when one network is attacked the damage doesn't cascade into others. In many industries, increasing buffering would involve moving away from just-in-time production processes. Firms would need to increase inventories of feedstocks and parts so production can continue even when the supply of these essential inputs is interrupted. Clearly this policy would reduce economic efficiency, but the extra security of more stable and resilient production networks could far outweigh this cost.

Circuit breakers would prove particularly useful in situations where crowd behavior and panic can get out of control. They have already been implemented on the New York Stock Exchange: Trading halts if the market plunges more than a certain percentage in a particular period of time. In the case of terrorism, one of the factors heightening public anxiety is the incessant barrage of sensational reporting and commentary by 24-hour news TV. As is true for the stock exchange, there might be a role for an independent, industry-based monitoring body here, a body that could intervene with broadcasters at critical moments, or at least provide vital counsel, to manage the flow and content of information. In an emergency, for instance, all broadcasters might present exactly the same information (vetted by the monitoring body and stated deliberately and calmly) so that competition among broadcasters doesn't encourage sensationalized treatment. If the monitoring body were under the strict authority of the broadcasters themselves, the broadcasters would—collectively—retain complete control over the content of the message, and the procedure would not involve government encroachment on freedom of speech.

If terrorist attacks continue, economic forces alone will likely encourage the dispersal of high-value assets. Insurance costs could become unsupportable for businesses and industries located in vulnerable zones. In 20 to 30 years, we may be astonished at the folly of housing so much value in the exquisitely fragile buildings of the World Trade Center. Again, dispersal may entail substantial economic costs, because we'll lose economies of scale and opportunities for synergy.

Yet we have to recognize that we face new circumstances. Past policies are inadequate. The advantage in this war has shifted toward terrorists. Our increased vulnerability—and our newfound recognition of that vulnerability—makes us more risk-averse, while terrorists have become more powerful and more tolerant of risk. (The September 11 attackers, for instance, had an extremely high tolerance for risk, because they were ready and willing to die.) As a result, terrorists have significant leverage to hurt us. Their capacity to exploit this leverage depends on their ability to understand the complex systems that we depend on so critically. Our capacity to defend ourselves depends on that same understanding.

Press extracts: More Species Slide to Extinction

RICHARD BLACK

Worry But Don't Panic Over Glacial Losses

RICHARD A. KERR

The following pieces illustrate one of the paradoxes of global environmental politics. For, despite overwhelming scientific evidence that indicates a global trend of increasing atmospheric and ocean temperatures, in the United States—a global leader in producing so-called greenhouse gases—significant numbers of people believe that "global warming" is a hoax. How might a politician who is opposed to enacting restrictions on greenhouse gas emissions use these articles to support his or her position? Using the same articles, what would be a counter-argument that stresses the need to restrict greenhouse emissions?

More Species Slide to Extinction

RICHARD BLACK

One fifth of animal and plant species are under the threat of extinction, a global conservation study has warned.

Scientists who compiled the Red List of Threatened Species say the proportion of species facing wipeout is rising.

But they say intensive conservation work has already pulled some species back from the brink of oblivion.

The report is being launched at the UN Biodiversity Summit in Japan, where governments are discussing how to better protect the natural world.

Launched at the UN Convention on Biological Diversity (CBD) meeting, the report says that amphibians remain the most threatened category of animals, with 41% of species at risk, while only 13% of birds qualify for Red-Listing.

The highest losses were seen in Southeast Asia, where loss of habitat as forests are cleared for agriculture, including biofuel crops, is fastest.

"More Species Slide to Extinction," by Richard Black (26 October 2010) © BBC News. http://www.bbc.co.uk/news/science-environment-11630355

"The 'backbone' of biodiversity is being eroded," said the eminent ecologist, Professor Edward O Wilson of Harvard University.

"One small step up the Red List is one giant leap forward towards extinction. This is just a small window on the global losses currently taking place."

However, the scientists behind the assessment - who publish their findings formally in the journal Science - say there is new evidence this time that conservation projects are having a noticeable global impact.

"Really focused conservation efforts work when we do them - many island birds are recovering, lots of examples like this," said Simon Stuart, chair of the Species Survival Commission with the International Union for the Conservation of Nature (IUCN).

"We can show for sure that when we focus conservation efforts and really address the threats and put enough money into it, then you see positive results."

Species that have benefited from such action include three bred in captivity and returned to the wild - the California condor and black-footed ferret of the US, and Przewalski's horse in Mongolia.

The ban on commercial whaling has led to such a swiftly increasing population of humpback whales that they have come off the Red List entirely.

Meanwhile, a parallel study, also published in Science, asks where trends of increased risk, but also increased conservation effort, will lead the natural world in future.

Researchers analysed a range of scientific studies and global assessments. Although projections varied, all found that fundamental changes are needed in order to avoid declining populations across many types of plant and animal species.

United Front

"There is no question that business-as-usual development pathways will lead to catastrophic biodiversity loss," said research leader Paul Leadley from the Universite Paris-Sud.

"Even optimistic scenarios for this century consistently predict extinctions and shrinking populations of many species."

This picture is, in large part, what the CBD meeting is supposed to prevent.

One of the many debates currently ongoing at the meeting here is what the global target for 2020 should be - to completely halt the loss of biodiversity, or something less ambitious.

Dr Leadley's analysis backs up the view of many that a complete halt is not feasible.

But governments do at least appear united in their desire to do something, according to Dr Stuart, one of a large IUCN team monitoring developments here.

"They've said that they want to see improvements in status, especially in those species that are most at risk," he told BBC News.

"That to us is a very good target - we think it's achievable with a lot of effort.

"There doesn't seem to be much disagreement between countries on that issue - on other issues, yes, but on the species issue they're pretty solid."

However, on financing for species protection there is a lot of disagreement.

Some developing countries want a 100-fold increase in current rates of spending by the West. Other nations are arguing for a 10-fold rise.

But given that the world is in recession, that climate change is also supposed to see a huge and rapid increase in spending, and that no-one knows what the current spend on biodiversity actually is, all bets are currently off on what wording delegates will eventually arrive at.

Worry But Don't Panic Over Glacial Losses

RICHARD A. KERR

With glaciers suddenly galloping to the sea in Greenland and the "weak underbelly" of Antarctic ice beginning to give way, it's hard to keep a cool head, but a couple of glaciologists at the meeting gave it a try. At least in the short term, they said, the situation, while bad, is not always quite as bad as it looks.

Glaciologist Ian Joughin of the University of Washington, Seattle, reported on his and his colleagues' study of the forces acting on the Jakobshavn Glacier of southern Greenland. Jakobshavn accelerated toward the sea early in the decade after warming ocean water destroyed part of its floating ice tongue that had been helping to restrain it.

Jakobshavn is still accelerating and thus increasing the rate of sea level rise—plenty of cause for worry—but Joughin cautioned that Jakobshavn is not totally off its leash. Judging by the glacier's behavior from season to season, restraining forces such as friction with rock at the glacier's sides will likely keep it from accelerating by more than a factor of 3 in this century, not the factor of 10 sometimes bandied about. And even at the slower rate, by 2100 it will have retreated up onto dry land, where friction must slow it greatly.

Still, glaciologist Richard Alley of Pennsylvania State University, University Park, saw cause for some worry as well. Glaciers draining the West Antarctic Ice Sheet are also flowing faster these days. New ocean warmth has melted the floating tongues of some glaciers there, loosening their hold on bumps on the sea floor that had been restraining glacier flow and accelerating ice loss. Flow will slow only when the ice again becomes stuck on a sea-floor bump somewhere farther upstream. Such pulses of ice loss are inevitable and for many glaciers unpredictable, Alley warned, because no one is sure where the bumps are.

If researchers are going to predict such glacial surges, "we'll need to understand what's under the ice," notes glaciologist Robert Bindschadler of NASA's Goddard Space Flight Center in Greenbelt, Maryland. In the meantime, he advises not focusing on just a few glaciers like Jakobshavn. "If we do," he says, "we're likely to get too excited when they accelerate and too relieved when they pause." His advice: Keep your eye on measures of the overall losses from an ice sheet. Those will be steadier, and plenty worrisome.

From Richard A. Kerr, "Worry But Don't Panic Over Glacial Losses," *Science*, Vol. 331, No. 6014 (14 Jan. 2011); page 143. Reprinted with permission from AAAS.

Useful Internet Resources

Arctic Monitoring and Assessment Programme (AMAP), http://www.amap.no
Convention on Biological Diversity, http://www.cbd.int/
Convention on Long-Range Transboundary Air Pollution, http://unece.org/env/Irtap/
Earth Day Footprint Quiz, http://www.myfootprint.org/
Global Environment Facility, http://gerweb.org/
Intergovernmental Panel on Climate Change (IPCC), http://www.ipcc.ch/
International Water Law Project, http://internationalwaterlaw.org/
Socioeconomic Data and Applications Center, http://sedac.ciesin.org/
U.S. Environmental Protection Agency, http://www.epa.gov/
United Nations Framework Convention on Climate Change, http://unfccc.int/2860.php
World Conservation Union, http://www.iucn.org

Discussion Questions and Activities

1. Has globalization ended the high politics/low politics distinction that once characterized the academic study of international relations? Explain your answer.
2. Imagine that you are a newly appointed political advisor to the leader of a country. What advice would you give your boss regarding security; the promoting of trade; the defending of human rights; and protecting the environment? Upon which academic theory that we have studied will you base your recommendations? Why?
3. Many analysts of global politics discuss the topics we studied in this part as polar opposites: for instance, security vs. human rights; trade vs. the environment. Do you agree with these dichotomies? Why? Why not? Use specific examples from the global press to support your answer.
4. In this part we studied issues related to security; trade and finance; human rights; and the environment. Which one issue is the most important topic facing global society today? Defend your answer with specifie examples from the global press.

APPENDIX ONE: GLOSSARY

Absolute gains: All states seek to gain more power and influence in the system to secure their national interests. This is absolute gain. Offensive neorealists are also concerned with increasing power relative to other states. One must have enough power to secure interests and more power than any other state in the system—friend or foe.

Adaptation strategies: A foreign policy based on reacting to international events and adjusting national goals to conform to the effects of events external to that state.

Advocacy networks: Groups of regional, national, and international NGOs bound together by shared values. They coordinate activity to frame political debate and to influence policy outcomes.

Al-Qaeda: Most commonly associated with now deceased Osama bin Laden, "The Base" (as it means in Arabic) is a religious-based group whose fighters swear an oath of fealty to bin Laden.

Americanization: The spread of American values, practices, popular culture, and way of life.

Anarchic system: A Realist description of the international system that suggests there is no common power or central governing structure.

Anarchy: A system operating in the absence of any central government. It does not imply chaos but, in Realist theory, the absence of political authority.

Appeasement: A policy of making concessions to a revanchist (or otherwise territorially acquisitive) state in the hope that settlement of more modest claims will assuage that state's expansionist appetites. Appeasement remains most (in)famously associated with British prime minister Neville Chamberlain's acquiescence to Hitler's incursions into Austria and then Czechoslovakia, culminating in the Munich Agreement of September 1938. Since then, appeasement has generally been seen as synonymous with a craven collapse before the demands of dictators—encouraging, not disarming, their aggressive designs.

Armistice: A cease-fire agreement between enemies in wartime. In the case of World War I, the armistice began at 11:00 a.m. on November 11, 1918.

Arms embargo: Similar to economic sanctions, an arms embargo stops the flow of arms from one country to another.

Arms race: This is a central concept in Realist thought. As states build up their military to address real or perceived threats to their national security, they may create insecurity in other states. These states, in turn, develop their military capacities and thus begin an arms race. This never-ending pursuit of security creates the condition we know as a security dilemma.

Association of Southeast Asian Nations (ASEAN): A geopolitical and economic organization of several countries located in Southeast Asia. Initially formed as a display of solidarity against communism, it has since redefined its aims and broadened to include the acceleration of economic growth and the promotion of regional peace. By 2005 the ASEAN countries had a combined GDP of about $884 billion.

Asymmetric conflict: In symmetric warfare, armies with comparable weapons, tactics, and organizational structures do battle. Wars are fought on near-equal terms. When stakes are high and those actors in conflict are not equal in terms of weapons and technology, the weaker side adopts asymmetric tactics. These include guerrilla warfare, roadside bombs, attacks on civilians, and other terrorist tactics.

Autarchy: The mercantilist recommendation that states strive for economic self-sufficiency by using trade protectionism or policies of complete isolation.

Balance of power: In Realist theory, this refers to an equilibrium between states; historical Realists regard it as the product of diplomacy (contrived balance), whereas structural Realists regard the system as having a tendency towards a natural equilibrium (fortuitous balance). It is a doctrine and an arrangement whereby the power of one state (or group of states) is checked by the countervailing power of other states.

Bipolar: A term to describe an international political order in which two states dominate all others. It is often used to describe the nature of the international system when the two superpowers, the USSR and the US, were dominant powers during the Cold War.

Blitzkrieg: The German term for "lightning war." This was an offensive strategy that used the combination of mechanized forces—especially tanks—and aircraft as mobile artillery to exploit breaches in an enemy's front line. The irony was that in 1940 the French army had more tanks than the German army. The French tanks, however, were spread among units along the front line, while the German commanders concentrated their tanks in a few units.

Bretton Woods System: The name given to the three institutions that make up the post–Second World War international political economic system. It is called Bretton Woods after the hamlet in northern New Hampshire where the leaders from the United States, the United Kingdom, and forty-two other countries met in July 1944.

Capacity building: Providing the funds and technical training to allow developing countries to participate in global environmental governance.

Capital controls: This is the monetary policy device that a government uses to regulate the flows into and out of a country's capital account (i.e., the flows of investment-oriented money into and out of a country or currency).

Capitalism: A system of production in which human labor and its products are commodities that are bought and sold in the marketplace.

Charter rights: Civil liberties guaranteed in a written document such as a constitution.

Civil society: (1) The totality of all individuals and groups in a society who are not acting as participants in any government institutions, or (2) all individuals and groups who are neither participants in government nor acting in the interests of commercial companies.

Civilization: The broadest construction of cultural identity to which individuals may subscribe. A number of broad cultures have emerged from world history, including the Western, Islamic, and Chinese civilizations.

Clandestine or "sleeper" cell: Usually a group of people, sent by an intelligence organization or terrorist network, that remains dormant in a target country until activated by a message to carry out a mission, which could include prearranged attacks.

Class: A social group that in Marxism is identified by its relationship with the means of production and the distribution of societal resources. Thus, we have the *bourgeoisie*, or the owners or upper classes, and the *proletariat*, or workers.

Climate change: A convention on climate was agreed to at the Rio Conference in 1992. Climate change represents a change in the statistical distribution of weather over periods of time that range from decades to millions of years. It can be a change in the average weather or a change in the distribution of weather events around an average (for example, greater or fewer extreme weather events). Climate change may be limited to a specific region, or it may occur across the whole Earth.

Coercive diplomacy: The use of diplomatic and military methods that force a state to concede to another state. These methods may include the threat of force and the actual mobilization of military forces so as to gradually "turn the screw" but exclude the actual use of force. The implication is that war is the next step if diplomacy fails.

Collective security: An arrangement in which memebers agree to treat aggression against one as an attack upon all.

Common security: At times called "cooperative security," it stresses noncompetitive approaches and cooperative approaches through which states—both friends and foes—can achieve security. Sometimes expressed as until all people are secure from threats of war, no one is secure.

Community: A human association in which members share common symbols and wish to cooperate to realize common objectives.

Concert of Europe: Five so-called great powers (Austria, Britain, France, Prussia, and Russia) created an informal institution and agreed on "rules of the game," including controlling revolutionary forces, managing the balance of power, and accepting interventions to keep current leaders in power. This system kept the peace in Europe until WWI.

Conditionality: When regional or international lending agencies require that recipient national governments accept certain policy conditions in order to receive a loan or some form of economic assistance.

Congress of Berlin: A meeting of the European states that had an interest in colonizing Africa. The Berlin conference redrew the existing political map of Africa, with a goal to avoid conflict between the Europeans in Africa.

Congress of Vienna: A meeting of major European leaders (1814–1815) that redrew the political map of Europe after the end of the Napoleonic Wars. The congress was an attempt to restore a conservative political order in the continent.

Constructivism: An approach to international politics that concerns itself with the centrality of ideas and human consciousness. As constructivists have examined world politics they have been broadly interested in how the structure constructs the actors' identities and interests, how their interactions are organized and constrained by that structure, and how their very interaction serves to either reproduce or transform that structure.

Containment: American political strategy for resisting perceived Soviet expansion, first publicly espoused by an American diplomat, George Kennan, in 1947 and aimed at limiting Soviet expansion in Europe. Containment became a powerful factor in American policy towards the Soviet Union for the next forty years, and a self-image of Western policy-makers. However, Kennan's view of containment did not include the aggressive militarization that brought the world closer to the brink of nuclear destruction.

Coordination: A form of cooperation requiring parties to pursue a common strategy in order to avoid the mutually undesirable outcome arising from the pursuit of divergent strategies.

Cosmopolitan culture: A pattern of relations within which people share the same goals and aspirations, generally to improve that culture for all members.

Cosmopolitan democracy: A condition in which international organizations, transnational corporations, and global markets are accountable to the peoples of the world.

Critical theory: Theories that are critical of the status quo and reject the idea that things can be fixed under the present system. These theories challenge core assumptions of the dominant paradigm and argue for transformation and not just reform.

Democratic deficit: Leaders have created many policy-making institutions at the global, regional, and national levels with policy-making power led by individuals who are appointed and not elected. Thus policy decisions are not subject to review by citizens.

Democratic peace: A central plank of Liberal-Internationalist thought, the democratic-peace thesis makes two claims: first, Liberal polities exhibit restraint in their relations with other Liberal polities (the so-called separate peace), but, second, they are imprudent in relations with authoritarian states. The validity of the democratic-peace thesis has been fiercely debated in the international relations literature.

Dependency theory: The world capitalist system divides the world into core, semiperiphery, and periphery states. The core states control both the economic and the political system and exploit the people and resources in the periphery and semiperiphery. The capitalist system is seen as impossible to reform, and only by withdrawing from the system can poor states break this dependency.

Deregulation: The removal of all regulation so that market forces, not government policy, control economic developments.

Desertification: This is the extreme deterioration of land in arid and dry subhumid areas due to loss of vegetation and soil moisture; desertification results chiefly from manmade activities and is influenced by climatic variations. This condition is principally caused by overgrazing, overdrafting of groundwater, and diversion of water from rivers for human consumption and industrial use—all of these processes fundamentally driven by overpopulation.

Détente: Relaxation of tension between East and West; Soviet–American détente lasted from the late 1960s to the late 1970s and was characterized by negotiations and nuclear arms control agreements.

Deterrence: The threat or use of force to prevent an actor from doing something the actor would otherwise do.

Development: In the orthodox view, top-down; reliance on "expert knowledge," usually Western and definitely external; large capital investments in large projects; advanced technology; expansion of the private sphere. In the alternative view, bottom-up; participatory; reliance on appropriate (often local) knowledge and technology; small investments in small-scale projects; protection of the commons.

Diplomacy: The process by which international actors communicate as they seek to resolve conflicts without going to war and find solutions to complex global problems.

Dollar standard: By 1947, the British pound and gold could no longer serve as the world's money. The only currency strong enough to be used to meet the demands for international liquidity was the US dollar. For both political and economic reasons, the US government was willing to become the world's central bank and use dollars for the key currency in the international monetary system.

Ecological footprint: Used to demonstrate the load placed on the Earth's carrying capacity by individuals or nations. It does this by estimating the area of productive land and water system required to sustain a population at its specified standard of living.

Ecologies: Communities of plants and animals in an environment that supplies raw materials for all living things.

Economic base: In the Marxist perspective the substructure of the society is the relationship between owners and workers. Capitalists own the means of production and control technology and resources. The workers are employed by the capitalists, and they are alienated, exploited, and estranged from their work and their society.

Economic sanctions: A tool of statecraft that seeks to get a state to behave by coercion of a monetary kind: for example, freeing banking assets, cutting aid programs, or banning trade.

Economic shock: An event that produces a significant change within an economy, despite occurring outside of it. Economic shocks are unpredictable and typically affect supply or demand throughout the markets. A sudden rise in commodity process and a devaluation of a currency are two examples of shocks that would hurt economic actors.

Ecosystem: A system of interdependent living organisms that share the same habitat, functioning together with all of the physical factors of the environment. Ecosystems can be permanent or temporary. The Convention on Biological Diversity (CBD)—ratified by more than 175 countries—defines the protection of ecosystems as natural habitats and the maintenance of viable populations of species in natural surroundings.

Electronic commerce: The buying and selling of products and services over the telephone or Internet. eBay and Amazon are examples of leaders in this area of commerce.

Empire: A distinct type of political entity, which may or may not be a state, possessing both a home territory and foreign territories. This may include conquered nations and colonies.

Enlightenment: Associated with rationalist thinkers of the eighteenth century. Key ideas (which some would argue remain mottoes for our age) include secularism, progress, reason, science, knowledge, and freedom.

Epistemic community: A knowledge-based transnational community of experts and policy activists.

Equity: Also called "stock" or "share"; a number of equal portions in the nominal capital of a company; the shareholder thereby owns part of the enterprise.

Ethic of responsibility: For historical Realists, an ethic of responsibility represents the limits of ethics in international politics; it involves the weighing up of consequences and the realization that positive outcomes may result from amoral actions.

European Union (EU): The EU was formally created in 1992 following the signing of the Maastricht Treaty. However, the origins of the EU can be traced back to 1951 and the creation of the European Coal and Steel Community, followed in 1957 with a broader customs union (the Treaty of Rome, 1958). Originally a grouping of six countries in 1957, "Europe" grew by adding new members in 1973, 1981, and 1986. Since the fall of the planned economies in Eastern Europe in 1989, the EU has grown and now includes twenty-seven member states.

Exceptionalism: The belief that a country has a unique set of domestic and foreign policy traditions. An implication is that other countries should embrace the same set of policies.

Export-led growth: An outward-oriented economy that is based on exploiting its own comparative advantages, such as cheap labor or resources, to capture a share of the world market in a given industry. Many of the countries in Asia took advantage of cheap labor to gain control of industries like electronics and textiles and thereby to control most of the exports to the world.

Extraterritoriality: When one government attempts to use domestic legal authority to control the global activities of its citizens or TNCs.

Failed (or failing) state: A state that does not command the primary loyalty of its citizens or subjects. These states have no monopoly of force at home and lack complete control over their own territory.

Feminism: A movement, a cause, and a research agenda to understand so as to change women's inequality, liberation, or oppression. For some, the aim is to move beyond gender, so that it no longer matters; for others, to validate women's interests, experiences, and choices; for others, to work for more equal and inclusive social relations overall. Feminist theories tend to be critical of the biases of the discipline. Many focus their research on the areas where women are excluded from the analysis of major international issues and concerns.

Fixed exchange rate: The price a currency will earn in a hard currency. Here a government is committed to keep it at a specific value.

Floating exchange rate: The market decides what the actual value of a currency is compared to other currencies.

Foreign direct investment (FDI): Capital speculation by citizens or organizations of one country into markets or industries in another country.

Foreign policy: The articulation of national interests and the means chosen to secure those interests, both material and ideational, in the international arena.

Foreign policy style: Often shaped by a state's political culture, history, and traditions, this describes how a country deals with other states and how it approaches any decision-making situation. For example, does it act unilaterally or multilaterally; does it seek consensus on an agreement or does it go with majority rule?

Fourteen Points: President Woodrow Wilson's vision of international society, first articulated in January 1918, included the principle of self-determination, the conduct of diplomacy on an open (not secret) basis, and the establishment of an association of nation-states to provide guarantees of independence and territorial integrity. Wilson's ideas exerted an important influence on the Paris Peace Conference, though the principle of self-determination was only selectively pursued when it came to American colonial interests.

Free market: A market ruled by the forces of supply and demand, where all buying and selling is not constrained by government regulations or interventions.

Free trade: An essential element of capitalism that argues for no barriers or minimal barriers to the exchange of goods, services, and investments between states.

Functionalism: An idea formulated by early proponents of European integration that suggests that cooperation should begin with efforts aimed at resolving specific regional or transnational problems. It is assumed that resolution of these problems will lead to cooperation, or spillover, in other policy areas.

Futures: Derivatives that oblige a buyer and seller to complete a transaction at a predetermined time in the future at a price agreed on today. Futures are also known as "forwards."

G-8 (Group of Eight): Established in 1975 as the G-5 (France, Germany, Japan, the UK, and the US); subsequently expanded as the G-7, to include Canada and Italy; and since 1998 the G-8, to include the Russian Federation. The G-8 conducts semiformal collaboration on world economic problems. Government leaders meet in annual G-8 summits, while finance ministers or their leading officials periodically hold other consultations.

Game theory: A branch of mathematics that explores strategic interaction.

Genocide: Deliberate and systematic extermination of an ethnic, national, tribal, or religious group.

Glasnost: Policy of greater openness pursued by Soviet leader Mikhail Gorbachev from 1985, involving greater toleration of internal dissent and criticism.

Global capital markets: These are banks, investment companies, insurance companies, trusts, hedge funds, and stock exchanges that transfer funds to industries and other commercial enterprises globally.

Global commons: Areas and resources not under national sovereignty that belong to no single country and are the responsibility of the entire world. The oceans beyond the 200-mile limit, outer space, and Antarctica are global commons areas.

Global environmental governance: Governance is the performance of regulative functions, often in the absence of a central government authority. Global environmental governance usually refers to the structure of international agreements and organizations but can also involve governance by the private sector or NGOs.

Global governance: Involves the regulation and coordination of transnational issue areas by nation-states, international and regional organizations, and private agencies through the establishment of international regimes. These regimes may focus on problem-solving or the simple enforcement of rules and regulations.

Global politics: The politics of global social relations in which the pursuit of power, interests, order, and justice transcends regions and continents.

Global sourcing: Obtaining goods and services across geopolitical boundaries. Usually the goal is to find the least expensive labor and raw material costs and the lowest taxes and tariffs.

Globalization: A historical process involving a fundamental shift or transformation in the spatial scale of human social organization that links distant communities and expands the reach of power relations across regions and continents.

Government: The people and agencies that have the power and legitimate authority to determine who gets what, when, where, and how within a given territory.

Great Depression: A byword for the global economic collapse that ensued following the US Wall Street stock market crash in October 1929. Economic shockwaves soon rippled around a world already densely interconnected by webs of trade and foreign direct investment, with the result that the events of October 1929 were felt in countries as distant as Brazil and Japan.

Great power: State that has the political, economic, and military resources to shape the world beyond its borders. In most cases such a state has the will and capacity to define the rules of the international system.

Gross domestic product (GDP): The sum of all economic activity that takes place within a country.

Guerrilla wars: Conflicts or insurgencies that involve irregular forces. Fighters in these wars use unconventional methods of warfare, such as sabotage, ambushes, roadside bombs, and sniping.

Hard power: The material threats and inducements leaders employ to achieve the goals of their state.

Hegemony: A system regulated by a dominant leader, or political (and/or economic) domination of a region, usually by a superpower. It is also means power and control exercised by a leading state over other states.

Holocaust: The term used to describe the attempts by the Nazis to murder the Jewish population of Europe. Some 6 million Jewish people were killed in concentration camps, along with a further million that included Soviet prisoners, Roma, Poles, communists, homosexuals, and the physically or mentally disabled.

Horizontal proliferation: An increase in the number of actors who possess nuclear weapons.

Human development: The notion that it is possible to improve the lives of people. Basically, it is about increasing the number of choices people have. These may include living a long and healthy life, access to education, and a better standard of living.

Human security: The security of people, including their physical safety, their economic and social well-being, respect for their dignity, and the protection of their human rights. Simply put, it is freedom from fear and freedom from want.

Humanitarian intervention: The use of military force by external actors to end a threat to people within a sovereign state.

Hybrid international organizations: Organizations that provide full membership and equality of status both to governmental actors and to transnational actors. They create policy to govern specific areas of international relations.

Hyperpower: A term meant to describe the situation of the United States after the Cold War ended. With the Soviet Union's military might greatly diminished and China having primarily only regional power-projecting capability, the United States was unchallenged in the world.

Idealism: Referred to by Realists as utopianism since it underestimates the logic of power politics and the constraints this imposes on political action. Idealism as a substantive theory of international relations is generally associated with the claim that it is possible to create a world of peace. Some idealists seek to apply liberal thinking in domestic politics to international relations—in other words, to institutionalize the rule of law.

Ideational/ideal interest: The psychological, moral, ethical goals of a state as it sets foreign and domestic policy.

Identity: The understanding of the self in relationship to an "other." Identities are social and thus always formed in relationship to others. Constructivists generally hold that identities shape interests; we cannot know what we want unless we know who we are. But because identities are social and produced through interactions, identities can change.

Immigration controls: When a government controls the number of people who may work, study, or relocate to its country. It may also include quotas for certain national groups for immigration.

Imperialism: The practice of foreign conquest and rule in the context of global relations of hierarchy and subordination. It can lead to the establishment of an empire.

Integration: A process of ever-closer union between states, in a regional or international context. The process often begins with cooperation to solve technical problems.

Intellectual property rights: Rules that protect the owners of content through copyright, patents, trademarks, and trade secrets. The World Intellectual Property Organization (WIPO) is the forum where states (184 members in 2010) discuss this issue.

Intercontinental Ballistic Missiles (ICBMs): Weapons system the US and USSR developed to threaten each other with destruction. The thirty- to forty-minute flight times of the missiles created a situation that is sometimes called "Mutually Assured Destruction (MAD)" or "the Balance of Terror."

Interdependence: A condition where states (or peoples) are affected by decisions taken by others. Interdependence can be symmetric (i.e., both sets of actors are affected equally) or it can be asymmetric, where the impact varies between actors. If political or economic costs of interdependence are high, a state is in a vulnerable position. If costs are low, it is a situation of sensitivity interdependence.

Intergovernmental organization (IGO): A formal, legally constituted organization established by states to handle common problems or issues; membership and decision-making authority are limited to governments.

International law: The formal rules of conduct that states acknowledge or contract between themselves.

International non-governmental organization (INGO): A formal international organization with transnational members from at least three countries. There are many different types, with membership from national NGOs, local NGOs, companies, political parties, or individual people. A few have other INGOs as members, and some have mixed membership structures.

International order: The normative and the institutional pattern in the relationship between states. The elements of this may be thought to include such things as sovereignty, the forms of diplomacy, international law, the role of the great powers, and the codes circumscribing the use of force. It is a shared value and condition of stability and predictability in the relations of states.

International organization: Any institution with formal procedures and formal membership from three or more countries. The minimum number of countries is set at three, rather than two, because multilateral relationships have significantly greater complexity than bilateral relationships.

International relations: In a traditional sense, this is the study of the interactions of states in the international system. It was initially considered a part of diplomatic history or political science. Today, departments of international relations include concentrations in international security, political economy, foreign policy, human rights, global governance, and environmental issues. The field now includes the study of other actors, including corporations and NGOs, and a wide variety of issues, such as culture, identity, and ethics.

Interparadigm debate: This is the debate between the two main theoretical approaches in the field of global politics: realism versus liberalism. Some present this debate as one between neo-realism and neo-liberalism. Critics argue that this is no real debate because the two theoretical approaches share many assumptions.

Intervention: Direct involvement within a state by an outside actor to achieve an outcome preferred by the intervening agency without the consent of the host state.

Intrafirm trade: International trade from one branch of a TNC to an affiliate of the same company in a different country.

Invisible hand: The concept found in the eighteenth-century writing of Adam Smith that proposed governments leave trade and financial sectors alone.

Jihad: In Arabic, *jihad* simply means "struggle." Jihad can refer to a purely internal struggle to be a better Muslim, or a struggle to make society more closely align with the teachings of the Koran.

League of Nations: The first permanent collective international security organization aimed at preventing wars and resolving global problems. The League failed due to the failure of the US to join and the inability of its members to commit to a real international community.

Legitimacy: A legitimate authority is respected and recognized by those it rules and by other rulers or leaders of other states. The source of legitimacy can be laws or a constitution and the support of the society.

Liberal democracy: States with democratic or representative governments and capitalist economies that are promoters of multilateralism and free trade. Domestic interests, values, and institutions shape foreign policy.

Liberal feminism: A position that advocates equal rights for women but also supports a more progressive policy agenda that would include social justice, peace, economic well-being, and ecological balance.

Liberal internationalism: A perspective that seeks to transform international relations to emphasize peace, individual freedom, and prosperity, and to replicate domestic models of liberal democracy at the international level.

Liberalism: A political philosophy that developed in Western Europe, beginning roughly in the 1600s. The movement sought to restrict the privileges of monarchs, replacing them with limited government and written constitutions guaranteeing the rights of individuals. Often associated with the rise of a middle class dominated by industrial interests that challenged the power of an aristocracy whose power was linked to the ownership of land. Key provisions included a right to own property, religious freedom, and freedom of expression.

Liberalization: Describes government policies that reduce the role of the state in the economy, such as the dismantling of trade tariffs and barriers, the deregulation and opening of the financial sector to foreign investors, and the privatization of state enterprises.

Market democracies: See "Liberal democracy."

Marshall Plan: Officially known as the European Recovery Program, it was a program of financial and other economic aid for Europe after WWII. Proposed by Secretary of State George Marshall in 1948, it was offered to all European states, including the Soviet Union, and these funds played a critical role in European recovery.

Marxism: A theory critical of the status quo or dominant paradigm. It is a critique of the capitalist political economy from the view of the revolutionary proletariat, or workers. The relations of production, or the relationship between workers and owners, is the determining factor in political relations. Marxists believe that those who own the means of production also control the political system. In capitalist systems, workers are exploited and thus alienated from both the economic and political systems. Marxists' ideal is a stateless and classless society.

Material interest: The tangible physical goals of state officials as they set foreign and domestic policy.

Materialism: In this context materialism means the spreading of a global consumer culture and popular-culture artifacts like music, books, and movies. Christopher Lasch called this the "ceaseless translation of luxuries into necessities." These elements are seen as undermining traditional cultural values and norms.

Modern state: Political unit within which citizens identify with the state and see the state as legitimate. This state has a monopoly over the use of force and is able to provide citizens with key services.

Monopoly capitalism: A term introduced by Lenin that suggested that competitive capitalism had been replaced by large corporations that control the market in specific sectors.

Most favored nation status: This is the status granted to most trading partners that says trade rules with that country will be the same as those given to their most favored trading partner.

Multilateralism: The process by which states work together to solve a common problem.

Multinational corporations or enterprises (MNCs/MNEs): A business or firm with administration, production, distribution, and marketing located in countries around the world. Such a business moves money, goods, services, and technology around the world depending upon where the firm can make the most profit.

Nation: An community of people who share a common sense of identity, which may be derived from language, culture, or ethnicity; this community may be a minority within a single country or may live in more than one country.

Nation-state: A political community in which the state claims legitimacy on the grounds that it represents the nation.

National interest: The combination of material and ideal goals that make up the goals of the government of a state.

National liberation: This was a doctrine promoted by the Soviet Union that encouraged anticolonial or anti-Western insurgencies in the developing world.

National security: A fundamental value in the foreign policy of states secured by a variety of tools of statecraft, including military actions, diplomacy, economic resources, and international agreements and alliances. It also depends on a stable and productive domestic society.

Nationalism: The idea that the world is divided into nations that provide the overriding focus of political identity and loyalty, which in turn should be the basis for defining the population of states. Nationalism also can refer to this idea in the form of a strong sense of identity (*sentiment*) or organizations and movements seeking to realize this idea (*politics*).

National self-determination: The right or desire of distinct national groups to become states and to rule themselves.

Natural law: The idea that humans have an essential nature, which dictates that certain kinds of human goods are always and everywhere desired; because of this, there are common moral standards that govern all human relations, and these common standards can be discerned by the application of reason to human affairs.

Neoclassical realism: A version of realism that combines both structural factors such as the distribution of power and unit-level factors such as the interests of states.

Neo-liberalism: Shaped by the ideas of commercial, republican, sociological, and institutional liberalism. Neo-liberals see the international system as anarchic but believe relations can be managed by the establishment of international regimes and institutions. Neo-liberals think that actors with common interests will try to maximize absolute gains.

New World Order: This refers to the post–Cold War rhetoric of President George Herbert Walker Bush, who called for a new world order based on neo-liberal values of democracy, capitalism, and the rule of law. After periods of turmoil or war, the victors often call for a new world order based on their values, beliefs, and interests.

Niche diplomacy: Every state has its national interests and its areas of comparative advantage over other international actors. This is its area of expertise and where it has the greatest interests. Hence, this is where the state concentrates its foreign policy resources.

Noncompliance: The failure of states or other actors to abide by treaties or rules supported by international regimes.

Nongovernmental organization (NGO): An organization with policy goals, but neither governmental nor corporate in its composition. These organizations make up global civil society—the space between governments and the corporate business world. An NGO is any group of people relating to each other regularly in some formal manner and engaging in collective action, provided the activities are noncommercial and nonviolent and are not on behalf of a government.

Nonintervention: The principle that external powers should not intervene in the domestic affairs of sovereign states.

Non–nuclear weapons state (NNWS): A state that is party to the Treaty on the Nonproliferation of Nuclear Weapons, meaning that it does not possess nuclear weapons.

Nonpolar world: A world in which there are many power centers and many of them are not nation-states. Power is diffused and is in many hands in many policy areas.

Non-state actor: Any participant in global politics that is neither acting in the name of government nor created and served by government. NGOs, terrorist networks, global crime syndicates, and multinational corporations are examples.

Normative theory: Systematic analyses of the ethical, moral, and political principles that either govern or ought to govern the organization or conduct of global politics. The belief that theories should be concerned with what ought to be, rather than merely diagnosing what is.

Norms: These specify general standards of behavior and identify the rights and obligations of states. So, in the case of the GATT, the basic norm is that tariffs and nontariff barriers should be reduced and eventually eliminated. Together, norms and principles define the essential character of a regime, and these cannot be changed without transforming the nature of the regime.

North Atlantic Treaty Organization (NATO): Organization established by treaty in April 1949 comprising twelve (later sixteen) countries from Western Europe and North America. The most important aspect of the NATO alliance was the American commitment to the defense of Western Europe. Today NATO has twenty-eight member states.

Nuclear deterrence: Defined by nuclear strategists as the possession of sufficient power to inflict unacceptable damage on a potential adversary. Nuclear deterrence must involve explicit threats in order to prevent a state from using weapons. These threats must be seen as credible and must be clearly communicated.

Nuclear terrorism: The use of or threat to use nuclear weapons or nuclear materials to achieve the goals of rogue states or revolutionary or radical organizations.

Nuclear weapon state (NWS): A state that is party to the Nonproliferation Treaty and has tested a nuclear weapon or other nuclear explosive device before January 1, 1967.

Offensive realism: A structural theory of Realism that views states as security maximizers.

Offshore finance centers: Extraterritorial banks that investors use for a range of reasons, including the desire to avoid domestic taxes, regulations, and law enforcement agencies.

Oligarchy: A term from ancient Greece to describe a political system in which a few people control a state.

Ostpolitik: The West German government's "Eastern Policy" of the mid- to late 1960s, designed to develop relations between West Germany and members of the Warsaw Pact.

Paradigm: A model, or example. In the case of international relations theory, the term is a rough synonym for "academic perspective." A paradigm provides the essential basis for a theory. It presents a comprehensive framework for the identification of factors that are referenced in the construction of theory. It tells us what is real and significant in a given area. Research questions fall within the paradigm. It provides a means of selecting what will be the object of theory.

Paradox: An absurd or self-contradictory statement.

Parsimony: A word that can mean "miserliness," in political science it refers to attempts to develop a paradigm or theory that explains events in the simplest way possible.

Patriarchy: A persistent society-wide structure within which gender relations are defined by male dominance and female subordination.

Peace dividend: The misplaced belief that the end of the Cold War would bring about a fundamental change in international relations and provide funds for domestic programs or even result in a reduction in taxes.

Peace enforcement: Designed to bring hostile parties to agreement; may occur without the consent of the parties.

Peace of Westphalia, 1648: The treaties of Osnabrück and Münster, which together form the Peace of Westphalia, ended the Thirty Years' War and were crucial in delimiting the political rights and authority of European monarchs.

Peace Treaty of Versailles, 1919: The Treaty of Versailles formally ended the First World War (1914–1918). The treaty established the League of Nations, specified the rights and obligations of the victorious and defeated powers, and created the "Mandate" system under which "advanced nation-states" were given legal tutelage over colonial peoples.

Peacekeeping: The interposition of third-party military personnel to keep warring parties apart.

Peacemaking: Active diplomatic efforts to seek a resolution to an international dispute that has already escalated.

Perestroika: Gorbachev's policy of restructuring, pursued in tandem with glasnost, and intended to modernize the Soviet political and economic system.

Pluralism: The political theory of pluralism holds that political power and influence in society does not belong just to the citizens, nor to elite groups in various sectors of society, but is distributed among a wide number of groups in the society. It can also mean a recognition of ethnic, racial, and cultural diversity.

Positivism and postpositivism: Positivists (social scientists) and postpositivists (critical and constitutive theorists) form the basis for fierce debates among scholars. At the core lies a disagreement about whether social science theory can be value-free. Positivists believe we can explain the social world as effectively as natural and physical scientists explain their phenomena. Postpositivists believe we cannot possibly be objective—value-free—observers since we are actively or passively a part of the events and issues unfolding before us.

Positivists: Analysts who use the scientific method to structure their research.

Post-conflict peace building: Activities launched after a conflict has ended that seek to end the condition that caused the conflict.

Post–Washington Consensus: A slightly modified version of the Washington Consensus, promoting economic growth through trade liberalization coupled with pro-poor growth and poverty-reduction policies.

Postmodern or new terrorists: Groups and individuals subscribing to millennial and apocalyptic ideologies and system-level goals. Most value destruction for its own sake, unlike most terrorists in the past, who had specific goals, usually tied to a territory.

Postmodern state: A political unit within which citizens are less nationalistic and more cosmopolitan in their outlook on both domestic and foreign policy. Policy-making authority for this kind of state is shared with a variety of actors at the local, national, regional, and international levels.

Postmodernity: The postmodern international system is one where domestic and international affairs are intertwined, national borders are permeable, and states have rejected the use of force for resolving conflict. The European Union is seen as an example of the evolution of the state-centric system.

Poverty: In the orthodox view, a situation suffered by people who do not have the money to buy food and satisfy other basic material needs. In the alternative view, a situation suffered by people who are not able to meet their material and nonmaterial needs through their own effort.

Premodern state: A state within which the primary identity of citizens or subjects is to national, religious, or ethnic communities. People think of themselves as members of the subnational group first, rather than the state.

Preventive diplomacy: Measures that states take to keep a disagreement from escalating.

Preventive war: Launching a war to eliminate a perceived threat from another country, often started prior to the escalation of a crisis or before the enemy is itself prepared to attack.

Protectionism: Not an economic policy but a variety of political actions taken to protect domestic industries from more-efficient foreign producers. Usually this means the use of tariffs, nontariff barriers, and subsidies to protect domestic interests.

Protestant Reformation: A social movement in reaction to the widespread perception that the Catholic Church had become corrupt and had lost its moral compass.

Public diplomacy: The use of media, the Internet, and other social culture outlets to communicate the message of a state.

Radical liberalism: This is the utopian side of liberalism best exemplified by the academic community called the World Order Models Project (WOMP). These scholars advocated a world in which states promote values like social justice, economic well-being, peace, and ecological balance. These scholars see the liberal order as predatory and clearly in need of transformation.

Rapprochement: Reestablishment of more friendly relations between the People's Republic of China and the United States in the early 1970s.

Ratification: The procedure by which a state approves a convention or protocol that it has signed. There will be rules in the treaty concerning the number of ratifications required before it can enter into force.

Realism: The theoretical approach that analyzes all international relations as the relation of states engaged in the pursuit of power. Realists see the international system as anarchic or without a common power, and they believe conflict is endemic in the international system.

Realpolitik: First used to describe the foreign policy of Bismarck in Prussia, it describes the practice of diplomacy based on the assessment of power, territory, and material interests, with little concern for ethical realities.

Reciprocity: A form of statecraft that employs retaliatory strategy, cooperating only if others do likewise.

Regimes: Sets of implicit or explicit principles, norms, rules, and decision-making procedures around which actors' expectations converge in a given area of international relations. Often simply defined as governing arrangements in a regional or global policy area.

Regulatory arbitrage: In the world of banking, the process of moving funds or business activity from one country to another in order to increase profits by escaping the constraints imposed by government regulations. By analogy, the term can be applied to any transfer of economic activity by any company in response to government policy.

Relative gains: One of the factors that Realists argue constrain the willingness of states to cooperate. States are less concerned about whether everyone benefits (absolute gains) and more concerned about whether someone may benefit more than someone else.

Responsibility to Protect: The 2001 final report of the International Commission on Intervention and State Sovereignty; a UN publication that asserted the moral obligation for states to intervene in a state when that state violates the human rights of people living there.

Revolution in military affairs (RMA): This is the effect generated by the marriage of advanced communications and information processing with state-of-the-art weapons and delivery systems. It is a means of overcoming the uncertainty and confusion that are part of any battle in war.

Security: Measures taken by states to ensure the safety of their citizens, the protection of their way of life, and the survival of their nation-state. Security can also mean the ownership of property that gives an individual the ability to secure the enjoyment or enforcement of a right or a basic human need.

Security community: A regional group of countries that have the same guiding philosophic ideals—usually liberal-democratic principles, norms, and ethics—and tend to have the same style of political systems.

Security dilemma: In an anarchic international system, one with no common central power, when one state seeks to improve its security it creates insecurity in other states.

Self-help: In Realist theory, in an anarchical environment, states cannot assume other states will come to their defense even if they are allies. *Each state must take care of itself.*

September 11, 2001: The day when Islamic terrorists in the United States hijacked four aircraft. Two destroyed the World Trade Center in New York, one partially destroyed the Pentagon, and a fourth crash-landed in a field in Pennsylvania.

Sex and gender: "Sex" is biological difference, born male or female; the sex act; sexual difference. "Gender" is what it means to be male or female in a particular place or time; the social construction of sexual difference.

Sharia law: Traditional Islamic law of the Koran ("al Qur'an") and the "Sunna," which are the interpretations of the life of the Prophet Muhammad.

Skyjacking: The takeover of a commercial airplane for the purpose of taking hostages and using these hostages to bargain for a particular political or economic goal.

Social movement: People with a diffuse sense of collective identity, solidarity, and common purpose that usually leads to collective political behavior. The concept covers all the different NGOs and networks, plus all their members and all the other individuals who share the common value(s). Thus, the women's movement and the environmental movement are much more than the specific NGOs that provide leadership and focus the desire for social change.

Social structure: An arrangement based on ideas, norms, values, and shared beliefs. According to constructivists, the social domain does not exist in nature but is constructed through processes of interaction and the sharing of meaning.

Soft power: Influence and authority deriving from the attraction that a country's political, social, and economic ideas, beliefs, and practices have for people living in other countries.

Sovereign equality: The idea that all countries have the same rights, including the right of noninterference in their internal affairs.

Sovereignty: The condition of a state being free from any higher legal authority. It is related to, but distinct from, the condition of a government being free from any external political constraints. It is the rightful entitlement to exclusive, unqualified, and supreme rule within a delimited territory.

Special Drawing Right (SDR): IMF members have the right to borrow this asset from the organization up to the amount that the country has invested in the IMF. The SDR is based on the value of a "basket" of the world's leading currencies: British pound, euro, Japanese yen, and US dollar.

Specialized agencies: International institutions that have a special relationship with the central system of the UN but are constitutionally independent, having their own assessed budgets, executive heads and committees, and assemblies of the representatives of all state members.

Standard operating procedures (SOPs): The prepared-response patterns that organizations create to react to general categories of events, crises, and actions.

Standards of civilization: A nineteenth-century European discourse about which values and norms made a country "civilized," or "barbaric" and "uncivilized." The conclusion was that civilized countries should colonize "barbaric regions" for the latter's benefit.

State: A legal territorial entity composed of a stable population and a government; it possesses a monopoly over the legitimate use of force; its sovereignty is recognized by other states in the international system.

State sovereignty: The concept that all countries are equal under international law and that they are protected from outside interference;

this is the basis on which the UN and other international and regional organizations operate.

State system: The regular patterns of interaction between states, but without implying any shared values between them. This is distinguished from the view of a "society" of states.

Statecraft: The methods and tools that national leaders use to achieve the national interests of a state.

Strategic Arms Reductions Treaty (START): Negotiations began in 1982 and progressed at a very slow pace over eight years. The US and the USSR debated these issues in twelve rounds of formal negotiations, thirteen foreign ministers' meetings, and six summit conferences. In May 1990, George H. W. Bush and Gorbachev agreed to a framework for arms reduction. A treaty was signed in Moscow in July 1991. This treaty reversed a forty-five-year-old strategic nuclear arms race. The treaty broke new ground because it called for a reduction of nuclear arms rather than just a limit on the growth of these weapons.

Summit diplomacy: A direct meeting between heads of government (of the superpowers in particular) to resolve major problems. The "summit" became a regular mode of contact during the Cold War.

Superstructure: In the Marxist perspective this is the government or political structure that is controlled by those who own the means of production.

Supranational global organization: An authoritative international organization that operates above the national state.

Supraterratoriality: Social, economic, cultural, and political connections that transcend territorial geography.

Sustainable development: Development that meets the needs of the present without compromising the ability of future generations to meet their own needs.

Tactics: The conduct and management of military capabilities in or near the battle area.

Technology transfer: The process of sharing skills, knowledge, technologies, methods of manufacturing, and facilities among governments and private actors (like corporations) to ensure that scientific and technological developments are accessible to a wider range of users for application in new products, processes, materials, or services.

Terrorism: The use of illegitimate violence by both state and nonstate groups to inspire fear, by attacking civilians or symbolic targets. This is done for purposes such as drawing widespread attention to a grievance, provoking a severe response, or wearing down an opponent's moral resolve, to effect political change. Determining when the use of violence is legitimate, which is based on the contextual morality of the act as opposed to its effects, is the source for disagreement over what constitutes acts of terrorism.

Theocracy: A state based on religion.

Theory: A proposed explanation of an event or behavior of an actor in the real world. Definitions range from "an unproven assumption" to "a working hypothesis that proposes an explanation for an action or behavior." In international relations we have intuitive theories, empirical theories, and normative theories.

Third-tier states: Sometimes called the "less-developed states" or the "premodern states." These countries fail to provide the basics, such as border protection, law and order, and maintenance of a functioning economy.

Thirty Years' War: The last of the great wars in Europe nominally for religion. Some historians believe that political leaders cynically used religious differences as an excuse to extend their kingdoms.

Trade liberalization: The removal or reduction of barriers to free trade such as tariffs or quotas on the trading of specific goods.

Transborder: Economic, political, social, or cultural activities crossing or extending across a border.

Transnational actor: Any nongovernmental actor, such as a multinational corporation or one country's religious humanitarian organization, that has relations with any actor from another country or with an international organization.

Transnational company/corporation (TNC): A company that has affiliates in a foreign country. The affiliates may be branches of the parent company, separately incorporated subsidiaries, or associates with large minority shareholdings.

Transnational nonstate actor: Any nonstate or nongovernmental actor from one country that has relations with any actor from another country or with an international organization.

Transnational terrorist networks: Terrorists use existing global or transnational economic, transportation, and communication systems to manage and maintain terrorist organizations around the world. These networks facilitate the movement of followers and material to locations around the world.

Trench warfare: From 1914 to 1918 the two sides in WWI dug elaborate defensive fortifications in the ground. Because of the power of weapons like machine guns and rapid-fire cannons, trenches often gave the advantage in battle to the defenders.

Triangulation: This occurs when trade or communication between two countries is routed indirectly via a third country. For example, in the early 1980s, neither the Argentine government nor the British government permitted trade between the two countries, but some companies simply sent their exports via Brazil or Western Europe.

Truman Doctrine: Statement made by US President Harry Truman in March 1947 that it "must be the policy of the United States to support free people who are resisting attempted subjugation by armed minorities or by outside pressures." Intended to persuade Congress to support limited aid to Turkey and Greece, the doctrine came to underpin the policy of containment and American economic and political support for its allies.

United Nations Charter (1945): The UN charter is the legal regime that created the UN as the world's only "supranational" organization. The charter defines the structure of the UN, the powers of its constitutive agencies, and the rights and obligations of sovereign states party to the charter. Among other things, the charter is the key legal document limiting the use of force to instances of self-defense and collective peace enforcement endorsed by the UN Security Council.

Vertical proliferation: An increase in the number of nuclear weapons a state possesses, and in other technologies used for delivery of weapons. Recently, concerns were raised about the production of tactical nuclear weapons like "bunker busters" that could be used to destroy caves and underground facilities in Afghanistan.

Veto power: The right of the five permanent members of the Security Council (United States, Russia, China, France, and Great Britain) to forbid any action by the UN.

Virtual jihad academy: The use of the Internet to plan, promote, and propagate physical and cyber attacks as well as train and educate future followers or jihadists.

Warsaw Pact: The Warsaw Pact was created in May 1955 in response to West Germany's rearmament and entry into NATO. It comprised the USSR and seven communist states (though Albania withdrew support in 1961). The organization was officially dissolved in July 1991.

Washington Consensus: The belief of key opinion-formers in Washington that global welfare would be maximized by the universal application of neoclassical economic policies that favor a minimalist state and an enhanced role for the market.

Weapons of mass destruction: A category defined by the UN in 1948 to include "atomic explosive weapons, radioactive material weapons, lethal chemical and biological weapons, and any weapons developed in the future which have characteristics comparable in destructive effects to those of the atomic bomb or other weapons mentioned above."

Widening school of international security: Sometimes called the Copenhagen School, this refers to authors who extend the definition of security to include economic, political, societal, and environmental policy areas.

World Bank Group: A collection of five agencies, the first established in 1945, with head offices in Washington, DC. The WBG promotes development in medium- and low-income countries with project loans, structural-adjustment programs, and various advisory services.

World order: This is a wider category of order than the "international." It takes as its units of order not states, but individual human beings, and assesses the degree of order on the basis of the delivery of certain kinds of goods (such as security, human rights, basic needs, or justice) for humanity as a whole.

World Trade Organization (WTO): Established in 1995 with headquarters in Geneva. Membership (2010) of 153 states. The WTO is a permanent institution to replace the provisional GATT. It has a wider agenda, covering services, intellectual property, and investment issues as well as merchandise trade. The WTO also has greater powers of enforcement through its dispute-settlement mechanism. The organization's Trade Policy Review Body conducts surveillance of members' commercial measures.

Zero-sum world: A pessimistic view of any interaction that suggests that another's gains are your losses.

APPENDIX TWO

Table of Theoretical Perspectives Discussed in Readings

	Primary Perspective Applied				
	Realism	**Liberalism**	**Marxist**	**Contructivist**	**Feminist**
Academic Sources					
Ahn		X			
Alagappa	X				
Amin			X		
Anderlini		X		X	X
Bedford					X
Behera	X	X			
Bin Laden					
Brocklehurst					X
Christoff				X	
Clark		X			
De Waal		X			
Der Derian				X	
Doyle		X			
el-Ojeili and Hayden				X	
Elshtain					X
Enloe					X
Falk		X			
Ferguson	X				
Gray, Kittilson, and Sandholtz		X			X
Hafner-Burton		X			X
Hardin					
Hashmi		X		X	
Homer-Dixon		X			
Huntington	X				
Keck and Sikkink		X			
Kindleberger		X			
Krugman		X			

(Continued)

Table of Theoretical Perspectives Discussed in Readings *(Continued)*

	Primary Perspective Applied				
	Realism	**Liberalism**	**Marxist**	**Contructivist**	**Feminist**
Academic Sources					
Lim		X	X		
Lipsky	X	X			
Magdoff			X		
Manjikian	X	X		X	
Morgenthau	X				
Ohmae	X	X			
Olson	X	X			
Ostrom	X	X			
Qutb	X				
Scott		X			
Singh			X		
Stiglitz		X			
Sylvester	X	X		X	X
Tang	X				
Tickner	X	X			X
Waltz	X				
Walzer	X				
Wendt				X	
Government or News Media Materials					
Applying European Values to Foreign Policy (The European Union)		X			
More Species Slide to Extinction (Black)					
National Military Strategy Plan for the War on Terrorism U.S. (Chairman of the Joint Chiefs of Staff)	X				
Obama (or Netanyahu) as Modern Moses! (Bishara)					
Need Versus Greed (Sachs)		X			
UN Expert Says Security Council Counterterrorism Measures Anti-Human Rights (Krastev)	X				
Worry But Don't Panic Over Glacial Losses (Kerr)				X	

INDEX